F. Scott
FITZGERALD'S
The Great Gatsby:

A Literary Reference

F. Scott
FITZGERALD'S

The Great Gatsby:

A Literary Reference

EDITED BY

MATTHEW J. BRUCCOLI

CARROLL & GRAF PUBLISHERS
NEW YORK

Still for Scottie

F. SCOTT FITZGERALD'S *THE GREAT GATSBY:*
A Literary Reference

Carroll & Graf Publishers
An Imprint of Avalon Publishing Group Incorporated
161 William Street, 16th Floor
New York, NY 10038

Copyright © 2000 by The Gale Group

First Carroll & Graf trade paperback edition 2002

Library of Congress Cataloging-in-Publication Data is available.

ISBN: 0-7867-0996-0

Printed in the United States of America
Distributed by Publishers Group West

Contents

Introduction

This is the first *Literary Reference* volume restricted to a single literary work. Why does *The Great Gatsby* merit an entire documentary history? How does this volume serve readers of *The Great Gatsby*? The second question can be restated as: what do you do with it? These are fair questions to ask about a reference book intended for the use of students and teachers, as well as nonacademic serious readers.

Gatsby is regarded as the most widely taught and widely read American literary classic, and its readers—especially those abroad—need help to fully enjoy and fully understand it. A classic is a work that continues to be read and becomes part of the equipment of educated people long after its willing or unwilling readers still know the things that the author knew. *Gatsby* is seventy-five years old. F. Scott Fitzgerald, like all authors, used the places, people, events, and details that he expected his readers to recognize and respond to. The proper way to read *Gatsby* or any other classic is to be placed in a time machine and transported to the day the book was published in order to respond to it with the knowledge, values, standards, and biases of the public the author was writing for. That statement is not a joke: all literary works that examine particular times go out of date. The older the book, the less readers understand about its world and its characters. One of the functions of this *Literary Reference* is to provide an illustrated gloss to the material of *Gatsby*. Fitzgerald declared in the 1934 introduction to the Modern Library reprint of his novel: "But, my God! it was my material, and it was all I had to deal with." This statement is true for every good writer.

Serious writers know what they are doing. Every detail is intentional. If that claim were not true, great books would not be worth the attention they require. The obligation of the serious reader of a great book is to approach as closely as possible the author's intentions in writing it. This task requires work; not all books are worth the effort. When a reader discovers one of those miraculous books that seems to have been written for him/her, the necessary tools ought to be available.

Since Fitzgerald preserved the manuscript and reworked proofs for his novel—and because his daughter, Scottie, kept them together and donated them to Princeton—it is possible to reconstruct the stages of writing, revision, and rewriting and thereby to understand how he fulfilled his intentions. Genius is the ability of a writer to express what is in his mind. This volume used in conjunction with the facsimiles of the manuscript, the first galley proofs, and the reworked proofs aids the reader to understand Fitzgerald's creative process for *Gatsby*. There are those who object that no work of literature merits this reader commitment. When in doubt, consult Samuel Johnson: "The minute changes made in their compositions by eminent writers are always a matter of both curiosity and instruction to literary men, however trifling and unimportant they may appear to blockheads."

The evident brilliance of *Gatsby* has interfered with the proper recognition and assessment of Fitzgerald's genius—his craftsmanship, his emotional capacity, his versatility, his taste, his devotion to writing. This novel should be considered as one element in his whole career. Correct appraisal of an author necessitates reading all—or nearly all—of his words. Fitzgerald wrote Scottie in 1939: "I am not a great man, but sometimes I think the impersonal and objective quality of my talent and the sacrifices of it, in pieces, to preserve its essential value has some sort of epic grandeur."

The Great Gatsby was the third novel of a writer in his twenties who mastered his craft during the process of writing it. *This Side of Paradise* and *The Beautiful and Damned* did not foreshadow the technical and structural achievement or the controlled point of view in *Gatsby*. It was—or should have been—the fulcrum of his career. Fitzgerald ruefully admitted to his daughter in 1940, the year of his death:

> What little I've accomplished has been by the most laborious and uphill work, and I wish now I'd never relaxed or looked back—but said at the end of *The Great Gatsby:* "I've found my line—from now on this comes first. This is my immediate duty—without this I am nothing."

It is not the case that Fitzgerald did not write another great novel. *Tender is the Night* (1934) is a greater work: more profound, more deeply felt, more moving—although less brilliant. The nine years between *Gatsby* and *Tender* were too long to sustain the loyalty of Fitzgerald's parishioners. Too many things happened to Fitzgerald, his readers, and America. Readers and reviewers who expected a son-of-*Gatsby* were disappointed. *The Great Gatsby* remains the work by which Fitzgerald is gauged: an imprecise gauge that fosters the impression among "general readers" or "common readers" that he died a has-been. F. Scott Fitzgerald died at forty-four writing *The Love of the Last Tycoon: A Western,* the most heartbreaking work-in-progress in American literature.

Acknowledgments

This book was produced by Bruccoli Clark Layman, Inc. Karen L. Rood is senior editor for the *Dictionary of Literary Biography* series. George P. Anderson and D. W. Thomas were the in-house editors.

Production manager is Philip B. Dematteis.

Administrative support was provided by Ann M. Cheschi, Tenesha S. Lee, and Joann Whittaker.

Accountant is Kathy Weston. Accounting assistant is Angi Pleasant.

Copyediting supervisor is Phyllis A. Avant. Senior copyeditor is Thom Harman. The copyediting staff includes Brenda Carol Blanton, James Denton, Worthy B. Evans, Melissa D. Hinton, William Tobias Mathes, and Jennifer S. Reid. Freelance copyeditor is Rebecca Mayo.

Editorial assistant is Margo Dowling.

Indexing was done by Alex Snead and Cory McNair.

Layout and graphics supervisor is Janet E. Hill. Graphics staff includes Karla Corley Brown and Zoe R. Cook.

Office manager is Kathy Lawler Merlette.

Photography editors are Charles Mims, Scott Nemzek, Alison Smith, and Paul Talbot. Digital photographic copy work was performed by Joseph M. Bruccoli and Zoe R. Cook.

SGML supervisor is Cory McNair. The SGML staff includes Tim Bedford, Linda Drake, Frank Graham, and Alex Snead.

Systems manager is Marie L. Parker.

Database manager is Kimberly Kelly.

Typesetting supenisor is Kathleen M. Flanagan. The typesetting staff includes Kimberly Kelly, Mark J. McEwan, and Patricia Flanagan Salisbury. Freelance typesetters are Wanda Adams and Vicki P. Grivetti.

Walter W. Ross and Steven Gross did library research. They were assisted by the following librarians at the Thomas Cooper Library of the University of South Carolina: Linda Holderfield and the interlibrary-loan staff; reference-department head Virginia Weathers; reference librarians Marilee Birchfield, Stefanie Buck, Stefanie DuBose, Rebecca Feind, Karen Joseph, Donna Lehman, Charlene Loope, Anthony McKissick, Jean Rhyne, and Kwamine Simpson; circulation-department head Caroline Taylor; and acquisitions-searching supervisor David Haggard.

These people rendered valuable aid and comfort: Chris Bryne (Harold Ober Associates), John Delaney (Princeton University Library), Catherine Fry (University of South Carolina Press), Glenn Horowitz (New York City), Michael L. Lazare (New Milford, Connecticut), Charles Scribner III (Simon and Schuster), and Cliff Tinder (*Playbill*).

Permissions

Louis Auchincloss for the section of *The Great Gatsby* from *Three "Perfect Novels" and What They Have in Common* (Bloomfield Hills, Mich.: Bruccoli Clark, 1981).

Jonathan Bishop for the John Peale Bishop letter to F. Scott Fitzgerald, 9 June 1925.

Cambridge University Press for Matthew J. Bruccoli, Introduction to *New Essays on* The Great Gatsby, edited by Bruccoli (Cambridge & New York, 1985).

Cambridge University Press and George Garrett for his "Fire and Freshness: A Matter of Style in *The Great Gatsby,*" in *New Essays on* The Great Gatsby, edited by Matthew J. Bruccoli (Cambridge & New York, 1985).

Chicago Tribune for Fanny Butcher, "New Fitzgerald Book Proves He's Really a Writer," 18 April 1925.

Crossroads Communications for Janet Maslin, "Ballantine's Scotch, Glemby Haircuts, White Suits, and White Teflon: Gatsby 1974," in *The Classic American Novel and the Movies,* edited by Gerald Peary and Roger Shatzkin (New York: Ungar, 1977).

Andre Deutsch for the extract from Cyril Connolly in *The Modern Movement* (London, 1965).

Doubleday Broadway Publishing Group for Lionel Trilling, "F. Scott Fitzgerald," in his *The Liberal Imagination* (Garden City, N.Y., 1950).

Enoch Pratt Library for the H. L. Mencken letter to Fitzgerald, 16 April 1925.

Farrar, Straus and Giroux for the Edmund Wilson letter to Fitzgerald, 11 April 1925, from *Letters on Literature and Politics, 1912–1972* (New York, 1977).

G. K. Hall for Robert Roulston, "Something Borrowed, Something New: A Discussion of Literary Influences on *The Great Gatsby,*" in *Critical Essays on* The Great Gatsby, edited by Scott Donaldson (Boston, 1984).

Holt, Rinehart and Winston for the excerpt from H. D. Piper, "*The Great Gatsby:* Finding a Hero," in his *F. Scott Fitzgerald: A Critical Portrait* (New York, 1962).

Levin and Gann for the Gertrude Stein letter to Fitzgerald, 22 May 1925.

The Nation for Joseph Wood Krutch, "Drama: Long Island Sentiment," 24 February 1926, and for Manny Farber, "Films," 13 August 1949.

The New Republic for Edmund Wilson, "Mürger and Wilde on the Screen," 24 March 1926.

The New Statesman for the unsigned review of *The Great Gatsby,* 27 March 1926.

The New Yorker for the unsigned review of *The Great Gatsby,* 23 May 1925, and for Penelope Gilliatt, "The Current Cinema: Courtly Love's Last Throw of the Dice," 1 April 1974.

The New York Times for J. Brooks Atkinson, "Careless People and Gatsby," 3 February 1926; for Atkinson, "From Novel to Stage," 7 February 1926; for Vincent Canby, "A Lavish 'Gatsby' Loses Book's Spirit," 28 March 1974~; for Bosley Crowther, "The Screen in Review: 'The Great Gatsby,'" 14 July 1949; for Mordaunt Hall, "The Screen: Gold and Cocktails," 22 November 1926; and for the unsigned articles "Explains 'The Great Gatsby' Closing," 4 May 1926, and "Not Wholly 'Lost,'" 24 December 1940.

The Observer for Kenneth Tynan, "Gatsby and The American Dream," 14 April 1974.

The Saturday Evening Post for Fitzgerald's "How to Live on $36,000 a Year," 5 April 1924.

Charles Scribner III for his "Celestial Eyes—from Metamorphosis to Masterpiece."

Simon and Schuster for "Absolution"; for the excerpt from *Ernest Hemingway: Selected Letters, 1917–1961,* edited by Carlos Baker (New York: Scribners, 1981); for Matthew J. Bruccoli, "A Brief Life of F. Scott Fitzgerald," in *The Short Stories of F. Scott Fitzgerald,* edited by Bruccoli (New York: Scribners, 1989); for selections from *Dear Scott/Dear Max: The Fitzgerald-Perkins Correspondence,* edited by John Kuehl and Jackson R. Bryer (New York: Scribners, 1971); and for excerpts from *The Great Gatsby* (New York: Scribners, 1925).

Permissions

Simon and Schuster and Charles Scribner III for Maxwell Perkins's letters to Fitzgerald.

Simon and Schuster and Harold Ober Associates for the Fitzgerald letter to H. L. Mencken, 4 May 1925; and for the excerpts from Fitzgerald's letters to Edmund Wilson, 25 May 1925, and to John Peale Bishop, August 1925.

Southern Illinois University Press for Richard O. Lehan, "*The Great Gatsby* and Its Sources," in his *F. Scott Fitzgerald and the Craft of Fiction* (Carbondale, Ill., 1966).

Sun Source for H. L. Mencken, "As H. L. M. Sees It," *Baltimore Evening Sun*, 2 May 1925.

Time for the unsigned review "Incorruptible Yegg," 11 May 1925.

Washington Post for Sally Quinn, "*The Great Gatsby:* Flack or Fiction," 29 March 1974.

Watkins Loomis Agency for the Edith Wharton letter to Fitzgerald, 8 June 1925.

Illustrations

Charles M. Schulz Creative Associates for the *Gatsby* strip from *Peanuts*.

Everett Collection for the photograph of Gilda Gray.

Harcourt Brace for the T. S. Eliot letter to Fitzgerald, 31 December 1925.

Harold Ober Associates for facsimiles of Fitzgerald's manuscripts, galleys, and *Ledger*.

The New Yorker for Miguel Covarrubias, "The Final Pot Shot at the Great Gatsby" (1926).

Photofest for the photograph of Joe Frisco.

Playbill for its cover for the Metropolitan Opera production of *The Great Gatsby*.

The Estate of John Held Jr., for the map of Great Neck, originally published in *The New Yorker*.

F. Scott
FITZGERALD'S
The Great Gatsby:

A Literary Reference

A Brief Life of F. Scott Fitzgerald

By Matthew J. Bruccoli

The compensation of a very early success is a conviction that life is a romantic matter.

–F. Scott Fitzgerald

The dominant influences on F. Scott Fitzgerald were aspiration, literature, Princeton, Zelda Sayre Fitzgerald, and alcohol.

Francis Scott Key Fitzgerald was born in St. Paul, Minnesota, on September 24, 1896, the namesake and second cousin three times removed of the author of the National Anthem. Fitzgerald's given names indicate his parents' pride in his father's ancestry. His father, Edward, was from Maryland, with an allegiance to the old South and its values. Fitzgerald's mother, Mary (Mollie) McQuillan, was the daughter of an Irish immigrant who became wealthy as a wholesale grocer in St. Paul. Both were Catholics.

Edward Fitzgerald failed as a manufacturer of wicker furniture in St. Paul, and he became a salesman for Procter & Gamble in Upstate New York. After he was dismissed in 1908, when his son was twelve, the family returned to St. Paul and lived comfortably on Mollie Fitzgerald's inheritance. Fitzgerald attended the St. Paul Academy; his first writing to appear in print was a detective story in the school newspaper when he was thirteen.

During 1911–1913 he attended the Newman School, a Catholic prep school in New Jersey, where he met Father Sigourney Fay, who encouraged his ambitions for personal distinction and achievement. As a member of the Princeton Class of 1917, Fitzgerald neglected his studies for his literary apprenticeship. He wrote the scripts and lyrics for the Princeton Triangle Club musicals and was a contributor to the *Princeton Tiger* humor magazine and the *Nassau Literary Magazine*. His college friends included Edmund Wilson and John Peale Bishop. On academic probation and unlikely to graduate, Fitzgerald joined the army in 1917 and was commissioned a second lieutenant in the infantry. Convinced that he would die in the war, he rapidly wrote a novel, "The Romantic Egotist"; the letter of rejection from Charles Scribner's Sons praised the novel's originality and asked that it be resubmitted when revised.

In June 1918 Fitzgerald was assigned to Camp Sheridan, near Montgomery, Alabama. There he fell in love with a celebrated belle, eighteen-year-old Zelda Sayre, the youngest daughter of an Alabama Supreme Court judge. The romance intensified Fitzgerald's hopes for the success of his novel, but after revision it was rejected by Scribners a second time. The war ended just before he was to be sent overseas; after his discharge in 1919 he went to New York City to seek his fortune in order to marry. Unwilling to wait while Fitzgerald succeeded in the advertisement business and unwilling to live on his small salary, Zelda broke their engagement.

In July 1919 Fitzgerald quit his job and returned to St. Paul to rewrite his novel as *This Side of Paradise;* it was accepted by editor Maxwell Perkins of Scribners in September. Set mainly at Princeton and described by its author as "a quest novel," *This Side of Paradise* traces the career aspirations and love disappointments of Amory Blaine.

In the fall–winter of 1919 Fitzgerald commenced his career as a writer of stories for the mass-circulation magazines. Working through agent Harold Ober, Fitzgerald interrupted work on his novels to write money-making popular fiction for the rest of his life. *The Saturday Evening Post* became Fitzgerald's best story market, and he was regarded as a "*Post* writer." His early commercial stories about young love introduced a fresh character: the independent, determined young American woman who appeared in "The Offshore Pirate" and "Bernice Bobs Her Hair." Fitzgerald's more ambitious stories, such as "May Day" and "The Diamond as Big as the Ritz," were published in *The Smart Set,* which had a small circulation.

The publication of *This Side of Paradise* on March 26, 1920, made the twenty-four-year-old Fitzgerald famous almost overnight, and a week later he married Zelda in New York. They embarked on an extravagant life as young celebrities. Fitzgerald endeavored to earn a solid literary reputation, but his playboy image impeded the proper assessment of his work.

After a riotous summer in Westport, Connecticut, the Fitzgeralds took an apartment in New York City; there he wrote his second novel, *The Beautiful and*

Damned, a naturalistic chronicle of the dissipation of Anthony and Gloria Patch. When Zelda became pregnant, they took their first trip to Europe in 1921 and then settled in St. Paul for the birth of their only child; Frances Scott (Scottie) Fitzgerald was born in October 1921.

Fitzgerald expected to become affluent from his play, *The Vegetable;* in the fall of 1922 they moved to Great Neck, Long Island, in order to be near Broadway. The political satire—subtitled "From President to Postman"—failed at its tryout in November 1923, and Fitzgerald wrote his way out of debt with short stories. The distractions of Great Neck and New York prevented Fitzgerald from making progress on his third novel. During this time his drinking increased. Fitzgerald was an alcoholic, but he wrote sober. Zelda regularly got "tight," but she was not an alcoholic. There were frequent domestic rows, usually triggered by drinking bouts.

Literary opinion-makers were reluctant to accord Fitzgerald full marks as a serious craftsman. His reputation as a drinker inspired the myth that he was an irresponsible writer; yet he was a painstaking reviser whose fiction went through layers of drafts. Fitzgerald's clear, lyrical, colorful, witty style evoked the emotions associated with time and place. When critics objected to Fitzgerald's concern with love and success, his response was: "But, my God! it was my material, and it was all I had to deal with." The chief theme of Fitzgerald's work is aspiration—the idealism he regarded as defining American character. Another major theme was mutability or loss. As a social historian Fitzgerald became identified with "The Jazz Age": "It was an age of miracles, it was an age of art, it was an age of excess, and it was an age of satire."

The Fitzgeralds went to France in the spring of 1924 seeking tranquillity for his work. He wrote *The Great Gatsby* during the summer and fall in Valescure near St. Raphael, but the marriage was damaged by Zelda's involvement with a French naval aviator. The extent of the affair—if it was in fact consummated—is not known. On the Riviera the Fitzgeralds formed a close friendship with Gerald and Sara Murphy.

The Fitzgeralds spent the winter of 1924–1925 in Rome, where he revised *The Great Gatsby;* they were en route to Paris when the novel was published in April. *The Great Gatsby* marked a striking advance in Fitzgerald's technique, utilizing a complex structure and a controlled narrative point of view. Fitzgerald's achievement received critical praise, but sales of *Gatsby* were disappointing, though the stage and movie rights brought additional income.

In Paris Fitzgerald met Ernest Hemingway—then unknown outside the expatriate literary circle—with whom he formed a friendship based largely on his admiration for Hemingway's personality and genius. The Fitzgeralds remained in France until the end of 1926, alternating between Paris and the Riviera.

Fitzgerald made little progress on his fourth novel, a study of American expatriates in France provisionally titled "The Boy Who Killed His Mother," "Our Type," and "The World's Fair." During these years Zelda's unconventional behavior became increasingly eccentric.

The Fitzgeralds returned to America to escape the distractions of France. After a short, unsuccessful stint of screenwriting in Hollywood, Fitzgerald rented "Ellerslie," a mansion near Wilmington, Delaware, in the spring of 1927. The family remained at "Ellerslie" for two years interrupted by a visit to Paris in the summer of 1928, but Fitzgerald was still unable to make significant progress on his novel. At this time Zelda commenced ballet training, intending to become a professional dancer. The Fitzgeralds returned to France in the spring of 1929, where Zelda's intense ballet work damaged her health and estranged them. In April 1930 she suffered her first breakdown. Zelda was treated at Prangins Clinic in Switzerland until September 1931, while Fitzgerald lived in Swiss hotels. Work on the novel was again suspended as he wrote short stories to pay for psychiatric treatment.

Fitzgerald's peak story fee of $4,000 from *The Saturday Evening Post* may have had in 1929 the purchasing power of $40,000 in 1994 dollars. Nonetheless, the general view of his affluence is distorted. Fitzgerald was not among the highest-paid writers of his time; his novels earned comparatively little, and most of his income came from 160 magazine stories. During the 1920s his income from all sources averaged under $25,000 a year—good money at a time when a schoolteacher's average annual salary was $1,299, but not a fortune. Scott and Zelda Fitzgerald did spend money faster than he earned it; the author who wrote so eloquently about the effects of money on character was unable to manage his own finances.

The Fitzgeralds returned to America in the fall of 1931 and rented a house in Montgomery. Fitzgerald made a second unsuccessful trip to Hollywood in 1931. Zelda suffered a relapse in February 1932 and entered Johns Hopkins Hospital in Baltimore. She spent the rest of her life as a resident or outpatient of sanitariums.

In 1932, while a patient at Johns Hopkins, Zelda rapidly wrote *Save Me the Waltz.* Her autobiographical novel generated considerable bitterness between the Fitzgeralds, for he regarded it as pre-empting the material that he was using in his novel-in-progress. Fitzgerald rented "La Paix," a house outside Baltimore, where he completed his fourth novel, *Tender Is the Night.* Published in 1934, his most ambitious novel was a commercial failure, and its merits were matters of critical dispute. Set in France during the 1920s, *Tender Is the Night* examines the deterioration of Dick Diver, a brilliant American psychiatrist, during the course of his marriage to a wealthy mental patient.

The 1935–1937 period is known as "the crack-up" from the title of an essay Fitzgerald wrote in 1936. Ill, drunk, in debt, and unable to write commercial stories, he lived in hotels in the region near Asheville, North Carolina, where in 1936 Zelda entered Highland Hospital. After Baltimore Fitzgerald did not maintain a home for Scottie. When she was fourteen, she went to boarding school, and the Obers became her surrogate family. Nonetheless, Fitzgerald functioned as a concerned father by mail, attempting to supervise Scottie's education and to shape her social values.

Fitzgerald went to Hollywood alone in the summer of 1937 with a six-month Metro-Goldwyn-Mayer contract at $1,000 a week. He received his only screen credit for adapting *Three Comrades* (1938), and his contract was renewed for a year at $1,250 a week. This $91,000 from M-G-M was a great deal of money during the late Depression years when a new Cheverolet

coupé cost $619, but, although Fitzgerald paid off his debts, he was unable to save. His trips East to visit Zelda were disastrous. In California Fitzgerald fell in love with movie columnist Sheila Graham. Their relationship endured despite his benders. After M-G-M dropped his option at the end of 1938, Fitzgerald worked as a freelance script writer and wrote short-short stories for *Esquire*. He began his Hollywood novel, *The Love of the Last Tycoon*, in 1939 and had written more than half of a working draft when he died of a heart attack in Graham's apartment on December 21, 1940. Zelda Fitzgerald perished in a fire in Highland Hospital in 1948.

F. Scott Fitzgerald died believing himself a failure. The obituaries were condescending, and he seemed destined for literary obscurity. The first phase of the Fitzgerald resurrection—"revival" does not properly describe the process—occurred between 1945 and 1950. By 1960 he had achieved a secure place among America's enduring writers: *The Great Gatsby,* a work that seriously examines the theme of aspiration in an American setting, defines the classic American novel.

–From *The Short Stories of F. Scott Fitzgerald*
(New York: Scribners, 1989)

The Great Gatsby

In my younger and more vulnerable years my father told me something that I've been turning over in my my mind ever since.

"When you feel like criticizing anyone," he said, "just remember that everyone in this world hasn't had the advantages that you've had."

He didn't say anymore but we've always been unusually communicative in a reserved way and I understood that he meant a great deal more than that. In consequence I'm inclined to reserve all judgements, a habit that has opened up many curious natures to me and also made me the victim of not a few colossal bores. The abnormal mind is quick to detect and attach itself to this quality when it appears in a normal person, and so it came about that in college I was unjustly accused of being of politician, because I was privy to the secret griefs of wild, unknown men. Most of the confidences were unsought — frequently I have feigned sleep, preoccupation or a hostile levity when I realized by some unmistakeable sign that an intimate revelation was quivering on the horizon — for the intimate revelations of young men or at any rate the terms in which they express them vary no more than the heavenly messages which reach us over the psychic radio. Reserving judgements is a matter of infinite hope. I am still a little afraid of missing something if I forget that, as my father snobbishly suggested and I snobbishly repeat, a sense of the fundamental decencies is parcelled out unequally at birth.

And, after boasting this way of my tolerance, I come to the admission that it has a limit. Conduct may be founded on the hard rock or the wet marshes but after a certain point I don't care what it's founded on. When I came back here from the east last autumn I felt that I wanted the world to be in uniform and at a sort of moral attention forever; I wanted no more riotous excursions with privileged glimpses into the human heart. It was only Gatsby himself that was exempted from my

First page of the manuscript (Princeton University Library)

Chronology

October 1921	Fitzgerald writes "The Diamond as Big as the Ritz" in St. Paul, Minnesota.
June 1922	Fitzgerald begins planning his third novel at White Bear Lake, Minnesota.
September 1922	Fitzgerald writes "Winter Dreams" in St. Paul.
October 1922	The Fitzgeralds move to Great Neck, Long Island.
June 1923	Fitzgerald begins writing the novel; he writes "Absolution."
November 1923	Fitzgerald writes "The Sensible Thing."
April 1924	*Ledger:* "Out of the woods at last + starting novel."
May 1924	The Fitzgeralds leave for the Riviera.
September 1924	The first draft is finished. *Ledger:* "Hard work sets in."
September–October 1924	Fitzgerald revises the typescript. *Ledger:* "Working at high pressure to finish."
November 1924	The typescript is sent to Maxwell Perkins. *Ledger:* "Novel off at last."
20 November 1924	Perkins responds to the typescript.
January–February 1925	Fitzgerald revises and rewrites galleys in Rome.
March 1925	Fitzgerald makes last revisions at Capri.
10 April 1925	Publication of *The Great Gatsby*.

Lieutenant F. Scott Fitzgerald met Zelda Sayre when he was stationed at Camp Sheridan, Alabama. His courtship inspired the account of Gatsby's love for Daisy.

CHAPTER 1:

BACKGROUNDS OF *THE GREAT GATSBY*

All great novels are great social history. F. Scott Fitzgerald was a social realist and a social historian, but his technique was not reportorial. He transmuted actual people, places, and events into fiction. Fitzgerald was concerned with evoking the sense of time and place associated with his characters' behavior. The material of his writing was recognizable in 1925 and identifiable now. He selected details for their power to generate reader confidence in the story and the characters—as do all first-rank authors. Accuracy for its own sake is essential; but Fitzgerald was much more concerned with the evocative power of detail. Thus the list of the people who attended Gatsby's parties includes no actual figures; yet their names and the impressionistic descriptions convey an overview of a social order—or social disorder—at a certain point in American history.

The chapter on the Backgrounds of The Great Gatsby *documents the sources for the novel as well as the circumstances of Fitzgerald's life while he was working on the book. The more the reader knows about the author's intentions and material, the better the reader responds to the work. Fitzgerald's best fiction conveys how it was and how it felt—especially how it felt. Thus he advised his daughter, Scottie, on writing: "But when in a freak moment you will want to give the low-down, not the scandal, not the merely <u>reported</u> but the <u>profound</u> essence of what happened at a prom or after it, perhaps that honesty will come to you—and then you will understand how it is possible to make even a forlorn Laplander <u>feel</u> the importance of a trip to Cartiers!" Or feel the importance of Gatsby's party.*

PEOPLE AND EVENTS

The Great Gatsby and Its Sources
Richard D. Lehan

In a letter to Maxwell Perkins from Rome, dated December 20, 1924, Fitzgerald discussed the creation of *The Great Gatsby,* which he was then in the process of revising. After mentioning Tom Buchanan, Gatsby, Daisy, and Myrtle, Fitzgerald says: "Jordan Baker of course was a great idea (perhaps you know it's Edith Cummings)."[1] Edith Cummings was . . . a close friend of Ginevra King, both in Chicago and at Westover where they were in the class of 1917.

Like Jordan Baker in *The Great Gatsby,* she was a famous golfer—playing out of the elegant Onwentsia Club in Chicago—and once winning the national woman's golf championship. Fitzgerald met Edith Cummings a number of times—both in Lake Forest and in New York—when he was dating Ginevra King.

. . . .

In August of 1916, Fitzgerald visited Ginevra in Lake Forest. Peg Cary, Edith Cummings, Courtney Letts—the old Westover crowd—were all there, and, according to Fitzgerald's Ledger, there was a "petting party" and many gay evenings. The Kings made it clear that they disapproved of Fitzgerald. In his Ledger, Fitzgerald wrote that someone at this time told him, "Poor boys shouldn't think of marrying rich girls."[2] If Mr. King would not put it this crudely, these were his sentiments.[3]

The next time that Fitzgerald saw Ginevra King was with Peg Cary at the Yale game in November of 1916. Ginevra met Fitzgerald once again in January of 1917, at which time she broke with him for good.

. . . .

In June of 1917, Fitzgerald suspected that Ginevra was engaged; in September of 1917, he wrote in his Ledger, "Oh Ginevra"; by June of 1918, while he was stationed at Camp Sheridan near Montgomery, Alabama, he found out that Ginevra King was to be married in September. She was marrying William Mitchell who . . . was "the current catch of Chicago." Mitchell was from an extremely wealthy family, long associated with Chicago banking—especially with the Continental Illinois Bank. After he married Ginevra, Mitchell became a director in the family firm of Mitchell, Hutchins & Co., and served on the boards of Balaban and Katz, Inland Glass, and Elgin Clock.

Ginevra King's father . . . went to Yale (class of 1894), and Charles King and William Mitchell both owned a string of polo ponies, Mr. King bringing his East to Long Island where he often rode with Louis E. Stoddard, who was on the American team that played England in the Twenties. The principal characters in *The Great Gatsby* thus

Edith Cummings, winner of the 1923 U.S. Women's Amateur golf championship, was identified by Fitzgerald as the model for Jordan Baker; but there is no evidence of her dishonesty. Cummings was a Lake Forest, Illinois, friend of Fitzgerald's first love, Ginevra King.

begin to emerge: a great deal of Ginevra King went into Fitzgerald's conception of Daisy Fay; Tom Buchanan—who came from a wealthy Chicago family, went to Yale, owned a string of polo ponies on Long Island—is the fusion of Mr. King and William Mitchell; Jordan Baker is Edith Cummings, a friend of Ginevra, just as Jordan is a friend of Daisy.

Fitzgerald came away from Ginevra with a sense of social inadequacy, a deep hurt, and longing for the girl beyond attainment. He expressed these sentiments first, not in *The Great Gatsby*, but in "Winter Dreams," published in December of 1922 in *Metropolitan Magazine*. In this story, the two lovers are separated by money—Dexter Green is the son of a grocer, just as Fitzgerald's maternal grandfather was in the grocery business—and Judy Jones's father is as wealthy as his Pierce-Arrow automobile indicates. When he is twenty-three, Dexter falls in love with Judy, who encourages and then drops him. At twenty-five Dexter is engaged to another girl, but he breaks his engagement when Judy once again shows interest in him. When Judy has proved to herself her complete power over Dexter, she dismisses him once and for all from her life. At thirty-two, Dexter is a Jay

Gatsby, preserving his "old" image of Judy, his "winter" dreams: Dexter learns at this time that Judy, who has since married, is having marital troubles and that she has "faded" and is considered "too old" for her husband. The news shocks him because suddenly he realizes that his youth is gone—and with it an ideal conception of perfect beauty that had kept the world resplendent and alive:

> He had thought that having nothing else to lose he was invulnerable at last—but he knew that he had just lost something more, as surely as if he had married Judy Jones and seen her fade away before his eyes.
> The dream was gone. Something had been taken from him. . . . For he had gone away and he could never go back any more. . . . Even the grief he could have borne was left behind in the country of illusion, of youth . . . where his winter dreams had flourished.
> "Long ago," he said, "long ago, there was something in me, but now that thing is gone. . . . I cannot cry. I cannot care. That thing will come back no more."[4]

As in "Winter Dreams," Fitzgerald gets his feelings of lost youth and beauty into *The Great Gatsby*. He also gets into the novel his sense of social inadequacy and his emotion of hurt when the dream is betrayed by lack of money. "'The whole idea of Gatsby,'" Fitzgerald said, "'is the unfairness of a poor young man not being able to marry a girl with money. This theme comes up again and again because I lived it.'"[5]

Fitzgerald had almost lost Zelda also because of his lack of money; but he finally won her. It was the wound over Ginevra that never healed (Fitzgerald described it "as the skin wound on a haemophile"). Fitzgerald kept all of Ginevra's letters to the end of his life. He even had them typed up and bound in a volume that runs 227 pages.

The "dreams" in "Winter Dreams" are an eternal yearning for the promise of summer and the fulfillment of romance. When Fitzgerald lost Ginevra, he came to believe that such yearning was an end in itself; he believed in the need to preserve a romantic state of mind where the imagination and the will are arrested—in a state of suspension—by an idealized concept of beauty and love. The loss creates an eternal striving, and keeps the world beautifully alive.

When Gatsby kisses Daisy his mind "would never romp again," his conception of beauty was fixed, and his will yearned eternally for that beauty. "It is sadder to find

> She was a slender, small-breasted girl with an erect carriage which she accentuated by throwing her body backward at the shoulders like a young cadet. Her grey sun-strained eyes looked back at me with polite reciprocal curiosity out of a wan, charming discontented face. It occurred to me now that I had seen her, or a picture of her, somewhere before.
>
> *—The Great Gatsby*, p. 12

Fitzgerald was doing something in *The Great Gatsby* that he had not done before. He was pushing his sense of experience away from the middle ground of verisimilitude toward extremes–toward two kinds of distortions. The dreamer distorted becomes Gatsby–a man whose hopelessly vulgar taste allows an eternal yearning for a meretricious beauty. The rich man distorted becomes Tom Buchanan–a man whose ruthlessness preserves his worldly comfort, and whose shoddy ideas keep intact his sense of superiority. Both Gatsby and Tom Buchanan are men without conscience. Gatsby is just as intent on taking Daisy from Tom as Tom is on keeping Daisy from Gatsby. Both caricature Fitzgerald's own experience–his own sense of combat: the dreamer in conflict with a rigid reality; the promises of youth in conflict with the ravages of time; and the man of suspect means in conflict with the established rich.

. . . .

Fitzgerald wrote out of his own sense of experience as openly in *The Great Gatsby* as he did in his earlier novels; but never before was he able to transmogrify that experience into forms that carried it beyond its own literal meaning–and never before was Fitzgerald able to use irony and descriptive detail to plumb the complexity of this life and to control his tendency to sentimentalize. *The Great Gatsby* is the most pure product of Fitzgerald's imagination that we have, a novel in which experience is metamorphosized–heightened and extended–and at the same time brilliantly under control.

–F. Scott Fitzgerald and the Craft of Fiction
(Carbondale: Southern Illinois University Press, 1966)

Ginevra King

the past again," Fitzgerald once wrote, "and find it inadequate to the present than it is to have it elude you and remain forever a harmonious conception of memory."[6]

As long as one cares, the loss can keep the world alive with expectation. Nick Carraway expresses Gatsby's loss of expectation when he surmises that perhaps Gatsby "no longer cared" and if so, then his sky must have suddenly become "unfamiliar," the leaves "frightening," and a rose "grotesque." As Daisy was the source of Gatsby's ideal beauty, Ginevra King was the source of Fitzgerald's. In October of 1937, when he was writing for Hollywood, Fitzgerald went up to Santa Barbara to see Ginevra who was there on a visit. He was overcome with fear because "She was the first girl I ever loved and I have faithfully avoided seeing her up to this moment to keep that illusion perfect."[7]

Fitzgerald saw the need for a "perfect illusion" as part of the creative impulse. In "The Pierian Spring and the Last Straw," an early (1917) short story, the author gets his girl and then no longer feels the need to write. Not only did Ginevra King go into *The Great Gatsby;* she was in many ways part of Fitzgerald's motive for writing the novel in the first place. Is it any wonder that at one point in *The Great Gatsby* Daisy Fay is described as "the king's daughter"?

. . . .

Notes

1. *The Letters of F. Scott Fitzgerald*, ed. Andrew Turnbull (New York: Scribners, 1963), p. 173.

2. Fitzgerald's Ledger, p. 70. The total context of these quotes as they appear in the Ledger are as follows: "Aug 1916–Lake Forest. Peg Carry. Petting Party. Ginevra Party. The bad day at the McCormicks. The dinner at Pegs. Disapointment. Mary Birlard Pierce. Little Marjorie King [Ginevra's sister] & her smile. Beautiful Billy Mitchell [whom Ginevra eventually married]. Peg Carry stands straight. "'Poor boys shouldn't think of marrying rich girls.'"

3. Mrs. Marjorie King Belden, Ginevra's sister, told me (February 21, 1965) that there were abrasive feelings between Fitzgerald and Charles King.

4. "Winter Dreams," *Metropolitan Magazine,* December, 1922; reprinted in *All the Sad Young Men* (New York: Scribners, 1926), p. 90. All further quotations from this story will be cited to this edition, page reference indicated in brackets after the quote.

5. Andrew Turnbull, *Scott Fitzgerald* (New York: Scribners, 1962), p. 150.

6. "Show Mr. and Mrs. F. to Number–," *Esquire,* May–June, 1934; reprinted in *The Crack-Up,* p. 50.

7. *Letters,* p. 19. This experience later became the basis for the story "Three Hours Between Planes," published in *Esquire,* July of 1941, and reprinted in *The Stories of F. Scott Fitzgerald,* pp. 464–69.

How to Live on $36,000 a Year

By F. Scott Fitzgerald

In 1923 the Fitzgeralds spent $36,000 at Great Neck, while he earned $28,760. This article in The Saturday Evening Post *(5 April 1924) humorously accounts for his financial debacle.*

The Fitzgeralds On Long Island

The Fitzgeralds moved from St. Paul, Minnesota, to Great Neck, Long Island, in October 1922. The ostensible reason for the move was to be near New York for the expected Broadway production of his play, The Vegetable; *but they were bored in St. Paul and wanted to be near the stimulation of New York. Great Neck is a suburb of the city and at that time was favored by show-business people. The social diversions in Great Neck interfered with Fitzgerald's writing, and his drinking increased. He described their life in "How to Live on $36,000 a Year."*

[Great Neck] is one of those little towns springing up on all sides of New York which are built especially for those who have made money suddenly but have never had money before.

. . . .

It was an exquisite summer and it became a habit with many world-weary New Yorkers to pass their week-ends at the Fitzgerald house in the country. Along near the end of a balmy and insidious August I realized with a shock that only three chapters of my novel were done.

. . . .

But the play was going into rehearsal in two months. To tide over the interval there were two courses open to me— I could sit down and write some short stories or I could continue to work on the novel and borrow the money to live on. Lulled into a sense of security by our sanguine anticipations I decided on the latter course, and my publishers lent me enough to pay our bills until the opening night.

So I went back to my novel, and the months and money melted away; but one morning in October I sat in the cold interior of a New York theater and heard the cast read through the first act of my play. It was magnificent; my estimate had been too low. I could almost hear the people scrambling for seats, hear the ghostly voices of the movie magnates as they bid against one another for the picture rights. The novel was now laid aside; my days were spent at the theatre and my nights in revising and improving the two or three little weak spots in what was to be the success of the year.

. . . .

The play opened in Atlantic City in November. It was a colossal frost. People left their seats and walked out, people rustled their programs and talked audibly in bored impatient whispers. After the second act I wanted to stop the show and say it was all a mistake but the actors struggled heroically on.

. . . .

Over our garage is a large bare room whither I now retired with a pencil, paper and the oil stove, emerging the next afternoon at five o'clock with a 7,000-word story. That was something; it would pay the rent and last month's overdue bills. It took twelve hours a day for five weeks to rise from abject poverty back into the middle class, but within that time we had paid our debts, and the cause for immediate worry was over.

* * *

The expression Break out
a comfortable but dangerous
and deteriorating year at
great heart. No ground under our feet.

Twenty six years old

Sept — Went New York from Commodore. Left Anna with Baby. Play rejected. Lived at Plaza. House hunting. The Boyds (Earliest) Anderson & Dos Passos. Twente

Oct — Took house on Gateway Drive, great neck. Zelda went west + got baby. Met Lardners, Bucks, Swopes. The Foxes
St. Patricks parade. Maury & ____ Bros + on steps of St Patricks a saturnine thursday of fat, favorite, secular priest.

Nov — More Ring Lardner. Wrote play over for third time. Janet. Bucks to Princeton. Selves + Val come out. Grace Flandreau out

Dec — A series of parties — The Boyds, Mary Blair, Chas + Katy. Charlie Towne.

1923 Jan — Hearst contract. Chas + Katy leave. Val Engalitcheff ill & nursing. My dream of the baseball player, football player + general to put me to sleep. Minimic girl at Milbank party. Two kids drunk whiskey. They ____ it.

Feb — Still drunk — story for Townsend. Reynolds and the outlet "Say Fitzgerald". William and Salley. Tom Smith + Dreser + Mencken + Anderson.

March — Sold This Side of Paradise + South to Montgomery. Dapper Dan. The Whitfields. Kalmans in new york. Party with The Boyds. Bunny marries. Eleanor Wylie William drunk ____. Fight et mon: Bill. Tom Boyds Book accepted

April — Third anniversary. On the wagon. Joined club here. Duncan Pell and his wife. Party with Barthelmess - another fight. Tearing drunk. Tom. I should have asked Julia Everson if he wanted the suitcase for the silver.

May — Play accepted by williams. Met Mrs Rumsey + Tommy Hitchcock + went to parties there. Visits from Biggs, Esther murphy. Katie Drewry and mary wristong. Fight with Helen Bucks brother in law.

June — Eleanor Browder came. Party at Clarence mackays. Began unwell. Squabble at Kings. Party in new york with _____ and nathan. Anita Loos out. The Coysystyns become obnoxious. Augustus Tolyus Laurette Taylor. _____ Edesco "Only write for intellectual"

July — Tootsie arrived. Intermittent work on a novel. Constant drinking. Some golf. Baby begins to talk. Parties at Allen Dwans. _____ Sibaurson and the movie crowd. Our party for Tootsie. The Perkins arrive. I drove into the lake.

Aug — Tootsie again. More drinking. Opening of Anita Loos play. Loe's party. Aunt Annabel + Don Stuart. Firpo-Dempsey fight

Fitzgerald's Ledger *(Washington, D.C.: Bruccoli Clark/Microcard Edition, 1972) includes a month-by-month catalogue of professional and personal events, organized by the years of his life (September to August). Each year is headed with Fitzgerald's judgment on his activities. Events and people that went into the gestation of* The Great Gatsby *are noted in the page above: his friendship with Ring Lardner and parties given by Herbert Bayard Swope, Allen Dwann, Clarence Mackay, and other Long Islanders.*

Monthly Expenditure 1923		
TAXES	200.00	
RENT	300.00	
FOOD	200.00	
COAL + WOOD	35.00	
ICE	8.50	
GAS	27.00	
LIGHT	14.50	
PHONE	25.00	
WATER	5.00	
SERVANTS	295.00	
DOCTORS	42.50	
DRUG STORE	32.50	
CLUB	105.50	
NEWSPAPERS	5.00	
BOOKS	14.50	
FLOWERS	9.00	
AUTO	23.00	
PLUMBER	13.50	
ELECTRIC	1.50	
COMUTATION	4.00	
SCOTT'S CLOTHES	33.00	
Zelda's CLOTHES	100.00	
BABY'S CLOTHES	25.00	
HOUSEHOLD AND MISSCLANEUS CHARGES	81.00	
TYPING	12.00	
	1620.40	

TRIPS, PLEASURE + PARTIES

		(apportioned per 1 mo)
House LIQUOR	80.00	"
PLAZA	26.50	"
ALABAMA	433.00	"
ATLANTIC CITY	10.00	"
THEATRE	20.00	"
BARBER	10.00	"
HAIR DRESSING	15.00	"
CHARITY	4.00	"
WILD PARTIES	100.00	"
Taxis	15.00	"
Gambling	33.00	"
LUNCHES (N.Y)	25.00	"
SUBWAY (ect)	29.00	"
Miscelaeneous Cash	276.00	"
	785.60	
	1620.40	
	2396.00	

Fitzgerald's budget for the cost of living in Great Neck. The rubric for "Subway (ect)" allowed for 580 New York City subway rides per month (Matthew J. and Arlyn Bruccoli Collection, University of South Carolina).

Ring Lardner in Great Neck with his sons: Ring Jr., James, David, and John—all of whom became writers

Ring Lardner

Fitzgerald formed a close friendship in Great Neck with Ring Lardner, the famous sports columnist, humorist, and short-story writer. Lardner, an alcoholic, may have been a source for Owl Eyes and was the model for Abe North in Tender Is the Night *(1934). Lardner maintained a mock courtship with Zelda and wrote that "F. Scott Fitzgerald is a novelist, and his wife is a novelty."*

Fitzgerald, who was concerned that Lardner was neglecting his career, brought him to his editor Maxwell Perkins. Scribners' publication of Lardner's collection How to Write Short Stories *(1924), which Fitzgerald probably titled, resulted in a critical reassessment of Lardner as a serious writer.*

When Lardner died in 1933, Fitzgerald wrote a moving tribute to his friend: "Let us not obscure him by the flowers, but walk up and look at that fine medallion, all abraded by sorrows that perhaps we are not equipped to understand."

For a year and a half, the writer of this appreciation was Ring Lardner's most familiar companion, after that, geography made separations and our contacts were rare. When my wife and I last saw him in 1931, he looked already like a man on his deathbed—it was terribly sad to see that six feet three inches of kindness stretched out ineffectual in the hospital room. His fingers trembled with a match, the tight skin on his handsome skull was marked as a mask of misery and nervous pain.

He gave a very different impression when we first saw him in 1921—he seemed to have an abundance of quiet vitality that would enable him to outlast anyone, to take himself for long spurts of work or play that would ruin any ordinary constitution. He had recently convulsed the country with the famous kitten-and-coat saga (it had to do with a world's series bet and with the impending conversion of some kittens into fur), and the evidence of the betting, a beautiful sable, was worn by his wife at the time. In those days he was interested in people, sports, bridge, music, the stage, the newspapers, the magazines, the books. But though I did not know it, the change in him had already begun—the impenetrable despair that dogged him for a dozen years to his death.

He had practically given up sleeping, save on short vacations deliberately consecrated to simple pleasures, most frequently golf with his friends, Grantland Rice or John Wheeler. many anight we talked over a case of Canadian ale until bright dawn, when Ring would rise and yawn: "Well, I guess the children have left for school by this time—I might as well go home."

–*"Ring"* (1933)

* * *

The Great Gatsby as Social History

Matthew J. Bruccoli

For a long time, *The Great Gatsby* was classified as "a book about the Roaring Twenties." It is one of those novels that so richly evoke the texture of their time that they become, in the fullness of time, more than literary classics; they become a supplementary or even substitute form of history. It is surprising that this statement should apply to a work by F. Scott Fitzgerald, for in certain ways the historiographer of the Jazz Age (which he named) was ill-equipped for the task.

He was not a documentary writer. John O'Hara paid him the tribute of declaring: "He always knew what he was writing about. . . . Scott Fitzgerald had the correct impressions because, quite apart from his gifts, the impressions were not those of a man who's never been there."[1] Although O'Hara carefully repeated the word "impressions," the implication that Fitzgerald was a master reporter is overgenerous. His control of detail was not as sharp or comprehensive as O'Hara's. The most famous car in American fiction is never identified. Fitzgerald may have felt that to stipulate its make would render the "circus wagon"/ "death car" less extraordinary—it would have become just a Pierce-Arrow or Stutz or Duesenberg. Instead, he treated the vehicle impressionistically: "It was a rich cream color, bright with nickel, swollen here and there in its monstrous length with triumphant hatboxes and supper-boxes and tool-boxes, terraced with a labyrinth of wind-shields that mirrored a dozen suns" (p. 51). He relied on style to evoke a car appropriate for Gatsby. (Note Fitzgerald's characteristic use of the surprising adjective in "*triumphant* hatboxes.")

The Great Gatsby provides little in the way of sociological or anthropological data. Three cars are identified: Gatsby's Rolls-Royce (not his personal car), Nick's Dodge, and the "dust-covered wreck of a Ford which crouched in a dim corner" at Wilson's garage (p. 22). Three celebrities are named: Joe Frisco, Gilda Gray, and David Belasco—all from show business. Two criminals—Charles Becker and Herman Rosenthal—are mentioned. Yet Fitzgerald's invented list of the attendees at Gatsby's party has become a source for students of Prohibition society. The laureate of the Jazz Age had little interest in jazz. His music was the popular songs of the era, six of which are mentioned in the novel: "The Sheik of Araby," "The Love Nest," "Ain't We Got Fun?" "Three O'Clock in the Morning," "The Rosary," and "Beale Street Blues" (a 1917 jazz work by W. C. Handy that was a popular dance tune).

Although he had a keen sense of history, Fitzgerald was indifferent to many of the causes of the twenties. Despite his call for political and social change annexed to *This Side of Paradise* (1920), he soon abandoned that concern. He ignored the Sacco and Vanzetti case, which enlisted his

literary friends. When Fitzgerald came to write his 1931 postmortum, "Echoes of the Jazz Age," he observed: "It was characteristic of the Jazz Age that it had no interest in politics at all."[2] This generalization doesn't hold, but it applies to Fitzgerald. His claim that he had been influenced by *The Decline of the West*—"I read him [Spengler] the same summer I was writing *The Great Gatsby* and I don't think I ever quite recovered from him"[3]—does not bear scrutiny. *The Decline of the West* was not available in English in the summer of 1924.

Another subject of interest in the Twenties that Fitzgerald was ignorant of was the stock market. Nevertheless, he was able to convey the Eldorado mood that provides the background for *The Great Gatsby*. Nick Carraway decides to enter the investment field because "Everybody I knew was in the bond business" (p. 6). When James B. ("Rot-Gut") Ferret left the gambling table at Gatsby's party, "it meant that he was cleaned out and Associated Traction would have to fluctuate profitably next day" (p. 50). Gatsby is involved with Meyer Wolfshiem in a securities swindle, as well as bootlegging; but Fitzgerald was unable to document this activity. When Maxwell Perkins read the unrevised typescript, he noted that Gatsby's criminal activities were

Joe Frisco, the comedian and dancer who perfected the Black Bottom

Gilda Gray, star of the Ziegfeld Follies, *invented the dance called the Shimmy. Nick mentions her along with Joe Frisco in his account of Gatsby's party: "Suddenly one of these gypsies in trembling opal seizes a cocktail out of the air, dumps it down for courage and moving her hands like Frisco dances out alone on the canvas platform. A momentary hush; the orchestra leader varies his rhythm obligingly for her and there is a burst of chatter as the erroneous news goes around that she is Gilda Gray's understudy from the 'Follies.' The party has begun" (p. 34).*

vague. Fitzgerald admitted that the flaw resulted from his own ignorance: "But I know now—and as a penalty for not having known first, in other words make sure, I'm going to tell more."[4] Although Fitzgerald subsequently reported to Perkins that "I've accounted for his money,"[5] he supplied only clues that Gatsby was involved in illegal endeavors. His source was a man in Rome who briefed him on the 1922 Fuller–McGee Case, in which the partners in a New York brokerage firm were charged with misappropriating clients' funds. Arnold Rothstein, the remote source for Wolfshiem, was implicated.

Writing to Corey Ford from Hollywood a dozen years after *The Great Gatsby,* Fitzgerald described his method of treating material:

In *This Side of Paradise* (in a crude way) and in *Gatsby* I selected the stuff to fit a given mood or "hauntedness" or whatever you might call it, rejecting in advance in *Gatsby,* for instance, all the ordinary material for Long Island, big

crooks, adultery theme and always starting from the *small* focal point that impressed me—my own meeting with Arnold Rothstein, for instance.[6]

Fitzgerald did not work directly from models; he did not attempt to copy life. He transmuted his impressions. "Whether it's something that happened twenty years ago or only yesterday, I must start out with an emotion—one that's close to me and that I can understand."[7]

The figure who controls Gatsby's mysterious wealth is a travesty of Rothstein. Fitzgerald attempted to document Wolfshiem's criminal background through his reminiscences of the 1912 Rosenthal–Becker murder case, but the facts are distorted to accommodate Wolfshiem's sentimentality. Except for the touch of menace provided by his human-molar cufflinks, Wolfshiem is a caricature racketeer—as is Gatsby in different ways. O'Hara, one of Fitzgerald's staunchest admirers, commented: "I fully believed Gatsby until I went to NY and met some of those mob people. Gatsby would not have lasted a week with the ones I met, let alone taken control."[8]

Despite inaccuracies and absurdities, *The Great Gatsby* has become a source for historians because of Fitzgerald's sense of time, of the emotions evoked by particular moments. Many writers have been distinguished by a sense of the past; Fitzgerald possessed a complex and delicate sense of the passing present. Malcolm Cowley has observed that Fitzgerald wrote as if surrounded by clocks and calendars.

Fitzgerald's primary concern was with the rhythms, the colors, the tones associated with time and place—often

Theater producer David Belasco, whose sets were notable for their realism. Owl Eyes refers to Gatsby as "a regular Belasco" (p. 38)

TIME (87)

night have the decency not to telephone him at dinner	time.	
true." She hesitated. "Well, I've had a very bad	time,	
"Ten o'clock," she remarked, apparently finding the	time	
remarked, apparently finding the time on the ceiling.	"Time	
I have been drunk just twice in my life, and the second	time	
been married. Mrs. Wilson had changed her costume some	time.	
shout, "most of these fellas will cheat you every	time.	
"These people! You have to keep after them all the	time."	
all in two days in the private rooms. We had an awful	time	
toward the park through the soft twilight, but each	time	
shoes, and I couldn't keep my eyes off him, but every	time	
looking with blind eyes through the smoke, and from	time	
with blind eyes through the smoke, and from time to	time	
for each other, found each other a few feet away. Some	time.	
said. "I never care what I do, so I always have a good	time?	
sport? Just near the shore along the Sound." "What	time?	
near the shore along the Sound." "What time?" "Any	time	
when Jordan looked around and smiled. "Having a gay	time	
formality of speech just missed being absurd. Some	time	
mornings. I was alone and it was almost two. For some	time	
raised voices. "Whenever he sees I'm having a good	time	
among the last to go, as if he had desired it all the	time,	
din from those in the rear had been audible for some	time,	
infinitely less than my personal affairs. Most of the	time	
who loitered in front of windows waiting until it was	time	
somewhere between his cocktails and his flowers. "One	time	
glass." Once I wrote down on the empty spaces of a	time	
who came to Gatsby's house that summer. It is an old	time	
of melody from its three-noted horn. It was the first	time	
agreed the policeman, tipping his cap. "Know you next	time,	
Queensboro Bridge is always the city seen for the first	time."	
a friend. I told you we'd talk about that some other	time	
in the car." There was the smile again, but this	time?	
in the world." "Have you known Gatsby for a long	time,	
a way that every young girl wants to be looked at some	time,	
You can hold your tongue, and, moreover, you can	time	
six weeks ago, she heard the name Gatsby for the first	time	
mouth smiled, and so I drew her up again closer, this	time	
would interest you. It wouldn't take up much of your	time	
floor, and peering toward the bleared windows from	time	
and peering toward the bleared windows from time to	time	
his watch as if there was some pressing demand on his	time	
central bay, spat meditatively into the garden. It was	time	
the poor get—children. In the meantime, In between	time,	
into it with a creative passion, adding to it all the	time,	
leaving them there together. CHAPTER VI ABOUT this	time,	
an hour. I suppose he'd had the same ready for a long	time,	
even faintly true. Moreover he told it to me at a	time	
me go," she whispered. "If you want to kiss me any	time	
she'd been alone with Gatsby she wasn't having a good	time.	
didn't like it," he insisted. "She didn't have a good	time."	
of lost words, that I had heard somewhere a long	time	
. . . and as for your bothering me about it at lunch	time,	
if he had just recognized her as someone he knew a long	time	
whereupon Jordan whispered, "Excuse me"—but this	time	
and insulting! "You must have gone there about the	time,	
meet. But both of us loved each other all that	time."	
I always come back, and in my heart I love her all the	time.	
little stunts. I picked him for a bootlegger the first	time	
was talking to him in a low voice and attempting, from	time	
to him in a low voice and attempting, from time to	time,	
into the path. I must have felt pretty weird by that	time,	
I can't be sure." I disliked him so much by this	time.	
slip from his shoulders. So he made the most of his	time.	
the use of doing great things if I could have a better	time.	
he sat with Daisy in his arms for a long, silent	time.	
dying orchids on the floor beside her bed. And all the	time	
if we'd been in ecstatic cahoots on that fact all the	time	
open for long distance from Detroit. Taking out my	time	
knew every object in it before morning—and from	time	
every object in it before morning—and from time to	time?	
Maybe even if you haven't been there for a long	time.	
Didn't you get married in a church?" "That was a long	time,	
look back into the room. But Wilson stood there a long	time,	
Wilson was gone. His movements—he was on foot all the	time	
Thus far there was no difficulty in accounting for his	time	
"had a way of finding out," supposed that he spent that	time	
he asked someone the way to Gatsby's house. So by that	time	
on Broadway, and I called Information, but by the	time	
and when he looked around him now for the first	time,"	
"You young men think you can force your way in here any	time	
office, remarking in a reverent voice that it was a sad	time	
because he couldn't buy some regular clothes. First	time	
7.00–9.00 " GENERAL RESOLVES No wasting	time	
for other cars. So did Gatsby's father. And as the	time	
from prep school and later from college at Christmas	time.	
understood nor desired, face to face for the last	time	

Don't you think?" Almost before I had grasped her	19.4
Nick, and I'm pretty cynical about everything."	20.25
on the ceiling. "Time for this good girl to go to	22.20
for this good girl to go to bed." "Jordan's going to	22.20
was that afternoon; so everything that happened has a	35.1
before, and was now attired in an elaborate afternoon	36.15
All they think of is money. I had a woman up here	37.1
She looked at me and laughed pointlessly. Then she	38.12
getting back, I can tell you. God, how I hated that	41.8
I tried to go I became entangled in some wild, strident	43.3
he looked at me I had to pretend to be looking at the	43.20
to time groaning faintly. People disappeared,	44.20
groaning faintly. People disappeared, reappeared, made	44.21
toward midnight Tom Buchanan and Mrs. Wilson stood face	44.24
When I was here last I tore my gown on a chair, and he	52.21
"Any time that suits you best." It was on the tip of	58.1
that suits you best." It was on the tip of my tongue	58.2
now?" she inquired. "Much better." I turned again to	58.5
before he introduced himself I'd got a strong	59.3
confused and intriguing sounds had issued from a long,	62.1
he wants to go home." "Never heard anything so selfish	63.14
"Good night, old sport. . . . Good night." But as I	65.9
and added to the already violent confusion of the	65.21
I worked. In the early morning the sun threw my shadow	68.18
for a solitary restaurant dinner—young clerks in the	69.27
he killed a man who had found out that he was nephew to	73.8
-table the names of those who came to Gatsby's house	73.12
-table now, disintegrating at its folds, and headed	73.14
he had called on me, though I had gone to two of his	76.14
Mr. Gatsby. Excuse me!" "What was that?" I	82.10
in its first wild promise of all the mystery and the	82.22
"I beg your pardon," said Mr. Wolfshiem, "I had a	85.18
I held out against it. "I don't like mysteries," I	86.4
I inquired. "Several years," he answered in a	86.27
and because it seemed romantic to me I have remembered	91.2
any little irregularity of your own so that everybody	94.3
in years. It was when I asked you—do you	94.9
to my face. CHAPTER V WHEN I came home to West Egg	97.8
and you might pick up a nice bit of money. It happens	100.10
to time as if a series of invisible but alarming	102.18
as if a series of invisible but alarming happenings	102.18
elsewhere. "I can't wait all day." "Don't be silly;	102.26
I went back. While the rain continued it had seemed	107.19
—" As I went over to say good-by I saw that the	115.29
decking it out with every bright feather that drifted	116.11
an ambitious young reporter from New York arrived one	117.2
even then. His parents were shiftless and	118.12
of confusion, when I had reached the point of believing	122.3
during the evening, Nick, just let me know and I'll be	126.15
We were at a particularly tipsy table. That was my	128.10
He was silent, and I guessed at his unutterable	132.17
ago. For a moment a phrase tried to take shape in my	134.23
I won't stand that at all!" "Holding down the	138.26
ago. "You resemble the advertisement of the man," she	142.22
no one laughed. "I'll pick it up," I offered. "I've	152.12
Biloxi went to New Haven." Another pause. A waiter	154.22
old sport, and you didn't know. I used to laugh	157.20
"You're revolting," said Daisy. She turned to me,	158.11
I saw him, and I wasn't far wrong." "What about it?"	161.6
to time, to lay a hand on his shoulder, but Wilson	167.11
to lay a hand on his shoulder, but Wilson neither	167.11
because I could think of nothing except the luminosity	172.6
that I didn't find it necessary to tell him he was	172.29
He took what he could get, ravenously and	178.18
telling her what I was going to do?" On the last	180.6
It was a cold fall day, with fire in the room and her	180.9
something within her was crying for a decision. She	181.23
His gorgeous pink rag of a suit made a bright spot of	185.9
-table, I drew a small circle around the three-fifty	187.2
to time sat down beside Wilson trying to keep him more	189.7
sat down beside Wilson trying to keep him more quiet.	189.7
Maybe I could call up the church and get a priest to	189.11
ago." The effort of answering broke the rhythm of his	189.19
his face close to the window pane, nodding into the	192.15
—were afterward traced to Port Roosevelt and then to	192.25
—there were boys who had seen a man "acting sort of	193.3
going from garage to garage thereabout, inquiring for a	193.9
he knew Gatsby's name. At two o'clock Gatsby put on	193.16
I had the number it was long after five, and no one	198.9
and saw the height and splendor of the hall and the	201.29
she scolded. "We're getting sickantired of it. When	205.9
for all of us, and offered me a cigar. "My memory goes	205.18
I saw him was when he come into Winebrenner's poolroom	205.25
at Shafters or [a name, indecipherable] No more	208.26
passed and the servants came in and stood waiting in	209.20
Those who went farther than Chicago would gather in	211.6
in history with something commensurate to his capacity	217.29

The noun "time" is the most frequently used theme-word in the novel, with eighty-seven appearances (Andrew Crosland, A Concordance to F. Scott Fitzgerald's The Great Gatsby *[Detroit: Bruccoli Clark/Gale, 1974]).*

James J. Hill (1838–1916), financier who organized the Great Northern Railway and the Northern Pacific. He was the leading figure in St. Paul, Minnesota, when Fitzgerald grew up there. Gatsby's father compares his son to Hill: "If he'd of lived he'd been a great man. A man like James J. Hill. He'd of helped build up the country" (p. 131).

expressed through synesthesia, as in "yellow cocktail music" (p. 34). Time and place are inseparable in Fitzgerald: not just how it was, but how it felt in "a transitory enchanted moment" (p. 140). He later wrote, "After all, any given moment has its value; it can be questioned in the light of after-events, but the moment remains."[9] His task was to fix and preserve evanescent experience. Fitzgerald's sense of mood was extraordinary: the summer twilight in New York, the riotous Long Island nights, the Chicago railroad station at holiday time (yet he stipulated the wrong station before Ring Lardner corrected it). These passages have become touchstones of American prose.

At the end of "Echoes of the Jazz Age" he observed: "and it all seems rosy and romantic to us who were young then, because we will never feel quite as intensely about our surroundings any more."[10] This theme is not the same as the familiar *ubi sunt* (Where are?) formula. Fitzgerald and his heroes do not yearn for the melted snows of yesteryear; they mourn for their lost capacity to respond to those snows: "the snow of twenty-nine wasn't real snow. If you didn't want it to be snow, you just paid some money."[11]

The strongest feeling generated by *The Great Gatsby* is regret. It is not regret keyed to mutability.

Fitzgerald evokes regret for depleted emotional capacity, a regret as intense as the emotions that inspired it were. While he was writing *The Great Gatsby*, Fitzgerald explained: "That's the whole burden of this novel—the loss of those illusions that give such color to the world that you don't care whether things are true or false as long as they partake of the magical glory."[12]

The Great Gatsby is time-haunted from "In my younger and more vulnerable years" to "borne back ceaselessly into the past." There are at least 450 time words in the novel.[13] Exclusive of character names, the second most frequent noun is *time*, with 87 occurrences. (*House* appears 95 times.) *Moment* or *moments* occur 73 times; *day* or *days*, 70; *minute* or *minutes*, 49; *hour* or *hours*, 47; *o'clock*, 26; *year*, 19; *past*, 18 (as against 5 appearances of *future*); *month* or *months*, 15; *week* or *weeks*, 15; *twilight*, 9; *clock*, 6; *watch* (noun), 5; *time-table*, 3. The first striking image in the novel is the Buchanans' lawn "jumping over sundials" (p. 9).

In Chapter 5, the fulcrum of the nine-chapter novel, when Gatsby is reunited with Daisy, his "head leaned back so far that it rested against the face of a defunct mantelpiece clock" (p. 68). A moment later Gatsby almost knocks the clock off the mantle, "whereupon he turned and caught it with trembling fingers and set it back in place" (p. 68). The irony of this symbolism may be too blatant: Gatsby, the time defier, rescues a defunct timepiece, but time will put him "back in place." When Gatsby takes Daisy to tour his house later in this chapter, Klipspringer plays the piano and Fitzgerald provides the lyric:

> In the morning,
> In the evening,
>   Ain't we got fun—
>
> . . .
>
> In the meantime,
> In between time—

And when Daisy leaves Gatsby's party in the next chapter, the orchestra is playing "Three O'Clock in the Morning"—"a neat, sad little waltz of that year" (p. 85).

Fitzgerald's treatment of time with the effect of simultaneous detachment and involvement—what Cowley described as "double vision"[14]—reinforces the permeation of realism and imagination that identifies his best fiction. Thus, Nick jots down the names of the people who came to Gatsby's parties on a timetable headed "This schedule in effect July 5th, 1922" (p. 49). Such horology fosters the impression of historical truth—which is not the same as straight history.

—Revised from "Introduction,"
New Essays on The Great Gatsby
(New York: Cambridge University Press, 1985)

Photograph of Max Gerlach printed in the New York Evening Journal *(18 January 1930), during a psittacosis scare*

Notes

1. John O'Hara, Introduction to *The Portable F. Scott Fitzgerald* (New York: Viking Press, 1945), p. xii.
2. *Scribner's Magazine* (November 1931): 459–465. Reprinted in *The Crack-Up*.
3. "To Maxwell Perkins," *The Letters of F. Scott Fitzgerald*, ed. Andrew Turnbull (New York: Scribners, 1963), pp. 289–290.
4. Turnbull, p. 173.
5. Turnbull, p. 177.
6. Turnbull, p. 551.
7. "One Hundred False Starts," *The Saturday Evening Post,* March 4, 1933, pp. 13, 65–66.
8. *Selected Letters of John O'Hara,* ed. Matthew J. Bruccoli (New York: Random House, 1978), p. 425.
9. "Six of One–," *Redbook,* 58 (February 1932): 22–25, 86, 88. Collected in *The Price Was High* (New York: Harcourt Brace Jovanovich/Bruccoli Clark, 1979).
10. See Jackson R. Bryer and G. T. Tanselle, "*The Great Gatsby*–A Study in Literary Reputation," *New Mexico Quarterly,* 33 (Winter 1963–1964): 409–425; also Bryer, *F. Scott Fitzgerald: The Critical Reception* (New York: Franklin, 1978).
11. "Babylon Revisited," *The Saturday Evening Post,* February 21, 1931, pp. 3–5, 82–84. Collected in *Taps at Reveille.*
12. To Ludlow Fowler, *Correspondence of F. Scott Fitzgerald,* ed. Matthew J. Bruccoli and Margaret Duggan (New York: Random House, 1980), p. 145.
13. Andrew T. Crosland, *Concordance to* The Great Gatsby (Detroit: Gale Research, 1975).
14. "Fitzgerald: The Double Man," *Saturday Review of Literature,* February 24, 1951, pp. 9–10, 42–44.

SOURCES FOR JAY GATSBY

"How Are You and the Family, Old Sport?" – Gerlach and Gatsby
Matthew J. Bruccoli

The connection between Jay Gatsby and a Long Island bootlegger named "von Guerlach or something" seems more likely with the identification of a 20 July 1923 note to F. Scott Fitzgerald from a Gerlach who, Gatsby-like, addressed him as *old sport*. Fitzgerald preserved this note, which was written on a newspaper photo of the Fitzgeralds, in his scrapbook.

Henry Dan Piper reports that near the end of her life Zelda Fitzgerald told him about "a neighbor named von Guerlach or something who was said to be General Pershing's nephew and was in trouble over bootlegging."[1] And Edmund Wilson's use of a "gentleman bootlegger named Max Fleischman" in his 1924 play "The Crime in the Whistle Room" originated from Fitzgerald's description of such a character to Wilson. In his copy of this play collected in Wilson's *This Room and This Gin and These Sandwiches* Fitzgerald noted: "I had told Bunny my plan for Gatsby."[2] A considerable search has failed to reveal little more about this Gerlach or von Gerlach.[3] In 1930 the *New York Evening Journal* ran a photo of "Max Gerlach, wealthy yachtsman" kissing his parrot during a psittacosis scare.[4] Since "yachtsman" was sometimes a euphemism for rumrunner, it is possible that this Max Gerlach was the man Fitzgerald knew.

In 1939 Max Gerlach, a used-car dealer in Flushing, New York, blinded himself in a suicide attempt. He died in 1958.[5]

Fitzgerald/Hemingway Annual 1975
(Englewood, Colo.: Microcard Editions, 1975)

Notes

1. Piper to Bruccoli, 22 April 1974. Since Zelda Fitzgerald supplied the name "von Gerlach" in conversation, Piper's spelling is conjectural.
2. Bunny was Edmund Wilson's nickname.
3. Joseph Corso did much of the searching.
4. 18 January 1930, p. 3. Courtesy of John Payne and Sally Leach, University of Texas Library.
5. The New York City Department of Health refuses to make Max von Gerlach's death certificate available. His probate file has not been located. In 1951 and 1954 Gerlach contacted Arthur Mizener offering information about Fitzgerald; Mizener failed to act on these opportunities.

Gatsby's defining expression, "old sport," was used by Max Gerlach in a 1923 note to Fitzgerald (Fitzgerald's Scrapbook, Princeton University Library). The earliest Oxford English Dictionary citation for "old sport" is from 1905.

James Gatz—that was really, or at least legally, his name. He had changed it at the age of seventeen and at the specific moment that witnessed the beginning of his career—when he saw Dan Cody's yacht drop anchor over the most insidious flat on Lake Superior. It was James Gatz who had been loafing along the beach that afternoon in a torn green jersey and a pair of canvas pants, but it was already Jay Gatsby who borrowed a row-boat, pulled out to the *Tuolomee* and informed Cody that a wind might catch him and break him up in half an hour. . . .

Cody was fifty years old then, a product of the Nevada silver fields, of the Yukon, of every rush for metal since Seventy-five. The transactions in Montana copper that made him many times a millionaire found him physically robust but on the verge of softmindedness, and suspecting this an infinite number of women tried to separate him from his money. The none too savory ramifications by which Ella Kaye, the newspaper woman, played Madame de Maintenon to his weakness and sent him to sea in a yacht, were common knowledge to the turgid journalism of 1902. He had been coasting along all too hospitable shores for five years when he turned up as James Gatz's destiny in Little Girl Bay.

To young Gatz, resting on his oars and looking up at the railed deck, that yacht represented all the beauty and glamor in the world. I suppose he smiled at Cody—he had probably discovered that people liked him when he smiled. At any rate Cody asked him a few questions (one of them elicited the brand new name) and found that he was quick, and extravagantly ambitious. A few days later he took him to Duluth and bought him a blue coat, six pair of white duck trousers and a yachting cap. And when the *Tuolomee* left for the West Indies and the Barbary Coast Gatsby left too.

—*The Great Gatsby*, pp. 76–78

Robert C. Kerr Jr. (courtesy of Doris Kerr Brown)

yacht would tilt more and more and probably break in two. So I rowed along side and yelled to one of the crew, "Hey, Mister, you're going to break your boat!"*

The Captain waved the boy away, but the owner told the boy to come on board.

"What do you do?" he asked, and I told him.

"How'd you like to work for me?" he next asked. "I'll give you $25 a week."

I was barefoot and in old clothes, tanned and dirty. . . . I had only old clothes at the beach . . . so he took me to Jim Bell's . . . and had me outfitted completely, with blue coat with brass buttons and white flannels. O, it was great!

These curiously familiar recollections might belong to a diary account by James Gatz of North Dakota, or to a draft of the scene F. Scott Fitzgerald put into Chapter VI of *The Great Gatsby*. But they are from a *Great Neck News* account of the adventures of fourteen-year-old Robert Crozier Kerr Jr. on Sheepshead Bay in Brooklyn, New York. The year was 1907 and the yacht belonged to Edward Robinson Gilman, general manager of Iron Clad Manufacturing Company of 23 Cliff Street, Brooklyn, New York.

*Fitzgerald wrote that "Jay Gatsby borrowed a row-boat, pulled out to the *Tuolomee* and informed Cody that the ebb-tide would catch him and break him up in half an hour." After Ring and Rex Lardner informed Perkins that there are no tides in Lake Superior, the editor emended the reading to "a wind might catch him" (p. 76). There are no clams or salmon in Lake Superior, but these readings were not emended.

Gatsby and Robert Kerr

Joseph Corso

The link between Jay Gatsby and Fitzgerald's Great Neck friend, Robert Kerr, was first explicated by Joseph Corso in his essay "One Not-Forgotten Summer Night: Sources for Fictional Symbols of American Character in The Great Gatsby*" (Fitzgerald/Hemingway Annual 1976). This revised version of the essay utilizes details from Brooke Kroeger's* Nellie Bly *(New York: Times Books, 1994).*

Fitzgerald's list of sources for The Great Gatsby *assigns "Bob Kerr's story" to Chapter VI.*

One day I was out in the Bay when I noticed a handsome, big yacht had come into the harbor—one of the finest I'd ever seen and, with a kid's curiosity, I made for it.

I noticed they'd run it in so the stern was up and I realized that when the tide ran out, as it was sure to do, the

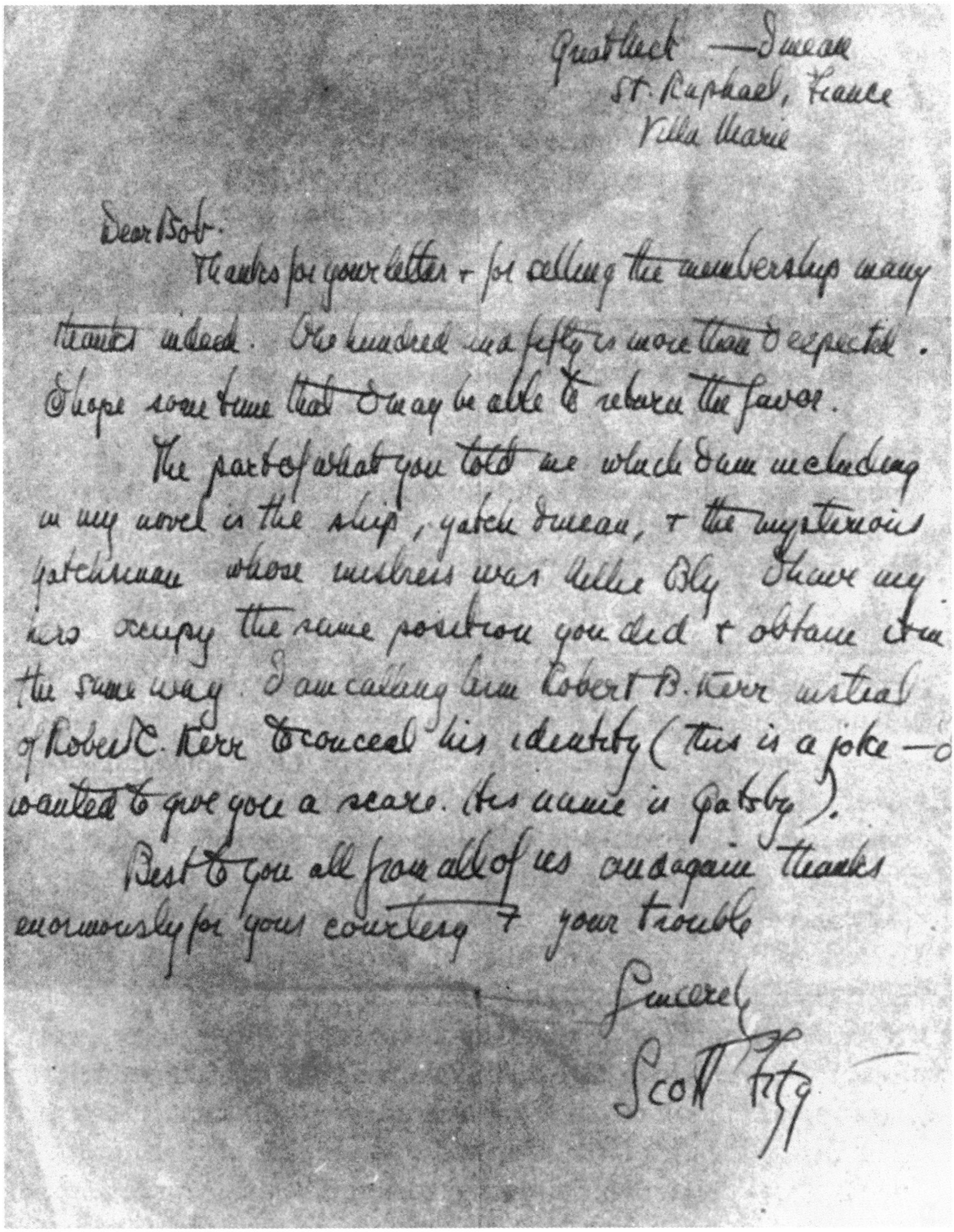

Great luck — Scott
St. Raphael, France
Villa Marie

Dear Bob:

Thanks for your letter + for selling the membership many thanks indeed. One hundred and fifty is more than I expected. I hope some time that I may be able to return the favor.

The part of what you told me which I am including in my novel is the ship, yacht Drean, + the mysterious patchman whose mistress was Nellie Bly. I have my hero occupy the same position you did + obtain it in the same way. I am calling him Robert B. Kerr instead of Robert C. Kerr to conceal his identity (this is a joke — I wanted to give you a scare. His name is Gatsby).

Best to you all from all of us and again thanks enormously for your courtesy + your trouble

Sincerely
Scott Fitzg

Fitzgerald's 1924 letter to Robert Kerr at the time The Great Gatsby *was in the early stages of composition (courtesy of Doris Kerr Brown)*

Kerr was a Great Neck resident who became Fitzgerald's friend during 1922–1923. Jeweler, philanthropist, singer, piano player, and engaging personality, Kerr exchanged stories with Fitzgerald, one of which the author immortalized. That situation is a vivid illustration of how Fitzgerald utilized such phenomena in his fiction.

In June 1975 the Great Neck Library sponsored an exhibition, "F. Scott Fitzgerald and Great Neck in the 1920's." I had the honor and pleasure of contributing to the exhibition and addressing Great Neck residents on the subject one evening. On the last night of the exhibition, I was approached by two women. One of them introduced herself, and she introduced the other: "Mr. Corso, I would like you to meet the daughter of The Great Gatsby."

In fact, I was introduced to Doris Brown, daughter of Robert C. Kerr Jr., who as a child had grown up amid the zany doings in Great Neck during the Roaring Twenties. The exhibition had brought Mrs. Brown out with some memorabilia that had once belonged to her father. She produced for me several documents that not only illuminate Fitzgerald's reference to "Bob Kerr's story" in his chapter outline but also provide significant insights into the creative process in the making of "Jay Gatsby of West Egg, Long Island."

The most significant is Fitzgerald's letter to Kerr, the date of which can be placed around July 1924, when the Fitzgeralds were living at the Villa Marie in Valescure. The reference in the first paragraph is to Fitzgerald's membership in a local country club. The balance of the letter reveals that Kerr had told Fitzgerald a story about a yacht and a "mysterious yachtsman whose mistress was Nellie Bly." To

further clarify her father's story, Mrs. Brown produced both an inscribed first printing of *Gatsby* acknowledging Fitzgerald's use of Kerr's material and clippings from two Great Neck newspaper articles.

According to the first news article, Kerr met Major Edward R. Gilman in Sheepshead Bay almost exactly the way James Gatz met Dan Cody in Little Girl's Bay on Lake Superior. The second article paraphrases some of the first but further states:

> Yes sir, it was regular Horatio Alger stuff. . . . That was "From Rags to Riches" for fair, from a dirty dory to an immaculate yacht. Bob Kerr lived on board the boat acting as his employer's secretary for three and a half years, until Mr. Gilman died. At that time he was getting $75 a week and found. In time he developed his skill at the piano and in singing. Mr. Gilman had a fine entertainer as well as secretary on board. Also the youth had a fine training in business.

Born in 1863, Edward Robinson Gilman was an 1885 West Point graduate, but the rank of major was probably self-conferred. His West Point biography reads as follows:

> He was the son of the late Colonel Jeremiah H. Gilman, of Class of 1856, and was appointed to the Military Academy from Maine, his father's native state. He entered the Academy July 1, 1881, graduated June 13, 1885, and was thereupon appointed Second Lieutenant, Fifth Infantry. He joined his regiment at Fort Keogh, Montana.
>
> He resigned in June 1888, to enter business at St. Paul, Minnesota, as representative of the Thompson-Houston Electric Company (now General Electric Company) and established a large and prosperous business for his company in the Northwest.
>
> In 1890 or 1891 he went to Chicago and there organized the Great Western Electric Supply Co., of which he was president and general manager. In the financial panic in 1893 the company went out of business. Following this he took up residence in New York City, and for a time was connected with the Merriam Publishing Co. In 1899 he was employed to re-organize the Iron Clad Manufacturing Co. of Brooklyn, NY, of which he became general manager in 1900 and later, also of the American Steel Barrel Co. With these two he remained until his death.
>
> He was Democratic candidate for Congress from the Sixth District of New York in 1908 and was defeated. The nomination again was offered to him in the fall of 1910, but his health made acceptance impossible.
>
> Mr. Gilman was a member of the Army and Navy Club and Lawyers' Club of New York City, New York Yacht Club, The Carnarsie Yacht Club, The Automobile Club of America, and the Aero Club. He was vice-president of the Brooklyn Demo-

---

Fitzgerald chose the name *Tuolomee* for Dan Cody's yacht. It was an apt choice since Tuolumne County in California was the scene of considerable gold mining in the 1850s and 1860s. The key to understanding Fitzgerald's choice lies in the awareness that Mark Twain once lived in a mining camp on Jackass Hill in Tuolumne County, which he wrote about in *Roughing It*. Fitzgerald was probably aware of a much-publicized event which took place at Jackass Hill on 10 June 1922 while he was at Dellwood Lake in Minnesota. The *St. Paul Dispatch* was the only twin cities paper to carry the story, headlining the A.P. dispatch "TWAIN'S CABIN DEDICATED. Author Lived in Shack During California Gold Rush." The largest gold mine south of the town of Tuolumne was the Buchanan mine.

—Joseph Corso

Robert Seaman, circa 1896

Major Edward R. Gilman, the yachtsman who hired Robert Kerr as his factotum (Brooke Kroeger, Nellie Bly, 1994). Gilman, a source for Dan Cody, was manager of the Iron Clad Manufacturing Company, which Bly inherited from her husband, Robert Seaman.

Reporter Elizabeth Jane Cochran, who wrote under the byline Nellie Bly and in 1890 beat Phileas Fogg's fictional feat of circling the globe in eighty days

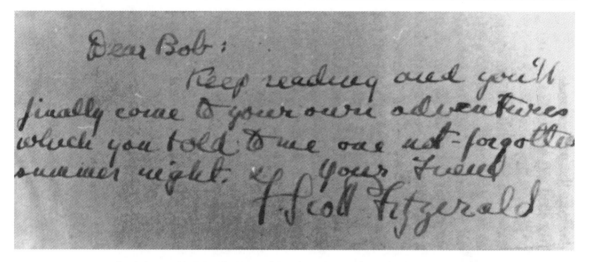

Inscription pasted in Robert Kerr's copy of The Great Gatsby *(courtesy of Doris Kerr Brown)*

cratic Club and president of the Waterway League of Greater New York and Long Island.

He never married, and was buried beside his father and mother, at Kensico, N.Y.

His sister Katherine, the wife of Dr. John E. MacKenty of New York City, survives him.

Edward Gilman died at Sheepshead Bay on 9 February 1911. He had a relationship with the most famous of early female reporters, Elizabeth Cochrane Seaman, popularly known as Nellie Bly. Fitzgerald's letter alludes to the alleged liaison, and his novel refers to "Ella Kaye, the newspaper woman" and her relationship with Dan Cody that was common knowledge to the turgid journalism of 1902. Nellie Bly was the most famous woman journalist of her time, celebrated for having emulated Phileas Fogg, the hero of Jules Verne's *Around the World in 80 Days*. In 1895 she had married Robert L. Seaman, the millionaire owner of the Iron Clad Manufacturing Company, which produced milk cans and other hardware items. He was seventy; she was thirty-one. At Seaman's death in 1904, his widow inherited the Iron Clad operation managed by Gilman, who had been hired by Seaman.

It is impossible to determine how much Kerr told Fitzgerald about Gilman. In the way that most novelists work, Fitzgerald combined Seaman (the elderly millionaire) with Gilman (the yachtsman who befriended Kerr) into Dan Cody. The novel stipulates that Cody was fifty, and Gilman was about forty-four when he employed Kerr.

When Robert Seaman died in 1904, very advanced in age and blind, Elizabeth Seaman was thirty-eight and Gilman was forty. Two wills were set forth within months of his death. According to *New York Times* articles of 17 June and 2 September 1904, Nellie Bly was able to claim everything Seaman left.

Bly had assumed her husband's responsibilities before his death, with the help of Gilman. The Iron Clad company steadily lost money after Seaman's death. When Gilman died it was discovered that he and others had looted and embezzled $450,000. A yacht valued at $25,000 was among the company's expenditures.

* * *

Gatsby and E. M. Fuller
Henry Dan Piper

Of all Fitzgerald's Long Island neighbors, the one whose outlines are most clearly discernible in *The Great Gatsby* was a certain Great Neck resident by the name of Edward M. Fuller. This was the Fuller of the "Fuller-McGee" case which Fitzgerald told Perkins he had studied until he felt he knew Gatsby better than he knew his own child. A thirty-nine-year-old bachelor and man about town, Fuller was president of the New York brokerage firm of E. M. Fuller and Co., with offices at 50 Broad Street. Of obscure origins, he had emerged suddenly on Wall Street in 1916 as a member of the Consolidated Stock Exchange and the head of his own company. Before long, he was being mentioned in the newspapers as one of a fashionable set that included Gertrude Vanderbilt, Charles A. Stoneham, the owner of the New York Giants baseball team, and Walter B. Silkworth, prominent clubman and president of the

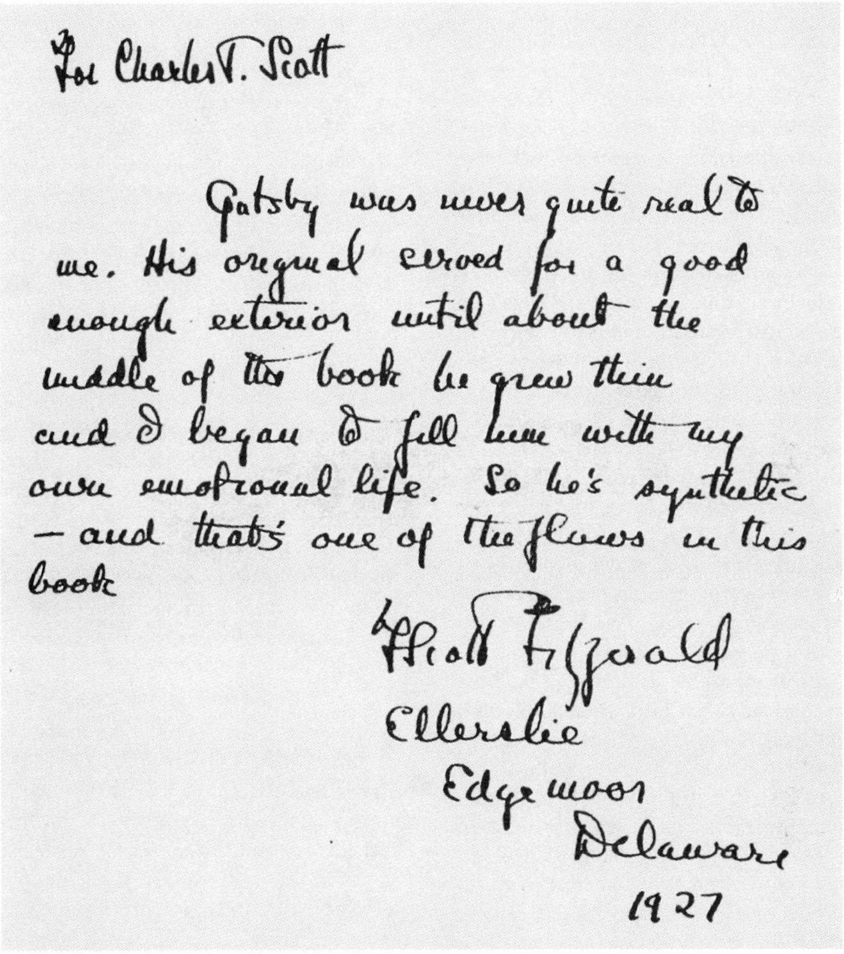

For Charles T. Scott

Gatsby was never quite real to
me. His original served for a good
enough exterior until about the
middle of the book he grew thin
and I began to fill him with my
own emotional life. So he's synthetic
— and that's one of the flaws in this
book

F Scott Fitzgerald
Ellerslie
Edgemoor
Delaware
1927

Fitzgerald responded to a fan letter with an admission of his dissatisfaction with the characterization of Gatsby (University of Michigan).

Consolidated Exchange. Fuller, an aviation enthusiast, was one of the first Long Island residents to commute weekly by airplane from his Great Neck estate to Atlantic City while the horse-racing season was on.

On June 22, 1922, however, E.M. Fuller and Co. declared itself bankrupt, with some six million dollars in debts and assets of less than seventy thousand dollars. Fuller and his vice-president, William F. McGee, were promptly indicted on a twelve-count charge that included operating a "bucket shop"–i.e., illegally gambling with their customers' funds. It took four trials to put them behind prison bars, and it is significant that the first opened two months after the Fitzgeralds moved to Great Neck, and ended several days later with a hung jury. The second trial, in December, ended in a mistrial after the state admitted its inability to produce a key witness, who had unaccountably disappeared. The third,

which began the following April, 1923, also resulted in a hung jury. During this trial it was revealed that Fuller's lawyer, a prominent New York attorney named William J. Fallon, had tried to bribe one of the jurors. For this Fallon was subsequently convicted and imprisoned, disgraced for life.

During this third trial, a leading state's witness was temporarily kidnapped by another of Fuller's attorneys, and vital records and other evidence also disappeared. By now the "Fuller-McGee" case was being featured on the front pages of the New York newspapers, and the fourth trial opened on June 11, 1923, amid a rash of rumors that Fuller and McGee were going to throw themselves on the mercy of the court and make a full confession. A deal had been arranged, it was reported, whereby they were to receive light sentences in exchange for confessions implicating a number of prominent New York officials, politicians, and businessmen with whom they had been associated in their financial ventures. Instead, however, both Fuller and McGee merely pleaded guilty to the more innocuous charges and were promptly sentenced to five years in Sing Sing– a sentence that was subsequently reduced to twelve months for "good behavior."

By coincidence, McGee's wife, a former New York showgirl named Louise Groody, arrived in Paris the same day that Fuller and her husband confessed their guilt. According to the Paris newspapers, Mrs. McGee disembarked from the liner at Cherbourg covered with diamonds and other jewels valued at several hundred thousand dollars. It was subsequently revealed that she had cashed a check of her husband's for $300,000 just a few hours before E. M. Fuller and Company went bankrupt.

Actually, the state of New York had difficulty establishing conclusive proof for most of the charges brought against Fuller and McGee. Nonetheless, it was obvious that they were part of a tangled web of corruption that included some of New York's wealthiest and most powerful business and political leaders. Fuller, according to his testimony, owed his business success mainly to his friendship with Charles A. Stoneham, another mysterious Gatsby-like figure who began life as a board boy in a broker's office and rose swiftly in the Wall Street financial hierachy, emerging eventually as president of the brokerage house of C. A. Stoneham and Company. In 1921, he had sold his firm's interest to E. M. Fuller and Co. and three other investment houses (E. D. Dier and Co., E. H. Clarke and Co., and Dillon and Co.) and plunged heavily into big-time gambling and sporting enterprises. Besides his controlling interest in the New York Giants baseball club, Stoneham owned a race track, a gambling casino, a newspaper, and other associated interests in Havana. By 1923, all four of the firms which had bought the assets of Stoneham and Co. had gone bankrupt, with debts totaling more than twenty million dollars.[1]

Fuller testified under oath that, after the dissolution of Stoneham and Co., Charles Stoneham had become a silent partner in the Fuller firm; he further claimed that his friend had advanced some two hundred thousand dollars in checks drawn against the Giants club, in a fruitless attempt to stave off Fuller and Co.'s impending bankruptcy. Stoneham insisted, however, that the money had merely been a private loan to Fuller, which he had advanced at the request of his friend Thomas F. Foley, former New York sheriff and Tammany Hall official. Foley, who had himself loaned Fuller $15,000, explained

that he had come to Fuller's assistance purely out of friendship for one of McGee's former wives, a certain Nellie Sheean, who had remarried and was now living in Paris (the residence, also, of the current Mrs. McGee).

Fuller and Company, it turned out, had a rather dubious financial history. In 1920, the firm was indicted for having systematically defrauded its customers over the past three years by sale of worthless oil securities, but the case was thrown out of court on the grounds of insufficient evidence. On February 24, 1923, while awaiting his third bankruptcy trial, Fuller was arrested on another charge along with seven other men and women, most of whom had criminal records. They were seized in a suite of the Hotel Embassy, where they were accused of having attempted to sell fraudulent securities over the telephone. It was further claimed by the police that Fuller and his friends were planning to organize a new securities firm for the purpose of selling worthless stocks. This case, however, was also dismissed by the court because of lack of evidence.

On June 13, 1922, Fuller had again been involved with the police, but under more romantic circumstances. On this occasion, his Broad Street offices had been invaded by "a fashionably dressed young lady" who, according to the New York *Times,* had threatened Fuller with severe bodily harm. Later, in the police court, the woman identified herself as Nellie Burke, twenty-seven, of 245 West Seventy-fifth Street. Miss Burke, who at the time of her arrest was wearing $20,000 worth of what she told newspaper reporters was "borrowed" jewelry, testified that she had become acquainted with Fuller in 1915, in the bar of the Hotel Knickerbocker. Their subsequent friendship had terminated in a breach-of-promise suit which she had brought against him in 1921. On June sixth of that year, she said, she had been visited by Fuller's friend and business associate, the notorious Arnold Rothstein, who had promised her $10,000 if she would sign a paper dropping the suit and agreeing not to pester Fuller any more. She had signed the paper and received $5,000 from Rothstein, but the rest of the money had been withheld. Her visit to Fuller's office the following June had, she claimed, been merely to collect the $5,000 in cash still due her. The magistrate found her guilty of assault but agreed to suspend sentence if she would promise not to give Fuller any more trouble. (Fuller's failure to pay her the additional $5,000 was explained several days later, on June twenty-second, when his firm went into bankruptcy!)

Many intimations of a mysterious tie between Fuller and the gambler, Arnold Rothstein, appeared during the Fuller trials, but the precise nature of this relationship was never fully clarified. Rothstein–"the walking bank, the pawnbroker of the underworld, the fugitive, unhealthy man who sidled along doorways," as Stanley Walker has described him in *The Night Club Era*–testified that Fuller owed him $336, 768, most of which consisted of unpaid gambling debts. Fuller countered this statement with the charge that Rothstein personally owed him some $385,000. In subsequent testimony, Rothstein admitted having borrowed $187,000 at one time from Fuller and Co., for which he had put up $25,000 worth of collateral. But Fuller and Co.'s financial records (those that could be located) were so confused that this testimony was of little significance. More informative was Rothstein's statement that Fuller was a shrewd gambler who usually won his bets. Beyond this, Rothstein refused to testify. It was generally suspected that the firm's assets had been squandered by Fuller, McGee, Rothstein, and their friends on racing, baseball, boxing, and other sporting interests. Rothstein was believed to have "fixed" the World Series in 1919, although, again, nothing conclusive was ever proved against him. He was also reputed to be engaged in numerous other criminal activities, including the operation of gambling houses, shops selling stolen gems, brothels, and a lucrative bootlegging business–enterprises which did not affect his social standing. Like Fuller, he was frequently seen in the company of respected New York business and society figures, whom he entertained lavishly in his expensive Park Avenue apartment.[2]

Another interesting friendship disclosed during the trials was that between Edward Fuller and William S. Silkworth, the president of the Consolidated Stock Exchange. For months prior to the collapse of Fuller and Company, Silkworth had repeatedly ignored requests from Fuller's customers that Fuller and Co. be suspended from the exchange for fraudulent practices. Silkworth's brother was one of Fuller's employees, and during the trial Silkworth himself was unable to account for $133,000 in his private banking account–$55,175 of which had been deposited in cash. After Fuller's and McGee's convictions, Silkworth was obliged to resign from his presidency of the Consolidated Exchange.

Fitzgerald borrowed more heavily from the newspaper accounts of Fuller's business affairs in creating Gatsby than he had from the details of Fuller's personality. For example, it seems unlikely that Fuller's friendship with Nellie Burke inspired Gatsby's idealistic attachment to Daisy Buchanan.

However, Charles Stoneham's paternal interest in young Fuller, as it came out during the trial, is paralleled in the novel by Dan Cody's friendship for Gatsby, and Meyer Wolfshiem obviously was suggested by Fuller's friend, Arnold Rothstein. From the newspaper accounts of Fuller's career Fitzgerald also borrowed such details as Gatsby's airplane, the young stock-and-bond salesmen who haunted his parties, his mysterious connections with "the oil business" as well as his efforts to find a "small town" in which to start up some new and unmistakably shady enterprise, and his connections with New York society people like Tom Buchanan's friend Walter Chase. "That drug store business was just small change," Tom says after he has investigated Gatsby's business connections with Chase, "but you've got something on now that Walter's afraid to tell me about." What that "something" was Fitzgerald had spelled out in more detail in one of the earlier drafts of *The Great Gatsby*. "Until last summer when Wolfshiem was tried (but not convicted) on charges of grand larceny, forgery, bribery, and dealing in stolen bonds," Nick Carraway says, "I wasn't sure what it all included." Later, however, Fitzgerald omitted this passage, preferring to leave most of the facts about his hero's business affairs to the reader's imagination.[3]

For after all, in a world where people like Tom and Daisy and Jordan Baker survived and continued to be admired, what difference did it make what crimes Gatsby had committed? Besides, who in the real world of the Twenties, or in the novel that mirrored it, was free of the universal stain? The files of the Fuller-McGee case prove concretely what *The Great Gatsby* implies indirectly: that society leaders, financial tycoons, politicians, magistrates, pimps, jurors, lawyers, baseball players, sheriffs, bond salesmen, debutantes, and prostitutes–all shared in some degree the responsibility for Gatsby's fate.

Gatsby's murder was a grimmer fate than that meted out to Edward Fuller, who successfully delayed going to Sing Sing for several years and who was then paroled at the end of a year. Even so, Fitzgerald's premonition that careers like Fuller's and Rothstein's were destined to end violently was borne out by later history. Rothstein was fated to die in almost exactly the same manner as Meyer Wolfshiem's friend Rosy Rosenthal, who was shot "three times in his full belly" at four A.M. in the morning outside the old Metropole, where he had spent the night plotting with five of his mobsters. Rothstein was finally killed by an anonymous gunman in 1928 just as he was leaving a conference of big-time bootleggers and gangsters in the Park Central Hotel. In Rothstein's case, however, there were no witnesses to eulogize the manner of his passing, as Wolfshiem did so lyrically for Rosy Rosenthal. Afterwards, the New York

Gambler Herman Rosenthal was the victim of the murder in Times Square that Meyer Wolfshiem recalls.

Police Lieutenant Charles Becker was executed for his role in the Rosenthal murder.

police were not only reluctant to investigate Rothstein's murder, but devoted their efforts instead to seizing and suppressing his papers, lest his connections with other prominent New Yorkers be brought to light. Ultimately it was the public hue and cry over the police's inability to solve the mystery of the Rothstein slaying that triggered the historic Seabury gradually compiled enough evidence to force the resignation of Mayor Jimmy Walker and his top officials, intimate ties were disclosed between money, politics, sports, crime, and business–ties which Fitzgerald had already described in *Gatsby* some years earlier. The further the 1920's recede, the more the novel emerges as one of the most penetrating criticisms of that incredible decade.

–From Fitzgerald's *The Great Gatsby:
The Novel, The Critics, The Background*
(New York: Scribners, 1970)

Notes

1. Feature article on Charles Stoneham, *New York Times,* September 9, 1923, VII:2:1, see also Gene Fowler, *The Great Mouthpiece: A Life Story of William J. Fallon* (New York: Blue Ribbon Books, 1931), 326–340.

2. Stanley Walker, *The Night Club Era* (New York: Fred A. Stokes Co., 1933), 10; Lloyd Morris, *Postscript to Yesterday* (New York: Random House, 1947), 75.

3. *Gatsby,* 161; pencil draft of *Gatsby* manuscript, 206, Princeton University Library.

"The old Metropole," brooded Mr. Wolfshiem gloomily. "Filled with faces dead and gone. Filled with friends gone now forever. I can't forget so long as I live the night they shot Rosy Rosenthal there. It was six of us at the table and rosy had eat and drunk a lot all evening. When it was almost morning the waiter came up to him with a funny look and says somebody wants to speak to him outside. 'All right' says Rosy and begins to get up and I pulled him down in his chair.

"'Let the bastards come in here if they want you, Rosy, but don't you, so help me, move outside this room.'

"It was four o'clock in the morning then and if we'd of raised the blinds we'd of seen daylight."

"Did he go?" I asked innocently.

"Sure he went,"–Mr. Wolfshiem's nose flashed at me indignantly–"He turned around in the door and says, 'Don't let that waiter take away my coffee!' Then he went out on the sidewalk and they shot him three times in his full belly and drove away."

"Four of them were electrocuted," I said, remembering.

"Five with Becker." His nostrils turned to me in an interested way. "I understand you're looking for a business gonnegtion."

–*The Great Gatsby*, p. 56

This group includes Whitey Lewis, Dago Frank, Lefty Louie, and Gyp the Blood, who were executed with Becker for the murder of Herman Rosenthal.

The Fuller-McGee Case

Fitzgerald had the failure of the Fuller brokerage firm in mind when he hinted at the mysterious stock-market activities of Gatsby and Wolfshiem. Arnold Rothstein was suspected of involvement in Fuller's peculations.

The New York Times, 28 June 1922

E. M. Fuller & Co., stock brokers, of 50 Broad Street, members of the Consolidated Stock Exchange, failed yesterday.

In a petition in bankruptcy filed in the United States District Court here, assets were tentatively estimated at $250,000 and liabilities at $500,000. No more definite estimate is expected for several days.

Information current in Chicago, following the crash here, was that there were only negligible assets to offset the claims of customers there totaling $1,250,000. This outlook, coupled with the fact that the firm also has branches with many customers in Boston, Cleveland, Pittsburgh and Uniontown, Pa.,

gave rise to a belief in Wall Street that total losses might be much greater than those intimated in the original petition.

The firm had accounts on its books here of from 1,500 to 1,800 men and women. In Chicago there were 2,100 customers. The number trading with other branches was not disclosed.

"Propaganda against Consolidated Exchange houses," with its resulting "pressure," was the cause assigned for the failure by James Louis Moore of Hays, St. John & Moore, 43 Exchange Place, attorneys for the firm. Added to this was a story circulated immediately after the failure became known, to the effect that an enemy of the concern had broken into its private files, rifled them of a list of customers and circulated an anonymous circular which frightened its traders. This story, attributed to a clerk employed by the firm, was furnished with the added details that since the files were pillaged a night watchman had guarded them.

The collapse of E. M. Fuller and Company made headlines.

Suspended From Exchange.

This general explanation of the cause of the failure, however, was flatly disputed by William S. Silkworth, President of the Consolidated Exchange, from which the Fuller concern was suspended yesterday. Public announcement from the rostrum of the Exchange attributed the dropping of the firm to failure to meet commitments and "reckless and unbusinesslike methods."

To that Mr. Silkworth added last night the declaration that one of the two partners, Edward M. Fuller, had been hard hit in Mexican Petroleum stock. Mr. Silkworth said that Fuller had speculated on the short side of the market. Within the last two weeks "Mex Pete" has undergone a sensational rise.

Mr. Fuller, who lives at Great Neck, L. I., refused to make any comment on the situation for himself. The other partner, William F. McGee, lived until recently at 55 East Seventy-third Street, the home of Miss Louise Groody, star of "Good Morning, Dearie," with whom McGee entered into a runaway marriage in Greenwich, Conn., on Feb. 20 last. Mr. McGee made no statement after the failure and could not be reached last night.

The house closed its doors yesterday under sensational circumstances. A big corps of clerks, stenographers, telegraphers, messengers and other employes reported to find the suite bare of virtually everything except furniture.

Books, papers and records had been removed so that the place resembled an office just being furnished in anticipation of doing business instead of one in which hundreds of customers had been trading daily. The employes milled around, at a loss to understand what had overtaken them. They were all the more puzzled when they found that the executives who could have explained the situation to them were not on hand.

Gradually the idea that they were out of a job began to filter through the minds of the staff and there was some good natured rejoicing that they all had been paid up to Saturday night, even if the customary formality of informing them that they were through had been omitted. Mixed with the philosophic chaff was the dismay of some to whom the sudden loss of employment was a serious if not an overwhelming happening.

Things were in that state and the excitement was growing when word came that an involuntary petition in bankruptcy had been filed, that the firm had consented to being adjudged bankrupt and that a receiver had been appointed. While the clerks and other employes were dispersing there came word of a most unusual procedure to explain the bareness of the offices.

The firm had taken its books, papers and records late on Monday night to the offices of its attorneys. Not until after the receiver had been appointed were their whereabouts disclosed. Then according to Carl J. Austrian of 27 Cedar Street, who, with Francis L. Kohlman, represented the petitioning creditors, they were surrendered to the receiver under a stipulation that they were not to be the basis of court proceedings against the firm other than those normal to a liquidation.

No one could be found after the failure was made public to explain this proceeding in detail or to answer the question whether any such stipulation would operate to stay the hand of any Federal or State authorities who might believe that they had found in the circumstances of the failure cause for official action. Nor could it be learned whether the pains taken to sequester the records and to surrender them only under a protecting stipulation had any connection with the fact that an indictment was returned in the United States District Court on June 24, 1920, charging the several defendants with conspiracy to defraud by using the United States mails in exploiting and selling the capital stock of the Crown Oil Company, a California concern.

The defendants named in this indictment were: The Crown Oil Company, Charles D. Pratt, no address; Benjamin V. Hole, Burlingham, Cal.; William P. Williams, no address; B. X. Dawson, 601 West 113th Street; Edward M. Fuller and W. F. McGee, 50 Broad Street.

All of the defendants in this case appeared in court and filed pleas of not guilty to the charge before Judge Learned Hand. The Court fixed bail at $5,000 each, which was given, and the defendants were released.

Case Never Tried.

This indictment followed an investigation conducted by Jerome Simmons, then an assistant to the United States Attorney. When Mr. Simmons retired from office the indictments which had been in his care were turned over to Sampson Selig, now in charge of this branch of criminal prosecution in Colonel Hayward's office. Mr. Selig, in commenting yesterday on the fact that the case had not been brought to trial, remarked that he inherited a mass of true bills, many of which he had not had time as yet to bring to trial. The indictment, according to the records, has been on file more than two years.

These questions were not answered in court before Judge Julius M. Mayer yesterday, where the proceedings were largely of a routine nature. The petitioning creditors were Walter A. Clifford, who has a claim for $15,000, money loaned; Seminole Printing Company with a claim for $800 for printing and materials, and John G. Kinzinger, who claims $250 for services rendered.

After Hays, St. John & Moore had consented to their client being adjudicated a bankrupt, the Court appointed Samuel Strasbourger, former Judge of the City Court, receiver with a bond of $25,000.

Soon after failure had become public and the partners had denied themselves to newpaper [*sic*] men, James L. Moore, on their behalf, made this statement:

"E. M. Fuller & Co., is the largest brokerage house on the Consolidated Exchange. The house is eight years old. There are only two members in the firm, Edward M. Fuller and W. F. McGee. They have two offices in New York, one at 50 Broad Street, and the other uptown. They have branch offices in Boston, Philadelphia, Chicago, Cleveland, Pittsburgh and Uniontown, Penn.

"It is impossible to give even an approximate estimate of the assets and liabilities at this time. It is hoped that the estate will be sufficient to pay a large part of the claims but it will take an audit, perhaps of months, to determine just what the assets are.

"The cause of the failure is due to the pressure which has been brought to bear upon Consolidated Stock Exchange houses in the past few months. Owing to propaganda which has appeared in the newspaper and magazines concerning houses connected with this exchange, customers have transferred accounts or closed out entirely, causing a steady drain on the brokerage houses. Fuller & Co. have paid out enormous sums since the first of the year, but at last it was found necessary to put themselves in the hands of the court for the protection of the remaining creditors. We shall work in co-operation with the receiver and his counsel, Francis L. Kohlman, to realize all that we possibly can from the assets for the benefit of the creditors."

Tells of Losses in Mex. Pete.

With Mr. Moore's version of the reasons for the collapse of the partnership in hand, information was sought from Mr. Silkworth after the Consolidated had acted to bar the E. M. Fuller & Company from further trading there. Amplifying his declaration that Fuller had lost heavily in "Mex Pete" in trades in other houses than his own, Mr. Silkworth said:

"Our committee of investigation has discovered that Mr. Fuller sustained some very serious losses in the shares of Mexican Petroleum Company. He was not doing this trading in his own office, but in other offices where he had connections."

Mr. Silkworth could not say the exact number of shares of stock Mr. Fuller had been short, the extent of the losses he had sustained in that security, or whether settlement of these losses had been made. Mexican Petroleum, in its recent upswing in the market advanced from the low of 133, less than two weeks ago, to 204½, the high point reached on Monday, a sheer advance of 71½ points. It is known that many sales of the stock were made on Mr. Fuller's account between $150 and $160 per share.

"The actual reason behind the suspension," said the President of the Consolidated Stock Exchange, "was that our investigations proved that members of the firm had been reckless in their dealings. We had had many complaints of late that they had been slow in settlement with their clients. In view of these complaints that we had received, we caused an investigation to be made of the affairs of the firm, particularly the manner in which their customers have been treated of late, and we deemed it advisable, at the conclusion of the investigation, to suspend them from the privileges of the New York Consolidated Exchange. Announcement to this effect was made from the rostrum of our trading floor Tuesday morning at the opening of business."

Mr. Silkworth added that the firm had been a member of the Exchange since early in 1920, and that while he had no figures at hand, he was under the impression that the number of customers carrying accounts with the firm would aggregate between 1,500 and 1,800 men and women.

Did Business Over Telephone.

One unusual effect of the failure was that it drew to the almost deserted rooms of the concern many customers who had never been there before.

These offices are in several rooms on the seventh floor of 50 Broad Street. Unlike many other brokerage houses which recently have been obliged to suspend, they were not luxuriously furnished and did not give the appearance of "ready money" that some concerns in the financial district regard as an asset. The firm had no board room and customers were not invited to headquarters. Practically all of the business was transacted over the telephone and one entire room was given to an exchange where operators could give instant information to inquirers about the state of stocks in which they might be interested.

The office furniture was particularly plain, and consisted of a long row of wooden desks, in one large hall-like room, at which a dozen or so stenographers and other clerical assistants performed their tasks. The offices of Mr. Fuller and Mr. McGee were in the rear of this room, were glass-enclosed and, like the outer offices, were simply and modestly furnished. The firm has been a tenant at 50 Broad Street all of the time it has been a member of the Consolidated Stock Exchange.

Edward M. Fuller, the senior partner, figured in the newspapers recently when he appeared as complainant in Tombs Court against a young woman named Nellie Black of 245 West Seventy-fifth Street on June 15. He charged Miss Black with disorderly conduct. Mr. Fuller alleged that the young woman had entered his office, refused to leave when ordered to do so and had threatened him with bodily harm. Magistrate Oberwager released her on suspended sentence.

Miss Black, a movie actress, testified that she and Fuller had been friends for seven years and that she had visited Fuller's office to collect $5,000 which she alleged Fuller had agreed to pay her when she signed an agreement presented to her by Arnold Rothstein on the broker's behalf. Fuller already had paid her $5,000, she said.

The other partner, William F. McGee, has had little publicity, aside from his runaway match with Miss Groody. A month before that occurred a "Mrs. McGee" sued Miss Groody for alienation of McGee's affections. McGee denied that the plaintiff was his wife. Interviewed on the occasion of his marriage, he said that he did not know what had become of the woman's suit.

* * *

Rothstein/Wolfshiem

Gambler Arnold Rothstein (1882–1928), the source for Meyer Wolfshiem, was suspected of having fixed the 1919 World Series. The extent of his involvement in the fix was never determined, but it was generally believed that he knew about it and bet accordingly.

Topics of the Times
The New York Times, 2 October 1920, p. 14

He Goes, but is Not Driven.

With patience at last exhausted, one Arnold Rothstein, who seems to be a man of commanding eminence in the circles where he moves, has decided to give no more excuse to the censorious. It seems that in the past, whenever by any possibility his name could be linked with a current scandal, somebody has done it. Naturally this has worn upon the nerves of a man with a nature as sensitive as his. As he puts it in a printed interview of a length proportioned to the importance of his determination, "it is not pleasant to be what some may call a 'social outcast,'" and so "I have made up my mind to retire from the gambling business." Hereafter "I am going to devote most of my time to the real estate business and to my racing stable."

It is interesting to note—and especially our police and the District Attorney's office should be regardful—that Mr. Rothstein's decision to retire from what he calls "the gambling business" is entirely an outcome of his own present preferences and desires. For years and years he has lived and prospered on the profits of what "some may call" criminal activities, and the only penalty has been the linking of his name with all the current scandals!

One easily can imagine how annoying that would be to him, but more serious inconveniences not infrequently

have been endured by persons who did not confess, even after conviction, their lawbreaking as frankly as does Mr. Rothstein. Evidently he has no fear that his revelation now will have effects any more troublesome than did his continuous conduct of a business which the law professes to hold criminal.

There is mystery here, but presumably the police will regard it with "that baffled look" which has come to be their usual, if not their habitual, expression.

* * *

ROTHSTEIN CLEARED IN BASEBALL FIXING
Gedeon Is Also Exonerated, but They Give Evidence
Tending to Convict Others.
The New York Times, 27 October 1920, p. 17

CHICAGO. Oct. 26.—Arnold Rothstein of New York and Joe Gedeon, St. Louis American League second baseman, testified today before the Cook County Grand Jury investigating the baseball scandal, which the State's Attorney's office afterward announced had "exonerated the two men from complicity in the throwing of games in the 1919 world's series, but had materially strengthened the cases against some of the men already indicted."

The jury completed today the taking of testimony in the investigation, which has lasted more than a month and resulted in true bills being voted against thirteen men on charges of conspiracy to do an illegal act, but it will hold a final session Friday to finish up clerical work. The jury will vote no more true bills, according to State officials.

Gedeon and Rothstein testified against Abe Attell, Hal Chase, William Burns and others on whom the jury already had acted. Their testimony probably will result in an attempt to have Attell brought back here from Canada for trial. Officials said it was believed here that he can be extradited.

Supplementing the announcement by the State's Attorney's office, President Ban Johnson of the American League declared he felt that Gedeon was "entirely innocent," and Alfred Austrian, attorney for the Chicago American League club, issued a statement declaring that "Rothstein, in his testimony today, had proved himself guiltless."

Gatsby hesitated, then added coolly: "He's the man who fixed the World's Series back in 1919."

"Fixed the World's Series?" I repeated.

The idea staggered me. I remembered of course that the World's Series had been fixed in 1919 but if I had thought of it at all I would have thought of it as a thing that merely *happened,* the end of some inevitable chain. It never occurred to me that one man could start to play with the faith of fifty million people—with the single-mindedness of a burglar blowing a safe.

—The Great Gatsby, p. 58

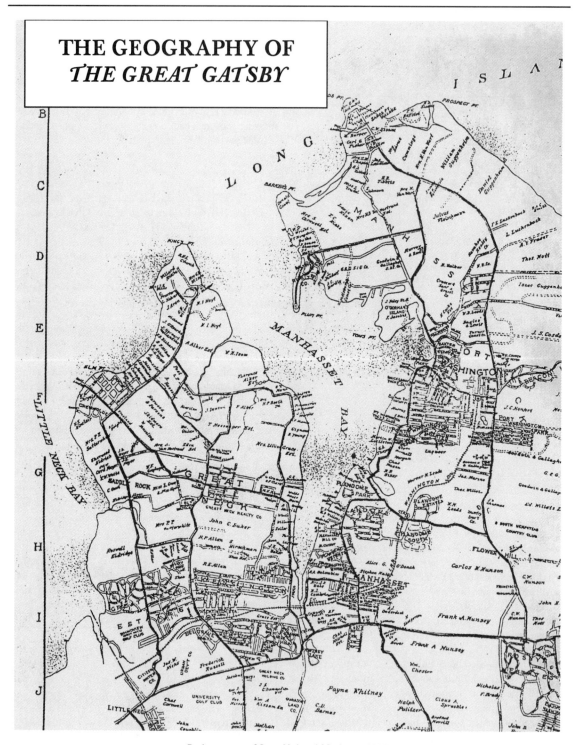

THE GEOGRAPHY OF *THE GREAT GATSBY*

Real estate map of Great Neck and Manhasset, 1922

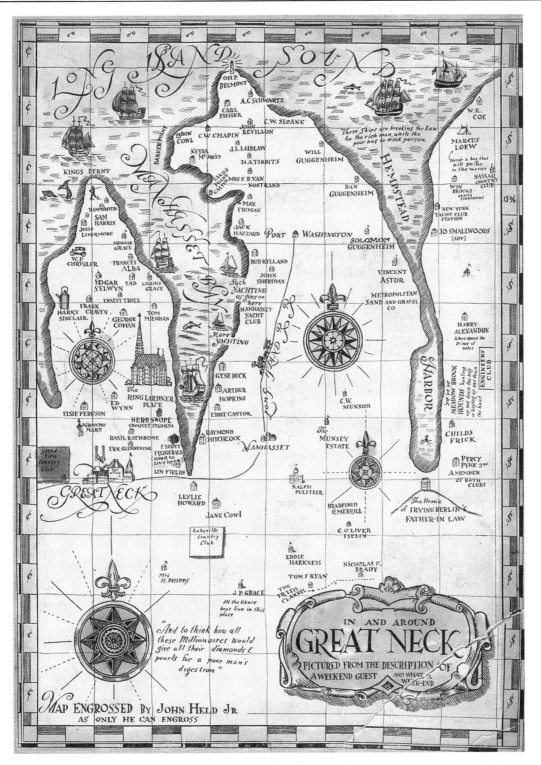

Map of the Great Neck area by John Held Jr. in The New Yorker *(1927). Held was the most popular illustrator of the 1920s, famous for his caricatures of flappers and sheiks.*

AN INVENTED LONG ISLAND

So successfully did Fitzgerald superimpose an imaginary geography on factual Long Island that maps of the actual area—showing no identical, almost perfectly oval peninsulas—now seem defective. West Egg and East Egg, fictional as to shape and name, otherwise correspond to Great Neck (where Fitzgerald lived in 1922–1924) and Manhasset Neck on the North Shore—the Long Island Sound side—of Long Island. The tip of Manhasset was an enclave of the fashionable respectably wealthy. Across Manhasset Bay to the west were the possessors of more adventurously acquired fortunes in Great Neck.

Fitzgerald imposed a fictional Long Island geography on the actual places. Long Island extends from Manhattan Island, with the New York City boroughs of Brooklyn and Queens at the western end (courtesy of University of South Carolina Press).

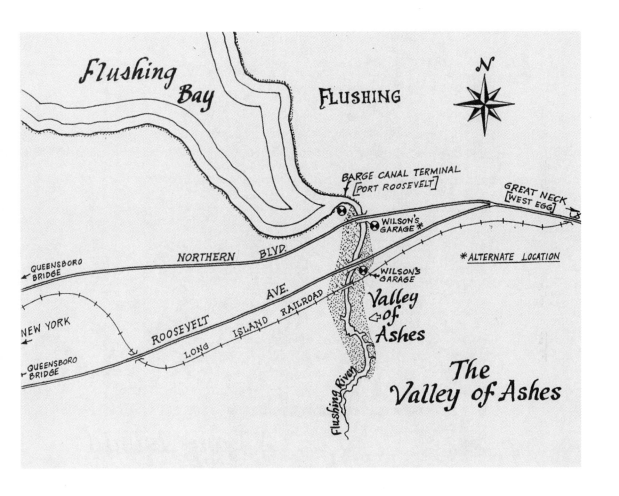

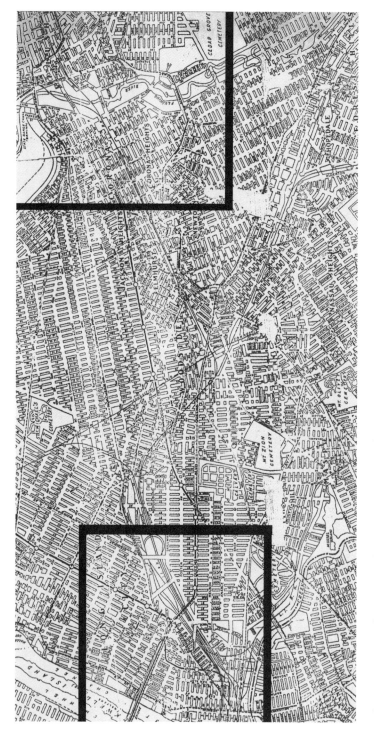

The Queensboro Bridge (Long Island City) to Corona, Queens, 1922. The New York City boroughs of Queens and Brooklyn are on the western end of Long Island. The drive to the Queensboro Bridge, which connected Northern Boulevard to the city at 59th Street, was—and is—through the district of Queens called Long Island City. Fitzgerald erred in having the drive through Astoria, the northernmost district of Queens; Astoria does not provide access to the Queensboro Bridge.

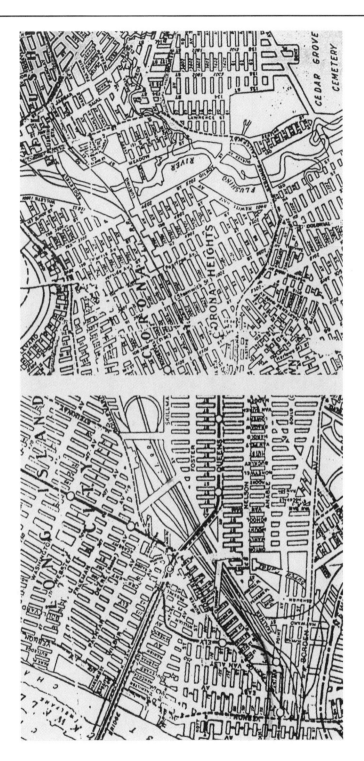

The site of the Valley of Ashes

Long Island City

About half way between West Egg and New York the motor-road hastily joins the railroad and runs beside it for a quarter of a mile so as to shrink away from a certain desolate area of land. This is a valley of ashes—a fantastic farm where ashes grow like wheat into ridges and hills and grotesque gardens, where ashes take the forms of houses and chimneys and rising smoke and finally, with a transcendent effort, of men who move dimly and already crumbling through the powdery air. Occasionally a line of grey cars crawls along an invisible track, gives out a ghastly creak and comes to rest, and immediately the ash-grey men swarm up with leaden spades and stir up an impenetrable cloud which screens their obscure operations from your sight.

—*The Great Gatsby*, p. 21

THE VALLEY OF ASHES

Traveling the twenty miles west to "the city" (the borough of Manhattan) via Northern Boulevard by automobile or by the Long Island Railroad it was necessary to cross the Corona dumps (now Flushing Meadows-Corona Park), a swamp that was landfill for garbage, horse manure, and ashes from coal-burning furnaces. Road and railroad were divergent there, however, rather than hastily joined "so as to shrink away from . . . a valley of ashes." Wilson's gas station beside Northern Boulevard is nearer the railroad drawbridge over the Flushing River than was in fact possible.

GATSBY'S MANSION

Fitzgerald did not base Gatsby's mansion on any particular Long Island structure, but several mansions contributed to the description in the novel.

> The one on my right was a colossal affair by any standard—it was a factual imitation of some Hôtel de Ville in Normandy, with a tower on one side, spanking new under a thin beard of raw ivy, and a marble swimming pool and more than forty acres of lawn and garden.
>
> —*The Great Gatsby*, p. 8

Harbor Hill, Clarence Mackay's French château at Roslyn, Long Island. Fitzgerald's Ledger *notes that he attended a party here in June 1923 (Monica Randall,* The Mansions of Long Island's Gold Coast*).*

Beacon Towers, August Belmont's mansion at Sands Point, Long Island (Monica Randall, The Mansions of Long Island's Gold Coast*)*

Land's End, Herbert Bayard Swope's house at Great Neck (Monica Randall, The Mansions of Long Island's Gold Coast*)*

"Oheka," the Otto Kahn estate at Cold Spring Harbor, Long Island (Monica Randall, The Mansions of Long Island's Gold Coast*)*

ARTIFACTS,
BUILDINGS, AND DOCUMENTS

"This idea is that we're Nordics. I am and you are and
you are and——" After an infinitesimal hesitation he
included Daisy with a slight nod and she winked at me
again, "——and we've produced all the things that go to
make civilization–oh, science and art and all that."

–The Great Gatsby, p. 14

When I came back they had disappeared so I sat down
discreetly in the living room and read a chapter of
"Simon Called Peter"–either it was terrible stuff or the
whiskey distorted things because it didn't make any
sense to me.

–The Great Gatsby, p. 26

THE
RISING TIDE OF COLOR

AGAINST WHITE WORLD-SUPREMACY

BY

LOTHROP STODDARD, A.M., PH.D. (Harv.)

AUTHOR OF "THE STAKES OF THE WAR,"
"PRESENT-DAY EUROPE: ITS NATIONAL STATES OF MIND,"
"THE FRENCH REVOLUTION IN SAN DOMINGO," ETC.

WITH AN INTRODUCTION BY
MADISON GRANT

CHAIRMAN NEW YORK ZOOLOGICAL SOCIETY; TRUSTEE AMERICAN
MUSEUM OF NATURAL HISTORY; COUNCILLOR AMERICAN GEOGRAPHICAL SOCIETY
AUTHOR OF "THE PASSING OF THE GREAT RACE"

NEW YORK
CHARLES SCRIBNER'S SONS
1922

SIMON CALLED
PETER

BY

ROBERT KEABLE

AUTHOR OF "THE DRIFT OF PINIONS,"
"STANDING BY," ETC.

NEW YORK
E. P. DUTTON & COMPANY
681 FIFTH AVENUE

*The reprinting of the 1920 book that prompts Tom Buchanan's racial
fears: "'Civilization's going to pieces,' broke out Tom violently. 'I've
gotten to be a terrible pessimist about things. Have you read "The
Rise of the Coloured Empires" by this man Goddard?'" (p. 14)*

*Title page for the novel Nick Carraway attempts to read in chapter 2.
Fitzgerald disapproved of this novel about the amatory experiences
of a World War I chaplain. Originally published in England,
it was a huge seller in America.*

Pennsylvania Station at 34th Street and Seventh Avenue, the Manhattan station for the Pennsylvania and Long Island Railroads

Trinity College Quad, Oxford, where Gatsby had been a student

"Then came the war, old sport. It was a great relief and I tried very hard to die but I seemed to bear an enchanted life. I accepted a commission as first lieutenant when it began. In the Argonne Forest I took two machine-gun detachments so far forward that there was a half mile gap on either side of us where the infantry couldn't advance. We stayed there two days and two nights, a hundred and thirty men with sixteen Lewis guns, and when the infantry came up at last they found the insignia of three German divisions among the piles of dead. I was promoted to be a major and every Allied government gave me a decoration—even Montenegro, little Montenegro down on the Adriatic Sea!"

—The Great Gatsby, p. 53

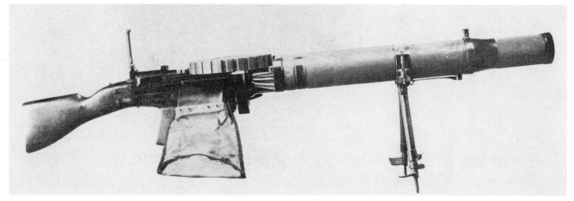

Lewis gun, used in World War I

He reached in his pocket and a piece of metal, slung on a ribbon, fell into my palm.

"That's the one from Montenegro."

To my astonishment the thing had an authentic look. *Orderi di Danilo,* ran the circular legend, *Montenegro, Nicolas Rex.*

"Turn it."

Major Jay Gatsby, I read, *For Valour Extraordinary.*

"Here's another thing I always carry. A souvenir of Oxford days. It was taken in Trinity Quad—the man on my left is now the Earl of Doncaster."

—The Great Gatsby, p. 53

Orderi di Danilo, the medal from "little Montenegro" that Gatsby shows Nick

THE SONGS
OF THE NOVEL

In the morning,
In the evening,
   Ain't we got fun—
. . . .
One thing's sure and nothing's surer
The rich get richer and the poor get—children.
In the meantime,
In between time—

   —The Great Gatsby, p. 75

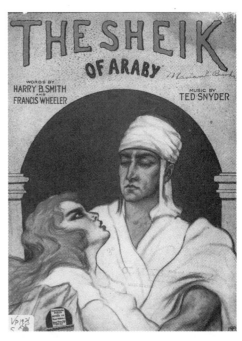

Sheet-music cover for the popular song Nick hears when he learns why Gatsby has bought a house just across the bay from Daisy. "I'm the Sheik of Araby, / Your love belongs to me. / At night when you're asleep, / Into your tent I'll creep—" (Matthew J. and Arlyn Bruccoli Collection, University of South Carolina).

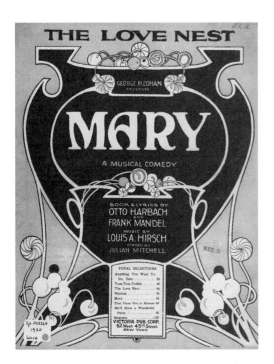

Sheet-music covers for the two popular songs that Klipspringer plays for Gatsby and Daisy at their reunion (Bagaduce Music Lending Library and Matthew J. and Arlyn Bruccoli Collection, University of South Carolina)

First page of sheet music for one of the two songs quoted in the novel

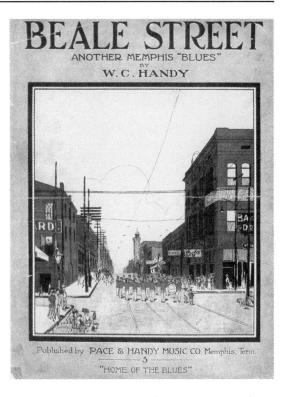

Published in 1919, this song was described as "a neat sad little waltz" in the novel (Matthew J. and Arlyn Bruccoli Collection, University of South Carolina).

Blues tune popular in Louisville before Daisy's marriage to Tom (Bagaduce Music Lending Library)

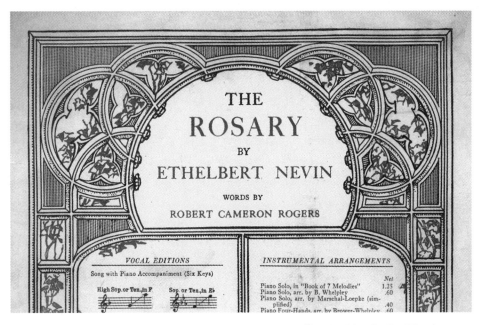

Although published in 1898, this song became popular in the 1920s (Bagaduce Music Lending Library).

Fitzgerald at the time he was writing The Great Gatsby *(Matthew J. and Arlyn Bruccoli Collection, University of South Carolina)*

CHAPTER 2:

WRITING *THE GREAT GATSBY*

Something Extraordinary and Beautiful and Simple + Intricately Patterned

Matthew J. Bruccoli

F. Scott Fitzgerald began planning the novel that became *The Great Gatsby* in June 1922 at White Bear Lake, Minnesota, after writing the first draft of *The Vegetable:*

> When I send on this last bunch of stories I may start my novel and I may not. Its locale will be the middle west and New York at 1885 I think. It will concern less superlative beauties than I run to usually + will be centered on a smaller period of time. It will have a catholic element. I'm not quite sure whether I'm ready to start it quite yet or not. I'll write next week + tell you more definate plans.[1]

From the start Fitzgerald wanted his third novel to be structurally significant. As early as July 1922 he declared to Maxwell Perkins: "I want to write something *new*—something extraordinary and beautiful and simple + intricately patterned."[2] "Winter Dreams," a short story written in September 1922, shows that the subject of a poor boy's ambitious love for a destructive rich girl was on Fitzgerald's mind—indeed, it was a subject that was always on his mind—and this story of success and disenchantment is clearly a preview of *The Great Gatsby*.

In October 1922 Fitzgerald moved to Great Neck, Long Island, from St. Paul. He was seeing Maxwell Perkins, his editor at Charles Scribner's Sons, so their correspondence is not entirely helpful for reconstructing the gestation of *The Great Gatsby*. Fitzgerald began writing the novel in June 1923 but interrupted work when he became involved in the production of *The Vegetable* in September. None of this draft survives except for the two pages he later sent to Willa Cather (see "'An Instance of Apparent Plagiarism'"). After the play failed

in its November 1923 tryout, Fitzgerald was compelled to devote the winter and spring of 1923–24 to writing short stories to pay off his debts ("'The Sensible Thing,'" "Rags Martin-Jones and the Pr-nce of W-les," "Gretchen's Forty Winks," "Diamond Dick and The First Law of Woman," "The Baby Party," "The Third Casket," "One of My Oldest Friends," "Absolution," "The Pusher-in-the-Face," "The Unspeakable Egg," "John Jackson's Arcady"). "'The Sensible Thing,'" another poor-boy/rich-girl story, written in November 1923, has close connections with *The Great Gatsby*.

By April 1924 Fitzgerald was back to full-time work on the novel; and on the seventh Perkins informed Fitzgerald that he had reservations about the proposed title, "Among the Ash-Heaps and Millionaires"–clear evidence that by this time Fitzgerald had found one of the central symbols of his novel. On 16 April Perkins asked for the title so that an advance dust jacket could be prepared for promotional use and noted, "I always thought that 'The Great Gatsby' was a suggestive and effective title . . ." The word *always* seems to indicate that "The Great Gatsby" was the title for the lost 1923 version. In early April 1924, after he had cleared his debts with short stories, Fitzgerald reported to Perkins that he was working on a "new angle"–by which he meant a new plot or a new narrative frame:

> While I have every hope + plan of finishing my novel in June you know how those things often come out. And even it takes me 10 times that long I cannot let it go out unless it has the very best I'm capable of in it or even as I feel sometimes, something better than I'm capable of. Much of what I wrote last summer was good but it was so interrupted that it was ragged + in approaching it from a new angle I've had to discard a lot of it–in one case 18,000 words (part of which will appear in The Mercury as a short story).

Fitzgerald's statement that he has discarded a lot of his summer 1923 work, part of which he has salvaged as a story for *The American Mercury,* indicates that "Absolution" was not—as is usually assumed—simply removed from *The Great Gatsby.* Rudolph Miller and Father Schwartz belong to the "catholic element" version of 1922–23.[3] Indeed, Jay Gatsby is not even a Roman Catholic: his funeral is conducted by a Lutheran minister.

Great Neck provided the setting and background material for Fitzgerald's "new angle." It was at that time a favored residence for show-business and promoter types; and Fitzgerald's neighbors included Ring Lardner, Lew Fields, Ed Wynn, Raymond Hitchcock, and Herbert Bayard Swope. A great place for parties. The Fuller-McGee Case, which resulted from the failure of E. M. Fuller & Co. in June 1922, was in the papers through 1922–23 and involved Arnold Rothstein, the man who was generally believed responsible for fixing the 1919 World Series. Rothstein was the source for Meyer Wolfshiem. Jay Gatsby's life-style may have been based on an actual Long Island bootlegger named Max Gerlach or von Gerlach. Fitzgerald discussed this bootlegger with Edmund Wilson, for Fitzgerald noted "I had told Bunny my plan for Gatsby" in the margin of his copy of Wilson's 1924 play, *The Crime in the Whistler Room,* where a character who resembles Fitzgerald has the following speech:[4]

He's a gentleman bootlegger: his name is Max Fleischman. He lives like a millionaire. Gosh, I haven't seen so much to drink since Prohibition. . . . Well, Fleischman was making a damn ass of himself bragging about how much his tapestries were worth and how much his bath-room was worth and how he never wore a shirt twice—and he had a revolver studded with diamonds. . . . And he finally got on my nerves—I was a little bit stewed—and I told him I wasn't impressed by his erminelined revolver: I told him he was nothing but a bootlegger, no matter how much money he made. . . . I told him I never would have come into his damn house if it hadn't been to be polite and that it was torture to stay in a place when everything was in such terrible taste.

The Fitzgeralds sailed for France in May 1924, where he worked steadily on *The Great Gatsby* on the Riviera during a summer of domestic unhappiness caused by Zelda Fitzgerald's interest in Edouard Jozan. By about 25 August, Fitzgerald was able to tell Perkins that the novel "will be done next week," but that he wouldn't send it before October because "Zelda and I are contemplating a careful revision."

Fizgerald's *Ledger* entries for September–October 1924 indicate that these months were devoted to revising the first draft: "Hard work sets in" and "Working at high pressure to finish." On 10 September he was able to inform Perkins that the penultimate draft was completed.

> Now for a promise—the novel will absolutely + definately be mailed to you before the 1st of October. I've had to rewrite practically half of it—at present its stored away for a week so I can take a last look at it + see what I've left out—there's some intangible sequence lacking somewhere in the middle + a break in interest there invariably means the failure of a book. It is like nothing I've ever read before.

Then in November the *Ledger* has "Novel off at last." It was Fitzgerald's habit to revise one or more secretarial typescripts (working on the ribbon copy and carbons) in pencil until he had achieved printer's copy. He did not type. The final typescript and carbon-copy were sent to Perkins and to Harold Ober at the Paul Revere Reynolds Agency for possible serial sale.[5]

Except for galley inserts, no typescript material survives for *The Great Gatsby.* There are the holograph first draft (Princeton University Library), a set of the unrevised proofs (Bruccoli Collection, University of South Carolina), and Fitzgerald's heavily reworked proofs (Princeton University Library). The unrevised proofs correspond to Fitzgerald's setting-copy revised typescript (with house-styling and any corrections Scribner editors may have made), but there is no way of determining how many layers of typescript preceded it. At the head of the first page of MS Chapter III there is this note in another hand: "3 exempl."—indicating that there were two or three carbons of the first working typescript, which was almost certainly retyped before submission to Scribners.[6]

Shortly before leaving the Riviera in early November to spend the winter of 1924–25 in Rome, Fitzgerald wrote Perkins expressing dissatisfaction with chapter 6 (the second Gatsby party) and chapter 7 (the confrontation between Gatsby and Tom). This letter also indicates his uncertainty about the title, which was "Trimalchio in West Egg"—an uncertainty that lasted for five months as he considered and rejected "Trimalchio," "Gold-Hatted Gatsby," "Gatsby," "The High-Bouncing Lover," and "On the Road to West Egg" before reluctantly returning to *The Great Gatsby* in December. Finally, on 19 March 1925 he cabled Perkins: "CRAZY ABOUT TITLE UNDER THE RED WHITE AND BLUE STOP WHART WOULD DELAY BE."[7] By then it was too late.

On 20 November 1924 Perkins wrote Fitzgerald his first detailed report on the novel, in which his principal criticism was that Gatsby was vague, a defect Perkins thought could be remedied by interpolating "little touches of various kinds, that would suggest that he

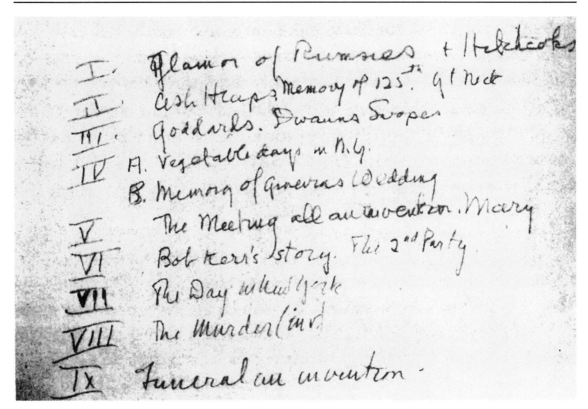

Fitzgerald made this list of sources for the Gatsby *chapters in a copy of Andre Malraux's* Man's Hope *(1938). "Rumsies" refers to the sculptor and polo player Charles Cary Rumsey, married to Mary Harriman; they had an estate at Westbury, Long Island. "Hitchcoks" refers to war hero and polo player Tommy Hitchcock (May 1923* Ledger *entry: "Met Mrs Rumsey + Tommy Hitchcock + went to parties there"). Fitzgerald placed him "in my pantheon of heroes." "Goddards" may refer to playwright Charles William Goddard or to wealthy Great Neck resident Charles Harold Goddard. "Dwanns" refers to moviedirector Allan Dwan (November 1923* Ledger *entry: "Parties at Allen Dwans"). "Swopes" refers to Herbert Bayard Swope, Executive Editor of the* New York World, *a Long Island neighbor of Fitzgerald's and celebrated host. Ginevra was Ginevra King, Fitzgerald's first serious love. Mary probably refers to actress Mary Hay. Bob Kerr was a Great Neck friend (Princeton University Library, by permission of the Estate of F. Scott Fitzgerald).*

was in some active way mysteriously engaged." He also expressed concern about the long biography of Gatsby in chapter 8, pointing out that it was a departure from the design of the book. He suggested that Fitzgerald "might find ways to let the truth of some of his claims like 'Oxford' and his army career come out bit by bit in the course of the actual narrative." Although these recommendations were in keeping with the narrative plan Fitzgerald had already built into the novel, Fitzgerald generously gave Perkins credit for the structural success of *The Great Gatsby*.[8] About 1 December 1924 Fitzgerald replied to these suggestions from Rome, saying that he knew how to fix chapters 6 and 7 and Gatsby's vagueness, but that he was uncertain about how to break up the biography in chapter 8. And around 20 December Fitzgerald wrote to Perkins expressing confidence in his ability "to make it perfect" in proof, although he admit-

ted that the confrontation between Gatsby and Tom in chapter 7 would never be right because "I can't quite place Daisy's reaction." As for Gatsby's vagueness, Fitzgerald explained that it resulted from his own ignorance: "If I'd known + kept it from you you'd have been *too impressed with my knowledge to protest.* . . . But I know now—and as a penalty for not having known first, in other words to make sure I'm going to tell more."[9]

The only set of the unrevised galley proofs (Bruccoli Collection, University of South Carolina) has the printed identification "Fitzgerald's Trimalchio" altered in pencil to "The Great Gatsby." The provenance of the unrevised galleys is unknown. They were auctioned at the Parke-Bernet Galleries sale of 18 May 1971 (sale #3209, item #22). By 24 January 1925 Fitzgerald had revised the first half of the galleys and returned them with replies to Perkins' queries. Of particular interest is his explanation of why he wants to retain "orgastic future" in Nick's closing meditation.[10]

Fitzgerald's set of revised proofs (Princeton University Library) reveals that *The Great Gatsby* achieved greatness through his proof revisions. Fitzgerald regarded galleys as a special kind of typescript or trial edition in which to rewrite whole scenes when necessary. The reworking of the novel in galleys is analyzed below, but it should be noted here that Fitzgerald revised only the first galleys, and that Perkins was responsible for seeing the book through the press. By about 18 February 1925 Fitzgerald returned the second batch of his revised galleys to Perkins with the report that he had solved the problems that bothered both of them.

Revised proofs were read at Scribners by Perkins, Roger Burlingame, and Charles Dunn. Rex and Ring Lardner supplied corrections of factual matters.[11]

The Great Gatsby was published 10 April 1925; on the 20th Perkins cabled Fitzgerald: "SALES SITUATION DOUBTFUL EXCELLENT REVIEWS." The first printing of 20,870 copies sold slowly, and there was a second printing of 3,000 in August. Except for the 1926 English printing by Chatto & Windus and the 1934 Modern Library printing, there were no further editions or printings in Fitzgerald's lifetime. The two Scribners printings brought the author about $6,700.

Fitzgerald wrote Perkins about 24 April that there were two reasons for the commercial failure of *The Great Gatsby:* the title is "only fair," and it has no important woman character. Around this time he explained to Edmund Wilson that the big fault of the novel is that "I gave no account (and had no feeling about or knowledge of) the emotional relations between Gatsby and Daisy from the time of their reunion to the catastrophe."[12] He made the same criticisms to H. L. Mencken on 4 May 1925.[13]

The Manuscript

The holograph draft of *The Great Gatsby*–so titled–consists of 264 leaves of unruled 8 3/8" (8 7/16") x 12 7/8" (13") paper written in pencil on the rectos. The paper has oxidized to a tannish hue, but it was probably originally off-white. It is wove paper, watermarked 'CASCADE BOND / U.S.A.'–of two weights.

Since the entire holograph draft is written on American-made paper, the idea suggests itself that Fitzgerald had arrived in France with a complete or substantially complete draft of the novel. However, his correspondence with Perkins makes it clear that this was

not the case; Fitzgerald apparently brought a supply to France.

MS I:	1–2, insert, 3–19, 19½, 20–26, insert, (27–29), 30, (31–32), 33–37. Corresponds to galleys 1–7 and to *Book Chapter 1*.
MS II:	38–62. Corresponds to galleys 12–19 and to *Book Chapter 3*–Gatsby's first party.
MS III:	63–65, insert, 66–67, insert, 68–85, cancelled page, 86–90. Corresponds to galleys 19–25 and to *Book Chapter 4*–Nick's trip to New York with Gatsby.
MS III:	1–6, insert, 7–29. Corresponds to galleys 7–12 and to *Book Chapter 2*–Myrtle's party.
MS V:	1–12, 12½, 13–14, insert, 15–17. Corresponds to galleys 25–30 and to *Book Chapter 5*–Gatsby's reunion with Daisy.
MS VI:	97–112. Corresponds to galleys 30–34 and to *Book Chapter 6*–Gatsby's second party.
MS VI:	1–16, 113–115, 117, insert 118, 109–116, 131½, 132–134, 134½, 135–137, 137½, 138–139, 139½, 140 140½, 28–29, 23, 31–40. Corresponds to galleys 34–35 and to *Book Chapter 7*–confrontation and accident.
MS VII:	1–22. Corresponds to galleys 45–51 and to *Book Chapter 8*–the murder.
MS VIII:	23–32, [33], 34–35. Corresponds to galleys 51–57 and to *Book Chapter 9*.

MS Fragment
Opening of Chapter III (*Book Chapter 4*)–the guest list: 5 unnumbered pages.

This manuscript is the last draft preceding the typescripts. Fitzgerald composed in holograph and turned the chapters over to a professional typist as each holograph chapter was completed, so at a given point he would be composing in holograph while revising one or more typed chapters. Fitzgerald never worked directly on a typewriter and did not make his own typescripts.

It is not possible to reconstruct every stage of the evolution of *The Great Gatsby* in manuscript. For one thing, none of the early-version *Gatsby* material survives in recognizable form. More to the point, it is clear that this manuscript draft consists of two or more conflated layers of manuscript. The most useful evidence for differentiating manuscript layers are the handwriting and the splices. In general, a small handwriting with few current revisions (i.e., revisions and corrections made during the initial composition rather than those made as a result of later review) indicates that the material has been re-copied by Fitzgerald. It is, however, impossible to differentiate current revisions from review revisions

First manuscript draft for the guest list (Princeton University Library)

From West Egg came the Chester Beckers and the Leeches and a man named Bunsen ~~who said Tom Buchanan played polo~~ that I knew at Yale and Dr. Webster Civet who was drowned last summer up in Maine. And the Hornbeams and the Willie Voltaires and a whole clan named Blackbuck who ~~a~~ always gathered in a corner ~~together~~ and ~~flipped~~ up their noses, like goats at whoever came near. And the Ismays and the Chrysties ~~and~~ (or rather Hubert Aurback and Chrystie's wife) and ~~G.P. Whitebait~~ Edgar Beaver whose hair they say turned cotton-white one winter afternoon for no good reason at all.

Clarence Endive was from West Egg ~~I~~ as I ~~think remember as~~ remember. He came only once in white knickerbockers and had a fight with a tough ~~nut~~ named Etty in the garden. From father out the Island came the ~~Dewars~~ Dewars and G.R.P. Schraeders and the Ripley Brewers and the Fishguards and the Snells — Snell was there three days before he was arrested, so drunk ~~that that~~ out on the gravel ~~path through Faty~~ drive mrs. Ullyses Swett's chauffeur run over his right hand. The Dancy's came too and ~~Edgar Beaver~~ G.P. Whitebait who was well over ~~sixty~~ and ~~Maurice~~ Hunk and the Hammerheads and Belugo the tobacco importer and Beluga's girls.

From East Egg came the Poles and the Mulreadys and Cecil Roebuck and Cecil Schoen and Gulick the state senator and ~~Richard~~ Newton Wepper who controlled Films par Excellence and Eeckhoust and Clyde Cohen and and ~~Hubert~~ Egbert Schwartze (the son) and Egbert M°Carthy who were all connected with the movies and some way or other. And the Catlins and Bembergs and the G. Earl Muldoons, brother to that Muldoon who afterwards ~~killed~~ strangled his wife. with a stocking Da Fontano the promoter came there and Ed Legros and and James B Ferret and the de Jongs and Earnest Lilly — they came to gamble and ~~nose~~ whenever ~~one of them~~ ~~was~~ Ferret wandered out ~~of it~~ into the garden people said it meant, he was cleaned out and ~~Associated~~ Traction would have to fluctuate ~~next~~ profitably next day.

~~Percy Clipspringer was there so often~~

~~Then there was~~

~~From New York came the Arthur G.~~ a man named ~~Lott~~ Clipspringer was there so often and so long that he became known as the boarder— I doubt if he had any other home. Of ~~people~~ ~~"connected" with the stage~~ theatrical people there were Gus Waize and Horace ~~Dorsey~~ O'Donovan and

Lester Myer and the Wombett brothers and George Duckweed and Francis Bull. Also from New York were The Chromes and the Backhyssons and Dennickers and Russel Betty and the ~~Myers~~ Corrigans and the Kellehers and the ~~Chadlys~~ Dewars and the Scullys and S. W. Belcher and the ~~Duckweeds~~ Smirkes and the ~~G~~ young Quinns, both divorced now, and ~~Percy~~ Henry L. Palmetto who killed himself by jumping in pront of a subway train in Times Square.

~~Benny~~ ~~Leupicke~~ McClenaham arrived always with four girls. ~~They differed often in person but their~~ ~~names were invariably~~ They were never quite the same ~~ones~~ in physical person but they were ~~almost~~ all so identical with one another that it seemed inevitable ~~that~~ they had been there before. I have forgotten their names — Marcia chiefly I think or else Jackeline or Gloria or ~~Edith or Charlotte or~~ Judy or June and their last names were either the melodious names of flowers and months or the sterner ones of the great American capitalists whose cousins if pressed they would confess themselves to be.

In addition to all these I can remember the
Ascott Jones there at Cannstonce and the
~~De Harren~~ Cockerell girls and ~~————~~
the
The ~~Malcolm~~ Metcalfs who had his arm shot off in the war. and ~~Mr.~~ Albruckshargen
and Miss Haag, his fiancée and ~~Henry~~ Ardita
Fitz Peters, and Miss Dewings, and a man reputed to be his chaufer and Mr.
Jewett ~~who was~~, once head of the American
Legion, and De Coursey Abrahams and a
Prince of something who we called Prince
and whose name if I ever knew it I have
forgotten.

All these people came to Gatsby's house in
the summer.

with certainty. A large handwriting with frequent current revision indicates a first draft. But, as Fitzgerald worked on a stint his handwriting gradually enlarged, so that there are handwriting differences do not differentiate re-copied sections from first drafts. For example—the first page of Chapter I is a re-copied page; the second page is re-copied, but with extensive review alterations; page 34 of Chapter I is a clear case of a first draft with current revisions. The splices—which are not to be confused with simple inserts—occur at places where two drafts have been connected by deletion and/or connecting words. Page 4 of Chapter I is a small-hand page that originally ended with a description of people in other cars looking at Nick; the last word, "curiously–," was followed by "people in Rolls-Royces" at the beginning of p. 10. Fitzgerald deleted the last two paragraphs on p. 4, added the words "My house was" to splice p. 4 to p. 5 (insert); he then deleted material at the beginning and end of p. 6 (note bigger handwriting) to splice pp. 5–7 together. Page 8 (originally numbered 7) and p. 9 are connecting inserts that complete the splice between pp. 4 and 10–again note that the handwriting on these two pages is the same.[14] A third kind of evidence is the name changes: Daisy was originally Ada, and Nick was originally Dud. Pages in which Ada or Dud are changed are almost certainly salvaged from the early drafts; unfortunately there are only a few cases–Ada: II, 57; III, 89–90; Dud: I, 26; I, (31–32).[15]

Because Fitzgerald did not number the pages of a chapter until he thought he was done with it, the usefulness of the numbering is somewhat limited. The different numbering systems do not reveal much about how each chapter evolved; but they do make it possible to determine the order in which the chapters were written, as well as the order in which they were originally to appear in the novel.[16]

The first chapters of this final holograph draft to be written were paged 1–90 (pp. 1–37, 38–62, 63–90–in simple form); designated I, II, III by Fitzgerald, but corresponding to chapters 1, 3, and 4 of the book. Of special interest in the opening chapter is the original version of Nick's peroration on p. 37 that became the coda for the novel. At this stage of composition, the Wilsons, the Valley of Ashes, and T. J. Eckleburg were introduced in manuscript Chapter III (book Chapter 4) when Nick and Gatsby stop for gas on their way to New York. Also note the conversation on manuscript p. 89 between Nick and Jordan about the ethics of bringing Daisy and Gatsby together–see the section of this introduction dealing with the typescript for discussion.

By the time Fitzgerald reached the opening of his manuscript Chapter III on p. 63, the first two chapters had been turned over to a typist, for this page has the note "(43 on typewriter)." As has been mentioned, it was Fitzgerald's custom to revise secretarial typescripts for earlier chapters while writing ahead on the manuscript. This fact is of the greatest importance in understanding the evolution of *The Great Gatsby,* for it must not be thought that this manuscript represents a single final working draft or that the unrevised proofs represent *the* typescript:–one or more revised typescripts (and their carbons) came between the manuscript and the printer's-copy typescript. The last typescripts were not mere fair copies; they were working drafts and were heavily reworked. There also survives a five-page unnumbered trial draft for the opening of manuscript chapter III, the superb guest list. Comparison of these pages with pp. 63–64 clearly shows the difference between the appearance of a first draft and Fitzgerald's recopying of it. It is noteworthy that this delicately controlled passage is so close to its final form in the manuscript draft.

Only after bringing the story through the first party at Gatsby's house and Nick's trip to New York with Gatsby did Fitzgerald write the account of Nick's day in New York with Tom and Myrtle that became chapter 2 (manuscript pp. 1–29). Since he headed this chapter "III," Fitzgerald planned to have it replace the original "III" (manuscript pp. 63–90)–positioning it between Gatsby's party and Nick's trip to New York with Gatsby. There is no manuscript Chapter IV, so it is clear that the original Chapter III became IV–which it is in the novel. The new Chapter III (Tom and Myrtle) ends with Nick's summary of his evenings in New York and his analysis of Jordan's dishonesty (pp. 26–29), which was moved in typescript to the end of book Chapter 3 as a bridge between Gatsby's party and Nick's trip with Gatsby to convey the impression of the passage of time.

The first section of the manuscript developed this way:

MS	corresponds to	Book
I		1
II		3
III		4
III (later insertion)		2

Manuscript Chapter V–the reunion of Daisy and Gatsby at Nick's house–corresponds to book chapter 5. It is paged 1–12, 12½, 13–14, insert, 15–17. This manuscript chapter is mostly re-copied, but spliced at the end.[17]

There are two manuscript chapters designated "VI"– one corresponding to book chapter 6 (2nd Gatsby party), and one corresponding to book chapter 7 (confrontation between Tom and Gatsby and death of Myrtle). It is impossible to tell which of these chapters was actually written first; but the logic of the plot obviously requires that Tom and Daisy's presence at Gatsby's party precedes the confrontation scene. When Fitzgerald wrote the second party chapter he knew that it would go between the reunion and the con-

Second manuscript draft for the guest list (Princeton University Library)

64.

Muldoon, brother to that Muldoon who afterwards strangled his wife. De Fontano the promoter came there and Ed Legros and James B. ("Rot-gut") Ferret and the de Gonzs and ~~Ernest~~ Ernest Lilly— there came to gamble and whenever Ferret wandered ~~out~~ into the garden ~~it~~ it meant he was cleaned out and Associated Traction would have to fluctuate profitably next day.

A man named Klipspringer was there so often and so long that he became known as "the boarder"— I doubt if he had any other home. Of theatrical people there were Gus Waize and Horace O'Donavan and Lester Myer and the Wombat brothers and George Duckweed and Francis Bull. Also from New York were the Chromes and the Backhyssons and the Dennickers and Russel Betty and the Corrigans and the Kellebers and the Dewars and the Scullys and S. W. Belcher and the Smirkes and the young Quinns, divorced now, and Henry ~~L.~~ Palmetto who killed himself by jumping in front of a subway train in Times Square.

Benny McClenahan arrived always with four girls. They were never quite the same ones in physical person but they were so identical with one another that it ~~always~~ inevitably ~~that~~ seemed they had been there before. I have forgotten their names—Jaqueline, I think, or else Consuella or Gloria or Judy or June, and their last names were either the melodious names of flowers and months or the sterner ones of the great American capitalists whose cousins, if pressed, they would confess themselves to be.

In addition to all these I can remember that the Ascott-Jones came there at least once and the Cockerell girls and young Metcalf who had his nose shot off in the war and Mr. Albrucksburger and Mrs Haag, his fiancé, and Ardita Fitz-Peters, and Mr. P. Jewett, once head of the American Legion, and Miss ~~Daisy~~ Claudia Hip with a man reputed to be her chauffer, and a Prince of something ~~of something~~ whom we called ~~Prince~~ Duke and whose name, if I ever knew it, I have forgotten.

All these people came to Gatsby's house in the summer.

At nine o'clock one ~~by~~ morning in June Gatsby's ~~called on the telephone and asked me to drive with him to town.~~ ~~"I'm leaving right away," he added,~~ "I'll take you along in the machine." In a few ~~minutes his~~ car lurched weightily ~~heavily on its silver~~

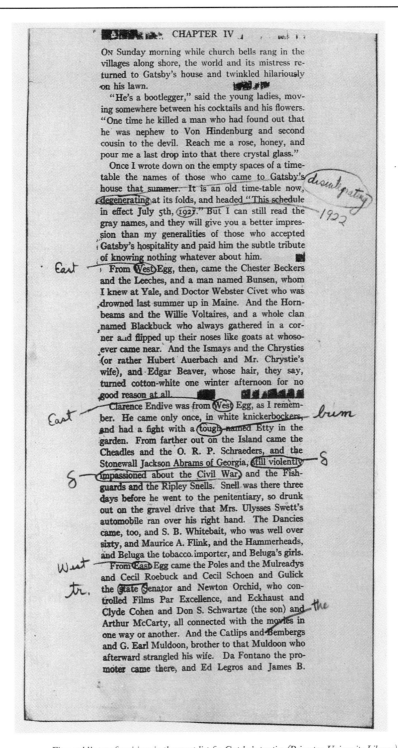

On Sunday morning while church bells rang in the villages along shore, the world and its mistress returned to Gatsby's house and twinkled hilariously on his lawn.

"He's a bootlegger," said the young ladies, moving somewhere between his cocktails and his flowers. "One time he killed a man who had found out that he was nephew to Von Hindenburg and second cousin to the devil. Reach me a rose, honey, and pour me a last drop into that there crystal glass."

Once I wrote down on the empty spaces of a time-table the names of those who came to Gatsby's house that summer. It is an old time-table now, *degenerating* [disintegrating] at its folds, and headed "This schedule in effect July 5th, 1927 [1922]." But I can still read the gray names, and they will give you a better impression than my generalities of those who accepted Gatsby's hospitality and paid him the subtle tribute of knowing nothing whatever about him.

From West [East] Egg, then, came the Chester Beckers and the Leeches, and a man named Bunsen, whom I knew at Yale, and Doctor Webster Civet who was drowned last summer up in Maine. And the Hornbeams and the Willie Voltaires, and a whole clan named Blackbuck who always gathered in a corner and flipped up their noses like goats at whosoever came near. And the Ismays and the Chrysties (or rather Hubert Auerbach and Mr. Chrystie's wife), and Edgar Beaver, whose hair, they say, turned cotton-white one winter afternoon for no good reason at all.

Clarence Endive was from West [East] Egg, as I remember. He came only once, in white knickerbockers, [*brim*] and had a fight with a *tough named* Etty in the garden. From farther out on the Island came the Cheadles and the O. R. P. Schraeders, and the Stonewall Jackson Abrams of Georgia, *still violently impassioned about the Civil War,* and the Fishguards and the Ripley Snells. Snell was there three days before he went to the penitentiary, so drunk out on the gravel drive that Mrs. Ulysses Swett's automobile ran over his right hand. The Dancies came, too, and S. B. Whitebait, who was well over sixty, and Maurice A. Flink, and the Hammerheads, and Beluga the tobacco importer, and Beluga's girls.

From East [West] Egg came the Poles and the Mulreadys and Cecil Roebuck and Cecil Schoen and Gulick the State Senator [tr.] and Newton Orchid, who controlled Films Par Excellence, and Eckhaust and Clyde Cohen and Don S. Schwartze (the son) and *the* Arthur McCarty, all connected with the movies in one way or another. And the Catlips and Bembergs and G. Earl Muldoon, brother to that Muldoon who afterward strangled his wife. Da Fontano the promoter came there, and Ed Legros and James B.

Fitzgerald's proof revisions in the guest list for Gatsby's parties (Princeton University Library)

Gal 20—Fitzgerald's Trimalchio—46725—12-14-3fE

("Rot-Gut") Ferret and the De Jongs and Ernest Lilly—they came to gamble, and when Ferret wandered into the garden it meant he was cleaned out and Associated Traction would have to fluctuate profitably next day.

A man named Klipspringer was there so often and so long that he became known as "the boarder" —I doubt if he had any other home. Of theatrical people there were Gus Waize and Horace O'Donavan and Lester Myer and George Duckweed and Francis Bull. Also from New York were the Chromes and the Backhyssons and the Dennickers and Russel Betty and the Corrigans and the Kellehers and the Dewars and the Scullys and S. W. Belcher and the Smirkes and the young Quinns, divorced now, and Henry L. Palmetto, who killed himself by jumping in front of a subway train in Times Square.

Benny McClenahan arrived always with four girls. They were never quite the same ones in physical person, but they were so identical with one another that it inevitably seemed they had been there before. I have forgotten their names—Jaqueline, I think, or else Consuela, or Gloria or Judy or June, and their last names were either the melodious names of flowers and months or the sterner ones of the great American capitalists whose cousins, if pressed, they would confess themselves to be.

In addition to all these I can remember that the Ascott-Jones came there at least once and the Cockrell girls and young Brewer, who had his nose shot off in the war, and Mr. Albrucksburger and Miss Haag, his fiancée and Ardita Fitz-Peters and Mr. P. Jewett, once head of the American Legion, and Miss Claudia Hip, with a man reputed to be her chauffeur, and a prince of something, whom we called Duke, and whose name, if I ever knew it, I have forgotten.

All these people came to Gatsby's house in the summer.

At nine o'clock, one morning late in July, Gatsby's gorgeous car lurched up the rocky drive to my door and gave out a burst of melody from its three-noted horn. It was the first time he had called on me, though I had gone to two of his parties, mounted in his hydroplane, and, at his polite invitation, made frequent use of his beach.

"Hello, old sport," he said, "you're having lunch with me in the city to-day, and I thought you might like to ride up now."

That formal caution that enveloped his every word was less perceptible in the daytime—as he stood balancing on the dashboard of his car he seemed very natural, after all. His body had about it that American resourcefulness of movement—a characteristic that is due, I suppose, to the absence of heavy lifting work in youth and, even more, to the formless grace of our nervous, sporadic games.

"I suppose you've seen my car?"

frontation. Party chapter VI is numbered 97–112, indicating that it was keyed to the typescript pagination. At the point when Fitzgerald wrote the first page of this chapter, the manuscript had been typed through p. 96–which would have been about right for five chapters, but probably too short for six chapters.

Page 99 has the first of only four appearances of "old sport" in the manuscript: VI, 100 (deleted); VI, 113; VIII, 37. Before p. 99, the expressions used by Gatsby are "old fellow" and "old man."[18] The decision to characterize Gatsby by this slightly absurd expression was made during the revision of the typescripts.

The second manuscript Chapter VI (book chapter 7) apparently gave Fitzgerald more trouble than any other surviving manuscript chapter. He was never satisfied with it and came to blame the commercial failure of *The Great Gatsby* on his inability to clarify Daisy's reactions in the Plaza Hotel scene. The pagination is 1–16, 113–115, 117, insert 118, 109–116, 131½, 132–134, 134½, 135–137, 137½, 138–139, 139½, 140, 140½, 28–29, 23, 31–40–which includes parts of at least three drafts. This chapter was originally paged manuscript 1–40 and typed; then the middle section was rewritten at least twice, with the holograph revisions keyed to the typescript pagination.

MS VI (Book Chapter 7)

Sequence A, pp. 1–16: Gatsby replaces servants; he tells Nick about Louisville courtship and sings his song (some of this material was moved to the book chapter 6); lunch at the Buchanan home; trip to New York with stop at Wilson's garage; arrival at Plaza.

Sequence B, pp. 113–115, 117, insert 118: Gatsby replaces servants; he describes courtship and sings song; he discusses his ambitions and his disappointment in Daisy. This sequence is later draft and is keyed to the typescript.

Sequence C, pp. 109–116: picks up after Tom has learned that Wilson is taking Myrtle away; Tom, Daisy, Gatsby, Nick, and Jordan go to Polo Grounds; confrontation between Tom and Gatsby at cafe in Central Park; departure from New York. Sequence C was written before sequence D.

Sequence D, pp. 131½, 132–134, 134½, 135–137, 137½, 138–139, 139½, 140, 140½: picks up after Tom has learned that Wilson is taking Myrtle away; confrontation in Plaza Hotel; departure from New York. This sequence is a later draft and is keyed to the typescript. The Plaza version of the confrontation is a replacement for the Polo-Grounds–Central-Park version in sequence C. The scene was rewritten in proof.

Sequence E, pp. 28–29, 23, 31–40: death of Myrtle; return to Buchanan home; Nick and Gatsby in driveway.

The middle section of the manuscript developed this way:

MS	corresponds to	Book
V		5
VI		6
VI		7

The last two chapters, manuscript VII (book chapter 8) and manuscript VIII (book chapter 9) are paged 1–22 and 23–45. Chapter VII is mostly recopied material, and is spliced at pp. 19–20. Chapter VIII is paged 23–45; although there are no splices, it combines recopied material with working draft. The information about Gatsby's criminal activities in the final chapter deserves attention–see the section of this introduction dealing with the typescript for discussion. The conclusion of the novel is clearly an early draft.

The Typescript & Unrevised Galleys

The lost typescript that Fitzgerald sent to Perkins in November 1924 was used to set the first proof; therefore the stage of typescript revision can be reconstructed by comparison of the manuscript with the unrevised galleys for "Fitzgerald's Trimalchio."

Unrevised galleys: chapter 1 (galleys 1–7); chapter 2 (galleys 7–12); chapter 3 (galleys 12–19); chapter 4 (galleys 19–25); chapter 5 (galleys 25–30); chapter 6 (galleys 30–34); chapter 7 (galleys 34–45–*N.B.* the length of this chapter); chapter 8 (galleys 45–51); chapter 9 (galleys 51–57).

The unrevised galleys conform to the general plan of the published novel. There are nine chapters which are ordered as in the book; but Fitzgerald subsequently revised the galleys heavily and rewrote chapters 6–8. The only significant structural alteration between manuscript and typescript–apart from the re-ordering of chapters 2–4, already discussed–occurs where Fitzgerald moved Nick's summary of his evenings in New York and Nick's analysis of Jordan's dishonesty from the end of the episode in Myrtle's apartment (book chapter 2; manuscript III, pp. 26–29) to follow Gatsby's party in book chapter 3.

Unrevised galleys (typescript) chapter 1 has two important revisions from manuscript: the green light at the end of Daisy's dock is added; and Nick's historical ruminations are deleted from the end of the manuscript chapter (p. 37) and augmented to become the conclusion of the novel.

Unrevised galleys (typescript) chapter 2 has Nick's bridge transposed from the end of manuscript chapter 2 to the end of galley chapter 3–described above. The added conversation in Myrtle's apartment between Catherine and Nick about Gatsby is worth noting, for it shows Fitzgerald's concern to build the reader's interest in Gatsby before the first party in the next chapter.

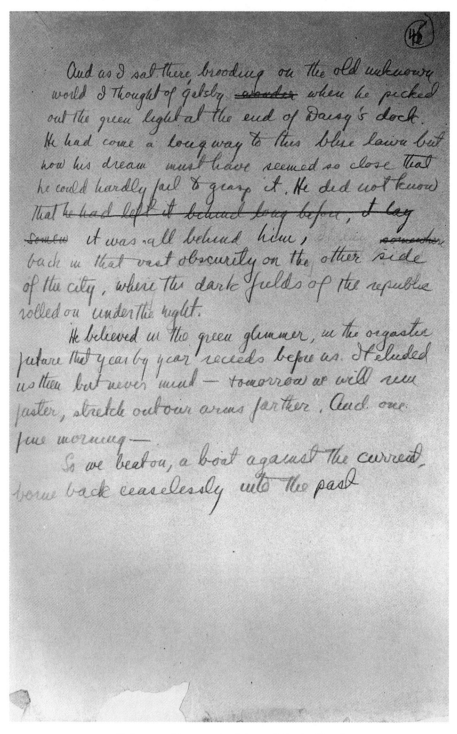

The last page of the manuscript (Princeton University Library)

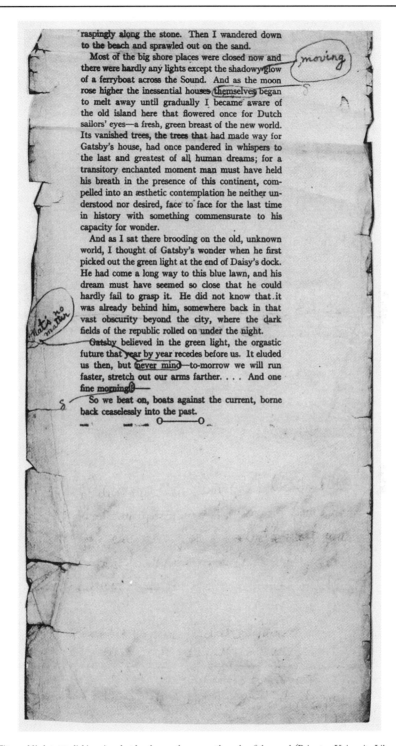

raspingly along the stone. Then I wandered down to the beach and sprawled out on the sand.

Most of the big shore places were closed now and there were hardly any lights except the shadowy glow of a ferryboat across the Sound. And as the moon rose higher the inessential houses themselves began to melt away until gradually I became aware of the old island here that flowered once for Dutch sailors' eyes—a fresh, green breast of the new world. Its vanished trees, the trees that had made way for Gatsby's house, had once pandered in whispers to the last and greatest of all human dreams; for a transitory enchanted moment man must have held his breath in the presence of this continent, compelled into an æsthetic contemplation he neither understood nor desired, face to face for the last time in history with something commensurate to his capacity for wonder.

And as I sat there brooding on the old, unknown world, I thought of Gatsby's wonder when he first picked out the green light at the end of Daisy's dock. He had come a long way to this blue lawn, and his dream must have seemed so close that he could hardly fail to grasp it. He did not know that it was already behind him, somewhere back in that vast obscurity beyond the city, where the dark fields of the republic rolled on under the night.

Gatsby believed in the green light, the orgastic future that year by year recedes before us. It eluded us then, but never mind—to-morrow we will run faster, stretch out our arms farther.... And one fine morning——

So we beat on, boats against the current, borne back ceaselessly into the past.

——— O———O———

Fitzgerald's latest polishings in what has become known as the coda of the novel (Princeton University Library)

Unrevised galleys (typescript) chapter 3 which ended in manuscript with the view of Gatsby saying goodnight to his guests has the new conclusion moved from the end of manuscript chapter 3. Since this material includes an analysis of Nick's probity and Jordan's dishonesty, an earlier reference to these matters was deleted from the manuscript (MS p. 50). Note that where in manuscript Nick describes himself as "one of the few decent people that I have ever known," the word *decent* is emended to *honest* in the unrevised galleys. The talk at the party about dope was cut in typescript; and a description of Gatsby was revised (MS p. 52). The long description of "The Jazz History of the World" was shortened between manuscript and unrevised galleys and then was shortened again in the revised galleys. Nick's view of Jordan and Gatsby talking in the library was deleted between manuscript and unrevised galleys. Lucille's account of Gatsby sending her a dress was added in typescript, as well as other bits of reported party conversation—some of which were later cut in the revised proof.

Unrevised galleys (typescript) chapter 4 has a very important revision: the manuscript's account of Gatsby and Nick encountering Myrtle at the Valley of Ashes on their way to New York was deleted, along with the connected appearance of Myrtle with Tom in the cafe where Nick lunches with Gatsby and Wolfshiem. As has been discussed, this revision resulted from Fitzgerald's decision to interpolate book chapter 2 into the manuscript. Nick's report of the rumors about Gatsby in the car was deleted between manuscript (p. 67) and unrevised galleys. The manuscript material about Meyer Wolfshiem was revised. Most interestingly, the cuff links of human molars were added in typescript—thereby setting up Nick's symbolic identification of Tom with Wolfshiem at the end of the novel ("Then he went into the jewelry store to buy a pearl necklace—or perhaps only a pair of cuff buttons . . ."). Fitzgerald removed Wolfshiem's lugubrious second speech about the Metropole (MS p. 79) between manuscript and unrevised galleys, and also corrected the facts about the Rosenthal murder.[19] An important difference between manuscript and unrevised galleys for chapter 4 involves Nick's ambiguous role in bringing Daisy and Gatsby together. For a man who insists on his disinclination to become involved with people, he certainly becomes deeply involved in Gatsby's life. At p. 89 of the manuscript Fitzgerald provided Nick with reasons for playing Pandarus—that he resents Tom's open unfaithfulness to Daisy, and that he is romantically impressed by the account of Gatsby's commitment to Daisy that Jordan has just related to him: "And besides an assignation becomes more than an assignation, becomes a ritual after five years." The word *assignation* is revealing, for it indicates that Nick is aware that he is setting up a love tryst—not a reunion. Fitzgerald cut this material in typescript because it blows Nick's cover as observer-narrator and converts him into an instigator-novelist. No reason is provided for Nick's complic-

ity in the published novel. In this same scene between Nick and Jordan there is an interesting revision of the phrase that Nick hears. The manuscript (p. 90) reads "Been everywhere, seen everything, done everything"; but the unrevised galleys have "There are only the pursued, the pursuing, the busy and the tired." The point of this change is to emphasize Nick's sense of the variety of life and his concomitant anxiety that he is being left out.

Unrevised galleys (typescript) chapter 5 adds Dan Cody—who was not mentioned in the manuscript chapter—as preparation for the true biography of James Gatz. At manuscript p. 14 Gatsby tells Daisy about the two green lights on her dock, but in the unrevised galleys there is just one green light.

Unrevised galleys (typescript) chapter 6 had one particularly interesting alteration. At manuscript p. 105 when Daisy asks Nick if she and Gatsby can sit on his steps, he offers her the key to his house. Again, it can be seen that one of Fitzgerald's concerns in revising the typescript was to remove evidence of Nick's active encouragement of Daisy's adultery. The unrevised galleys also play down Daisy's obvious sense of superiority to Gatsby's second party. Much of chapter 6 was rewritten in proof.

Unrevised galleys (typescript) chapter 7—the longest in the novel, and the chapter that gave Fitzgerald the most trouble—was thoroughly revised. The most interesting difference between manuscript and unrevised galleys comes near the beginning of the chapter when Gatsby tells Nick that Daisy wants to run off with him. In both the manuscript and unrevised galleys Gatsby seems weak and consumed with self-pity, as well as manifesting a degree of self-absorption that undercuts his "romantic readiness." Between manuscript (p. 114) and unrevised galleys Fitzgerald deleted Gatsby's complaints to Nick about Daisy's failure to understand his ambitions: "'Jay Gatsby!' he cried suddenly in a ringing voice, 'There goes the great Jay Gatsby! That's what people are going to say—wait and see, I'm only thirty-two now.'" Fitzgerald added to the typescript a description of Gatsby sobbing because Daisy doesn't understand that he wants her to tell Tom that she never loved him. But this typescript addition is counter-balanced by deletion of the manuscript account of Gatsby's absurdly sentimental song on pp. 4–5. There is an important change at the end of the chapter in the way Nick learns the truth about Myrtle's death. In the manuscript (p. 38) Gatsby volunteers the information that Daisy was driving; but in the unrevised galleys Nick guesses the truth, which Gatsby then admits—a clear improvement, because the reader's belief in the intensity of Gatsby's love for Daisy would be weakened by Gatsby's readiness to reveal Daisy's guilt. Most of chapter 7 was rewritten in proof.

Unrevised galleys (typescript) chapter 8 was not revised significantly from the manuscript, but of some interest is the alteration from manuscript third-person to first-person in the account of Gatsby's early career. In the manuscript it is biography reported by Nick (pp. 2–6), but in the unrevised galleys it is autobiography. When Fitzgerald moved the material from chapter 8 to chapter 6 in the revised galleys, he restored the third-person point-of-view. Obviously, he was undecided about how much of the spotlight to put on Gatsby. The effect of the third-person biographical form is to strengthen Nick as narrator and to obscure Gatsby's voice. Indeed, Gatsby speaks very little in the novel; Nick reports most of what Gatsby says to him—but in Nick-ese, not in Gatsby-ese.

Unrevised galleys (typescript) chapter 9 has one important addition: the passage in which Nick has the grotesque vision of the East as "a night scene by El Greco." Just before this new material, Fitzgerald deleted Nick's rejection of Eastern ways: "I don't like casualness, I don't like waters that close over your head without a bubble or a ripple when you go. The feeling that they shouldn't became a sort of obsession, then finally a horror to me . . ." (MS p. 39). After Nick's break with Jordan, the unrevised galleys add his summing up: "'I'm thirty,' I said. 'It's five years too late for me to lie to myself and call it honor.'" In the typescript Fitzgerald was still uncertain about how to handle Gatsby's association with Wolfshiem, and he excised Nick's explanation of Gatsby's criminal activities from manuscript p. 32 ("It was such luck that he should have run into Wolfshiem . . ."). Gatsby's success schedule is slightly revised between manuscript and unrevised galleys. The manuscript passage (p. 37) in which Nick seems to hear Gatsby at the funeral was deleted. Finally, in Nick's closing peroration, the manuscript's "green glimmer" became "green light" in the unrevised galleys: "Gatsby believed in the green light. . . ."

The Revised Galleys

Proof Revisions

MS revisions for galleys 13, 15, 17, 20–21, 26, 28 (Chapters 3, 4, 5): pp. 1–8.
MS (with carbon-copy typescript) revisions for galley 30 (opening of Chapter 6): pp. 1, 3, 1–5, 5½, 6.
MS (with carbon-copy typescript) revisions for galleys 34, 37, 39, 40, 42, 44 (Chapters 7 and 8): pp. 1–21.

The revised galley proofs at the Princeton University Library consist of 57 galleys, with chapters 6, 7, and 8 rewritten. That these revised galleys are the set Fitzgerald retained after sending another revised set to Perkins is clear, for the Princeton set includes the late revisions—in Fitzgerald's hand—that he sent to Perkins in letters. Since it is manifestly impossible for Fitzgerald—who was in Rome and Capri—to have made revisions on the galleys after they arrived in New York, it follows that he retained a duplicate set in which he entered these late changes. Moreover, there are no

editorial or compositorial marks on this set of revised galleys, and it is clear from the Fitzgerald/Perkins correspondence that Perkins had made queries on the master galleys. The master set of revised galleys sent to Perkins is presumably lost. In addition to the corrections written on the galleys, Fitzgerald pasted on them typed slips with longer insertions, which were themselves revised in holograph. His system for making these insertions was to write them in holograph and then have them typed on slips of paper. But, again, there are layers of galley revision. There survive with the manuscript revised carbon-copies of some of the insertions for the galley; since the pasted-on typed slips are carbon-copies, the sequence for some of the slips is: manuscript6typescript A & carbon (revised in holograph)6typescript B & carbon (revised and pasted to galleys).

The revised first galleys that Fitzgerald returned to Scribners marked the end of this real work on *The Great Gatsby*. Page proofs were sent to Fitzgerald (Perkins to Fitzgerald, 19 March), but he did not rework them. Fitzgerald did, however, send Perkins corrections and spot-revisions through March–April 1925—some of which were made in the second printing.[20] The revised galleys—after house-styling and correction by Perkins and the Scribners editors—became the text of the published novel.[21]

Chapter I (galleys 1–7): Every galley revised, but no major deletions or insertions.

Chapter II (galleys 7–12): Every galley revised, but no major deletions or insertions.

Chapter III (galleys 12–19): Hungry Englishmen shifted on galley 13 (book p. 35) and orchid-like movie actress removed. Conversation with mush-mouth men removed on galley 14. Description of Gatsby's smile and conversation about him inserted on galley 15 (book p. 40). Description of "Jazz History of the World" cut on galley 16. Account of director kissing actress deleted, and Jordan's good-night to Nick inserted on galley 17.

Chapter IV (galleys 19–25): Conversation between Nick and Gatsby in car rewritten on galleys 20–21 (book pp. 51–53).

Chapter V (galleys 25–30): Gatsby's offer to help Nick make money added on galley 26 (book p. 65). Conversation between Nick and Gatsby about Gatsby's wealth added on galley 28 (book p. 71). Phone call about Gatsby's business added on galley 29 (book p. 73).

Chapter VI (galleys 30–34): Killed and completely rewritten in proof. The most important change is that pieces of Gatsby's biography as related by Nick were moved to book chapter 6 from typescript chapters 7 and 8. The account of Gatsby's association with Dan Cody was shifted to the opening of book chapter 6 from typescript chapter 8; and Gatsby's conversation with Nick about Daisy after the party was shifted there from typescript chapter 7.

This major reorganization resulted from Perkins' suggestion that the large block of material about Gatsby's past in typescript chapter 8 be broken up. In the unrevised galleys for chapter 6 there is a detailed description of the second Gatsby party, which was a costume affair. The typescript and unrevised galleys had interesting material about the relationship between Daisy and Gatsby at this stage of their affair, particularly about Daisy's strong sense of superiority to Gatsby's guests. For example, there was an episode in which the orchid-like movie actress asks Gatsby for the name of Daisy's hairdresser—which he considers an enormous compliment and Daisy treats as absurd. The great exchange between Nick and Gatsby about repeating the past is new (book p. 86). Fitzgerald deleted the reference to Daisy's jealousy of Gatsby at the end of proof chapter 6: "or perhaps some authentically radiant young girl who, with one fresh glance at Gatsby, one moment of magical encounter, would blot out those five years of unwavering devotion."

Chapter VII (galleys 34–45): Given a new opening in proof. Galley 34 and 2/3 of galley 35 were killed and replaced with a shorter opening. The account of Gatsby's courtship originally here had already been transposed to chapter 6. The end of galley 37 was replaced by a new material in which Tom tells Nick and Jordan that he has been investigating Gatsby (book p. 95). Galleys 39–41–the confrontation scene in the Plaza Hotel–were rewritten in proof. This key scene, the fulcrum of the novel, concerned Fitzgerald the most in each stage of revision; and he felt that he never managed to get Daisy's reaction exactly right. The function of the galley revisions for this scene is twofold: to remove Gatsby's weakness and to make Tom's defeat of Gatsby more convincing. Tom does not really know what Gatsby's extra-legal activities are, but he knows enough to bluff Gatsby and scare Daisy. In the typescript Tom merely accuses Gatsby of being mixed up with Wolfshiem; but in the revised galleys Tom knows about Gatsby's bootlegging and his involvement with Walter Chase—which produces "that unfamiliar yet recognizable look" on Gatsby's face (book p. 105). The material about Biloxi was added on galley 39. Nick's ruminations on being thirty were revised on galley 42. As discussed above in the section of this introduction dealing with the typescript, Fitzgerald changed the revelation that Daisy was responsible for Myrtle's death on galley 44 from Gatsby's disclosure to Nick's guess.

Sequence in MS & TS (unrevised galleys)	Sequence in Book (revised galleys)
MS VI (TS 6)	6
	Biography of Gatsby (Cody)
Tom & friends visit Gatsby	Tom & friends visit Gatsby
Buchanans attend party	Buchanans attend party
	Gatsby tells Nick about love for Daisy
MS VI (TS 7)	7
Gatsby replaces servants	Gatsby replaces servants
Gatsby tells Nick about love for Daisy	
Lunch at Buchanan home	Lunch at Buchanan home
Tom stops for gas	Tom stops for gas
[Polo Grounds-Central Park & confrontation]	
Plaza & confrontation	Plaza & confrontation
Death of Myrtle	Death of Myrtle
Nick & Gatsby outside Buchanan home	Nick & Gatsby outside Buchanan home
MS VII (TS 8)	8
Biography of Gatsby (Cody)	
Gatsby's courtship & Daisy's marriage	Gatsby's courtship & Daisy's marriage
Nick & Jordan	Nick & Jordan
Flashback to garage	Flashback to garage
Murder of Gatsby	Murder of Gatsby

A. Galley 15

He smiled understandingly --- much more than understandingly.
It was one of those rare smiles with a quality of eternal reassurance
in it, that you may come across four or five times in life. It faced --
or seemed to face -- the whole eternal world for an instant, and
then concentrated on you with an irresistable prejudice in your favor.
It understood you just so far as you wanted to be understood, believed
in you as you would like to believe in yourself and assured you that
it had precisely that impression that, at your best, you hoped to
convey. Just at that point it vanished -- and I was looking at
an elegant young roughneck, a year or two over thirty, whose
elaborate formality of speech just missed being absurd. Some time
before he introduced himself I'd got a strong

(Join on to TP in galley)

A. galley 15

He smiled understandingly — much more than understandingly.
It was one of those rare smiles with a quality of eternal
reassurance in it that you may come across four or five
times in life. It faced — or seemed to face — the whole eternal
world for an instant, and then concentrated on you with an
irresistable prejudice in your favor. It understood you just
so far as you wanted to be understood, believed in you as
you would like to believe in yourself and assured you
that it had precisely that impression that, at your best, you
hoped to convey. Just at that point it vanished — and I
was looking at an elegant young roughneck, a year or
two over thirty, whose elaborate formality of speech just
missed being absurd. Some time before he introduced himself
I'd got a strong ...

(Join on to TP in galley) *B. galley 15* *Florida*

my surprise. I had expected that Mr. Gatsby would be a florid
and corpulent person in his middle years.
"Who is he?" I demanded, "Do you know?"
"He's just a man named Gatsby."
"Where is he from, I mean? And what does he do?"
"Now you've started on the subject," she answered with a
wan smile, "Well, — he told me once he was an Oxford man."
A dim background started to take shape behind him but at the
next remark it faded away.
"However, I don't believe it."
"Why not? "
"I don't know," she insisted, " I just don't think he went
there."
Something in her tone reminded me of the other girl's "I
think he killed a man," and had the effect of stimulating my
curiosity. I would have accepted without question the information
that Gatsby sprang from the swamps of Louisiana or the lower east
side of New York. That was comprehensible. But young men didn't --
at least in my provincial inexperience I believed they didn't --
drift coolly out of nowhere and buy a palace on Long Island Sound.
"Anyhow he gives large parties," said Jordan, changing the
subject with an urban distaste for the concrete. And I like large
parties. They're so intimate. At small parties there isn't any
privacy."
There was the boom of a base drum, and the voice of the
orchestra leader rang out suddenly above the chatter of the garden.

Fitzgerald revised the Gatsby *galleys by writing inserts and replacements in hand and then attaching the revised typed slips to the galleys. Here he rewrote Nick's first impression of Gatsby (Princeton University Library).*

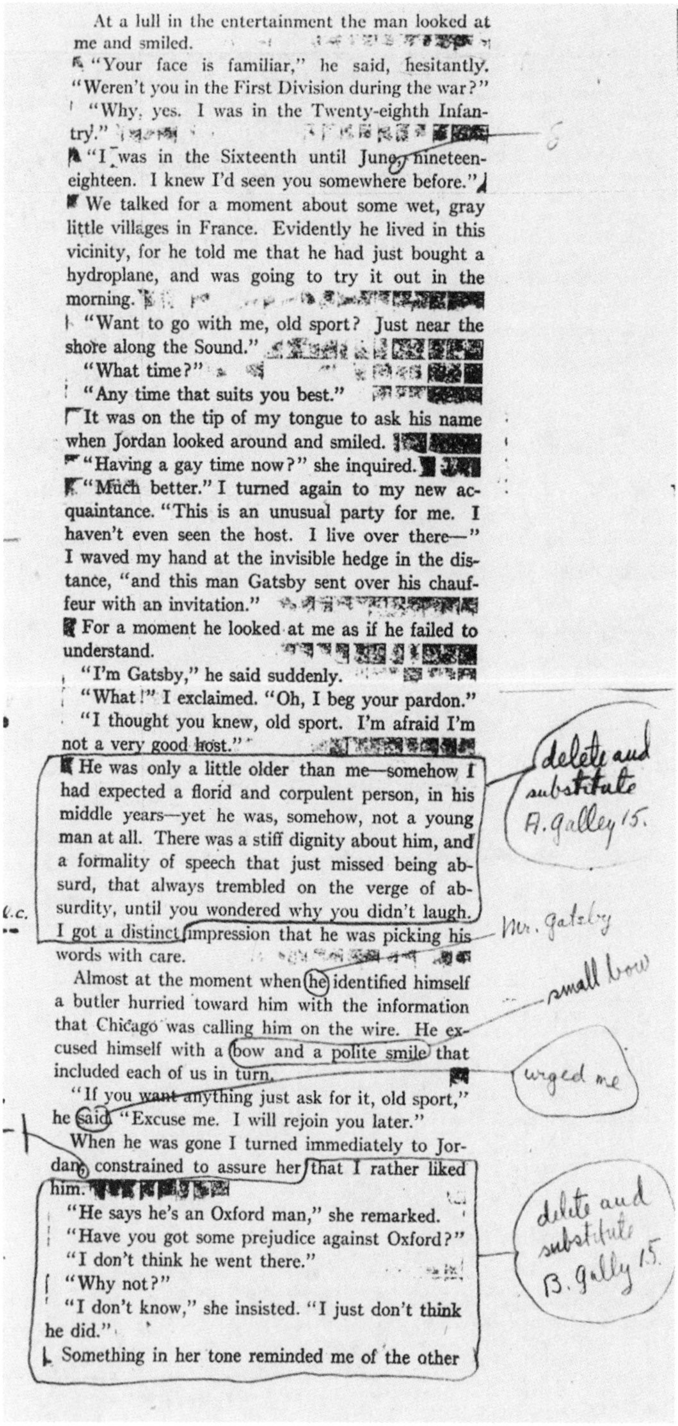

At a lull in the entertainment the man looked at me and smiled.

"Your face is familiar," he said, hesitantly. "Weren't you in the First Division during the war?"

"Why, yes. I was in the Twenty-eighth Infantry."

"I was in the Sixteenth until June, nineteen-eighteen. I knew I'd seen you somewhere before."

We talked for a moment about some wet, gray little villages in France. Evidently he lived in this vicinity, for he told me that he had just bought a hydroplane, and was going to try it out in the morning.

"Want to go with me, old sport? Just near the shore along the Sound."

"What time?"

"Any time that suits you best."

It was on the tip of my tongue to ask his name when Jordan looked around and smiled.

"Having a gay time now?" she inquired.

"Much better." I turned again to my new acquaintance. "This is an unusual party for me. I haven't even seen the host. I live over there—" I waved my hand at the invisible hedge in the distance, "and this man Gatsby sent over his chauffeur with an invitation."

For a moment he looked at me as if he failed to understand.

"I'm Gatsby," he said suddenly.

"What!" I exclaimed. "Oh, I beg your pardon."

"I thought you knew, old sport. I'm afraid I'm not a very good host."

He was only a little older than me—somehow I had expected a florid and corpulent person, in his middle years—yet he was, somehow, not a young man at all. There was a stiff dignity about him, and a formality of speech that just missed being absurd, that always trembled on the verge of absurdity, until you wondered why you didn't laugh. I got a distinct impression that he was picking his words with care.

Almost at the moment when he identified himself a butler hurried toward him with the information that Chicago was calling him on the wire. He excused himself with a bow and a polite smile that included each of us in turn.

"If you want anything just ask for it, old sport," he said. "Excuse me. I will rejoin you later."

When he was gone I turned immediately to Jordan, constrained to assure her that I rather liked him.

"He says he's an Oxford man," she remarked.

"Have you got some prejudice against Oxford?"

"I don't think he went there."

"Why not?"

"I don't know," she insisted. "I just don't think he did."

Something in her tone reminded me of the other

[handwritten annotations in margins:]
delete and substitute A. Galley 15.
l.c.
Mr. Gatsby
small bow
urged me
delete and substitute B. Galley 15.

Chapter VIII (galleys 45–51): Deletion of Gatsby's biography on galleys 45–47, which had already been shifted to chapter 6. On galley 48 (book p. 119) Fitzgerald inserted Gatsby's attempt to convince Nick that Daisy never loved Tom ("In any case . . . it was just personal") and Nick's thoughts about the intensity of Gatsby's commitment to Daisy.

Chapter IX (galleys 51–57): Insertion of the phone call from Slagle about the arrest of Young Parke (book p. 129), which is counterbalanced by the deletion on galley 54 of Nick's report of Wolfshiem's later trial "(but not conviction) on ten charges, ranging from simple bribery to dealing in stolen bonds." As we know, when Perkins questioned the mysteriousness of Gatsby's presumed criminal activities in the typescript, Fitzgerald admitted that at that point he had not known himself what Gatsby was supposed to be involved in. It was imperative that Fitzgerald account for Gatsby's money in a way that would neither cheapen nor harden him for the reader. Gatsby can't be in something like dope or prostitution, and he can't be a Caponetype gangster. In a rejected holograph revision for chapter 7 Tom states that Gatsby and Wolfshiem had been squeezing money out of "taxi drivers and drunks and the poor bums that hang around the streets"–a mean racket that would have cost Gatsby reader sympathy. Bootlegging was virtually respectable in the twenties, and stolen securities at least have a certain class. It is noteworthy that there are only five substantive proof revisions in Nick's coda, the richest passage of the novel.

After Fitzgerald dispatched the final batch of corrected galleys to Perkins from Rome on 18 February 1925, before departing for Capri, he sent a few spot-changes and insertions.[22] On 5 March Perkins wired: "All proofs and corrections received." Since the novel was published on 10 April, there was no time to send second galleys or page proofs back and forth across the Atlantic. Perkins and the editorial staff at Scribners did a remarkable job in producing the book from the revised galleys in less than a month, for whole chapters had to be reset.

In 1934 F. Scott Fitzgerald wrote an introduction for the Modern Library reprint of *The Great Gatsby* in which he declared: "Now that this book is being reissued, the author would like to say that never before did one try to keep his artistic conscience as pure as during the ten months put into doing it." And he went on to state that "What I cut out of it both physically and emotionally would make another novel!" This statement has been accepted at face value by critics who have postulated a much longer draft that Fitzgerald converted into a selective short novel. But if Fitzgerald's statement about physical cuts is to be taken literally, it can only apply to the 19th-century-midwest-Catholic pre-*Gatsby*–

from which nothing survives, except possibly "Absolution." It is clear from the surviving evidence that "physically" should be understood to mean that Fitzgerald left out material that he could have written–not that he actually excised material he had written.

The Great Gatsby is "extraordinary and beautiful and simple + intricately patterned" because F. Scott Fitzgerald was a genius and a craftsman.

–Revised from the Introduction to
The Great Gatsby: A Facsimile of the Manuscript
(Washington, D.C.: Bruccoli Clark/Microcard Editions, 1973), pp. xiii–xxxv.

Notes

1. Fitzgerald to Maxwell E. Perkins, c. 20 June 1922. Unless otherwise located, all Fitzgerald/Perkins letters referred to in this introduction are in *Dear Scott/Dear Max*, ed. Jackson Bryer and John Kuehl (New York: Scribners, 1971). An instructive article is Kenneth Eble's "The Craft of Revision: *The Great Gatsby*," *American Literature,* 36 (November 1964), 315–326.

2. Charles Scribner's Sons Archives, Princeton University Library.

3. Fitzgerald's *Ledger* specifies June 1923 for the writing of "Absolution," which was published in *The American Mercury* for June 1924. In 1934 Fitzgerald informed John Jamieson: "It might interest you to know that a story of mine, called 'Absolution'. . . was intended to be a picture of his [Gatsby's] early life, but that I cut it because I preferred to preserve the sense of mystery"–*The Letters of F. Scott Fitzgerald*, ed. Andrew Turnbull (New York: Scribners, 1963).

4. In *This Room and This Gin and These Sandwiches* (New York: New Republic, 1937); Wilson's play was first performed in October 1924.

5. After serial rights to *The Great Gatsby* were declined by Ray Long of the Hearst magazines and John Wheeler of *Liberty,* H. N. Swanson offered $10,000 in January 1925 for serial publication by *College Humor*. Fitzgerald rejected it because he did not want to delay book publication for less than $20,000, and because he thought that serialization in *College Humor* would give the book a frivolous image. For the Fitzgerald/Ober correspondence bearing on these negotiations see *As Ever, Scott Fitz–*, ed. Matthew J. Bruccoli and Jennifer McC. Atkinson (New York & Philadelphia: Lippincott, 1972).

6. A note on the manuscript reads: "Returne a Institut Gaudeo 19 Avenue de la Victoire Nice"–almost certainly the typing agency.

7. Charles Scribner's Sons Archives, Princeton University Library.

8. "Max, it amuses me when praise comes in on the 'structure' of the book–because it was you who fixed up the structure, not me" (c. 10 July 1925).

9. Compare Hemingway's "my new theory that you could omit anything if you knew that you omitted and the omitted part would strengthen the story and make people feel something more than they understood"–*A Moveable Feast* (New York: Scribners, 1964, p. 75). *Gatsby* was published

before Fitzgerald met Hemingway.

10. "'Orgastic' is the adjective from 'orgasm' and it expresses exactly the intended ecstasy." The first edition read "orgastic"; but all subsequent American editions, beginning with the 1941 *Last Tycoon-Great Gatsby* volume, have "orgiastic." The case is complicated by the fact that Fitzgerald's corrected copy of *Gatsby* includes the change to "orgiastic"; but it is impossible to determine that the inserted "i" is in his hand. See Jennifer E. Atkinson, "Fitzgerald's Marked Copy of *The Great Gatsby*," *Fitzgerald/Hemingway Annual 1970*.

11. Ring Lardner's brother Rex was a *Liberty* editor and read *The Great Gatsby* in proof when it was being considered for serialization. He called Perkins's attention to the fact that Dan Cody's yacht could not have been threatened by tides in Lake Superior (Perkins to Fitzgerald, 19 March 1925). Ring Lardner also read the novel in page proof and informed Fitzgerald that he had provided Perkins with "a brief list of what I thought were errata": "On Pages 31 and 46 you spoke of the news-stand on the *lower level,* and the cold waiting room on the *lower level* of the Pennsylvania Station. There ain't any lower level at that station and I suggested substitute terms for same. On Page 82, you had the guy driving his car under the elevated at Astoria, which isn't Astoria, but Long Island City. On Page 118 you had a tide in Lake Superior and on Page 209 you had the Chicago Milwaukee & St. Paul running out of the LaSalle Street Station" (24 March 1925–Princeton University Library). Only the tides and the LaSalle Street Station were corrected.

12. *Letters*, p. 341.

13. *Letters*, p. 480.

14. Other obvious splices in the manuscript are at I, 12–15; I, 18–20; I, 24–26; I, (31–32)–33; II, 40–41; III, 72–73; V, 15–17; VII, 19–20.

15. On p. 83 of MS III Daisy Fay Buchanan's maiden name is given as *Machen,* which was Zelda Fitzgerald's mother's maiden name.

16. For a study of Fitzgerald's writing habits, see Bruccoli, *The Composition of Tender Is the Night* (Pittsburgh: University of Pittsburgh Press, 1963).

17. On p. 2 of MS chapter V occurs the only instance when Fitzgerald left a space in the manuscript for a word to be inserted later: "–there was a sharp line where my ragged lawn ended and the darker, well-kept   of his began." The word he wanted was "expanse."

18. The first "old sport" in the book occurs at p. 57 when Gatsby invites Nick to try out his hydroplane.

19. Herman Rosenthal was murdered outside the Metropole Hotel on 43rd Street off Times Square in 1912. At manuscript p. 76 Fitzgerald mistakenly has Wolfshiem identify Jack Rose–not Rosenthal–as the victim; but Rose was actually implicated in the murder. Wolfshiem could not have been eating with Rosenthal, for Rosenthal was alone at the Metropole table when he was called outside. Arnold Rothstein–the model for Wolfshiem–was not involved in the Rosenthal murder. However, Rothstein was an enemy of police captain Becker, one of the five men electrocuted for the murder; and Rothstein was at that time a close friend of Herbert Bayard Swope, then a young reporter whose coverage of the case helped to make him famous.

When Fitzgerald was working on *The Great Gatsby* he lived near Swope at Great Neck.

20. The August 1925 printing had six plate changes: 60.16 chatter [echolalia; 119.22 northern [southern; 165.16 it's [its; 165.29 away [away.; 205.9–10 sick in tired [sickantired; 211.7–8 Union Street station [Union Station. For the publication history of *The Great Gatsby*, see Bruccoli, *F. Scott Fitzgerald: A Descriptive Bibliography* (Pittsburgh: University of Pittsburgh Press, 1972).

21. It is important to recognize that Fitzgerald did not resist house-styling: he expected and welcomed it. The texture of the punctuation in *The Great Gatsby* represents a collaboration between author and editors.

22. On 18 February 1925–the day he mailed the final batch of galleys–Fitzgerald wired Perkins: "HOLD UP GALLEY FORTY FOR BIG CHANGE," the Plaza Hotel confrontation scene. Other late alterations for which undated correspondence survives in the Charles Scribner's Sons Archives (Princeton University Library) involve the insertion of Gatsby's suggestion that he and Nick use the pool on galley 25 (book 98.21–23); the insertion of a description of Gatsby on galley 16 (book 61.1–4); the revision of "Just" to "Precisely" (galley 15; book 58.28); the insertion of "toward" (galley 25; book 98.18); the correction of "demanding" to "demanded" (galley 53; book 202.28); the emendation of "November" to "December" (galley 55; book 211.8); the correction of the typo "gounds" (galley 28; book 112.16); the emendation of "chatter" to "echolalia" (galley 15; book 60.16–made in second printing); the emendation of "unsubstantial" to "short-winded" (galley 1; book 3.5); the deletion of "the" in "the West Egg Village" (galley 1; book 4.24); the emendation of "shadow" to "silhouette" (galley 7; book 25.22); the emendation of "sick in tired" to "sickantired" (book 205.9–10–made in second printing).

CLUSTER STORIES

For a long time Fitzgerald's short stories were studied apart as separate from his novels. Because they appeared in mass-circulation magazines that paid him very well, Fitzgerald's "commercial" stories were branded as hackwork or pot-boilers that consumed writing time he should have conserved for serious work. The relationship between the stories and novels is now better understood. The stories written before and during the gestation and composition of The Great Gatsby and Tender Is the Night often have close thematic connections with those novels; therefore they have been designated as "cluster stories"–the narratives that cluster around a novel and in which Fitzgerald was testing material and ideas. Five of his 1922–1924 stories constitute the Gatsby cluster: "The Diamond as Big as the Ritz" (1922), "Winter Dreams" (1922), "Dice, Brassknuckles & Guitar" (1923), "Absolution" (1924), and "'The Sensible Thing'" (1924). These stories variously deal with the aspiration for and the corruption of wealth, the love of a poor boy for an unattainable girl, and the connection between love and money. The Gatsby-related stories may be read as works-in-progress toward the novel.

Fitzgerald wrote in the room over the garage at 6 Gateway Drive, Great Neck.

THE DIAMOND AS BIG AS THE RITZ

Fitzgerald's long story "The Diamond as Big as the Ritz" was published in June 1922 by The Smart Set *after the mass-circulation magazines rejected it as blasphemous. Fitzgerald explained in his annotated contents page for* Tales of the Jazz Age *(1926), the volume in which he collected the story, that "I was in a mood characterized by a perfect craving for luxury, and the story began as an attempt to feed that craving on imaginary foods."*

Full in the light of the stars, an exquisite château rose from the borders of the lake, climbed in marble radiance half the height of an adjoining mountain, then melted in grace, in perfect symmetry, in translucent feminine languor, into the massed darkness of a forest of pine. The many towers, the slender tracery of the sloping parapets, the chiselled wonder of a thousand yellow windows with their oblongs and hectagons and triangles of golden light, the shattered softness of the intersecting planes of starshine and blue shade, all trembled on John's spirit like a chord of music. On one of the towers, the tallest, the blackest at its base, an arrangement of exterior lights at the top made a sort of floating fairyland—and as John gazed up in warm enchantment the faint acciaccare sound of violins drifted down in a rococo harmony that was like nothing he had ever heard before. Then in a moment the car stopped before wide, high marble steps around which the night air was fragrant with a host of flowers. At the top of the steps two great doors swung silently open and amber light flooded out upon the darkness, silhouetting the figure of an exquisite lady with black, high-piled hair, who held out her arms toward them.

"Mother," Percy was saying, "this is my friend, John Unger, from Hades."

Afterward John remembered that first night as a daze of many colors, of quick sensory impressions, of music soft as a voice in love, and of the beauty of things, lights and shadows, and motions and faces. There was a white-haired man who stood drinking a many-hued cordial from a crystal thimble set on a golden stem. There was a girl with a flowery face, dressed like Titania with braided sapphires in her hair. There was a room where the solid, soft gold of the walls yielded to the pressure of his hand, and a room that was like a platonic conception of the ultimate prism—ceiling, floor, and all, it was lined with an unbroken mass of diamonds, diamonds of every

(Matthew J. and Arlyn Bruccoli Collection, University of South Carolina Library)

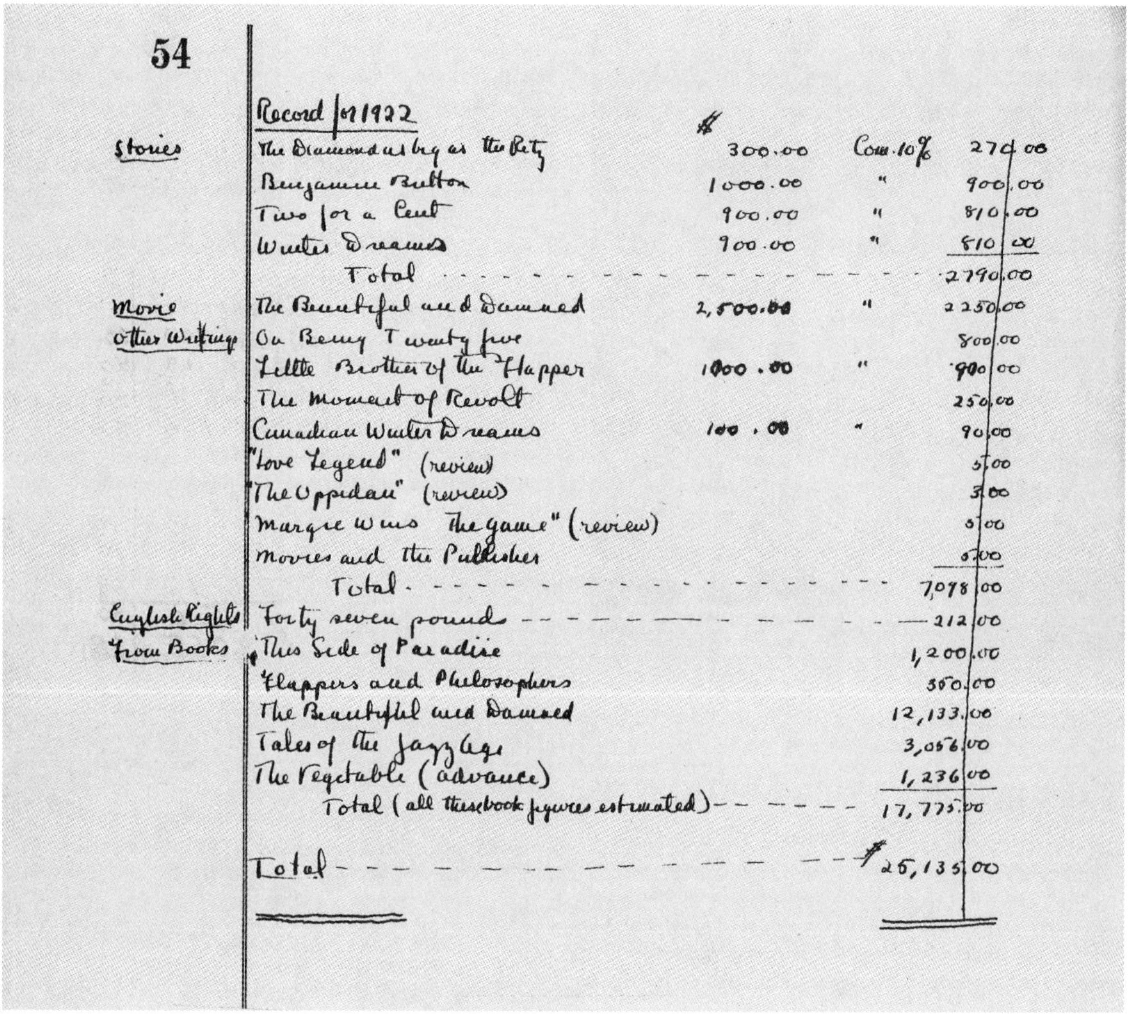

54

	Record for 1922	$		
Stories	The Diamond as big as the Ritz	300.00	Com. 10%	270.00
	Benjamin Button	1000.00	"	900.00
	Two for a Cent	900.00	"	810.00
	Winter Dreams	900.00	"	810.00
	Total			2,790.00
Movie	The Beautiful and Damned	2,500.00	"	2,250.00
Other Writings	On Being Twenty five			800.00
	Little Brother of the Flapper	1000.00	"	900.00
	The Moment of Revolt			250.00
	Canadian Winter Dreams	100.00	"	90.00
	"Love Legend" (review)			5.00
	"The Oppidan" (review)			5.00
	"Margie Wins the Game" (review)			5.00
	Movies and the Publisher			5.00
	Total			7,078.00
English Rights	Forty seven pound			212.00
From Books	This Side of Paradise			1,200.00
	Flappers and Philosophers			350.00
	The Beautiful and Damned			12,133.00
	Tales of the Jazz Age			3,056.00
	The Vegetable (advance)			1,236.00
	Total (all these book figures estimated)			17,775.00
	Total			$25,135.00

Fitzgerald's Ledger *entry for the year he began planning his third novel notes the publication of "Winter Dreams" and "The Diamond as Big as the Ritz."*

size and shape, until, lit with tall violet lamps in the corners, it dazzled the eyes with a whiteness that could be compared only with itself, beyond human wish or dream.

Through a maze of these rooms the two boys wandered. Sometimes the floor under their feet would flame in brilliant patterns from lighting below, patterns of barbaric clashing colors, of pastel delicacy, of sheer whiteness, or of subtle and intricate mosaic, surely from some mosque on the Adriatic Sea. Sometimes beneath layers of thick crystal he would see blue or green water swirling, inhabited by vivid fish and growths of rainbow foliage. Then they would be treading on furs of every texture and color or along corridors of palest ivory, unbroken as

though carved complete from the gigantic tusks of dinosaurs extinct before the age of man. . . .

    —Tales of the Jazz Age

WINTER DREAMS

Fitzgerald described "Winter Dreams" (Metropolitan, *December 1922; collected in* All the Sad Young Men) *as "a miniature of Gatsby."*

Some of the caddies were poor as sin and lived in one-room houses with a neurasthenic cow in the front yard, but Dexter Green's father owned the second best grocery-store in Black Bear—the best one was "The

Hub," patronized by the wealthy people from Sherry Island—and Dexter caddied only for pocket-money.

In the fall when the days became crisp and gray, and the long Minnesota winter shut down like the white lid of a box, Dexter's skis moved over the snow that hid the fairways of the golf course. At these times the country gave him a feeling of profound melancholy—it offended him that the links should lie in enforced fallowness, haunted by ragged sparrows for the long season. It was dreary, too, that on the tees where the gay colors fluttered in summer there were now only the desolate sand-boxes knee-deep in crusted ice. When he crossed the hills the wind blew cold as misery, and if the sun was out he tramped with his eyes squinted up against the hard dimensionless glare.

In April the winter ceased abruptly. The snow ran down into Black Bear Lake scarcely tarrying for the early golfers to brave the season with red and black balls. Without elation, without an interval of moist glory, the cold was gone.

Dexter knew that there was something dismal about this Northern spring, just as he knew there was something gorgeous about the fall. Fall made him clinch his hands and tremble and repeat idiotic sentences to himself, and make brisk abrupt gestures of command to imaginary audiences and armies. October filled him with hope which November raised to a sort of ecstatic triumph, and in this mood the fleeting brilliant impressions of the summer at Sherry Island were ready grist to his mill. He became a golf champion and defeated Mr. T. A. Hedrick in a marvellous match played a hundred times over the fairways of his imagination, a match each detail of which he changed about untiringly—sometimes he won with almost laughable ease, sometimes he came up magnificently from behind. Again, stepping from a Pierce-Arrow automobile, like Mr. Mortimer Jones, he strolled frigidly into the lounge of the Sherry Island Golf Club—or perhaps, surrounded by an admiring crowd, he gave an exhibition of fancy diving from the spring-board of the club raft. . . . Among those who watched him in open-mouthed wonder was Mr. Mortimer Jones.

And one day it came to pass that Mr. Jones—himself and not his ghost—came up to Dexter with tears in his eyes and said that Dexter was the—best caddy in the club, and wouldn't he decide not to quit if Mr. Jones made it worth his while, because every other—caddy in the club lost one ball a hole for him—regularly—

"No, sir," said Dexter decisively, "I don't want to caddy any more." Then, after a pause: "I'm too old."

"You're not more than fourteen. Why the devil did you decide just this morning that you wanted to quit? You promised that next weed you'd go over the the State tournament with me."

"I decided I was too old."

Dexter handed in his "A Class" badge, collected what money was due him from the caddy master, and walked home to Black Bear Village.

"The best—caddy I ever saw," shouted Mr. Mortimer Jones over a drink that afternoon. "Never lost a ball! Willing! Intelligent! Quiet! Honest! Grateful!"

The little girl who had done this was eleven—beautifully ugly as little girls are apt to be who are destined after a few years to be inexpressibly lovely and bring no end of misery to a great number of men. The spark, however, was perceptible. There was a general ungodliness in the way her lips twisted down at the corners when she smiled, and in the—Heaven help us!—in the almost passionate quality of her eyes. Vitality is born early in such women. It was utterly in evidence now, shining through her thin frame in a sort of glow.

She had come eagerly out on to the course at nine o'clock with a white linen nurse and five small new golf-clubs in a white canvas bag which the nurse was carrying. When Dexter first saw her she was standing by the caddy house, rather ill as ease and trying to conceal the fact by engaging her nurse in an obviously unnatural conversation graced by startling and irrelevant grimaces from herself.

"Well, it's certainly a nice day, Hilda," Dexter heard her say. She drew down the corners of her mouth, smiled, and glanced furtively around, her eyes in transit falling for an instant on Dexter.

Then to the nurse:

"Well, I guess there aren't very many people out here this morning, are there?"

The smile again—radiant, blatantly artificial—convincing.

"I don't know what we're supposed to do now," said the nurse, looking nowhere in particular.

"Oh, that's all right. I'll fix it up."

Dexter stood perfectly still, his mouth slightly ajar. He knew that if he moved forward a step his stare would be in her line of vision—if he moved backward he would lose his full view of her face. For a moment he had not realized how young she was. Now he remembered having seen her several times the year before—in bloomers.

Suddenly, involuntarily, he laughed, a short abrupt laugh—then, startled by himself, he turned and began to walk quickly away.

"Boy!"

Dexter stopped.

"Boy—"

Beyond question he was addressed. Not only that, but he was treated to that absurd smile, that preposterous smile—the memory of which at least a dozen men were to carry into middle age.

METROPOLITAN

Winter Dreams
by F. Scott Fitzgerald

Illustrations by Arthur William Brown

"I don't know what's the matter with me. Last night I thought I was in love with a man and to-night I think I'm in love with you—"

ARTHUR WILLIAM BROWN —'22

SOME of the caddies were poor as sin and lived in one-room houses with a neurasthenic cow in the front yard, but Dexter Green's father owned the second best grocery store in Dillard—the best one was "The Hub," patronized by the wealthy people from Lake Erminie—and Dexter caddied only for pocket-money.

In the fall when the days became crisp and grey and the long Minnesota winter shut down like the white lid of a box, Dexter's skis moved over the snow that hid the fairways of the golf course. At these times the country gave him a feeling of profound melancholy—it offended him that the links should lie in enforced gallowness, haunted by ragged sparrows for the long season. It was dreary, too, that on the tees where the gay colors fluttered in summer there were now only the desolate sand-boxes knee-deep in crusted ice. When he crossed the hills the wind blew cold as misery, and if the sun was out he tramped with his eyes squinted up against the hard dimensionless glare.

In April the winter ceased abruptly. The snow ran down into Lake Erminie scarcely tarrying for the early golfers to brave the season with red and black balls. Without elation,

Readers of the mass-circulation magazines in the 1920s expected short stories to be illustrated. Fitzgerald liked Arthur William Brown's work.

"Boy, do you know where the golf teacher is?"

"He's giving a lesson."

"Well, do you know where the caddy-master is?"

"He isn't here yet this morning."

"Oh." For a moment this baffled her. She stood alternately on her right and left foot.

"We'd like to get a caddy," said the nurse. "Mrs. Mortimer Jones sent us out to play golf, and we don't know how without we get a caddy."

Here she was stopped by an ominous glance from Miss Jones, followed immediately by the smile.

"There aren't any caddies here except me," said Dexter to the nurse, "and I got to stay here in charge until the caddy-master gets here."

"Oh."

Miss Jones and her retinue now withdrew, and at a proper distance from Dexter became involved in a heated conversation, which was concluded by Miss Jones taking one of the clubs and hitting it on the ground with violence. For further emphasis she raised it again and was about to bring it down smartly upon the nurse's bosom, when the nurse seized the club and twisted it from her hands.

"You damn little mean old *thing*!" cried Miss Jones wildly.

Another argument ensued. Realizing that the elements of the comedy were implied in the scene, Dexter several times began to laugh, but each time restrained the laugh before it reached audibility. He could not resist the monstrous conviction that the little girl was justified in beating the nurse.

The situation was resolved by the fortuitous appearance of the caddy-master, who was appealed to immediately by the nurse.

"Miss Jones is to have a little caddy, and this one says he can't go."

"Mr. McKenna said I was to wait here till you came," said Dexter quickly.

"Well, he's here now." Miss Jones smiled cheerfully at the caddy-master. Then she dropped her bag and set off at a haughty mince toward the first tee.

"Well?" The caddy-master turned to Dexter. "What you standing there like a dummy for? Go pick up the young lady's clubs."

"I don't think I'll go out today," said Dexter.

"You don't—"

"I think I'll quit."

The enormity of his decision frightened him. He was a favorite caddy, and the thirty dollars a month he earned through the summer were not to be made elsewhere around the lake. But he had received a strong emotional shock, and his perturbation required a violent and immediate outlet.

It is not so simple as that, either. As so frequently would be the case in the future, Dexter was unconsciously dictated to by his winter dreams.

II

Now, of course, the quality and the seasonability of these winter dreams varied, but the stuff of them remained. They persuaded Dexter several years later to pass up a business course at the State university—his father, prospering now, would have paid his way—for the precarious advantage of attending an older and more famous university in the East, where he was bothered by his scanty funds. But do not get the impression, because his winter dreams happened to be concerned at first with musings on the rich, that there was anything merely snobbish in the boy. He wanted not association with glittering things and glittering people—he wanted the glittering things themselves. Often he reached out for the best without knowing why he wanted it—and sometimes he ran up against the mysterious denials and prohibitions in which life indulges. It is with one of those denials and not with his career as a whole that this story deals.

He made money. It was rather amazing. After college he went to the city from which Black Bear Lake draws its wealthy patrons. When he was only twenty-three and had been there not quite two years, there were already people who liked to say, "Now *there's* a boy—" All about him rich men's sons were peddling bonds precariously, or investing patrimonies precariously, or plodding through the two dozen volumes of the "George Washington Commercial Course," but Dexter borrowed a thousand dollars on his college degree and his confident mouth, and bought a partnership in a laundry.

It was a small laundry when he went into it but Dexter made a speciality of learning how the English washed fine woolen golf-stockings without shrinking them, and within a year he was catering to the trade that wore knickerbockers. Men were insisting that their shetland hose and sweaters go to his laundry just as they had insisted on a caddy who could find golf balls. A little later he was doing their wives' lingerie as well—and running five branches in different parts of the city. Before he was twenty-seven he owned the largest string of laundries in his section of the country. It was then that he sold out and went to New York. But the part of his story that concerns us goes back to the days when he was making his first big success.

When he was twenty-three Mr. Hart—one of the gray-haired men who like to say "Now there's a boy"—gave him a guest card to the Sherry Island Golf Club for a weekend. So he signed his name one day on the register, and that afternoon played golf in a foursome with Mr. Hart and Mr. Sandwood and Mr. T. A. Hedrick. He did not consider it necessary to remark that he had once carried Mr. Hart's bag over this same links, and that he knew every trap and gully with his eyes shut—but he found himself glancing at the four caddies who trailed them, trying to catch a gleam or gesture that would remind him of himself, that would lessen the gap which lay between his present and his past.

It was a curious day, slashed abruptly with fleeting, familiar impressions. One minute he had the sense of being a trespasser—in the next he was impressed by the tremendous superiority he felt toward Mr. T. A. Hedrick, who was a bore and not even a good golfer any more.

Then, because of a ball Mr. Hart lost near the fifteenth green, an enormous thing happened. While they were searching the stiff grasses of the rough there was a clear call of "Fore!" from behind a hill in their rear. And as they all turned abruptly from their search a bright new ball sliced abruptly over the hill and caught Mr. T. A. Hedrick in the abdomen.

"By Gad!" cried Mr. T. A. Hedrick, "they ought to put some of these crazy women off the course. It's getting to be outrageous."

A head and a voice came up together over the hill:

"Do you mind if we go through?"

"You hit me in the stomach!" declared Mr. Hedrick wildly.

"Did I?" The girl approached the group of men. "I'm sorry. I yelled 'Fore!'"

Her glance fell casually on each of the men—then scanned the fairway for her ball.

"Did I bounce into the rough?"

It was impossible to determine whether this question was ingenuous or malicious. In a moment, however, she left no doubt, for as her partner came up over the hill she called cheerfully:

"Here I am! I'd have gone on the green except that I hit something."

As she took her stance for a short mashie shot, Dexter looked at her closely. She wore a blue gingham dress, rimmed at throat and shoulders with a white edging that accentuated her tan. The quality of exaggeration, of thinness, which had made her passionate eyes and down-turning mouth absurd at eleven, was gone now. She was arrestingly beautiful. The color in her cheeks was centered like the color in a picture—it was not a "high" color, but a sort of fluctuating and feverish warmth, so shaded that it seemed at any moment it would recede and disappear. This color and the mobility of her mouth gave a continual impression of flux, of

intense life, of passionate vitality—balanced only partially by the sad luxury of her eyes.

She swung her mashie impatiently and without interest, pitching the ball into a sand-pit on the other side of the green. With a quick, insincere smile and a careless "Thank you!" she went on after it.

"That Judy Jones!" remarked Mr. Hedrick on the next tee, as they waited—some moments—for her to play on ahead. "All she needs is to be turned up and spanked for six months and then to be married off to an old-fashioned cavalry captain."

"My God, she's good-looking!" said Mr. Sandwood, who was just over thirty.

"Good-looking!" cried Mr. Hedrick contemptuously, "she always looks as if she wanted to be kissed! Turning those big cow-eyes on every calf in town!"

It was doubtful if Mr. Hedrick intended a reference to the maternal instinct.

"She'd play pretty good golf if she'd try," said Mr. Sandwood.

"She has no form," said Mr. Hedrick solemnly.

"She has a nice figure," said Mr. Sandwood.

"Better thank the Lord she doesn't drive a swifter ball," said Mr. Hart, winking at Dexter.

Later in the afternoon the sun went down with a riotous swirl of gold and varying blues and scarlets, and left the dry, rustling night of Western summer. Dexter watched from the veranda of the Golf Club, watched the even overlap of the waters in the little wind, silver molasses under the harvest-moon. Then the moon held a finger to her lips and the lake became a clear pool, pale and quiet. Dexter put on his bathing suit and swam out to the farthest raft, where he stretched dripping on the wet canvas of the spring-board.

There was a fish jumping and a star shining and the lights around the lake were gleaming. Over on a dark peninsula a piano was playing the songs of last summer and of summers before that—songs from "Chin-Chin" and "The Count of Luxemburg" and "The Chocolate Soldier"—and because the sound of a piano over a stretch of water had always seemed beautiful to Dexter he lay perfectly quiet and listened.

The tune the piano was playing at that moment had been gay and new five years before when Dexter was a sophomore at college. They had played it at a prom once when he could not afford the luxury of proms, and he had stood outside the gymnasium and listened. The sound of the tune precipitated in him a sort of ecstasy and it was with that ecstasy he viewed what happened to him now. It was a mood of intense appreciation, a sense that, for once, he was magnificently attune to life and that everything about him was radiating a brightness and a glamour he might never know again.

A low, pale oblong detached itself suddenly from the darkness of the Island, spitting forth the reverberate sound of a racing motor-boat. Two white streamers of cleft water rolled themselves out behind it and almost immediately the boat was beside him, drowning out the hot tinkle of the piano in the drone of its spray. Dexter raising himself on his arms was aware of a figure standing at the wheel, of two dark eyes regarding him over the lengthening space of water—then the boat had gone by and was sweeping in an immense and purposeless circle of spray round and round in the middle of the lake. With equal eccentricity one of the circles flattened out and headed back toward the raft.

"Who's that?" she called, shutting off her motor. She was so near now that Dexter could see her bathing suit, which consisted apparently of pink rompers.

The nose of the boat bumped the raft, and as the latter tilted rakishly he was precipitated toward her. With different degrees of interest they recognized each other.

"Aren't you one of those men we played through this afternoon?" she demanded.

He was.

"Well, do you know how to drive a motor-boat? Because if you do I wish you'd drive this one so I can ride on the surf-board behind. My name is Judy Jones"—she favored him with an absurd smirk—rather, what tried to be a smirk, for, twist her mouth as she might, it was not grotesque, it was merely beautiful—"and I live in a house over there on the Island, and in that house there is a man waiting for me. When he drove up at the door I drove out of the dock because he says I'm his ideal."

There was a fish jumping and a star shining and the lights around the lake were gleaming. Dexter sat beside Judy Jones and she explained how her boat was driven. Then she was in the water, swimming to the floating surf-board with a sinuous crawl. Watching her was without effort to the eye, watching a branch waving or a sea-gull flying. Her arms, burned to butternut, moved sinuously among the dull platinum ripples, elbow appearing first, casting the forearm back with a cadence of falling water, then reaching out and down, stabbing a path ahead.

They moved out into the lake; turning, Dexter saw that she was kneeling on the low rear of the now uptilted surf-board.

"Go faster," she called, "fast as it'll go."

Obediently he jammed the lever forward and the white spray mounted at the bow. When he looked around again the girl was standing up on the rushing board, her arms spread wide, her eyes lifted toward the moon.

"It's awful cold," she shouted. "What's your name?"

He told her.

"Well, why don't you come to dinner tomorrow night?"

His heart turned over like the fly-wheel of the boat, and, for the second time, her casual whim gave a new direction to his life.

III

Next evening while he waited for her to come downstairs, Dexter peopled the soft deep summer room and the sun-porch that opened from it with the men who had already loved Judy Jones. He knew the sort of men they were—the men who when he first went to college had entered from the great prep schools with graceful clothes and the deep tan of healthy summers. He had seen that, in one sense, he was better than these men. He was newer and stronger. Yet in acknowledging to himself that he wished his children to be like them he was admitting that he was but the rough, strong stuff from which they eternally sprang.

When the time had come for him to wear good clothes, he had known who were the best tailors in America, and the best tailors in America had made him the suit he wore this evening. He had acquired that particular reserve peculiar to his university, that set if off from other universities. He recognized the value to him of such a mannerism and he had adopted it; he knew that to be careless in dress and manner required more confidence that to be careful. But carelessness was for his children. His mother's name had been Krimslich. She was a Bohemian of the peasant class and she had talked broken English to the end of her days. Her son must keep to the set patterns.

At a little after seven Judy Jones came downstairs. She wore a blue silk afternoon dress, and he was disappointed at first that she had not put on something more elaborate. This feeling was accentuated when, after a brief greeting, she went to the door of a butler's pantry and pushing it open called: "You can serve dinner, Martha." He had rather expected that a butler would announce dinner, that there would be a cocktail. Then he put these thoughts behind him as they sat down side by side on a lounge and looked at each other.

"Father and mother won't be here," she said thoughtfully.

He remembered the last time he had seen her father, and he was glad the parents were not to be here tonight—they might wonder who he was. He had been born in Keeble, a Minnesota village fifty miles farther north, and he always gave Keeble as his home instead of Black Bear Village. Country towns were well enough

"The name is Judy Jones. Ghastly reputation but enormously popular." She favored him with an absurd smirk—rather, what tried to be a smirk, for, twist her mouth as she might, it was not grotesque, it was merely beautiful

This passage from "Winter Dreams" was revised in the book text.

to come from if they weren't inconveniently in sight and used as footstools by fashionable lakes.

They talked of his university, which she had visited frequently during the past two years, and of the near-by city which supplied Sherry Island with its patrons, and whither Dexter would return next day to his prospering laundries.

During dinner she slipped into a moody depression which gave Dexter a feeling of uneasiness. Whatever petulance she uttered in her throaty voice worried him. Whatever she smiled at—at him, at a chicken liver, at nothing—it disturbed him that her smile could have no root in mirth, or even in amusement. When the scarlet corners of her lips curved down, it was less a smile than an invitation to a kiss.

Then, after dinner, she led him out on the dark sun-porch and deliberately changed the atmosphere.

"Do you mind if I weep a little?" she said.

"I'm afraid I'm boring you," he responded quickly.

"You're not. I like you. But I've just had a terrible afternoon. There was a man I cared about, and this afternoon he told me out of a clear sky that he was poor as a church-mouse. He'd never even hinted it before. Does this sound horrible mundane?"

"Perhaps he was afraid to tell you."

"Suppose he was," she answered. "He didn't start right. You see, if I'd thought of him as poor—well, I've been mad about loads of poor men, and fully intended to marry them all. But in this case, I hadn't thought of him that way, and my interest in him wasn't strong enough to survive the shock. As if a girl calmly informed her fiancé that she was a widow. He might not object to widows, but—

"Let's start right," she interrupted herself suddenly. "Who are you, anyhow?"

For a moment Dexter hesitated. Then:

"I'm nobody," he announced. "My career is largely a matter of futures."

"Are you poor?"

"No," he said frankly, "I'm probably making more money than any man my age in the Northwest. I know that's an obnoxious remark, but you advised me to start right."

There was a pause. Then she smiled and the corners of her mouth drooped and an almost imperceptible sway brought her closer to him, looking up into his eyes. A lump rose in Dexter's throat, and he waited breathless for the experiment, facing the unpredictable compound that would form mysteriously from the elements of their lips. Then he saw—she communicated her excitement to him, lavishly, deeply, with kisses that were not a promise but a fulfillment. They aroused in him not hunger demanding renewal but surfeit that

would demand more surfeit . . . kisses that were like charity, creating want by holding back nothing at all.

It did not take him many hours to decide that he had wanted Judy Jones ever since he was a proud, desirous little boy.

IV

It began like that—and continued, with varying shades of intensity, on such a note right up to the dénouement. Dexter surrendered a part of himself to the most direct and unprincipled personality with which he had ever come in contact. Whatever Judy wanted, she went after with the full pressure of her charm. There was no divergence of method, no jockeying for position or premeditation of effects—there was a very little mental side to any of her affairs. She simply made men conscious to the highest degree of her physical loveliness. Dexter had no desire to change her. Her deficiencies were knit up with a passionate energy that transcended and justified them.

When, as Judy's head lay against his shoulder that first night, she whispered, "I don't know what's the matter with me. Last night I thought I was in love with a man and tonight I think I'm in love with you—"—it seemed to him a beautiful and romantic thing to say. It was the exquisite excitability that for the moment he controlled and owned. But a week later he was compelled to view this same quality in a different light. She took him in her roadster to a picnic supper, and after supper she disappeared, likewise in her roadster, with another man. Dexter became enormously upset and was scarcely able to be decently civil to the other people present. When she assured him that she had not kissed the other man, he knew she was lying—yet he was glad that she had taken the trouble to lie to him.

He was, as he found before the summer ended, one of a varying dozen who circulated about her. Each of them had at one time been favored above all others—about half of them still basked in the solace of occasional sentimental revivals. Whenever one showed signs of dropping out through long neglect, she granted him a brief honeyed hour, which encouraged him to tag along for a year or so longer. Judy made these forays upon the helpless and defeated without malice, indeed half-unconscious that there was anything mischievous in what she did.

When a new man came to town everyone dropped out—dates were automatically cancelled.

The helpless part of trying to do anything about it was that she did it all herself. She was not a girl who could be "won" in the kinetic sense—she was proof against cleverness, she was proof against charm; if any of these assailed her too strongly she would immediately resolve the affair to a physical basis, and under the magic of her physical splendor the strong as well as the brilliant played her game and not their own. She was entertained only by the gratification of her desires and by the direct exercise of her own charm. Perhaps from so much youthful love, so many youthful lovers, she had come, in self-defense, to nourish herself wholly from within.

Succeeding Dexter's first exhilaration came restlessness and dissatisfaction. The helpless ecstasy of losing himself in her was opiate rather than tonic. It was fortunate for his work during the winter that those moments of ecstasy came infrequently. Early in their acquaintance it had seemed for a while that there was a deep and spontaneous mutual attraction—that first August, for example—three days of long evenings on her dusky veranda, of strange wan kisses through the late afternoon, in shadowy alcoves or behind the protecting trellises of the garden arbors, of mornings when she was fresh as a dream and almost shy at meeting him in the clarity of the rising day. There was all the ecstasy of an engagement about it, sharpened by his realization that there was no engagement. It was during those three days that, for the first time, he had asked her to marry him. She said "maybe some day," she said "kiss me," she said "I'd like to marry you," she said "I love you"—she said—nothing.

The three days were interrupted by the arrival of a New York man who visited at her house for half September. To Dexter's agony, rumor engaged them. The man was the son of the president of a great trust company. But at the end of a month it was reported that Judy was yawning. At a dance one night she sat all evening in a motor-boat with a local beau, while the New Yorker searched the club for her frantically. She told the local beau that she was bored with her visitor, and two days later he left. She was seen with him at the station, and it was reported that he looked very mournful indeed.

On this note the summer ended. Dexter was twenty-four, and he found himself increasingly in a position to do as he wished. He joined two clubs in the city and lived at one of them. Though he was by no means an integral part of the stag-lines at these clubs, he managed to be on hand at dances where Judy Jones was likely to appear. He could have gone out socially as much as he liked—he was an eligible young man, now, and popular with downtown fathers. His confessed devotion to Judy Jones had rather solidified his position. But he had no social aspirations and rather despised the dancing men who were always on tap for the Thursday or Saturday parties and who filled in at dinners with the younger married set. Already he was playing with the idea of going East to New York. He

wanted to take Judy Jones with him. No disillusion as to the world in which she had grown up could cure his illusion as to her desirability.

Remember that—for only in the light of it can what he did for her be understood.

Eighteen months after he first met Judy Jones he became engaged to another girl. Her name was Irene Scheerer, and her father was one of the men who had always believed in Dexter. Irene was light-haired and sweet and honorable, and a little stout, and she had two suitors whom she pleasantly relinquished when Dexter formally asked her to marry him.

Summer, fall, winter, spring, another summer, another fall—so much he had given of his active life to the incorrigible lips of Judy Jones. She had treated him with interest, with encouragement, with malice, with indifference, with contempt. She had inflicted on him the innumerable little slights and indignities possible in such a case—as if in revenge for having ever cared for him at all. She had beckoned him and yawned at him and beckoned him again and he had responded often with bitterness and narrowed eyes. She had brought him ecstatic happiness and intolerable agony of spirit. She had caused him untold inconvenience and not a little trouble. She had insulted him, and she had ridden over him, and she had played his interest in her against his interest in his work—for fun. She had done everything to him except to criticize him—this she had not done—it seemed to him only because it might have sullied the utter indifference she manifested and sincerely felt toward him.

When autumn had come and gone again it occurred to him that he could not have Judy Jones. He had to beat this into his mind but he convinced himself at last. He lay awake at night for a while and argued it over. He told himself the trouble and the pain she had caused him, he enumerated her glaring deficiencies as a wife. Then he said to himself that he loved her, and after a while he fell asleep. For a week, lest he imagined her husky voice over the telephone or her eyes opposite him at lunch, he worked hard and late, and at night he went to his office and plotted out his years.

At the end of a week he went to a dance and cut in on her once. For almost the first time since they had met he did not ask her to sit out with him or tell her that she was lovely. It hurt him that she did not miss these things—that was all. He was not jealous when he saw that there was a new man tonight. He had been hardened against jealousy long before.

He stayed late at the dance. He sat for an hour with Irene Scheerer and talked about books and about music. He knew very little about either. But he was beginning to be master of his own time now, and he had a rather priggish notion that he—the young and already fabulously successful Dexter Green—should know more about such things.

That was in October, when he was twenty-five. In January, Dexter and Irene became engaged. It was to be announced in June, and they were to be married three months later.

The Minnesota winter prolonged itself interminably, and it was almost May when the winds came soft and the snow ran down into Black Bear Lake at last. For the first time in over a year Dexter was enjoying a certain tranquillity of spirit. Judy Jones had been in Florida, and afterward in Hot Springs, and somewhere she had been engaged, and somewhere she had broken it off. At first, when Dexter had definitely given her up, it had made him sad that people still linked them together and asked for news of her, but when he began to be placed at dinner next to Irene Scheerer people didn't ask him about her any more—they told him about her. He ceased to be an authority on her.

May at last. Dexter walked the streets at night when the darkness was damp as rain, wondering that so soon, with so little done, so much of ecstasy had gone from him. May one year back had been marked by Judy's poignant, unforgivable, yet forgiven turbulence—it had been one of those rare times when he fancied she had grown to care for him. That old penny's worth of happiness he had spent for this bushel of content. He knew that Irene would be no more than a curtain spread behind him, a hand moving among gleaming teacups, a voice calling to children . . . fire and loveliness were gone, the magic of nights and the wonder of the varying hours and seasons . . . slender lips, down-turning, dropping to his lips and bearing him up into a heaven of eyes. . . .The thing was deep in him. He was too strong and alive for it to die lightly.

In the middle of May when the weather balanced for a few days on the thin bridge that led to deep summer he turned in one night at Irene's house. Their engagement was to be announced in a week now—no one would be surprised at it. And tonight they would sit together on the lounge at the University Club and look on for an hour at the dancers. It gave him a sense of solidity to go with her—she was so sturdily popular, so intensely "great."

He mounted the steps of the brownstone house and stepped inside.

"Irene," he called.

Mrs. Scheerer came out of the living room to meet him.

"Dexter," she said, "Irene's gone upstairs with a splitting headache. She wanted to go with you but I made her go to bed."

"Nothing serious, I—"

"Oh, no. She's going to play golf with you in the morning. You can spare her for just one night, can't you, Dexter?"

Her smile was kind. She and Dexter liked each other. In the living room he talked for a moment before he said good-night.

Returning to the University Club, where he had rooms, he stood in the doorway for a moment and watched the dancers. He leaned against the door-post, nodded at a man or two—yawned.

"Hello, darling."

The familiar voice at his elbow startled him. Judy Jones had left a man and crossed the room to him—Judy Jones, a slender enamelled doll in cloth of gold: gold in a band at her head, gold in two slipper points at her dress's hem. The fragile glow of her face seemed to blossom as she smiled at him. A breeze of warmth and light blew through the room. His hands in the pockets of his dinner-jacket tightened spasmodically. He was filled with a sudden excitement.

"When did you get back?" he asked casually.

"Come here and I'll tell you about it."

She turned and he followed her. She had been away—he could have wept at the wonder of her return. She had passed through enchanted streets, doing things that were like provocative music. All mysterious happenings, all fresh and quickening hopes, had gone away with her, come back with her now.

She turned in the doorway.

"Have you a car here? If you haven't, I have."

"I have a coupé."

In then, with a rustle of golden cloth. He slammed the door. Into so many cars she had stepped—like this—like that—her back against the leather, so—her elbow resting on the door—waiting. She would have been soiled long since had there been anything to soil her—except herself—but this was her own self outpouring.

With an effort he forced himself to start the car and back into the street. This was nothing, he must remember. She had done this before, and he had put her behind him, as he would have crossed a bad account from his books.

He drove slowly downtown and, affecting abstraction, traversed the deserted streets of the business section, peopled here and there where a movie was giving out its crowd or where consumptive or pugilistic youth lounged in front of pool-halls. The clink of glasses and the slap of hands on the bars issued from saloons, cloisters of glazed glass and dirty yellow light.

She was watching him closely and the silence was embarrassing, yet in this crisis he could find no casual word with which to profane the hour. At a convenient turning he began to zigzag back toward the University Club.

"Have you missed me?" she asked suddenly.

"Everybody missed you."

He wondered if she knew of Irene Scheerer. She had been back only a day—her absence had been almost contemporaneous with his engagement.

"What a remark!" Judy laughed sadly—without sadness. She looked at him searchingly. He became absorbed in the dashboard.

"You're handsomer than you used to be," she said thoughtfully. "Dexter, you have the most rememberable eyes."

He could have laughed at this, but he did not laugh. It was the sort of thing that was said to sophomores. Yet it stabbed at him.

"I'm awfully tired of everything, darling." She called everyone darling, endowing the endearment with careless, individual comaraderie. "I wish you'd marry me."

The directness of this confused him. He should have told her now that he was going to marry another girl, but he could not tell her. He could as easily have sworn that he had never loved her.

"I think we'd get along," she continued, on the same note, "unless probably you've forgotten me and fallen in love with another girl."

Her confidence was obviously enormous. She had said, in effect, that she found such a thing impossible to believe, that if it were true he had merely committed a childish indiscretion—and probably to show off. She would forgive him, because it was not a matter of any moment but rather something to be brushed aside lightly.

"Of course you could never love anybody but me," she continued. "I like the way you love me. Oh, Dexter, have you forgotten last year?"

"No, I haven't forgotten."

"Neither have I!"

Was she sincerely moved—or was she carried along by the wave of her own acting?

"I wish we could be like that again," she said, and he forced himself to answer:

"I don't think we can."

"I suppose not. . . . I hear you're giving Irene Scheerer a violent rush."

There was not the faintest emphasis on the name, yet Dexter was suddenly ashamed.

"Oh, take me home," cried Judy suddenly; "I don't want to go back to that idiotic dance—with those children."

Then, as he turned up the street that led to the residence district, Judy began to cry quietly to herself. He had never seen her cry before.

The dark street lightened, the dwellings of the rich loomed up around them, he stopped his coupé in front of the great white bulk of the Mortimer Joneses' house, somnolent, gorgeous, drenched with the splendor of the damp moonlight. Its solidity startled him. The strong walls, the steel of the girders, the breadth and beam and pomp of it were only to bring out the contrast with the young beauty beside him. It was sturdy to accentuate her slightness—as if to show what a breeze could be generated by a butterfly's wing.

He sat perfectly quiet, his nerves in wild clamor, afraid that if he moved he would find her irresistibly in his arms. Two tears had rolled down her wet face and trembled on her upper lip.

"I'm more beautiful than anybody else," she said brokenly, "why can't I be happy?" Her moist eyes tore at his stability—her mouth turned slowly downward with an exquisite sadness: "I'd like to marry you if you'll have me, Dexter. I suppose you think I'm not worth having, but I'll be so beautiful for you, Dexter."

A million phrases of anger, pride, passion, hatred, tenderness fought on his lips. Then a perfect wave of emotion washed over him, carrying off with it a sediment of wisdom, of convention, of doubt, of honor. This was his girl who was speaking, his own, his beautiful, his pride.

"Won't you come in?" He heard her draw in her breath sharply.

Waiting.

"All right," his voice was trembling, "I'll come in."

V

It was strange that neither when it was over nor a long time afterward did he regret that night. Looking at it from the perspective of ten years, the fact that Judy's flare for him endured just one month seemed of little importance. Nor did it matter that by his yielding he subjected himself to a deeper agony in the end and gave serious hurt to Irene Scheerer and to Irene's parents, who had befriended him. There was nothing sufficiently pictorial about Irene's grief to stamp itself on his mind.

Dexter was at bottom hard-minded. The attitude of the city on his action was of no importance to him, not because he was going to leave the city, but because any outside attitude on the situation seemed superficial. He was completely indifferent to popular opinion. Nor, when he had seen that it was no use, that he did not possess in himself the power to move fundamentally or to hold Judy Jones, did he bear any malice toward her. He loved her, and he would love her until the day he was too old for loving—but he could not have her. So he tasted the deep pain that is reserved only for the strong, just as he had tasted for a little while the deep happiness.

Even the ultimate falsity of the grounds upon which Judy terminated the engagement that she did not want to "take him away" from Irene–Judy, who had wanted nothing else–did not revolt him. He was beyond any revulsion or any amusement.

He went East in February with the intention of selling out his laundries and settling in New York–but the war came to America in March and changed his plans. He returned to the West, handed over the management of the business to his partner, and went into the first officers' training-camp in late April. He was one of those young thousands who greeted the war with a certain amount of relief, welcoming the liberation from webs of tangled emotion.

VI

This story is not his biography, remember, although things creep into it which have nothing to do with those dreams he had when he was young. We are almost done with them and with him now. There is only one more incident to be related here, and it happens seven years farther on.

It took place in New York, where he had done well–so well that there were no barriers too high for him. He was thirty-two years old, and, except for one flying trip immediately after the war, he had not been West in seven years. A man named Devlin from Detroit came into his office to see him in a business way, and then and there this incident occurred, and closed out, so to speak, this particular side of his life.

"So you're from the Middle West," said the man Devlin with careless curiosity. "That's funny–I thought men like you were probably born and raised on Wall Street. You know–wife of one of my best friends in Detroit came from your city. I was an usher at the wedding."

Dexter waited with no apprehension of what was coming.

"Judy Simms," said Devlin with no particular interest; "Judy Jones she was once."

"Yes, I knew her." A dull impatience spread over him. He had heard, of course, that she was married–perhaps deliberately he had heard no more.

"Awfully nice girl," brooded Devlin meaninglessly, "I'm sort of sorry for her."

"Why?" Something in Dexter was alert, receptive, at once.

"Oh, Lud Simms has gone to pieces in a way. I don't mean he ill-uses her, but he drinks and runs around–"

"Doesn't she run around?"

"No. Stays at home with her kids."

"Oh."

"She's a little too old for him," said Devlin.

"Too old!" cried Dexter. "Why, man, she's only twenty-seven."

He was possessed with a wild notion of rushing out into the streets and taking a train to Detroit. He rose to his feet spasmodically.

"I guess you're busy," Devlin apologized quickly. "I didn't realize–"

"No, I'm not busy," said Dexter, steadying his voice. "I'm not busy at all. Not busy at all. Did you say she was–twenty-seven? No, I said she was twenty-seven."

"Yes, you did," agreed Devlin dryly.

"Go on, then. Go on."

"What do you mean?"

"About Judy Jones."

Devlin looked at him helplessly.

"Well, that's–I told you all there is to it. He treats her like the devil. Oh, they're not going to get divorced or anything. When he's particularly outrageous she forgives him. In fact, I'm inclined to think she loves him. She was a pretty girl when she first came to Detroit."

A pretty girl! That phrase struck Dexter as ludicrous.

"Isn't she–a pretty girl, any more?"

"Oh, she's all right."

"Look here," said Dexter, sitting down suddenly, "I don't understand. You say she was a 'pretty girl' and now you say she's 'all right.' I don't understand what you mean–Judy Jones wasn't a pretty girl, at all. She was a great beauty. Why, I knew her, I knew her. She was–"

Devlin laughed pleasantly.

"I'm not trying to start a row," he said. "I think Judy's a nice girl and I like her. I can't understand how a man like Lud Simms could fall madly in love with her, but he did." Then he added: "Most of the women like her."

Dexter looked closely at Devlin, thinking wildly that there must be a reason for this, some insensitivity in the man or some private malice.

"Lots of women fade just like *that*," Devlin snapped his fingers. "You must have seen it happen. Perhaps I've forgotten how pretty she was at her wedding. I've seen her so much since then, you see. She has nice eyes."

A sort of dullness settled down upon Dexter. For the first time in his life he felt like getting very drunk. He knew that he was laughing loudly at something Devlin had said, but he did not know what it was or why it was funny. When, in a few minutes, Devlin went, he lay down on his lounge and looked out the window at the New York sky-line into which the sun was sinking in dull lovely shades of pink and gold.

He had thought that having nothing else to lose he was invulnerable at last—but he knew that he had just lost something more, as surely as if he had married Judy Jones and seen her fade away before his eyes.

The dream was gone. Something had been taken from him. In a sort of panic he pushed the palms of his hands into his eyes and tried to bring up a picture of the waters lapping on Sherry Island and the moonlit verandah, and gingham on the golf-links and the dry sun and the gold color of her neck's soft down. And her mouth damp to his kisses and her eyes plaintive with melancholy and her freshness like new fine linen in the morning. Why, these things were no longer in the world! They had existed and they existed no longer.

For the first time in years the tears were streaming down his face. But they were for himself now. He did not care about mouth and eyes and moving hands. He wanted to care, and he could not care. For he had gone away and he could never go back any more. The gates were closed, the sun was gone down, and there was no beauty but the gray beauty of steel that withstands all time. Even the grief he could have borne was left behind in the country of illusion, of youth, of the richness of life, where his winter dreams had flourished.

"Long ago," he said, "long ago, there was something in me, but now that thing is gone. Now that thing is gone, that thing is gone. I cannot cry. I cannot care. That thing will come back no more."

—All the Sad Young Men

"Magnificently Attuned to Life": The Value of "Winter Dreams"

Clinton S. Burhans Jr.

Fitzgerald once described "Winter Dreams" as "A sort of first draft of the Gatsby idea," and it seems too bad that he did. In discussing the story, writers on Fitzgerald have apparently accepted his comment as a First Principle, with results that often seem unjust appraisals of the story itself as well as inaccurate understandings of its relationship to *The Great Gatsby*. On both counts, therefore, "Winter Dreams" is well worth careful study.

Whether praising the story as do Arthur Mizener, Henry Dan Piper, and Charles Shain or, on balance, attacking it as do K. G. W. Cross, Sergio Perosa, James

E. Miller, Jr., and Robert Sklar, most critics base their interpretations on the magnitude of Dexter Green's response to learning that Judy Jones's beauty is fading and that she has become just another housewife. Mr. Piper believes that Dexter's tears stem from his sudden realization that he cannot repeat the past; Messrs. Cross, Miller, and Perosa argue that he has lost the illusion of eternal beauty. Mr. Mizener and Mr. Shain think he cries because he has lost the ability to feel deeply; Messrs. Mizener, Perosa, and Sklar point to Dexter's forced awareness of the destructiveness of time. The first two views suggest a reading backwards from Gatsby to Dexter rather than a concern with Dexter himself and with his particular dreams, and the latter two are plausible but only partially and superficially true. None of them seems sufficiently based either on Dexter, his dreams, and his relationship to them; or on what Judy Jones really represents to him.

Son of a middle-class storekeeper and of a mother with a peasant background, Dexter dreams of better things. He caddies in an upper-class country club, and all summer long his mind fills with images of wealth and position and privilege. These images become the substance of his winter dreams: "October filled him with hope which November raised to a sort of ecstatic triumph, and in this mood the fleeting brilliant impressions of the summer at Sherry Island were ready grist to his mill" [*Babylon Revisited and Other Stories* (New York, 1960), p. 115. Subsequent page references will be to this edition]. Now, there is nothing either Platonic or idealistic about Dexter's dreams. Taken separately or together, they simply add up to a way of life that seems to him obviously richer, both literally and figuratively, than his own; that is to say, Dexter Green has a clear-eyed perception and a hard-headed understanding that, all else being equal, it is better to be wealthy than to be poor, better to have money than not to have it, better to have a great deal of money than only a little.

Consequently, Dexter dreams not of some ineffable gaudiness, some intangible perfection, some eternal beauty, but rather of what in his young experience seems the best this world can offer—wealth and position and privilege and the infinite possibilities they promise. "The quality and the seasonability of these winter dreams varied, but the stuff of them remained. . . . But do not get the impression, because his winter dreams happened to be concerned at first with musings on the rich, that there was anything merely snobbish in the boy. He wanted not association with glittering things and glittering people—he wanted the glittering things themselves. Often he reached out for the best without knowing why he wanted it . . ." (p. 118). His dreams are no reflections of transcendental urgings, no gleams in the wake of immortal longings. They are highly specific images of personal superiority—of golf championships and fancy diving before admiring crowds, of expensive clothes and luxury cars, of excellence in everything his life may touch. He reaches out for the best simply because it is the best, because the best is clearly more worth having than second or third best. Unlike so many other Fitzgerald heroes, therefore, no tension or conflict exists between Dexter's dreams and either their particular embodiments or the means he employs in pursuing them.

Ambitious, intelligent, hard-headed, pragmatic, and hard-working, Dexter builds his life on the blueprint of his winter dreams. He attends one of the best universities in the East instead of the less expensive state university not from snobbishness but because he is fully aware that the Eastern degree will open doors for him that the state university degree never could and that it will give him a background and manners to help him function more successfully within those doors. And so it proves: with the help of his degree, he borrows enough money to buy into a small laundry that he rapidly expands and then sells, taking his money to New York, where he becomes a successful financier. In the midst of this growing success, however, he becomes entangled with Judy Jones, who turns out to be one of "the mysterious denials and prohibitions in which life indulges." (p. 118)

Dexter first meets Judy when he is fourteen and she is eleven and "beautifully ugly as little girls are apt to be who are destined after a few years to be inexpressibly lovely and bring no end of misery to a great number of men" (p. 115). There is "a general ungodliness" in her smile and "in the almost passionate quality of her eyes" (pp. 115–16). Dexter is "treated to that absurd smile, that preposterous smile—the memory of which at least a dozen men were to carry into middle age" (p. 116); and suddenly, surprising even himself, he quits his job rather than caddy for her. "As so frequently would be the case in the future, Dexter was unconsciously dictated by his winter dreams" (p. 118). Intense, full of vitality, beautiful, and imperious, Judy Jones becomes for Dexter without his realizing it one of the "glittering things" that form the stuff of his dreams; and he is therefore unable to accept a relationship in which he is inferior to her.

Nine years later, in the process of achieving his first success, Dexter meets Judy again and falls completely in love with her. Twenty now, she has become "arrestingly beautiful . . . a continual impression of flux, of intense life, of passionate vitality . . . " (p. 120). She makes "men conscious to the highest degree of her physical loveliness," and her "exquisite excitability" is irresistible. "Her deficiencies were knit up with a passionate energy that transcended and justified them" (p. 125). Kissing her for the first time, Dexter waits "breathless for the experiment, facing the unpredictable compound that would form mysteriously from the elements of their lips. Then he saw—she communicated her excitement to him, lavishly, deeply, with kisses that were not a promise but a fulfillment" (p. 124). Before long, Dexter realizes "that he had wanted Judy Jones ever since he was a proud, desirous little boy," and he surrenders " a part of himself to the most direct and unprincipled personality with which he had ever come in contact." (p. 125)

At first, there are "mornings when she was fresh as a dream" (p. 126), but soon Dexter becomes just another in the long line of those who have loved Judy only to lose her. Men are playthings for Judy, passing tributes to her beauty and desirability, and she wearies of them as soon as they become hers. She brings Dexter "ecstatic happiness and intolerable agony of spirit" until finally "it occurred to him that he could not have Judy Jones" (p. 127). In time, he meets and becomes engaged to Irene Scheerer; but Judy, finding her discarded toy in the hands of someone else, reclaims it, only to throw it away again a month later. Dexter had not hesitated to break his engagement to Irene; he "was at bottom hard-minded. . . . Nor, when he had seen that it was no use, that he did not possess in himself the power to move fundamentally or to hold Judy Jones, did he bear any malice toward her. He loved her, and he would love her until the day he was too old for loving—but he could not have her. So he tasted the deep pain that is reserved only for the strong, just as he had tasted for a little while the deep happiness." (p. 132)

In loving Judy Jones as well as in his responses to losing her, Dexter is once again "unconsciously dictated to by his winter dreams." The most beautiful and desirable girl in his world, she is one of the "glittering things" he has dreamed of having; and when he accepts the fact that she is beyond his grasp, he continues to love her and no one else. In loving her, he had "reached out for the best," and nothing less will do.

The end of the story occurs seven years later. Now a wealthy Wall Street financier, Dexter has realized all his winter dreams except Judy, and he has neither seen her nor heard much about her during those years. A business visitor from Detroit mentions that the wife of his best friend had come from Dexter's home town, and Dexter learns what has become of Judy Jones. When she had first come to Detroit,

Devlin remarks, she had been "'pretty'"; now she is "'fading'" but "'all right.'" She is "'awfully nice,'" and people are "'sorry for her'"; she is "'a little too old'" for her husband, who drinks and is unfaithful to her. She loves him nevertheless and "'stays at home with her kids'"; and "'when he's particularly outrageous she forgives him.'" Dexter's visitor "'likes'" her but can't understand how his friend "'could fall madly in love with her.'" Most damning of all, even "'the women like her.'" Dexter is stricken by this new incomprehensible image of Judy; and after Devlin leaves, he lies on his office lounge and cries:

> He had thought that having nothing else to lose he was invulnerable at last—but he knew that he had just lost something more, as surely as if he had married Judy Jones and seen her fade away before his eyes.
>
> The dream was gone. Something had been taken from him. In a sort of panic he pushed the palms of his hands into his eyes and tried to bring up a picture of the waters lapping on Sherry Island and the moonlit veranda, and gingham on the golf-links and the dry sun and the gold color of her neck's soft down. And her mouth damp to his kisses and her eyes plaintive with melancholy and her freshness like new fine linen in the morning. Why, these things were no longer in the world! They had existed and they existed no longer.
>
> For the first time in years the tears were streaming down his face. But they were for himself now. He did not care about mouth and eyes and moving hands. He wanted to care, and he could not care. For he had gone away and he could never go back any more. The gates were closed, the sun was gone down, and there was no beauty but the gray beauty of steel that withstands all time. Even the grief he could have borne was left behind in the country of illusion, of youth, of the richness of life, where his winter dreams had flourished.
>
> "Long ago," he said, "long ago, there was something in me, but now that thing is gone. Now that thing is gone, that thing is gone. I cannot cry. I cannot care. That thing will come back no more." (133–35)

Men like Dexter Green do not cry easily; his tears and the language explaining them therefore point either to melodrama or to a complex significance. The difficulty lies in understanding precisely what Dexter has lost and whether its loss justifies the prostration of so strong and hard-minded a man. It seems clear that he is not mourning a new loss of Judy herself, the final extinction of lingering hopes; he had long ago accepted as irrevocable the fact that he could never have her. Nor has he lost the ability to feel deeply, at least not in any general sense: Fitzgerald makes it clear that Dexter has lost only the single and specific ability to respond deeply to images of Judy and of their moments together; and he is certainly able to feel deeply the loss of this response. Similarly, he is not crying over the loss of any illusions of eternal youth or beauty. Given his character, the nature of his dreams, and the history of his striving to achieve them, Dexter is simply not the kind of man to have such illusions. And in the unlikely event that he could somehow entertain them, he is even less the kind of man to weep over the loss of abstractions. Hardly more plausible are the views that he is shocked by a sudden awareness of the destructiveness of time or of the impossibility of repeating the past. Again, it seems unlikely that this man, especially at thirty-two, could have missed the reality of time and the finality of the past.

What is it, then, that Devlin's description of Mrs. Lud Simms has destroyed in Dexter Green? To begin with, Devlin has taken from Dexter's image of Judy the same things he would have lost if he had married her and seen her suddenly "fade away before his eyes": the specific features and qualities that comprised her unparalleled beauty and desirability, her appeal to him as one of the "glittering things," one of the "best." These had been the basis of his love for her—not her reflection of eternal youth or beauty but their physical and perishable realities. Once before, in turning from Judy to Irene Scheerer, he had found almost unendurable the loss of these tangible and emotional qualities: "fire and loveliness were gone, the magic of nights and the wonder of the varying hours and seasons . . . slender lips, down-turning, dropping to his lips and bearing him up into a heaven of eyes. . . . The thing was deep in him. He was too strong and alive for it to die lightly" (p. 129). At first glance, *thing* may seem a strange and imprecise word for Dexter's profound and encompassing love, but it is more consistent and apt than it might appear. His love for Judy is no more Platonic than his other winter dreams; it is sensuous and emotional, and "thing" suggests this tangible reality as well as the nature of what he has lost. Moreover, Fitzgerald's conscious use of the term for these purposes is reflected in his repetition of it nine times in the final passage of the story.

Paradoxically, in finally giving up all hope of Judy and in going to New York, Dexter is able to have her in a way he never could had they married. With the real Judy out of his life, the girl he had dreamed of having can remain alive in his imagination, unchanging in the images of her youthful beauty and desirability. More importantly, these images keep alive in Dexter the "thing" they had originally so deeply stirred in him—his love for Judy and his dream of having her. It is all this that Devlin kills in Dexter by forcing on him a new and intolerable image of Judy.

In Devlin's description of her as Mrs. Lud Simms, Fitzgerald carefully strips away every feature and every quality of the Judy Jones Dexter had known and still loves in his images of her. His "'great beauty'" (p. 134) becomes an ordinarily pretty woman; the unique and imperious paragon courted by worshippers becomes a conventional and submissively put-upon housewife; the queen of his love and dreams becomes a rather mousy commoner he could not conceivably love. No wonder Dexter is devastated. Having accepted the loss of the real Judy Jones, he had thought himself safe from further hurt; now, with every word of Devlin's, he finds himself not only losing her again but what is worse losing the ability to go on loving her.

As long as Dexter knows little or nothing new about Judy, she can stay alive and immediate in his imagination; thus, the real past continues unchanged as the imaginative present. Responding to these images of Judy Jones, Dexter can continue to love her as he had in the beginning, when the dream of having this "glittering thing" and the striving for her could still be part of that love. But Devlin destroys the time-suspending equation. When he tells Dexter what has happened to Judy, when he forces him to imagine her as the older and fading Mrs. Lud Simms, then the young and vibrant girl Dexter had loved disappears into the wax museum of the irredeemable past. The real present supplants the imaginative present and forces the past to become only the past.

For Dexter, "the dream was gone"; when he tries to recall his images of the earlier Judy, they come to him not as a continuing present but as a completed past, as "things . . . no longer in the world," things that "had existed and . . . existed no longer." Now they are only memories of a girl he had known and loved who has unaccountably become Mrs. Lud Simms, and they no longer have the power to stir his love or his dreams. "He did not care about mouth and eyes and moving hands. He wanted to care, and he could not care." Dexter wants desperately to care because these images have been the source of his love for Judy Jones and the means of keeping it alive. The end of their power to stir him is therefore the end of that love, and his tears are a bitter mourning for a second and this time total loss of Judy Jones. "'Long ago,' he said, 'long ago, there was something in me, but now that thing is gone. . . . That thing will come back no more.'"

Dexter cries with good reason, then, but he has even more reason to cry. When his images of Judy Jones no longer create an imaginative present, he loses not only his ability to go on loving her but also something else equally and perhaps even more shattering. Gone, too, is a part of himself also deeply associated with and still alive in these images: the fragile moment in time when youth and his winter dreams were making his life richer and sweeter than it would ever be again.

Fitzgerald makes it clear that the story centers on this moment in time and its significance. The story is not Dexter's "biography . . . although things creep into it which have nothing to do with those dreams he had when he was young" (p. 133). Specifically, Fitzgerald writes, "the part of his story that concerns us goes back to the days when he was making his first big success" (p. 119). These are the years between twenty-three and twenty-five, the years just after college and just before New York. "When he was only twenty-three . . . there were already people who like to say: "Now *there's* a boy—'" (p. 118). Already Dexter is making a large amount of money and receiving guest cards to the Sherry Island Golf Club, where he had been a caddy and had indulged his winter dreams (p. 119). At twenty-four he finds "himself increasingly in a position to do as he wished" (p. 126), and at twenty-five he is "beginning to be master of his own time" as "the young and already fabulously successful Dexter Green . . ." (p. 128).

This progress towards making his winter dreams come true is not, however, unqualified. Almost from the beginning, disillusion casts strange shadows on Dexter's bright successes. He had dreamed of being a golf champion and defeating Mr. T. A. Hedrick "in a marvellous match played a hundred times over the fairways of his imagination" (p. 115); now, as a guest playing in a foursome on the real fairways of the Sherry Island Golf Club, Dexter is "impressed by the tremendous superiority he felt toward Mr. T. A. Hedrick, who was a bore and not even a good golfer any more" (p. 119). A year later, "he joined two clubs in the city and lived at one of them. . . . He could have gone out socially as much as he liked—he was an eligible young man, and popular with the down-town fathers . . . But he had no social aspirations and rather despised the dancing men who were always on tap for Thursday or Saturday parties and who filled in at dinners with the younger married set." The farther he moves into the world of his winter dreams, the more he is disillusioned with it. (pp. 126–127)

Significantly, and again reflecting Fitzgerald's central concern with the relationship between reality and the imagination, the only one of Dexter's winter dreams with which he is not ultimately disillusioned is the only one he cannot have in the real world and time–Judy Jones. After quitting his job rather than caddy for her, he doesn't see her again until she plays through his foursome on the afternoon when he is a guest at the Sherry Island Golf Club. That evening they meet again and Fitzgerald carefully creates a scene in which Judy becomes identified with this particular moment in Dexter's life. "'There was a fish jumping and a star shining and the lights around the lake were gleaming" (p. 121). Lying on a raft, Dexter is listening to a piano across the lake playing a popular song, a song he had heard "at a prom once when he could not afford the luxury of proms, and he had stood outside the gymnasium and listened. The sound of the tune precipitated in him a sort of ecstasy and it was with that ecstasy he viewed what happened to him now. It was a mood of intense appreciation, a sense that, for once, he was magnificently attune to life and that everything about him was radiating a brightness and a glamour he might never know again." (p. 121)

For Dexter, the melody drifting over the water fuses the past and the present, the years of struggle just behind and the fulfillment just beginning. This is the magic moment when dreaming and striving reach out to grasp realization, the time of rapture before the fullness of achievement brings its seemingly inevitable disillusion. Suddenly, a motor-boat appears beside the raft, "drowning out the hot tinkle of the piano in the drone of its spray" (*ibid.*), and Judy Jones becomes part of this moment in which Dexter is "magnificently attune to life" as he wil never be again. She asks him to take her surf-boarding; and highlighting her association with Dexter's "mood of intense appreciation," Fitzgerald repeats the line with which he had begun the scene. As Dexter joins Judy in the boat, "there was a fish jumping and a star shining and the lights around the lake were gleaming" (p. 122). When she invites him to dinner on the following night, "his heart turned over like the fly-wheel of the boat, and, for the second time, her casual whim gave a new direction to his life." (*ibid.*)

This is the night Dexter realizes he is in love with Judy, and her identification with his sense of being "magnificently attune to life" deepens. "'Who are you, anyhow?'" she asks him. "'I'm nobody,' he announced. 'My career is largely a matter of futures.'" He is "'probably making more money than any man my age in the Northwest'" (p. 124); and with all the "glittering things" shining just ahead of him, Dexter realizes that he has wanted Judy since boyhood. She "communicated her excitement to him" (*ibid.*), and her youthful beauty thus becomes both a part of his dreams as well as the embodiment of his "intense appreciation" of life at the beginning of their fulfillment.

As the next two years bring him increasing success and his first disillusion with its products, Dexter's love for Judy remains constant. "No disillusion as to the world in which she had grown up could cure his illusion as to her desirability" (p. 126). Not even her roller-coaster inconstancy can diminish his love for her or disillusion him with her. In Judy, he continues to find the excitement and anticipation that had made the striving for his winter dreams and the threshold of their fulfillment somehow better than their realization was proving to be. When he first loses her and becomes engaged to Irene, he wonders "that so soon, with so little done, so much of ecstasy had gone from him" (p. 128). And when Judy returns to him, "all mysterious happenings, all fresh and quickening hopes, had gone away with her, come back with her now" (p. 130). In finally giving up all hope of having her, Dexter is thereafter safe from being disillusioned with Judy and thus can keep imaginatively alive the excitement and anticipation she represents for him not only in herself but also in her identification with his youthful winter dreams.

Against this background, Dexter's tears are even more comprehensible. At thirty-two, he finds that all his winter dreams, except for Judy Jones, have come true, and there are "no barriers too high for him" (p. 133). But the world he has won has lost the brightness it had had in his dreams; realizing them has cost him the illusions that were their most precious dimension. Now, having long ago accepted the loss of Judy and with his illusions gone, he thinks he has "nothing else to lose" and is therefore "invulnerable at last." Devlin's detailed picture of Judy as Mrs. Simms strips away this last illusion.

Because Judy Jones and his love for her had become so closely associated with the untarnished richness of his youthful winter dreams, the imaginative present in which she remains alive for Dexter also preserves that youthful richness. When Devlin destroys this imaginative present, Dexter finally and forever loses not only Judy and his love for her but also his ability to keep alive in his imagination the best part of his youth and its winter dreams. He has "gone away and he could never go back any more." Devlin has wrought a kind of death in Dexter's imagination, and "even the grief he could have borne was left behind in the country of illusion, of youth, of the richness of life, where his winter dreams had flourished." Dexter's tears are justifiably for himself, then: he has lost even more than his love for Judy Jones. In realizing his winter dreams, he has discovered that their greatest value was in the dreaming; and now he has lost the only way left to preserve that priceless capacity.

In this complex and moving conclusion, "Winter Dreams" becomes a story with many values. In itself, it is an interesting and often profound treatment of the ironic winner-take-nothing theme, the story of a man who gets nearly everything he wants at the cost of nearly everything that made it worth wanting. In its relationship to Fitzgerald's other writing, "Winter Dreams" makes a valuable prologue to *The Great Gatsby* and reflects several of the themes that characterize Fitzgerald's view of the human condition.

Because of Fitzgerald's explicit linking of the two works, it is common to parallel Dexter Green and Jay Gatsby, but the difference between them are even more instructive than the similarities. Both men have generally similar economic and social backgrounds: Dexter's family is higher on the socio-economic scale than Jimmy Gatz's shiftless parents, but neither boy starts out anywhere near the wealthy upper class or social elite. Both boys are bright and ambitious, dream of wealth and position, and associate their dreams with a rich and beautiful young girl. Both achieve wealth at an early age, only to find its products strangely disillusioning; each loses the girl he loves and thereafter makes her the center of his imaginative life.

Nevertheless, the differences between Dexter Green and Jay Gatsby are essential and revealing: they not only point up the separate interest of the story but also illuminate by contrast many of the complexities of the novel. Dexter, for example, is from beginning to end Dexter Green; he wants not a different self but a richer life, and his dreams are mundane and specific. Jimmy Gatz, however, rejects Jimmy Gatz in favor of a "Platonic conception of himself"; he is "a son of God," and he dreams of "a universe of ineffable gaudiness." Similarly, Judy Jones is *part* of Dexter's dreams, one of the "glittering things" he dreams of having who also embodies his reasons for wanting them. But Daisy is the *incarnation* of Gatsby's dreams, the ineffable made flesh and therefore no longer ineffable.

Dexter gains his wealth by conventional and respectable means entirely consistent with his dreams, and indeed, largely indistinguishable from them. Gatsby's means are apparently corrupt; but, even if they weren't, no earthly means could be any more consistent with the nature of his dreams than is his incarnation of them in a mortal form. Dexter keeps alive his love for Judy Jones and the brightness of his youthful winter dreams in the only way the past can remain alive—by fixing its images out of time and the real world in an imaginative present. Gatsby tries to recapture the past by regaining the real Daisy and through her repeating in the real world the actual moment in time and the actual situation in which his dreams started to become "confused and disordered."

In effect, then, Dexter Green succeeds in recapturing the past only to lose it when new images from the real world and the real present destroy his imaginative present. Gatsby fails to repeat the past and therefore never loses the illusion that he can; his failure is only a temporary setback making even more necessary and stronger his resolve to regain and thereby reshape the past. In his tears, Dexter realizes what Gatsby never learns—that his dreams are forever "behind him, somewhere back in that vast obscurity beyond the city, where the dark fields of the republic rolled on under the night," back in "the country of illusion, of youth," where dreaming was still untouched by the bruising fall of coming true. Dexter survives with most of his limited dreams realized but having lost twice and forever the richest dimension of those dreams; primarily, he symbolizes the power and also the tragic fragility of the imaginative present. Gatsby is killed, but he dies with his illimitable dreams apparently intact; ultimately, he symbolizes man's unquenchable and tragic capacity for imagining a perfection he not only can never achieve but also inevitably destroys in pursuing.

Beyond its useful relationship to Fitzgerald's masterpiece, "Winter Dreams" is also valuable in its early reflection of the themes that characterize most of his significant writing. The dream-and-disillusion motif in the story appears in varying forms and degrees from its intermittent emergence in *This Side of Paradise* to its central exploration in *The Last Tycoon;* it is Fitzgerald's major theme. Dexter Green's painful recognition that the richest part of dreams is not their fulfillment but the dreaming of and striving for them appears implicitly in many other works; related to this theme and even more important in Fitzgerald's thought and art is the central stress of the story on the power and value of imaginative life and time. Taken together, these themes reflect the essentially tragic vision of the human condition working at the core of Fitzgerald's serious writing: his increasing concern with man as a creature whose imagination creates dreams and goals his nature and circumstances combine to doom. For any reader, then, "Winter Dreams" can be a fertile and challenging story; for a student of Fitzgerald, its careful analysis is a rewarding necessity.

—Studies in Short Fiction,
Summer 1969, pp. 401–412

* * *

55

Stories	Record for 1923				
	Option from Hearsts	$ 1500.00	Com. 10%	# 1350	00
	"Dice, Brassknuckles and Guitar"	1500.00	"	1350	00
	Hot and Cold Blood	1500.00	"	1350	00
	"Diamond Dick"	1500.00	"	1350	00
	"Our Own Movie Queen" (Ruth Talmadge)	1000.00	"	900	00
	Gretchen's Forty Winks	1200.00	"	1080	00
	Winter Dreams (English Rights)	125.00	"	112	50
	Total			7,492	50

Movies			
	This Side of Paradise	10,000	00
	The Camel's Back	1,000	00
	Grit	2,000	00
	Filler for Glimpses of the Moon	500	00
	Total	13,500	00

Play Advance		500.00	Com. 10%	450	00

Other Writing					
	Imagination and a few Mothers	1000.	Com 10%	900	00
	The Cruise of the Rolling Junk	300.	"	270	00
	Making Monogamy Work	300.	"	270	00
	Our Irresponsible Rich	350.	"	315	00
	The Most Disgraceful Thing I ever did			20	00
	Review of "Being Respectable"			15	00
	" " Many Marriages			5	00
	" " Through the Wheat			5	00
	Total			1,800	00
	Syndicate Returns	74. 75	Com 10%	67	28

Books			
	This Side of Paradise	880	00
	Flappers and Philosophers	98	00
	The Beautiful and Damned	292	00
	Tales of the Jazz Age	270	43
	Total (figures estimated)	1,510	00
	Advance on New Novel (The Great Gatsby)	3,939	00
	Total	5,450	00

	Total	# 28,759	78

Page from Fitzgerald's Ledger *listing his earnings during the year he wrote "Dice, Brassknuckles & Guitar"*

A Typical Fitzgerald Story

Dice, Brassknuckles & Guitar

By F. Scott Fitzgerald

Illustrations by Frederic Dorr Steele

PARTS of New Jersey, as you know, are under water, and other parts are under continual surveillance by the authorities. But here and there lie patches of garden country dotted with old-fashioned frame mansions, which have wide shady porches and a red swing on the lawn. And perhaps, on the widest and shadiest of the porches there is even a hammock left over from the hammock days, stirring gently in a mid-Victorian wind.

When tourists come to such last-century landmarks they stop their cars and gaze for a while and then mutter: "Well, thank God, this age is joined on to something," or else they

to paint the hood yellow but unfortunately had been called away when but half through the task.

As the gentleman and his body-servant were passing the house where Amanthis lay beautifully asleep in the hammock, something happened—the body fell off the car. My only apology for stating this so suddenly is that it happened very suddenly indeed. When the noise had died down and the dust had drifted away master and man arose and inspected the two halves.

"Look-a-there," said the gentleman in disgust, "the doggone thing got all separated that time."

"She bust in two," agreed the body-servant.

This story was the first published under Fitzgerald's contract with Hearst's International.

DICE, BRASSKNUCKLES & GUITAR

This Gatsby *cluster story, a humorous treatment of the cruelty of the rich, was published in the May 1923 issue of* Hearst's International *magazine. Fitzgerald did not include this story in one of his collections.*

"It's a sort of Academy. And I'm the head of it. I invented it."

He flipped a card from his case as though he were shaking down a thermometer.

"Look."

She took the card. In large lettering it bore the legend

James Powell; J. M.
"Dice, Brassknuckles and Guitar"

She stared in amazement.

"Dice, Brassknuckles and Guitar?" she repeated in awe.

"Yes mamm."

"What does it mean? What—do you *sell* 'em?"

"No mamm, I teach 'em. It's a profession."

"Dice, Brassknuckles and Guitar? What's the J. M.?"

"That stands for Jazz Master."

"But what *is* it? What's it about?"

"Well, you see, it's like this. One night when I was in New York I got talkin' to a young fella who was drunk. He was one of my fares. And he'd taken some society girl somewhere and lost her."

"*Lost* her?"

"Yes mamm. He forgot her, I guess. And he was right worried. Well, I got to thinkin' that these girls nowadays—these society girls—they lead a sort of dangerous life and my course of study offers a means of protection against these dangers."

"You teach 'em to use brassknuckles?"

"Yes mamm, if necessary. Look here, you take a girl and she goes into some café where she's got no business to go. Well then, her escort he gets a little too much to drink an' he goes to sleep an' then some other fella comes up and says 'Hello, sweet mamma' or whatever one of those mashers says up here. What does she do? She can't scream, on account of no real lady'll scream nowadays—no—She just reaches down in her pocket and slips her fingers into a pair of Powell's defensive brassknuckles, débutante's size, executes what I call the Society Hook, and *Wham!* that big fella's on his way to the cellar."

"Well—what—what's the guitar for?" whispered the awed Amanthis. "Do they have to knock somebody over with the guitar?"

"No, *mamm!*" exclaimed Jim in horror. "No mamm. In my course no lady would be taught to raise a guitar against anybody. I teach 'em to play. Shucks! you ought to hear 'em. Why, when I've given 'em two lessons you'd think some of 'em was colored."

"And the dice?"

"Dice? I'm related to a dice. My grandfather was a dice. I teach 'em how to make those dice perform. I protect pocket-book as well as person."

* * *

HEARST'S International

℃, *Amanthis laid her hand softly on Jim's shoulder. "I understand,"*
she said. "You're better than all of them put together, Jim."

This line from "Dice, Brassknuckles & Guitar," here used as a caption, anticipates Nick's judgment on Gatsby:
"You're worth the whole damn bunch put together."

This portrait of the Fitzgeralds appeared in the issue of the magazine that published "Dice, Brassknuckles & Guitar." The statement that "all of F. Scott Fitzgerald's new fiction will appear in HEARST'S INTERNATIONAL" is untrue; he became dissatisfied with the Hearst arrangement and broke the contract.

ABSOLUTION

"Absolution," first published in The American Mercury *(June 1924), relates the encounter between an imaginative poor boy and a deranged priest. The story was salvaged from a lost early draft of the novel that became* The Great Gatsby. *It was collected in* All the Sad Young Men.

There was once a priest with cold, watery eyes, who, in the still of the night, wept cold tears. He wept because the afternoons were warm and long, and he was unable to attain a complete mystical union with our Lord. Sometimes, near four o'clock, there was a rustle of Swede girls along the path by his window, and in their shrill laughter he found a terrible dissonance that made him pray aloud for the twilight to come. At twilight the laughter and the voices were quieter, but several times he had walked past Romberg's Drug Store when it was dusk and the yellow lights shone inside and the nickel taps of the soda-fountain were gleaming, and he had found the scent of cheap toilet soap desperately sweet upon the air. He passed that way when he returned from hearing confessions on Saturday nights, and he grew careful to walk on the other side of the street so that the smell of the soap would float upward before it reached his nostrils as it drifted, rather like incense, toward the summer moon.

But there was no escape from the hot madness of four o'clock. From his window, as far as he could see, the Dakota wheat thronged the valley of the Red River. The wheat was terrible to look upon and the carpet pattern to which in agony he bent his eyes sent his thought brooding through grotesque labyrinths, open always to the unavoidable sun.

One afternoon when he had reached the point where the mind runs down like an old clock, his housekeeper brought into his study a beautiful, intense little boy of eleven named Rudolph Miller. The little boy sat down in a patch of sunshine, and the priest, at his walnut desk, pretended to be very busy. This was to conceal his relief that someone had come into his haunted room.

Presently he turned around and found himself staring into two enormous, staccato eyes, lit with gleaming points of cobalt light. For a moment their expression startled him—then he saw that his visitor was in a state of abject fear.

"Your mouth is trembling," said Father Schwartz, in a haggard voice.

The little boy covered his quivering mouth with his hand.

"Are you in trouble?" asked Father Schwartz, sharply. "Take your hand away from your mouth and tell me what's the matter."

The boy—Father Schwartz recognized him now as the son of a parishioner, Mr. Miller, the freight-agent—moved his hand reluctantly off his mouth and became articulate in a despairing whisper.

"Father Schwartz—I've committed a terrible sin."

"A sin against purity?"

"No, Father . . . worse."

Father Schwartz's body jerked sharply.

"Have you killed somebody?"

"No—but I'm afraid—" the voice rose to a shrill whimper.

"Do you want to go to confession?"

The little boy shook his head miserably. Father Schwartz cleared his throat so that he could make his voice soft and say some quiet, kind thing. In this moment he should forget his own agony, and try to act like God. He repeated to himself a devotional phrase, hoping that in return God would help him to act correctly.

"Tell me what you've done," said his new soft voice.

The little boy looked at him through his tears, and was reassured by the impression of moral resiliency which the distraught priest had created. Abandoning as much of himself as he was able to this man, Rudolph Miller began to tell his story.

"On Saturday, three days ago, my father he said I had to go to confession, because I hadn't been for a month, and the family they go every week, and I hadn't been. So I just as leave go, I didn't care. So I put it off till after supper because I was playing with a bunch of kids and father asked me if I went, and I said 'no,' and he took me by the neck and he said 'You go now,' so I said 'All right,' so I went over to church. And he yelled after me: 'Don't come back till you go.' . . ."

II

"On Saturday, Three Days Ago."

The plush curtain of the confessional rearranged its dismal creases, leaving exposed only the bottom of an old man's old shoe. Behind the curtain an immortal soul was alone with God and the Reverend Adolphus Schwartz, priest of the parish. Sound began, a labored whispering, sibilant and discreet, broken at intervals by the voice of the priest in audible question.

Rudolph Miller knelt in the pew beside the confessional and waited, straining nervously to hear, and yet not to hear what was being said within. The fact that the priest was audible alarmed him. His own turn came next, and the three or four others who waited

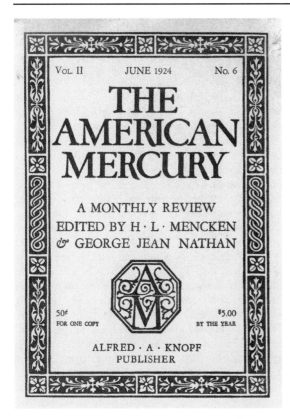

Vol. II   JUNE 1924   No. 6

THE AMERICAN MERCURY

A MONTHLY REVIEW
EDITED BY H·L·MENCKEN
& GEORGE JEAN NATHAN

50¢
FOR ONE COPY

$5.00
BY THE YEAR

ALFRED·A·KNOPF
PUBLISHER

"Absolution" was an uncommercial story; it was published in this iconoclastic magazine edited by Fitzgerald's friends H. L. Mencken and George Jean Nathan (Matthew J. and Arlyn Bruccoli Collection, University of South Carolina Library).

might listen unscrupulously while he admitted his violations of the Sixth and Ninth Commandments.

Rudolph had never committed adultery, nor even coveted his neighbor's wife—but it was the confession of the associate sins that was particularly hard to contemplate. In comparison he relished the less shameful failings away—they formed a grayish background which relieved the ebony mark of sexual offenses upon his soul.

He had been covering his ears with his hands, hoping that his refusal to hear would be noticed, and a like courtesy rendered to him in turn, when a sharp movement of the penitent in the confessional made him sink his face precipitately into the crook of his elbow. Fear assumed solid form, and pressed out a lodging between his heart and his lungs. He must try now with all his might to be sorry for his sins—not because he was afraid, but because he had offended God. He must convince God that he was sorry and to do so he must first convince himself. After a tense emotional struggle he achieved a tremulous self-pity, and decided that he was

now ready. If, by allowing no other thought to enter his head, he could preserve this state of emotion unimpaired until he went into that large coffin set on end, he would have survived another crisis in his religious life.

For some time, however, a demoniac notion had partially possessed him. He could go home now, before his turn came, and tell his mother that he had arrived too late, and found the priest gone. This, unfortunately, involved the risk of being caught in a lie. As an alternative he could say that he *had* gone to confession, but this meant that he must avoid communion next day, for communion taken upon an uncleansed soul would turn to poison in his mouth, and he would crumple limp and damned from the altar-rail.

Again Father Schwartz's voice became audible.

"And for your—"

The words blurred to a husky mumble, and Rudolph got excitedly to his feet. He felt that it was impossible for him to go to confession this afternoon. He hesitated tensely. Then from the confessional came a tap, a creak, and a sustained rustle. The slide had fallen and the plush curtain trembled. Temptation had come to him too late. . . .

"Bless me, Father, for I have sinned. . . . I confess to Almighty God and to you, Father, that I have sinned. . . . Since my last confession it has been one month and three days. . . . I accuse myself of—taking the Name of the Lord in vain. . . ."

This was an easy sin. His curses had been but bravado—telling of them was little less than a brag.

". . . of being mean to an old lady."

The wan shadow moved a little on the latticed slat.

"How, my child?"

"Old lady Swenson," Rudolph's murmur soared jubilantly. "She got our baseball that we knocked in her window, and she wouldn't give it back, so we yelled 'Twenty-three, Skidoo,' at her all afternoon. Then about five o'clock she had a fit, and they had to have the doctor."

"Go on, my child."

"Of—of not believing I was the son of my parents."

"What?" The interrogation was distinctly startled.

"Of not believing that I was the son of my parents."

"Why not?"

"Oh, just pride," answered the penitent airily.

"You mean you thought you were too good to be the son of your parents?"

"Yes, Father." On a less jubilant note.

"Go on."

"Of being disobedient and calling my mother names. Of slandering people behind my back. Of smoking—"

Rudolph had now exhausted the minor offenses, and was approaching the sins it was agony to tell. He held his fingers against his face like bars as if to press out between them the shame in his heart.

"Of dirty words and immodest thoughts and desires," he whispered very low.

"How often?"

"I don't know."

"Once a week? Twice a week?"

"Twice a week."

"Did you yield to these desires?"

"No, Father."

"Were you alone when you had them?"

"No, Father. I was with two boys and a girl."

"Don't you know, my child, that you should avoid the occasions of sin as well as the sin itself? Evil companionship leads to evil desires and evil desires to evil actions. Where were you when this happened?"

"In a barn in back of—"

"I don't want to hear any names," interrupted the priest sharply.

"Well, it was up in the loft of this barn and this girl and—a fella, they were saying things—saying immodest things, and I stayed."

"You should have gone—you should have told the girl to go."

He should have gone! He could not tell Father Schwartz how his pulse had bumped in his wrist, how a strange, romantic excitement had possessed him when those curious things had been said. Perhaps in the houses of delinquency among the dull and hard-eyed incorrigible girls can be found those for whom has burned the whitest fire.

"Have you anything else to tell me?"

"I don't think so, Father."

Rudolph felt a great relief. Perspiration had broken out under his tight-pressed fingers.

"Have you told any lies?"

The question startled him. Like all those who habitually and instinctively lie, he had an enormous respect and awe for the truth. Something almost exterior to himself dictated a quick, hurt answer.

"Oh, no, Father, I never tell lies."

For a moment, like the commoner in the king's chair, he tasted the pride of the situation. Then as the priest began to murmur conventional admonitions he realized that in heroically denying he had told lies, he had committed a terrible sin—he had told a lie in confession.

In automatic response to Father Schwartz's "Make an act of contrition," he began to repeat aloud meaninglessly:

"Oh, my God, I am heartily sorry for having offended Thee. . . ."

He must fix this now—it was a bad mistake—but as his teeth shut on the last words of his prayer there was a sharp sound, and the slat was closed.

A minute later when he emerged into the twilight the relief in coming from the muggy church into an open world of wheat and sky postponed the full realization of what he had done. Instead of worrying he took a deep breath of the crisp air and began to say over and over to himself the words "Blatchford Sarnemington, Blatchford Sarnemington!"

Blatchford Sarnemington was himself, and these words were in effect a lyric. When he became Blatchford Sarnemington a suave nobility flowed from him. Blatchford Sarnemington lived in great sweeping triumphs. When Rudolph half closed his eyes it meant that Blatchford had established dominance over him and, as he went by, there were envious mutters in the air: "Blatchford Sarnemington! There goes Blatchford Sarnemington."

He was Blatchford now for a while as he strutted homeward along the staggering road, but when the road braced itself in macadam in order to become the main street of Ludwig, Rudolph's exhilaration faded out and his mind cooled, and he felt the horror of his lie. God, of course, already knew of it—but Rudolph reserved a corner of his mind where he was safe from God, where he prepared the subterfuges with which he often tricked God. Hiding now in this corner he considered how he could best avoid the consequences of his misstatement.

At all costs he must avoid communion next day. The risk of angering God to such an extent was too great. He would have to drink water "by accident" in the morning, and thus, in accordance with a church law, render himself unfit to receive communion that day. In spite of its flimsiness this subterfuge was the most feasible that occurred to him. He accepted its risks and was concentrating on how best to put it into effect, as he turned the corner by Romberg's Drug Store and came in sight of his father's house.

III

Rudolph's father, the local freight-agent, had floated with the second wave of German and Irish stock to the Minnesota-Dakota country. Theoretically, great opportunities lay ahead of a young man of energy in that day and place, but Carl Miller had been incapable of establishing either with his superiors or his subordinates the reputation for approximate immutability which is essential to success in a hierarchic industry. Somewhat gross, he was nevertheless, insufficiently hard-headed and unable to take fundamental relationships for granted, and this inability made him suspicious, unrestful, and continually dismayed.

His two bonds with the colorful life were his faith in the Roman Catholic Church and his mystical worship of the Empire Builder, James J. Hill. Hill was the apotheosis of that quality in which Miller himself was deficient—the sense of things, the feel of things, the hint of rain in the wind on the cheek. Miller's mind worked late on the old decisions of other men, and he had never in his life felt the balance of any single thing in his hands. His weary, sprightly, undersized body was growing old in Hill's gigantic shadow. For twenty years he had lived alone with Hill's name and God.

On Sunday morning Carl Miller awoke in the dustless quiet of six o'clock. Kneeling by the side of the bed he bent his yellow-gray hair and the full dapple bangs of his mustache into the pillow, and prayed for several minutes. Then he drew off his night-shirt—like the rest of his generation he had never been able to endure pajamas—and clothed his thin, white, hairless body in woollen underwear.

He shaved. Silence in the other bedroom where his wife lay nervously asleep. Silence from the screened-off corner of the hall where his son's cot stood, and his son slept among his Alger books, his collection of cigar-bands, his mothy pennants—"Cornell," "Hamlin," and "Greetings from Pueblo, New Mexico"—and the other possessions of his private life. From outside Miller could hear the shrill birds and the whirring movement of the poultry, and, as an undertone, the low, swelling click-a-tick of the six-fifteen through-train for Montana and the green coast beyond. Then as the cold water dripped from the wash-rag in his hand he raised his head suddenly—he had heard a furtive sound from the kitchen below.

He dried his razor hastily, slipped his dangling suspenders to his shoulder, and listened. Someone was walking in the kitchen, and he knew by the light footfall that it was not his wife. With his mouth faintly ajar he ran quickly down the stairs and opened the kitchen door.

Standing by the sink, with one hand on the still dripping faucet and the other clutching a full glass of water, stood his son. The boy's eyes, still heavy with sleep, met his father's with a frightened, reproachful beauty. He was barefooted, and his pajamas were rolled up at the knees and sleeves.

For a moment they both remained motionless—Carl Miller's brow went down and his son's went up, as though they were striking a balance between the extremes of emotion which filled them. Then the bangs of the parent's mustache descended portentously until they obscured his mouth, and he gave a short glance around to see if anything had been disturbed.

The kitchen was garnished with sunlight which beat on the pans and made the smooth boards of the floor and table yellow and clean as wheat. It was the center of the house where the fire burned and the tins fitted into tins like toys, and the steam whistled all day on a thin pastel note. Nothing was moved, nothing touched—except the faucet where beads of water still formed and dripped with a white flash into the sink below.

"What are you doing?"

"I got awful thirsty, so I thought I'd just come down and get—"

"I thought you were going to communion."

A look of vehement astonishment spread over his son's face.

"I forgot all about it."

"Have you drunk any water?"

"No—"

As the word left his mouth Rudolph knew it was the wrong answer, but the faded indignant eyes facing him had signalled up the truth before the boy's will could act. He realized, too, that he should never have come downstairs; some vague necessity for verisimilitude had made him want to leave a wet glass as evidence by the sink; the honesty of his imagination had betrayed him.

"Pour it out," commanded his father, "that water!"

Rudolph despairingly inverted the tumbler.

"What's the matter with you, anyways?" demanded Miller angrily.

"Nothing."

"Did you go to confession yesterday?"

"Yes."

"Then why were you going to drink water?"

"I don't know—I forgot."

"Maybe you care more about being a little bit thirsty than you do about your religion."

"I forgot." Rudolph could feel the tears straining in his eyes.

"That's no answer."

"Well, I did."

"You better look out!" His father held to a high, persistent, inquisitory note: "If you're so forgetful that you can't remember your religion something better be done about it."

Rudolph filled a sharp pause with:

"I can remember it all right."

"First you begin to neglect your religion," cried his father, fanning his own fierceness, "the next thing you'll begin to lie and steal, and the *next* thing is the *reform* school!"

Not even this familiar threat could deepen the abyss that Rudolph saw before him. He must either tell all now, offering his body for what he knew would be a ferocious beating, or else tempt the thunderbolts by receiving the Body and Blood of Christ with sacrilege upon his soul. And of the two the former seemed more terrible—it was not so much the beating he dreaded as the savage ferocity, outlet of the ineffectual man, which would lie behind it.

"Put down that glass and go upstairs and dress!" his father ordered, "and when we get to church, before you go to communion, you better kneel down and ask God to forgive you for your carelessness."

Some accidental emphasis in the phrasing of this command acted like a catalytic agent on the confusion and terror of Rudolph's mind. A wild, proud anger rose in him and he dashed the tumbler passionately into the sink.

His father uttered a strained, husky sound, and sprang for him. Rudolph dodged to the side, tipped over a chair, and tried to get beyond the kitchen table. He cried out sharply when a hand grasped his pajama shoulder, then he felt the dull impact of a fist against the side of his head, and glancing blows on the upper part of his body. As he slipped here and there in his father's grasp, dragged or lifted when he clung instinctively to an arm, aware of sharp smarts and strains, he made no sound except that he laughed hysterically several times. Then in less than a minute the blows abruptly ceased. After a lull during which Rudolph was tightly held, and during which they both trembled violently and uttered strange, truncated words, Carl Miller half-dragged, half-threatened his son upstairs.

"Put on you clothes!"

Rudolph was now both hysterical and cold. His head hurt him, and there was along, shallow scratch on his neck from his father's finger-nail, and he sobbed and trembled as he dressed. He was aware of his mother standing at the doorway in a wrapper, her wrinkled face compressing and squeezing and opening out into new series of wrinkles which floated and eddied from neck to brow. Despising her nervous ineffectuality and avoiding her rudely when she tried to touch his neck with witch-hazel, he made a hasty, choking toilet. Then he followed his father out of the house and along the road toward the Catholic church.

IV

They walked without speaking except when Carl Miller acknowledged automatically the existence of passers-by. Rudolph's uneven breathing alone ruffled the hot Sunday silence.

His father stopped decisively at the door of the church.

"I've decided you'd better go to confession again. Go in and tell Father Schwartz what you did and ask God's pardon."

"You lost your temper, too!" said Rudolph quickly.

Carl Miller took a step toward his son, who moved cautiously backward.

"All right, I'll go."

"Are you going to do what I say?" cried his father in a hoarse whisper.

"All right."

Rudolph walked into the church, and for the second time in two days entered the confessional and knelt down. The slat went up almost at once.

"I accuse myself of missing my morning prayers."

"Is that all?"

"That's all."

A maudlin exultation filled him. Not easily ever again would he be able to put an abstraction before the necessities of his ease and pride. An invisible line had been crossed, and he had become aware of his isolation—aware that it applied not only to those moments when he was Blatchford Sarnemington but that it applied to all his inner life. Hitherto such phenomena as "crazy" ambitions and petty shames and fears had been but private reservations, unacknowledged before the throne of his official soul. Now he realized unconsciously that his private reservations were himself—and all the rest a garnished front and a conventional flag. The pressure of his environment had driven him into the lonely secret road of adolescence.

He knelt in the pew beside his father. Mass began. Rudolph knelt up—when he was alone he slumped his posterior back against the seat—and tasted the consciousness of a sharp, subtle revenge. Beside him his father prayed that God would forgive Rudolph, and asked also that his own outbreak of temper would be pardoned. He glanced sidewise at his son, and was relieved to see that the strained, wild look had gone from his face and that he had ceased sobbing. The Grace of God, inherent in the Sacrament, would do the rest, and perhaps after Mass everything would be better. He was proud of Rudolph in his heart, and beginning to be truly as well as formally sorry for what he had done.

Usually, the passing of the collection box was a significant point for Rudolph in the services. If, as was often the case, he had no money to drop in he would be furiously ashamed and bow his head and pretend not to see the box, lest Jeanne Brady in the pew behind should take notice and suspect an acute family poverty. But today he glanced coldly into it as it skimmed under his eyes, noting with casual interest the large number of pennies it contained.

When the bell rang for communion, however, he quivered. There was no reason why God should not stop his heart. During the past twelve hours he had committed a series of mortal sins increasing in gravity, and he was now to crown them all with a blasphemous sacrilege.

"*Domine, non sum dignus, ut intres sub tectum meum: sed tantum dic verbo, et sanabitur anima mea. . . .*"

There was a rustle in the pews, and the communicants worked their ways into the aisle with downcast eyes and joined hands. Those of larger piety pressed together their finger-tips to form steeples. Among these latter was Carl Miller. Rudolph followed him toward the altar-rail and knelt down, automatically taking up the napkin under his chin. The bell rang sharply, and the priest turned from the altar with the white Host held above the chalice:

"*Corpus Domini nostri Jesu Christi custodiat animam tuam in vitam æternam.*"

A cold sweat broke out on Rudolph's forehead as the communion began. Along the line Father Schwartz moved, and with gathering nausea Rudolph felt his heart-valves weakening at the will of God. It seemed to him that the church was darker and that a great quiet had fallen, broken only by the inarticulate mumble which announced the approach of the Creator of Heaven and Earth. He dropped his head down between his shoulders and waited for the blow.

Then he felt a sharp nudge in his side. His father was poking him to sit up, not to slump against the rail; the priest was only two places away.

"*Corpus Domini nostri Jesu Christi custodiat animam tuam in vitam aeternam.*"

Rudolph opened his mouth. He felt the sticky wax taste of the wafer on his tongue. He remained motionless for what seemed an interminable period of time, his head still raised, the wafer undissolved in his mouth. Then again he started at the pressure of his father's elbow, and saw that the people were falling away from the altar like leaves and turning with blind downcast eyes to their pews, alone with God.

Rudolph was alone with himself, drenched with perspiration and deep in mortal sin. As he walked back to his pew the sharp taps of his cloven hoofs were loud upon the floor, and he knew that it was a dark poison he carried in his heart.

V

"Sagitta volante in die"

The beautiful little boy with eyes like blue stones, and lashes that sprayed open from them like flower-petals had finished telling his sin to Father Schwartz—and the square of sunshine in which he sat had moved forward half an hour into the room. Rudolph had become less frightened now; once eased of the story a reaction had set in. He knew that as long as he was in the room with this priest God would not stop his heart, so he sighed and sat quietly, waiting for the priest to speak.

Father Schwartz's cold watery eyes were fixed upon the carpet pattern on which the sun had brought out the swastikas and the flat bloomless vines and the pale echoes of flowers. The hall-clock ticked insistently toward sunset, and from the ugly room and from the afternoon outside the window arose a stiff monotony, shattered now and then by the reverberate clapping of a faraway hammer on the dry air. The priest's nerves were strung thin and the beads of his rosary were crawling and squirming like snakes upon the green felt of his table top. He could not remember now what it was he should say.

Of all the things in this lost Swede town he was most aware of this little boy's eyes—the beautiful eyes, with lashes that left them reluctantly and curved back as though to meet them once more.

For a moment longer the silence persisted while Rudolph waited, and the priest struggled to remember something that was slipping farther and farther away from him, and the clock ticked in the broken house. Then Father Schwartz stared hard at the little boy and remarked in a peculiar voice:

"When a lot of people get together in the best places things go glimmering."

Rudolph started and looked quickly at Father Schwartz's face.

"I said—" began the priest, and paused, listening. "Do you hear the hammer and the clock ticking and the bees? Well, that's no good. The thing is to have a lot of people in the center of the world, wherever that happens to be. Then"—his watery eyes widened knowingly—"things go glimmering."

"Yes, Father," agreed Rudolph, feeling a little frightened.

"What are you going to be when you grow up?"

"Well, I was going to be a baseball-player for a while," answered Rudolph nervously, "but I don't think that's a very good ambition, so I think I'll be an actor or a Navy officer."

Again the priest stared at him.

"I see *exactly* what you mean," he said, with a fierce air.

Rudolph had not meant anything in particular, and at the implication that he had, he became more uneasy.

"This man is crazy," he thought, "and I'm scared of him. He wants me to help him out some way, and I don't want to."

"You look as if things went glimmering," cried Father Schwartz wildly. "Did you ever go to a party?"

"Yes, Father."

"And did you notice that everybody was properly dressed? That's what I mean. Just as you went into the party there was a moment when everybody was properly dressed. Maybe two little girls were standing by the door and some boys were leaning over the banisters, and there were bowls around full of flowers."

"I've been to a lot of parties," said Rudolph, rather relieved that the conversation had taken this turn.

"Of course," continued Father Schwartz triumphantly, "I knew you'd agree with me. But my theory is that when a whole lot of people get together in the best places things go glimmering all the time."

Rudolph found himself thinking of Blatchford Sarnemington.

"Please listen to me!" commanded the priest impatiently. "Stop worrying about last Saturday. Apostasy implies an absolute damnation only on the supposition of a previous perfect faith. Does that fix it?"

Rudolph had not the faintest idea what Father Schwartz was talking about, but he nodded and the priest nodded back at him and returned to his mysterious preoccupation.

"Why," he cried, "they have lights now as big as stars—do you realize that? I heard of one light they had in Paris or somewhere that was as big as a star. A lot of people had it—a lot of gay people. They have all sorts of things now that you never dreamed of."

"Look here—" He came nearer to Rudolph, but the boy drew away, so Father Schwartz went back and sat down in his chair, his eyes dried out and hot. "Did you ever see an amusement park?"

"No, Father."

"Well, go and see an amusement park." The priest waved his hand vaguely. "It's a thing like a fair, only much more glittering. Go to one at night and stand a little way off from it in a dark place—under dark trees. You'll see a big wheel made of lights turning in the air, and a long slide shooting boats down into the water. A band playing somewhere, and a smell of peanuts—and everything will twinkle. But it won't remind you of anything, you see. It will all just

hang out there in the night like a colored balloon—like a big yellow lantern on a pole."

Father Schwartz frowned as he suddenly thought of something.

"But don't get up close," he warned Rudolph, "because if you do you'll only feel the heat and the sweat and the life."

All this talking seemed particularly strange and awful to Rudolph, because this man was a priest. He sat there, half terrified, his beautiful eyes open wide and staring at Father Schwartz. But underneath his terror he felt that his own inner convictions were confirmed. There was something ineffably gorgeous somewhere that had nothing to do with God. He no longer thought that God was angry at him about the original lie, because He must have understood that Rudolph had done it to make things finer in the confessional, brightening up the dinginess of his admissions by saying a thing radiant and proud. At the moment when he had affirmed immaculate honor a silver pennon had flapped out into the breeze somewhere and there had been the crunch of leather and the shine of silver spurs and a troop of horsemen waiting for dawn on a low green hill. The sun had made stars of light on their breastplates like the picture at home of the German cuirassiers at Sedan.

But now the priest was muttering inarticulate and heart-broken words, and the boy became wildly afraid. Horror entered suddenly in at the open window, and the atmosphere of the room changed. Father Schwartz collapsed precipitously down on his knees, and let his body settle back against a chair.

"Oh, my God!" he cried out, in a strange voice, and wilted to the floor.

Then a human oppression rose from the priest's worn clothes, and mingled with the faint smell of old food in the corners. Rudolph gave a sharp cry and ran in a panic from the house—while the collapsed man lay there quite still, filling his room, filling it with voices and faces until it was crowded with echolalia, and rang loud with a steady, shrill note of laughter.

Outside the window the blue sirocco trembled over the wheat, and girls with yellow hair walked sensuously along roads that bounded the fields, calling innocent, exciting things to the young men who were working in the lines between the grain. Legs were shaped under starchless gingham, and rims of the necks of dresses were warm and damp. For five hours now hot fertile life had burned in the afternoon. It would be night in three hours, and all along the land there would be these blonde Northern girls and the tall young men form the farms lying out beside the wheat, under the moon.

—All the Sad Young Men

* * *

The relationship between "Absolution" and The Great Gatsby, *and the connection between Rudolph Miller and James Gatz, remain matters of dispute among scholars. Fitzgerald's response to a fan letter provides a clue.*

April 15, 1934

Dear Mr. Jamieson:

Thank you, immensely, for sending me your article. I agree with you entirely, as goes without saying, in your analysis of Gatsby. He was perhaps created on the image of some forgotten farm type of Minnesota that I have known and forgotten, and associated at the same moment with some sense of romance. It might interest you to know that a story of mine, called "Absolution," in my book *All the Sad Young Men* was intended to be a picture of his early life, but that I cut it because I preferred to preserve the sense of mystery.

Again, thanks!

With very best wishes,

Yours,
Scott Fitzgerald

***

"Absolution" and *The Great Gatsby*

Lawrence D. Stewart

It is no secret that Scott Fitzgerald's short story, "Absolution," began as a prologue to *The Great Gatsby* but was dropped because, as Fitzgerald himself wrote in 1934, "I preferred to preserve the sense of mystery."[1] The merit of this revision has been much debated: it is unlikely that Mrs. Wharton knew of "Absolution's" connection with the novel, but her letter of 8 June 1925 to Fitzgerald—which Fitzgerald called one of the few "intelligable" criticisms his book had received—would seem to argue for inclusion of the short story.[2] Other critics hold to judicative indecisiveness, observing either that "Actually the book gains as well as loses by the blurredness of Gatsby; it gains in mystery what it loses in definition,"[3] or that "The blurring of Gatsby, if it is a defect, is also a virtue, in that it renders his fantastic illusion more believable."[4]

Such statements—including the one by Fitzgerald—sound as though the omission of "Absolution" had been a matter of taste. If the *Gatsby* prologue was much like the published short story, however, I think that Fitzgerald was compelled to eliminate it; for "Absolution" and *The Great Gatsby,* though they share a few superficial similarities, are basically irreconcilable.[5]

I

The manuscripts and galley proofs of "Absolution" seem to have disappeared; Fitzgerald's records, however, indicate that the story was written in June 1923.[6] The only extant manuscript of *The Great Gatsby* makes no allusion to "Absolution"; therefore, the only evidence for what the story was is what the story is. First published in the June 1924 *American Mercury*—nearly a year before the novel came out—it was in 1926 included in *All the Sad Young Men,* Fitzgerald's third collection of short stories. For this volume, Fitzgerald made incidental verbal revisions in sixteen places, only one or two of them suggesting any change in his intention.[7]

The published story shows certain clear affinities to *The Great Gatsby:* both Mr. Gatz and Mr. Miller greatly admire James J. Hill; neither Rudolph Miller nor Jimmy Gatz believes himself the son of his parents, each having invented an alter ego; the imagery of rundown clocks and falling leaves is common to both accounts; and there is even occasionally heard the same voice as storyteller: "Perhaps in the houses of delinquency among the dull and hardeyed incorrigible girls can be found those for whom has burned the whitest fire" must be Carraway speaking, the same man who once said of Tom and Daisy (in the manuscript, in lines not published), "they didn't seem quite so remotely rich if they enjoyed the supposition that I was possessed by the flowery lust. After all they too had once walked in all innocence through the charmed garden."

We might best try "Absolution" as an adjunct to *The Great Gatsby* if we view the novel's protagonist as an Alger hero and find "the deepness of the roots of Gatsby's dream in the deprivations of his past."[8] But the hypothesis will not stand the testing; for how do the deprivations in Rudolph's life account for the preposterous expression Gatsby gives his dreams?

Only once in "Absolution" did Fitzgerald even momentarily suggest that Rudolph's fancies could evolve into Gatsby's dreams. The passage comes after the boy's second lie in confession:

> An invisible line had been crossed, and he had become aware of his isolation—aware that it applied not only to those moments when he was Blatchford Sarnemington but that it applied to all his inner life. Hitherto such phenomena as "crazy" ambitions and petty shames and fears had been but private reservations, unacknowledged before the throne of his official soul. Now he realized unconsciously that his private reservations were himself—and all the rest a garnished front and a conventional flag (124).

But Fitzgerald did not end his paragraph with notions of Rudolph's uniqueness. Instead, he concluded: "The pressure of his environment had driven him into the lonely secret road of adolescence"—and we pass from the individual to the universal. The eleven-year-old boy is already moving toward "the air cushions that lie on the asphalts of fourteen," Fitzgerald's *This Side of Paradise* survey of the road through adolescence.

In the worlds of "Absolution" and *The Great Gatsby* few characters worship the same god; certainly Rudolph Miller and Jay Gatsby do not stand before the same god. Orthodox religion threatens and terrifies Rudolph, and his consuming fear of God makes his shift defensively into feelings of superiority to the Divinity. The priest's madness confirms his suspicion that "There was something ineffably gorgeous somewhere that had nothing to do with God" (131)–this, the outcome of his earlier practice of reserving "a corner of his mind where he was safe from God, where he prepared the subterfuges with which he often tricked God" (117). Ultimately, "He no longer thought God was angry at him about the original lie, because He must have understood that Rudolph had done it to make things finer in the confessional, brightening up the dinginess of his admissions by saying a thing radiant and proud" (131). He never felt identification with God, and the last remark suggests the shaky alliance he formed with the Divinity.

Jay Gatsby, however, "sprang from his Platonic conception of himself. He was a son of God–" and his dreams develop in Biblical imagery: Jacob's ladder, the confrontation in the Temple, the Platonism of the Gospel of John. With respect to this parallelism between Christ and Gatsby we can ironically appreciate Fitzgerald's use of "mystery" as an explanation for the story's cancellation, for we learn of Gatsby's life only at selected moments, in the same way that we know of Christ's at isolated intervals. Little in either account tells us of the protagonists except when their actions are fulfillments of their inspired purposes. We cannot therefore legitimately want "more" about Gatsby's childhood when "more" would violate this aspect of Fitzgerald's intention. Even if that objection were met, "Absolution" itself never would have served: for in the use of religious imagery and ideas, Jay Gatsby has his predecessor not in the small boy, Rudolph, but in the priest, Father Schwartz.

II

With an account of the priest's plight we begin "Absolution"; with a final vision of his despair, we leave it. Assuredly, the story is much concerned with "the transition in Rudolph,"[9] but desire to connect the story to the novel has deflected attention from the equally important, dedicated man "who, in the still of the night, wept cold tears . . . because the afternoons were warm and long, and he was unable to attain a complete mystical union with out Lord" (109).

The priest is driven mad by contacts with this world, and he finds the shrill laughter of girls "a terrible dissonance," the scent of cheap toilet soap "desperately sweet," the Dakota wheat fields "terrible to look upon," and four o'clock of the afternoon a "hot madness." The only thing in the world lovely to him is an amusement part, because "it won't remind you of anything, you see. It will all just hang out there in the night like a colored balloon–like a big yellow lantern on a pole" (130). But even it must be regarded circumspectly–"a little way off from it in a park place–under dark trees . . . But

don't get up close . . . because if you do you'll only feel the heat and the sweat and the life" (130). He never forgets his own repeated admonition: "my theory is that when a whole lot of people get together in the best places things go glimmering all the time" (129). It is a curiously inappropriate conversation to hold with a child; no wonder Rudolph thinks the priest is mad.

But nothing indicates that Fitzgerald himself regarded the priest's dilemma with amusement. One of the revisions he made in the story after its first publication was the alteration of the priest's concluding words with Rudolph: once "inarticulate and dim and terrible," they are now "inarticulate and heart-broken" (131); it is a small revision, but it suggests Fitzgerald's increasing sympathy for the priest as we see him–significantly, not through Rudolph's uncomprehending eyes.

The priest's disappointed desire for "a complete mystical union with our Lord" balances with his awareness of the physical unions which are presumably everywhere possible. Living in a world where all is ripeness, he finds denied him the one union he desires. Sexual frustration probably does contribute to the involutions in his behavior, but surely it is an oversimplification to dismiss Father Schwartz's problem as "the incoherent frustrations of the old Catholic priest, celibate by profession."[10] Certainly Fitzgerald's treatment of the man encourages another interpretation.

Was it not Fitzgerald's intention to use the language of physical fulfillment in a mystical sense, to suggest the priest's permanent three o'clock in the morning? The priest desperately needs an object to symbolize his yearning for God, and finds it, ironically, in a glittering amusement part because "it won't remind you of anything, you see." Only by comprehending his character can we understand how he has changed a "vast, vulgar, and meretricious beauty" into a mystical symbol. But this was to be the practice too of Jay Gatsby when he converted the tawdriness of the world into his secret symbols: a green light into a girl, a girl's voice into magical money, a girl herself into a manifestation of the Divine.

Until the creation of Jay Gatsby, Father Schwartz remained Fitzgerald's best example of the tragic, dream-haunted man. Because Father Schwartz is a Father, Fitzgerald can take these longings and, through the character of the man, transform them into a gaudy, glittering symbol without implying that the dreams themselves are worthless. With Gatsby, Fitzgerald worked conversely: cheap and obvious dreams were spoken of in religious language to point up Gatsby's devotion without implying that the objects ever became what the hero saw in them. We always keep a double vision with these committed men. We know the amusement park is sordid; but we also appreciate how to Father Schwartz it is pure. We know the worthlessness of Daisy and all of Gatsby's pursuits; but because we look through his eyes too, we see her and them as he would have us do.

"Absolution" stands as prologue to *The Great Gatsby* only as the harbinger of tragedy: the destruction of the priest foreshadows what must inevitably happen to Gatsby and his more intense dreams. But the short story alleged Gatsby-as-boy is a child who has no awareness of Father Schwartz's dilemma and who uses the priest's behavior as justification for developing quite different notions. It takes uncommon faith to believe that Rudolph could have evolved into the man who gave his name to Fitzgerald's most polished novel.

—*Fitzgerald/Hemingway Annual 1973*

Notes

1. *Letters of F. Scott Fitzgerald,* ed. Andrew Turnbull (New York: Scribners, 1963), p. 509. Ten years earlier, on 18 June 1924, Fitzgerald had told Max Perkins the story "was to have been the prologue of the novel but it interfered with the neatness of the plan" (p. 164). Recently Henry Dan Piper in his *Fitzgerald's "The Great Gatsby": The Novel, The Critics, The Background* (New York: Scribners, 1970) has said that "Absolution" served at one stage as the first chapter of a discarded early version of the novel" (p. 1) and that Fitzgerald "intended 'Absolution' at one time to be the opening chapter of an early version of *The Great Gatsby*" (p. 83). Prof. Piper gives no evidence justifying the translation of Fitzgerald's term, "prologue," into either "first chapter" or "opening chapter."

2. F. Scott Fitzgerald, *The Crack-Up,* ed. Edmund Wilson (New York: New Directions, 1945), p. 309; however, Mrs. Wharton appears to have been interested more in the first years of the newly-created Jay Gatsby than she was in the formative years of Jimmy Gatz. Fitzgerald's editor similarly complained about the vagueness of Gatsby's history when he first read the manuscript; cf. letter of Maxwell Perkins to Fitzgerald, 20 November 1924, asking for more details about Gatsby's present as well as past (*Editor to Author: The Letters of Maxwell E. Perkins,* ed., John Hall Wheelock [New York: Scribners, 1950], p. 39).

3. Malcolm Cowley (ed.), *The Stories of F. Scott Fitzgerald* (New York: Scribners, 1951), p. xviii.

4. James E. Miller, Jr., *F. Scott Fitzgerald: His Art and His Technique* (New York: New York University Press, 1964), p. 116. Also cf. Robert Sklar, *F. Scott Fitzgerald: The Last Laocoon* (New York: Oxford University Press, 1967), p. 174: "there was a plan, and its form required that the hero's origins remain mysterious to the end." Cf. also pp. 223–24.

5. For an interpretation that sees Gatsby growing out of "Absolution," and not irreconciliable to it, cf. Henry Dan Piper, *F. Scott Fitzgerald: A Critical Portrait* (New York: Holt, Rinehart & Winston, 1965), pp. 13, 103–7. Also cf. Henry Dan Piper, "The Untrimmed Christmas Tree: The Religious Background of *The Great Gatsby*," in *Fitzgerald's "The Great Gatsby,"* pp. 93–100. Also cf. Sklar, pp. 159–60, 173–74, 186.

6. Piper, *Fitzgerald: Critical Portrait,* p. 103.

7. Rudolph's father originally was described as being "Somewhat gross and utterly deficient in curiosity. . . ." Fitzgerald recast this to "Somewhat gross he was, nevertheless, insufficiently hard-headed . . . " (118). (All parenthetical page references are to F. Scott Fitzgerald, *All the Sad Young Men* [New York: Scribners, 1926]). The punctuation of the two versions differs considerably. Fitzgerald revised primarily to smooth the flow of his rhetoric. One small change recalls his fascination for certain words: in 1925, after the first printing of *Gatsby* had come from the press in April, "echolalia" began reverberating in Fitzgerald's mind. Before the second printing in August 1925 he had

the plates amended to replace "the chatter of the garden" (p. 60) with "the echolalia of the garden." Originally, "Absolution" neared its conclusion with the priest collapsed upon the floor, "filling his room, filling it with voices and faces until it was crowded with shadowy movements, and rang loud with a steady, shrill note of laughter." *For All the Sad Young Men,* Fitzgerald converted "shadowy movements" to "echolalia."

8. Miller, p. 115.

9. Miller, p. 103. Arthur Mizener, *The Far Side of Paradise* (Boston: Houghton Mifflin, 1965; revised ed.), p. 214 sees the story as a contrast between "a romantic young man, who has a bad conscience and dreams of himself as a worldly hero named Blatchford Sarnemington, with a spoiled priest, who is filled with piety and a maddening dream of a life like an eternal amusement park."

10. Miller p. 104. Piper, *Fitzgerald: Critical Portrait,* pp. 106–7, insists: "Rudolph is so much more attractive a character than Father Schwartz that it is hard to accept the foolish priest as an appropriate symbol of the faith he so unworthily serves. Fitzgerald's personal dislike obscures the priest's aesthetic function in the story. He was undoubtedly a portrait of someone Fitzgerald had known, and it is pretty clear that Schwartz's treatment of Rudolph is connected in some way with Schwartz's latent homosexuality." I know of no evidence that will support these assumptions.

Cover for the issue of the mass-circulation magazine that published Fitzgerald's story "'The Sensible Thing.'" Liberty declined to serialize The Great Gatsby *because the novel was too racy for its readers and did not divide into suspenseful installments.*

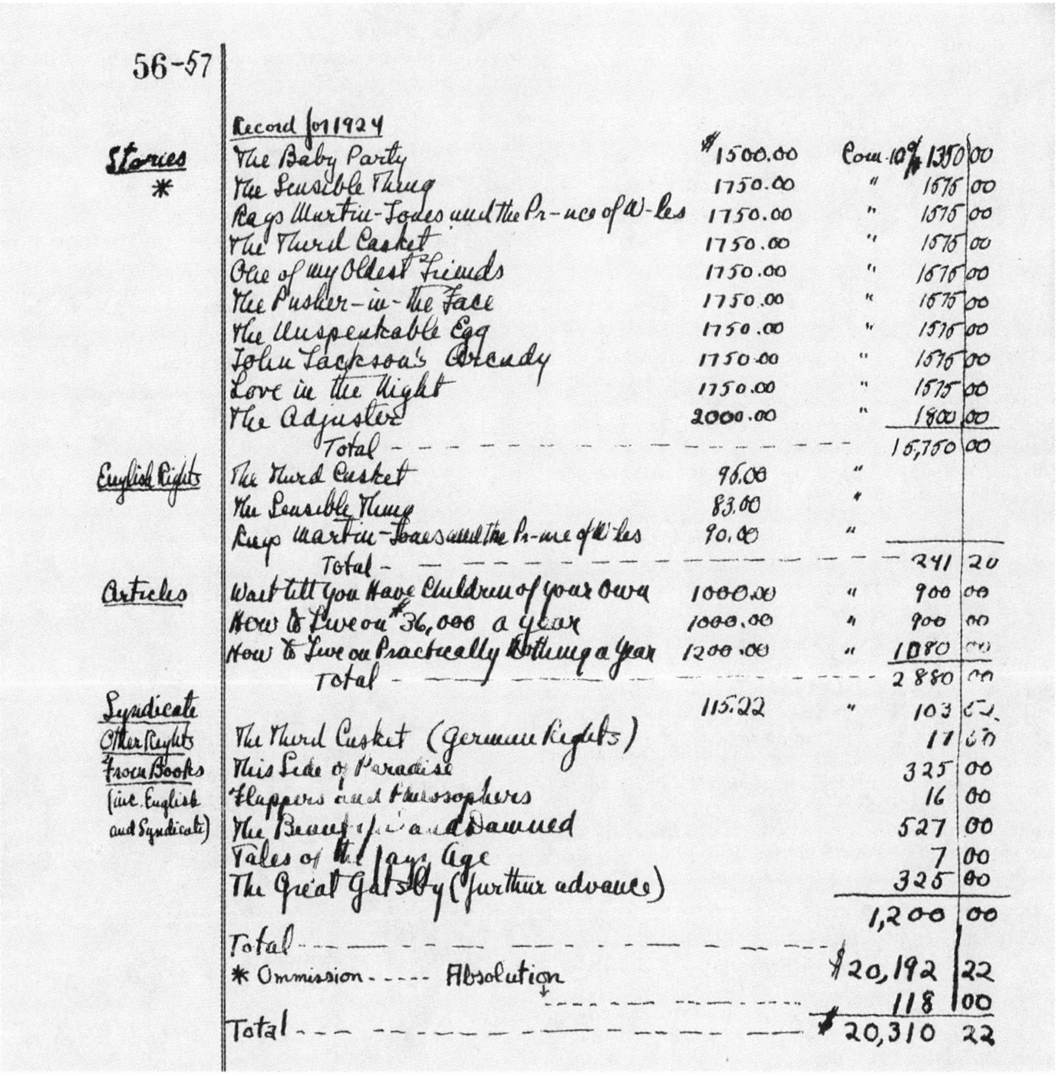

56-57

Record for 1924

Stories ***	The Baby Party	$1500.00	Com .10% 1350 00
	The Sensible Thing	1750.00	" 1575 00
	Rags Martin-Jones and the Pr-nce of W-les	1750.00	" 1575 00
	The Third Casket	1750.00	" 1575 00
	One of my Oldest Friends	1750.00	" 1575 00
	The Pusher-in-the Face	1750.00	" 1575 00
	The Unspeakable Egg	1750.00	" 1575 00
	John Jackson's Arcady	1750.00	" 1575 00
	Love in the Night	1750.00	" 1575 00
	The Adjuster	2000.00	" 1800 00
	Total		15,750 00
English Rights	The Third Casket	96.00	"
	The Sensible Thing	83.00	"
	Rags Martin-Jones and the Pr-nce of W-les	90.00	"
	Total		241 20
Articles	Wait till you Have Children of your Own	1000.00	" 900 00
	How to Live on $36,000 a year	1000.00	" 900 00
	How to Live on Practically Nothing a Year	1200.00	" 1080 00
	Total		2880 00
Syndicate		115.22	" 103 62
Other Rights	The Third Casket (German Rights)		11 60
From Books	This Side of Paradise		325 00
(inc. English and Syndicate)	Flappers and Philosophers		16 00
	The Beautiful and Damned		527 00
	Tales of the Jazz Age		7 00
	The Great Gatsby (further advance)		325 00
			1,200 00
Total			$20,192 22
*** Ommission ----- Absolution			118 00
Total			$20,310 22

Page from Fitzgerald's Ledger *listing his earnings during the year he wrote "'The Sensible Thing'" and commenced steady work on his novel*

"THE SENSIBLE THING"

"'The Sensible Thing'" is one of the strongest Gatsby *cluster stories. Drawing on his courtship of Zelda Sayre, Fitzgerald wrote about a young man who loses a Southern girl because of his poverty. After one of the sudden reversals of fortune that characterize Fitzgerald's stories, George O'Kelley comes back for Jonquil Cary a year later with money and a promising future. Now she is ready to marry him; but O'Kelley realizes that during the year something has been irretrievably lost:*

All the time in the world—his life and hers. But for an instant as he kissed her he knew that though he search through eternity he could never recapture those lost April hours. He might press her close now till the muscles knotted on his arms—she was something desirable and rare that he had fought for and made his own—but never again an intangible whisper in the dark, or on the breeze of night. . . .

Well, let it pass he thought; April is over, April is over. There are all kinds of love in the world, but never the same love twice.

O'Kelley can accept the mutability of love, but Gatsby insists on nothing less than total restoration: he wants the same love twice.

* * *

110

He had lost an eyebrow somewhere, and he still wore a bandage on his arm, but he was too young not to realize that on the steamer many women had looked at him with unusual tributary interest.

Illustrations from "'The Sensible Thing'"

LITERARY INFLUENCES ON *THE GREAT GATSBY*

Joseph Conrad

Conrad's preface to The Nigger of the Narcissus *was republished as* Joseph Conrad on the Art of Writing *(1914). Many writers have acknowledged the influence of the lines "My trick which I am trying to achieve is, by the power of the written word to make you hear, to make you feel—it is, before all, to make you see." Fitzgerald greatly respected Conrad's work and read it carefully. It is generally agreed that Fitzgerald was indebted to Conrad's writing for the technique of Nick as partially involved narrator in Gatsby. There is an undocumented anecdote that Fitzgerald and Ring Lardner attempted to pay homage to Conrad by performing a dance when he was visiting his American publisher on Long Island.*

Excerpt from Conrad's Preface

Fiction—if it at all aspires to be art—appeals to temperament. And in truth it must be, like painting, like music, like all art, the appeal of one temperament to all the other innumerable temperaments whose subtle and resistless power endows passing events with their true meaning, and creates the moral, the emotional atmosphere of the place and time. Such an appeal to be effective must be an impression conveyed through the senses; and, in fact, it cannot be made in any other way, because temperament, whether individual or collective, is not amenable to persuasion. All art, therefore, appeals primarily to the senses, and the artistic aim when expressing itself in written words must also make its appeal through the senses, if its high desire is to reach the secret spring of responsive emotions. It must strenuously aspire to the plasticity of sculpture, to the colour of painting, and to the magic suggestiveness of music—which is the art of arts. And it is only through complete, unswerving devotion to the perfect blending of form and substance; it is only through an unremitting never-discouraged care for the shape and ring of sentences that an approach can be made to plasticity, to colour, and that the light of magic suggestiveness may be brought to play for an evanescent instant over the commonplace surface of words: or the old, old words, worn thin, defaced by ages of careless usage.

The sincere endeavour to accomplish that creative task, to go as far on that road as his strength will carry him, to go indeterred by faltering, weariness, or reproach, is the only valid justification for the worker in prose. And if his conscience is clear, his answer to those who, in the fullness of a wisdom which looks for immediate profit, demand specifically to be edified, consoled,

Joseph Conrad

amused; who demand to be promptly improved, or encouraged, or frightened, or shocked, or charmed, must run thus: My task which I am trying to achieve is, by the power of the written word to make you hear, to make you feel—it is, before all, to make you *see*. That—and no more, and it is everything. If I succeed, you shall find there according to your deserts: encouragement, consolation, fear, charm—all you demand—and, perhaps, also that glimpse of truth for which you have forgotten to ask.

To snatch in a moment of courage, from the remorseless rush of time, a passing phase of life, is only the beginning of the task. The task approached in tenderness and faith is to hold up unquestioningly, without choice and without fear, the rescued fragment before all eyes in the light of a sincere mood. It is to show its vibration, its colour, its form; and through its movement, its form, and its colour, reveal the substance of its truth—disclose its inspiring secret: the stress and passion within the core of each convincing moment. In a single-minded attempt of that kind, if one be deserving and fortunate, one may perchance attain to such clearness of sincerity that at last the presented vision of regret or pity, of terror or mirth, shall awaken in the hearts of the beholders that feeling of unavoidable solidarity; of the solidarity in mysterious origin, in toil, in joy, in hope, in uncertain fate, which binds men to each other and all mankind to the visible world.

It is evident that he who, rightly or wrongly, holds by the convictions expressed above cannot be faithful to any one of the temporary formulas of his craft. The enduring part of them—the truth which each only imperfectly veils—should abide with him as the most precious of his possessions, but they all: Realism, Romanticism, Naturalism, even the unofficial sentimentalism (which, like the poor, is exceedingly difficult to get rid of), all these gods must, after a short period of fellowship, abandon him—even on the very threshold of the temple—to the stammerings of his conscience and to the outspoken consciousness of the difficulties of his work. In that uneasy solitude the supreme cry of Art for Art, itself, loses the exciting ring of its apparent immorality. It sounds far off. It has ceased to be a cry, and is heard only as a whisper, often incomprehensible, but at times and faintly encouraging.

* * *

"An Instance of Apparent Plagiarism": F. Scott Fitzgerald, Willa Cather, and the First *Gatsby* Manuscript
Matthew J. Bruccoli

Willa Cather

The Princeton University Library has a letter from F. Scott Fitzgerald to Willa Cather enclosing two pages from a working manuscript of *The Great Gatsby*. Concerned that he had inadvertently echoed wording in Cather's short novel, *A Lost Lady*, Fitzgerald explained in late March or early April 1925 that his evocation of Daisy's voice, which resembles Cather's description of Marian Forrester, had been written before he read *A Lost Lady*.

Hotel Tiberio, Capri, Italy
My Dear Miss Cather:
    As one of your greatest admirers—an admirer particularly of *My Antonia, A Lost Lady, Paul's Case* and *Scandal* I want to write to explain an instance of apparent plagiarism which some suspicious person may presently bring to your attention.
    To begin with, my new book *The Great Gatsby* will appear about the time you receive this letter (I am sending you the book besides). When I was in the middle of the first draft *A Lost Lady* was published and I read it with the greatest delight. One of the finest passages is the often quoted one toward the end which includes the

phrases "she seemed to promise a wild delight that he has not found in life. . . "I could show you" . . . ect (all misquoted here as I have no copy by me).
    Well, a month or two before I had written into my own book a parallel and almost similar idea in the description of a woman's charm—an idea I'd had for several years. Now my expression of this was neither so clear, nor so beautiful, nor so moving as yours but the essential similarity was undoubtedly there. I was worried because I hated the devil to cut mine out so I went to Ring Lardner and several other people and showed them mine and yours and finally decided to retain it. Also I've kept the pages from my first draft to show you and am enclosing them here. The passage as finally worked out is in my Chapter One. Hoping you will understand my motive in communicating this to you I am
    With Best Wishes and Most Sincere Admiration
                                F. Scott Fitzgerald

The passage Fitzgerald quoted from memory appears on pp. 171-172 of *A Lost Lady* (New York: Knopf, 1923):

113

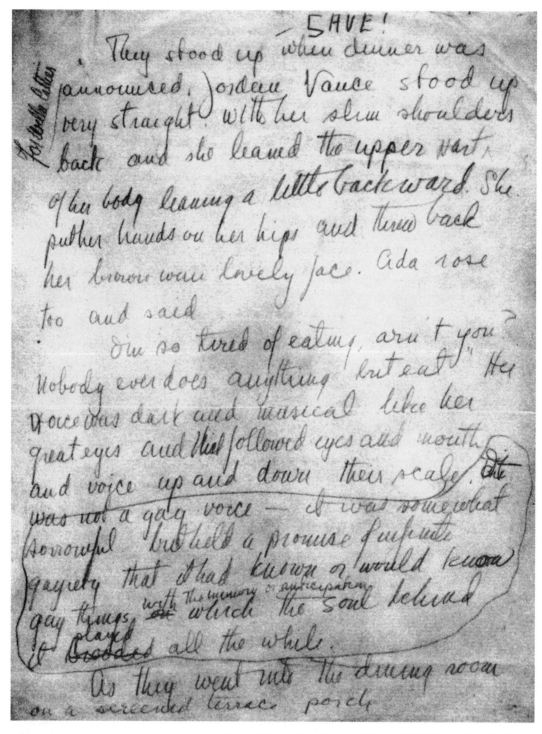

Manuscript pages Fitzgerald sent to Cather in 1925 (Princeton University Library)

SAVE!

It was a dark sad face with bright things in it like children playing in a house of death. The ~~was~~ curve of the mouth and the ~~was~~ singing ~~compellingness~~ compulsion of the voice. The "listen" ~~whispering~~ ~~isn't~~ now richness of it which seem to proceed every word — the words changed their notes. The sentences were songs. There are no words to describe such voices but there is a promise of gay things in them of something magical done or yet to do.

About the ~~the~~ rest of her Caraway felt ~~rather than~~ was aware of a diminishing of vitality since he first knew her. ~~He supposed~~ There was a strain in an intensely strong vital man like ~~Kay~~

Her eyes, when they laughed for a moment into one's own, seemed to promise a wild delight that he had not found in life. "I know where it is," they seemed to say, "I could show you!" He would like to call up the shade of the young Mrs. Forrester, as the witch of Endor called up Samuel's, and challenge it, demand the secret of that ardour; ask her whether she had really found some ever-blooming, ever-burning, ever-piercing joy, or whether it was all fine play-acting. Probably she had found no more than another; but she had always the power of suggesting things much lovelier than herself, as the perfume of a single flower may call up the whole sweetness of spring.

As published, the description of Daisy's voice on p. 11 of *The Great Gatsby* reads:

Her face was sad and lovely with bright things in it, bright eyes and a bright passionate mouth, but there was an excitement in her voice that men who had cared for her found difficult to forget: a singing compulsion, a whispered "Listen," a promise that she had done gay, exciting things just a while since and that there were gay, exciting things hovering in the next hour.

On 28 April 1925, Willa Cather replied, saying that she had enjoyed reading *Gatsby* before she received Fitzgerald's letter and that she had not detected any duplication of *A Lost Lady*. She acknowledges that many authors have tried to say that same thing, but none has succeeded. The only way to describe beauty is to describe its effect, and not the person. Fitzgerald pasted this letter in his scrapbook.[1]

Apart from demonstrating Fitzgerald's scrupulous literary honesty as well as the care with which he had read Willa Cather, these documents provide a significant supplement to our knowledge about the composition of *Gatsby*: they are the only known pages from the working draft that preceded the complete 1924 manuscript now in the Princeton University Library.

Since Fitzgerald notes that he "was in the middle of the first draft" of his novel when he read *A Lost Lady* soon after publication on 14 September 1923, it now seems probable that Fitzgerald was working on the final plot of *Gatsby* earlier than has been thought. Until the discovery of the pages he sent Cather, it had appeared that Fitzgerald did not conceive the Gatsby-Daisy-Nick plot until Spring 1924. These manuscript pages attest to the existence of at least a partial working draft in 1923 which Fitzgerald then completely rewrote—not revised—in 1924. Apart from the name changes (Jordan Vance became Jordan Baker, and Ada became Daisy), the crucial difference between the drafts is that the 1923 draft was written from the point of view of the omniscient author. Nick Carraway did not become the narrator until Fitzgerald rewrote the novel in 1924. Moreover,

Title page for the novel published in 1923

the evidence of the paper reinforces the separation of these drafts. The pages Fitzgerald sent to Cather are on 8½ x 11 paper watermarked SHAMROCK TYPEWRITER LINER, whereas the complete 1924 draft is on 8 3/8 x 12 7/8 paper watermarked CASCADE BOND / U.S.A.

On the basis of two pages it is impossible to tell how close to the published novel the plot of the 1923 draft actually was. Fitzgerald was living in Great Neck, Long Island, in 1922–1924 and seeing Maxwell Perkins regularly, so there is little editorial correspondence about *Gatsby* during this period. The original conception of the novel, which Fitzgerald reported to Perkins in June 1922, was for a novel set in the Midwest and New York in 1885 with "a catholic element." No manuscript survives for this version.

In April 1924, Fitzgerald informed Perkins that he had decided to rewrite the novel from a "new angle": "Much of what I wrote last summer was good but it was so interrupted that it was ragged + in approaching it from a new angle I've had to discard a lot of it—in one case 18,000 words (part of which will appear in The Mercury as a short story).[2] The two manuscript pages Fitzgerald sent Willa Cather indicate that the plot of the 1923 draft of *Gatsby* was probably close to the plot of the published novel.

Fitzgerald's rapid progress with *The Great Gatsby* on the Riviera in the summer of 1924 was aided by an earlier working draft. Since Fitzgerald usually exaggerated his progress on a novel, his claim to Willa Cather that he was "in the middle of the first draft" in September 1923 may be regarded with suspicion. Even if this draft was half-written, there is no evidence that it was ever finished. The existence of the 1923 draft—of whatever extent—in no way diminishes Fitzgerald's achievement in completely rewriting *The Great Gatsby* between June and September 1924. The process did not end there, of course. He rewrote and revised the typescript and galleys until February 1925.

—*The Princeton University Library Chronicle,* Spring 1978

Notes

1. Because of restrictions in Cather's will, the text of her letter to Fitzgerald cannot be published.
2. "Absolution," *The American Mercury,* June 1924.

* * *

Fitzgerald's Jay Gatz and Young Ben Franklin
Floyd C. Watkins

According to many recent critics, one of the features of the works of F. Scott Fitzgerald, especially *The Great Gatsby,* is an awareness of the American historical tradition. Jay Gatsby is not only a representative of the Roaring Twenties in which he lived; he also, according to Lionel Trilling, "comes inevitably to stand for America itself." In an article in the *Pacific Spectator,* Charles S. Holmes has shown that Fitzgerald was "concerned with the generic American character, the national 'style,' and the native tradition." According to his biographer, Arthur Mizener, "The substance out of which Fitzgerald constructed his stories . . . was American, perhaps more completely American than that of any other writer of his time." John Peale Bishop has seen Gatsby as "the Emersonian man brought to completion and eventually to failure." And this documentation of Fitzgerald and Gatsby as personifications of America and the American dream could be carried to much greater length.

In *The Great Gatsby,* Fitzgerald was certainly aware of the American tradition as it was being developed by his contemporaries in the Twenties. Describing the very symbolical ash dumps, Fitzgerald in one sentence

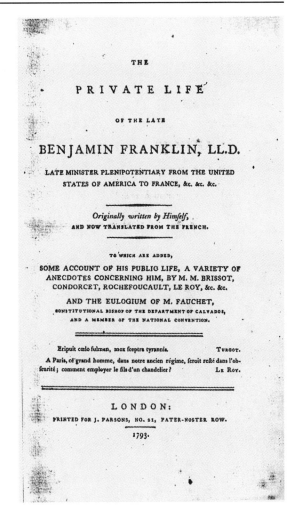

Benjamin Franklin's rules for success were assembled in his Autobiography, *which became a classic statement of the American success ethic (The Lilly Library, Indiana University). Gatsby's rules in his copy of Clarence E. Mulford's* Hopalong Cassidy *(1910) imitate Franklin's prescription.*

alluded to two contemporary works that attempted to place the period in an historical frame of reference: "The only building in sight was a small block of yellow brick sitting on the edge of the waste land, a sort of compact Main Street ministering to it, and contiguous to absolutely nothing." Here the meaning of his description is very much in tone with the works to which he refers, Eliot's *The Waste Land* and Lewis' *Main Street.* The most important linking of the novel to the American past, however, is accomplished at the end of the book, where Fitzgerald speaks of Manhattan as "the old island here that flowered once for Dutch sailors' eyes—a fresh green breast of the new world. Its vanished trees,

Hopalong Cassidy

BY

Clarence E. Mulford
Author of "Bar-20" and "The Orphan"

WITH FIVE ILLUSTRATIONS IN COLOR
BY
Maynard Dixon

CHICAGO
A. C. McCLURG & CO.
1910

Fitzgerald's reference to this popular cowboy novel incorrectly assigns it to 1906 (The Lilly Library, Indiana University)

the trees that had made way for Gatsby's house, had once pandered in whispers to the last and greatest of all human dreams. . . ." The import of this passage lies in the implied comparison of Gatsby's incorruptible dream to the dream of the New World.

There is one other significant connection between *The Great Gatsby* and the American past, and it has been only vaguely noted heretofore. Mr. Holmes has described Gatsby as "devoted . . . to the success maxims of the Ben Franklin tradition." Mr. Charles Weir quotes entirely the schedule that Jay Gatsby as the young Jay Gatz had copied into "a ragged old copy of a book called *Hopalong Cassidy*." Then he exclaims: "What childhood dreams of Franklin or Edison lay behind the scrawl, what lectures on self-improvement, what tradition that every Ameri-

can boy could make a million dollars or become President!"

The source is not nearly so much Edison as it is Franklin, that early American whom Carlyle called "the Father of all Yankees" and who was to Sinclair Lewis' Babbitt "this solid American citizen." Most of the resolutions of Fitzgerald's hero can be traced either to Franklin's own schedule or to his list of thirteen virtues to which he gives "a week's strict attention" in order to attain moral perfection. Thus by five o'clock in his daily timetable Franklin wrote "Rise," and at six o'clock Gatsby intended to "Rise from bed." The early American intended to "prosecute the present study" before eight o'clock, and the modern American planned to "Study electricity, etc." from 7:15 until 8:15; thus Gatsby did not devote himself to study of the philosophers as Franklin had, but to one of the most practical (and American) aspects of his model's career. Whereas Franklin wrote "Work" by the hours from eight to twelve and from two to six, with an hour out for lunch, young Jay Gatz recorded, "Work . . . 8:30–4:30 P.M." Fitzgerald gave Gatsby one greater virtue than Franklin: he was earlier to bed. Gatsby slept from nine until six; Franklin, from ten to five. Franklin's reputation as inventor might have caused the resolve by the later American to "Study needed inventions" from seven to nine.

Many of the "GENERAL RESOLVES" listed at the bottom of Gatsby's schedule can be traced to Franklin's list of thirteen virtues, and the result of the comparison is often comic as well as pathetic. Franklin's "Cleanliness" becomes for Gatsby "Bath every other day"; "Industry" is "No wasting time at Shafters or [a name, indecipherable]"; "Frugality" is "Save $5.00 [crossed out] $3.00 per week"; "Temperance" is "No more smoking or chewing"; "Sincerity. Use no hurtful deceit" and "Justice. Wrong none by doing injuries, or omitting the benefits that are your duty" possibly become for Gatsby more specific and less inclusive: "Be better to parents." Perhaps a source for Gatsby's "Read one improving book or magazine per week" may be found in Franklin's scheduled notation to "Read" during his noon hour. From five to six o'clock during the day Gatsby plans to "Practice elocution, poise and how to attain it," but in this resolution he remembered none of the virtue to be found in Franklin's description of "Sincerity": "think innocently and justly, and, if you speak, speak accordingly." In every single parallel Gatsby took Franklin's general virtue and listed in its stead one concrete and very specific resolution which was less demanding than that found in his source. These parallels leave only two activities or resolves that are scheduled by Gatsby and that are not to be found in Franklin: "Dumbbell exercise and wall-scaling," from 6:15 to 6:30 in the morning; and "Baseball and sports," from 4:30 to 5:00 in the afternoon. The earlier American's recreations, "Music or diversion, or conversation," were too inactive and intellectual for his follower.

Such close parallels as these surely indicate that Fitzgerald had Franklin's *Autobiography* either in front of him or in his mind when he wrote the schedule of Jay Gatz. It is my opinion that he closely followed Franklin in order to give concreteness to the historical tradition of Gatsby and to make Gatsby something beyond a mere member of the lost generation: an American who was a personification of the national dream as it had been corrupted.

—New England Quarterly, June 1954

Excerpt from Benjamin Franklin's *Autobiography*

It was about this time I conceived the bold and arduous project of arriving at moral perfection. I wished to live without committing any fault at any time; I would conquer all that either natural inclination, custom, or company might lead me into. As I knew, or thought I knew, what was right and wrong, I did not see why I might not *always* do the one and avoid the other. But I soon found I had undertaken a task of more difficulty than I had imagined. While my attention was taken up in guarding against one fault, I was often surprised by another; habit took the advantage of intention; inclination was sometimes too strong for reason. I concluded, at length, that the mere speculative conviction that it was our interest to be completely virtuous was not sufficient to prevent our slipping; and that the contrary habits must be broken, and good ones acquired and established, before we can have any dependence on a steady, uniform rectitude of conduct. For this purpose I therefore contrived the following method.

In the various enumerations of the moral virtues I had met with in my reading, I found the catalogue more or less numerous, as different writers included more or fewer ideas under the same name. Temperance, for example, was by some confined to eating and drinking, while by others it was extended to mean the moderating every other pleasure, appetite, inclination, or passion, bodily or mental, even to our avarice and ambition. I proposed to myself, for the sake of clearness, to use rather more names, with fewer ideas annexed to each, than a few names with more ideas; and I included under thirteen names of virtues all that at that time occurred to me as necessary or desirable, and annexed to each a short precept, which fully expressed the extent I gave to its meaning.

These names of virtues with their precepts were:

1. TEMPERANCE
Eat not to dullness; drink not to elevation.

2. SILENCE
Speak not but what may benefit others or yourself; avoid trifling conversation.

3. ORDER
Let all your things have their places; let each part of your business have its time.

4. RESOLUTION
Resolve to perform what you ought; perform without fail what you resolve.

5. FRUGALITY
Make no expense but to do good to others or yourself; *i.e.,* waste nothing.

6. INDUSTRY
Lose no time; be always employed in something useful; cut off all unnecessary actions.

7. SINCERITY
Use no hurtful deceit; think innocently and justly; and, if you speak, speak accordingly.

8. JUSTICE
Wrong none by doing injuries, or omitting the benefits that are your duty.

9. MODERATION
Avoid extremes; forbear resenting injuries so much as you think they deserve.

10. CLEANLINESS
Tolerate no uncleanness in body, clothes, or habitation.

11. TRANQUILLITY
Be not disturbed at trifles, or at accidents common or unavoidable.

12. CHASTITY
Rarely use venery but for health or offspring; never to dullness, weakness, or the injury of your own or another's peace or reputation.

13. HUMILITY
Imitate Jesus and Socrates.

My intention being to acquire the *habitude* of all these virtues, I judged it would be well not to distract my attention by attempting the whole at once, but to fix it on one of them at a time; and, when I should be master of that, then to proceed to another, and so on, till I should have gone through the thirteen; and as the previous acquisition of some might facilitate the acquisition of certain others, I arranged them with that view, as they stand above. *Temperance* first, as it tends to procure that coolness and clearness of head, which is so necessary where constant vigilance was to be kept up, and guard maintained against the unremitting attraction of ancient habits, and the force of perpetual temptations. This being acquired and established, *Silence* would be more easy; and my desire being to gain knowledge at the same time that I improved in virtue, and considering that in conversation it was obtained rather by the use of the ears than of the tongue, and therefore wishing to break a habit I was getting into of prattling, punning, and joking, which only made me acceptable to trifling company, I gave *Silence* the second place. This and the next, *Order,* I expected would allow me more time for attending to my project and my studies. *Resolution,* once become habitual, would keep me firm in my endeavors to obtain all the subsequent virtues; *Frugality* and *Industry,* by freeing me from my remaining debt, and producing affluence and independence, would make more easy the practice of *Sincerity* and *Justice,* etc., etc. Conceiving then, that, agreeable to the advice of Pythagoras in his Golden Verses, daily examination would be necessary, I contrived the following method for conducting that examination.

I made a little book, in which I allotted a page for each of the virtues. I ruled each page with red ink, so as to have seven columns, one for each day of the week, marking each column with a letter for the day.

I crossed these columns with thirteen red lines, marking the beginning of each line with the first letter of one of the virtues, on which line, and in its proper column, I might mark, by a little black spot, every fault I found upon examination to have been committed respecting that virtue upon that day.

I determined to give a week's strict attention to each of the virtues successively. Thus, in the first week, my great guard was to avoid even the least offense against *Temperance,* leaving the other virtues to their ordinary chance, only marking every evening the faults of the day. Thus, if in the first week I could keep my first line, marked T, clear of spots, I supposed the habit of that virtue so much strengthened, and its opposite weakened, that I might venture extending my attention to include the next, and for the following week keep both lines clear of spots. Proceeding thus to the last, I could go through a course complete in thirteen weeks, and four courses in a year. And like him who, having a garden to weed, does not attempt to eradicate all the bad herbs at once, which would exceed his reach and his strength, but works on one of the beds at a time, and, having accomplished the first, proceeds to a second, so I should have, I hoped, the encouraging pleasure of seeing on my pages the progress I made in virtue, by clearing successively my lines of their spots, till in the end, by a number of courses, I should be happy in viewing a clean book, after a thirteen weeks' daily examination.

This my little book had for its motto these lines from Addison's *Cato:*

Here will I hold. If there is a power above us
(And that there is, all nature cries aloud
Through all her works), He must delight in virtue;
And that which he delights in must be happy.

Another from Cicero,

"O vitæ Philosophia dux! O virtutum indagatrix, expultrixque vitiorum! Unus dies bene, et ex præceptis tuis actus, peccanti immortalitati est anteponendus."

[Oh philosophy, guide of life! Oh searcher out of virtues and expeller of vices! One day lived well and according to thy precepts is to be preferred to an eternity of sin.]

Another from the Proverbs of Solomon, speaking of wisdom or virtue:

"Length of days is in her right hand, and in her left hand riches and honor. Her ways are ways of pleasantness, and all her paths are peace." iii. 16, 17.

TEMPERANCE

Eat not to Dulness.
Drink not to Elevation.

	S.	M.	T.	W.	T.	F.	S.
T.							
S.	* *		*	*		*	
O.	*	*	*		*	*	*
R.			*			*	
F.		*			*		
I.			*				
S.							
J.							
M.							
Cl.							
T.							
Ch.							
H.							

And conceiving God to be the fountain of wisdom, I thought it right and necessary to solicit his assistance for obtaining it; to this end I formed the following little prayer, which was prefixed to my tables of examination, for daily use.

O powerful Goodness! bountiful Father! merciful Guide! Increase in me that wisdom which discovers my truest interests. Strengthen my resolutions to perform what that wisdom dictates. Accept my kind offices to thy other children as the only return in my power for thy continual favors to me.

I used also sometimes a little prayer which I took from Thomson's poems, viz.:

Father of light and life, thou Good Supreme!
O teach me what is good; teach me Thyself!
Save me from folly, vanity, and vice,
From every low pursuit; and fill my soul
With knowledge, conscious peace, and virtue pure;
Sacred, substantial, never-fading bliss!

The precept of *Order* requiring that *every part of my business should have its allotted time,* one page in my little book contained the following scheme of employment for the twenty-four hours of a natural day.

I entered upon the execution of this plan for self-examination, and continued it with occasional intermissions for some time. I was surprised to find myself so much fuller of faults that I had imagined; but I had the satisfaction of seeing them diminish. To avoid the trouble of renewing now and then my little book, which, by scraping out the marks on the paper of old faults to make room for new ones in a new course, became full of holes, I transferred my tables and precepts to the ivory leaves of a memorandum book, on which the lines were drawn with red ink, that made a durable stain, and on those lines I marked my faults with a black lead pencil, which marks I could easily wipe out with a wet sponge. After a while I went through one course only in a year, and afterwards only one in several years, till at length I omitted them entirely, being employed in voyages and business abroad, with a multiplicity of affairs that interfered; but I always carried my little book with me.

–Houghton Mifflin, 1966

* * *

THE MORNING *Question*. What good shall I do this day?	5 6 7	Rise, wash, and address *Powerful Goodness!* Contrive day's business, and take the resolution of the day; prosecute the present study, and breakfast.
	8 9 10 11	Work.
NOON.	12 1	Read, or overlook my accounts, and dine.
	2 3 4 5	Work.
EVENING. *Question*. What good have I done to-day?	6 7 8 9	Put things in their places. Supper. Music or diversion, or conversation. Examination of the day.
NIGHT.	10 11 12 1 2 3 4	Sleep.

"Look here, this is a book he had when he was a boy. It just shows you."

He opened it at the back cover and turned it around for me to see. On the last fly-leaf was printed the word SCHEDULE, and the date September 12th, 1906. And underneath:

Rise from bed . . . . 6.00   A.M.

Dumbbell exercise and wall-scaling. . . . . 6.15–6.30   "

Study electricity, etc. . . . . 7.15–8.15   "

Work. . . . . 8.30–4.30   "

Baseball and sports . . . . 4.30–5.00   "

Practice elocution, poise and how to attain it 5.00–6.00   "

Study needed inventions . . . . 7.00–9.00   "

GENERAL RESOLVES

No wasting time at Shafters or [a name, indecipherable]
No more smoking or chewing
Bath every other day
Read one improving book or magazine per week
Save $5.00 [crossed out] $3.00 per week
Be better to parents

–*The Great Gatsby,* pp. 134–135

Something Borrowed, Something New: A Discussion of Literary Influences on *The Great Gatsby*

Robert Roulston

Surely few twentieth-century works have been credited with a larger and more diverse literary lineage than *The Great Gatsby*. In the three decades that F. Scott Fitzgerald has been the object of more than sporadic scholarly attention, critics have detected in his third novel influences ranging from Chaucer's to Rafael Sabatini's. A catalog of the authors whose writings have supposedly left traces on *The Great Gatsby* is as full of bizarre incongruities as Nick Carraway's list of guests at Gatsby's parties. Flaubert is there with Stephen Leacock and Dreiser with Edith Wharton. There too are Charles Dickens and Ford Madox Ford, Joseph Conrad and Anthony Hope, Coleridge and Clarence E. Mulford, Thackeray and Harold Bell Wright, T. S. Eliot and George Eliot, Petronius and Stendahl, Mark Twain and Emily Brontë, Herman Melville and Horatio Alger, Oswald Spengler and Willa Cather, John Keats and the anonymous creator of Diamond Dick, H. G. Wells and his nemesis Henry James, and poor John Lawson Stoddard, who finds himself confused with the racist Theodore Lothrop Stoddard. And not far from the center, as conspicuous as he would have wished, is the sage of Baltimore, H. L. Mencken.[1]

We have here, surely, more than the perverse fancies of desperate academics. In truth, *The Great Gatsby* invites influence studies the way William Faulkner's fiction invites myth and symbol analyses. (*The Great Gatsby* has elicited its share of the latter as well.) To begin with, Fitzgerald's own sometimes unreliable hints offer clues that scholarly sleuths evidently find irresistible. Furthermore, Fitzgerald's almost miraculous artistic maturation during the brief interval between the completion of his second novel, *The Beautiful and Damned,* and the writing of *The Great Gatsby,* cries out for an explanation. Back in the 1950s, James E. Miller, Jr., offered such an explanation by attributing the superiority of *The Great Gatsby* over its predecessors to Fitzgerald's shift of allegiance from the sprawling novels of H. G. Wells, Compton Mackenzie, Theodore Dreiser, and Frank Norris to the more controlled, selectively textured fiction of subtler writers, especially Joseph Conrad.[2] Later studies have attempted to provide more evidence for the impact of the same authors or have argued for the influence of different and often quite dissimilar writers.

Obviously no all these claims are equally impressive. Some of the purported parallels seem

fortuitous. And, as might be expected, critics occasionally damage valid arguments by overstating them. What is more, there has been some inevitable quibbling over just what Fitzgerald read, when he read it, and whether concrete evidence of his having read a work is necessary to establish an influence when the circumstantial indications that he did are compelling.

Since this paper cannot examine all the putative sources of *The Great Gatsby,* it will concentrate upon those writers whose influence on the novel either is very pronounced or has been a subject of illuminating controversy. Of the latter authors, Oswald Spengler has exemplified more than any other both the pitfalls and the possibilities for expanded insights which can confront the seeker of literary influences. Fitzgerald himself acknowledged Spengler as a major influence, avowing in a letter to Maxwell Perkins that he was under Spengler's spell during the summer of 1924 while writing *The Great Gatsby.* Nothing would seem more conclusive.[3] And so, not surprisingly, discussions of Spenglerian themes in the novel were forthcoming, most notably those of Robert W. Stallman and Richard Lehan. Then in 1967, Robert Sklar derided such enterprises by observing that Spengler's *The Decline of the West* did not appear in an English translation until a year after the publication of *The Great Gatsby;* consequently, Fitzgerald, who was ignorant of German, could not knowingly have used Spenglerian motifs in his novel.

Not so, rejoined Dalton Gross: in July 1924 a summary of Spengler's ideas appeared in *Yale Review,* the sort of magazine Fitzgerald perused "to keep abreast of current literary developments." Unchastened, Richard Lehan leapt back into the fray, first in 1970, then in 1980. In his later offering he observed that at least nine articles or review-essays on *The Decline of the West* were published in English between 1922 and 1924, including a lengthy piece in the summer of 1924 in one of Fitzgerald's favorite periodicals, the *Century.* Lehan proceeded to amplify his earlier discussion of parallels between Spengler and *The Great Gatsby.* And Lehan is right: the parallels do exist. Gatsby is a Spenglerian "Faustian" man—a product of a simpler, more dynamic milieu crushed by the post-Enlightenment, urban, moneyed Caesar—Tom Buchanan.[4] Indubitably the New York Fitzgerald depicts is analogous to Spengler's Rome, which taught "the Classical World. . . . the *pre-eminence of money*" in an age when the vitality of artistic creativity had waned along with heroic values.[5] Lehan is no less correct in his contention that to insist that someone can be influenced only by the ideas of an author with whose writings he has intimate first-hand knowledge is naive and pedantic. One need not have read a page of *Das Kapital* to know something about Marx's surplus value theory or a syllable of Carl Jung to converse coherently and even accurately about archetypes and personae. It should be equally self-evident that a person need not read a novel or a poem to acquire some notion of both its contents and its technical innovations. And—especially with a mind as wide-ranging, wayward, and retentive as Fitzgerald's—influences are as likely to come from conversations, second- and third-hand published accounts, or from a derivative minor work as from direct familiarity with an apparent "source"— a fact, no doubt, vexing to poor souls who crave precision and certainty.

One writer with whom Fitzgerald was certainly familiar, however, was T. S. Eliot. "The greatest of living poets," Fitzgerald proclaimed him in an inscription in the copy of *The Great Gatsby* he sent to Eliot in 1925—an opinion he was to repeat the following year in a letter to Maxwell Perkins.[6] In the inscription he also designated himself as Eliot's "enthusiastic worshipper." We need not find as much significance in the analogues between Fitzgerald's novel and Eliot's poems as some critics have found to recognize that Fitzgerald's imagery in the "valley of ashes" episodes is reminiscent of Eliot's "The Waste Land." So also are the juxtapositions of banal details about contemporary life with objects having grand historical resonances such as those Robert Emmet Long has noted in the second chapter of *The Great Gatsby*.[7] Furthermore, many of the Spenglerian aspects of *The Great Gatsby* have counterparts in "The Waste Land," whose author, unlike Fitzgerald, read German and who was much more likely to have known Spengler's book well, and to have been familiar with an entire corpus of continental writing about the collapse of cultures in general and of modern Europe in particular.

In truth, anyone in the 1920s with a taste for apocalyptic visions did not have to reach back to Richard Wagner's *Götterdämmerung,* or out to Spengler's *Decline of the West* and Hermann Hesse's *A Glimpse into Chaos* (cited by Eliot in his notes to "The Waste Land"), or to Eliot's favorite French journalist, Charles Maurras. Such a person had merely to descend to Tom Buchanan's level and read such alarmist offerings as Madison Grant's *The Passing of a Great Race* or Theodore Lothrop Stoddard's *The Rising Tide of Color*.[8] The anti-Semitic smudges in *This Side of Paradise* and *The Beautiful and Damned,* as well as the slurs against blacks, Italians, and orientals in *Tender Is The Night,* indicate that Fitzgerald would have been less hostile to such racist fare than Nick Carraway's comments about Tom's nibbling "at the edge of stale ideas" suggest.[9] Indeed, Fitzgerald had merely to regard his own failures of will and waning energy to decay all about him, for as far back as 1921 he had written to Maxwell Perkins: "I'm sick of the flabby, semi-intellectual softness in which I flounder with my generation."[10] In short, Eliot, Spengler, and even racist pessimists like Stoddard were providing an intellectual scaffolding or useful details to support what he, Fitzgerald, perceived intuitively in himself and his contemporaries.

When in the mood for particulars about the failings of his countrymen, though, Fitzgerald had to seek no farther than the writings and conversations of his friend, mentor, and sometime publisher—that berater of the "boobus-Americanus" and the plutocracy, H. L. Mencken. As editor, first of *The Smart Set* and later of *The American Mercury,* Mencken had ushered into print such important stories by Fitzgerald as "May Day," "The Diamond as Big as the Ritz," and "Absolution," as well as such negligible ones as "Porcelain and Pink," "Mister Icky," and "Tarquin of Cheapside." More important, Mencken, with his formidable wit and even more formidable certitude, imposed upon Fitzgerald, as upon so many younger readers in the early 1920s, some of his own literary preferences. James R. Miller, Jr., has examined how decisively Mencken shaped Fitzgerald's artistic development by luring him away from his youthful entrancement with writers like Compton Mackenzie and Robert W. Chambers and by instilling in him an appreciation of Theodore Dreiser, Frank Norris, and Joseph Conrad.[11] Fitzgerald, moreover, was not simply flattering Mencken when he wrote to him in 1920: "I have already adopted many of your views."[12] Throughout Fitzgerald's second novel, the impact of Mencken's tastes and ideas is ubiquitous—a fact Fitzgerald himself was aware of. By spring of 1924, however, he had come to regard *The Beautiful and Damned* as "a false lead . . . a concession to Mencken."[13] All the illblended mixture in *The Beautiful and Damned* of gritty Dreiserian realism and of a whimsical cynicism redolent of *The Smart Set* reveals, as Arthur Mizener points out, that Mencken's influence was not entirely salutary and that Fitzgerald was correct in regarding certain aspects of it as qualities to be outgrown.[14] But when Mencken, after praising the writing in *The Great Gatsby,* complained that the story seemed "trivial" and hardly more than an anecdote, Fitzgerald defended its narrow focus and its omission of the kind of detail Mencken admired in *This Side of Paradise* and *The Beautiful and Damned* by evoking as a precedent Mencken's favorite living novelist, Joseph Conrad. Fitzgerald also chided Mencken's preference for sprawling fiction and added: "It is in protest against my own formless two novels, and Lewis' and Dos Passos' that this [*The Great Gatsby*] was written."[15]

Although by 1924 Fitzgerald had begun to exorcise Mencken's spell, *The Great Gatsby* nonetheless reflects Mencken's attitudes toward both the incompetent poor like George Wilson and the plutocratic rich like Tom Buchanan, as well as toward the kind of plebian vulgarity embodied by Myrtle Wilson and the McKees. But the novel also expresses contrary values, as we shall see.

Deferring for awhile the more complex question of Joseph Conrad's influence upon *The Great Gatsby*, Fitzgerald's novel shows the impact of at least two other of Mencken's favorite authors, Theodore Dreiser and Willa Cather. Although Dreiser's influence upon Fitzgerald reached its apogee in *The Beautiful and Damned*, the parallels between Dreiser's "Vanity, Vanity Saith the Preacher" and *The Great Gatsby* cited by Maxwell Geismar and Eric Solomon suggest that the influence may have lingered on into the middle of the 1920s.[16] More noteworthy are the similarities between *The Great Gatsby* and the writings of Willa Cather, of whose *My Ántonia* Mencken asserted: "No romantic novel ever written in America, by man or woman, is one-half so beautiful."[17] Like *My Ántonia*, *The Great Gatsby* has a narrator who interprets—as he recounts in a series of impressionistic scenes—the fortunes and misfortunes of a protagonist at least outwardly unlike himself. Both works, too, are pervaded with a bittersweet nostalgia, and both are written in finely crafted, evocative prose which, as Mencken observed of Cather's novel, "proves . . . that careful and penetrating representation is itself the source of a rare and wonderful beauty."[18]

Although Cather's language may be less beautiful in *A Lost Lady* than in *My Ántonia*, Fitzgerald not only read the former "with great delight"; he also duplicated a passage from her book closely enough to fear she might accuse him of plagiarism. In a letter he assured her that he had written his own passage a month or two before reading hers and that, therefore, the similarity is a coincidence.[19] Matthew J. Bruccoli may be correct in concluding that, since in the same letter he claimed to have been in the middle of the first draft of *The Great Gatsby* while reading *A Lost Lady*, Fitzgerald "began work on the final plot

earlier than has been supposed."[20] But, even allowing that Fitzgerald's memory about dates here was accurate, he wrote enough of his novel after his exposure to *A Lost Lady* for the latter to have had some effect upon *The Great Gatsby*. Neil Herbert's fascination with the beautiful Marian Forrester is similar enough to Jay Gatsby's obsession with Daisy Fay to justify Miller's suggestion that Cather's novel may have influenced Fitzgerald. So too are the parallels between Neil's efforts to reconcile Mrs. Forrester's resplendence with her amorality and Nick Carraway's attempts to resolve his own ambiguous feelings toward Gatsby. And if Long is correct in identifying Cather as the source of the East-West contrast which is so important to the thematic scheme of *The Great Gatsby*, then Fitzgerald's debt to her was indeed considerable.[21]

Yet Fitzgerald's antithesis between a crude but innocent West and a sophisticated, sinister East certainly has resonances of an author who rarely deigned to cast his vision beyond the western shore of the Hudson River. That writer, one of Mencken's *bête noires*, was of course Henry James. In novel after novel and story after story, from the beginning to the end of his long career, James had posed just such an antithesis—not, to be sure, between the East Coast and the Middle West as Fitzgerald does, but between complex, corrupt Europe and a simpler, more innocent America. In a sense, therefore, the geographical symbolism of *The Great Gatsby* is that of James, shifted four-thousand miles westward. There is well-nigh universal agreement that little evidence exists of Fitzgerald's having read James before writing *The Great Gatsby*. Yet the parallels Henry Dan Piper cites between Fitzgerald's novel and James's *The American* and *Daisy Miller* are pronounced enough to indicate that Fitzgerald was probably familiar with them.[22] And surely the theme and story of *Daisy Miller*, in particular, were known widely enough for anyone interested in literature to have been familiar with the work's main features. That the heroine of Fitzgerald's novel is named Daisy; that the hero of "Absolution," which was originally to have served as an introduction to *The Great Gatsby*, is named Rudolph Miller; and that Daisy Miller's brother is Randolph—all may be trivial resemblances. But trivial or not they suggest that Fitzgerald was acquainted with at least the cast of characters in James's novel.

There seems to be much less doubt that Fitzgerald has read Edith Wharton. Furthermore, his sending her an inscribed copy of *The Great Gatsby* in 1925 hardly implies that he shared the disdain toward her of his erstwhile mentor, Mencken, who tended to regard her as a Henry James in skirts. Commenting on Wharton's objections to the lack of information about Jay Gatsby, Michael Millgate has shown how she had used a similar technique herself in *The Custom of the Country*. While unwilling to assert categorically that *The Custom of the Country* directly influenced *The Great Gatsby,* Millgate agrees with Frederick J. Hoffman that Fitzgerald may have derived narrative techniques from Wharton's *Ethan Frome*–a view endorsed by Henry Dan Piper. The principal points of resemblance are, of course, the first-person narrator who, in a sequence of brief scenes, tells a story leading to a violent climax. Parallels have also been noted between *The Great Gatsby* and Wharton's *The Spark*.[23]

Nearly everyone who has addressed himself in print to this matter agrees that Joseph Conrad had some effect upon *The Great Gatsby*. Agreement vanishes, however, over how decisive that effect was and over which of Conrad's works exercised it. Although he later minimized the importance of the influence, Arthur Mizener noted its presence back in 1951. Mizener at the same time regretted what he regarded as the "not always fortunate echoes of Conrad's phrasing."[24] Apparently, though, the traces he detected there of Conrad's method of narration seemed less unfortunate to him. For Robert W. Stallman a few years later there was nothing either unfortunate or equivocal about Conrad's influence on *The Great Gatsby*.[25] Theme, characters, plot, narrative method, settings–all reflect Fitzgerald's entrancement with *Nostromo, Lord Jim,* and *Heart of Darkness*. Gatsby sometimes is Conrad's Jim in a pink suit; at other times Nostromo in a cream-colored limousine or an American Kurtz sinking into a New York no less dark at its heart than Kurtz's African counterpart. And there, reporting it all, is Fitzgerald's version of Marlow, Nick Carraway, albeit Nick's mind "lacks Marlow's range and points of curiosity," and his "provincial squeamishness" makes him a less sympathetic observer than Marlow.[26] Jerome Thale and Harold Hurwitz have found still other parallels.[27] Hurwitz makes much of apparent similarities between Marlow's conversation with Kurtz's fiancée and Nick's scene with Gatsby's father, observing that, in both instances, a narrator tries explaining a protagonist to a listener who is under an illusion about the person being discussed. The resulting irony, according to Hurwitz, is compounded in both instances by the ambivalence of the narrator's feelings about the protagonist.

For James E. Miller, Jr., Conrad gave Fitzgerald more than hints for mere themes or for the delineation of characters; Conrad provided an aesthetic theory which enabled him to transform himself in an incredibly short time from the author of sprawling cluttered novels into the creator of the brilliantly compact *The Great Gatsby*.[28] Indeed, Conrad is the true hero of Miller's book, which depicts Conrad's preface to *The Nigger of the "Narcissus"* as the guide which led Fitzgerald away from the baneful influence of the formless or cluttered writings of Wells, Dreiser, and Norris. Thanks to that preface as well as to the model provided by Conrad's own fiction, Fitzgerald could leave behind the vices of what Henry James, citing Wells as an example, had called the novel of "saturation": and could embrace the virtues of writing novels of "selection."

Although they do not go as far as Miller does, Sklar, Piper, and Perosa all regard Conrad as a major influence upon *The Great Gatsby*. Sklar maintains that Fitzgerald derived from Conrad not techniques, but an "attitude toward human hopes and human history."[29] Yet he also tries to deny the significance of some of the parallels cited by Stallman and Thale by contending that the only works of Conrad Fitzgerald had read before writing *The Great Gatsby* were *Nostromo, Victory,* "Youth," *The Nigger of the "Narcissus,"* and *A Mirror of the Sun*. (Sklar's assertion that Fitzgerald had not read *Lord Jim* seems to be refuted by the reference to the book in Fitzgerald's 1923 review of Sherwood Anderson's *Many Marriages*.[30])

As we have seen, however, a dearth of evidence of a first-hand knowledge by Fitzgerald of a work rarely has deterred a determined seeker of literary influences from considering it a possible source for *The Great Gatsby*. Thus Andrew Crosland, while admitting there is no proof Fitzgerald actually read Conrad's *The Secret Agent*, maintains that the similarities between it and *The Great Gatsby* are striking enough to make one "think Fitzgerald . . . had consciously echoed certain parts of it in order to generate subtle ironies and to help define character."[31] By far the most assiduous hunter of parallels between *The Great Gatsby* and works by other writers has been Robert Emmet Long. Long's most productive labors have been expended upon the Conrad-Fitzgerald connection. In addition to finding hitherto undetected resemblances between *The Great Gatsby* and *Heart of Darkness, Nostromo,* and *Lord Jim,* Long discusses affinities between Fitzgerald's novel and *An Outcast of the Islands, The Rescue,* "Youth," and, in considerable detail, *Almayer's Folly*.[32] Indeed, Conrad's tropical dreamer seems to become a veritable prototype for Jay Gatsby as Long cites similar words used by both writers to describe their protagonists. Long also finds significance in the way the illusions of both heroes are embodied in their houses and in how both houses are located near water and across from the homes of more securely established opponents. He also indicates analogues between Gatsby's and Almayer's backgrounds and believes that Dan Cody's yacht serves the same function as Captain Lingard's ship—to launch the protagonist into a splendid future that will become ultimately anything but splendid.

Where does all this leave us? Nick Carraway's function does resemble Marlow's. But it also resembles the function of narrators used by Edith Wharton, Willa Cather, and even, as I have argued elsewhere, of George Ponderevo in what was once Fitzgerald's favorite novel, H. G. Wells's *Tono-Bungay*.[33] *The Great Gatsby,* to be sure, is developed through a series of short dramatic scenes as are several of Conrad's works. But so are *My Ántonia* and *Ethan Frome.* And if analogues exist between Gatsby and Kurtz, Nostromo, Jim, and Almayer, they also exist between Gatsby and a whole range of fictional characters from Trimalchio to Horatio Alger's heroes. As for Fitzgerald's avowal that in *The Great Gatsby* he was an imitator of Conrad, he also declared that he was influenced by Thackeray. Yet the latter influence has received relatively little attention, despite resemblances between *The Great Gatsby* and *Vanity Fair* such as the parallel between Gatsby's preoccupation with Daisy and Bobbin's mooning over Amelia and the similarity between Fitzgerald's guest list and a comparable comic catalog in *Vanity Fair*.[34] And the reason for all but ignoring the Thackeray connection is obvious: whatever Fitzgerald may have appropriated from Thackeray, *The Great Gatsby* is so dissimilar to *Vanity Fair* in tone, pacing, style, and texture, that any similarity between the works seems of peripheral significance. The problem with the links between *The Great Gatsby* and the writings of Conrad is that they are numerous and important enough to tempt us to regard Fitzgerald as a disciple of Conrad who unfortunately lacks his master's profundity and deep moral seriousness.

The temptation should be resisted. Whether we accept Lawrence Thornton's suggestion that Ford Madox Ford exerted a more decisive influence on Fitzgerald than Conrad did, we must recognize the validity of Thornton's objections to regarding Conrad as the paramount model for *The Great Gatsby.* As Thornton points out, Fitzgerald's sensibility and values differed enormously from Conrad's.[35] For the brooding Pole the past is where fatal errors have been made and where evil has had its genesis. Thus it is through probing his own past or the past of

some kindred soul like Jim or Kurtz that Conrad's Marlow arrives at self-knowledge and the strength to endure the tragic farce of life. Little could be more remote from what Fitzgerald informed Roger Burlingame was the unifying emotion of *The Great Gatsby:* "I was tremendously pleased that it [*The Great Gatsby*] moved you in that way 'made you want to be back somewhere so much' because that describes so much better than I could have put it myself, either in regard to the temperment [*sic*] of Gatsby himself or my own mood while writing it."[36] Now, it seems unlikely that *Lord Jim* has ever made anyone want to be aboard the sinking *Patna* or that *Heart of Darkness* has induced a desire to share the nightmarish experiences that have led the dying Kurtz to exclaim "The horror! The horror!" Yet Fitzgerald's dazzling prose and romantic vision invest Gatsby's dreams and aspirations, memories, and delusions with such a glow that for Gatsby, even more than for John Dryden's Antony or Cleopatra, the world seems "well lost." Moreover, for all their fatuous vulgarity Gatsby's parties are amusing—something that can be said for very few occurrences in Conrad.

What an undue concentration upon the influence of any single author on *The Great Gatsby* can obscure is the multi-faceted quality of Fitzgerald's novel. Just as, according to Fitzgerald, "the test of a first-rate intelligence is the ability to hold two opposed ideas at the same time, and still retain the ability to function,"[37] so the test of a perceptive critic is his ability to recognize in *The Great Gatsby* the presence not only of opposed ideas but of the influence of writers radically dissimilar from each other. It is even more important to perceive the truth of Fitzgerald's boast about *The Great Gatsby:* "It is unlike anything I have ever read before."[38] And apprehending the originality of the novel obviously entails recognizing how the novel differs from works to which it bears certain resemblances.

Just as, despite its Conradian gestures, *The Great Gatsby* is not fundamentally an exercise in Conradian moralizing, neither is it a prolonged wallow in that romantic tradition which rejects the real world as a painful sham to be shunned or transcended. To be sure, elements of that tradition are present. But whether Fitzgerald derived them from Flaubert, Stendhal, John Keats, or Ford Madox Ford[39] is less important than the way Fitzgerald combines the disillusionment of Nick Carraway with an avidity for experience so that the book as a whole justifies Nick's assertion: "I was within and without, simultaneously enchanted and repelled by the inexhaustible variety of life" (p. 36). The enchantment is no less integral to the work than the repulsion, and a failure to grasp it blinds one to at least half of the book's magic.

Gatsby's actions may be as foolish or self-destructive as Emma Bovary's. But whereas Flaubert's measured prose mocks Emma's rebellion while relentlessly exposing the coarseness of her provincial milieu, Fitzgerald's exuberant lyricism does the exact opposite. As Michael Millgate has stated: "At the end of Fitzgerald's brilliant display of advocacy we stand, despite all the evidence, with Gatsby,"[40] And standing with Gatsby requires sharing at least provisionally Gatsby's awed response toward Daisy, the world of the rich, and New York.

The Great Gatsby, of course, also satirizes these things. Indeed, the most depressing aspect of some of the scholarship about the novel is how it misses not merely the satire but the humor. As Long has noted, Meyer Wofshiem, for all his evil, is a genuinely comic character. So are Myrtle Wilson, McKee, Klipspringer, and, as I have maintained elsewhere, Tom Buchanan.[41] Yet despite the jabs, comic or otherwise, at New York's gaudiness and seaminess, the city hardly emerges from the book as H. L. Mencken's third-rate Babylon on the Hudson.

Mencken's reservations about the worth of *The Great Gatsby*, in fact, may have resulted not merely from Fitzgerald's failure to adhere in it to Mencken's aesthetic dictates, but also from the way the novel treats respectfully things Mencken scorned—among them the American Dream. Despite his illustrious Maryland forebears, Fitzgerald was too much the parvenu to be altogether comfortable with Mencken's diagnosis that "the capital defect of culture in These States is the lack of a civilized aristocracy, secure in its position."[42]

Down the list of influences on *The Great Gatsby* we could go, observing in each instance a profound divergence for every resemblance. Thus for instance, if Fitzgerald, like Cather, could invoke the West against the corrupt East, he was no prairie primitivist, as Cather sometimes pretended to be. And whatever Fitzgerald's "valley of ashes" may owe to Eliot's "The Waste Land," Gatsby's New York is too glamorous and dynamic to be Eliot's catatonic "unreal city." Then too one can imagine the withering contempt with which Eliot would have depicted Gatsby with his flashy car and bogus Norman "Hôtel de Ville." Fitzgerald's affection for such a character would have been even more alien to Henry James and Edith Wharton. James's self-made millionaires like Christopher Newman and Adam Verver, having made their fortunes before arriving in the great centers of civilization, seem downright patrician compared to Gatsby. Edith Wharton's Ethan Frome may be a dignified yeoman, but it is hard to imagine her

treating the vulgar Gatsby with less hauteur than she treats Simon Rosedale in *The House of Mirth*. As for Oswald Spengler, although Fitzgerald shared his forebodings about Western civilization, he also expressed in *The Great Gatsby* a joie de vivre absent from Spengler's somber tome.

As a book that soars and laughs no less than it laments, *The Great Gatsby* is no more a Conradian tragedy than it is Cather-like celebration of the frontier, a Mencken-like exposé of America, a Jamesian study of fine sensibilities, a Dreiserian pageant of personal disintegration, a Flaubertian exercise in aesthetics, or a romantic flight from life. It is sui generis, not an eclectic hodgepodge or a clever reworking of one particular source—a fact not even the most convincing influence study should ever permit us to forget.

—*Critical Essays on F. Scott Fitzgerald's The Great Gatsby*, (Boston: G. K. Hall, 1984)

Notes

1. Nancy Y. Hoffman, "*The Great Gatsby*: Troilus and Criseyde Revisited?" *Fitzgerald/Hemingway Annual 1971*, pp. 148–58; Robert E. Morsberger, "The Romantic Ancestry of *The Great Gatsby*," *Fitzgerald/Hemingway Annual 1972*, pp. 119–30 (Sabatini, Hope, Brontë, et al.); Leslie F. Chard, II, "Outward Forms and the Inner Life: Coleridge and *Gatsby*," *Fitzgerald/Hemingway Annual 1973*, pp. 189–94; Ralph Curry and Janet Lewis, "Stephen Leacock: An Early Influence on F. Scott Fitzgerald," *Canadian Review of American Studies*, 8 (1976), 5–14; Taylor Alderman, "*The Great Gatsby* and *Hopalong Cassidy*," *Fitzgerald/Hemingway Annual 1975*, pp. 75–87 (Mulford); Dale B. J. Randall, "The 'Seer' and 'Seen' Themes in *Gatsby* and Some of their Parallels in Eliot and Wright," *Twentieth Century Literature*, 10 (1964), 51–63; Paul A. Makurath, Jr., "Another Source for 'Gatsby,'" *Fitzgerald/Hemingway Annual 1975*, pp. 115–16 (George Eliot); "*The Great Gatsby* and Trimalchio," *The Classical Journal*, 45 (1950), 307–14; Horst H. Kruse, "'Gatsby' and 'Gadsby,'" *Modern American Studies*, 15 (1969–70), 539–41 (Twain); John Schroeder, "Some Unfortunate Idyllic Love Affairs: The Legends of Taji and Jay Gatsby," *Books at Brown*, 22 (1968), 143–53 (Melville); Gary Scharnhorst, "Scribbling Upward: Fitzgerald's Debt of Honor to Horatio Alger, Jr.," *Fitzgerald/Hemingway Annual 1978*, pp. 26–35; James Ellis, "The Stoddard Lectures' in *The Great Gatsby*," *American Literature*, 44 (1972), 470–71; Daryl E. Jones, "Fitzgerald and Pulp Fiction: From *Diamond Dick* to *Gatsby*," *Fitzgerald/Hemingway Annual 1978*, pp. 137–39. Others will be cited later.

2. James E. Miller, Jr., *The Fictional Techniques of Scott Fitzgerald* (The Hague: Martinus Nijhoff, 1957), pp. 129–33.

3. 6 June 1940, *The Letters of F. Scott Fitzgerald*, ed. Andrew Turnbull (New York: Scribner's, 1963), pp. 289–90.

4. Robert W. Stallman, "Gatsby and the Hole in Time," *Modern Fiction Studies*, 1 (1955), 2–16; Richard Lehan, *F. Scott Fitzgerald and the Craft of Fiction* (Carbondale:

Southern Illinois University Press, 1966), pp. 30–36; "Focus on F. Scott Fitzgerald's *The Great Gatsby:* The Nowhere Hero," in *American Dreams, American Nightmares,* ed. David Madden (Carbondale: Southern Illinois University Press, 1970), pp. 106–14; "F. Scott Fitzgerald and Romantic Destiny," *Twentieth Century Literature,* 26 (1980), 137–56; Robert Sklar, *F. Scott Fitzgerald: The Last Laocoön* (New York: Oxford University Press, 1967), p. 24; Dalton Gross, "F. Scott Fitzgerald's *The Great Gatsby* and Oswald Spengler's *The Decline of the West,*" *Notes and Queries,* 17 (1970), 476.

5. Oswald Spengler, *The Decline of the West,* trans. Charles F. Atkins, I (New York: Knopf, 1926), 36.

6. *Correspondence of F. Scott Fitzgerald,* ed. Matthew J. Bruccoli and Margaret M. Duggan (New York: Random House, 1980), p. 180.

7. Robert Emmet Long, *The Achieving of The Great Gatsby: F. Scott Fitzgerald, 1920–1925* (Lewisburg: Bucknell University Press, 1979), pp. 126, 211–12. See also Randall, pp. 51–56, and Philip Young, "Scott Fitzgerald's Waste Land," *Filologia e Letteratura,* 10 (1964), 113–20.

8. Lewis A. Turlish, "*The Rising Tide of Color:* A Note on the Historicism of *The Great Gatsby,*" *American Literature,* 43 (1971), 442–44. See also Stallman, pp. 2–12.

9. *The Great Gatsby* (New York: Scribner's, 1925), p. 21. Cited hereafter in the text in parentheses.

10. 25 August 1921, *Letters,* p. 167.

11. Miller, pp. 39–43.

12. To Mencken, 20 March 1920, *Correspondence,* p. 55.

13. To Moran Tudury, 11 April 1924, *Correspondence,* p. 139.

14. *The Far Side of Paradise* (Boston: Houghton, 1951), pp. 138–39.

15. To Mencken, 4 May 1925, *Letters,* p. 480.

16. Maxwell Geismar, "Theodore Dreiser," *Rebels and Ancestors: The American Novel, 1890–1915: Frank Norris, Stephen Crane, Jack London, Ellen Glasgow, Theodore Dreiser* (Boston: Houghton Mifflin, 1953), p. 342; Eric Solomon, "Source for Fitzgerald's *The Great Gatsby,*" *Modern Language Notes,* 73 (1938), 186–88.

17. "The Novel," *Prejudices: Third Series* (New York: Knopf, 1922), pp. 210–11.

18. Ibid., p. 210.

19. Late March/Early April 1925, *Correspondence,* pp. 155–56.

20. "An Instance of Apparent Plagiarism: F. Scott Fitzgerald, Willa Cather and the First *Gatsby* Manuscript," *Princeton University Library Chronicle,* 3 (1978), 176.

21. Long, p. 181.

22. *F. Scott Fitzgerald: A Critical Portrait* (New York: Holt, 1965), pp. 128–29.

23. Frederick J. Hoffman, "Points of Moral Reference: A Comparative Study of Edith Wharton and F. Scott Fitzgerald," *English Institute Essays* (New York: Columbia University Press, 1950), pp. 147–76; Michael Millgate, *American Social Fiction: James to Cozzens* (London: Olivier & Boyd, 1964), pp. 110–11; Michael A. Peterman, "A Neglected Source for *The Great Gatsby:* The Influence of Edith Wharton's *The Spark,*" *Canadian Review of American Studies,* 8 (1977), 26–35.

24. Mizener, p. 170.

25. "Conrad and *The Great Gatsby,*" *Twentieth Century Fiction,* I (1955), 5–11.

26. Ibid., p. 11.

27. Jerome Thale, "The Narrator as Hero," *Twentieth Century Literature,* 3 (1955), 69–73; Harold Hurwitz, "*The Great Gatsby* and 'The Heart of Darkness,'" *Fitzgerald/Hemingway Annual 1969,* pp. 27–34.

28. Miller, pp. 67–114.

29. Sklar, p. 152. See also Piper, pp. 129–33.

30. Reprinted in *F. Scott Fitzgerald: In His Own Time: A Miscellany,* ed. Matthew J. Bruccoli and Jackson R. Bryer (New York: Popular Library, 1971), p. 138.

31. "*The Great Gatsby* and *The Secret Agent,*" *Fitzgerald/Hemingway Annual 1975,* p. 75.

32. Long, pp. 88–96.

33. "Traces of *Tono-Bungay* in *The Great Gatsby,*" *Journal of Narrative Technique,* 10 (1980), 68–76.

34. See Stephen Curry and Peter L. Hays, "Fitzgerald's *Vanity Fair,*" *Fitzgerald/Hemingway Annual 1977,* pp. 63–75; Long, p. 214; and Fitzgerald's letter to John Jamieson, 7 April 1934, *Letters,* p. 509.

35. "Ford Madox Ford and *The Great Gatsby,*" *Fitzgerald/Hemingway Annual 1975,* pp. 57–71.

36. 19 April 1925, *Correspondence,* pp. 159–60.

37. *The Crack-up,* ed. Edmund Wilson (New York: New Directions, 1945), p. 67.

38. To Maxwell Perkins, 10 September 1924, *Correspondence,* p. 146.

39. Long, p. 119, and Thornton, p. 60, suggest a possible influence of Flaubert through either Conrad or Ford. Mizener insists that similarities between Fitzgerald and Stendhal are "immeasurably more important" than any between Fitzgerald and either Eliot or Conrad; but Mizener avers that there is no evidence Fitzgerald ever read Stendhal: Preface to the Vintage Edition of *The Far Side of Paradise* (New York: Vintage, 1959), pp. vii–viii. In a letter to Holger Lundbergh in 1923, however, Fitzgerald claimed to have just finished *The Red and the Black* (*Correspondence,* p. 133). On Keats see Dan McCall, 'The Self-Same Song That Found a Path': Keats and *The Great Gatsby,*" *American Literature,* 42 (1971), 521–30; Joseph B. Wagner, "Gatsby and John Keats: Another Version, *Fitzgerald/Hemingway Annual 1979,* pp. 91–98.

40. Millgate, p. 110.

41. "Tom Buchanan: Patrician in Motley," *Arizona Quarterly,* 34 (1978), 101–11.

42. "American Culture," *A Mencken Chrestomathy,* ed. H. L. Mencken (New York: Knopf, 1949), p. 178.

* * *

The Yacht Club,
White Bear Lake.

Dear Mr. Perkins:
Glad you liked the addenda to the Table of Contents. I feel quite confident the book will go. How do you think *The Love Legend* will sell? You'll be glad to know that nothing has come of the movie idea + I'm rather glad myself. At present I'm working on my play — the same one. Trying to arrange for an Oct. production in New York. Bunny Wilson (Edmund Wilson Jr.) says that it's without doubt the best American comedy to date (That's just between you and me.)

Did you see that in that Literary Digest contest I stood 6th among the novelists? Not that it matters. I suspect you of having been one of the voters.

Will you see that the semi-yearly account is mailed to me by the 1st of the month — or before if it is ready? I want to see where I stand. I want to write something *new* — something extraordinary and beautiful and simple + intricately patterned.

As usual
F Scott Fitzgerald

In the final sentence of this letter to editor Maxwell Perkins (mid July 1922) Fitzgerald declares his ambition for the novel that became The Great Gatsby *(Princeton University Library).*

Maxwell Perkins in his office at Charles Scribner's Sons. He believed that wearing a hat indoors aided his hearing. Perkins had championed This Side of Paradise *at Scribners, and his personal and editorial relationship with Fitzgerald grew increasingly close. The composition and rewriting of* The Great Gatsby *are documented in their correspondence between 1922 and 1925.*

THE COMPOSITION OF A CLASSIC

Maxwell E. Perkins, head of the Scribners editorial department, remains the most celebrated literary editor in American publishing history. It was he who overcame the opposition of Charles Scribner II to publishing This Side of Paradise. *Fitzgerald brought his friends Ring Lardner and Ernest Hemingway to Perkins and Scribners. Perkins's services to Fitzgerald went far beyond editorial help. He became Fitzgerald's most loyal friend, banker, and surrogate father.*

Because of Perkins's editorial labors with Thomas Wolfe it has been incorrectly assumed that he performed the same services for Fitzgerald. Their correspondence concerning the writing and rewriting of The Great Gatsby *establishes that their work was not collaborative. Fitzgerald worked alone. Perkins's role was to advise Fitzgerald, who acted on his editor's advice about structure and character.*

These letters are in the Charles Scribner's Sons Archives and the F. Scott Fitzgerald Papers at the Princeton University Library.

From Fitzgerald to Perkins

The Yatch Club, White Bear Lake, Minn
June 1922

When I send on this last bunch of stories I may start my novel and I may not. Its locale will be the middle west and New York of 1885 I think. It will concern less superlative beauties than I run to usually + will be centered on a smaller period of time. It will have a catholic element. I'm not quite sure whether I'm ready to start it quite yet or not. I'll write next week + tell you more definate plans.

* * *

April 1924
Great Neck

Dear Max:

A few words more relative to our conversation this afternoon. While I have every hope + plan of finishing my novel in June you know how those things often come out. And even it takes me 10 times that long I cannot let it go out unless it has the very best I'm capable of in it or even as I feel sometimes, something better than I'm capable of. Much of what I wrote last summer was good but it was so interrupted that it was ragged + in approaching it from a new angle I've had to discard a lot of it—in one case 18,000 words (part of which will appear in the Mercury as a short story). It is only in the last four months that I've realized how much I've—well, almost <u>deteriorated</u> in the three years since I finished the Beautiful and Damned. The last four months of course I've worked but in the two years—over two years—before that, I produced exactly <u>one</u> play, <u>half a dozen</u> short stories and three or four articles,—an average of about <u>one hundred</u> words a day. If I'd spent this time reading or travelling or doing anything—even staying healthy—it'd be different but I spent it uselessly, niether in study nor in contemplation but only in drinking and raising hell generally. If I'd written the B + D at the rate of 100 words a day it would have taken me <u>4 years</u> so you can imagine the moral effect the whole chasm had on me.

What I'm trying to say is just that I'll have to ask you to have patience about the book and trust me that at last, or at least for the 1st time in years, I'm doing the best I can. I've gotten in dozens of bad habits that I'm trying to get rid of

1. Laziness
2. Referring everything to Zelda—a terrible habit, nothing ought to be referred to anybody until its finished
3. Word consciousness + self doubt

ect. ect. ect. ect.

I feel I have an enormous power in me now, more than I've ever had in a way but it works so fitfully and with so many bogeys because I've <u>talked so much</u> and not lived enough within myself to develop the nessessary self reliance. Also I don't know anyone who has used up so [much] personal experience as I have at 27. Copperfield + Pendennis were written at past forty while This Side of Paradise was three books + the B. + D. was two. So in my new novel I'm thrown directly on purely creative work—not trashy imaginings as in my stories but the sustained imagination of a sincere and yet radiant world. So I tread slowly and carefully + at times in considerable distress. This book will be a consciously artistic acheivement + must depend on that as the 1st books did not.

If I ever win the right to any liesure again I will assuredly not waste it as I wasted this past time. Please believe me when I say that now I'm doing the best I can.

Yours Ever
Scott F———

* * *

April 16, 1924

Dear Scott:

I delayed answering your letter because I wanted to answer it at length. I was delighted to get it. But I have been so pressed with all sorts of things that I have not had time to write as I meant and I am not doing so now. I do not want to delay sending some word on one or two points.

For instance, I understand exactly what you have to do and I know that all these superficial matters of exploitation and so on are not of the slightest consequence along side of the importance of your doing your very best work the way you want to do it;- that is, according to the demands of the situation. So far as we are concerned, you are to go ahead at just your own pace, and if you should finish the book when you think you will, you will have performed a very considerable feat even in the matter of time, it seems to me.

My view of the future is - particularly in the light of your letter - one of very great optimism and confidence.

The only thing is, that if we had a title which was likely, but by no means sure to be the title, we could prepare a cover and a wrap and hold them in readiness for use. In that way, we would gain several weeks if we should find that we were to have the book this fall. We would be that much to the good. Otherwise we should have done no harm. If we sold the book under a title which was later changed, no harm would have been done either. I always thought that "The Great Gatsby" was a suggestive and effective title,- with only the vaguest knowledge of the book, of course. But anyway, the last thing we want to do is to divert you to any degree, from your actual writing, and if you let matters rest just as they are now, we shall be perfectly satisfied. The book is the thing and all the rest is inconsiderable beside it.

Yours,

* * *

The Fitzgeralds' passports, dated 29 April 1924 (Matthew J. and Arlyn Bruccoli Collection, University of South Carolina Library). The Fitzgeralds moved to France to economize and to escape the distractions of Great Neck. They did not live inexpensively, but he was able to concentrate on writing his novel.

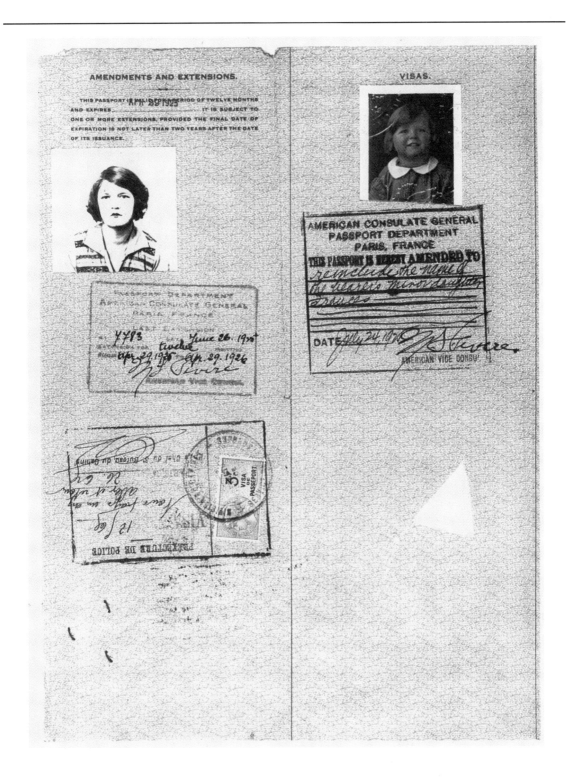

178

The most miserable year since
I was nineteen, full of terrible
failures and acute miseries
but the hard work fairly well accomplished
in the latter end and starting to do better.

Twenty-seven years old

Sept. High hopes for the play. A new schedule + more work on the novel. Ball game (worlds series)

Oct. The Boyds come to Great Neck. The Notre Dame game. Floyd Hooper. Beginning rehearsals. Firing Lee Patrick. Sam Forrest. Meeting Ernest Truex. Bunny's Baby

Nov. Rehearsal. Short of Money. Excitement. More Rumsey parties. Atlantic City. The Failure + dismal return. On the wagon. Writing story in one day. Scribners in Newark.

Dec. Still on the wagon. Fell off Xmas. Party Goldberg. Deterioration.

1924 Jan. Party with Gloria Swanson. Read Dostoiefski. Ring's book. Grand fight with Hovey + buying back stories.

Feb. Struggling with Money. Wrote all night on Baby Party. Success of the Kauffman play

Mar. Tired of Boyds, Townsend ect. Generally bored + feeling bad. Ring at Hot Springs. Father + Mother came to visit

April Out of the woods at last + starting novel. Gloria Swanson's party. Kauffman's party. Decision on 15th to go to Europe Miss Bruyn, William + Sally. Bunny + Ring talk all night. The "one-day" story again. Leland Hayward + Connie Bennet. Enter Murphy's party.

May Sailed. Bunny Burgers. The Captain's table. Paris. Tootsie + her husband. Hyeres + Grimms Park Hotel. Trip to Cannes Bishop. Edith Wharton's garden. Monsieur Astier. A night at Mont Martre

June Settled at St. Raphael at Villa Marie (Valescure) Bought Car. Josanne and Silve. Trip to Nice. Mr. + Mrs. Ring. Mrs. Nellone. Miss Wity Bobby Crozier. Gave 1st dinner + sat up all night. Pickie Miss Maddox

July The Big crisis — 13th of July. Sad Trip to Monte Carlo gave dinner. Pauline Paris, Trips of San Maximin. Mrs. Dougherty. Zelda swimming every day. Getting brown. Wore Olive Burgess. Ring's book big success. House rented in Great Neck.

Aug On the wagon on Wed 6th Sldes and Amanda arrive the 4th Trip to Monte Carlo again + often to Antibes. Good work on novel. Zelda and I close together. Rows Miss Maddox. The Murphys, Dos Passos. Almost go to Antibes

Sept Fred Gresse, the Barrys, Avignon, The novel finished, Ring coming. Trouble clearing away

The April 1924 entry in Fitzgerald's Ledger *notes "starting novel" and the decision to go to France.*

From Perkins to Fitzgerald
5 June 1924

I read your story* in the Mercury and it seemed to me very good indeed, and also different from what you had done before,- it showed a more steady and complete mastery, it seemed to me. Greater maturity might be the word. At any rate it gave me a more distinct sense of what you could do,- possibly because I have not read any of your other stories in the magazines except "How to Live on Thirty-six Thousand" which of course was a trifle. This seemed to show a remarkable strength and resource. I was greatly impressed by it.

*"Absolution"

> We were going to the Old World to find a new rhythm for our lives, with a true conviction that we had left our old selves behind for ever-and with a capital of just over seven thousand dollars.
> —"How to Live on Practically Nothing a Year," *The Saturday Evening Post*

* * *

From Fitzgerald to Perkins

Villa Marie, Valescure
St. Raphael, France
June 18, 1924

We are idyllicly settled here + the novel is going fine-it ought to be done in a month-though I'm not sure as I'm contemplating another 16,000 words which would make it about the length of Paradise-not quite though even then.

I'm glad you liked Absolution. As you know it was to have been the prologue of the novel but it interfered with the neatness of the plan.

> I remember our last conversation and it makes me sad. I feel old too, this summer—I have ever since the failure of my play a year ago. Thats the whole burden of this novel—the loss of those illusions that give such color to the world so that you don't care whether things are true or false as long as they partake of the magical glory.
>
> Fitzgerald to Ludlow Fowler, August 1924

* * *

From Fitzgerald to Perkins

August 1924
Villa Marie, Valescure
St. Raphael, France

(1.)The novel will be done next week. That doesn't mean however that it'll reach America before October 1st. as Zelda and I are contemplating a careful revision after a weeks complete rest.

. . . .

(6)For Christs sake don't give anyone that jacket you're saving for me. I've written it into the book.

(7)I think my novel is about the best American novel ever written. It is rough stuff in places, runs only to about 50,000 words + I hope you won't shy at it

(8)Its been a fair summer. Ive been unhappy but my work hasn't suffered from it. I am grown at last.

* * *

The Villa Marie, Valescure, where the manuscript of The Great Gatsby *was completed (Matthew J. and Arlyn Bruccoli Collection, University of South Carolina)*

Fitzgerald and Scottie at the Villa Marie, 1924 (Matthew J. and Arlyn Bruccoli Collection, University of South Carolina)

From Perkins to Fitzgerald

September 10, 1924

There is certainly not the slightest risk of our giving that jacket to anyone in the world but you. I wish the manuscript of the book would come, and I don't doubt it is something very like the best American novel.

* * *

October 27, 1924
Villa Marie, Valescure
St. Raphael, France
(After Nov. 3d Care of American Express Co, Rome Italy)
Dear Max:

Under separate cover I'm sending you my third novel:

<u>The Great Gatsby</u>

(I think that at last I've done something really my own), but how good "my own" is remains to be seen.

I should suggest the following contract.

15% up to 50,000
20% after 50,000

The book is only a little over fifty thousand words long but I believe, as you know, that Whitney Darrow has the wrong psychology about prices (and about what class constitute the bookbuying public now that the lowbrows go to the movies) and I'm anxious to charge two dollars for it and have it a <u>full size book</u>.

The Fitzgeralds in their Renault NN on the Riviera, summer 1924. Scottie is in the back seat with her nanny (Matthew J. and Arlyn Bruccoli Collection, University of South Carolina)

Of course I want the binding to be absolutely uniform with my other books—the stamping too—and the jacket we discussed before. This time I don't want any signed blurbs on the jacket—not Mencken's or Lewis' or Howard's or anyone's. I'm tired of being the author of <u>This Side of Paradise</u> and I want to start over.

About serialization. I am bound under contract to show it to Hearsts but I am asking a prohibitive price, Long hates me and its not a very serialized book. If they should take it—they won't—it would put of publication in the fall. Otherwise you can publish it in the spring. When Hearst turns it down I'm going to offer it to Liberty for $15,000 on condition that they'll publish it in ten weekly installments before April 15th. If they don't want it I shan't serialize. <u>I am absolutely positive Long won't want it.</u>

I have an alternative title:

<u>Gold-hatted Gatsby</u>

After you've read the book let me know what you think about the title. Naturally I won't get a nights sleep until I hear from you but do tell me the absolute truth, <u>your first impression of the book</u> + tell me anything that bothers you in it.

I'd rather you wouldn't call Reynolds as he might try to act as my agent.

Would you send me the N.Y. World with the accounts of Harvard-Princeton and Yale-Princeton games?

As Ever

* * *

November 1924
Hotel Continental, St. Raphael, France
(Leaving Tuesday)

Dear Max:

By now you've recieved the novel. There are things in it I'm not satisfied with in the middle of the book—Chapters 6 + 7. And I may write in a complete new scene in proof. I hope you got my telegram.

I have now decided to stick to the title I put on the book.

<u>Trimalchio in West Egg</u>

The only other titles that seem to fit it are <u>Trimalchio</u> and <u>On the Road to West Egg</u>. I had two others <u>Gold-hatted Gatsby</u> and <u>The High-bouncing Lover</u> but they seemed too light.

We leave for Rome as soon as I finish the short story I'm working on.

As ever,
Scott

* * *

Nov. 18, 1924

Dear Scott:

I think the novel is a wonder. I'm taking it home to read again and shall then write my impressions in full;- but it has vitality to an extraordinary degree, and <u>glamour</u>, and a great deal of underlying thought of unusual quality. It has a kind of mystic atmosphere at times that you infused into parts of "Paradise" and have not since used. It is a marvelous fusion, into a unity of presentation, of the extraordinary incongruities of life today. And as for sheer writing, it's astonishing.

Now deal with this question: various gentlemen here don't like the title,- in fact none like it but me. To me, the strange incongruity of the words in it sound the note of the book. But the objectors are more practical men than I. Consider as quickly as you can the question of a change.

But if you do not change, you will have to leave that note off the wrap.* Its presence would injure it too much;- and good as the wrap always seemed, it now seems a masterpiece for this book. So judge of the value of the title when it stands alone and write or cable your decision the instant you can.

With congratulations, I am,

Yours,

Possibly an identification of the title.

* * *

November 20, 1924

Dear Scott:

I think you have every kind of right to be proud of this book. It is an extraordinary book, suggestive of all sorts of thoughts and moods. You adopted exactly the right method of telling it, that of employing a narrator who is more of a spectator than an actor: this puts the reader upon a point of observation on a higher level than that on which the characters stand and at a distance that gives perspective. In no other way could your irony have been so immensely effective, nor the reader have been enabled so strongly to feel at times the strangeness of human circumstance in a vast heedless universe. In the eyes of Dr. Eckleberg various readers will see different significances; but their presence gives a superb touch to the whole thing: great unblinking eyes, expressionless, looking down upon the human scene. It's magnificent!

I could go on praising the book and speculating on its various elements, and meanings, but points of criticism are more important now. I think you are right in feeling a certain slight sagging in chapters six and seven, and I don't know how to suggest a remedy. I hardly doubt that you will find one and I am only writing to say that I think it does need something to hold up

Memorandum of Agreement, *made this* twenty-second *day of* December 19 24

between F. SCOTT FITZGERALD

of *hereinafter called "the* AUTHOR,"

and CHARLES SCRIBNER'S SONS, *of New York City, N. Y., hereinafter called "the* PUBLISHERS." *Said* - - F. Scott Fitzgerald - - *being the* AUTHOR *and* PROPRIETOR *of a work entitled:*

THE GREAT GATSBY

in consideration of the covenants and stipulations hereinafter contained, and agreed to be per-formed by the PUBLISHERS, *grants and guarantees to said* PUBLISHERS *and their successors the exclusive right to publish the said work in all forms during the terms of copyright and renewals thereof, hereby covenanting with said* PUBLISHERS *that he is the sole* AUTHOR *and* PROPRIETOR *of said work.*

Said AUTHOR *hereby authorizes said* PUBLISHERS *to take out the copyright on said work, and further guarantees to said* PUBLISHERS *that the said work is in no way whatever a violation of any copyright belonging to any other party, and that it contains nothing of a scandal-ous or libelous character; and that* he *and* his *legal representatives shall and will hold harmless the said* PUBLISHERS *from all suits, and all manner of claims and proceedings which may be taken on the ground that said work is such violation or contains anything scandalous or libelous; and* he *further hereby authorizes said* PUBLISHERS *to defend at law any and all suits and proceedings which may be taken or had against them for infringement of any other copy-right or for libel, scandal, or any other injurious or hurtful matter or thing contained in or alleged or claimed to be contained in or caused by said work, and pay to said* PUBLISHERS *such reasonable costs, disbursements, expenses, and counsel fees as they may incur in such defense.*

Said PUBLISHERS, *in consideration of the right herein granted and of the guarantees aforesaid, agree to publish said work at their own expense, in such style and manner as they shall deem most expedient, and to pay said* AUTHOR, *or* - *his* - *legal representatives,* FIFTEEN (15) ———————— *per cent. on their Trade-List (retail) price, cloth style, for* the first forty thousand (40,000) copies of said work sold by them in the United States and TWENTY (20) per cent. for all copies sold thereafter. *Provided, nevertheless, that one-half the above named royalty shall be paid on all copies sold out-side the United States; and provided that no percentage whatever shall be paid on any copies destroyed by fire or water, or sold at or below cost, or given away for the purpose of aiding the sale of said work.*

It is further agreed that the profits arising from any publication of said work, during the period covered by this agreement, in other than book form shall be divided equally between said PUBLISHERS *and said* AUTHOR.

The contract for the novel establishes that The Great Gatsby *was the working title at the end of 1924. The 15% royalty brought Fitzgerald 30 cents per copy sold. The 20,870 copies in the first printing earned Fitzgerald about $6,200—less the cost of proof alterations, which he was required to pay—cancelling his $6,000 debt to Scribners for borrowings. The sales did not reach 40,000. The last paragraph on page one covers subsidiary rights: profits from non-book rights (such as movies and dramatic versions) were equally divided between Fitzgerald and Scribners. During the Twenties these sub-rights earned more than book sales of the novel.*

Expenses incurred for alterations in type or plates, exceeding twenty per cent. of the cost of composition and electrotyping said work, are to be charged to the AUTHOR'S *account.*

The first statement shall not be rendered until six months after date of publication; and thereafter statements shall be rendered semi-annually, on the AUTHOR'S *application therefor, in the months of February and August; settlements to be made in cash, four months after date of statement.*

If, on the expiration of five *years from date of publication, or at any time thereafter, the demand for said work should not, in the opinion of said* PUBLISHERS, *be sufficient to render its publication profitable, then, upon written notice by said* PUBLISHERS *to said* AUTHOR, *this contract shall cease and determine; and thereupon said* AUTHOR *shall have the right, at his option, to take from said* PUBLISHERS, *at cost, whatever copies of said work they may then have on hand; or, failing to take said copies at cost, then said* PUBLISHERS *shall have the right to dispose of the copies on hand as they may see fit, free from any percentage or royalty, and to cancel this contract.*

Provided, also, that if, at any time during the continuance of this agreement, said work shall become unsalable in the ordinary channels of trade, said PUBLISHERS *shall have the right to dispose of any copies on hand, paying to said* AUTHOR – fifteen (15) – *per cent. of the net amount received therefor, in lieu of the percentage hereinbefore prescribed.*

In consideration of the mutuality of this contract, the aforesaid parties agree to all its provisions, and in testimony thereof affix their signatures and seals.

Witness to signature of
Charles Scribner's Sons

[L. S.]

Witness to signature of
F. Scott Fitzgerald

The Fitzgeralds in Rome, winter 1924–1925, where The Great Gatsby *was revised and rewritten in proof (Matthew J. and Arlyn Bruccoli Collection, University of South Carolina)*

here to the pace set, and ensuing. I have only two actual criticisms: -

One is that among a set of characters marvelously palpable and vital– I would know Tom Buchanan if I met him on the street and would avoid him– Gatsby is somewhat vague. The reader's eyes can never quite focus upon him, his outlines are dim. Now everything about Gatsby is more or less a mystery i.e. more or less vague, and this may be somewhat of an artistic intention, but I think it is mistaken. Couldn't he be physically described as distinctly as the others, and couldn't you add one or two characteristics like the use of that phrase "old sport",- not verbal, but physical ones, perhaps. I think that for some reason or other a reader– this was true of Mr. Scribner and of Louise*– gets an idea that Gatsby is a much older man than he is, although you have the writer say that he is little older than himself. But this would be avoided if on his first appearance he was seen as vividly as Daisy and Tom are, for instance;- and I do not think your scheme would be impaired if you made him so.

The other point is also about Gatsby: his career must remain mysterious, of course. But in the end you make it pretty clear that his wealth came through his connection with Wolfsheim. You also suggest this much earlier. Now almost all readers numerically are going to be puzzled by his having all this wealth and are going to feel entitled to an explanation. To give a distinct and definite one would be, of course, utterly absurd. It did occur to me though, that you might here and there interpolate some phrases, and possibly incidents, little touches of various kinds, that would suggest that he was in some active way mysteriously engaged. You do have him called on the telephone, but couldn't he be seen once or twice consulting at his parties with people of some sort of mysterious significance, from the political, the gambling, the sporting world, or whatever it may be. I know I am floundering, but that fact may help you to see what I mean. The total lack of an explanation through so large a part of the story does seem to me a defect;- or not of an explanation, but of the suggestion of an explanation. I wish you were here so I could talk about it to you for then I know I could at least make you understand what I mean. What Gatsby did ought never to be definitely imparted, even if it could be. Whether he was an innocent tool in the hands of somebody else, or to what degree he was this, ought not to be explained. But if some sort of business activity of his were simply adumbrated, it would lend further probability to that part of the story.

There is one other point: in giving deliberately Gatsby's biography when he gives it to the narrator you do depart from the method of the narrative in some degree, for otherwise almost everything is told, and beautifully told, in the regular flow of it,- in the succession of events or in accompaniment with them. But you can't avoid the biography altogether. I thought you might find ways to let the truth of some of his claims like "Oxford" and his army career come out bit by bit in the course of actual narrative. I mention the point anyway for consideration in this interval before I send the proofs.

The general brilliant quality of the book makes me ashamed to make even these criticisms. The amount of meaning you get into a sentence, the dimensions and intensity of the impression you make a paragraph carry, are most extraordinary. The manuscript is full of phrases which make a scene blaze with life. If one enjoyed a rapid railroad journey I would compare the number and vividness of pictures your living words suggest, to the living scenes disclosed in that way. It seems in reading a much shorter book than it is, but it carries the mind through a series of experiences that one would think would require a book of three times its length.

The presentation of Tom, his place, Daisy and Jordan, and the unfolding of their characters is unequalled so far as I know. The description of the valley of ashes adjacent to the lovely country, the conversation and the action in Myrtle's apartment, the marvelous catalogue of those who came to Gatsby's house,- these are such things as make a man famous. And all these things, the whole pathetic episode, you have given a place in time and space, for with the help of T. J. Eckleberg and by an occasional glance at the sky, or the sea, or the city, you have imparted a sort of sense of eternity. You once told me you were not a <u>natural</u> writer— my God! You have plainly mastered the craft, of course; but you needed far more than craftsmanship for this.

As Ever,
Maxwell E. Perkins

P.S. Why do you ask for a lower royalty on this than you had on the last book where it changed from 15% to 17% after 20,000 and to 20% after 40,000? Did you do it in order to give us a better margin for advertising? We shall advertise very energetically anyhow and if you stick to the old terms you will sooner overcome the advance. Naturally we should like the ones you suggest better, but there is no reason you should get less on this than you did on the other.

*Mrs. Perkins

* * *

Hotel des Princes
Piazza di Spagna
Rome, Italy

December 1924
Dear Max:

Your wire + your letters made me feel like a million dollars– I'm sorry I could make no better response than a telegram whining for money. But the long siege of the novel winded me a little + I've been slow on starting the stories on which I must live.

I think all your critisisms are true

(a) About the title. I'll try my best but I don't know what I can do. Maybe simply "Trimalchio" or "Gatsby." In the former case I don't see why the note shouldn't go on the back.

(b) Chapters VI + VII I know how to fix

(c) Gatsby's business affairs I can fix. I get your point about them.

(d) His vagueness I can repair by <u>making more pointed</u>–this doesn't sound good but wait and see. It'll make him clear

(e) But his long narrative in Chap VIII will be difficult to split up. Zelda also thought I was a little out of key but it is good writing and I don't think I could bear to sacrifice any of it.

(f) I have 1000 minor corrections which I will make on the proof + several more large ones which you didn't mention

Your critisisms were excellent + most helpful + you picked out all my favorite spots in the book to praise as high spots. Except you didn't mention my favorite of all-the chapter where Gatsby + Daisy meet.

. . . .

Another point– in Chap. II of my book when Tom + Myrte go into the bedroom while Carraway reads Simon called Peter– is that raw? Let me know. I think its pretty nessessary.

I made the royalty smaller because I wanted to make up for all the money you've advanced these two years by letting it pay a sort of interest on it. But I see by calculating I made it too small–a difference of 2000

THE SATYRICON OF
PETRONIUS ARBITER

Complete and unexpurgated translation by W. C.
Firebaugh, in which are incorporated the
forgeries of Nodot and Marchena, and
the readings introduced into the text
by De Salas. Illustrations by
Norman Lindsay.

VOLUME ONE

New York: 1922. Published for Private
Circulation Only by Boni & Liveright

This edition was limited to 1,250 copies (Matthew J. and Arlyn Bruccoli Collection, University of South Carolina).

dollars. Let us call it 15% up to 40,000 and 20% after that. That's a good fair contract all around.

. . . .

Anyhow thanks + thanks + thanks for your letters. I'd rather have you + Bunny like it than anyone I know. And I'd rather have you like it than Bunny. If its as good as you say, when I finish with the proof it'll be perfect.

Remember, by the way, to put by some cloth for the cover uniform with my other books.

As soon as I can think about the title I'll write or wire a decision. Thank Louise for me, for liking it. Best Regards to Mr. Scribner. Tell him Galsworthy is here in Rome

As Ever,
Scott

* * *

The Satyricon

Two of the working titles for the novel were "Trimalchio" and "Trimalchio in West Egg," referring to the nouveau riche party-giver in Petronius's Latin novel, The Satyricon *(before 66 A.D.). The 1922 illustrated translation of* The Satyricon, *published by Boni & Liveright and edited by Fitzgerald's friend T. R. Smith, was charged with obscenity by the New York Society for the Suppression of Vice.*

CHAPTER THE THIRTY-THIRD. Picking his teeth with a silver quill, "Friends," said he, "it was not convenient for me to come into the dining-room just yet, but for fear my absence should cause you any inconvenience, I gave over my own pleasure: permit me, however, to finish my game." A slave followed with a terebinth table and crystal dice, and I noted one piece of luxury that was superlative; for instead of black and white pieces, he used gold and silver coins. He kept up a continual flow of various coarse expressions. We were still dallying with the relishes when a tray was brought in, on which was a basket containing a wooden hen with her wings rounded and spread out as if she were brooding. Two slaves instantly approached, and to the accompaniment of music, commenced to feel around in the straw. They pulled out some pea-hen's eggs, which they distributed among the diners. Turning his head, Trimalchio saw what was going on. "Friends," he remarked, "I ordered pea-hen's eggs set under the hen, but I'm afraid they're addled, by Hercules I am: let's try them anyhow, and see if they're still fit to suck." We picked up our spoons, each of which weighed not less than half a pound, and punctured the shells, which were made of flour and dough, and as a matter of fact, I very nearly threw mine away for it seemed to me that a chick had formed already, but upon hearing an old experienced guest vow, "There must be something good here": I broke open the shell with my hand and discovered a fine fat fig-pecker, imbedded in a yolk seasoned with pepper.

CHAPTER THE THIRTY-FOURTH. Having finished his game, Trimalchio was served with a helping of everything and was announcing in a loud voice his willingness to join anyone in a second cup of honied wine, when, to a flourish of music, the relishes were suddenly whisked away by a singing chorus, but a small dish happened to fall to the floor, in the scurry, and a slave picked it up. Seeing this, Trimalchio ordered that the boy be punished by a box on the ear, and made him throw it down again; a janitor followed with his broom and swept the silver dish away among the litter. Next followed two long-haired Ethiopians, carrying small leather bottles, such as are commonly seen in the hands of those who sprinkled sand in the arena, and poured wine upon our hands, for no one offered us water. When complimented upon these elegant extras, the host cried out, "Mars loves a fair fight: and so I ordered each one a separate table: that way these stinking slaves won't make us so hot with their crowding." Some glass bottles carefully sealed with gypsum were brought in at that instant; a label bearing this inscription was fastened to the neck of each one:

OPIMIAN FALERNIAN
ONE HUNDRED YEARS OLD.

While we were studying the labels, Trimalchio clapped his hands and cried, "Ah me! To think that wine lives longer than poor little man. Let's fill 'em up! There's life in wine and this is the real Opimian, you can take my word for that. I offered no such vintage yesterday, though my guests were far more respectable." We were tippling away and extolling all these elegant devices, when a slave brought in a silver skeleton, so contrived that the joints and movable vertebræ could be turned in any direction. He threw it down upon the table a time or two, and its mobile articulation caused it to assume grotesque attitudes, whereupon Trimalchio chimed in:

"Poor man is nothing in the scheme of things
And Orcus grips us and to Hades flings
Our bones! This skeleton before us here
Is as important as we ever were!
Let's live then while we may and life is dear."

CHAPTER THE THIRTY-FIFTH. The applause was followed by a course which, by its oddity, drew every eye, but it did not come up to our expectations. There was a circular tray around which were displayed the signs of the zodiac, and upon each sign the caterer had placed the food best in keeping with it. Ram's vetches on Aries, a piece of beef on Taurus, kidneys and lamb's fry on Gemini, a crown on Cancer, the womb of an unfarrowed sow on Virgo, an African fig on Leo, on Libra a balance, one pan of which held a tart and the other a cake, a small seafish on Scorpio, a bull's eye on Sagittarius, a sea lobster on Capricornus, a goose on Aquarius and two mullets on Pisces. In the middle lay a piece of cut sod upon which rested a honeycomb with the grass arranged around it. An Egyptian slave passed bread around from a silver oven and in a most discordant voice twisted out a song in the manner of the mime in the musical farce called Laserpitium. Seeing that we were rather depressed at the prospect of busying ourselves with such vile fare, Trimalchio urged us to fall to: "Let us fall to, gentlemen, I beg of you, this is only the sauce!"

CHAPTER THE THIRTY-SIXTH. While he was speaking, four dancers ran in to the time of the music, and removed the upper part of the tray. Beneath, on what seemed to be another tray, we caught sight of stuffed capons and sows' bellies, and in the middle, a hare equipped with wings to resemble Pegasus. At the corners of the tray we also noted four figures of Marsyas and from their bladders spouted a highly spiced sauce upon fish which were swimming about as if in a tide-race. All of us echoed the applause which was started by the servants, and fell to upon these exquisite delicacies, with a laugh. "Carver," cried Trimalchio, no less delighted with the artifice practised upon us, and the carver appeared immediately. Timing his strokes to the beat of the music he cut up the meat in such a fashion as to lead you to think that a gladiator was fighting from a chariot to the accompaniment of a water-organ. Every now and then Trimalchio would repeat "Carver, Carver," in a low voice, until I finally came to the conclusion that some joke was meant in repeating a word so frequently, so I did not scruple to question him who reclined about me. As he had often experienced byplay of this sort he explained, "You see that fellow who is carving the meat, don't you? Well, his name is Carver. Whenever Trimalchio says Carver, carve her, by the same word, he both calls and commands!"

CHAPTER THE THIRTY-SEVENTH. I could eat no more, so I turned to my whilom informant to learn as much as I could and sought to draw him out with far-fetched gossip. I inquired who that woman could be who was scurrying about hither and yon in such a fashion. "She's the wife of Trimalchio, and she measures her money by the peck. And only a little while ago, what was she! May your genius pardon me, but you would not have been willing to take a crust of bread from her hand. Now, without rhyme or reason, she's in the seventh heaven and is Trimalchio's factotum, so much so that he would believe her if she told him it was dark when it was broad daylight! As for him, he don't know how rich he is, but this harlot keeps an eye on everything and where you least expect to find her, you're sure to run into her. She's temperate, sober, full of good advice, and has many good qualities, but she has a scolding tongue, a very magpie on a sofa, those she likes, she likes, but those she dislikes, she dislikes! Trimalchio himself has estates as broad as the flight of a kite is long, and piles of money. There's more silver plate lying in his steward's office than other men have in their whole fortunes! And as for slaves, damn me if I believe a tenth of them knows the master by sight. The truth is, that these stand-a-grapes are so much in awe of him that any one of them would step into a fresh dunghill without ever knowing it, at a mere nod from him!

CHAPTER THE THIRTY-EIGHTH. "And don't you get the idea that he buys anything; everything is produced at home, wool, pitch, pepper, if you asked for hen's milk you would get it. Because he wanted his wool to rival other things in quality, he bought rams at Tarentum and sent 'em into flocks with a slap on the arse. He had bees brought from Attica, so he could produce Attic honey at home, and, as a side issue, so he could improve the native bees by crossing with the Greek. He even wrote to India for mushroom seed one day, and he hasn't a single mule that wasn't sired by a wild ass. Do you see all those cushions? Not a single one but what is stuffed with either purple or scarlet wool! He hasn't anything to worry about! Look out how you criticise those other fellow-freedmen-friends of his, they're all well heeled. See the fellow reclining at the bottom of the end couch? He's worth his 800,000 any day, and he rose from nothing! Only a short while ago he had to carry faggots on his own back. I don't know how true it is, but they say that he snatched off an Incubo's hat and found a treasure! For my part, I don't envy any man anything that was given him by a god. He still carries the marks of his ox on the ear, and he isn't wishing himself any bad luck! He posted this notice, only the other day:

CAIUS POMPONIUS DIOGENES HAS
PURCHASED A HOUSE
THIS GARRET FOR RENT AFTER
THE KALENDS OF JULY.

What do you think of the fellow in the freedman's place? He has a good front, too, hasn't he? And he has a right to. He saw his fortune multiplied tenfold, but he lost heavily through speculation at the last. I don't think he can call his very hair his own, and it is no fault of his either by Hercules, it isn't. There's no better fellow anywhere: his rascally freedmen cheated him out of everything. You know very well how it is; everybody's business is nobody's business, and once let business affairs start to go wrong, your friends will stand from under! Look at the fix he's in, and think what a fine trade he had! He used to be an undertaker. He dined like a king, boars roasted whole in their shaggy hides, bakers' pastries, birds, cooks and bakers! More wine was spilled under his table than another has in his wine cellar. His life was like a pipe dream, not like an ordinary mortal's. When his affairs commenced go to wrong, and he was afraid his creditors would guess that he was bankrupt, he advertised an auction and this was his placard:

JULIUS PROCULUS WILL SELL AT
AUCTION HIS SUPERFLUOUS
FURNITURE."

CHAPTER THE THIRTY-NINTH. Trimalchio broke in upon this entertaining gossip, for the course had been removed and the guests, happy with wine, had started a general conversation: lying back upon his couch, "You ought to make this wine go down pleasantly," he said, "the fish must have something to swim in. But I say, you didn't think I'd be satisfied with any such dinner as you saw on the top of that tray? 'Is Ulysses no better known?' Well, well, we shouldn't forget our culture, even at dinner. May the bones of my patron rest in peace, he wanted me to become a man among men. No one can show me anything new, and that little tray has proved it. This heaven where the gods live, turns into as many different signs, and sometimes into the Ram: therefore, whoever is born under that sign will own many flocks and much wool, a hard head, a shameless brow, and a sharp horn. A great many school-teachers and rambunctious butters-in are born under that sign." We applauded the wonderful penetration of our astrologer and he ran on, "then the whole heaven turns into a bull-calf and the kickers and herdsmen and those who see to it that their own bellies are full, come into the world. Teams of horses and oxen are born under the Twins, and well-hung wenchers and those who be-dung both sides of the wall. I was born under the Crab and therefore stand on many legs and own much property on land and sea, for the crab is as much at home on one as he is in the other. For that reason, I put nothing on that sign for fear of weighing down my own destiny. Bulldozers and gluttons are born under the Lion, and women and fugitives and chain-gangs are born under the Virgin. Butchers and perfumers are born under the Balance, and all who think that it is their business to straighten things out. Poisoners and assassins are born under the Scorpion. Cross-eyed people who look at the vegetables and sneak away with the bacon, are born under the Archer. Horny-handed sons of toil are born under Capricorn. Bartenders and pumpkin-heads are born under the Water-Carrier. Caterers and rhetoricians are born under the Fishes: and so the world turns round, just like a mill, and something bad always comes to the top, and men are either being born or else they're dying. As to the sod and the honeycomb in the middle, for I never do anything without a reason, Mother Earth is in the centre, round as an egg, and all that is good is found in her, just like it is in a honeycomb."

CHAPTER THE FORTIETH. "Bravo!" we yelled, and, with hands uplifted to the ceiling, we swore that such fellows as Hipparchus and Aratus were not to be compared with him. At length some slaves came in who spread upon the couches some coverlets upon which were embroidered nets and hunters stalking their game with boar-spears, and all the paraphernalia of the chase. We knew not what to look for next, until a hideous uproar commenced, just outside the dining-room door, and some Spartan hounds commenced to run around the table all of a sudden. A tray followed them, upon which was served a wild boar of immense size, wearing a liberty cap upon its head, and from its tusks hung two little baskets of woven palm fibre, one of which contained Syrian dates, the other, Theban. Around it hung little suckling pigs made from pastry, signifying that this was a brood-sow with her pigs at suck. It turned out that these were souvenirs intended to be taken home. When it came to carving the board, our old friend Carver, who had carved the capons, did not appear, but in his place a great bearded giant, with bands around his legs, and wearing a short hunting cape in which a design was woven. Drawing his hunting-knife, he plunged it fiercely into the boar's side, and some thrushes flew out of the gash; fowlers, ready with their rods, caught them in a moment, as they fluttered around the room and Trimalchio ordered one to each guest, remarking, "Notice what fine acorns this forest-bred boar fed on," and as he spoke, some slaves removed the little baskets from the tusks and divided the Syrian and Theban dates equally among the diners.

. . . .

CHAPTER THE SEVENTY-FIRST. Trimalchio was hugely tickled at this challenge. "Slaves are men, my friends," he observed, "but that's not all, they sucked the same milk that we did, even if hard luck has kept them down; and they'll drink the water of freedom if I live: to make a long story short, I'm freeing all of them in my will. To Philargyrus, I'm leaving a farm, and his bedfellow, too. Carrio will get a tenement house and his twentieth, and a bed and bedclothes to boot. I'm making Fortunata my heir and I commend her to ally my friends. I announce all this in public so that my household will love me as well now as they will when I'm dead." They all commenced to pay tribute to the generosity of their master, when he, putting aside his trifling, ordered a copy of his will brought in, which same he read aloud from beginning to end, to the groaning accompaniment of the whole household. Then, looking at Habinnas, "What say you, my dearest friend," he entreated; "you'll construct my monument in keeping with the plans I've given you, won't you? I earnestly beg that you carve a little bitch at the feet of my statue, some wreaths and some jars of perfume, and all of the fights of Petraites. Then I'll be able to live even after I'm dead, thanks to your kindness. See to it that it as a frontage of one hundred feet and a depth of two hundred. I want fruit trees of every kind planted around my ashes; and plenty of vines, too, for it's all wrong for a man to deck out his house when he's alive, and then have no pains taken with the one he must stay in for a longer time, and that's the reason I particularly desire that this notice be added:

–THIS MONUMENT DOES NOT–
–DESCEND TO AN HEIR–

In any case, I'll see to it through a clause in my will, that I'm not insulted when I'm dead. And for fear the rabble comes running up into my monument, to crap, I'll appoint one of my freedmen custodian of my tomb. I want you to carve ships under full sail on my monument, and me, in my robes of office, sitting on my tribunal, five gold rings on my fingers, pouring out coin from a sack for the people, for I gave a dinner and two dinars for each guest, as you know. Show a ban-quet-hall, too, if you can, the people in it having a good time. On my right, you can place a statue of Fortunata holding a dove and leading a little bitch on a leash, and my favorite boy, and large jars sealed with gypsum, so the wine won't run out; show one broken and a boy crying over it. Put a sun-dial in the middle, so that whoever looks to see what time it is must read my name whether he wants to or not. As for the inscription, think this over carefully, and see if you think it's appropriate:

HERE RESTS G POMPEIUS TRIMALCHIO
FREEDMAN OF MAECENAS DECREED
AUGUSTAL SEVIR IN HIS ABSENCE
HE COULD HAVE BEEN A MEMBER OF
EVERY DECURIA OF ROME BUT WOULD
NOT CONSCIENTIOUS BRAVE LOYAL HE
GREW RICH FROM LITTLE AND LEFT
THIRTY MILLION SESTERCES BEHIND
HE NEVER HEARD A PHILOSOPHER
FAREWELL TRIMALCHIO
FAREWELL PASSERBY"

* * *

The New York Times, *28 September 1922, p. 11*

John S. Summer, Secretary of the New York Society for the Suppression of Vice, suffered another defeat in his literature crusade when Magistrate Charles A. Oberwager, in Harlem Court, yesterday dismissed the summons against Boni & Liveright, Inc., whose publication of "The Satyricon of Petronius Arbiter," Summer charged was in violation of Section 1141 of the Penal Law. The court also found Harry J. Salsberg, co-defendant with the publishing house, not guilty of offering the classic for sale.

Magistrate Oberwager rendered a comprehensive opinion of thirteen pages, quoting from the Encyclopedia Britannica and several other authorities on literature, decisions of higher courts and his own conviction as to the contribution of the book to present-day thought.

He asserted that the Legislature, through the statute in question, scarcely intended "to destroy literature or to anathematize all historical manners and morals different from our own or to close the treasure house of the past."

Another significant statement made by the Court, in its decision, came as a blow to Mr. Summer whose efforts toward censorship have been most pronounced in recent months.

Scope of Powers Conferred by Act.

"The Legislature did not intend to confer upon any individual or society general powers of censorship over literary works," declared Magistrate Oberwager, "for if such were the case the power could easily be abused and the destruction of the freedom of speech as well as the freedom of press would be resultant effects of such a statute. Works of art, the masterpieces of ancient ages, scientific works, aye, the daily press, would be subjected to a censorship that would cause the destruction of our free institutions. One who is not content with repressing scandalous excesses, but demands austere piety will soon discover that not only has the rendering of an impossible service to the cause of virtue been attempted, but that vice has thereby been aided."

It is generally believed by scholars that the book in question was written by the Roman in the time of Nero. The English translation, which the New York publishing house printed in a limited edition of 1,200 copies, was offered to their subscribers at $30 a set for the two volumes.

"Petronius," said the Magistrate in his opinion, "is generally thought to have lived in the time of Nero and according to tradition was the arbiter of elegance and dictator of fashion in the Court of Nero. The Satyricon is a keen satire on the vulgarity of mere wealth, its vanity and its grossness, and constitutes a fragment containing parts of two books out of a total of sixteen. The author was interested in the intellectual pursuits, as well as in the vices and follies of his own evil time. The worship of the flesh and its lusts alternately disgusted and fascinated him.

"The book portrays an important part of the history of civilization, and the prosecution gives rise to the question whether the record of civilization can be supressed.

"With this prosecution the Society for the Suppression of Vice seeks to impose a duty upon the Court to exercise a censorship over literature with a view of suppressing a work of literary merit which has lived for nineteen hundred years.

But such is not the duty of the courts, irrespective of the character of the book, unless its publication or circulation is accomplished in violation of the criminal statues."

Value of Book Long Recognized.

"It must be admitted," he said, "that the Satyricon is a part of the body of classical literature. Its value has been recognized both from the historical and literary viewpoint. It has been assigned the place of prototype of picaresque literature and critics have avowed its influence upon such greater writers as Ster, Fielding, Smollett and Rabelais.

"Its value to the student and the scholar is such that it would be too serious a matter to deny access to it, for ancient literature enlarges and enriches the mind.

"Time has determined that this work must survive, and were it simply a piece of obscenity it would have perished long since and never have reached the portals of this tribunal."

Among the authorities on the value and place in literature of the Satyricon, quoted by the Magistrate, were Sir Samuel Dill, in his "Roman Society From Nero to Marcus Aurelius," Charles Whibley's "Studies in Frankness," William Young Stellar writing in the Encyclopedia Britannica, Professor Harry T. Peck's translation of "Trimalchio's Dinner" and Frank Frost Abbott writing in Classical Philology.

If the Satyricon is to fall, the contemporaries of Petronicus such as Ovid, Juvenal, Horace, Martial and Tacitus must come under the ban, declared the Magistrate, adding, "If one is to condemn simply because of the existence of isolated passages of obscenity, we are to condemn to a fate of obliteration and oblivion Shakespeare, Chaucer, Voltaire, Rousseau, Boccaccio, Balzac, Flaubert, de Maupassant, Zola, Poe and even the Bible."

Augmenting his prepared opinion by a resumé of how he arrived at it, the Court declared that he had spent many hours in public libraries and in universities before making up his mind. He thanked Mr. Summer for bringing the complaint, because, as he said, "it took me back to school days once more."

Mr. Summer took exception to the decision, asserted that now the publishing house can issue it in unlimited quantities and indiscriminately, and asked that new summonses be issued, because, as the Court admitted, certain passages were obscene. The Magistrate asked Sumner to make his request in writing. Arthur G. Hays, counsel for Mr. Liveright, asked that warrants be issued instead of summonses, so that he can have redress if the case is thrown out.

Horace Liveright later announced that he intended instituting suit for $25,000 against Summer and his Vice Society for libel. Summer said in the public press, according to the publisher, that his limited editions were not limited in any way and could be purchased by any one who was willing to pay.

* * *

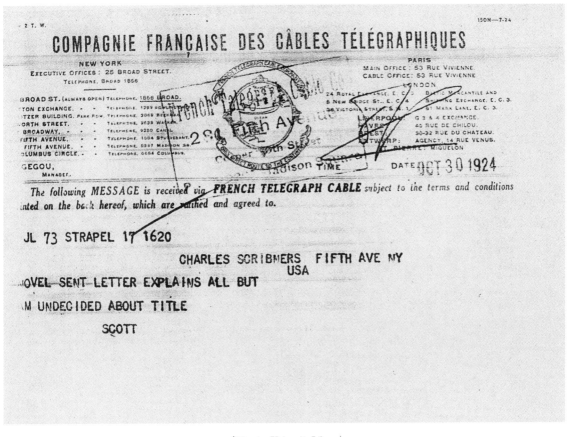

COMPAGNIE FRANÇAISE DES CÂBLES TÉLÉGRAPHIQUES

DATE OCT 30 1924

The following MESSAGE is received via *FRENCH TELEGRAPH CABLE* subject to the terms and conditions printed on the back hereof, which are ratified and agreed to.

JL 73 STRAPEL 17 1620

CHARLES SCRIBNERS FIFTH AVE NY
USA

NOVEL SENT LETTER EXPLAINS ALL BUT

AM UNDECIDED ABOUT TITLE

SCOTT

(Princeton University Library)

THE TITLE

Although "The Great Gatsby" was a provisional title for his third novel almost from the beginning, Fitzgerald never liked it, and he claimed that it would damage the novel commercially.

* * *

Dec. 16, 1924

Dear Scott:

Your cable changing the title to "The Great Gatsby" has come and has been followed; and as I just now cabled, we have deposited the seven hundred and fifteen.*

. . . .

I hope you are thinking over "The Great Gatsby" in this interval and will add to it freely. The most important point I think, is that of how he comes by his wealth,- some sort of suggestion about it. He was supposed to be a bootlegger, wasn't he, at least in part, and I should think a little touch here and there would give the reader the suspicion that this was so and that is all that is needed.

. . . .

The request for $750 and the title change were contained in a cable dated December 15th.

* * *

Dec. 19, 1924

Dear Scott:

When Ring Lardner came in the other day I told him about your novel and he instantly balked at the title.* "No one could pronounce it," he said;- so probably your change is wise on other than typographical counts. Certainly it is a <u>good</u> title.

*"Trimalchio"

* * *

WESTERN UNION
CABLEGRAM

Form 2006

NEWCOMB CARLTON, PRESIDENT   GEORGE W. E. ATKINS, FIRST VICE-PRESIDENT

Received at

385N FAZ CABLE

ROMA 27 15

LCD SCRIBNERS   545

597 FIFTH NYK

TITLE THE GREAT GATSBY, IF YOU DEPOSIT SEVENHUNDRED AND FIFTEEN

GUARANTY TRUST FIFTH AVENUE IT MAKES FIVE THOUSAND ADVANCED AND

RELIEVE ANXIE-TIES

(NOT SIGNED)

610P

RB/OK

Deposit Marstille changed

Fitzgerald to Perkins, 15 December 1924; the note is in Perkins's hand (Princeton University Library).

Scott

P.S. Im returning the proof of the title page ect. It's O.K. but my heart tells me I should have named it *Trimalchio*. However against all the advice I suppose it would have been stupid and stubborn of me. *Trimalchio in West Egg* was only a compromise. *Gatsby* is too much like *Babbit* and *The Great Gatsby* is weak because there's no emphasis even ironically on his greatness or lack of it. However let it pass.

Fitzgerald to Perkins, 24 January 1925 (Princeton University Library)

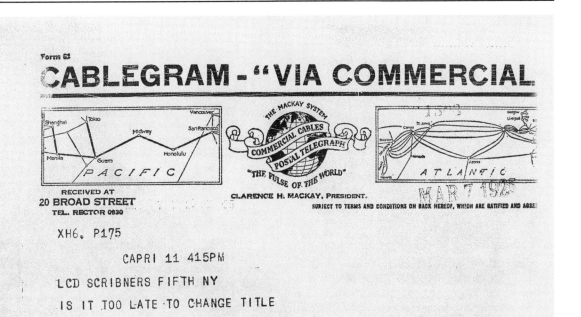

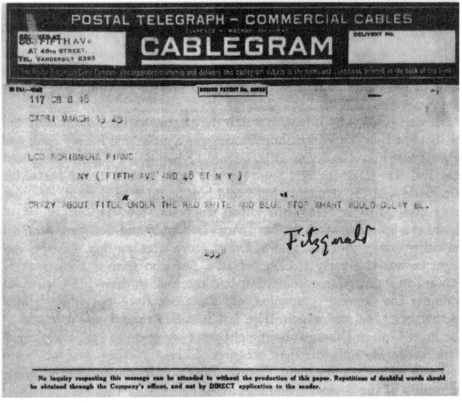

(Princeton University Library)

Fitzgerald's last proposed change to the title came too late. The book had been advertised and sold for publication on 10 April 1925
(Princeton University Library).

PROOF REVISION/REWRITING
AND PUBLICATION

Hotel des Princes, Piazza di Spagna, Rome
December 1924
Dear Max:

. . . .

I can now make it perfect but the proof (I will soon get the immemorial letter with the statement "We now have the book in hand and will soon begin to send you proof" [what is 'in hand'–I have a vague picture of everyone in the office holding the book in the right and and reading it]) will be one of the most expensive affairs since Madame Bovary. Please charge it to my account. If its possible to send a second proof over here I'd love to have it. Count on 12 days each way – four days here on first proof + two on the second. I hope there are other good books in the spring because I think now the public interest in books per se rises when there seems to be a group of them as in 1920 (spring + fall), 1921 (fall), 1922 (spring). Ring's + Tom's (first) books, Willa Cathers Lost Lady + in an inferior, cheap way Edna Ferber's are the only American fiction in over two years that had a really excellent press (say, since Babbit).

With the aid you've given me I can make "Gatsby" perfect. The chapter VII (the hotel scene) will never quite be up to mark – I've worried about it too long + I can't quite place Daisy's reaction. But I can improve it a lot. It isn't imaginative energy that's lacking – its because I'm automaticly prevented from thinking it out over again because I must get all those characters to New York in order to have the catastrophe on the road going back + I must have it pretty much that way. So there's no chance of bringing the freshness to it that a new free conception sometimes gives.

The rest is easy and I see my way so clear that I even see the mental quirks that queered it before. Strange to say my notion of Gatsby's vagueness was O.K. What you and Louise + Mr Charles Scribner found wanting was that:

I myself didn't know what Gatsby looked like or was engaged in + you felt it. If I'd known + kept it from you you'd have been too impressed with my knowledge to protest. This is a complicated idea but I'm sure you'll understand. But I know now – and as a penalty for not having known first, in other words to make sure I'm going to tell more.

It seems of almost mystical significance to me that you thot he was older – the man I had in mind, half

unconsciously, was older (a specific individual) and evidently, without so much as a definate word, I conveyed the fact. – or rather, I must qualify this Shaw-Desmond-trash by saying that I conveyed it without – I – a word that I can at present and for the life of me, trace. (I think Shaw Desmond* was one of your bad bets – I was the other)

Anyhow after careful searching of the files (of a man's mind here) for the Fuller Magee case + after having had Zelda draw pictures until her fingers ache I know Gatsby better than I know my own child. My first instinct after your letter was to let him go + have Tom Buchanan dominate the book (I suppose he's the best character I've ever done – I think he and the brother in "Salt" + Hurstwood in "Sister Carrie" are the three best characters in American fiction in the last twenty years, perhaps and perhaps not) but Gatsby sticks in my heart. I had him for awhile then lost him + now I know I have him again. I'm sorry Myrtle is better that Daisy. Jordan of course was a great idea (perhaps you know its Edith Cummings) but she fades out. Its Chap VII thats the trouble with Daisy + it may hurt the book's popularity that it's a man's book.

Anyhow I think (for the first time since The Vegetable failed) that Im a wonderful writer + its your always wonderful letters that help me to go on believing in myself.

Now some practical, very important questions. Please answer every one.

1. Montenegro has an order called The Order of Danilo. Is there any possible way you could find out for me there what it would look like – whether a courtesy decoration given to an American would bear an English inscription – or anything to give versimilitude to the medal which sounds horribly amateurish.

2. Please have no blurbs of any kind on the jacket!!! No Mencken or Lewis or Sid Howard or anything. I don't believe in them one bit any more.

3. Don't forget to change name of book in list of works

4. Please shift exclamation point from end of 3d line to end of 4th line in title page poem. Please! Important!

5. I thought that the whole episode (2 paragraphs) about their playing the Jazz History of the world at Gatsby's first party was rotten. Did you? Tell me frank reaction – personal. don't think! We can all think!

Always Yours
Scott Fitz–––

Irish author

* * *

The year of Zelda's sickness and re-sulting depression. Drink, loafing the Murphys

Twenty—eight years Old   179

Sept — Yves leaves. Hard work sets in. Zelda reads Roderick Hudson. Decides on Rome. Another welcome departure of a friend! Swimming over. On the Plage at night.

Oct — Working at high pressure to finish. Colder. Man at King's bank. Champagne with Jean. Man to Hotel. Last sight of Josanne. Touring Club de France.

Nov — Novel offballast. René. Crossing the border. Pan Remo, Nellbone fairs, Genoa, Pisa, Arretyo, Orvietto, Rome. Miss Gibson, Hungry, the English lady, Opera, Egyptian, Housekeeping, Herbert Howe and the movies, Harden + his daughter, Kathleen Key, Dipping with Zelda, Perkins wire, Reynolds, The Beg bust, Collatzo

Dec — Hotel des Princes, Dark glasses, thieving waiters, Osborne, Castelli Caesari, Depression, Proof arrives (later) Movie party, Hungry, Row in café, Zelda's doll, Sue, Xmas row, Kellys, Reconciliation, Water Wagon. New Years douce. My nose. the nigger

1925 Jan — Gillespie. Sickness for both. American Restaurant. Tivoli, Frascati, the donkey, Mrs Jackson, Herbert Howe. Pincio. Movies

Feb — Trip to Capri, Naples, Sorrento, Excelsior, Chapman, Zelda sick, Paranci, Blue grot. M'Kenzie + his wife, Tiberio, Boat, Naples bust up, rows + conductor. Sickness, Proof off, Miss Normand, Capri, Cuomo, Spirelli, the sister

Mar — Miss Normand, Aunt Annabel, Zelda better then relapse, the Russians, Mrs Hatton, Wilmington + Detroit girls, Zelda's lessons, E. F. Benson and Ellingham Brooks, German Beer, Golding, The New Zealanders, Nanny and Mr Ming.

Apr — Zelda painting, my drinking, Mary Roberts Rinehart, Quia capri, Brett Young and the fairy. The Captain too and Mrs M'Kenzie, The boat question, nervous collapse, Sorrento to Naples, Naples to Marseille eat.

May — We abandon trip with broken car in Lyon, Zelda's hairdresser, Paris - the Florida, B. Kauffman, Hemingway, Pawley, Ordway and a million Americans. Lyon with Ernest. Brisky. Stephen. Mad Boyd. appartment 1 – 3 Ave. Kleber. Gertrude Stein.

June — Murphys, Esther, Teddy Chandler, Trinty, Famous Ritz Party, Bob Handly, Noel, the Wymans, Mary Hay, 1000 parties and no work. Edith Wharton. Parker q ten Morning in the Bois, Ritz Bar, The Johnsons. Carol; Joanne

July — Party at Alice Delemers on 14th, 4th with Sapt. Fud. Legolliere (Eva) Again 1000 parties and no work — until last ten days. Capelane + Tootsie, Kiki Allen Preston.

Aug — Left for Antibes, Hamelton, M'Slushes, Brockets manners, Open hearted tent. Diving, Tadmans, Gordon, Myndred, The lighthouse, Murphy's garden - Trip down the accident, Orange, Sap to Monte Carlo, Sailing, Benchleys. Conceive novel. St Sol. Elaine Duncan, Hookes, Wonderful nights, Zelda drugged, Virginia Reel

Sept — Reaches Paris. Forrestal night eat. Trip to Verdun (no! Oct!) Rue Tilsit house Begin work

Fitzgerald's Ledger *entries for 1924–1925 record his completion of the novel in France, his work on the proofs in Rome and Capri, and his first encounter with Ernest Hemingway in Paris.*

American Express Co,
Rome.

January 1925
Dear Max:

Proof hasn't arrived yet. Have been in bed for a week with grippe but I'm ready to attack it violently. Here are two important things.

(1.) In the scene in Myrtes appartment – in the place where <u>Tom + Myrtle dissapear for awhile</u> noticably raw. Does it stick out enough so that the censor might get it. Its the only place in the book I'm in doubt about on that score. Please let me know right away.

(2.) Please have <u>no quotations from any critics whatsoever on the jacket</u> – simply your own blurb on the back and don't give away too much of the idea – especially don't connect Daisy + Gatsby (I need the quality of surprise there) Please be <u>very general.</u>

. . . .

As Ever Scott

* * *

Jan. 20, 1925
Dear Scott:

I am terribly rushed for time so I am answering your letter as briefly and rapidly as I can,- but I will have a chance to write to tell you the news, etc. etc., soon.

First as to the jazz history of the world:- that did jar on me unfavorably. And yet in a way it pleased me as a tour de force, but one not completely successful. Upon the whole, I should probably have objected to it in the first place except that I felt you needed something there in the way of incident, something special. But if you have something else, I would take it out.

You are beginning to get me worried about the scene in Myrtle's apartment for you have spoken of it several times. It never occurred to me to think there was any objection to it. I am sure there is none. No censor could make an issue on that,- nor I think on anything else in the book.

I will be sure not to use any quotations and I will make it very general indeed, because I realize that not much ought to be said about the story. I have not thought what to say, but we might say something very brief which gave the impression that nothing need any longer be said.

I certainly hope the proofs have got to you and that you have been at work on them for some time. If not you had better cable. They were sent first-class mail. The first lot on December 27th and the second lot on December 30th.

Yours,

P.S. The mysterious hand referred to in the immemorial phrase is that of the typesetter.

* * *

Fitzgerald annotated this postcard (Princeton University Library).

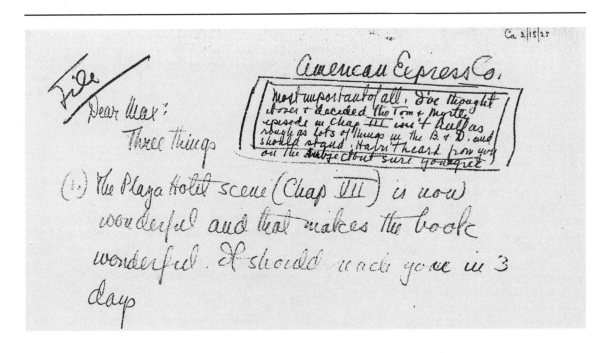

Ca 2/15/25

Dear Max:
    Three things

American Express Co.

Most important of all, I've thought
it over + decided the Tom + Myrtle
episode in Chap III isn't as
rough as lots of things in the B. & D. and
should stand. Haven't heard from you
on the subject but sure you agree

(1) The Plaza Hotel scene (Chap VII) is now
wonderful and that makes the book
wonderful. It should reach you in 3
days

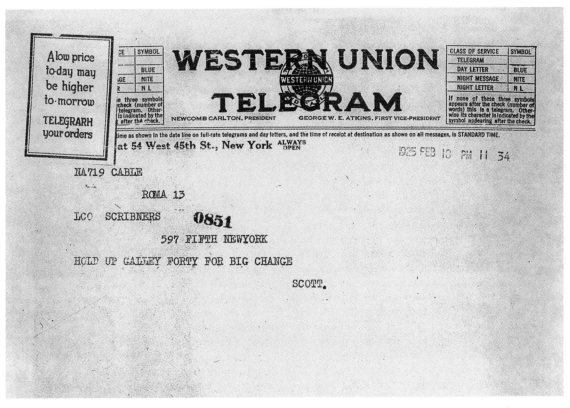

	SYMBOL			CLASS OF SERVICE	SYMBOL
CE				TELEGRAM	
	BLUE			DAY LETTER	BLUE
GE	NITE			NIGHT MESSAGE	NITE
R	N L			NIGHT LETTER	N L

WESTERN UNION TELEGRAM

NEWCOMB CARLTON, PRESIDENT   GEORGE W. E. ATKINS, FIRST VICE-PRESIDENT

A low price to-day may be higher to-morrow

TELEGRARH your orders

three symbols check (number of telegram. Otherwise is indicated by the after the check.

If none of these three symbols appears after the check (number of words) this is a telegram. Otherwise its character is indicated by the symbol appearing after the check.

time as shown In the date line on full-rate telegrams and day letters, and the time of receipt at destination as shown on all messages, is STANDARD TIME.

at 54 West 45th St., New York ALWAYS OPEN

1925 FEB 18 PM 11 34

NA719 CABLE

ROMA 13

LCO SCRIBNERS   **0851**

597 FIFTH NEWYORK

HOLD UP GALLEY FORTY FOR BIG CHANGE

SCOTT.

Fitzgerald's letter and cable in which he alerts Scribners that he is changing the Plaza Hotel confrontation between Jay Gatsby and Tom Buchanan (Princeton University Library)

Hotel des Princes,
Rome, Italy.

January 24th. = 1925
(But address the American Express
Co. because its damn cold here
and we may leave any day.

Dear Max:

This is a most important letter so I'm having it typed. Guard it as your life.

1) Under a separate cover I'm sending the first part of the proof. While I agreed with the general suggestions in your first letters I differ with you in others. I <u>want</u> Myrtle Wilson's breast ripped off —its exactly the thing, I think, and I don't want to chop up the good scenes by too much tinkering. When Wolfshiem says "sid" for "said", it's deliberate. "Orgastic" is the adjective from "orgasm" and it expresses exactly the intended ecstasy. It's not a bit dirty. I'm much more worried about the disappearance of Tom and Myrtle on Galley 9– I think it's all right but I'm not sure. If it isn't please wire and I'll send correction.

2) Now about the page proof —under certain conditions never mind sending them (unless, of course, there's loads of time, which I suppose there isn't. I'm keen for late March or early April publication)

<u>The conditions are two.</u>

a) That someone reads it <u>very carefully twice</u> to see that every one of my inserts are put in correctly. There are so many of them that I'm in terror of a mistake.

b) That no changes <u>whatsoever</u> are made in it except in the case of a misprint so glaring as to be certain, and that only by you.

If there's some time left but not enough for the double mail send them to me and I'll simply wire O.K. which will save two weeks. However don't postpone for that. In any case send me the page proof as usual just to see.

3) Now, many thanks for the deposit. Two days after wiring you I had a cable from Reynolds that he'd sold two stories of mine for a total of $3,750. but before that I was in debt to him and after turning down the ten thousand dollars from College Humor* I was afraid to borrow more from him until he'd made a sale. I won't ask for any more from you until the book has earned it. My guess is that it will sell about 80,000 copies but I may be wrong. Please thank Mr. Charles Scribner for me. I bet he thinks he's caught another John Fox** now for sure. Thank God for John Fox. It would have been awful to have had no predecessor

4) This is very important. Be sure not to give away <u>any</u> of my plot in the blurb. Don't give away that Gatsby <u>dies</u> or is a <u>parvenu</u> or a <u>crook</u> or anything. Its a part of the suspense of the book that all these things are in doubt until the end. You'll watch this won't you? And remember about having no quotations from critics on the jacket – <u>not even about my other books</u>!

. . . .

Do answer every question and keep this letter until the proof comes. Let me know how you like the changes. I miss seeing you, Max, more than I can say.

As ever,
Scott

*For serial rights.
**Nineteenth-century Scribner author.

* * *

Feb. 1st, <u>1925</u>

Dear Max:

Here's another correction for part one of the galley which must have reached you by now. This in <u>very</u> important so will you see that its put in right. Its second individual correction I've sent. Did the first arrive. I'm sorry to trouble you so much. Did the first arrive?

. . . .

Wouldn't it be safer to make this insert in the galley if not too late. I'm afraid if its made in the page proof it might get in the wrong place + spoil the rythm of the prose. I know I'm fussy as an old woman but I feel horribly helpless so far away.

The rest of the corrected proof will be sent to you in about 6 days.

As Ever
Scott

* * *

New Adress { Hotel Tiberius
            { Capri

18 February 1925

Dear Max:

After six weeks of uninterrupted work the proof is finished and the last of it goes to you this afternoon. On the whole its been very successful labor

(1.) I've brought Gatsby to life

(2.) I've accounted for his money

(3.) I've fixed up the two weak chapers (VI and VII)

(4.) I've improved his first party

(5.) I've broken up his long narrative in Chap. VIII

This morning I wired you to <u>hold up the galley of chap 40</u>. The correction —and God! its important because in my other revision I made Gatsby look too mean—is enclosed herewith. Also some corrections for the page proof.

We're moving to Capri. We hate Rome. I'm behind financially and have to write three short stories. Then I try another play, and by June, I hope, begin my new novel.

Had long interesting letters from Ring and John Bishop. Do tell me if all corrections have been received. I'm worried

I hope you're setting publication date at first possible moment.

* * *

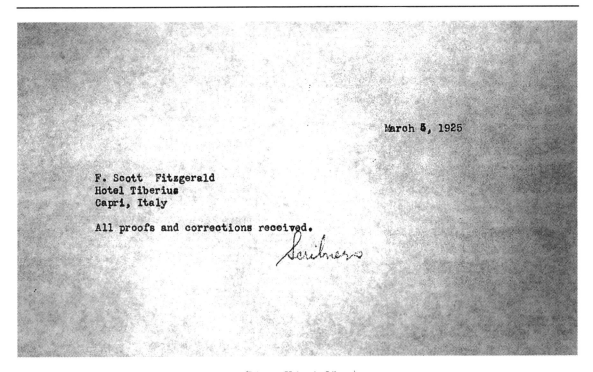

March 5, 1925

F. Scott Fitzgerald
Hotel Tiberius
Capri, Italy

All proofs and corrections received.

Scribners

(Princeton University Library)

Feb. 24, 1925

Dear Scott:

I congratulate you on resisting the $10,000. I don't see how you managed it. But it delighted us, for otherwise book publication would have been deferred until too late in the spring. Now we are getting the first twenty-five or so galleys into pages with the additional changes you wrote about in your notes (one dated February first) incorporated; and I'm expecting the other galleys any day.- Don't worry because they have not come yet. They travel much more slowly than do letters. Galley 40 I shall hold out for the later changes of which you wrote. Those you have made do wonders for Gatsby,- in making him visible and palpable. You're right about the danger of meddling with the high spots—instinct is the best guide there. I'll have the proofs read twice, once by Dunn and once by Roger,* and shall allow no change unless it is certain the printer has blundered. I know the whole book so well myself that I could hardly decide wrongly. But I won't decide anything if there is ground for doubt.

Charles Dunn and Roger Burlingame, Scribners editors.

* * *

March 19, 1925

Dear Scott:

This is not a letter, but a sort of bulletin. All the correc-tions came safely, I am sure, and all have been rightly made. I had to make two little changes: there are no tides in Lake Superior, as Rex Lardner told me and I have verified the fact, and this made it necessary to attribute the danger of the yacht to wind. The other change was where in describing the dead Gatsby in the swimming pool, you speak of the "leg of transept". I ought to have caught this on the galleys. The transept is the cross formation in a church and surely you could not figuratively have referred to this. I think you must have been thinking of a transit, which is an engineer's instru-ment. It is really not like compasses, for it rests upon a tripod, but I think the use of the word transit would be psychologi-cally correct in giving the impression of the circle being drawn. I think this must be what you meant, but anyway it could not have been transept. You will now have page proofs and you ought to deal with these two points and make them as you want them, and I will have them changed in the next printing. Otherwise we found only typographical errors of a perfectly obvious kind. I think the book is a won-der and Gatsby is now most appealing, effective and real, and yet altogether original. We publish on April 10th.

. . . .

As ever,

* * *

155

March 25, 1925

Dear Scott:

. . . .

As for your own book,- it is a magical book. I have not read it through again, but all your corrections I read in the context. All my criticisms vanished before them. I am sure that all corrections came, and both Dunn and Roger read the final page proof and compared it with the corrected proof. Can't you send us a new picture of yourself? The royalty report I enclose,- regretfully; but Gatsby ought to do much for his creator.

* * *

Hotel Tiberius, Capri

31 March 1925

Dear Max:

As the day approaches my nervousness increases. Tomorrow is the 1st and your wire say the 10th. I'll be here until the 25th, probably later, so if the book prospers I'll expect some sort of cable before I leave for Paris.

. . . .

Yours in a Tremble
Scott

* * *

April 10th

Dear Max:

The book comes out today and I am overcome with fears and forebodings. Supposing women didn't like the book because it has no important woman in it, and critics didn't like it because it dealt with the rich and contained no peasants borrowed out of Tess in it and set to work in Idaho? Suppose it didn't even wipe out my debt to you— why it will have to sell 20,000 copies even to do that! In fact all my confidence is gone–I wouldn't tell you this except for the fact that by the this reaches you the worst will be known. I'm sick of the book myself–I wrote it over at least five times and I still feel that what should be the strong scene (in the Hotel) is hurried and ineffective. Also the last chapter, the burial, Gatsby's father ect is faulty. Its too bad because the first five chapters and parts of the 7th and 8th are the best things I've ever done.

"The best since Paradise". God! if you you knew how discouraging that was. That was what Ring said in his letter together with some very complementary remarks. . . .

Now as to the changes I don't think I'll make any more for the present. Ring suggested the correction of certain errata–if you made the changes all right–if not let them go. Except on Page 209 old dim La Salle Street Station should be old dim Union Station and should be

changed in the second edition. Transit will do fine though of course I really meant compass. The page proofs arrived and seemed to be O.K. though I don't know how the printer found his way through those 70,000 corrections. The cover (jacket) came too and is a delight. Zelda is mad about it (incidently she is quite well again).

When you get this letter adress me c/o Guaranty Trust Co. 1 Rue des Italennes, Paris.

Another thing–I'm convinced that Myers* is all right but have him be sure and keep all trite phrases as "Surely the book of the Spring!" out of the advertising. That one is my pet abomination. Also to use no quotations except those of unqualified and exceptionally entheusiastic praise from eminent individuals. Such phrases as

"Should be on everyones summer list"

Boston Transcript

"Not a dull moment . . . a thoroughly sound solid piece of work"

havn't sold a copy of any book in three years. I thought your advertising for Ring was great.

. . . .

Life in New Cannan sounds more interesting than life in Plainfield. I'm sure anyhow that at least two critics Benet** + Mary Column will have heard about the book. I'd like her to like it–Benet's opinion is of no value whatsoever.

And thanks mightily for the $750.00 which swells my debt to over $6000.00

When should my book of short stories be in?

Scott

P. S.

I had, or rather saw, a letter from my uncle who had seen a preliminary announcement of the book. He said:

"It sounded as if it were very much like his others."

This is only a vague impression, of course, but I wondered if we could think of some way to advertise it so that people who are perhaps weary of assertive jazz and society novels might not dismiss it as "just another book like his others." I confess that today the problem baffles me–all I can think of is to say in general to avoid such phrases as "a picture of New York life" or "modern society"–though as that is exactly what the book is its hard to avoid them. The trouble is so much superficial trash has sailed under those banners. Let me know what you think

Scott

*Scribmers advertising manager.
**William Rose Benét

* * *

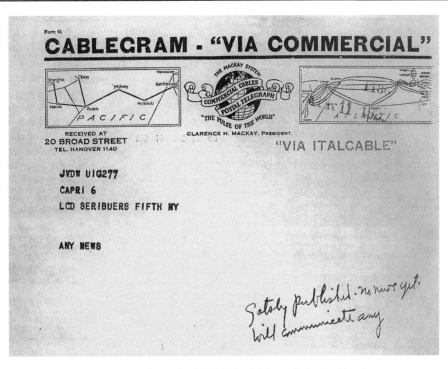

11 April 1925. The note is in Perkins's hand (Princeton University Library).

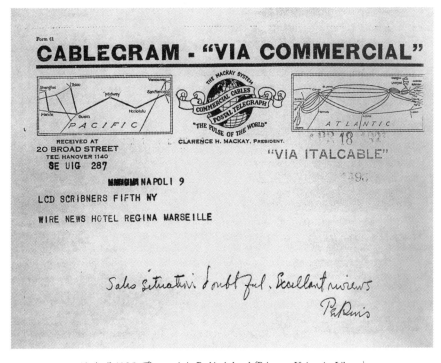

18 April 1925. The note is in Perkins's hand (Princeton University Library).

April 20, 1925

Dear Scott:

I wired you today rather discouragingly in the matter of the sales and I could send no qualifications in a cable. A great many of the trade have been very skeptical. I cannot make out just why. But one point is the small number of pages in the book,- an old stock objection which I thought we had got beyond. To attempt to explain to them that the way of writing which you have chosen and which is bound to come more and more into practice is one where a vast amount is said by implication, and that therefore the book is as full as it would have been if written to much greater length by another method, is of course utterly futile. The small number of pages, however, did in the end lead a couple of big distributors to reduce their orders immensely at the very last minute. The sale if up to the public and that has not yet had time to reveal itself fully. On the other hand, we have had a very good review, a very conspicuous one, in the Times, and an excellent one also in the Tribune from Isabelle Patterson. William Rose Benet has announced preliminary to a review in the Saturday Review, that this is distinctly your best book. And the individuals whom I encounter like Gilbert Seldes (who will write also), Van Wyck Brooks, John Marquand, John Bishop, think this too. Marquand and Seldes were both quite wild about it. These people understand it fully, which even the Times and Tribune reviewers did not.

I will send you anything that has much significance by cable. I know fully how this period must try you: it must be very hard to endure, because it is hard enough for me to endure. I like the book so much myself and see so much in it that its recognition and success mean more to me than anything else in sight at the present time,- I mean in any department of interest, not only that of literature. But it does seem to me from the comments of many who yet feel its enchantment, that it is over the heads of more people than you would probably suppose.

In the course of this week when they have had time to accumulate, I will get together ads. and reviews and send them on. The situation has really not developed sufficiently yet to say anything decisive, but you can at least have the satisfaction of knowing that I shall watch it with the greatest anxiety imaginable in anyone but the author.

Yours,

* * *

Early April 1925

Dear Max:

Your telegram depressed me–I hope I'll find better news in Paris and am wiring you from Lyons. There's nothing to say until I hear more. If the book fails commercially it will be from one of two reasons or both

1st The title is only fair, rather bad than good.

2nd And most important–the book contains no important woman character and women controll the fiction market at present. I don't think the unhappy end matters particularly.

It will have to sell 20,000 copies to wipe out my debt to you. I think it will do that all right–but my hope was it would do 75,000. This week will tell.

. . . .

In all events I have a book of good stories for this fall. Now I shall write some cheap ones until I've accumulated enough for my my next novel. When that is finished and published I'll wait and see. If it will support me with no more intervals of trash I'll go on as a novelist. If not I'm going to quit, come home, go to Hollywood and learn the movie business. I can't reduce our scale of living and I can't stand this financial insecurity. Anyhow there's no point in trying to be an artist if you can't do your best. I had my chance back in 1920 to start my life on a sensible scale and I lost it and so I'll have to pay the penalty. Then perhaps at 40 I can start writing again without this constant worry and interruption

Yours in great depression
Scott

* * *

April 25, 1925

Dear Scott:

I sent you just now a rather meaningless cable. The fact is that not enough time has passed to disclose much. I have been very keenly conscious of your inevitable anxiety–which I have myself largely shared I can tell you, on account of the early appearance of the enclosed review by Ruth Hale and the one from the World by a man of no importance–and I would have sent you a word, and tried to think of what I could say in a cable. But in reality there was nothing decisive to say. I enclose a lot of other reviews and while most of the reviewers seem rather to fumble with the book, as if they did not fully understand it, they praise it very highly, and better still, they all show a kind of excitement which they

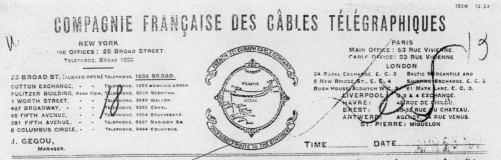

April 24, 1925

F. Scott Fitzgerald
Hotel Regina
Marseilles,France

Developments favorable   Reviews excellent   Must still wait

Perkins

(Princeton University Library)

COMPAGNIE FRANÇAISE DES CÂBLES TÉLÉGRAPHIQUES

The following *MESSAGE* is received *via* **FRENCH TELEGRAPH CABLE** subject to the terms and conditions printed on the back hereof, which are ratified and agreed to.

DWPL16

AVIGNON 12

LCD SCRIBNEKS FIFTH NYK

PLEASE WIRE APPROXIMATE NUMBER SOLD HOTEL CLOCHE DIJON

Ten Thousand. Reviews coming beginning.
Remember public need 3 week to know of book.

To reduce the risk of errors or delays, please file any answer to this message at one of the Company's own offices. Messengers may be summoned by Telephone for Cablegrams *FREE OF CHARGE.*

15 April 1925. The note is in Perkins's hand (Princeton University Library).

caught from its vitality. Of course none of the best people have reviewed yet and I have no doubt at all of their enthusiasm so that in the matter of reviews the situation will keep improving;- for people who will be heard from are those who will really understand and grasp it, and so far nobody has done that.

As to the sales situation, we have met a curious opposition in the trade.- Of course based upon an opposition they assume to exist in the public. But a very encouraging indication comes from Womrath in whose stores the popular reaction is first felt:- he ordered at first, 100. The next week he ordered in 25s, daily. In the next two days he ordered 100s and yesterday he ordered 200. Whenever I see anything of real significance, I will send you a wire.

At any rate, one thing I think, we can be sure of: that when the tumult and shouting of the rabble of reviewers and gossipers dies, "The Great Gatsby" will stand out as a very extraordinary book. Perhaps it's not perfect! It is one thing to ride a sleepy cob of a talent to perfection and quite another to master a wild young thoroughbred of a talent. That's the way I see it.

Yours,

* * *

Guaranty Trust Co.
Paris. May 1st

Dear Max:

There's no use for indignation against the long suffering public when even a critic who likes the book fails to be fundamentally held—that is Stallings who has written the only intelligent review so far*—but its been depressing to find how quick one is forgotten, especially unless you repeat yourself <u>ad nauseam</u>. Most of the reviewers floundered around in a piece of work that obviously they completely failed to understand and tried to give it reviews that committed them neither <u>pro</u> or <u>con</u> until some one of culture had spoken. Of course I've only seen the <u>Times</u> and the <u>Tribune</u>—and, thank God, Stallings, for I had begun to believe no one was even glancing at the book.

. . . .

Many Thanks to Mr. Scribner and to all the others and to you for all you've done for me and the book. The jacket was a hit anyhow

Scott

*Laurence Stallings's review appeared in the 22 April issue of the New York World.

* * *

Cugat's copy of the jacket painting. Gouache on paper (Arlyn Bruccoli Collection).

THE DUST JACKET

Celestial Eyes—from Metamorphosis to Masterpiece
Charles Scribner III

Little is known about Francis Cugat (or F. Coradel-Cugat): he was born in Spain in 1893 and raised in Cuba; he was the brother of orchestra leader Xavier Cugat; he worked in Hollywood as a designer for Douglas Fairbanks and as a technicolor consultant; he had a one-man New York show in 1942. No other Cugat book jackets have been identified.

Francis Cugat's painting for F. Scott Fitzgerald's *The Great Gatsby* is the most celebrated—and widely disseminated—jacket art in twentieth-century American literature, and perhaps of all time. After appearing on the first printing in 1925, it was revived more than a half-century later for the "Scribner Library" paperback edition in 1979; over a decade (and several million copies) later it may be seen in classrooms of virtually every high school and college throughout the country. Like the novel it embellishes, this Art Deco tour-de-force has firmly established itself as a classic. At the same time, it

160

Cugat's preliminary sketch of railroad scene. Charcoal with pen-and-ink, watercolor, and gouache on paper (Arlyn Bruccoli Collection).

Second, enlarged version of railroad scene. Charcoal with pen-and-ink, watercolor, and gouache on paper (Arlyn Bruccoli Collection).

represents a most unusual–in my view, unique–form of "collaboration" between author and jacket artist. Under normal circumstances, the artist illustrates a scene or motif conceived by the author; he lifts, as it were, his image from a page of the book. In this instance, however, the artist's image *preceded* the finished manuscript and Fitzgerald actually maintained that he had "written it into" his book.[1] But what precisely did he mean by this claim?

Cugat's rendition is not illustrative, but symbolic, even iconic: the sad, hypnotic, heavily outlined eyes of a woman beam like headlights through a cobalt night sky. Their irises are transfigured into reclining female nudes. From one of the eyes streams a green luminescent tear; brightly rouged lips complete the sensual triangle. No nose or other discernable facial contours are introduced in this celestial visage; a few dark streaks

across the sky (behind the title) suggest hairlines. Below, on earth, brightly colored carnival lights blaze before a metropolitan skyline.

It has been alleged that Fitzgerald's symbolic billboard eyes of Dr. T. J. Eckleburg derived from Cugat's jacket. Fitzgerald describes them as "blue and gigantic–their retinas[2] are one yard high. They look out of no face, but, instead, from a pair of enormous yellow spectacles which pass over a non-existent nose." If this hypothetical source is valid, then we are clearly not dealing here with a literal translation from graphic imagery into prose: there can be no mistaking of Cugat's seductive visage for the grotesque, bespectacled eyes of the optician's billboard. Yet each is, in its own way, both ethereal and mystical; each is explicitly abstracted from a face, in each case with the nose "edited out." As we would expect from a writer of

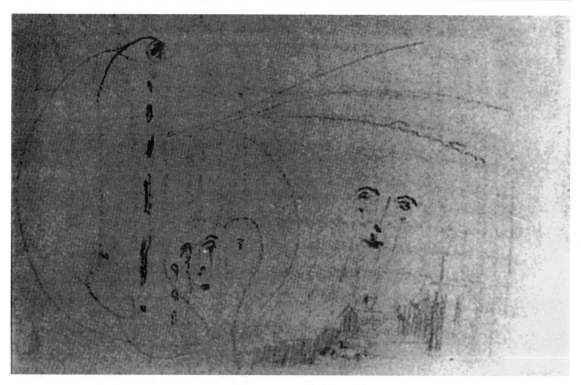

Sketch of face over house, with details of weeping eye. Pencil and crayon on paper (Arlyn Bruccoli Collection).

Fitzgerald's imagination, he thoroughly transforms his visual sources, or background images, into his own creation: that is to say, one symbol *evolves* into another.

To those who still find the derivation troublesome, an alternative has recently been proposed for Fitzgerald's acknowledged debt to Cugat: Nick Carraway's image of Daisy as the "girl whose disembodied face floated along the dark cornices and blinding signs" of New York at night.[3] This citation at the close of chapter four appears to correspond perfectly with the final jacket. But, at the same time, it raises the question of how far we may reasonably seek interrelations between the jacket art and the text of *Gatsby*. In other words, what did Cugat know of the novel before he illuminated its jacket; and what did the novelist know of Cugat's artwork before he completed his manuscript? Fortunately, Matthew J. Bruccoli's recent discovery of Cugat's preparatory studies and sketches for the design sheds new light on these questions as well as on the creative evolution of his iconographic masterpiece.

In the editor-author correspondence between Maxwell Perkins and Fitzgerald there are several references to the *Gatsby* jacket art. These comments are more intriguing than clarifying. The first occurs on April 1, 1924:

Perkins asks whether Fitzgerald has finally decided on a title for his new novel-in-progress so that Scribners might proceed to design a "wrap," or jacket, in anticipation of its publication on Scribners' fall list. (Fitzgerald's *Ledger* entry for that month begins "out of woods at last and starting novel."[4]) Six days later, Perkins writes that he does not like Fitzgerald's proposed title "Among the Ash Heaps and Millionaires" although he likes the general idea it seeks to convey: "The weakness is in the words 'Ash Heaps' which do not seem to me to be a sufficiently definite and concrete expression of that part of the idea." This reaction evidently prompts either a phone call or a meeting, and is followed by Fitzgerald's confessional letter of circa April 10th ("A few words more relative to our conversation this afternoon. . . .") in which he explains that he has "every hope + plan of finishing my novel in June" but that it may take "10 times that long." In any event, the new novel will be "a consciously artistic achievement + must depend on that as the first books did not." Perkins replies on the 16th: "The only thing is, that if we had a title which was likely, but by no means sure to be the title, we could prepare a cover and a wrap and hold them in readiness for use. In that way, we would gain several weeks if we should find that we were to have the book this fall. . . ."

Sketch of face over Long Island Sound. Pencil and crayon on paper (Arlyn Bruccoli Collection).

Sketch of face over New York skyline. Pencil, crayon, charcoal, and gouache on paper (Arlyn Bruccoli Collection).

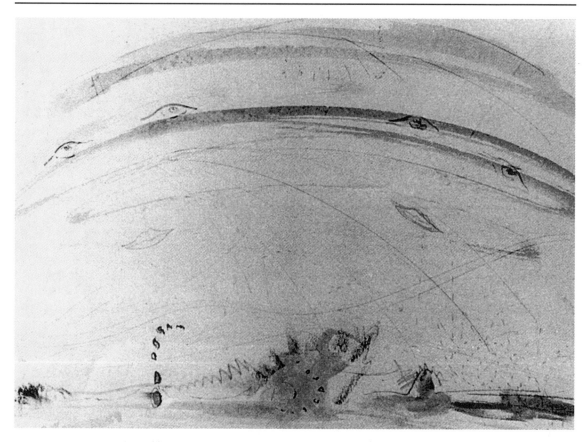

Study of faces over carnival lights. Pencil and watercolor on paper (Arlyn Bruccoli Collection).

On April 15th, Scott and Zelda decided to move to Europe. There is no further correspondence on the subject of a title or jacket art before they set sail in early May. The next written reference indicates a *fait accompli;* it appears in Fitzgerald's long itemized letter sent from France sometime in August. (Perkins acknowledged it on the 27th, and it took at least ten days for mail to travel by sea from the Villa Marie in St. Raphael to the Scribner offices in New York.) Item six: "For Christs sake don't give anyone that jacket you're saving for me. I've written it into the book." This seemingly straightforward request has provoked much speculation among scholars: what did he mean by "don't *give* anyone"? That Perkins should keep it secret? But that would nullify the very purpose in commissioning such art in advance, which was—then as now—to create promotional materials. The answer is simpler, and may be deduced from the context, or sequence, of the correspondence between editor and author.

In a letter of July 15th Perkins writes: "I suppose it will be here in a month or six weeks. . . . In any case,

your book could not now wisely be published this fall and the spring will be a good season with us because there is no other book of fiction that will have a large sale then. . . ." From these remarks, Fitzgerald must have inferred (correctly) that since his new novel had been taken off the "rush" list for fall 1924 and would not be published for at least another nine months, there was no longer a current need to have jacket art for its advance promotion. Perhaps he feared that Cugat's artwork might therefore be given to another book—or perhaps even to *Scribner's Magazine,* for which it would have made a striking poster—rather than being held in abeyance for several more months. Perkins immediately puts this worry to rest in his response of September 10th: "There is certainly not the slightest risk of our giving that jacket to anyone in the world but you. I wish the manuscript of the book would come, and I don't doubt it is something very like the best American novel." Two things are clear: that Perkins still had yet to read any of it, and that he would reserve for it the previously designed jacket art.

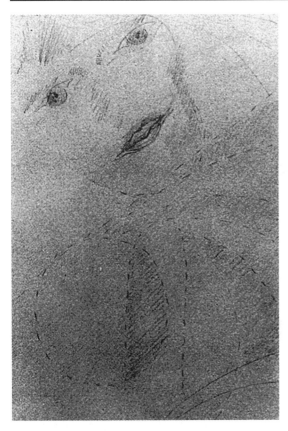

Study of face and geometric patterns. Pencil on paper (Arlyn Bruccoli Collection).

On October 27, Fitzgerald writes that he is finally sending *The Great Gatsby*. (He offers as an alternate title "Gold-hatted Gatsby.") He follows up a week or so later with a letter in which he says:

> I have now decided to stick to the title I put on the book. *Trimalchio in West Egg*. The only other titles that seem to fit it are *Trimalchio* and *On the Road to West Egg*. I had two others *Gold-hatted Gatsby* and *The High-bouncing Lover* but they seemed too light.

On November 14th Perkins replies that none of his Scribner colleagues likes the "Trimalchio" title, and urges him to change it. Significantly, he adds: "But if you do not change, you will have to leave that note off the wrap. Its presence would injure it too much;— and good as the wrap always seemed, it now seems a masterpiece for this book." Fitzgerald replies: "About the title. I'll try my best but I don't know what I can do. Maybe simply 'Trimalchio' or 'Gatsby.' In the former case I don't see why the note shouldn't go on the back." Fitzgerald's typescript no

longer exists; but the first set of the proofs is slugged "Trimalchio" at the top of each galley. We can only guess at the length and content of the note explaining Trimalchio's source in Petronius's *Satyricon*. That ancient Roman host of extravagantly decadent feasts did indeed offer a worthy prototype for Fitzgerald's Gatsby—but would readers or booksellers have been able to pronounce it, much less spell it?

Fitzgerald was never satisfied with the title *The Great Gatsby*. Yet when the first copy of the book arrived he wrote to Perkins that he "thought the new jacket was *great*." No doubt this concise compliment conveyed not only his approval of all its elements— illustration, flap copy, typography, and back ad—but also something of an inside joke. To the author, it was "new" in so far as it incorporated for the first time an actual title, from which Fitzgerald quoted the adjective—perhaps with pointed irony, since he had earlier denigrated to Perkins its titular connection with Jay Gatsby: "*The Great Gatsby* is weak because there's no emphasis even ironically on his greatness or lack of it. However, let it pass."

Was the jacket "new" to Fitzgerald in other ways? The payment card in the Scribner art files confirms that Cugat designed only one jacket, for which he was paid one hundred dollars. If the original jacket painting that Perkins had promised to save for Fitzgerald had in fact been replaced by a new one, there would be some indication of it on the card, as well as the payment of an additional fee to the artist. It is inconceivable that Perkins would have allowed such a substitution without further comment to the author after his written promise and, equally important, after his declaring the original design "a masterpiece." On the other hand, it is entirely conceivable that Fitzgerald had never seen Cugat's final, finished artwork, the magnificent gouache painting today preserved in the Princeton University Library.[5] Since there were at most a couple of weeks between the commission and Fitzgerald's departure to France, it is likely that what he had seen—and "written into the book"—was one or more of Cugat's preparatory sketches which were probably shown to him at Scribners for his comments before he set sail. We may now turn to the sketches themselves in search of a plausible scenario.

In the first, Cugat has rendered in charcoal and pen-and-ink, washed with watercolor and gouache, a scene of a train passing through a deserted depot amidst a bleak, grey landscape with distant hills. Over the green building at the far left a faint, crude image of a face emerges from the dark sky. Cugat proceeded to enlarge this sketch, altering

Sketch of nocturnal carnival. Crayon over oil on board (Arlyn Bruccoli Collection).

some of the architecture, transforming the central track into an undulating curve, and adding two significant elements that leave no doubt as to the connection between this watercolor and Fitzgerald's novel-in-progress. The red coal cars are lettered "Long Island Railroad," and over this ashen scene float, like so many balloons, a series of sad, feminine eyes and mouths—all without noses or other physionomic features. Signed at the bottom right, this sheet clearly represents a *modello,* or demonstration piece, for the advance jacket and derives its conception from Fitzgerald's originally proposed title, "Among the Ash Heaps and Millionaires." Cugat probably based this scene on an oral briefing—either by the art director or by Perkins himself—that included Fitzgerald's explanation to Perkins of the "valley of ashes," as it would eventually appear in chapter two: "About half way between West Egg and New York the motor road hastily joins the railroad and runs beside it for a quarter of a mile, so as to shrink away from a certain desolate area of land. . . ." The fact that in Cugat's sketch there is no indication of a billboard, much less the bespectacled eyes of Doctor Eckleburg, suggests that Fitzgerald had yet to conceive his optical symbol—or at least, had yet to share it with either his editor or the artist. We are left then with the enticing possibility that

Fitzgerald's arresting image was originally prompted by Cugat's fantastic apparitions over the valley of ashes; in other words, that the author derived his inventive metamorphosis from a recurrent theme of Cugat's trial jackets, one which the artist himself was to reinterpret and transform through subsequent drafts.

The next stage, a quick pencil and crayon sketch, adapts structural elements (rooflines, poles, automobile) from the "valley of ashes" watercolors, but the geography is unclear. The emphasis has shifted upward to the celestial eyes—now weeping—with outlined eyebrows, rouged lips, and what appear to be asymmetrical nostrils completing the hovering visage. A second face, or perhaps alternate pose, is sketched at the left and framed by a schematic heart that devolves into a sort of calligraphic kite's tail. Above, Cugat has drawn an enlarged version of the left eye, from which streams the broken, staccato trail of a tear, and which serves as the starting point for an expansive, purely abstract sweep of a circle breaking into three radiating lines—a variation on motifs already suggested by the cursive improvisations in the sky above the valley of ashes.

The focus on a single weeping eye links this rough draft with Cugat's next, and innovative, conception of the jacket: the pencil and crayon drawing of the female countenance, now reduced to one eye with parted red lips and viewed in profile—as he has noted on the sheet. The schematic tear falls into the Long Island Sound, with the New York skyline (labeled "cityscape") in the background and five prominent pilings directly below. Cugat's anatomical license is reminiscent of Egyptian hieroglyphics, if not Picasso. His invention—a beacon-like and beckoning eye of what Shakespeare called "the constant image" of the beloved—suggests an iconographic prefiguration of that "enchanted object" of Gatsby's, the green light "of colossal significance" at the end of Daisy's dock which had seemed as near to her "as the star to the moon."

The next and penultimate version is rendered in pencil, crayon, charcoal and gouache. Cugat here returns to his original image of a celestial visage seen straight on. Two full, bright blue eyes now hover over the expanded cityscape. Their hooded gaze alone expresses their sorrow; the trailing tear is integrated into a pattern of lines that punctuate the urban sky like so many flares or shooting stars. At some point between this sketch and the finished gouache painting the decision was made to enliven the somber skyline of bricks and mortar by superimposing a dazzling carnival of lights, as though Manhattan had been relegated to a backdrop for riotous Coney Island. The remaining three working sketches (as distinct from *modelli,* or display models) offer glimpses into this final transmutation. The first is a graphic impromptu or fantasia. Through tentative, faint pencil outlines and quick broad strokes of colored wash Cugat explores the dramatic juxtaposition of the heavenly serene faces, alternatively inclined, and the pyrotechnical explosion of swirling lights below. On a separate sheet, in pencil, he further refined the idealized physiognomy, enlarging the pupils and filling out the sensual lips; below, he improvised in dotted rhythms his basic geometric motifs—the circle, a steep parabola, and cascading arcs. Then, in a murky oil and crayon sketch, he experimented with the background from which his light show was to burst forth. In the center we find again the schematic Ferris wheel which in the final gouache would be suggested by an incomplete series of yellow bursts.

Cugat's carnival imagery is especially intriguing in view of Fitzgerald's pervasive use of light motifs throughout his novel; specifically, in metaphors for the latter-day Trimalchio, whose parties were illuminated by "enough colored lights to make a Christmas tree of Gatsby's enormous garden." Nick sees "the whole corner of the peninsula . . . blazing with light" from Gatsby's house "lit from tower to cellar." When he tells Gatsby that his place "looks like the World's Fair," Gatsby proposes that they "go to Coney Island." Fitzgerald had already introduced his amusement-park symbolism in his short story "Absolution." Written in 1923 as part of an early draft of the novel and published separately in 1924, it was originally intended to serve as the prologue illustrating an important facet of the Midwestern, Catholic youth of the central character who eventually developed into Jay Gatsby. At the conclusion of the story, a deranged priest encourages the guilt-ridden boy to go see an amusement park—"a thing like a fair only much more glittering" with "a big wheel made of lights turning in the air." But "don't get too close," he cautions, "because if you do you'll only feel the heat and the sweat and the life." The evocation of this passage in Cugat's jacket design suggests that someone had conveyed to the artist the symbolic light motif that defined Gatsby's life.[6]

Daisy's face, says Nick, was "sad and lovely with bright things in it, bright eyes and a bright passionate mouth." In Cugat's final painting, her celestial eyes enclose reclining nudes and her streaming tear is green—like the light "that burns all night" at the end of her dock, reflected in the water of the Sound that separates her from Gatsby. What Fitzgerald in fact drew directly from Cugat's art and "wrote into" the novel must of course remain an open question. What is beyond doubt is that Perkins hit the mark when, having finally read the completed typescript, he declared the jacket "a masterpiece." Yet Cugat's name never appears again in the Scribner art file. He was not a regular contributor to Scribners. Who commissioned him? Nowhere is Cugat ever mentioned by either Fitzgerald or Perkins. The credit must almost certainly go to some anonymous angel in the Scribner art department.

On the art file card, there is a handwritten notation that Cugat's gouache painting for *Gatsby* (mistakenly described as a watercolor: it does indeed look like one) was given to Fitzgerald on April 2, 1927. If so, he either gave it back to his publisher or left it behind when he returned home to Delaware, where he was struggling to make progress on the new novel that would become *Tender Is the Night.*[7]

Five days later, on April 7th, Perkins wrote to Fitzgerald: "I do not want to harass you about your book, which might be bad for it. But if we could by any possibility have the title, and some text, and enough of an idea to make an effective wrap, by the middle of April, we could get out a dummy. And even if all these things had to be changed, it would be worth doing this." We come full circle. April is not always the cruelest month. Three years earlier, Fitzgerald had planted with Perkins "enough of an idea to make an effective wrap." And reaped a unique visual harvest.

—This essay was separately published in 1991 to celebrate the critical edition of The Great Gatsby.

Notes

1. The Fitzgerald-Perkins correspondence is preserved in the Charles Scribner's Sons Archives at the Princeton University Library; most of the letters are published in J. Kuehl and J. R. Bryer, eds., *Dear Scott/Dear Max* (New York: Scribners, 1971). For a complete discussion of the composition and publications of the novel, see Matthew J. Bruccoli, ed., *The Great Gatsby* (Critical Edition; London and New York: Cambridge University Press, 1991). For biographical background, see Bruccoli, *Some Sort of Epic Grandeur: The Life of F. Scott Fitzgerald* (New York: Harcourt Brace Jovanovich, 1981).

2. Fitzgerald was referring to *irises* or *pupils*.

3. This observation was made by Mary Jo Tate.

4. Bruccoli, ed., *F. Scott Fitzgerald's Ledger* (Washington: Bruccoli Clark/NCR Microcard Editions, 1973).

5. Cugat liked his work so well that he painted a copy for himself (Arlyn Bruccoli Collection).

6. For an analysis of light imagery and religious metaphors in Fitzgerald's work, see Joan M. Allen, *Candles and Carnival Lights: The Catholic Sensibility of F. Scott Fitzgerald* (New York: NYU Press, 1978), especially pp. 93–116.

7. Decades later, my cousin George Schieffelin discovered it at Scribners in a trash can of publishing "dead matter" and preserved it for posterity. Eventually I inherited the painting, enjoyed it at home for several years, then donated it to Princeton University for its graphic arts collection.

* * *

THE DETAILS IN *THE GREAT GATSBY*

F. Scott Fitzgerald's classic fictions are accepted as documents of American social history by readers all over the world in every printed language. The Great Gatsby is read as a record of American life at a certain time and place. Gatsby is more real than Calvin Coolidge. Yet the 1925 first printing was flawed by incorrect details.

Getting It Right
Matthew J. Bruccoli

The decision to emend an internal error can be especially difficult because the distinction between intentional and unintentional inconsistencies may not be as clear as for verifiable external errors. In Chapter I of *Gatsby*, set in June 1922, Nick records Daisy's statement that her daughter is three years old. Daisy married Tom Buchanan in June 1919. If her child is indeed three, then Daisy was nine months pregnant at her wedding. The emendation of Pammy Buchanan's age to two is necessary in Chapter I. Determined exegetes might challenge this correction by arguing that the age of the child is a clue, planted by Fitzgerald, to Daisy's premarital promiscuity or even an indication that Pammy is Gatsby's child. Gatsby was sent to overseas in 1917 after he "took Daisy one still October night," and Tom did not meet Daisy until 1919; therefore, the father of her three-year-old child would have had to be some unidentified lover. It might also be asserted that Daisy's mistake in Pammy's age was intended by Fitzgerald to indicate her indifference to the child. The best explanation is that Fitzgerald fumbled his arithmetic, as he did in other instances. Further evidence for attributing this crux to authorial inadvertence is provided by Nick's indication in Chapter IV that, in the summer of 1922, Daisy has been married for five years ("He had waited five years and bought a mansion") and for four years in Chapter VI ("After she had obliterated four years").

In Chapter I Nick states that he "came back from the East last autumn"—that is, after Gatsby's murder, which occurred around Labor Day 1922. At the end of the novel Nick remarks that he remembers the events of the day of the murder "after two years." This inconsistency is probably Fitzgerald's lapse; but it is barely possible that he added a year to the time scheme to account for the time Nick was writing his recollections.

The oculist's billboard in *Gatsby*'s valley of ashes was presumably invented, but Fitzgerald's description includes a correctable error: "The eyes of Doctor T. J. Eckleburg are blue and gigantic—their retinas are one yard high." Impossible—the retina is at the back of the eye. Fitzgerald meant *pupils* or *irises*—probably irises. It has been objected that emendation here is improper because the editor is required to decide between two possible corrections—*pupils* or *irises*. The selection of either correct reading is preferable to perpetuating a distracting error. It has also been claimed that since the novel is narrated by Nick Carraway, this and other factual errors characterize him and bear on the question of his reliability. According to this perverse argument, some of Nick's errors may have been deliberately planted by Fitzgerald and should therefore be retained. Nevertheless, it is impossible to explain why Nick's misuse of *retinas* would have been meaningfully intended by Fitzgerald. The claim that the author may have liked the sound of *retinas* is unsatisfactory.[1]

Putative authorial errors can be deliberate and meaningful. A geographical crux in *Gatsby* involves the character named Biloxi who is "from Biloxi, Tennessee." There is no Biloxi in Tennessee, although there is a Biloxi in Mississippi. It is remotely possible that Fitzgerald was characterizing this rather mysterious figure by means of a geographical absurdity. Such problems are especially tricky in editing Fitzgerald. Because he had trouble getting things right, it is difficult to credit him with purposefully getting things wrong. Gatsby's claim to be a midwesterner from San Francisco indicates his autobiographical unreliability and should be retained; but many readers have regarded it as Fitzgerald's blunder.

When Edmund Wilson edited *The Great Gatsby* in 1941 he emended the celebrated line "Gatsby believed in the green light, the orgastic future, that year by year recedes before us." He subsequently explained: "The word *orgastic,* on the last page I took to be Scott's mistake for *orgiastic*—he was very unreliable about words." But Fitzgerald's intention is certain. Perkins had queried *orgastic,* and Fitzgerald replied that "it expresses exactly the intended ecstasy." Wilson's emendation to "orgiastic future" became the standard reading in later editions of the novel.

Fitzgerald is regarded as an orthographic phenomenon on the basis of his manuscripts ("yatch," "apon," "facinating"); but he, not unreasonably, expected proofreaders to do their jobs. Because of the scores of misspellings and usage errors printed in *The Side of Paradise* (1920), Fitzgerald's career was launched with the stigma of irresponsibility or illiteracy that remained attached to him and has influenced editorial thinking about his work. Wilson hyperbolically described that first novel as "one of the most illiterate books of any merit ever published (a fault which the publisher's wretched proof-reading apparently made no effort to correct)." Assessing the extent of Scribners' responsibility for textual details is essential to establishing policy for re-editing Fitzgerald.

Fitzgerald's sense of direction was unreliable, and his arithmetic was approximate—especially in calculating the ages of characters. These handicaps do not diminish his genius—which did not depend on navigation or mathematics—but they blemished his texts and provided ammunition for detractors.

Fitzgerald was not indifferent to the errors in his published work and their effects on his reputation.

Despite the close personal and literary relationship between Fitzgerald and Perkins, the now-legendary editor did not take responsibility for vetting Fitzgerald's facts. Charles Scribner, Jr., the former head of the house, wrote: "Perkins was totally useless when it came to copy editing or correcting a text. Such details meant very little to him. Consequently, the early editions of books such as Scott Fitzgerald's *The Great Gatsby* were textually corrupt to a nauseating degree." Since the edited setting-copy typescript and the master galleys for *Gatsby* have not survived, there is no record of the queries Perkins or other Scribners editors may have made for Fitzgerald to consider. Malcolm Cowley attributed the errors in Fitzgerald's books to Perkins's "aristocratic disregard for details so long as a book was right in its feeling for life."

Fitzgerald was a painstaking reviser who polished his work through multiple drafts and layers of typescript; because of his custom of revising and rewriting in proof, the production stages of *Gatsby* and *Tender* were rushed. In *Gatsby,* which was rewritten in galleys, Scribners' ability to make proof queries and Fitzgerald's power to make final corrections were restricted by the time required for boat mail between New York and Italy. If Fitzgerald received the reset galleys or page proofs, it was after the book had been published.

Fitzgerald's annotated copy of *Gatsby* includes some forty revisions and corrections; the military units in which Nick and Gatsby served are altered; the hotel in Louisville is corrected from the *Muhlbach* to the *Sealbach* (i.e., the *Seelbach*). Corrections were made in the second printing of the novel at Fitzgerald's instruction: St. Olaf's (i.e., St. Olaf) was moved from *northern* to *southern* Minnesota.

Ring Lardner sent Fitzgerald corrections on 24 March 1925:

> . . . I acted as volunteer proof reader and gave Max a brief list of what I thought were errata. On Pages 31 and 46 you spoke of the news-stand on the *lower level,* and the cold waiting room on the *lower level* of the Pennsylvania Station. There ain't any lower level at the station and I suggested substitute terms for same. On Page 82, you had the guy driving his car under the elevated at Astoria, which isn't Astoria, but Long Island City. On Page 118 you had a tide in Lake Superior and on Page 209 you had the Chicago, Milwaukee & St. Paul running out of the La Salle Street Station. These things are trivial, but some of the critics pick on trivial errors for lack of anything else to pick on.

WRITING *THE GREAT GATSBY*

The Queensboro Bridge connects 59th Street and Second Avenue in Manhattan with Long Island City in Queens.
The bridge spans the East River and Blackwell's Island.

Only the tides and the La Salle Street Station were corrected. The waiting room in Pennsylvania Station was in the main level; but the Long Island Railroad had a ticket counter below the waiting room, which Nick refers to as "the lower level."

The "Astoria" reading is a laboratory specimen of Fitzgerald's geographical lapses and provides a test case for the rationale of factual emendation in his work. The Queensboro Bridge crosses the East River between Manhattan's 59th Street and Long Island City (which is not a city, but a section of the borough to Queens). The Queensboro Bridge does not connect with Astoria (another section of Queens). It might be imagined that Fitzgerald liked the sound of "Astoria" and deliberately substituted Astoria for Long Island City, or that Astoria was intended as an oblique reference to John Jacob Astor and therefore to the history of great American fortunes. Other frivolous suppositions might be offered. The obvious explanation is that Fitzgerald did not know the name of the section of Queens he had frequently driven through between fall 1922 and spring 1924–an explanation that is consistent with other place-name confusions in his work. There is no evidence that Fitzgerald purposefully moved the bridge or meaningfully renamed the section of Queens. The fictional characters are in the real borough of Queens crossing the real Queensboro Bridge into the real borough of Manhattan.* Fitzgerald did not make the correction in his marked copy of the novel.

Gatsby is described as "beating his way along the south shore of Lake Superior as a clam-digger and salmon-fisher." There are no clams or salmon in Lake Superior, but emendation to "a deck-hand and trout-fisher" would be an improper intervention. Fitzgerald's readings must be retained here at the risk of misinforming readers about the fishery resources of the Great Lakes.

–Excerpted from "Getting It Right," in *Essays in Honor of William B. Todd*, compiled by Warner Barnes and Larry Carver, edited by Dave Oliphant (Copyright 1991 by Harry Ransom Humanities Research Center, The University of Texas at Austin).

Notes

1. The Cambridge University Press critical edition of *The Great Gatsby* retains the unemended readings "retinas" and "Astoria" because two of the Trustees of the Fitzgerald estate exercised their contractual right of approval and overruled the third Trustee, the General Editor. He became increasingly ashamed of his capitulation and subsequently resigned as editor of the edition.

2. In 1926 Ernest Hemingway sent Fitzgerald a parody description of *The Sun Also Rises:* "The hero, like Gatsby, is a Lake Superior Salmon Fisherman. (There are no salmon in Lake Superior)"; Bruccoli, *Fitzgerald and Hemingway* (New York: Carroll & Graf, 1994), p. 59. The lake trout may have been locally known as "land-locked salmon."

* * *

FITZGERALD'S STYLE

The Great Gatsby *marked an advance in every way over Fitzgerald's previous work. If he could develop so rapidly in the five years since* This Side of Paradise, *if he could write so brilliantly before he was thirty, his promise seemed boundless. Instead of addressing the reader, as he had done in* The Beautiful and Damned, *Fitzgerald utilized the resources of style to convey the meanings of* The Great Gatsby. *The values of the story are enhanced through imagery as detail is used with poetic effect. Thus the description of the Buchanans' house reveals how Fitzgerald's images stimulate the senses: "The lawn started at the beach and ran toward the front door for a quarter of a mile, jumping over sun-dials and brick walks and burning gardens—finally when it reached the house drifting up the side in bright vines as though from the momentum of its run." In his richest prose there is an impression of movement; here the lawn runs, jumps, and drifts. Again and again, sentences are made memorable by a single word—often a color word, as in "now the orchestra is playing yellow cocktail music."*

The technique in Gatsby *is scenic and symbolic. There are scenes and descriptions that have become touchstones of American prose: the first description of Daisy and Jordan, Gatsby's party, the shirt display, the guest list, Nick's recollection of the Midwest. Within these scenes Fitzgerald endows details with so much suggestiveness that they acquire symbolic force to extend the meanings of the story.*

The elevated structure at Long Island City, Queens, where Gatsby shows the motorcycle policeman his card from the commissioner

> . . . What little I've accomplished has been by the most laborious and uphill work, and I wish now I'd *never* relaxed or looked back-but said at the end of *The Great Gatsby:* "I've found my line-from now on this comes first. This is my immediate duty-without this I am nothing.". . .
>
> —F. Scott Fitzgerald to Frances Scott Fitzgerald, 12 June 1940

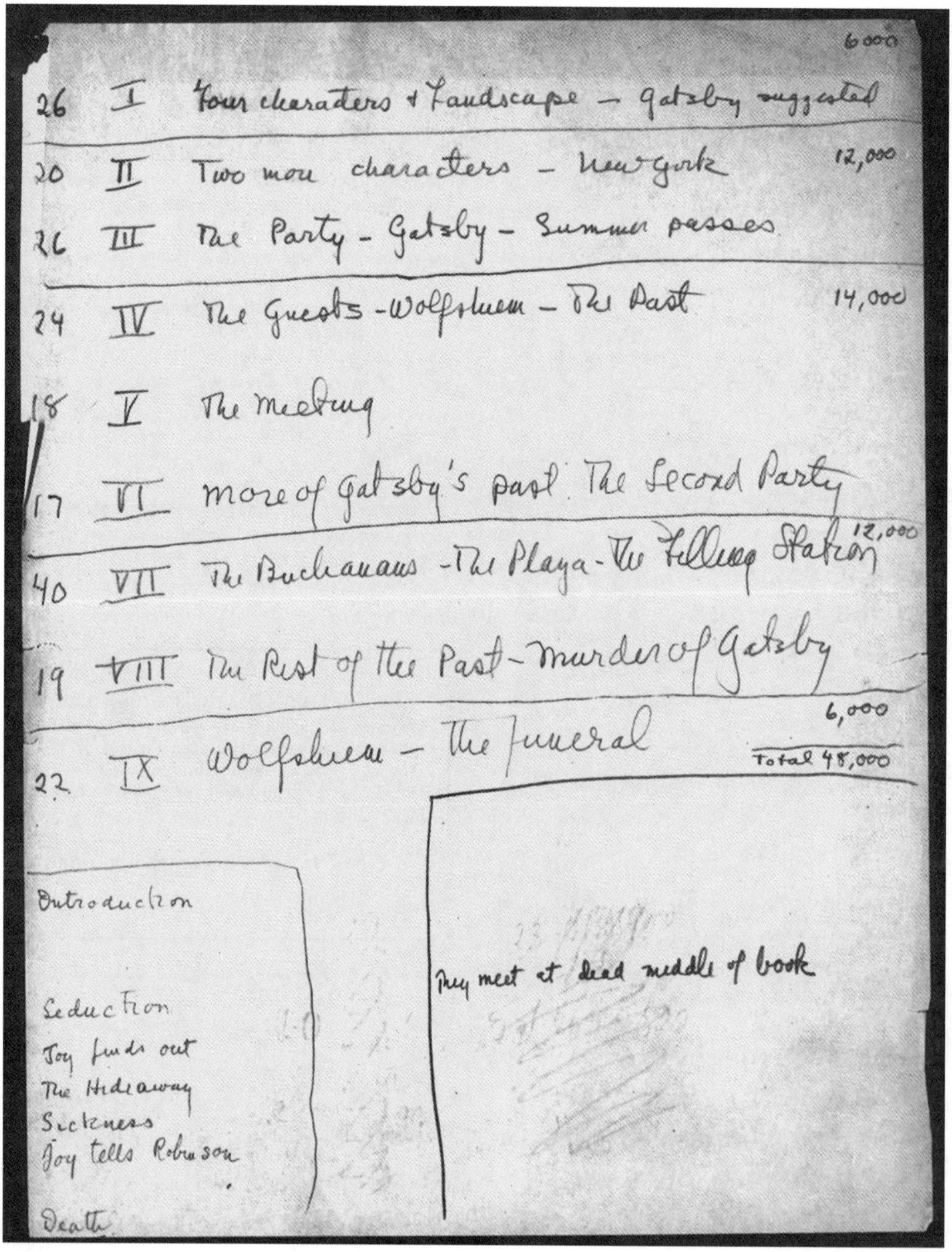

6000

26	I	Four characters + Landscape — Gatsby suggested	
20	II	Two more characters — New York	12,000
26	III	The Party — Gatsby — Summer passes	
24	IV	The Guests — Wolfshiem — The Past	14,000
18	V	The meeting	
17	VI	More of Gatsby's past. The Second Party	
40	VII	The Buchanans — The Plaza — The Filling Station	12,000
19	VIII	The Rest of the Past — Murder of Gatsby	
22	IX	Wolfshiem — The Funeral	6,000

Total 48,000

Introduction

Seduction
Joy finds out
The Hideaway
Sickness
Joy tells Robinson

Death

They meet at dead middle of book

Outline for The Great Gatsby *made by Fitzgerald at the time he was planning* The Love of the Last Tycoon, *circa 1939. The boxed notes at the bottom of the page refer to his Hollywood novel (by permission of the Fitzgerald Estate; Princeton University Library).*

The Scribner Building, 597 Fifth Avenue

F. Scott Fitzgerald on the Riviera: poster for the Fitzgerald Centenary celebration at the University of South Carolina (art by Kimberly L. Hamner)

CHAPTER 3:

THE GREAT GATSBY: RECEPTION, 1925–1926

Initial reviewers and initial readers are usually wrong about a novel. Literary history is a record of bad critical judgments. Most of the reviews of The Great Gatsby *were favorable; but the novel did not sell well in 1925: two printings totaling 23,870 copies—of which some were unsold when Fitzgerald died in 1940. Despite their general praise, none of the reviewers recognized* Gatsby *as a great American novel; Gilbert Seldes was the only one who identified Fitzgerald as one of the best living American writers. Fitzgerald was pleased by the praise from the literary friends he respected: H. L. Mencken, Edmund Wilson, and John Peale Bishop.*

Fitzgerald had expectations that the novel would be a best-seller and relieve him from the pressure to write short stories. He attributed the poor sales to the circumstance that women were the principal buyers of novels, and Gatsby *includes no admirable female character. The title worried Fitzgerald before and after publication, and he believed that it had damaged the novel's reception.*

The ten best-selling novels of 1925 were Soundings *by A. Hamilton Gibbs,* The Constant Nymph *by Margaret Kennedy,* The Keeper of the Bees *by Gene Stratton Porter,* Glorious Apollo *by E. Barrington,* The Green Hat *by Michael Arlen,* The Little French Girl *by Anne Douglas Sedgwick,* Arrowsmith *by Sinclair Lewis,* The Perennial Bachelor *by Anne Parish,* The Carolinian *by Rafael Sabatini, and* One Increasing Purpose *by A. S. M. Hutchinson (six were by American authors.)* Arrowsmith *was awarded the Pulitzer Prize, which Lewis declined.*

CORRESPONDENCE

The Great Gatsby *elicited letters from Fitzgerald's literary friends and from writers to whom he had sent copies.*

Edmund Wilson

Critic Edmund Wilson had been at Princeton with Fitzgerald, who came to regard him as his "intellectual con-

science." *Wilson was later the key figure in launching the Fitzgerald revival, following his death in 1940.*

11 April 1925

Dear Scott: Your book came yesterday and I read it last night. It is undoubtedly in some ways the best thing you have done—the best planned, the best sustained, the best written. In fact, it amounts to a complete new departure in your work. The only bad feature of it is that the characters are mostly so unpleasant in themselves that the story becomes rather a bitter dose before one has finished with it. However, the fact that you are able to get away with it is the proof of its brilliance. It is full of all sorts of happy touches—in fact, all the touches are happy—there is not a hole in it anywhere. I congratulate you—you have succeeded here in doing most of the things that people have always scolded you for not doing. I wish, in your next, you would handle a more sympathetic theme. (Not that I don't admire Gatsby and see the point of the whole thing, but you will admit that it keeps us inside the hyena cage.) Yours as ever, EW

I particularly enjoyed the man who takes the oculist's advertisement for the eyes of God.

—*Letters on Literature and Politics, 1912–1972*

TO: Edmund Wilson, May 1925
Dear Bunny:

Thanks for your letter about the book. I was awfully happy that you liked it and that you approved of its design. The worst fault in it, I think is a Big Fault: I gave no account (and had no feeling about or knowledge of) the emotional relations between Gatsby and Daisy from the time of their reunion to the catastrophe. However the lack is so astutely concealed by the retrospect of Gatsby's past and by blankets of excellent prose that no one

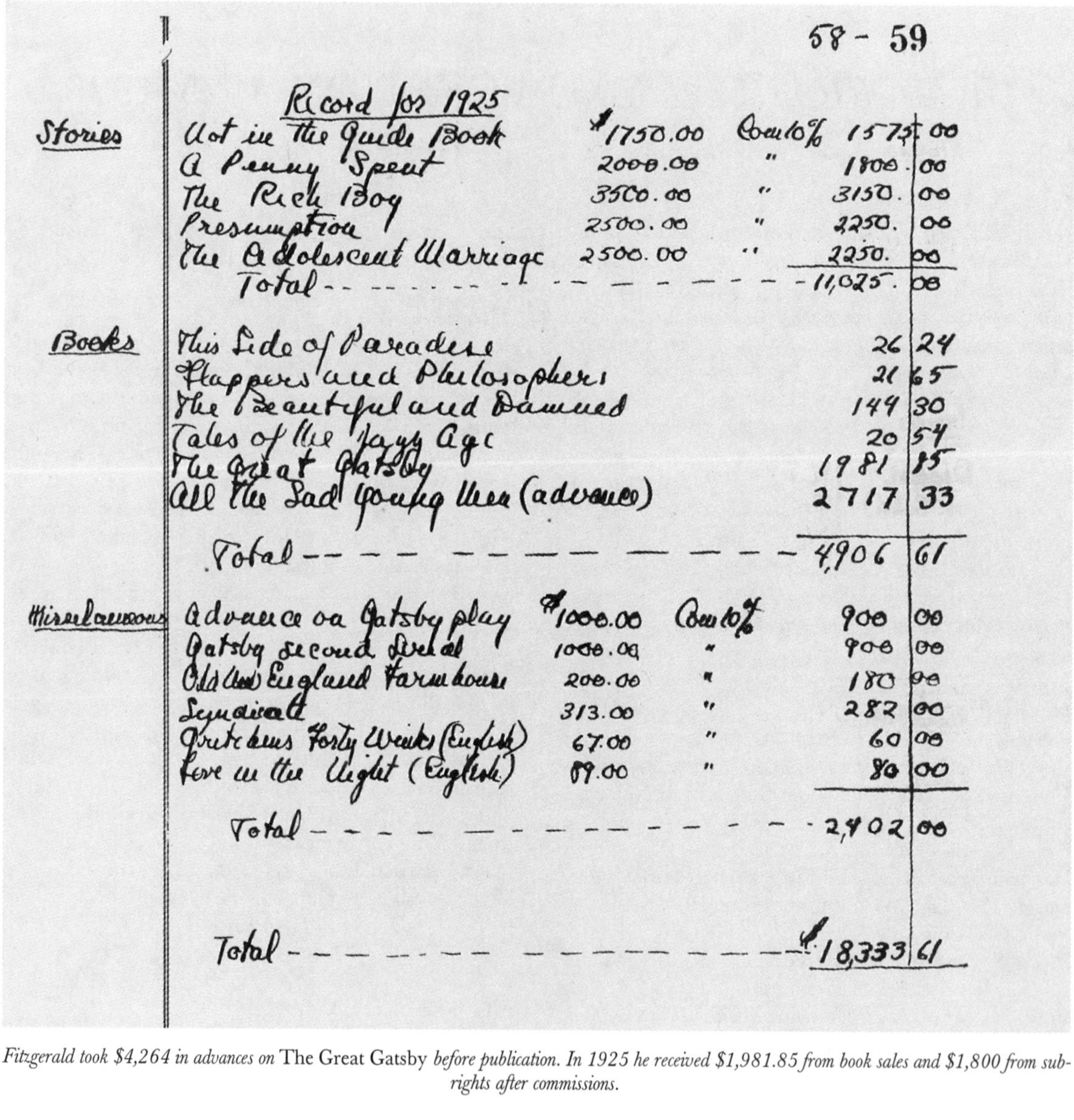

58 - 59

Record for 1925

Stories
Not in the Guide Book — $1750.00 — Com 10% — 1575.00
A Penny Spent — 2000.00 — " — 1800.00
The Rich Boy — 3500.00 — " — 3150.00
Presumption — 2500.00 — " — 2250.00
The Adolescent Marriage — 2500.00 — " — 2250.00
Total — — — — — — — — — — 11,025.00

Books
This Side of Paradise — 26 | 24
Flappers and Philosophers — 21 | 65
The Beautiful and Damned — 149 | 30
Tales of the Jazz Age — 20 | 54
The Great Gatsby — 1981 | 85
All the Sad Young Men (advance) — 2717 | 33
Total — — — — — — — — 4,906 | 61

Miscellaneous
Advance on Gatsby play — $1000.00 — Com 10% — 900 | 00
Gatsby second serial — 1000.00 — " — 900 | 00
Old New England Farmhouse — 200.00 — " — 180 | 00
Syndicate — 313.00 — " — 282 | 00
Gretchens Forty Winks (English) — 67.00 — " — 60 | 00
Love in the Night (English) — 89.00 — " — 80 | 00
Total — — — — — — — — — 2,402 | 00

Total — — — — — — — — — — $18,333 | 61

Fitzgerald took $4,264 in advances on The Great Gatsby *before publication. In 1925 he received $1,981.85 from book sales and $1,800 from sub-rights after commissions.*

60

	Record for 1926				
Stories	Your Way and Mine	$1750.00	Com 10%	1575	00
	The Dance	2000.00	"	1800	00
	Total			3375	00
English Rights	Love in the Night (Supraroupage)	91.75	Com 15%	78	00
	One of Our Oldest Friends	97.00	"	83	45
	A Penny Spent	76.38	"	61	92
	The Adolescent Marriage	76.23	"	64	80
	Total			288	17
Syndicate ect.	Adjuster, Pusher in the Face, Oldest Friends	239.19	Com 10% + 7.50	222	68
Article	How to Waste Material	100.00	"	90	00
Books	This Side of Paradise			44	00
(inc. English)	Flappers and Philosophers			35	80
	The Beautiful and Damned			33	10
	Tales of the Jazz Age			21	20
	The Great Gatsby			508	25
	All the Sad Young Men			1181	25
	Total			2033	20
Foreign	Danish and Swedish Rights to Gatsby			213	00
Moving Picture	The Great Gatsby	16,666.00	Com 10% (twice)	13500	00
Play	New York Run (Deduct last years advance)	3907.76	Com 6%	2616	98
(The Great Gatsby)	Chicago "	2971.07	"	2673	97
	Road Run "	751.38	"	673	26
	(Detroit, Brklyn, Balt, St. Louis, Chi, Denver, Phila)			5964	21
Total			$	25,686	05

Love in the Night (refund) — 97 | 75

In 1926 Gatsby *brought Fitzgerald $508.25 in royalties from book sales; however, income from movie and play rights was $19,667.21 after commissions* (Ledger).

Edmund Wilson

Scott
Thanks again for your cheering letter.
— *F. Scott Fitzgerald: A Life in Letters*

H. L. Mencken

Fitzgerald greatly respected H. L. Mencken, The Sage of Baltimore, who edited The American Mercury. *Mencken wrote Fitzgerald a letter of congratulation to which Fitzgerald responded with an assessment of his career. The two reviews by Mencken praise the quality of Fitzgerald's writing and the structure but dismiss the plot as unimportant.*

16 April 1925
Dear Fitz:—

"The Great Gatsby" fills me with pleasant sentiments. I think it is incomparably the best piece of work you have done. Evidences of careful workmanship are on every page. The thing is well managed, and has a fine surface. My one complaint is that the basic story is somewhat trivial—that it reduces itself, in the end, to a sort of anecdote. But God will forgive you for that.

Yours in Xt.,
H L Mencken
—Fitzgerald's Scrapbook, Princeton University Library

H. L. Mencken, "The Baltimore Anti-Christ," portrait by Stephen Longstreet (Arlyn Bruccoli Collection)

has noticed it—tho everyone has felt the lack and called it by another name. Mencken said (in a most entheusiastic letter received today) that the only fault was that the central story was trivial and a sort of anecdote (that is because he has forgotten his admiration for Conrad and adjusted himself to the sprawling novel.) and I felt that what he really missed was the lack of any emotional backbone at the very height of it.

Without makeing any invidious comparisons between Class A. and Class C. if my novel is an anectdote so is *The Brothers Karamazoff*. From one angle the latter could be reduced into a detective story. However the letters from you and Mencken have compensated me for the fact that of all the reviews, even the most enthusiastic, not one had the slightest idea what the book was about and for the even more depressing fact that it was, in comparison with the others, a financial failure (after I'd turned down fifteen thousand for the serial rights!). I wonder what Rosenfeld thought of it?

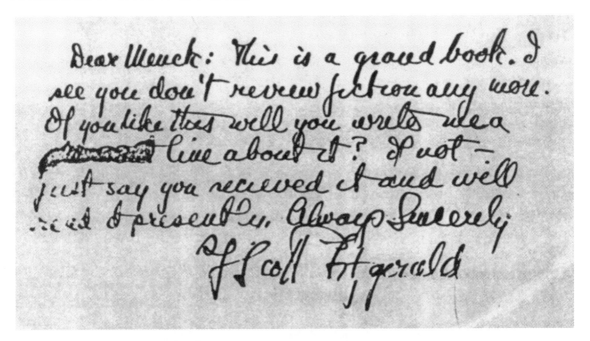

Dear Menck: This is a grand book. I
see you don't review fiction any more.
If you like this well you write me a
~~...~~ line about it? If not—
just say you recieved it and will
~~...~~ it present... Always Sincerely;
F Scott Fitgerald

Fitzgerald was in Europe when his novel was published; he supplied Scribners with inscription slips that were pasted in complimentary copies (H. L. Mencken Collection, Enoch Pratt Free Library).

TO: H. L. Mencken, 4 May 1925

Dear Menk—

Your letter was the first outside word that reached me about my book. I was tremendously moved both by the fact that you liked it and by your kindness in writing me about it. By the next mail came a letter from Edmund Wilson and a clipping from Stallings, both bulging with interest and approval, but as you know I'd rather have you like a book of mine than anyone in America.

There is a tremendous fault in the book–the lack of an emotional presentment of Daisy's attitude toward Gatsby after their reunion (and the consequent lack of logic or importance in her throwing him over.) Everyone has felt this but no one has spotted it because its concealed beneath elaborate and overlapping blankets of prose. Wilson complained: "The characters are so uniformly unpleasant," Stallings: "a sheaf of gorgeous notes for a novel" and you say: "The story is fundamentally trivial." I think the smooth, almost unbroken pattern makes you feel that. Despite your admiration for Conrad you have lately–perhaps in reaction against the merely well-made novels of James' imitators–become used to the formless. It is in protest against my own formless two novels, and Lewis' and Dos Passos' that this was written. I admit that in comparison to *My Antonia* and *The Lost Lady** it is a failure in what it tries to do but I think in comparison to *Cytherea* or *Linda Condon*** it is a success. At any rate I have learned a lot from writing it and the influence on it has been the masculine one of *The Brothers Karamazov* a thing of incomparable form, rather than the feminine one of *The Portrait of a Lady*. If it seems trivial or "anecdotal" (sp) it is because of an aesthetic fault, a failure in one very important episode and not a frailty in the theme–at least I don't think so. Did you ever know a writer to calmly take a just critisism and shut up?

–F. Scott Fitzgerald: A Life in Letters

*Novels by Willa Cather
**Novels by Joseph Hergesheimer

Gertrude Stein

Fitzgerald and Gertrude Stein met in Paris and were on friendly terms, but he did not become a member of her coterie and was not influenced by her experimental prose.

22 May 1925

My dear Fitzgerald

Here we are and have read your book and it is a good book. I like the melody of your dedica-

Gertrude Stein (left) with her companion Alice B. Toklas
(UCLA Library)

tion* it shows that you have a background of beauty and tenderness and that is a comfort. The next good thing is that you write naturally in sentences and that too is a comfort. You write naturally in sentences and one can read all of them and that among other things is a comfort. You are creating the contemporary world much as Thackery did his in Pendennis and Vanity Fair and this isn't a bad compliment. You make a modern world and a modern orgy strangely enough it never was done until you did it in This Side of Paradise. My belief in This Side of Paradise was alright. This is as good a book and different and older and that is what one does, one does not get better but different and older and that is always a pleasure. Best of good luck to you always, and thanks so much for the very genuine pleasure you have given me. We are looking forward to seeing you and Mrs. Fitzgerald when we get back in the Fall. Do please remember me to her and to you always
Gtde Stein.

I find that at the last moment of departure I did not copy your address into my address book, and so am sending this care of Hemingway. Do give it to me again.
G.S.

    −Fitzgerald's Scrapbook, Princeton University Library

*The Great Gatsby *was dedicated:* ONCE AGAIN TO ZELDA.

Edith Wharton

Although Edith Wharton acknowledged receipt of The Great Gatsby *by referring to herself as a representative of an older tradition,* The Age of Innocence *and* This Side of Paradise *were both published in 1920. Fitzgerald reportedly knelt in homage when he met Wharton in the Scribner offices.*

8 June 1925
Dear Mr. Fitzgerald,
    I have been wandering for the last weeks and found your novel−with its friendly dedication−awaiting me here on my arrival, a few days ago.

make me augur still greater things!—Thank you again.

Yrs. Sincerely,

Edith Wharton

—Fitzgerald's Scrapbook, Princeton University Library

This name should be Wolfshiem.

John Peale Bishop

Poet John Peale Bishop and Fitzgerald were classmates at Princeton; Fitzgerald credited Bishop with developing his understanding of poetry when they were undergraduates.

9 June 1925

Dear Scott, I have delayed unpardonably in acknowledging your letter and the book, having waited to get some inkling of your spring and summer address. All I know is that you can't be in Rome at this season, and yet it is to Rome that I suppose this will have to go.

I might begin as regards the Great Gatsby by telling you that I had dinner with Seldes and Van Wyck Brooks last night, and that Seldes is reviewing the GG

Edith Wharton

I am touched at your sending me a copy, for I feel that to your generation, which has taken such a flying leap into the future, I must represent the literary equivalent of tufted furniture & gas chandeliers. So you will understand that it is in a spirit of sincere deprecation that I shall venture, in a few days, to offer you in return the last product of my manufactory.

Meanwhile, let me say at once how much I like Gatsby, or rather His Book, & how great a leap I think you have taken this time—in advance upon your previous work. My present quarrel with you is only this: that to make Gatsby really Great, you ought to have given us his early career (not from the cradle—but from his visit to the yacht, if not before) instead of a short résumé of it. That would have situated him, & made his final tragedy a tragedy instead of a "fait divers" for the morning papers.

But you'll tell me that's the old way, & consequently not *your* way; & meanwhile, it's enough to make this reader happy to have met your *perfect* Jew, & the limp Wilson, & assisted at that seedy orgy in the Buchanan flat, with the dazed puppy looking on. Every bit of that is masterly—but the lunch with Hildesheim,* and his every appearance afterward,

Poet John Peale Bishop, the model for the character Thomas Parke D'Invilliers in Fitzgerald's This Side of Paradise. *The epigraph poem in* The Great Gatsby, *though credited to D'Invilliers, was written by Fitzgerald.*

A day or two after the trip Scott brought his book over. It had a garish dust jacket and I remember being embarrassed by the violence, bad taste and slippery look of it. It looked the book jacket for a book of bad science fiction. Scott told me not to be put off by it, that it had to do with a billboard along a highway in Long Island that was important in the story. He said he had liked the jacket and now he didn't like it. I took it off to read the book.

When I had finished the book I knew that no matter what Scott did, nor how he behaved, I must know it was like a sickness and be of any help I could to him and try to be a good friend. He had many good, good friends, more than anyone I knew. But I enlisted as one more, whether I could be of any use to him or not. If he could write a book as fine as *The Great Gatsby* I was sure that he could write an even better one. I did not know Zelda yet, and so I did not know the terrible odds that were against him. But we were to find them out soon enough.

—Ernest Hemingway, *A Moveable Feast*

in the Dial saying that you have written a grand book which leaves all your contemporaries behind (contemporaries specifically including Lewis and Cather, not to mention the Stevie-dear Benéts etc and in the hogswill) Brooks admitted modestly and with characteristic quietness that he had read the book and liked it.

On all sides, in fact, I gather that you have rather bowled them all over, intelligentsia and the more or less intelligent public. Johnson, the famous players gent who occasionally gives me some money for doing captions, thinks it one of the greatest books of all time etc.

As for myself, I think that you have definitely in this book, as you never did in its predecessors, crossed the line which distinguishes the artist from whatever you like, but not-artist. It has all the old fire, the instinctive gift of the novelist, which Godknows you've always had but it has also, what you never before showed, a fine and rigorous control, a clear sense of planning and an execution quite up to the plan. In brief you have got rid of your worst enemy, your ungodly facility. But—I could go on showering compliments on you quite as fervently as those you have already received and are about to receive. But as you'll undoubtedly get more of those than you can possibly have need for, I am going to put down, very briefly what I've got against the book. If I do, please don't think that I don't admire it with the most ardent; I do, but I also think that having come over the aforementioned line into the artist class you have got to be taken seriously and scrupulously to task for shortcomings which before were pardonable enough.

In the first place, I object to the inaccuracy of a great deal of the writing. For instance, in the paragraph in which

you introduce the two girls buoyed up by the sofa, the first impression is a stroke of genius, but as you go on, you in one phrase add and in the next detract from that impression. I am not here talking about the strict Dictionary, Edmund Wilson, use of words, I am talking about a quality of clear visualization. You admit things into that paragraph which could not, the first conditions being granted, have been seen. There are details which could not have been as you describe them. This may seem a picayune point, but it is, to my mind, the final distinction of good writing, accuracy at once to the emotion of the scene and its sensible fact. My own feeling is that you would profit by doing what Joyce, James etc, have done, taking notes on the spot, working them up as practice descriptions, and then carefully analyzing the result. This may seem like an amateur advising a professional, and it is. For there are a number of things which you can do already which no amount of note-taking will teach you or another. But I still think that you would gain by a very strict consideration of the elements which go into a description, whether of things only seen or of things felt. Different as they are, both Joyce and James are superbly accurate writers. The one is true to a visual, the other a nervous experience. Your own experience of things outside your self still seems to me a bit blurred, whether considered as a thing felt or a thing seen. This may seem to you splitting hairs that had better be left in the horse's tail, or surrounding the horse's ass. But I assure you that though a great many people will pass over such inaccuracies as I have noted, practically all of them will feel the gain in intensity of a complete realization of the thing—person, object, scene, situation—which in the GG now seems to me not quite there.

I feel this lack of complete realization also in the broader aspects of the book—in the character of Gatsby and in his relation to the girl. What you have got is all right as far as it goes, but it does not, to my mind, go far enough. I grant of course that Gatsby should remain a vague mysterious person to the end, but though he is seen through a mist, always, one should feel his solidity behind that mist. And it's because you don't entirely "get" him, that the violent end seems abrupt. Emotionally it is beautifully prepared for, but it does to me seem in action just a little "willed." Everything of Gatsby is specified, but it is though you saw him in patches instead of getting casual glimpses of what is after all a complete man. Great characters—Falstaff or Bloom or the Baron de Charlus—continually offer new and surprising aspects of themselves (somehow James characters don't, and I am inclined to think that this is one of the reasons why one resents James' overelaboration); so does Gatsby, but the transition, not in the scene but in the character, is not quite managed. The only way out of this is I suppose, a more lengthy preparation before writing another novel—after it is conceived and the characters placed in your mind.

> Gatsby was far from perfect in many ways but all in all it contains such prose as has never been written in America before. From that I take heart. From that I take heart and hope that some day I can combine the verve of Paradise, the unity of the Beautiful + Damned and the lyric quility of Gatsby, its aesthetic soundness, into something worthy of the admiration of those few—
> —God, I am inextricably intangled in that sentence, and the only thing to do is to start a new one. Anyhow, thanks.
>
> —Fitzgerald to Hazel McCormack, 15 May 1925,
> *F. Scott Fitzgerald: A Life in Letters*

I think too that the book is too short. I remember what you said to me in Paris about the excessive length of modern novels, and guess that you deliberately imposed the present length on your book. I grant the virtues you have gained by this; the impression of complete control, of nothing that is not strictly necessary, of the ultimate concision possible to your tale. Still I think the book would have gained by a greater elaboration and a slower tempo in the early portions. Your end is so violent that it seems to me you should have done, what Dickens and Conrad both do when they are working toward a bloody and extravagant end, so set the characters in a commonplace attitude, in everyday situations, that the reader completely accepts them, and hence, ultimately anything they may do or suffer.

But you have done wonders both as a writer and as a social critic. And you have, a thing after all, very few novelists succeed in doing, broken new ground. Gatsby is a new character in fiction, and, as everybody is now saying, a most familiar one in life. You have everything ahead of you; Gatsby definitely admits you to importance. For god's sake take your new place seriously. Scrutinize your own impressions, distrusting your facility which will continue to work anyhow as far as it is needful, and cultivate the acquaintance of writers who are both subtle and accurate, especially those who are different in temper from yourself. A little more subtlety, a little more accuracy, and you'll have every living American novelist, and most of the dead ones, wiped off the critic's slate.
John.
—Fitzgerald's Scrapbook, Princeton University Library

TO: John Peale Bishop, c. 9 August 1925
Dear John:
Thank you for your most pleasant, full, discerning and helpful letter about *The Great Gatsby.* It is about the only critisism that the book has had which has been intelligable, save a letter from Mrs. Wharton. I shall duly ponder, or rather I have pondered, what you say about accuracy–I'm afraid I haven't quite reached the ruthless artistry which would let me cut out an exquisite bit that had no place in the context. I can cut out the almost exquisite, the adequate, even the brilliant–but a true accuracy is, as you say, still in the offing. Also you are right about Gatsby being blurred and patchy. I never at any one time saw him clear myself–for he started as one man I knew and then changed into myself–the amalgam was never complete in my mind.
Scott

—Princeton University Library

T. S. Eliot

The most widely cited acknowledgment is T. S. Eliot's statement that the novel "seems to me to be the first step that American fiction has taken since Henry James." Eliot did not elaborate on this. Fitzgerald greatly admired The Waste Land *and The Valley of Ashes in* Gatsby *may have derived from Eliot's poem.*

T. S. Eliot

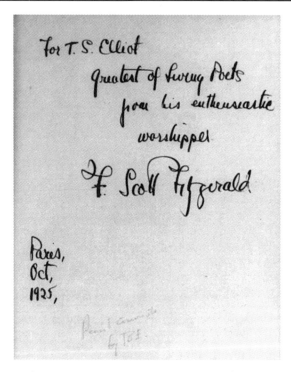

Fitzgerald sent T. S. Eliot an inscribed copy of The Great Gatsby *(Collection of Dan Siegel).*

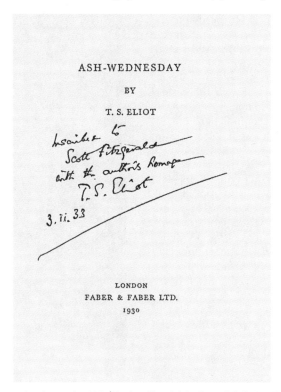

Eliot inscribed Fitzgerald's copy when they met in 1933 (Matthew J. and Arlyn Bruccoli Collection, University of South Carolina).

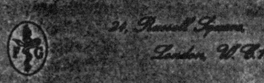

FABER and GWYER Ltd.
PUBLISHERS

TELEPHONE: MUSEUM 9543

24, Russell Square,
London, W.C.1.

31st December, 1925.

F. Scott Fitzgerald, Esqre.,
C/o Charles Scribners & Sons,
New York City.

Dear Mr Scott Fitzgerald,

"The Great Gatsby" with your charming and overpowering inscription arrived the very morning that I was leaving in some haste for a sea voyage advised by my doctor. I therefore left it behind and only read it on my return a few days ago. I have, however, now read it three times. I am not in the least influenced by your remark about myself when I say that it has interested and excited me more than any new novel I have seen, either English or American, for a number of years.

When I have time I should like to write to you more fully and tell you exactly why it seems to me such a remarkable book. In fact it seems to me to be the first step that American fiction has taken since Henry James.

I have recently become associated in the capacity of a director with the publishing firm whose name you see above. May I ask you, if you have not already committed yourself to publish "The Great Gatsby" with some other publishing house in London, to let us take the matter up with you? I think that if we published the book we could do as well by you as anyone.

By the way, if you ever have any short stories which you think would be suitable for the CRITERION I wish you would let me see them.

With many thanks,

I am,

Yours very truly, T. S. Eliot

P.S. By a coincidence,
Gilbert Seldes in his New York
Chronicle in the CRITERION for January 14th has chosen
your book for particular mention.

Eliot wrote this letter in his capacity as editor for an English publishing house (Fitzgerald's Scrapbook, Princeton University Library; by permission of Mrs. T. S. Eliot and Harcourt Brace).

Earliest dust jacket for the first printing. The lower-case j in "jay Gatsby" on the back was hand-corrected (Matthew J. and Arlyn Bruccoli Collection, University of South Carolina).

DESCRIPTIVE BIBLIOGRAPHY
The first edition: A11.1.a

The following section from the standard bibliography of Fitzgerald's published writings retains the identification numbers by which his works are identified in catalogues. Thus A11.1.a indicates the first edition and the first printing (1.a) of the eleventh book (A11) by Fitzgerald.

An edition includes all the printings or reprintings from the same typesetting. A printing or reprinting consists of the copies produced in a press run.

[i–vi] 1–218

[1–14]⁸

Contents: p. i: half title; p. ii: 'BY F. SCOTT FITZGER-ALD | [six titles]'; p. iii: title; p. iv: copyright; p. v: 'ONCE AGAIN | TO | ZELDA'; p. vi: blank; pp. 1–218: text, headed 'THE GREAT GATSBY | CHAP-TER 1'.

Typography and paper: 12 point on 14, Old Style. 5⁹/₁₆" (5¹³/₁₆") x 3½"; twenty-nine lines per page. Running heads: rectos and versos, 'THE GREAT GATSBY'. Wove paper.

Binding: Dark bluish green (#165) B cloth (linen-like grain). Front blind-stamped: 'THE GREAT | GATSBY | 'By F. Scott Fitzgerald'. Spine gold-stamped: 'THE | GREAT | GATSBY | [rule] | Fitzgerald | SCRIBNERS'.

White wove endpapers of sized stock. Top and bottom edges trimmed.

Dust jacket: Front has painting of woman's face above amusement park night scene, signed by F. Cugat: '[white lettering] [swash] The [roman] GREAT GATSBY | F – SCOTT – FITZGERALD'. Spine lettered in white: '[swash] The | [roman] GREAT | GATSBY | FITZGERALD | SCRIBNERS'. Back has blurb for *GG*. In first printing of jacket there is a lowercase 'j' in 'jay Gatsby' on the back at line 14; it is hand-corrected in ink in most copies seen. (The second printing of the jacket corrects this error.) Front flap lists books by Fitzgerald; back flap lists books by Ring W. Lardner. A later printing of the jacket quotes from reviews on the flaps and back.

Publication: 20,870 copies of the first printing. Published 10 April 1925. $2.00. Copyright #855444.

Printing: Composed and printed by the Scribner Press; plates made by the New York Electrotyping Co. Bound by the Scribner Press.

Locations: LC (deposited 2 June 1925); Lilly; MJB (dj with hand-corrected lowercase 'j', dj with capital 'J', dj with reviews); NjP (Fitzgerald's marked copy); OKentU (dj with capital'J'); PSt; ViU.

Note One: For studies of the text, see Bruce Harkness, "Bibliography and the Novelistic Fallacy," in *Bibliography and Textual Criticism,* ed. O M Brack, Jr., and Warner Barnes (Chicago: University of Chicago Press, [1969]),

THE GREAT GATSBY

BY
F. SCOTT FITZGERALD

Then wear the gold hat, if that will move her;
If you can bounce high, bounce for her too,
Till she cry "Lover, gold-hatted, high-bouncing lover,
I must have you!"
—Thomas Parke D'Invilliers.

NEW YORK
CHARLES SCRIBNER'S SONS
1925

Title page and copyright page of the first printing of the first edition

Copyright, 1925, by
CHARLES SCRIBNER'S SONS

Printed in the United States of America

From Matthew J. Bruccoli, F. Scott Fitzgerald: A Descriptive Bibliography, Revised Edition *(Pittsburgh: University of Pittsburgh Press, 1987)*

pp. 23–40; Bruccoli, "A Further Note on the First Printing of *The Great Gatsby,*" *Studies in Bibliography,* 16 (1961), 244; Bruccoli, "'A Might Collation': Animadversions on the Text of F. Scott Fitzgerald," in *Editing Twentieth Century Texts,* ed. Francess G. Halpenny (Toronto: University of Toronto Press, [1972]), pp. 28–50; Jennifer E. Atkinson, "Fitzgerald's Marked Copy of *The Great Gatsby,*" *Fitzgerald/Hemingway Annual 1970,* pp. 28–33; "Editorial," ibid., p. 265.

There are six textual variants between the first and second printings.

60.16 chatter [echolalia
119.22 northern [southern
165.16 it's [its
165.29 away [away.
205.9–10 sick in tired [sickantired
211.7–8 Union Street station [Union Station

Note two: the novel was serialized after book publication in *Famous Story Magazine,* 3 (April, May, June, July, August 1926). It was reprinted in England in *Argosy,* 22 (August 1937), 54–93. *GG* may have been serialized by the Bell Syndicate in 1926 (see *Dear Scott/Dear Max,* p. 119). An edited version of *GG* was published as "The Sunday Novel" supplement of the *Philadelphia Inquirer/Public Ledger* (23 May 1937), pp. 1–15.

Note three: *GG* was dramatized by Owen Davis. It opened at the Ambassador Theatre in New York on 2 February 1926 and ran for 112 performances. The play version was not published; but a typescript is at LC (PS$_{3507}$/.A$_{745}$G$_7$/Rare Bk. Coll.) See Burns Mantle, *The Best Plays of 1925–26* (New York: Dodd, Mead, 1926).

Note four: Thomas Parke D'Invilliers, to whom the title-page verse is attributed, is a character in *TSOP.*

A11.1.b
Second printing: New York: Scribners, 1925. Not differentiated on copyright page. August 1925. 3,000 copies. Locations: Lilly; MJB; ViU.

Identical with first printing, except for the six textual variants listed above. The second printing retains the Scribners seal on the copyright page.

AMERICAN REVIEWS

In 1925, more than now, American literary reputations were made in New York because in the pre-electronic-media era critical judgements were relayed only in print. The best newspapers had book columnists and book pages or weekly literary sup- *plements. The most influential periodicals and opinion-makers were New York based. Certain now-defunct newspapers had strong followings among serious readers—especially the* New York World, *which reviewed* Gatsby *both scathingly and admiringly. Other prominent venues where* Gatsby *received a warm welcome were* The New York Evening Post Literary Review *and* The Saturday Review of Literature. *Undercurrents in the reviews of* Gatsby *are the reviewers' concerns about Fitzgerald's commitment to his craft, their suspicion of his "facility," and their worry that he was giving in to the temptations of commercial writing. The favorable reviews recognized the novel as a fulfillment of the promise of his previous novels and expressed hope for his continuing development.*

F. Scott Fitzgerald's Latest a Dud
New York World, 12 April 1925

F. Scott Fitzgerald's new novel confirms the belief that there should be a consolidation of reviewers of average books and the selectors of scenarios. "The Great Gatsby" is another one of the thousands of modern novels which must be approached with the point of view of the average tired person toward the movie-around-the-corner, a deadened intellect, a thankful resigning of the attention, and an aftermath of wonder that such things are produced.

Mr. Fitzgerald shows the average wealthy American couple. The husband is a college-hero athlete, the wife an attractive nonentity. Each develops a love affair until between them they roll up a bill for one death by accident, one murder and one suicide. Gatsby is the wife's embryo lover, presumably a swindler on a swagger scale, burning with a steady devotion. But there is no important development of his character and many other titles would be equally appropriate. In fact with the telling of the plot "The Great Gatsby" is, in newspaper parlance, covered.

* * *

The Chicago Tribune *was the leading midwestern newspaper; its book review editor Fanny Butcher—whose taste was for conventional fiction—had a loyal readership.*

New Fitzgerald Book Proves He's Really a Writer
Fanny Butcher
Chicago Daily Tribune, 18 April 1925

F. Scott Fitzgerald, whose "This Side of Paradise" was the flaming skyrocket of its season, and whose photograph appeared in all of the exclusive journals as the picture of the hope of young America, the first person to turn the spotlight on the flapper in the back seat on a lonely road, has written his third novel. It is called "The Great Gatsby," and it is as different from the other two as experience is from innocence. The quality which "This Side of Paradise" glowed with was youth. It was about youth, written by youth and it had the combined innocence and bravado of adolescence, not in subject matter, but in the point of view of the author.

No one will ever be again so old as he is in his early twenties. No one will ever look upon life with the same secret eagerness and spoken cynicism that is in his eyes at twenty. Scott Fitzgerald got that bubble, stabbed with words, but never really pricked, into his book. It was inevitable that he should lose that quality in his work. It looked for a while in his next novel, "The Beautiful and the [*sic*] Damned," as if he were going to grow into the ordinary rather dull writer who chooses unhappiness and sodden souls to write about because he thinks such stories are "strong." "The Beautiful and the [*sic*] Damned" nearly did for him forever in the eyes of some readers.

"The Great Gatsby" proves that Scott Fitzgerald is going to be a writer, and not just a man of one book. It is bizarre. It is melodramatic. It is, at moments, dime novelish. But it is, despite its faults, a book which is not negligible as any one's work, and vastly important as Scott Fitzgerald's work. . . .

The story is sharp, ironical, in its framework. Its flesh and blood is the amusing, jaunty, sophisticated chatter of an idle, pleasure knowing group, and contrasted with it the silence of the great Gatsby, a man of 30 or so, immoderately rich, and unacceptably so because he did not inherit his gold, host to hundreds who used his great house as a roadhouse and told fantastic tales about him even to his face, for many of them never took the trouble to know Gatsby except as a name and a free bar.

* * *

The Scribners trade catalogue (Spring 1925) provided information to persuade retail booksellers to order The Great Gatsby.

The first Scribners advertisement for the novel on the day after publication accorded it more attention than the other books on the spring list.

Ruth Hale was an active feminist who was married to columnist Heywood Broun.

The Paper Knife
Ruth Hale
Brooklyn Daily Eagle, 18 April 1925

F. Scott Fitzgerald is a strange little bird. I can't make head or tail of him. I did not read "This Side of Paradise" until I had had my head talked off about it, so that it fell a little short of what I had been led to expect, through no fault of Mr. Fitzgerald's. In order to set myself straight about him, I read all his other books the moment they came out, and they did seem to me to be terrible. Now I have just read "The Great Gatsby," published by Scribner's, with a note on the book jacket to the effect that "it is a magical, living book, blended of irony, romance and mysticism." Well, of course, I suppose the Scribner jacket-writer wants to sell as many books as he can, otherwise I swear I would think he had gone completely mad. Find me one chemical trace of magic, life, irony, romance or mysticism in all of "The Great Gatsby" and I will bind myself to read one Scott Fitzgerald book a week for the rest of my life. The boy is simply puttering around. It is all right as a diversion for him, probably. He does, obviously, like to use hifalutin words and hifalutiner notions to concoct these tales. There may be those who like to read him. But why he should be called an author, or why any of us should behave as if he were, has never been explained satisfactorily to me.

* * *

Isabel Paterson reviewed Gatsby *again in June 1925 for* McNaught's Monthly, *a Canadian periodical, where she concluded that Fitzgerald had proved himself "a serious artist."*

Up to the Minute
Isabel Paterson
New York Herald Tribune Books, 19 April 1925

For a reviewer with a conscience, here is a nice problem—to give Scott Fitzgerald's new novel its just due without seeming to overpraise it, or, contrariwise, to say plainly that it is neither profound nor durable, without producing the impression that it is insignificant (which it is not).

This is like announcing a decision on points, when the public has been expecting a knock-out. The former method of winning is quite as honorable, but not so showy. "This Side of Paradise" was put over with a punch of a very special kind. But "The Great Gatsby" is the first convincing testimony that Mr. Fitzgerald is also an artist.

The reason why "This Side of Paradise" created such a furore was not its intrinsic literary worth, but its rare combination of precocity and true originality. The universal difficulty for beginning novelists is to use what they know. Fiction must be shaped to a pattern. Life appears to be formless, incoherent, fantastically irrelevant. In the individual experience episodes don't seem to hang together; cause and effect are not even on speaking terms; apparently things just happen. The technical tricks of foreshortening for perspective, of working to scale, of selecting and composing, and, above all, of using documentary facts simply as a painter employs a model for his imaginative figure paintings, these things are usually learned by a long process of trial and error. For this reason youth has seldom been articulate of its own emotions and ideas. The young are busy drawing from casts, from "the antique," learning the craft. By the time they have skill enough to work from the life—the first fine, careless rapture has faded. It has to be done from memory.

Mr. Fitzgerald managed somehow to pour his glowing youth on the page before it could escape forever. His natural facility was so extraordinary that he could get along with a minimum of conscious technique. Even the inevitable crudities and banalities of his first novel were a part of its authenticity. They were genuine echoes of the gaucheries of his age and environment. The smart, swaggering, callow cubs of 1915 (was it?) were like that; such were their amusements, catchwords, standards and point of view.

It was really a sociological document. Not even a personal confession, in the main, but a snapshot of one aspect of the crowd mind.

So is "The Great Gatsby" in a sense. But it is first and foremost a novel, which its predecessor wasn't. It is beautifully and delicately balanced; its shapeliness is the more praiseworthy for the extreme fragility of the material. It is an almost perfectly fulfilled intention. There is not one accidental phrase in it, nor yet one obvious or blatant line.

And to work at all with such people, such types and backgrounds, is something of a feat. They are the froth of society, drifting sand, along the shore. Can one twist ropes of sand? Decidedly not; but one may take the sand and fuse it in the warmth of fancy, and with skill enough one may blow it into enchanting bubbles of iridescent glass.

"The Great Gatsby" is just such an imponderable and fascinating trifle. Gatsby himself is the archetype of the species of ephemerides who occupy the whole tale. He was a man from nowhere, without roots or background, absolutely self-made in the image of an obscure and undefined ideal. You could not exactly call him an impostor; he was himself an artist of sorts, trying to remold himself. His stage was a Long Island summer colony, where he came in contact with the realities of his dream and was broken by them.

That he was a bootlegger, a crook, maybe a killer (all on the grand scale) is part of the irony of things; for it wasn't his sins he paid for, but his aspirations. He was an incurable romanticist (I would draw a distinction between that and a romantic, as between sentimentality and sentiment), and his mistake was to accept life at its face value.

There, too, is the chief weakness of Mr. Fitzgerald as a novelist. In reproducing surfaces his virtuosity is amazing. He gets the exact tone, the note, the shade of the season and place he is working on; he is more contemporary than any newspaper, and yet he is (by the present token) an artist. But he has not, yet, gone below that glittering surface except by a kind of happy accident, and then he is rather bewildered by the results of his own intuition. Observe how he explains the duration and intensity of Gatsby's passion for Daisy Buchanan. He says it was because of Daisy's superior social status, because she was a daughter of wealth—Gatsby "hadn't realized how extraordinary a 'nice' girl could be"; and the revelation dazzled him, made him Daisy's slave forever. Pooh, there is no explanation of love. Daisy might have been a cash girl or a mill hand, and made as deep a mark—it is Carmen and Don Jose over again. There isn't any why about that sort of thing.

Again, Mr. Fitzgerald identifies the strange rout who came of Gatsby's incredible parties as "the East," in contrast to a more solid, integrated society of the Middle West. But these drunken spenders and migratory merrymakers exist proportionately everywhere; there are more of them in and around New York because there is more of New York, and they congregate chiefly where there is easy money—like midges dancing over a pool. And they come from all quarters. They are not even peculiar to this age; they made up the guests at Trimalchio's supper, and Lucian satirized them.

But Gatsby hasn't the robust vitality of the vulgar Trimalchio. He and his group remain types. What has never been alive cannot very well go on living; so this is a book of the season only, but so peculiarly of the season, that it is in its small way unique.

* * *

Laurence Stallings's review appeared ten days after the unsigned negative review in the same newspaper.

The First Reader—Great Scott
Laurence Stallings
New York World, 22 April 1925

In this new book he is another fellow altogether. *The Great Gatsby* evidences an interest in the color and sweep of prose, in the design and integrity of the novel, in the development of character, like nothing else he has attempted. If you are interested in the American novel this is a book for your list.

Lawrence Stallings, who co-authored with Maxwell Anderson the World War I play What Price Glory?

Even the staid fellows who shrugged at Fitzgerald's stuff when he first brutally rang the bell of notoriety in *This Side of Paradise* must have known, and fearsomely too, that the child would some day be father to the novelist.

He was, in writing, something like the prodigals of his fiction: bursting with a gorgeous zest of life, interesting, highly diverting, above all possessed of a streak of talent as broad as it was erratic.

The Great Gatsby is no spontaneous burst of erratic divertissement proffered with an insolent grace. It is a novel written with pace and fine attention. Above all, handling the most exaggerated social scheme in the new world, it never once overdoes the thing.

I do not think for one moment in reading this book that "here is a great novel" or even, that "here is a fine book." The novelist has not brought it off in grand style; has, in fact, supplied little more than a sheaf of notes on a gorgeous plan for a novel on the topside life about us.

But in this, even though it not be God's plenty, there is more worth than in all his other work. One reading it knows that the fair-haired boy of American fiction will not sink gracefully into the sort of middle-aged precocity who once rang the bell. There is a sincerity of feeling for Gatsby, put forward with a delicacy of irony pointed with occasional lapses into brutality, which is distinguished, and worth many better matured novels.

* * *

Scott Fitzgerald's Novel
Herbert S. Gorman
New York Sun, 2 May 1925

Mr. F. Scott Fitzgerald was the trumpeter or saxophonist, as you choose, of the jazz age. He was intensely desirous of remaining well this side of Paradise, of mingling with the beautiful and damned, of conversing rather breathlessly with flappers and philosophers. But the temperament that gave so ample an illustration of the sophisticated buoyancy of a congenitally blase youth was marked apart from the average run of "smart" writers by a sensitiveness that revealed itself in flashes of profundity, poignancies of understanding and instinctive comments.

It was perceptible that an artist struggled in the depths of young Mr. Fitzgerald, an artist, that all too infrequently broke through the glittering crust of smartness that had fashioned his work into such popular pabulum. Wits and sophisticates, worse luck, we have with us always, but artists are not strewn about so plentifully as to arouse no more than a brief and yawning observance. And comprehending this, certain critics have waited impatiently for the artist that was indubitably in Mr. Fitzgerald to reveal himself. Perhaps "The Great Gatsby" is the first definite stir of that artist. Anyway, it is a novel that cannot be classified with "This Side of Paradise" or "The Beautiful and Damned."

For once the writer has passed beyond that sophistication that is an end in itself. There is still a sparkle and certain crispness in portions of "The Great Gatsby," but it is subdued; the fireworks are not so fanciful; the syncopation has been lowered to a minor key. Jay Gatsby, the mysterious millionaire, who is part hopeful and romantic boy and part unscrupulous adventurer, is the hub about which circles this periphery of an unstabilized and decadent society. Of all the personages in the book he attains a certain respect in the reader's mind, for he alone is sufficiently endowed with illusions and the romantic attitude to carry on for a consistently glimmering mirage, a goal of shadowy substance for which he deliberately attunes his gorgeous and reckless existence. . . .

In telling his story Mr. Fitzgerald has adopted a style that is slightly oblique. Indeed, in certain aspects it is Jamesian—the building up of a figure through the observations of a participator in the action and the adornment of this figure through meditative analysis. Gatsby gradually evolves as scene after scene reveals more and more of his real self and his purpose. The other personages are flung more swiftly upon the reader's consciousness. Tom Buchanan, carrying on his illicit affair with the wife of Wilson, the automobile dealer, is understandable from the first, and so, too, is that symbol of the New Age, Jordan Baker. In them we witness two broad facets of the febrilities of this contemporaneous life that has stripped so many illusions from the dubious task of existing. Tom is the sensualist of the bad-gin-and-fool-the-wife era. Jordan is the modern girl to whom nothing is surprising any more.

It is possible that some readers will find an unhealthy note in "The Great Gatsby," a vigorous shoving before them of frustrated and reckless personalities, with the intimation on the part of the author that this is the way smart life is carried on to-day, that this is what he has witnessed on that narrow tongue of land called Long Island. Gin parties, extravagant entertainments, love nests in the Bronx, illicit parleyings, dishonesties, and a lost spiritual integrity, all these things find their place in "The Great Gatsby," and yet, making use of them, perhaps, but untouched by them in his essential self, strides the figure of Jay Gatsby, who found an objective in life and lived and died in the pursuit of it. In spite of his mysterious dealings with the gambler, Meyer Wolfsheim, and the shady business of stolen bonds, there is vastly more sufficiency and integrity to him than to any other person in the book. At least, that is what the author conveys and somehow it satisfies the reader.

The book has certain plain deficiencies. It is so compactly written at times that the theme seems rather skeletonized. The swift strokes might have been enlarged somewhat without injury to the construction of the novel. Perhaps the author was a trifle tentative with his subject, comprehending it well enough but a little agitated about so unusual a departure on his part.

But these things do not militate against the awareness of a decisive advance by F. Scott Fitzgerald in the art of the novel. It is the most excellently formed work that he has undertaken and it should be the prelude to still finer things. The author has grown older and perhaps there is more bitterness in his adjustment to contemporary life, but these traits should be distinct adjuncts to him as he proceeds. "The Great Gatsby" is, perhaps, more important for its revelation of a noticeable growth in F. Scott Fitzgerald than it is as a work of art in itself. It is limited, but its limitations are of the sort that increasing maturity will remove. The ebullience and impertinence of "This Side of Paradise" is decidedly lessened, but taking their place are admirable qualities (not the least of them the ability to build up impressive characterizations) that were no more than hinted in the earlier works of F. Scott Fitzgerald.

* * *

As H.L.M. Sees It

H. L. Mencken

Baltimore Evening Sun, 2 May 1925; *The Chicago Tribune,* 24 May 1925

Scott Fitzgerald's new novel, *The Great Gatsby,* is in form no more than a glorified anecdote, and not too probable at that.

This story is obviously unimportant, and though, as I shall show, it has its place in the Fitzgerald canon, it is certainly not to be put on the same shelf with, say, *This Side of Paradise.* What ails it, fundamentally, is the plain fact that it is simply a story—that Fitzgerald seems to be far more interested in maintaining its suspense than in getting under the skins of its people. It is not that they are false; it is that they are taken too much for granted. Only Gatsby himself genuinely lives and breathes. The rest are mere marionettes—often astonishingly lifelike, but nevertheless not quite alive.

What gives the story distinction is something quite different from the management of the action or the handling of the characters; it is the charm and beauty of the writing. In Fitzgerald's first days it seemed almost unimaginable that he would ever show such qualities. His writing, then, was extraordinarily slipshod—at times almost illiterate. He seemed to be devoid of any feeling for the color and savor of words. He could see people clearly and he could devise capital situations, but as writer qua writer he was apparently little more than a bright college boy. The critics of the Republic were not slow to discern the fact. They praised *This Side of Paradise* as a story, as a social document, but they were almost unanimous in denouncing it as a piece of writing.

It is vastly to Fitzgerald's credit that he appears to have taken their caveats seriously and pondered them to good effect. In *The Great Gatsby* the highly agreeable fruits of that pondering are visible. The story, for all its basic triviality, has a fine texture, a careful and brilliant finish. The obvious phrase is simply not in it. The sentences roll along smoothly, sparkingly, variously. There is evidence in every line of hard and intelligent effort. It is a quite new Fitzgerald who emerges from this little book and the qualities that he shows are dignified and solid. *This Side of Paradise,* after all, might have been merely a lucky accident. But *The Great Gatsby,* a far inferior story at bottom, is plainly the product of a sound and stable talent, conjured into being by hard work.

. . . .

These are the defects that he has now got rid of. *The Great Gatsby,* I seem to recall, was announced a long while ago. It was probably several years on the stocks. It shows on every page the results of that laborious effort. Writing it, I take it, was painful. The author

wrote, tore up, rewrote, tore up again. There are pages so artfully contrived that one can no more imagine improvising a fugue. They are full of little delicacies, charming turns of phrase, penetrating second thoughts. In other words, they are easy and excellent reading—which is what always comes out of hard writing.

* * *

Jazz Parties on Long Island– But F. Scott Fitzgerald is Growing Up

Walter Yust

New York Evening Post Literary Review, 2 May 1925

It has been said that Robert Frost is the poet of gray New England gone or going to seed. I read this novel with a parallel notion that F. Scott is the poet of that portion of society which crashes madly enough along the border line between culture that money brings and vulgarity that money scarcely ever either conceals or dissipates—a portion of society that embodies disillusion and practices, out of caprice and indifference, a harshness in camaraderie cheaply tragic. This portion of society may be entirely fictitious. That is, there may be on the whole of Long Island no one like any of the personalities of this story. But it doesn't matter. The dissolution, the tawdry tragedy of much of life, as revealed in these pages, is bitterly true.

The Great Gatsby is, for me, Mr. Fitzgerald's most carefully devised story; his always assured, and sometimes prodigal, pen—but he, of all artists, must use the typewriter—is here more often restrained; from the opening page to the last, he has held successfully to one tone, to one vision—that of a group of people whom he perhaps sees in the composite figure of a clown, half-crazed by his own fripperies, laughing, blatant, weak, pitiable. He has admirably laid beneath livid colors the torture of horror.

The Great Gatsby is the story of a man who is gratuitously called great—a young man who grasps desperately after his especial brand of beauty, a tatterdemalion of romantic graces. . . .

Irony tinctures the story, as alcohol tinctures the personalities in it. Here in pungent solution are the ideals, the hopes and the pleasures of people. Once Mr. Fitzgerald's flappers and jellybeans, they are flappers and jellybeans no longer, they are less innocent, less naive, a little older and wiser—if wisdom be the name for disillusion. Alcohol—bootleg—in a manner symbolizes their decay, not that they are all of them drunkards, but that they use liquor, and imitation liquor to boot, when less vivid persons prime themselves in conventional fashion with

"A New Scott Fitzgerald Emerges" from

The Great Gatsby

Wm. Rose Benét in the Saturday Review:

"Reveals thoroughly matured craftsmanship. It has structure. It has high occasions of felicitous, almost magic phrase. . . . Perhaps you have gathered that we like the book. We do. It is written with concision and precision and mastery of material."

Laurence Stallings in the New York World:

"If you are interested in the American novel, this is a book for your list. . . . The talent is here aplenty; the erratic streak is curbed; the impudence takes on the civilized urbanity of the man at ease in art."

Alexander Woolcott in the New York Sun:

"New and striking and fine, rebuttal evidence aplenty that Scott Fitzgerald had a clear and seeing eye in his head when he was loitering on post-war Long Island, of which the book is a vivid, crystalline picture. I put it down with a new and profound respect for its astonishing author."

Fanny Butcher in the Chicago Tribune:

"Proves that Scott Fitzgerald is a writer and not just a man of one book. . . . As different from his other two books as experience is from innocence."

H. L. Mencken in the Baltimore Sun:

"It is a quite new Fitzgerald who emerges. . . . The qualities he shows are dignified and solid. . . . There are pages . . . full of little delicacies, charming turns of phrase, penetrating second thoughts."

Llewellyn Jones in the Chicago Evening Post:

"F. Scott Fitzgerald has got his second wind, and the people who were dolefully shaking their heads over him some time ago are going to be fooled."

Isabel Paterson in the New York Herald-Tribune:

'Beautifully and delicately balanced. . . . An almost perfectly fulfilled intention."

$2.00 at all bookstores

CHARLES SCRIBNER'S SONS, FIFTH AVENUE, NEW YORK

Scribners promoted Gatsby *with a series of ads in* The Saturday Review of Literature, *but sales did not improve.*

the comfortable unbottled illusion of a quiet home, hard work, dreams for the future, the consciousness of purpose in life.

Gatsby, mounting by questionable Wallingford* practices the ladder to the social heights of East Egg, seems, of all the represented characters of the story, to be the only one with fixed aim, with a clear and distinct notion that he can do something and that there *is* something for men and women to do, with life. His friends are surface lights and darknesses; their interminable jamborees, their nervous spasmodic enthusiasms, their exaggerated and violent expressions of a well-being they neither feel nor especially desire—beyond these he describes a beauty, whole, clear-cut, three-dimensional. A frightful accident, the ironic gesture of indifferent fate, snuffs him and his ideal out. F. Scott appears at this point a little willful, and indeed sentimental—but he casts his calculated glamour. Gatsby is actually as incapable of tragedy as Daisy is, or Tom, or Myrtle, all of whom meet irritations and pain with bad liquor, hectic parties, cynicisms. Tragedy would annihilate them. They couldn't bear up under it. And Gatsby is better wilfully dead.

The novel is one that refuses to be ignored. I finished it in an evening, and had to. Its spirited tempo, the motley of its figures, the suppressed, undersurface tension of its dramatic moments, held me to the page. The stark vulgarity of Myrtle's friends, the unhealthy sinister excitements of Gatsby's, invited as intense and as impersonal an interest as the panic of crawling things under a suddenly lifted moss-grown stone. It is not a book which might, under any interpretation, fall into the category of those doomed to investigation by a vice commission, and yet it is a shocking book—one that reveals incredible grossness, thoughtlessness, polite corruption, without leaving with the reader a sense of depression, without being insidiously provocative.

It is an extraordinary book in more ways than one—none more extraordinary than in its power to throw a spell over the reader. I think of the novel now with increasing surprise. The impression grows that while there is no incredible personality in the book, there is no memorable one. The figures fit the pattern of the story easily; they have been cut out for it. But there seems to be no one of them that remains, not even Gatsby himself, to convince me that I have followed his movements with some excitement for weeks and weeks. Four hours I knew them all; watched them with complete absorption. But now the book is ended, they are quite gone—vanished.

It was not my intention in the beginning to make any comparison between Frost and Fitzgerald. Since the names have been placed side by side, however, they might serve to indicate a distinction. Mr. Frost expresses his New England locality and tragedy through richly drawn personality. Mr. Fitzgerald expresses another kind of decay, not through individuals so much as through crowds. The party in Myrtle's apartment is as raw and vulgar and pulsing and unforgettable as life itself and the hectic assemblies on Gatsby's lawns are. Groups of persons live in the pages of Mr. Fitzgerald's book as no one person ever does. A poet of discords, he gives us starkly the asymmetry, the motley, the cacophony of crowds—whether they are crowds of three or of a hundred and three.

Reference to George Randolph Chester's Get-Rich-Quick Wallingford *(1908).*

* * *

Books on Our Table
H. B.
New York Post, 5 May 1925

F. Scott Fitzgerald's new novel will surprise a great many people who have read his earlier books. It did us. We had not read a half-dozen pages before we were saying: "Why, the man's perfectly at his ease in a serious piece of writing. His style fairly scintillates, and with a genuine brilliance; he writes surely and soundly." The rest of the book confirmed the impression. It does not seem to us a great novel, but as an index of the direction in which one of our young writers is going, it is of prime value. We must confess to the previous belief that Mr. Fitzgerald would be forgotten as soon as the vogue for the cocktail-flapper-jazz novel had vanished, that he might go on writing clever and mildly amusing stories; but that he could turn his hand to a social study as important in its implications as "The Great Gatsby," never once occurred to us. But he's done it. And in addition to demonstrating an admirable mastery of his medium both in style and construction, he has written a story that at its best is very, very good.

"The Great Gatsby" is a tale of present-day life on Long Island. Gatsby is an enormously wealthy unknown, who takes a vast house, stocks the cellar, hires innumerable servants, and gives a sort of continuous party to which people of all kinds flock in droves. Nobody knows anything about his antecedents; nobody cares. The quality of his liquor is excellent, so why worry about anything else? He has had a love affair with a girl in Louisville, Ky., while in an officers' training camp. The girl appears on the scene as the unhappy wife of a famous polo player and society man. Her husband has a mistress, which makes it easy for her to enter into a liaison with Gatsby. From this situation arises a terrific, smashing tragedy, told with a brutal directness that makes the reader shudder—as powerful a piece of writing as we have met for a long time and really the high spot in the novel from an artistic standpoint. Other tragedies follow rapidly until Gatsby is shot to death and buried, with all his fair-weather friends vanished. . . .

The plot and its developments work out too geometrically and too perfectly for "The Great Gatsby" to be a great novel, but Mr. Fitzgerald manipulates his people and his situations with a master hand, and it is not until the book has been finished and put aside that the sense of the stage director managing his puppets comes to temper one's admiration. In a way the book is as perfectly constructed as a good short story, and even the best short stories have something of the managed and diagrammed about them. But the handling is excellent, and one cannot withhold admiration from the creation of atmosphere which Mr. Fitzgerald does so well, nor from his blending of a cold and aloof irony with a sort of compassion for every one involved in the curious tangle, even for the great Gatsby, who has come up from nothing at all to the position of a famous Long Island host. He is unsparing with his characters, and for the most part they are a pretty rotten lot—true enough to life, though. Too true. . . .

We shall have more to say about "The Great Gatsby" later. With it Mr. Fitzgerald definitely deserts his earlier fiction which brought him a lot of money and a certain kind of renown, and enters into the group of American writers who are producing the best serious fiction. On the basis of this book alone Mr. Fitzgerald gives about as much promise as any young writer we have, and that is a thoughtful opinion.

To the reader, who cares less for such technical matters than for the story itself, we may well add that "The Great Gatsby" is fascinating. If you begin it you'll go straight through to the end, and you will be conscious that you have read an excellent piece of writing. Mr. Fitzgerald will bear watching.

* * *

An Admirable Novel
William Rose Benét
Saturday Review of Literature, 9 May 1925

The book finished, we find again, at the top of page three, the introductory remark:

William Rose Benét, editor of The Saturday Review of Literature, *was a former professor of English whose critical judgments were respected.*

No—Gatsby turned out all right at the end; it was what preyed on Gatsby, what foul dust floated in the wake of his dreams that temporarily closed out my interest in the abortive sorrows and short-winded elations of men.

Scott Fitzgerald's new novel is a remarkable analysis of this "foul dust." And his analysis leads him, at the end of the book, to the conclusion that all of us "beat on, boats against the current, borne back ceaselessly into the past." There is depth of philosophy in this.

The writer—for the story is told in the first person, but in a first person who is not exactly the author, but rather one of the number of personalities that compose the actual author,—the hypothecated chronicler of Gatsby is one in whose tolerance all sorts and conditions of men confided. So he came to Gatsby, and the history of Gatsby, obscured by the "foul dust" aforementioned, "fair sickened" him of human nature.

The Great Gatsby is a disillusioned novel, and a mature novel. It is a novel with pace, from the first word to the last, and also a novel of admirable "control." Scott Fitzgerald started his literary career with enormous facility. His high spirits were infectious. The queer charm, color, wonder, and drama of a young and reckless world beat constantly upon his senses, stimulated a young and intensely romantic mind to a mixture of realism and extravaganza shaken up like a cocktail. Some people are born with a knack, whether for cutting figure eights, curving an in-sheet, picking out tunes on the piano, or revealing some peculiar charm of their intelligence on the typewritten page. Scott Fitzgerald was born with a knack for writing. What they call "a natural gift." And another gift of the fairies at his christening was a reckless confidence in himself. And he was quite intoxicated with the joy of life and rather engagingly savage toward an elder world. He was out "to get the world by the neck" and put words on paper in the patterns his exuberant fancy suggested. He didn't worry much about what had gone before Fitzgerald in literature. He dreamed gorgeously of what there was in Fitzgerald to "tell the world."

And all these elements contributed to the amazing performance of *This Side of Paradise,* amazing in its excitement and gusto, amazing in phrase and epithet, amazing no less for all sorts of thoroughly bad writing pitched in with the good, for preposterous carelessness, and amazing as well as for the sheer pace of the narrative and the fresh quality of its oddly pervasive poetry. Short stories of flappers and philosophers displayed the same vitality and flourished much the same faults. *Tales of the Jazz Age* inhabited the same glamour. *The Beautiful and Damned,* while still in the mirage, furnished a more valuable document concerning the younger generation of the first quarter of the Twentieth Century. But brilliant, irrefutably brilliant as were certain passages of the novels and tales of which the "boy wonder" of our time was so lavish, arresting as were certain gleams of insight, intensely promising as were certain observed facilities, there remained in general, glamour, glamour everywhere, and, after the glamour faded, little for the mind to hold except an impression of this kinetic glamour.

There ensued a play, in which the present writer found the first act (as read) excellent and the rest as satire somehow stricken with palsy, granted the cleverness of the original idea. There ensued a magazine phase in which, as was perfectly natural, most of the stories were negligible, though a few showed flashes. But one could discern the demands of the "market" blunting and dulling the blade of that bright sword wildly whirled. One began to believe that Fitzgerald was coming into line with the purveyors of the staple product. And suddenly one wanted him back in the phase when he was writing so well and, at the same time, writing so very badly. Today he was writing, for the most part, on an even level of magazine acceptability, and on an even level of what seemed perilously like absolute staleness of mind toward anything really creative.

But *The Great Gatsby* comes suddenly to knock all that surmise into a cocked hat. *The Great Gatsby*

reveals thoroughly matured craftsmanship. It has structure. It has high occasions of felicitous, almost magic, phrase. And most of all, it is out of the mirage. For the first time Fitzgerald surveys the Babylonian captivity of this era unblinded by the bright lights. He gives you the bright lights in full measure, the affluence, the waste, but also the nakedness of the scaffolding that scrawls skeletons upon the sky when the gold and blue and red and green have faded, the ugly passion, the spiritual meagreness, the empty shell of luxury, the old irony of "fair-weather friends."

Gatsby remains. The mystery of Gatsby is a mystery saliently characteristic of this age in America. And Gatsby is only another modern instance of the eternal "fortunate youth." His actual age does not matter, in either sense. For all the cleverness of his hinted nefarious proceedings, he is the coney caught. For he is a man with a dream at the mercy of the foul dust that sometimes seems only to exist in order to swarm against the dream, whose midgedance blots it from the sky. It is a strange dream. Gatsby's,–but he was a man who had hope. He was a child. He believed in a childish thing.

It is because Fitzgerald makes so acid on your tongue the taste of the defeat of Gatsby's childishness that his book, in our opinion, "acquires merit." And there are parts of the book, notably the second chapter, that, in our opinion, could not have been better written. There are astonishing feats that no one but Fitzgerald could have brought off, notably the catalogue of guests in Chapter IV. And Tom Buchanan, the "great, big hulking specimen," is an American university product of almost unbearable reality.

Yet one feels that, though irony has entered into Fitzgerald's soul, the sense of mere wonder is still stronger. And, of course, there is plenty of entertainment in the story. It arises in part from the almost photographic reproduction of the actions, gestures, speech of the types Fitzgerald has chosen in their moments of stress. Picayune souls for the most part, and Gatsby heroic among them only because he is partly a crazy man with a dream. But what does all that matter with the actual narration so vivid and graphic? As for the drama of the accident and Gatsby's end, it is the kind of thing newspapers carry every day, except that here is a novelist who has gone behind the curt paragraphs and made the real people live and breathe in all their sordidness. They are actual, rich and poor, cultivated and uncultivated, seen for a moment or two only or followed throughout the story. They are memorable individuals of today–not types.

"*Mencken is right:*"

says JOSEPH HERGESHEIMER

"*it is beautifully written and saturated with a sharp, unforgettable emotion. It gathers up all his early promise surprisingly soon, and what he subsequently does must be of great interest and importance.*"

MR. HERGESHEIMER IS REFERRING TO

The Great Gatsby

By
Scott Fitzgerald

Here is an excellent summary of the merits of "The Great Gatsby," written by Herschel Brickell in the New York Evening Post:

"We had not read a half-dozen pages before we were saying: 'Why, the man's perfectly at his ease in a serious piece of writing. His style fairly scintillates, and with a genuine brilliance; he writes surely and soundly.' The rest of the book confirmed the impression. . . . A social study . . . important in its implications. . . . In addition to demonstrating an admirable mastery of his medium both in style and construction, he has written a story that at its best is very, very good. . . . Mr. Fitzgerald manipulates his people and his situations with a master hand. . . . The handling is excellent, and one cannot withhold admiration from the creation of atmosphere which Mr. Fitzgerald does so well, nor from his blending of a cold and aloof irony with a sort of compassion for every one involved in the curious tangle. . . . Mr. Fitzgerald's prose is distinguished, nothing short of it. It has color, richness, an abundance of imagery, and a fine sense of the picturesque. . . . With it, Mr. Fitzgerald . . . enters into the group of American writers who are producing the best serious fiction. On the basis of this book alone Mr. Fitzgerald gives about as much promise as any young writer we have, and that is a thoughtful opinion. . . . If you begin it you'll go straight through to the end, and you will be conscious that you have read an excellent piece of writing. Mr. Fitzgerald will bear watching."

$2.00 *at all bookstores*

CHARLES SCRIBNER'S SONS, NEW YORK

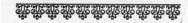

The Saturday Review of Literature, *23 May 1925*

Perhaps you have gathered that we like the book! We do. It has some miscues, but they seem to us negligible. It is written with concision and precision and mastery of material.

* * *

Prophets of the New Age
Harvey Eagleton
Dallas Morning News, 10 May 1925

The most outstanding characteristic of the work of F. Scott Fitzgerald is the ability of the older generation to understand what it is all about. When "This Side of Paradise" appeared, it was greeted with enthusiasm by one group, that of Mr. Fitzgerald, and interrogation by another, that of Mr. Fitzgerald's papa and mamma. Said the latter, "It is all very clever and witty and amusing, but, of course not true to life. People aren't like that." Said the former, "Hurrah, here we are in a book. These are the things we think; these are the things we do. We might have written it ourselves if we had only thought about it first."

Mr. Fitzgerald having thought course, not the first college novel; better, perhaps, a fad, that of the college novel. [*sic!*]

"This Side of Paradise" was, of course, not the first college novel, there was "Stover of Yale" years before and "Tom Brown at Oxford," for that matter, but it was the first college novel to find itself surrounded by a group of imitators, and it is undoubtedly the best college novel. With the exception of the Montross' book, "Town and Gown," no more careful, accurate, and realistic picture of undergraduate life and the undergraduate mind has been given us.

One may not approve of the picture, the papas and mammas of Mr. Fitzgerald's flappers and philosophers do not, partly because the picture is a reflection upon themselves and the manner in which they have reared their young, partly because of the ostrich tendency in all of us to hide our heads at what frightens us a little and to try and pretend that the frightening object is not there after all; but to anyone who knows undergraduate life in our great American institutions of higher learning, the picture of that life as drawn in "This Side of Paradise" and "Town and Gown" is only too true. Mr. Fitzgerald jerks his flappers and jelly-beans before us and says somewhat cynically, "Here you are. What are you going to do about it?" He offers no solution to the problem, and admittedly it is one, at least to the educator if not to the papas and mammas; he merely presents it.

But Mr. Fitzgerald, for all his attack on reform and reformers in "The Beautiful and the [*sic*] Damned," is essentially a reformer himself. Most young men with

a newly discovered literary talent have also newly discovered the evils of the world, and they use the one to portray the other, loudly calling the attention of the old heads to the strange creatures they have discovered unaided and alone, much to the amusement of the old heads who knew the strange creatures were there all along. It is only a sophomoric stage of development which sometimes last over into maturity, witness Byron, Shelley and Jean Jacques Rousseau. Mr. Fitzgerald is neither a Byron, a Shelley, nor a Jean Jacques Rousseau, but his agitation and lack of poise show him to belong to the same type, a type representing a peculiarly arrested mental development. Mr. Fitzgerald doesn't approve of his flappers and jelly-beans. He is secretly very much shocked by them. He assures us he is of them, that his wife, who is incidentally his own heroine, wearing sometimes black hair, sometimes brown, sometimes red, is of them, that his little daughter will be of them, but it is not because he approves of them. It is rather the attitude of the cheap evangelist who tells how hideously he sinned before he got religion in order to impress his hearers with the fact that he knows what he is talking about.

"The Beautiful and the [*sic*] Damned," Mr. Fitzgerald's second novel, was written purely in the spirit of reform. First he is a reformer of reformers. He has a natural and healthy dislike of gentlemen of Anthony Comstock's ilk, and he attacks them with all the savagery of youth. He doesn't believe in prohibition as a law, but he doesn't believe in drinking either, and he has his hero, a man of promise, completely destroy that promise and almost drink himself to death, giving us to understand that this is what the best of our young men and women are doing, and, hinting darkly that it is all due to modern education and the decay of the church in the face of science. Then he is distressed about the ugliness of life, and he shows us picture after picture, scene after scene, of this ugliness, hoping that we shall see it too and do something about it. And there is the weakness of the book, of all Fitzgerald's books, the weakness that prevents them from ever being more than "popular fiction" of the most ephemeral variety. We are to do something about it, but what the something is he knows no more than did Shelley, who was equally seriously concerned about similar matters.

The omission of the constructive in Fitzgerald's work is an indication of his fundamental lack of imagination, for in spite of all his cleverness, and his wit, he has no creative faculty. He has a photographic mind. He can not create beyond himself nor imagine experience very different from his own. He is continuously autobiographic. His heroine, as I have said, is his wife, and his hero is himself. He graduates from college; he writes a novel of college life. He marries; he writes a novel of young married life. He has a little girl, and she appears in "The Great Gatsby." We know these things because when he can not think of a simple plot on which he can hang his experience, he writes articles about himself and sells them to the American Magazine, the Saturday Evening Post and the Woman's Home Companion.

Having created a type of book, however, which has been so widely imitated, Mr. Fitzgerald suddenly finds himself crowded in his own field, a field too small to hold both himself and his followers, and so, in his latest novel, "The Great Gatsby," he has attempted to get out of his own field and either into a new one or into somebody's else not so crowded as his own. The results have not been happy. He gets into no particular field at all, but hangs up on the fence, leaning, perhaps, in the direction of Mr. Van Vechten's sterile and worthless acres: witness the characteristically unnecessary two-page list of the visitors to the Gatsby Long Island estate and the "literary allusions."

The novel has no plot to mention. Jay Gatz, later changed to Gatsby, from Minnesota, a young man of ability but no opportunity, is filled with the urge to make something of himself. The urge gets him started, but midway in career, when in training in Louisville during the World War, he meets Daisy whom he comes to love passionately. While he is in France winning his way to a captaincy by acts of "high daringdo," Daisy marries another man, and Jay's life is blighted. He comes back to America, makes an enormous fortune by dishonest means, leads a hectic and artificial life, surrounded by noise and vulgarity on his Long Island estate, longing always for Daisy, and finally is shot because he is blamed for Daisy's running over and killing a woman on the road from New York. The book is highly sensational, loud, blatant, ugly, pointless. There seems to be no reason for its existence. Mr. Fitzgerald thinks, quite obviously, that Gatsby is a great and tragic figure, but he merely succeeds in making the reader see him as a rather unbalanced young man who has become a clever crook. The story is told in first person, Mr. Fitzgerald, calling himself Mr. Carraway.

One finishes "The Great Gatsby" with a feeling of regret, not for the fate of the people in the book, but for Mr. Fitzgerald. When "This Side of Paradise" was published, Mr. Fitzgerald was hailed as a young man of promise, which he certainly appeared to be. But the promise, like so many, seems likely to go unfulfilled. The Roman candle which sent out a few gloriously colored balls at the first lighting seems to be ending in a fizzle of smoke and sparks.

* * *

Time, *the first news magazine, was launched in 1923. This review was unsigned.*

Incorruptible Yegg
Time, 11 May 1925
Still the brightest boy in the class, Scott Fitzgerald holds up his hand. It is noticed that his literary trousers are longer, less bell-bottomed, but still precious. His recitation concerns Daisy Fay who, drunk as a monkey the night before she married Tom Buchanan, muttered: "Tell 'em all Daisy's chang' her mind." A certain penniless Navy lieutenant was believed to be swimming out of her emotional past. They gave her a cold bath, she married Buchanan, settled expensively at West Egg, L. I., where soon appeared one lonely, sinister Gatsby, with mounds of mysterious gold, ginny habits and a marked influence on Daisy. He was the lieutenant, of course, still swimming. That he never landed was due to Daisy's baffled withdrawal to the fleshly, marital mainland. Due also to Buchanan's disclosure that the mounds of gold were ill-got. Nonetheless, Yegg Gatsby remained Daisy's incorruptible dream, unpleasantly removed in person toward the close of the book by an accessory in oil-smeared dungarees.

* * *

The Nation *had a limited circulation but was read by intellectuals.*

Fitzgerald on the March
Carl Van Vechten
The Nation, 20 May 1925
Mr. Fitzgerald is a born story-teller; his words, phrases, and sentences carry the eye easily through to the end of his books. Further, his work is imbued with that rare and beneficent essence we hail as charm. He is by no means lacking in power, as several passages in the current opus abundantly testify, and he commands a quite uncanny gift for hitting off character or presenting a concept in a striking and memorable manner. The writer he most resembles, curiously enough, despite the dissimilarity in their choice of material and point of attack, is Booth Tarkington, but there exits at present in the work of Mr. Fitzgerald a potential brutality, a stark sense of reality, set off in his case by an ironic polish, that suggests a comparison with the Frank Norris of *Vandover and the Brute,* or *McTeague.*

* * *

Novelist Carl Van Vechten was a warm friend of the Fitzgeralds at the time he reviewed Gatsby

The New Yorker *had commenced publication in 1925 and was struggling to continue.*

The New Yorker, 23 May 1925

It happened that we were one of the first readers of Scott Fitzgerald's first novel, which anybody could criticize to pieces, yet which—allowing for differences in the class-room furnishings of the minds and the impressiveness of the egos—struck us hard as being pretty much the prose beginning an American Byron born at the time of the Spanish War would make. And we thought, and think now, that a Byron would be a good thing for American writing, and we waited to see what young Fitzgerald would do next. He did "The Beautiful and Damned."

His third, "The Great Gatsby," revives our interest, though not in a Byronic promise he probably never had. He still reveres and pities romantic

constancy, but with detachment. Gatsby, its heroic victim, is otherwise a good deal of a nut, and the girl who is its object is idealized only by Gatsby. You are not, however, prepared for the mechanical but effective upset that makes her turn out to be an eligible member of sty-and-trough society, and Gatsby the vulgarian to be something of a grand gentleman.

The story has Fitzgerald's extravagance but a new maturity, as well as any amount of flash and go. Parts are solidly good; all has to be read. The young man is not petering out.

* * *

Harry Hansen had written a review of This Side of Paradise *proclaiming, "My, how that boy Fitzgerald can write!"*

Lots of Good Things
Harry Hansen
Chicago Daily News, 27 May 1925

Through a series of circumstances I came to read "The Great Gatsby," by F. Scott Fitzgerald, only this week, after all the other reviewers in Chicago had already acclaimed it. And I agree that this is a book one cannot afford to miss. It is only Fitzgerald's third novel. The reason that "This Side of Paradise" seems so far away is because the author has allowed several books of short stories to intervene. "The Great Gatsby" more than ever proves the vitality of Fitzgerald's fine talent. Here it is, blossoming out in a finely conceived American novel, firmly controlled and developed by this brilliant young man whose first book turned the tables on readers and sired a string of novels that looked the age in the face and called it by its right name. "The Great Gatsby" is American to the core, modern to the hour, sophisticated—with the little air of pretense that makes up so much of our sophistication—in other words Fitzgerald knows his times and his people. But it is spiced with richly ironic humor and with a discriminating observation of people and their ways, told in vivid, living language. To express a modern age demands modern methods in writing. Fitzgerald provides them. Moreover in his method Fitzgerald is one step in advance of most of his contemporaries who are trying to capture the mood of modern America. He is able to depict his people without covering them everywhere with his contempt. The author's sneer, so obvious in many books in which young writers deal with their so-called inferiors, is absent in Fitzgerald, and yet it is doubtful whether richer satire on our bootlegging, jazzing, wasting age, is being written. Who was the great Gatsby? The author tells you of this forlorn American who entertained lavishly every week-end in his tremen-

With the best of London, Vienna, Paris, Rome —

"He has produced something which approaches perilously near a masterpiece. . . . It can be put on the same book-shelf with the best of London, Vienna, Paris, or Rome. . . . One reads almost with a sense of elation, the elation with which one hears strongly emotional music or studies a perfectly poised painting."

This is quoted from William Curtis, writing in Town and Country of

Scott Fitz-gerald's

The Great Gatsby

$2.00 at all bookstores

H. L. Mencken says:

"A fine texture, a careful and brilliant finish. The obvious phrase is simply not in it. The sentences roll along smoothly, sparklingly, variously. There is evidence in every line of hard and intelligent effort. It is a quite new Fitzgerald who emerges from this little book and the qualities that he shows are dignified and solid. . . . Plainly the product of a sound and stable talent, conjured into being by hard work. . . . There is certainly no sign of petering out in Fitzgerald. . . . There are pages so artfully contrived that one can no more imagine improvising them than one can imagine improvising a fugue. They are full of little delicacies, charming turns of phrase, penetrating second thoughts."

Joseph Hergesheimer says: "Mencken is right":

"Mencken is right: it is beautifully written and saturated with a sharp, unforgettable emotion. It gathers up all his early promise surprisingly soon, and what he subsequently does must be of great interest and importance."

Charles Scribner's Sons, New York

The Saturday Review of Literature, *30 May 1925*

dous "period" house on Long Island, where few of the guests actually knew their host and none ever quite solved the secret of his wealth; of the interplay of personalities; of folk who live under the protective coloration of great wealth, whose amusements are imbecilic, whose lives are just one moment after another. None has bettered Fitzgerald in describing futile drinking parties. His is a look into life as it is lived on this continent, in these our times—and the crowd he describes is still on Long Island moving restlessly between East Egg and West Egg. "The Great Gatsby" has in it the challenge of modernity. Fitzgerald has style and his adjectives—in new combinations—are a delight. If you want to know what a first class American satirical novel is like you'd better hurry to get it.

* * *

Literature—and Less
John McClure
New Orleans Times-Picayune, 31 May 1925

Mr. F. Scott Fitzgerald is one of the Wednesday-and-Thursday boys. His books are the cleverest of the week, sometimes of the month or the year. He is satisfied to be one of the bright young people of the season, which is much like being a devil in one's own home town.

Literature is a long panorama. The republic of letters is old, large, rich, and populous. Its naturalized citizens do not die easily, and Plato, Aristophanes, Apuleius, Montaigne and Conrad are still walking about the streets. The year 1925 is as insignificant, in point of size, in the panorama of literary history as Possum Center in the United States or Bornhofen on the Rhine in Europe. It is a mere dot on the map. To be one of the brightest fellows in Bornhofen does not mean a great deal in Berlin, and means still less in Paris. It is a pity Mr. Fitzgerald is satisfied to be one of the bright young people of Bornhofen. He has the innate capacity, one is tempted to believe, to be a citizen of the larger world.

"The Great Gatsby," Mr. Fitzgerald's new book and probably his best, is one of the cleverest books of the year. That is what is the matter with it. Mr. Fitzgerald is simply too bright. He is such a clever conversationalist that he falls into the error of being merely a raconteur. He makes clever remarks, some spontaneous, many smacking of the notebook, to such an extent that you lose the sense of unity demanded in a work of literary art. Worse, he is so addicted to the use of Wednesday-and-Thursday terms (words which mean something this week but may mean something else before fall, new words that everybody else is using, just as everybody hums the momentary popular song) that the style is raw. The use of new words—colloquialisms or slang—is difficult. Unless they are used with consummate skill they are objectionable as new paint, slick, shiny, crude and glar-

ing. They grate on the nerves. Mr. Fitzgerald, in using an up-to-the-minute vocabulary, pays the penalty of crudeness. His style is often like new chrome yellow. He describes Gatsby: "I was looking at an elegant young roughneck, a year or two over thirty." This is hometown stuff, very clever this week—in Possum Center—but will it sound clever next week when we have ceased calling hicks roughnecks? This slick seasonal superficiality of expression permeates Mr. Fitzgerald's style to the core. Often it is merely a matter of intonation or the use of prepositions. But "The Great Gatsby," certainly, is written in the style of 1925. Now the 1925 model, in literature or automobile, is likely to be supplanted by a later model. Genuinely good writing (Mark Twain's or Flaubert's, as you please) does not reflect the fads of the season's conversation. Its texture is less superficial.

The pity is that Mr. Fitzgerald has very genuine talent. He has a fresh vision, a surprising flair for imagery, and a real enthusiasm for life. He has, too, an intense feeling for words which needs only to be disciplined. There are excellent passages in "The Great Gatsby," passages so excellent that one believes Mr. Fitzgerald ought to be able to do a fine book. This one is half-baked. All of his clever work, so far, has been half-baked.

Even in conception and construction "The Great Gatsby" seems a little raw. It is not convincing as a whole. Its finest spots are more convincingly clever than convincingly dramatic. The book has merit. Flashes of description, episodes of conduct, snatches of conversation are often striking. There is a feeling for life in the rendering.

"The Great Gatsby," though recommended to those who are interested in the art of literature only as a work of promise, is recommended to readers of current fiction as one of the best novels of the year. With all its deficiencies it is far above the average.

Mr. Fitzgerald is still where he was five years ago. He is developing in character very favorably; acquiring a broader view of life. But as a literary craftsman he still faces the necessity of a decision between writing in the fashion like Mr. Rupert Hughes, or according to his inner lights like James Branch Cabell and Sherwood Anderson.

* * *

Mencken reconsidered Gatsby *in a collective review that also commented on Ellen Glasgow's* Barren Ground, *Margaret Kennedy's* The Constant Nymph, *and Francis Brett Young's* Sea Horses.

New Fiction
H. L. Mencken
American Mercury, July 1925

Of these novels, the one that has given me most pleasure is Fitzgerald's, if only because it shows the author to be capable of professional advancement. He is still young and he has had a great success: it is a combination that is fatal to nine beginning novelists out of ten. They conclude at once that the trick is easy–that it is not worth while to sweat and suffer. The result is a steady and melancholy decline; presently the best-selling *eminentissimo* of yesterday vanishes and is heard of no more. I could adorn this page with a list of names, but refrain out of respect for the dead. Most of the novelists who are obviously on solid ground today had heavy struggles at the start: Dreiser, Cabell, Hergesheimer, Miss Cather. Fitzgerald, though he had no such struggle, now tries to make it for himself. "The Great Gatsby" is full of evidences of hard, sober toil. All the author's old slipshod facility is gone; he has set himself rigorously to the job of learning how to write. And he shows quick and excellent progress. "The Great Gatsby" is not merely better written than "This Side of Paradise"; it is written in a new way. Fitzgerald has learned economy of words and devices; he has begun to give thought to structure; his whole attitude has changed from that of a brilliant improvisateur to that of a painstaking and conscientious artist. I certainly don't think much of "The Great Gatsby" as a story. It is in part too well-made and in part incredible. But as a piece of writing it is sound and laudable work.

* * *

Thomas Caldecot Chubb was a prominent book reviewer who often wrote for The Forum, *a journal of cultural opinion.*

Bagdad-on-Subway
Thomas Caldecot Chubb
The Forum, August 1925

In a short career, even now amounting to only five years, Scott Fitzgerald has already found time to do a great many things. He has written the most brilliant novel of the younger generation. He has written one of the two best novels of the younger generation. He has written probably the worst play of any generation. He has scattered very close to half a hundred short stories in all the better-paying receptacles for facile fiction. He has told,–and presumably based the telling on his own experience,–how it is possible to live on $30,000 a year. Latterly he has been responsible for *The Great Gatsby,* a fable in the form of a realistic novel, an Arabian Nights' tale of the environs of what O. Henry used to call Bagdad-on-Subway, a hasheesh dream for a romantic minded inhabitant of Nassau County, and incidently his most attractive book.

The publishers assure us that Jay Gatsby would only be possible in this age and generation. We beg respectfully to inform them that he would be possible in any age and generation and impossible in all of them. We beg to inform them that there is something of Jay Gatsby in every man, woman, or child that ever existed. But also we beg to inform them that their particular Jay Gatsby of West Egg,

Long Island, and Oggsford, England, is a figment of the imagination. Just as that illustrious nature myth Jurgen,–so the critics tell us,–never left his pawnshop, so Jay Gatsby is James Gatz' dream of himself after he had poured down half a dozen synthetic drinks.

Here is a fragment of the story. Seventeen years old James Gatz is wandering out on the shore of Lake Superior. Up to the shore steams the yacht of Dan Cody, gambler and financier. Inventing the name of Jay Gatsby as he rows out to it, Gatz warns Cody that it would be dangerous to leave his yacht there. Cody is struck with him, makes him his steward, secretary and often jailer. Then, having given young Gatz a taste for extravagance, dies.

While he is still poor as an Irishman on Sunday morning, Gatz, now Gatsby, meets Dorothy [*sic*] Fay, a belle of Louisville. Since he is a soldier and it is during the war, she entertains him. Gatz, who is not unused to women, finds that she is just as amenable as any other. But she represents the dazzling security of a "nice" girl, and he falls in love with her. When he comes back from the war hoping to marry her, he finds that she has given up waiting for him and has married Ted [*sic*] Buchanan, ex football star. Out of the bitterness of her marriage to Ted the great Gatsby is born.

All this, however, is merely background. The story takes place at West Egg, Long Island, where the enormously wealthy Gatsby, "big Bootlegger", so it is rumored, and friend of Meyer Wolfsheim, "the man who fixed the world series in 1919" and incidentally who was dining with the gambler Rosenthal the night he was shot, has bought an enormous mansion simply to be able to gaze at the green light that flashes from the end of Daisy Buchanan's pier. And when the story does take place it is at once a tragedy and an extraordinarily convincing love tale and an extravaganza that is better than Michael Arlen because there is more control to it. Curiously enough in this day of studies it is actually a story, so I will not disclose it. It is the story of the green light.

Scott Fitzgerald is intellectually hard. He does not carry any baggage of sentimentality. He knows a great deal. And so he is not afraid of the sentimental because he realizes that it is part of the life he is considering. Gatsby is a sentimentalist. Daisy Buchanan is a sentimentalist. Ted [*sic*] Buchanan is a sentimentalist. Even the cool Jordan Baker, who is as cleanly drawn a feminine character as there is in modern fiction, and Nick Carraway the teller of the story have hearts that, even if only at moments, beat erratically under the glazed ice of their suave understanding of everything. To recommend this book on the ground of technical excellence is of course superfluous. I recommend it as a study of these sentimentalists by one whose heart does not ever beat erratically. In *The Great Gatsby* Scott Fitzgerald has every bit of the brilliance that we associate with hard surfaces.

* * *

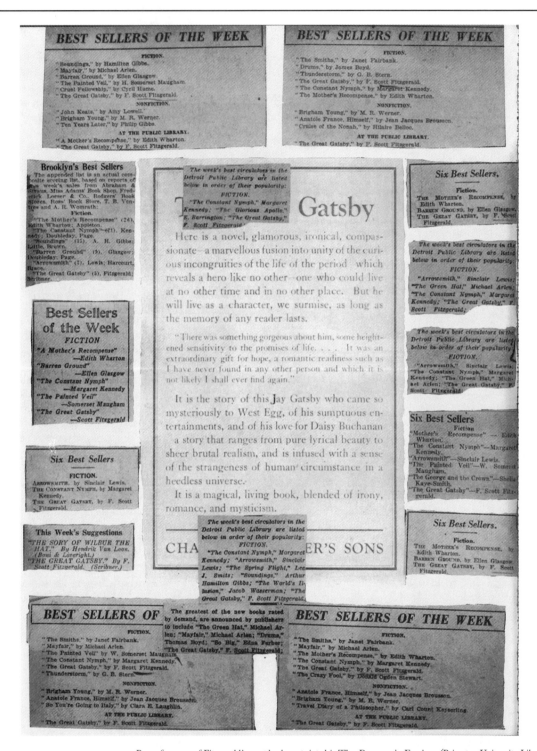

Pages from one of Fitzgerald's scrapbooks, reprinted in The Romantic Egoists *(Princeton University Library)*

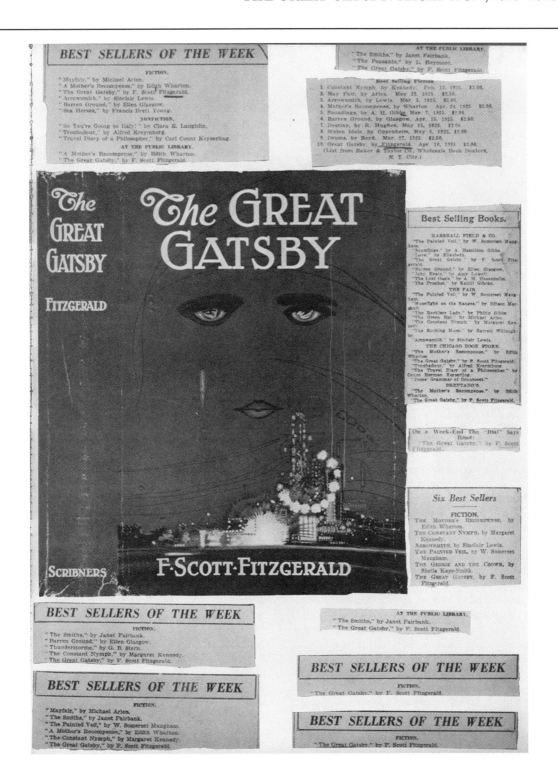

The strongest review of The Great Gatsby *was written by Fitzgerald's friend Gilbert Seldes in* The Dial, *a literary journal that promoted modernism. This review angered Ernest Hemingway, who claimed that it had ruined Fitzgerald by setting impossible goals for him. Seldes wrote another review for* The New Criterion *(4 January 1926), an English Journal, stating that "his talent is only beginning to mature; and until now, it has appeared to be the most abundant talent, most casually wasted, in American fiction."*

Scott told me that he had heard from Maxwell Perkins that the book was not selling well but that it had very fine reviews. I do not remember whether it was that day, or much later, that he showed me a review by Gilbert Seldes that could not have been better. It could only have been better if Gilbert Seldes had been better. Scott was puzzled and hurt that the book was not selling well but, as I said, he was not at all bitter then and he was both shy and happy about the book's quality.

–Ernest Hemingway, *A Moveable Feast*

Spring Flight
Gilbert Seldes
The Dial, August 1925

There has never been any question of the talents of F. Scott Fitzgerald; there has been, justifiably until the publication of *The Great Gatsby,* a grave question as to what he was going to do with his gifts. The question has been answered in one of the finest of contemporary novels. Fitzgerald has more than matured; he has mastered his talents and gone soaring in a beautiful flight, leaving behind him everything dubious and tricky in his earlier work, and leaving even farther behind all the men of his own generation and most of his elders.

In all justice, let it be said that the talents are still his. The book is even more interesting, superficially, than his others; it has an intense life, it must be read, the first time, breathlessly; it is vivid and glittering and entertaining. Scenes of incredible difficulty are rendered with what seems an effortless precision and crowds and conversation and action and retrospects–everything comes naturally and persuasively. The minor people and events are threads of colour and strength, holding the principal things together. The technical virtuosity is extraordinary.

All this was true of Fitzgerald's first two novels, and even of those deplorable short stories which one feared were going to ruin him. *The Great Gatsby* adds many things, and two above all: the novel is composed as an artistic structure, and it exposes, again for the first time, an interesting temperament. "The vast juvenile intrigue" of *This Side of Paradise* is just as good subject-matter as the intensely private intrigue of *The Great Gatsby*; but Fitzgerald racing over the country, jotting down whatever was current in college circles, is not nearly as significant as Fitzgerald regarding a tiny section of life and reporting it with irony and pity and a consuming passion. *The Great Gatsby* is passionate as *Some Do Not* is passionate, with such an abundance of feeling for the characters (feeling their integral reality, not hating or loving them objectively) that the most trivial of the actors in the drama are endowed with vitality. The concentration of the book is so intense that the principal characters exist almost as essences, as biting acids that find themselves in the same golden cup and have no choice but to act upon each other. And the *milieux* which are brought into such violent contact with each other are as full of character, and as immitigably compelled to struggle and to debase one another.

The book is written as a series of scenes, the method which Fitzgerald derived from Henry James through Mrs. Wharton, and these scenes are reported by a narrator who was obviously intended to be much more significant than he is. The author's appetite for life is so violent that he found the personality of the narrator an obstacle, and simply ignored it once his actual people were in motion, but the narrator helps to give the feeling of an intense unit which the various characters around Gatsby form. Gatsby himself remains a mystery; you know him, but not by knowing about him, and even at the end you can guess, if you like, that he was a forger or a dealer in stolen bonds, or a rather mean type of bootlegger. He had dedicated himself to the accomplishment of a supreme object, to restore to himself an illusion he had lost; he set about it, in a pathetic American way, by becoming incredibly rich and spending his wealth in incredible ways, so that he might win back the girl he loved; and a "foul dust floated in the wake of his dreams." Adultery and drunkenness and thievery and murder make up this dust, but Gatsby's story remains poignant and beautiful.

This means that Fitzgerald has ceased to content himself with a satiric report on the outside of American life and has with considerable irony attacked the spirit underneath, and so has begun to report on life in its most general terms. His tactile apprehension remains so fine that his people and his settings are specifically of Long Island; but now he meditates upon their fate, and they become universal

Gilbert Seldes

also. He has now something of extreme importance to say; and it is good fortune for us that he knows how to say it.

The scenes are austere in their composition. There is one, the tawdry afternoon of the satyr, Tom Buchanan, and his cheap and "vital" mistress, which is alive by the strength of the lapses of time; another, the meeting between Gatsby and his love, takes place literally behind closed doors, the narrator telling us only the beginning and the end. The variety of treatment, the intermingling of dialogue and narrative, the use of a snatch of significant detail instead of a big scene, make the whole a superb impressionistic painting, vivid in colour, and sparkling with meaning. And the major composition is as just as the treatment of detail. There is a brief curve before Gatsby himself enters; a longer one in which he begins his movement toward Daisy; then a succession of carefully spaced shorter and longer movements until the climax is reached. The plot works out not like a puzzle with odd bits falling into place, but like a tragedy, with every part functioning in the completed organism.

Even now, with *The Great Gatsby* before me, I cannot find in the earlier Fitzgerald the artistic integrity and the passionate feeling which this book possesses. And perhaps analysing the one and praising the other, both fail to convey the sense of elation which one has in reading his new novel. Would it be better to say that even *The Great Gatsby* is full of faults, and that that doesn't matter in the slightest degree? The cadences borrowed from Conrad, the occasional smartness, the frequently startling, but ineffective adjective—at last they do not signify. Because for the most part you know that Fitzgerald has consciously put these bad and half-bad things behind him, that he trusts them no more to make him the white-headed boy of *The Saturday Evening Post,* and that he has recognized both his capacities and his obligations as a novelist.

* * *

You could write such a damn fine book—What held you up and constipated you more than anything was that review of Seldes in the Dial—After that you became self conscious about it and knew you must write a masterpiece. Nobody but Fairies ever writes Maspertieces or Masterpieces consciously—Anybody else can only write as well as they can going on the system that if this one when it's done isn't a Masterpiece maybe the next one will be. You'd have written two damned good books by now if it hadn't been for that Seldes review.

—Ernest Hemingway to Fitzgerald, 4 September 1929

Collier's was a mass-circulation magazine that competed with The Saturday Evening Post; *Grant Overton was a popular writer on literary subjects.*

Have You Read–?
Grant Overton
Collier's, 8 August 1925

Twenty-nine on September 24th—that's the age of F. Scott Fitzgerald, author of "This Side of Paradise" and of a new novel, "The Great Gatsby."

It is five years since "This Side of Paradise" appeared.

One of the best ways to describe "The Great Gatsby" is to say that for the first time in reading Scott Fitzgerald you forget his age.

"This Side of Paradise," as one man said, had every imaginable fault except the fault that would have been fatal. It lived; the people in it lived and you lived as you read it.

Fitzgerald's second novel, "The Beautiful and Damned," had moments. But when it was finished it was just a second novel by the author of "This Side of Paradise."

"The Great Gatsby" really comes off. Without being anything more than memorable among the novels of the season or the year, the book is the most thrilling of 1925 so far in one direction: It unveils an author.

One novel does not make a writer any more than one swallow makes a summer drink. Show me a brilliant novel by a youngster and you show me a brilliant novel by a youngster—but you show me nothing more.

The infant prodigy exists in music and chess as a force to be reckoned with, but not in fiction. In judging "The Great Gatsby" you have to take into account how severely handicapped Scott Fitzgerald was simply from the fact of having written "This Side of Paradise" at twenty-three.

"The Great Gatsby" is not necessarily a novel of wide appeal. I don't even know whether it is fully intelligible to anyone who has not had glimpses of the kind of life it depicts. That life I should describe as the froth on the wave of the city washing out into the edges of the countryside. It is a mixture of iridescent bubbles and scum. It is silly, empty, bursting and beautiful. It leaves a dirty mark on the ground. You stare at the stain and wonder which is real, the glint of loveliness that you saw or the smear that is left.

And the answer, of course, is that both are real, real as life itself, the queer mixture of beauty and pain, courage and cruelty that blows bubbles continually for all of us. . . .

Well, if you had lived on western Long Island or in Westchester County, N.Y., or just outside Chicago or San Francisco or any other sizable city, you will recognize everything in "The Great Gatsby.". . .

You pick up your morning paper and see a headline: NAMES NEIGHBOR IN SOCIETY DIVORCE, or NEW EVIDENCE IN SMART SET'S MURDER. "The Great Gatsby" is a perfect picture of the life that produces those headlines. It is the story that the morning paper never gives you.

Please don't get the idea, however, that the book is melodramatic. It contains murder and sudden death, but off stage. You get what went before, and you get the consequences.

That is why I say this novel is thrilling. That is why I say it reveals a man who can write (and "write" here means go on writing and growing). Mr. Fitzgerald has said something like this to himself:

"Let the morning paper supply 'kick.' I am not a reporter; I am a novelist. My job is not to supply the reader with a kick; my job is to make him feel an emotion.

"The newspaper tells him what happened, but it never makes it clear enough. The reader wants to know *why* it happened. He wants to know how in thunder such a thing *could* happen. I'll show him how!"

If Scott Fitzgerald were a horse, I would back him now in anything where he had to go a good distance.

* * *

Edward Shenton drew the illustrations for Tender Is the Night *(1934).*

The Great Gatsby Establishes Scott Fitzgerald as an Artist

Edward Shenton

Anatole France believed a book review should be an appreciation. Other critics have other methods. One may be detached and hand down from the ivory tower a carefully balanced, precise estimate, or depend upon an immense gusto, a sort of personal broadcasting of loves and hatreds. Abstractedly the ivory tower intrigues us; temperamentally the first method seems most alluring.

"The Great Gatsby" is Scott Fitzgerald's latest and best work. It is a mature conception, adroitly planned, executed with great cunning, incredibly alive, written with economy, with subtle feeling for beauty. Fitzgerald has retained all the distinction of the best parts of "This Side of Paradise." To them he has added restraint, skill, a new power. In a few years he has discovered how to mould a story and then conceal the structure.

Scott Fitzgerald is a romanticist, if this means the desire to have life as it should be; but he sees too clearly to dwindle into a romantic novelist. The only course left is satire. Unable to achieve isolation, his satire is diluted by contempt, hatred, despair. This may reduce somewhat one effect of "The Great Gatsby," but it gives an additional vitality, a personal appeal; a characteristic more ponderous authors cannot achieve.

A strange glow of life pervades each page of the book. It is disturbing, fascinating, an under-rhythm of longing; the desire of youth for all things lovely to be truly so. "The wrong of unshapely things is a wrong too great to be told"; but Fitzgerald must tell this wrong because the things are unshapely beneath. On the surface they are beautiful. The people in "The Great Gatsby" have beauty, money, leisure. Fitzgerald wants them to be as charming as they look. He envelopes them in a glamorous texture from his own mind, and then sees them to be false. In fury he discloses their true selves. They appear selfish, vain, empty; liars and cowards. All but Gatsby, the nobody. Love gives him dignity. For a moment he is great.

The story progresses with amazing rapidity, in a febrile round of parties, a continuous squandering of beauty. Below, the current of life moves with a certain grandeur, culminating in the last dozen pages. The characters are like rockets exploding in the darkness. The gold and scarlet stars flare and fade, the glory of the night remains. Fitzgerald has caught this ephemeral brilliancy and related it to enduring things.

"The Great Gatsby" contains passages difficult to better; there are descriptive paragraphs when the scene is perfect. When Nick Carraway calls upon Daisy Bucha-nan and Jordan Baker:

–"We walked through a high hallway into a bright rosy-colored space, fragilely bound into the house by French windows at either end. The windows were ajar and gleaming white against the fresh grass outside that seemed to grow a little way into the house. A breeze blew thru the room, blew curtains in at one end and out the other like pale flags, twisting them up toward the frosted wedding-cake of the ceiling, and then rippling over the wine-colored rug, making a shadow on it as wind does on the sea. The only completely stationary object in the room was an enormous couch on which two young women were buoyed up as tho upon an over-head balloon. They were both in white, and their dresses were rippling and fluttering as if they had just been blown back in after a short flight around the house"–

"The Great Gatsby" is among the most absorbing books published this year, and not to be missed by those interested in the career of one of the most important younger writers. The Jazz Age is over. Scott Fitzgerald is definitely established as an artist.

–Unidentified clipping in Fitzgerald's Scrapbook

DESCRIPTIVE BIBLIOGRAPHY

The First English Printing of the American Edition

A11.1.c

Copyright page: 'PUBLISHED 1926 | PRINTED IN GREAT BRITAIN | ALL | RIGHTS RESERVED'.

Same pagination and collation as first Scribners printing.

Contents: p. i: half title; p. ii: blank; p. III: title; p. iv: copyright; p. v: dedication; p. vi: blank; pp. 1-218: text, headed 'THE GREAT GATSBY | CHAPTER I'.

Paper: Laid unwatermarked paper. Vertical chain lines 1" apart.

Binding: Dark blue (#183) paper-covered boards in V pattern. Spine gold-stamped: 'THE GREAT | GATSBY | F. | SCOTT FITZGERALD | CHATTO & WINDUS'. Also deep yellowish brown (#75) V cloth (fine linen-like grain), spine blackstamped. Also strong purplish blue (#196) paper-covered boards in B pattern, spine blackstamped. *The English Catalogue of Books* notes that 350 copies were sold in a cheaper binding.

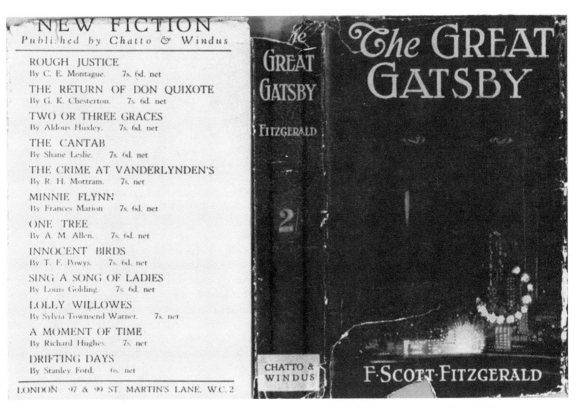

Dust jacket for the English reprint of the American edition, with remainder label (Matthew J. and Arlyn Bruccoli Collection, University of South Carolina)

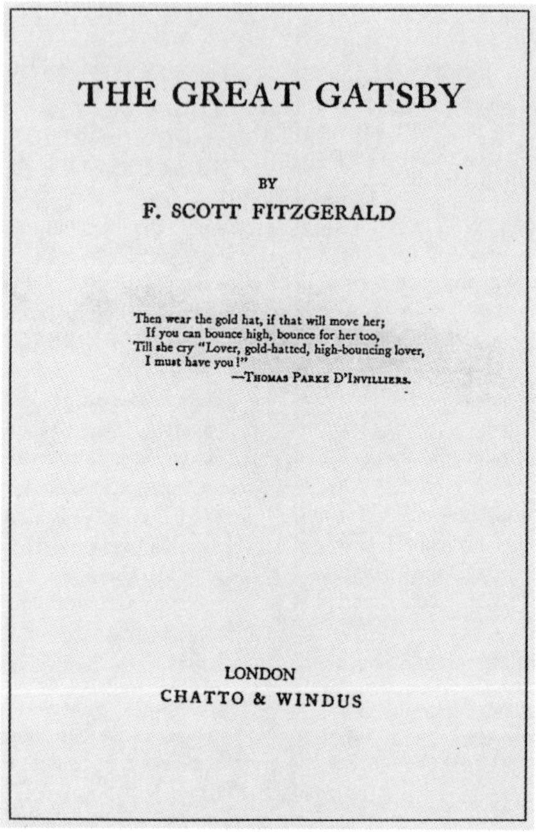

THE GREAT GATSBY

BY

F. SCOTT FITZGERALD

Then wear the gold hat, if that will move her;
If you can bounce high, bounce for her too,
Till she cry "Lover, gold-hatted, high-bouncing lover,
I must have you!"
—THOMAS PARKE D'INVILLIERS.

LONDON
CHATTO & WINDUS

Title page: A11.1.c (Matthew J. and Arlyn Bruccoli Collection, University of South Carolina)

Dust jacket: Front same as Scribners. Spine same as Scribners, with substitution of 'CHATTO & | WINDUS' imprint. Back printed in black on white: 'NEW FICTION' [12 titles beginning with *Rough Justice*]. Front flap: '7S.NET'. Back flap blank. Remainder jackets have price trimmed from front flap and on spine a rectangular '2/6NET' label or a circular '2/–' label.

Publication: Unknown number of copies of the first English printing. Published February 1926. 7s.

Locations: BL (10 FEB 26–blue boards); Bod (FEB 15 1926–blue boards); C. Burden (blue boards, dj); MJB (brown cloth, dj with 2/6 label); MJB (blue boards, dj with 2s label).

ENGLISH REVIEWS

The Great Gatsby *was published in 1926 by Chatto and Windus in London. The number of copies in this*

single printing is unknown, but the book did not sell. Copies of the 7s. book were remaindered at 2s.6d. and 2s. The novel was not widely reviewed in Britain, but the reviews were mainly respectful.

Seldes's second review of Gatsby *appeared in a literary journal edited by T. S. Eliot.*

Gilbert Seldes
New Criterion, January 1926

... The Great Gatsby is a brilliant work, and it is also a sound one; it is carefully written, and vivid; it has structure, and it has life. To all the talents, discipline has been added. The form is again derived from James through Mrs. Wharton, and there are cadences direct from the pages of Conrad; but I feel that Fitzgerald has at last made his borrowings his own, and that they nowhere diminish the vitality of his work. The subject, too, ought to be of interest outside America; it is a drama of an intense passion played on Long Island, the summer home of wealth, and even, in spots, of Society, near

212

New York. Fitzgerald has no feeling for Main Street; his satire is not that of reformer; and he has certainly the best chance, at this moment, of becoming our finest artist in fiction. The press has not been too enthusiastic about *The Great Gatsby;* Mencken has notably discovered it virtues, but so intense is our preoccupation with the drab as subject, that this story of a Long Island Trimalchio has been compared to the preposterous stories of high-life written by Robert W. Chambers. . . .

* * *

The Times Literary Supplement, *which published unsigned reviews, was the most influential English critical journal at that time. The* TLS *reviewer erred in stating that Fitzgerald's previous books had not been published in Britain.*

Times Literary Supplement, 18 February 1926

F. Scott Fitzgerald, author of *The Great Gatsby,* is a young American novelist whose work has not hitherto reached England. We understand that with his previous novels, one of which had a university setting, he has won a large amount of popularity in his own country, and that the present novel, his latest, is an effort in a rather different direction from that of ordinary American popular fiction. However this may be, *The Great Gatsby* is undoubtedly a work of art and of great promise. Mr. Fitzgerald has grasped the economical construction of a story, and his power of telling conciseness enables him, without being obscure, to compass a great deal in a short space. He uses words like living things, instead of like dead counters.

Gatz, or Gatsby, is a Conradian hero—one of those beings, like Almayer or the hero of *Heart of Darkness,* who are lifted above all the evil that they do or seek, above all the dirty trails that shoddy souls leave over the world, and above all the tragedy or destruction in which they finally sink, by some great elemental loyalty to a dream that, in a different world, would have been beautiful. Mr. Fitzgerald has imagined a son of broken-down and shiftless farm folk who, in his youth, found a platonic conception of himself and "invented just the sort of Jay Gatsby that a seventeen-year-old boy would be likely to invent, and to this conception he was faithful to the end." His dream universe of "ineffable gaudiness," realized partially by five years of secretaryship to a dissolute old millionaire, is enriched by an experience of love when, as a young officer, he had had a month of Daisy Buchanan and known an almost superhuman ecstasy. Daisy, then unmarried,

belonged to his dream universe of beauty, money, and ease; penniless Gatsby, having illicitly entered it in the disguise of uniform, comes back after brilliant service in the war to find himself still outside it and Daisy married. By the mouth of Mr. Carraway, who is related to Daisy and visits her home on Long Island, there is told what Gatsby did in order to enter into his dream again. All passes in one summer. Gatsby, wealthy through lending himself to nameless corruptions, keeps open house upon the shore of West Egg, because the green light of the Buchanans' dock, on the opposite shore of East Egg, twinkles to him in the darkness. All the lavish show of drunken vulgarity is simply kept up to bring that green light nearer. Through Carraway Gatsby meets Daisy again—the weak, shallow creature who loves only by moments—and their meeting, which culminates in Daisy's weeping over Gatsby's exhibition of multitudinous shirts in his wardrobe, is an admirable piece of writing. And so Gatsby, steadfast in all his corruption, becomes involved in the life of Daisy Buchanan and her sensual savage of a husband Tom, whose typical outing with his mistress, the wife of a seedy garage keeper, throws a queer light on the manners of New York. Tragedy is not long in coming, for Tom suspects Gatsby, and on the amazing afternoon when Gatsby tells him to his face that Daisy no longer loves him, it is Daisy's tawdriness that brings the dream to the ground with a crash. Daisy, having shattered Gatsby's life, can do no more than wrap him finally in death and dishonor. Mr. Fitzgerald finally maintains, besides his hard, sardonic realism, the necessary emotional intensity, but we must admit that it needs perhaps an excess of intensity to buoy up the really very unpleasant characters of this story.

* * *

L. P. Hartley published his first novel in 1925 and was at the beginning of a long career as an admired literary figure.

L. P. Hartley
Saturday Review, 20 February 1926

Mr. Scott Fitzgerald deserves a good shaking. Here is an unmistakable talent unashamed of making itself a motley to the view. *The Great Gatsby* is an absurd story, whether considered a romance, melodrama, or plain record of New York high life. An adventurer of shady antecedents builds a palace at a New York seaside resort, entertains on a scale which Lucullus would have marvelled at but could not have approved, and spends untold sums of money, all to catch the eye of his one time sweetheart, who lives on an island opposite, unhappily but very successfully married. At last, after superhuman feats of ostentation and display, the fly walks into the web. A train of disasters follows, comparable in quantity and quality with the scale of the Great Gatsby's prodigies of hospitality. Coincidence leaps to the helm and throws a mistress under a motor-car. The car does not stop, which, all things considered, is the most natural thing that happens in the book. An injured husband finds the Great Gatsby in suicidal mood sitting on a raft in his artificial lake and (apparently) forestalls him; anyhow they are both discovered dead. The elder Gatsby is unearthed and gives a pathetic account of his son's early years. All the characters behave as if they were entitled to grieve over a great sorrow, and the book closes with the airs of tragedy. Mr. Fitzgerald seems to have lost sight of O. Henry and hitched his wagon to Mr. Arlen's star. It is a great pity, for even in this book, in the dialogue, in many descriptive passages, there are flashes of wit and insight, felicities of phrase and a sense of beauty. His imagination is febrile and his emotion over-strained; but how good, of its kind, is his description of Gatsby's smile, which:

> faced—or seemed to face—the whole eternal world for an instant, and then concentrated on *you* with an irresistible prejudice in your favour. It understood you just as far as you wanted to be understood, believed in you as you would like to believe in yourself, and assured you that it had precisely the impression of you that, at your best, you hoped to convey.

The Great Gatsby is evidently not a satire; but one would like to think that Mr. Fitzgerald's heart is not in it, that it is a piece of mere naughtiness.

* * *

The New Statesman *was a journal of British political opinion.*

The New Statesman, 27 March 1926
Mr. Fitzgerald's story of New York's Bohemian and Smart Sets has qualities that remove it from the ruck of such novels. The Great Gatsby himself is drawn with spirit and insight and humour, a man who, though many kinds of rogue, is yet an idealist and dreamer of dreams. When we first meet him, Gatsby is the centre of a flamboyant society that sponges upon, despises and slanders him. He is living in an enormous and pretentious mansion on Long Island where he keeps open house. We soon learn that this ostentation of wealth

American poet Conrad Aiken's review recognized the lyrical qualities of Fitzgerald's prose

is but the means to an end. During the war Gatsby, a young officer with nothing but his pay, had met and loved a young woman of the established rich and his love had been returned. This girl is now married to a wealthy man of her own class who is notoriously unfaithful to her. They are living on Long Island, and Gatsby is there to meet her. He does, and for a time it seems that he will succeed in winning her from her husband, but in the end she cheats him, and he is killed in error by a man whom the husband has wronged. Mr. Fitzgerald is a satirist with a pretty thick velvet glove. When the narrator of the story tells the unhappy Gatsby that he is the best of the bunch, we agree.

* * *

Conrad Aiken
New Criterion, October 1926
In *The Great Gatsby* Mr. Fitzgerald has written a highly colored and brilliant little novel which, by

214

grace of one cardinal virtue, quite escapes the company of most contemporary American fiction–it has excellence of form. It is not great, it is not large, it is not strikingly subtle; but it is well imagined and shaped, it moves swiftly and neatly, its scene is admirably seized and admirably matched with the theme, and its hard bright tone is entirely original. Technically, it appears to owe much to the influence of the cinema; and perhaps also something to Henry James–a peculiar conjunction, but not so peculiar if one reflects on the flash-backs and close-ups and paralleled themes of that "little experiment in the style of Gyp," *The Awkward Age*. Mr. Fitzgerald's publishers call *The Great Gatsby* a satire. This is deceptive. It is only incidentally a satire, it is only in the *setting* that it is satirical, and in the tone provided by the minor characters. The story itself, and the main figure, are tragic, and it is precisely the fantastic vulgarity of the scene which gives to the excellence of Gatsby's soul its finest bouquet, and to his tragic fate its sharpest edge. All of Mr. Fitzgerald's people are real–but Gatsby comes close to being superb. He is betrayed to us slowly and skillfully, and with a keen tenderness which in the end makes his tragedy a deeply moving one. By so much, therefore, *The Great Gatsby* is better than a mere satire of manners, and better than Mr. Fitzgerald's usual sort of superficial cleverness. If only he can refrain altogether in future from the sham romanticism and sham sophistication which the magazines demand of him, and give another turn of the screw to the care with which he writes, he may well become a first-rate novelist.

* * *

Edward Shanks was a member of the Georgian group of English poets and was an active book reviewer.

Edward Shanks
London Mercury, April 1926

The shadow of the War hangs a little over Mr. Scott Fitzgerald as well. At any rate, this was the immediate cause which shot "the great Gatsby" into social circles other than those in which he was born. But Jimmy Gatz, caterpillar to the subsequent sinister and bewildered butterfly, would probably have achieved his metamorphosis somehow even if that occasion had been lacking.

The story leaves one with a queer nightmarish idea of the possibilities of life in America, but with no doubt as to Mr. Fitzgerald's talents. He handles his grotesque material with an artist's discretion and astonishes one sometimes by his moderation. Where he might well be flamboyant, he is dry: where he might be ragingly sentimental, he is full of commonsense. And Gatsby's hopeless, fatal passion for Daisy remains in the reader's mind at the end as something bizarre and, on the whole unimportant, but also as something which the author has made to yield the last scrap of significance. Cocktails, midnight parties, wildly driven cars, irregular sexual relations, base finance and a little banditry–these are queer, unpromising threads, but they are woven into an interesting texture. This is Mr. Fitzgerald's best book so far, and it suggests that he is getting away from models which were much too easy for him to copy.

The author of The Great Gatsby

CHAPTER 4:

REPUTATION OF *THE GREAT GATSBY*

The history of The Great Gatsby *fulfills F. Scott Fitzgerald's 1920 boast that he wrote for "the youth of his own generation, the critics of the next, and the schoolmasters of ever afterward." The Fitzgerald Revival—it more closely resembled a resurrection—raised him from a position of neglect and condescension to a secure position among the greatest American writers.* The Great Gatsby *was the focus of this reassessment and consequently became a serious contender for "the great American novel."*

The Fitzgerald Revival evolved through four stages from 1940–1941 to around 1960. In the first stage following his death the mostly patronizing obituaries and the tributes by his literary friends singled out Gatsby *for recognition, typically indicating that he had not fulfilled the expectations aroused by this novel. Edmund Wilson was the most influential figure at this point. He organized* The New Republic *tributes in 1941, and that year he edited* The Last Tycoon, *with which he packaged* The Great Gatsby.

Serious revivals result from active readership—not just from critical appreciation—which requires the availability of books. The Fitzgerald Revival was essentially a reader-driven revival, not critic-driven or professor-driven. Readers bought and read his books, and that resulted in the printing of more copies. Stage two of the revival came in 1945, and it was a Gatsby *year. The Armed Services Editions gave away some 150,000 copies of* Gatsby; *the novel was among the first ten Bantam paperbacks, priced at 25¢; it was included in* The Portable F. Scott Fitzgerald, *edited by Dorothy Parker with introduction by John O'Hara; it was reprinted by New Directions (dated 1946) with an influential introduction by Lionel Trilling. Grosset & Dunlap published an inexpensive hardbound* Gatsby *in 1949.*

The revival accelerated in 1950–1951—a decade after Fitzgerald's death. The first biography of Fitzgerald, Arthur Mizener's The Far Side of Paradise *(1951), was accompanied by Budd Schulberg's novel based on Fitzgerald in Hollywood,* The Disenchanted *(1950). Malcolm Cowley was instrumental in getting Fitzgerald's work republished. His selection of* The Stories of F. Scott Fitzgerald *(1951) included previously uncollected stories, and his edition of "The Author's*

Final Version" of Tender Is the Night *(1951) elicited a reappraisal of that then-underrated masterpiece. Nonetheless,* Gatsby *continued to lead the parade. The Bantam paperback was reprinted an undetermined number of times during the Fifties.* Gatsby *first appeared in the widely distributed English Penguin line in 1950 and remains there after more than sixty-eight printings.*

After 1960 The Great Gatsby *was firmly positioned among the masterpieces of American literature. It continued to be the most widely read and admired Fitzgerald work, and it became a classroom staple. In 1960* Gatsby *became the first volume in the paperback Scribner Library, and in 1961 it was reprinted as a Scribner School Edition intended for high schools. Since the 1960s Scribners has continued to repackage* Gatsby *in textbook series and in collections.* Gatsby *is the first volume in the Cambridge University Press critical edition of the works of Fitzgerald which commenced publication in 1991.*

STAGE AND SCREEN ADAPTATIONS IN THE 1920s

Play: *The Great Gatsby*

Ambassador Theatre, New York, 2 February 1926

Careless People and Gatsby

J. Brooks Atkinson

The New York Times Theater Reviews, 3 February 1926

Of the several attempts to portray on the stage these restless moderns, whose cynicisms and infidelities keep the calamity-howlers hoarse, none has been more able or moving than "The Great Gatsby," mounted last evening at the Ambassador. After the several counterfeits by Michael Arlen and his school of bogus sociologists this approach to the whirling, baffled folk who cherish no loyalties, none even to themselves, becomes conspicuous at once for its perspective and sincerity. As a novel from the facile pen of F. Scott Fitzgerald it found

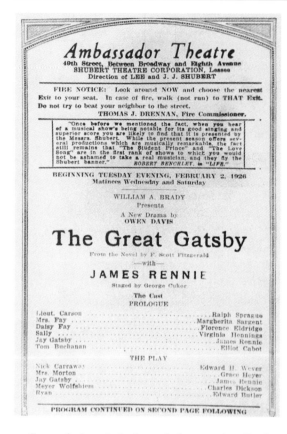

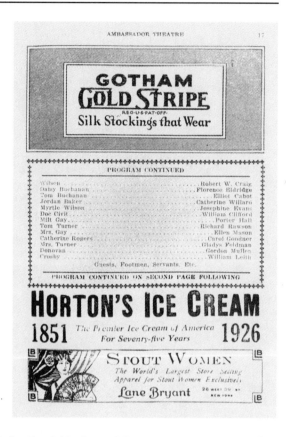

Program for the production that ran for fourteen weeks on Broadway (Matthew J. and Arlyn Bruccoli Collection, University of South Carolina)

immediate favor last season; the dramatic version by Owen Davis retains most of the novel's peculiar glamour. Both novel and play subordinate the meretricious cleverness inherent in this material to the task of telling a story and keeping the characters in true focus. In spite of certain rough edgings in the play composition, awkwardness in the exposition, looseness in some of the scenes, "The Great Gatsby" provides something more substantial than an evening's entertainment.

If the play loses some of the perfect nuances of the novel's comedy and character that cannot be translated in terms of the theatre, that are essential properties of literary style, it gains distinctly in criticism of the material. By use of people in the flesh, speaking and acting, the play accents the telling contrasts between Gatsby, the romantic swindler, positive and honorable according to his precedents, and the Buchanans and Bakers and people of quality who have a high sense of honor and cheat it continually. After a prologue rehearsing the furious romance between Second Lieutenant Gatsby and Daisy Fay in 1917, just before the war, the play begins its chron-

icle of West Egg, Long Island, life in the Summer of 1925. On the one side is Daisy, now married to Tom Buchanan of her "own class," bored, unsettled and frantic at her husband's infidelities with the chauffeur's wife. On the other is Gatsby, now fabulously and mysteriously wealthy, and quite solid personally in the midst of the superficial and cynical revelries of the people who throng to his gay parties.

Driven to desperate extremes by the blatancy of her husband's amours, Daisy flies to Gatsby as the one way out. But since his affection is more substantial than any familiar in her society, he is not content with the easy compromise she suggests. In fact, his idealism places her in a tremendously exalted position. In the final act, she is on the point of leaving her husband for good, has, in fact, made her choice deliberately between the two, when Buchanan exposes Gatsby as a bootlegger, a forger and criminal in general. Before the bewilderment has subsided, the cuckold chauffeur, led astray in his suspicions by Buchanan's sniveling duplicity, shoots Gatsby in mistaken revenge for the affront upon his domestic honor. "He was the best of the lot," says one of those present as the epitaph.

The motivations for murder are not too strong in the novel. In the play they are even more flimsy; the identification by a cigarette holder is scarcely convincing. But the situation so quickly brought about is bitter and ironical, for thus Gatsby is slain in cold blood for the sins of Buchanan which, psychologically, have made the one a man and the other a scoundrel. And this final catastrophe is the distillation of all the social contrasts between Gatsby and the careless, well-bred people who surround him. Beyond the drama of characterization, "The Great Gatsby" is also a romance. By cherishing his essential ideal Gatsby is forgiven his career of crime. To become the social equal of the woman he loves he has lifted himself by his bootstraps, and all that he has done he justifies by the reality of his affection. The virtue of the play is that it makes this new alignment of social values creditable for the time being at the pawns of characterization.

Mr. Rennie gives plausibility to the part of Gatsby in the roughness and fullness of his voice and in the solidity of his presence. It is the truest portrait in the first act when he covers these qualities with a slight film of social uneasiness in the presence of suaver people. In the emotion of the last two acts he plays a "straight part" that gives Gatsby a polite equality not strictly in keeping with the role. Miss Eldridge portrays Daisy Buchanan with fidelity; she is the distraught, thin, weak-willed young woman, drawn two ways at once. Miss Willard catches the indolence in Jordan Baker.

Mr. Dickson portrays the cautious loyalties of the professional gambler Meyer Wolfshiem. As the "rotter," Tom Buchanan, Mr. Cabot remains faithful to the motives of his part, and in the last act discovers a touch of tenderness beneath a general surface of boorishness. Mr. Wever likewise fits his part into the design of the play. The local color of the Gatsby party is tawdry and conventional. Indeed, in some respects the play has remained too faithful to the book. Although Mr. Davis is a good stage craftsman, his eagerness to catch as much of the book as possible is obviously responsible for much clumsiness in the ordering of the material, occasional bare spots and frequent confusing shifts of mood.

* * *

The Stage: Great Scott
Alexander Woollcott
New York World, 3 February 1926

Florence Eldridge and James Rennie (Matthew J. and Arlyn Bruccoli Collection, University of South Carolina)

While the younger Brady was loftily sponsoring a revival of "Little Eyolf" yesterday afternoon, the old block was busy putting the finishing touches on his own production for the day—the dramatization of "The Great Gatsby," which was formally presented to a bulging audience last night at the Ambassador.

This is the play which, with a kind of cunning that would also come in handy in working out jig-saw puzzles, Owen Davis has fashioned from the fine, vivid novel by Scott Fitzgerald. He has carried the book over on to the stage with almost the minimum of spilling: the result is a steadily interesting play, with a cast chosen with a good deal of shrewdness and then goaded into giving a vociferous performance.

"The Great Gatsby" is, to my notion, an engrossing book written with fine art. It is notable for its portrait of the shiny bounder, Gatsby, a portrait painted with humor and with compassion. It is notable, too, for its acute sensitiveness to the changing complexion of the times, its almost journalistic report on the post-war manners of Great Neck, which is plausibly credited with having inspired its gaudy West Egg, Long Island.

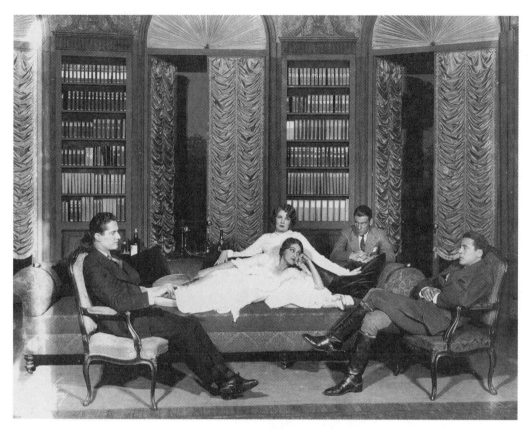

James Rennie, Florence Eldridge, Catherine Willard, Edward H. Wever, and Elliot Cabot (Matthew J. and Arlyn Bruccoli Collection, University of South Carolina)

This novel, wherewith Master Fitzgerald conquered new territory, has now been done into a play that adopts its substance without its sequence, and for its purposes, makes only one small shift in personnel. For the convenience of a playwright who did not want to pick up his play and go traipsing all over Long Island with it, the obscure fellow with whose wife Buchanan dallies so disastrously is now given a job as chauffeur under Buchanan's own roof and so moves into the play, bag and, as you might say, baggage.

Gatsby, as you ought to know already, old sport, is a young climber out of the unclassified Middle West who, in the freemasonry of the training camps, when all doors were open to personable young officers, caught a glimpse of the kind of interior and the kind of girl he might never even have dreamed of had they really kept us out of war. The play employs a prologue to reveal a moment out of that inciting 1917 prelude to his tragedy. Then, in the post-war scenes it devotes itself to his crude, bold reach for the place in this world and the things of this

world he thought would lift him to her level. It is a study of the rise/and fall of the great Gatsby, that criminal, childlike, grotesque, pathetic great Gatsby.

James Rennie proved, I think, a felicitous choice for this role—this made-while-you-wait gentleman of Fitzgerald's imagining. Then Elliott Cabot and Edward H. Wever afforded the most nicely graded contrast to bring out Gatsby's weakness, and to bring out Gatsby's strength. And there were good bits well managed by Catherine Willard, Charles Dixon and Charles W. Craig.

How much all that unfolded on the Ambassador's stage may have seemed clear and interesting to those who brought no knowledge of the play with them to the theatre, I cannot say. To those of us who had done our home-work it was an interesting evening. At the risk of seeming captious I should like to point out, however, that people from Louisville do not call it Loo-ee-vil. They call it Loo-a-vl.

* * *

From Novel to Stage

J. Brooks Atkinson

The New York Times Theater Reviews, 7 February 1926

As compared with the novel, the theatre places its characters boldly on the stage where their features and manners are brutally exposed and their voices leave definite impressions. And although this makes for vividness, and establishes a definite central post upon which all the subordinate impressions must be hung, it destroys the fine web of mystery that a good novelist may spin by tricks of style and technique. Owen Davis's dramatization of "The Great Gatsby" transposes F. Scott Fitzgerald's novel to the stage remarkably well, and retains not only the contours of the story, but the essences of the characterization. Indeed, it sharpens the foreground, if not the background, and it draws up the conflicts of the main characters in more orderly array. And just as "The Great Gatsby" as a novel surpassed its superficial relatives in organization and understanding, so the play improves upon its jazz-mad, gin-mad contemporaries.

Nevertheless, the novelist's lightness of touch, the detachment of the "first person singular," and the art of deft suggestion cannot endure the glare of the footlights. For instance the germ of the Dionysian orgy in the second act of the play is doubtless this paragraph in the novel:

By midnight the hilarity had increased. A celebrated tenor had sung in Italian, and a notorious contralto had sung in jazz, and between the numbers people were doing "stunts" all over the garden, while happy vacuous bursts of laughter rose toward the Summer sky. A pair of stage twins, who turned out to be the girls in yellow, did a baby act in costume, and champagne was served in glasses bigger than fingerbowls. The moon had risen higher, and floating in the Sound was a triangle of silver scales, trembling a little to the stiff, tinny drop of the banjoes on the lawn.

In the raucous and leering party of the second act, the play does not reproduce the slight touch of unworldliness in this impersonal description. But the most flagrant disillusionment in all novel dramatizations is the personification of side-remarks in which the novelist comments upon his theme. When in the third act Gatsby makes a clean breast of his much-doubted Oxford connection, Nick Carraway cries: "Good for you, Gatsby!", or words to that effect. The basis of that exclamation in the novel is much finer and much fuller because it is unexpressed: "I wanted to get up and slap him on the back. I had one of these renewals of complete faith in him that I'd experienced before." Again, one of the most searching observations in the novel, brilliant because it is at once broadly true and thoroughly casual, is this characterization of the rudderless

married couple: "They were careless people, Tom and Daisy—they snarled up things and creatures and then retreated back into their money or their vast carelessness, or whatever it was that kept them together, and let other people clean up the mess they had made." As dialogue in the drama, this line passes as casually as it is written; we of the audience have no time to digest it before the next line starts ringing in our ears.

By placing the characters on the stage and supplying details of their personalities left by the novel to the reader's imagination, the play gives a much more penetrating sense of contrast. In the precise terminology of the courts, this Gatsby is a master criminal. In the conception of the play, however, he is an idealist. As he protests in the last act when the sordid details of his business come to the surface, all the bootlegging plots and marketing of forged bonds do not matter. It is the virtue of true romance that infractions of the public code are justified by heroic idealism. Everything done in the interests of love is purified by that allegiance. It is likewise the virtue of true romance that the passionate lover exalts his lady to a plane far above her true reality. Whatever crimes Gatsby may have committed to raise himself socially, he is nevertheless the true romantic swain by virtue of his idealization.

Mr. Fitzgerald could have found no better device for exposing the shabby people of whom he is writing. While Gatsby's crimes belong properly to the realm of the legal code, theirs are social; and in the comparison of personal traits, personal honor, Gatsby the impostor excels in every respect. No play has exhibited more pungently, by implication and contrast, the instability and abortive neutrality of these "well-bred" people; restless futile, incurably dishonest, with a basic insincerity. Played and directed excellently, "The Great Gatsby" emerges—quite unintentionally—as the most disinterested commentary on this flask-and-flash era that has come to the stage this season. And chiefly, one suspects, because nothing was further from the author's intention. Mr. Fitzgerald and Mr. Davis, respectively were engrossed in writing marketable drama.

* * *

Long Island Sentiment

Joseph Wood Krutch

The Nation, 122 (24 February 1926)

F. SCOTT FITZGERALD was born into the flapper age with exactly the qualities and the defects which would enable him to become its accredited historian. Though granted just enough detachment to make him undertake the task of describing, he is by temperament too much a part of the things described to view them with any very penetratingly critical eye and he sees flap-

THE NEW YORKER   21

THE FINAL POT SHOT AT THE GREAT GATSBY

How Owen Davis makes Drama out of Scott Fitzgerald's romantic vulgarian, the great bootlegger and the near-great lover, at the Ambassador Theatre. Here depicted are James Rennie writhing in the noble agonies of his small catastrophe and Florence Eldridge whooping large whoops in an effort to get away without too much Long Island mud on her reputation.

Caricature by Miguel Covarrubias

pers, male and female, much as they see themselves. Sharing to a very considerable extent in their psychological processes, he romanticizes their puerilities in much the same fashion as they do; and when he pictures the manners of the fraternity house or the Long Island villa he pictures them less as they are than as their practitioners like to imagine them. He makes cocktails and kisses seem thrillingly wicked; he flatters the younger generation with the solemn warning that it is leading the world straight to the devil; and as a result he writes The Flapper's Own History of Flapperism. Thus he becomes less the genuine historian of a phase of social development than one of the characteristic phenomena of that development itself, and his books are seen to be little more than documents for the study of the thing which they purport to treat.

His works, like the works of Michael Arlen, illustrate the Nemesis of sophistication, which in their case turns out to be an abysmal if disguised sentimentality. Cynicism and disillusion are qualities which require ripening to develop and fortitude to bear if they are to constitute more than a pose. The youth who leaps gaily after them cannot live comfortably in the harsh world which they create, so that sentimentality, disguised or perverted, almost inevitably reenters by way of offering a compensation. All the old falsities reappear and constitute the chief charm of the writer for that portion of his audience which finds itself the victim of the same conflict between intellectual pose and emotional need which generates his work. Cynicism is modish, but sentimentality is comfortable."

"The Great Gatsby" (Ambassador Theater) has been fashioned by Owen Davis from Mr. Fitzgerald's novel of the same name, and the play has the same elements of popularity as the book. Here is that ever-intriguing figure the romantic criminal brought absolutely up to date; here, that is to say, is Robin Hood reincarnated as a bootlegger, and here too is the sauce of contemporary smartness supplying in liberal measure an additional piquancy to the dish. Thanks to the talent which he has for evoking the general atmosphere which is supposed to invest the smart set Mr. Fitzgerald can give to this naïve and sentimental story an air of sophistication, and in that fact lies the secret of his popularity. In its essence "The Great Gatsby" is a preposterously maudlin tale of the efforts of a poor boy to become rich enough to "make himself worthy" of a girl with whom he had had a war-time flirtation; in its accidents it purports to be a sophisticated picture of flapper morality; and as a result of these two elements it presents an excellent opportunity for that large portion of the population—which loves sentimentality, but is ashamed to indulge its taste—to enjoy itself thoroughly.

In the beginning the play promises something a little better than it eventually gives. The smart dialogue is brightly written and the characters, excellently interpreted by a uniformly capable cast which includes Florence Eldridge and James Rennie, are at least clear cut and recognizable types. Even the conception of Gatsby himself includes its strokes of truth and of pathos, for there is material for a real study in the story of this man who aspires wistfully toward a world into which he has not been born. But as the piece develops it grows steadily more meretricious. It takes its colors less and less from reality and more and more from a sort of servant-girl's dream world until it ends in sheer and tawdry melodrama. "The Great Gatsby" has the humor which "The Green Hat" in its dramatic form so completely lacks, but it belongs to a related genre.

* * *

Edmund Wilson
New Republic, 24 March 1926

The dramatization of Scott Fitzgerald's novel, The Great Gatsby, is a very agreeable entertainment. It has the usual theatrical deficiencies of stories not originally conceived for the stage; but Owen Davis has adapted it very adroitly, keeping as much of the original dialogue as possible and filling in the gaps with intelligence and a happy invention. In one place, indeed, he has actually succeeded in improving on Fitzgerald: where Fitzgerald has Gatsby, in his embarrassment, knock over the clock on the mantelpiece, Davis makes him tip over a high-ball glass and then apologize for upsetting "the vase." He has resisted obvious temptations in the direction of melodrama and has, in fact, erred, if at all, in keeping the action in too quiet a key.

What is most remarkable about The Great Gatsby is the extent to which Fitzgerald's characters have come to life on the stage. This is, of course, to a very great extent, the work of the actors and the producer, who have caught the color and the spirit of the novel with surprising success. But for the quality of an author to possess itself of the imaginations of actors and producers, that quality must have strength as well as individuality. We realize, in watching The Great Gatsby, how much vitality and how much enchantment Fitzgerald has put into his work. In none of his books are the characters more disreputable nor the events more disagreeable than they are in The Great Gatsby: some rich and stupid Middle-Westerners, a woman tennis champion suspected of cheating, a bootlegger who also sells bad bonds; an intrigue with a garage-keeper's wife and a drunken motor accident. To have treated these materials with some ruthlessness and at the same time invested them with glamor, at once to have made the bootlegger ridiculous and to have compelled us to accept him as a tragic hero from which the rest of the elements of the story derive their chief romance, required the sensibility and the imagination of a genuine poet. Mr. James Rennie perhaps makes Gatsby a little more attractive and personable than he appeared in the novel; yet he is authentically a Scott Fitzgerald character. We are delighted to find him come to life. And of the characters of how many other contemporary American novelists should we say the same?

* * *

> "The Great Gatsby" will close at the Ambassador Theatre on Saturday night. William A. Brady explained that the sudden closing of the Owen Davis–F. Scott Fitzgerald play is due to the illness in England of the mother of Lillian and Dorothy Gish, the motion picture stars. James Rennie, leading man of "The Great Gatsby," is the husband of Dorothy Gish, and he will sail immediately to join his wife, who is at her mother's bedside.
>
> —*The New York Times,* Tuesday, 4 May 1926

Movie: *The Great Gatsby* (Paramount, 1926)

No print of the silent movie version of The Great Gatsby *has been found. It is assumed that the nitrate film self-destructed.*

The Screen: Gold and Cocktails
Mordaunt Hall
The New York Times, 22 November 1926

It is a rare achievement for a director to have three pictures running simultaneously in Broadway theatres. This feat has been accomplished by Herbert Brenon, whose film version of "Beau Geste" is drawing capacity audiences at the Criterion. The new Paramount Theatre opened with Mr. Brenon's photoplay conception of "God Gave Me Twenty Cents," and at the Rivoli there is his pictorial translation of F. Scott Fitzgerald's novel, "The Great Gatsby," on which Owen Davis based his successful play.

The screen version of the "The Great Gatsby" is quite a good entertainment, but at the same time it is obvious that it would have benefited by more imaginative direction. Although Mr. Brenon has

included the tragic note at the end, he has succumbed to a number of ordinary movie flashes without inculcating much in the way of subtlety. Neither he nor the players have succeeded in fully developing the characters.

Warner Baxter fills the role of Jay Gatsby and Lois Wilson plays Daisy Buchanan. They both give conscientious performances but are handicapped by the incidental movie intrusions. Daisy is seen in one episode assuaging her disappointment in life by drinking absinthe. She takes enough of this beverage to render the average person unconscious. Yet she appears only mildly intoxicated, and soon recovers.

Cocktails are an important feature in this picture, after Gatsby returns from the war. Mr. Brenon makes the most of these insidious stimulants, and even has the girls in a swimming pool snatching at cocktails while they are swimming. To give the impression of Gatsby's recklessness with money there is a sequence in which this man of sudden means tosses twenty-dollar gold pieces into the water, and you see a number of the girls diving for the coins. A clever bit of comedy is introduced by a girl asking what Gatsby is throwing into the water, and as soon as this creature hears that they are real gold pieces she unhesitatingly plunges into the pool to get a share. Gatsby appears to throw the money into the water with a good deal of interest, whereas it might perhaps have been more effective to have him appear a little bored as he watched the scramble of the men and women.

Gatsby is unknown to most of his guests, and some of them are surprised that any one should want to meet the host. They are a hard lot, satisfied with the entertainment offered to them—modernists who have no gratitude or affection in their souls.

Daisy, who had been in love with Gatsby before he went to fight, married Tom Buchanan (Hale Hamilton). When Gatsby appears as the mysteriously wealthy individual she goes to Nick Carraway's house to meet him. Here one perceives a regular movie deluge of rain. The reckless driving that results in the death of Myrtle Wilson serves to bring out a sterling trait in Gatsby's character.

William Powell, while not quite in his element, gives an unerring portrayal of the chauffeur. Miss Wilson in a number of the scenes excels anything she has hitherto attempted on the screen. Hale Hamilton is competent as Buchanan, Daisy's faithless husband. Neil Hamilton's work is most artificial. Georgia Hale, who triumphed in Charlie Chaplin's comedy "The Gold Rush," is satisfactory in the role of Myrtle, the girl for whom Buchanan betrays a passionate admiration.

* * *

Lobby card for the lost silent movie (Matthew J. and Arlyn Bruccoli Collection, University of South Carolina)

The Great Gatsby

Abel

Variety, 24 November 1926

Paramount presentation of Herbert Brenon production, featuring Warner Baxter, Lois Wilson, Neil Hamilton and Georgia Hale in screen version of F. Scott Fitzgerald's novel, which Owen Davis dramatized last season. Screen play by Becky Gardner; adapted by Elizabeth Meehan. Footage, 7,296; 80 minutes. At Rivoli, New York, week Nov. 20.

Jay Gatsby	Warner Baxter
Daisy Buchanan	Lois Wilson
Nick Carraway	Neil Hamilton
Myrtle Wilson	Georgia Hale
George Wilson	William Powell
Tom Buchanan	Hale Hamilton
Charles Wolf	George Nash
Jordan Baker	Carmelita Geraghty
Lord Digby	Eric Blore
Bert	"Gunboat" Smith
Catherine	Claire Whitney

"The Great Gatsby" is serviceable film material, a good, interesting, gripping cinema exposition of the type certain to be readily acclaimed by the average fan, with the usual Long Island parties and the rest of those high-hat trimmings thrown in to clinch the argument.

Comes Warner Baxter, cast in a sympathetic role with a doubtful touch. Despite the vague uncertainty of Gatsby's illegal fortune from bootlegging (and Volstead violating in these post-prohibition days is not generally deemed a heinous crime despite the existence of a federal statute which declares it so), the title player has all the sympathies with him.

Lois Wilson and Warner Baxter in the shirt scene (Matthew J. and Arlyn Bruccoli Collection, University of South Carolina)

Then there is Hale Hamilton as the husband, a player who has been invariably cast on stage and screen as a manly and almost impossibly righteous husband or very dear, dear old friend of the family, and who is similarly cast here as the sire of the Buchanan household. He is the husband of Daisy (Lois Wilson), first betrothed to Gatsby.

The audience, in view of the general tenor of the triangular player's previous characterizations, finds itself somewhat befuddled. Along toward the last 20 minutes the wife calmly states she does not love her husband and that her affections are with Gatsby, from whom she was parted by the Great War. With that established, the audience's collective viewpoints are directed anew to the ultimate reunion of the wife of Buchanan and Gatsby, her first lover, particularly in view of Buchanan's apparent perfidy with a light lady.

The vacillating shades and touches make one wonder whether Brenon (or his scenarist) had not started out to alter the original Scott Fitzgerald story for screen purposes and was confronted with contractual obligations to the author, or other circumstances that prohibited such liberties. This is but a theory, since Fitzgerald is sufficiently established to command such special terms if he so elected.

The picture is no reflection on the original novel, an excellent volume, which, because of its literary form, permits a more faithful adherence to reality than the movies.

As a general entity the screen version of "The Great Gatsby" is good stuff. Fitzgerald will certainly have no quarrel with the filmization of his novel. All the niceties and un-niceties of fast Long Island life of the type Fitzgerald dotes on criticizing and exposing are capable of elaborate exposition. And where the exhibitor may look askance at the overlength of 80 minutes running time and be tempted to apply the shears to the swimming pool orgies, etc., it is cautioned against this because for the average layman that footage will be most appealing.

The casting is excellent as far as the cast's personations of their roles are concerned. Baxter as Gatsby leaves nothing wanting. Neil Hamilton as Nick Carraway, cousin of the leading feminine character and a sort of disinterested onlooker, has an easy time of it.

Lois Wilson and Hale Hamilton are the uncertainties. Miss Wilson did her role too faithfully, it seems. After all, she is what parallels the "heroine" of a screen story, and she might have softened it up in general. With the trueness of her personation there is naught to be found, but for the paradoxical criticism it is too well done. Ditto for Hamilton. It may be a director's fault, of course. Georgia Hale as the free-and-easy wife did well.

The average screen reviewer, it should be mentioned here, is generally the type that is a stickler for any nicety in any flicker production. The artistic, to him or her (generally a her), represents the crux of cinema attainment, without any idea or eye to the box office end. From the artistic reviewer's viewpoint, therefore, "The Great Gatsby" would fetch something akin to a "rave." For a commercial commentator, the conflicting emotions from the audience reaction are something to be regarded.

"The Great Gatsby" has in its favor the general sophisticated tenor of the adaptation, intelligent handling of all the opportunities, and the novel's and play's additional prestige. Withal, it's a worthwhile program release.

* * *

The Great Gatsby
Life, 16 December 1926

Herbert Brenon has tried hard to do the right thing by F. Scott Fitzgerald's novel, "The Great Gatsby." Like "What Price Glory," this was a story which, unless materially altered in plot and in point of view, would prove offensive to the notoriously tender sensibilities of the average movie fan.

Mr. Brenon, aided by an excellent cast (Warner Baxter and William Powell are the best), has avoided the prescribed alterations wherever possible. But he has not been

*Lois Wilson, Warner Baxter, Hale Hamilton, and Neil Hamilton (Matthew J. and
Arlyn Bruccoli Collection, University of South Carolina)*

able to make "The Great Gatsby" more than moderately interesting. In attempting to satisfy the limited group who have applauded Fitzgerald's novel, and also the unlimited group who wouldn't read the book on a bet, Mr. Brenon has fallen between two stools.

* * *

Novelist Likes the Film Translation
John O'Hara
New York Herald Tribune, 18 May 1958

Twenty-two years ago, as the decades fly, I made a rather pathetic attempt to buy *The Great Gatsby* from Paramount. I acted through a paid emissary, but I had done some investigating on my own before opening negotiations. I had learned, for instance, that Paramount did not even have a usable print of the F. Scott Fitzgerald novel, film version. I had also learned that a well-known dramatist had done a talking-picture script that Paramount did not like, and that Paramount considered

the property unsuitable for further development, and therefore presumably would let the story go for a price I could pay. I had allowed myself to be encouraged in the project as a result of a conversation with Clark Cable, who I thought (and still think) would make a perfect Gatsby. And I had been told that Paramount would be willing to sell the rights.

But as soon as I, or my emissary, made what was later to become known as a film offer, the price was not doubled; it was quadrupled. I was knocked back on my heels, but I made one more effort to do business: I went to 20th Century-Fox, which was not then, as it is now, my home lot, but where I had a connection, and tried to get a man there to buy *The Great Gatsby* from Paramount. No cigar.

Thus ended my only effort to engage in writing-producing. Paramount, as you may recall, did make a talking-picture version of *The Great Gatsby*, starring Alan Ladd, but I never went to see it, and not entirely because I was bitter. Mr. Ladd may

Glass slide (Matthew J. and Arlyn Bruccoli Collection, University of South Carolina)

have given a good performance in "Shane," but it only convinced me that I was right in not wanting to see him do Gatsby.

The reason I wanted to write a talking-picture version of the Fitzgerald novel was that I had seen the silent version and had admired it enormously. Warner Baxter was a good, if not a great, Gatsby, and Bill Powell as the garage-keeper gave a performance that made his later successes in the Thin Man series seem like kid stuff, which they were. Others in the cast were Lois Wilson, Neil Hamilton, and Hale Hamilton. All good. But even now I can remember my exultation at the end of the picture when I saw that Paramount had done an honest job, true to the book, true to what Fitzgerald had intended. My favorite Fitzgerald novel had not yet been written, but the movies had done right by Our Boy with the best he had written to date. Roughly ten years later I was sure that I could do

an even better job through the new camera techniques and audible dialogue.

* * *

I was rereading *The Great Gatsby* last night, after I had been going through my page proofs, and thinking with depression how much better Scott Fitzgerald's prose and dramatic sense were than mine. If I'd only been able to give my book the vividness and excitement, and the technical accuracy, of his! Have you ever read *Gatsby*? I think it's one of the best novels that any American of his age has done. Of course, he'd had to pass through several immature and amateurish phases before he arrived at that one, and writing, like everything else, is partly a matter of expertness—

—Edmund Wilson to Hamilton Basso, 9 May 1929

EARLY STAGES OF REVIVAL: CRITICISM AND THE SECOND MOVIE (1949)

The Fitzgerald Revival, 1941–1953
Malcolm Cowley

It is true that Fitzgerald died in something close to popular and critical neglect. Max Perkins once told me that, contrary to Fitzgerald's own belief, his books were still in print when he died. In other words, there were copies of them in the Scribner warehouse, as of December 1940, but nobody was buying them. Edmund Wilson worked more effectively to revive his reputation than anyone else in the wide, wide world. First, he arranged for the garland of tributes that appeared in *The New Republic* in the winter of 1941. (I was out of the office on a leave of absence and had asked Edmund to take my place for three months, just as I had taken *his* place ten years before.) Then he was given charge of Fitzgerald's papers and prepared his unfinished novel, *The Last Tycoon,* for publication in a 1941 volume that also contained five of the best stories and *The Great Gatsby.* Then finally he edited *The Crack-Up,* which Scribners decided not to publish, to their lasting regret, and which New Directions published in 1945. The book aroused very wide interest and the Fitzgerald revival was under way.

Wilson then dropped out of the parade, after leading the band. I have a question about Wilson's part in it. In later years did he feel that Fitzgerald was being praised too highly and unreservedly? I don't know, I don't know, butWilson didn't join in the later chorus.

Who persuaded the Viking Press to do a Portable Fitzgerald in 1945? That may have been Dorothy Parker, who made the selections, but didn't supply an introduction. John O'Hara was the logical man to write this, since his stories were carrying on the social-history side of the Fitzgerald tradition. *The Portable Fitzgerald* was No. 14 in the series and its early sale was considerably less than that of the Hemingway (No. 6), but rather more than that of the Faulkner (No.18). The book was published under a five-year lease from Scribners, and—to Viking's sorrow—the lease was not renewed when it ran out in 1950. "We want to bring Fitzgerald's books under one roof," Scribners explained.

Until that time Scribners had shown something less than an all-absorbing interest in Fitzgerald. They had chosen not to publish *The Crack-Up* and they had allowed Arthur Mizener's biography, *The Far Side of Paradise,* to go to another publisher. I don't know when Mizener started working on the book; perhaps it was as early as 1946. He published extracts from the Fitzgerald papers (*Furioso,* 1947; *Kenyon Review,* 1948). By the time his biography was finished, in 1950, Budd Schulberg

Malcolm Cowley

had published a best-selling novel, *The Disenchanted,* in which everybody recognized Fitzgerald as the alcoholic hero. *The Disenchanted* was dedicated to Arthur and Rosemary Mizener. While it was still being widely read, *The Far Side of Paradise* was being serialized in *The Atlantic Monthly,* then summarized in an article for *Life.* The book was extraordinarily successful when it appeared in the spring of 1951; I heard that it had sold more than fifty thousand copies in the first year.

So one can mention Wilson, Schulberg, Mizener as leaders of the Fitzgerald revival, the latter two because they made the story accessible. It was a story that appealed to something deep in the American psyche. "Success" and "failure" had been two weighted words for generations. "Will I be a success?" young Americans had kept asking themselves; and then, "Mightn't it be better to be a failure, that is, to fall from some dizzy height and yet in the end to be better than those who kept on rising?" By 1950 Scott and Zelda had become the hero and heroine of an American legend.

In that same year Scribners decided to put his books back into print, and they asked me, as a beginning, to

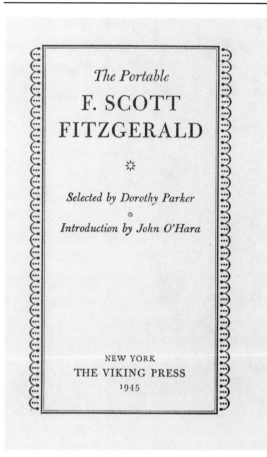

The Portable

F. SCOTT FITZGERALD

✴

Selected by Dorothy Parker

✿

Introduction by John O'Hara

NEW YORK
THE VIKING PRESS
1945

Title page for the influential collection that included The Great Gatsby *and* Tender Is the Night

He always knew what he was writing about, which is so, so untrue of so, so many so-so writers. It may not seem like much in 1945, when it is done all the time, but twenty-five years ago it was delightful to find a writer who would come right out and say Locomobile instead of high-powered motor car, Shanley's instead of gay cabaret, and George, instead of François, the *chasseur* at the Paris Ritz. These touches guaranteed that the writer knew what he has talking about and was not getting his information from Mr. Carnegie's local contribution to culture.

–John O'Hara, *"An Artist Is His Own Fault"* (1977)

Fitzgerald and John O'Hara, Encino, California, 1940 (photograph by Belle O'Hara; Matthew J. and Arlyn Bruccoli Collection, University of South Carolina)

All he was was our best novelist, one of our best novella-ists, and one of our finest writers of short stories.

–John O'Hara, *The Portable F. Scott Fitzgerald*

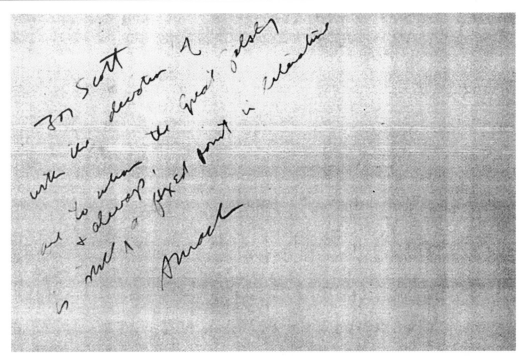

Inscription in Archibald Macleish's 1937 work The Fall of the City *(Matthew J. and Arlyn Bruccoli Collection, University of South Carolina)*

make a selection from his magazine stories. I took the assignment seriously, read everything in print, and worked among the Fitzgerald papers at Princeton, which at the time were opened freely to scholars. I had been writing about Fitzgerald for a long time—actually since I reviewed *All the Sad Young Men* in 1926—and now I wanted to bring everything together. *The Stories of F. Scott Fitzgerald* appeared in the spring of 1951. It contained twenty-eight stories—not enough; I wanted to include at least ten more, but the publishers said there wasn't space for them—besides a long introduction, parts of which had appeared in magazines. The book was very well received and continued to have a sale year after year.

In the Princeton Library I had also come across the copy of *Tender Is the Night* that Fitzgerald had revised and rearranged in the hope that it would be republished. "Let him have his wish," I said to Scribners, and they agreed to

issue the new edition. Whether his second version of the novel is better than the first is a question that has been debated since that time. In 1951 the weight of critical opinion was on the side of the first version, but it seems to me that the weight has been shifting in recent years. I prefer the second, for reasons explained in the introduction, but with the proviso that neither version is the perfect novel that Fitzgerald wanted to write; both are flawed, but deeply appealing.

Still later, in 1953, I prepared a new edition of *Gatsby*, with an introduction that contributed to the critical discussion. Except for some further work on the stories, which went into the only collected edition of Fitzgerald—the one published in London by Bodley Head—that has been my complete share in the revival. It was doubtless a real share, but later and less than Wilson's or Mizener's. Isn't it wrong, moreover, to explain the revival by putting the emphasis on critics and biographers rather than on Fitzgerald himself; on his life, on his writings? He dramatized an age and its aftermath, and his books can also be read—I wrote long ago—"as the intimate journal of an author whose story, observed with his own sharp eyes and judged by his conscience, is more impressive than any book about him that others can write."

—*Fitzgerald/Hemingway Annual 1974*, pp. 11–13

This is the first damned fan letter I've ever tried, but I've just reread "Gatsby" for the first time in five years, and if that isn't the most memorable novel of our generation, then the hell with writing one.

—Corey Ford to F. Scott Fitzgerald, 7 March 1937

* * *

The Great Gatsby
Peter Quennell

It would be doing Scott Fitzgerald a grave injustice to suggest that his novel was merely an essay in social satire, with special reference to the abuses of the capitalist system. His strictures on the worlds he describes are implied, not stated. *The Great Gatsby* is one of the most typical and also one of the most brilliant products of that exciting, disappointing period which witnessed the birth and extinction of so many hopes and crashed at last into the doldrums of a vast depression. It is a period piece with an unusual degree of permanent value, having the sadness and the remote jauntiness of a Gershwin tune, the same touches of slightly bogus romanticism—"the stiff tinny drip of the banjoes on the lawn"; the headlights of departing cars which wheel like long golden antennae across the obscurity of the "soft black morning"—the same nostalgic appeal to be taken seriously, a plea that in Scott Fitzgerald's case has, I think, succeeded. A large number of American mannerisms start with Scott Fitzgerald (who somehow never repeated that early triumph, though many of his long short stories are well worth reading) and not a few modern novelists are his unconscious imitators. Today when the Bum is a best-selling hero—the Share-Cropper, the vagrant Okie, the landless Poor White—it is refreshing to read this romantic tract on the sorrows of Dives.

—*New Statesman and Nation,* 1 February 1941

* * *

Writers who rewrite and rewrite until they reach the perfection they are after consider anything less than that perfection nothing at all. They would not as a rule, show it to their wives or to their most valued friends. Fitzgerald's perfection of style and form, as in "The Great Gatsby," has a way of making something that lies between your stomach and your heart quiver a little.

–James Thurber, *New Republic,* 9 February 1942

F. Scott Fitzgerald
Lionel Trilling

"'So be it! I die content and my destiny is fulfilled,' said Racine's Orestes; and there is more in his speech than the insanely bitter irony that appears on the surface. Racine, fully conscious of this tragic grandeur, permits Orestes to taste for a moment before going mad with grief the supreme joy of a hero; to assume his *exemplary* role." The heroic awareness of which André Gide speaks in his essay on Goethe was granted to Scott Fitzgerald for whatever grim joy he might find in it. It is a kind of seal set upon his heroic quality that he was able to utter his vision of his own fate publicly and aloud and in *Esquire* with no lessening of his dignity, even with an enhancement of it. The several essays in which Fitzgerald examined his life in crisis have been gathered together by Edmund Wilson—who is for many reasons the most appropriate editor possible—and published, together with Fitzgerald's notebooks and some letters, as well as certain tributes and memorabilia, in a volume called, after one of the essays, *The Crack-Up.* It is a book filled with the grief of the lost and the might-have-been, with physical illness and torture of mind. Yet the heroic quality is so much here, Fitzgerald's assumption of the "exemplary role" is so proper and right that it occurs to us to say, and not merely as a piety but as the most accurate expression of what we really do feel, that

> Nothing is here for tears, nothing to wail
> Or knock the breast, no weakness, no contempt,
> Dispraise, or blame, nothing but well and fair,
> And what may quiet us in a death so noble.

. . . .

It is hard to overestimate the benefit which came to Fitzgerald from his having consciously placed himself in the line of the great. He was a "natural," but he did not have the contemporary American novelist's belief that if he compares himself with the past masters, or if he takes thought—which, for a writer, means really knowing what his predecessors have done—he will endanger the integrity of his natural gifts. To read Fitzgerald's letters to his daughter—they are among the best and most affecting letters I know—and to catch the tone in which he speaks about the literature of the past, or to read the notebooks he faithfully kept, indexing them as Samuel Butler had done, and to perceive how continuously he thought about literature, is to have some clue to the secret of the continuing power of Fitzgerald's work.

The Great Gatsby, for example, after a quarter-century is still as fresh as when it first appeared; it has even gained in weight and relevance, which can be said of very few American books of its time. This, I think, is to be attributed to the specifically intellectual courage with which it was conceived and executed, a courage which implies Fitzgerald's grasp—both in the sense of awareness and of appropriation—of the traditional resources available to him. Thus, *The Great Gatsby* has its interest as a record of contemporary manners, but this might only have served to date it, did not Fitzgerald take the given moment of history as something more than a mere circumstance, did he not, in the manner of the great French novelists of the nineteenth century, seize the given moment as a moral fact. The same boldness of intellectual grasp accounts for the success of the conception of its hero—Gatsby is said by some to be not quite credible, but the question of any literal credibility he may or may not have becomes trivial before the large significance he implies. For Gatsby, divided between power and dream, comes inevitably to stand for America itself. Ours is the only nation that prides itself upon a dream and gives its name to one, "the American dream." We are told that "the truth was that Jay Gatsby of West Egg, Long Island, sprang from his Platonic conception of himself. He was a son of God—a phrase which, if it means anything, means just that—and he must be about His Father's business, the service of a vast, vulgar, an meretricious beauty." Clearly it is Fitzgerald's intention that our mind should turn to the thought of the nation that has sprung from its "Platonic conception" of itself. To the world it is anomalous in America, just as in the novel it is anomalous in Gatsby, that so much raw power should be haunted by envisioned romance. Yet in that anomaly lies, for good or bad, much of the truth of our national life, as, at the present moment, we think about it.

Then, if the book grows in weight of significance with the years, we can be sure that this could not have happened had its form and style not been as right as they are. Its form is ingenious—with the ingenuity, however, not of the craft but of intellectual intensity. The form, that is, is not the result of careful "plotting"—the form of a good novel never is—but is rather the result of the necessities of the story's informing idea, which require the sharpness of radical foreshortening. Thus, it will be observed, the characters are not "developed": the wealthy and brutal Tom Buchanan, haunted by his "scientific" vision of the doom of civilization, the vaguely guilty, vaguely homosexual Jordan Baker, the dim Wolfsheim, who fixed the World Series of 1919, are treated, we might say, as if they were ideographs, a method of economy that is reinforced by the ideographic use that is made of the Washington Heights flat, the terrible "valley of ashes" seen from the Long Island Railroad, Gatsby's incoherent parties, and the huge sordid eyes of the oculist's advertising sign. (It is a technique which gives the novel an affinity with *The Waste Land,* between whose author and Fitzgerald there existed a reciprocal admiration.) Gatsby himself, once stated, grows only in the understanding of the narrator. He is allowed to say very little in his own person. Indeed, apart from the famous "Her voice is full of money," he says only one memorable thing: when he is forced to admit that his lost Daisy did perhaps love her

---

In The Lost Weekend, *Charles Jackson's 1944 novel, protagonist Don Birnam fantasizes lecturing to a literature class:*

He took down *The Great Gatsby* and ran his finger over the fine green binding, "There's no such thing," he said aloud, "as a flawless novel. But if there is, this is it." He nodded. The class looked and listened in complete attention, and one or two made notes. . . . "People will be going back to Fitzgerald one day as they now go back to Henry James." He walked back and forth, tapping the book in his hand. "Pay no attention, either, to those who care for his writing merely; who speak of 'the texture of his prose' and other silly and borrowed and utterly meaningless phrases. True, the writing is the finest and purest, the most entertaining and most readable, that we have in America today . . . but it's the content that counts in literature. . . . Apart from his other gifts, Scott Fitzgerald has the one thing that a novelist needs: a truly seeing eye."

---

husband, he says, "In any case it was just personal." With that sentence he achieves an insane greatness, convincing us that he really is a Platonic conception of himself, really some sort of Son of God.

What underlies all success in poetry, what is even more important than the shape of the poem or its wit of metaphor, is the poet's voice. It either give us confidence in what is being said or it tells that we do not need to listen; and it carries both the modulation and the living form of what is being said. In the novel no less than in the poem, the voice of the author is the decisive factor. We are less consciously aware of it in the novel, and, in speaking of the elements of a novel's art, it cannot properly be exemplified by quotation because it is continuous and cumulative. In Fitzgerald's work the voice of his prose is of the essence of his success. We hear in it at once the tenderness toward human desire that modifies a true firmness of moral judgment. It is, I would venture to say, the normal or ideal voice of the novelist. It is characteristically modest, yet it has in it, without apology or self-consciousness, a largeness, even a stateliness, which derives from Fitzgerald's connection with a tradition and with mind, from his sense of what has been done before and the demands which this past accomplishment makes. " . . . I became aware of the old island here that flowered once for Dutch sailors' eyes—a fresh green breast of the new world. Its vanished trees, the trees that had made way for Gatsby's house, had once pandered in whispers to the last and greatest of all human dreams; for a transitory and enchanted moment man must have held his breath in the presence of this continent, compelled into an aesthetic contemplation he neither understood nor desired, face to face for the last time in history with something commensurate to his capacity for wonder." Here, in the well-known passage, the voice is a little dramatic, a little *intentional,* which is not improper to a passage in climax and conclusion, but it will the better suggest in brief compass the habitual music of Fitzgerald's seriousness.

Fitzgerald lacked prudence, as his heroes did, lacked that blind instinct of self-protection which the writer needs and the American writer needs in double measure. But that is all he lacked—and it is the generous fault, even the heroic fault. He said of his Gatsby, "If personality is an unbroken series of successful gestures, there was something gorgeous about him, some heightened sensitivity to the promises of life, as if he were related to one of those intricate machines that register earthquakes ten thousand miles away. This responsiveness had nothing to do with that flabby impressionability which is dignified under the name of 'the creative temperament'—it was an extraordinary gift for hope, a romantic readiness such as I have never found in any other person and which it is not likely I shall ever find again." And it is so that we are drawn to see Fitzgerald himself as he stands in his exemplary role.

—*The Liberal Imagination* (Garden City, N.Y.: Doubleday, 1950)

* * *

Fitzgerald was perhaps the last notable writer to affirm the Romantic Fantasy, descended from the Renaissance, of personal ambition and heroism, of life committed to, or thrown away for, some ideal of self.

—Lionel Trilling, *The Liberal Imagination*

F. Scott Fitzgerald: The Romance of Money
Malcolm Cowley

Although Fitzgerald regarded himself, and was regarded by others, as a representative figure of the age, there was one respect in which he did not represent its serious writers. In that respect he was much closer to the men of his college year who were trying to get ahead in the business world; like them he was fascinated by the process of earning and spending money. The young businessmen of the 1920s were bitterly determined to be successful and, much more than their successors of a later generation, they had been taught to measure success, failure, and even virtue in monetary terms. They had learned in school and Sunday school that virtue was rewarded with money and that viciousness was punished by the loss of money; apparently

their only problem was to earn lots of it fast. Yet money was merely a convenient and inadequate symbol for what they dreamed of earning. The best of them were like Jay Gatsby in having "some heightened sensitivity to the promise of life"; or they were like another Fitzgerald hero, Dexter Green—of "Winter Dreams"—who "wanted not association with glittering things and glittering people —he wanted the glittering things themselves." Their real dream was that of achieving a new status and a new essence, of rising to a loftier place in the mysterious hierarchy of human worth.

The serious writers also dreamed of rising to a loftier status, but — except for Fitzgerald — they felt that money-making was the wrong way to rise. They liked money if it reached them in the form of gifts or legacies or publishers' advances, but they were afraid of high earned incomes because of what the incomes stood for: obligations, respectability, time lost from their own work, expensive habits that would drive them to earn still higher incomes; in short, a series of involvements in the commercial culture that was hostile to art. "If you want to ruin a writer," I used to hear them saying, "just give him a big magazine contract or a job at ten thousand a year." Many of them tried to preserve their independence by earning only enough to keep them alive while writing; a few liked to regard themselves as heroes of poverty and failure.

Their attitude toward money went into the texture of their work, which was noncommercial in the sense of being written in various new styles that the public was slow to accept. The 1920s were the great age of literary experiment, when the new writers were moving in all directions simultaneously. Some of them tried to capture in words the effects of modern painting (like E. E. Cummings); some used the older literary language with Shakespearian orotundity (like Thomas Wolfe); some worked at developing a new language based on Midwestern speech (like Hemingway). Some tried to omit all but the simplest adjectives (again like Hemingway); some used five or six long adjectives in a row (like Faulkner); some ran adjectives and adverbs together in a hurryconfusing fashion (like Dos Passos). Some approached their characters only from the outside, while others gave only their inmost thoughts, their streams of subconsciousness, so that the extremes of objectivity and subjectivity were reached at the same moment. Some broke a story into fragments, some told it backwards, some circled around it as if the story were a tiger in an impenetrable swamp; a few tried to dispense with stories. They were all showing the same spirit of adventure and exploration in fiction that their contemporaries were showing in the business world. That spirit made them part of the age, but at the same time they were trying to criticize and escape from it, and many of them looked back longingly to other ages when, so they liked to think, artists had wealthy patrons and hence were able to live outside the economic system.

Fitzgerald, on the other hand, immersed himself in the age and always remained close to the business world which the others were trying to evade. That world was the background of his stories and they performed a business function in themselves, by supplying the narration that readers followed like a thread through the labyrinth of advertising in the slick-paper magazines. He did not divorce himself from readers by writing experimental prose or by inventing new methods of telling or refusing to tell a story. His very real originality was a matter of mood and subject rather than form and it was more evident in his novels than in his stories, good as the stories often were. Although he despised the trade of writing for magazines – or despised it with part of his mind – he worked at it honestly. It yielded him a large income, twenty-five or thirty thousand dollars a year, which he couldn't have earned in any other fashion, and the income was necessary to his self-respect.

Fitzgerald kept an accurate record of his earnings – in the big ledger where he also recorded his deeds and misdeeds, as if to strike a book-keeper's balance between them – but he was vague about his expenditures and was usually vague about his possessions, including his balance in the bank. Once he asked the cashier, "How much money have I got?" The cashier looked in a big book and answered without even scowling, "None." Fitzgerald resolved to be more thrifty, knowing that he would break the resolution. "All big men have spent money freely," he said in a letter to his mother. "I hate avarice or even caution." He had little interest in money for itself and less in the physical objects it would buy. On the other hand, he had a great interest in earning money, lots of it fast, because that was a sort of gold medal awarded with the blue ribbon for competitive achievement. Once the money was earned he and Zelda liked to spend lots of it fast, usually for impermanent things: not for real estate, fine motorcars, or furniture, but for traveling expenses, the rent of furnished houses, the wages of nurses and servants; for entertainments, party dresses, and feather fans of five colors. Zelda was as proudly careless about money as an Eighteenth Century nobleman's heir. Scott was more practical and had his penny-pinching moments, as if in memory of his childhood, but at other times he liked to spend without counting in order to enjoy a feeling of careless potency.

He was expressing the spirit of an age when conspicuous accumulation was giving way to conspicuous earning and spending. It was an age when gold was

> I still don't see how he could like a phony book like [Hemingway's *A Farewell to Arms*] and still like that one by Ring Lardner or that other one he's so crazy about, *The Great Gatsby*. . . . I was crazy about *The Great Gatsby*. Old Gatsby. Old Sport. That killed me.
>
> –Holden Caulfield speaking of his brother in J. D. Salinger's *The Catcher in the Rye* (1951)

melted down and became fluid; when wealth was no longer measured in possessions – land, buildings, livestock, machinery – but rather in dollars per year, as a stream is measured by its flow; when for the first time the expenses of government were being met by income taxes more than by customs and excise taxes; and when the new tax structure was making it more difficult to accumulate a solid fortune. Such fortunes still existed at the hardly accessible peak of the social system, defended by cliffs of ice, but the romantic figures of the age were not capitalists properly speaking. They were salaried executives and advertising men, they were promoters, salesmen, stock gamblers, or racketeers, and they were millionaires in a new sense – not men each of whom owned a million dollars' worth of property, but men who lived in rented apartments and had nothing but stock certificates and insurance policies (or nothing but credit and the proper connections), while spending more than the income of the old millionaires.

The change went deep into the texture of American society and deep into the feelings of Americans as individuals. Fitzgerald is its most faithful recorder, not only in the stories that earned him a place in the new moneyed class, but also in his personal confessions. He liked to describe his vitality and his talent in pecuniary terms, and when both of them temporarily disappeared – in his crack-up of the years 1935-36 – he pictured the event as a bankruptcy. He wrote (but without my italics), "I began to realize that for two years my life had been a *drawing on resources* that I did not possess, that I had been *mortgaging myself* physically and spiritually up to the hilt." Again he wrote, "When a new sky cut off the sun last spring, I didn't at first relate it to what had happened fifteen or twenty years ago. Only gradually did a certain family resemblance come through – an over-extension of the flank, a burning of the candle at both ends; a call upon physical resources that I did not command, *like a man overdrawing at his bank* . . . . There were plenty of counterfeit coins around that I could pass off instead of these" – that is, in spite of the honest emotions he had lost – "and I knew where I could get them at a nickel on the dollar."

"Where was the leak," Fitzgerald asked, "through which, unknown to myself, my enthusiasm and my vitality had been steadily and prematurely trickling away?" Vitality was something liquid and it was equated with money, which was also liquid. The attitude is different from that which prevailed before World War I, when people spoke of saving money as "piling up the rocks," instead of filling the tank, and when the millionaire in the funny papers was "Mr. Gotrocks." In Freud's great system, which is based on his observation of Nineteenth Century types, money is something solid, gold or silver, and the bodily product it suggests is excrement. Thus the accumulation of money for its own sake develops from anal eroticism and Freud observes that the miser is almost always a physically constipated man. Very few of Freud's disciples have noted that money is losing its old symbolic value and that, in the American subconcious, it is becoming identified with other bodily products like urine ("he just pissed it away"), blood, sperm, or nourishing milk. In this respect Fitzgerald was a better observer than most of the professional analysts. He uses the new imagery in much of his confessional writing and notably in a free-verse poem, "Our April Letter," which he wrote during his crack-up. Three lines of the poem read:

I have asked a lot of my emotions – one hundred and twenty stories. The price was high, right up with Kipling, because there was one little drop of something – not blood, not a tear, not my seed, but me more intimately than these, in every story, it was the extra I had. Now it has gone and I am just like you now.
Once the phial was full – here is the bottle it came in. Hold on, there's a drop left there. . . . No, it was just the way the light fell.

Note that the something more intimate than blood or tears or sperm – though suggested by all of these – had a monetary value and was being sold to the magazines at a price right up with what Kipling had been paid. Note also that in its absence Fitzgerald was no longer able to write saleable stories, so that he identified spiritual emptiness with financial bankruptcy. In that black year 1936 he owed more than forty thousand dollars to his literary agent, his publisher, and his friends, but he kept a careful record of his debts and later paid off most of them, by living in a modest fashion while he was earning a big salary in Hollywood. When he had recovered his financial standing, he found that he was once again capable of doing his best work – though he no longer wrote about young men mountain-climbing to a fortune. In his earlier novels and stories, most of which are concerned with the romance of money, he was not only presenting an intimate truth but was also dealing with the central theme of his American age. He pictured his countrymen as swimmers kept afloat by their earning power. "Americans," he liked to say, "should be born with fins and perhaps they were – perhaps money was a form of fin."

2.

One of his remarks about his work has always puzzled his critics. "D.H. Lawrence's great attempt to synthesize animal and emotional – things he left out," Fitzgerald wrote in his notebook, then added the comment, "Essential pre-Marxian. Just as I am essentially Marxian." He was never Marxian in any sense of the word that Marxians of whatever school would be willing to accept. It is true that he finally read *Das Kapital* and was impressed by "the terrible chapter," as he called it, on "The Working Day"; but there was no trace in his work of Marx's central belief in the mission of the proletariat. Fitzgerald's picture of proletarian life was of something alien to his own background, crudely vital, mysterious, threatening, and even criminal. It seems to have been symbolized in some of his stories by the riverfront strip in St. Paul that languished in the shadow of the big houses along the bluff, on Summit Avenue. He described the strip as a gridiron of mean streets where consumptive or pugilistic youths lounged in front of poolrooms, their skins turned livid by the neon lights. One story, "A Short Trip Home," ends with an excursion into the supernatural. A gambler comes out of the strip and tries to seduce the daughter of a Summit Avenue family. When the gambler dies, the girl has to be saved from his ghost, which has become the discarnation of evil – and also, one suspects, the threat of her losing social position and being forced to descend into the riverfront strip.

In *The Great Gatsby* Fitzgerald must have been thinking about the lower levels of American society when he described the valley of ashes between West Egg and New York – "a fantastic farm," he called it, "where ashes grow like wheat into ridges and hills and grotesque gardens; where ashes take the forms of houses and chimneys and rising smoke and, finally with a transcendent effort, of men who move dimly and already crumbling through the powdery air." One of his early titles for the novel was "Among Ash Heaps and Millionaires" –as if he were setting the two against each other while suggesting a vague affinity between them. In Fitzgerald's work as a whole, there could be no conflict between this ash-gray proletariat and the bourgeoisie. On the other hand, there could be a different struggle and on that the author must have regarded, for a time, as essentially Marxian. It was the struggle I have already suggested, between wealth as fluid income and wealth as a solid possession – or rather, since Fitzgerald is not an essayist but a story-teller, it is between a man

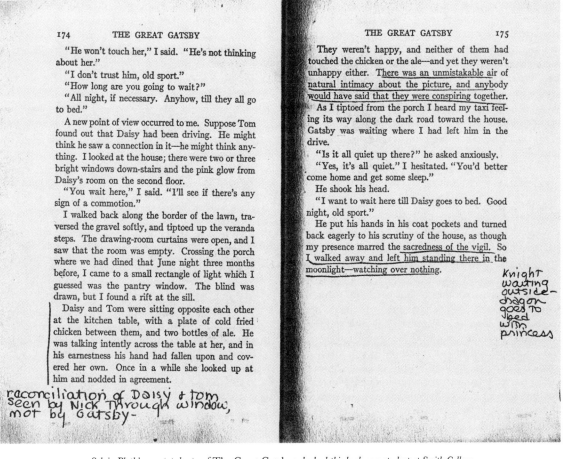

and a woman as representatives of the new and the old moneyed classes.

We are not allowed to forget that they are representatives. The man comes from a family with little or no money, but he manages to attend an Eastern universtiy – usually Harvard or Yale, to set a distance between the hero and the Princeton author. He then sets out to earn a fortune equal to those of his wealthy classmates. What he earns is not a fortune but an impressively large income, after he has become a success in his chosen field – which may be engineering or architecture or advertising or the laundry business or bootlegging or real estate or even, in one story, frozen fish; the heroes are never writers like himself, although one of them is described as a popular dramatist. When they are halfway to success, they fall in love.

The woman – or rather the girl – in a Fitzgerald story is younger and richer than the man and the author makes it even clearer that she represents her social class. "In children's books," he says, "forests are sometimes made out of all-day suckers, boulders out of peppermints and rivers out of gently flowing, rippling molasses taffy. Such books are less fantastic than they sound, for such localities exist, and one day a girl, herself little more than a child, sat dejected in the middle of one. It was all hers, she owned it; she owned Candy Town." Another heroine was "a stalk of ripe corn," he says, "bound not as cereals are but as a rare first edition, with all the binder's art. She was lovely and expensive and about nineteen." When still another heroine first appears, "Her childish beauty was wistful and sad about being so rich and sixteen." Later, when her father loses his money, the hero pays her a visit in London. "All around her," Fitzgerald says, "he could feel the vast Mortmain fortune melting down, seeping back into the matrix whence it had come." The hero thinks that she might marry him, now that she has fallen almost to his financial level; but he finds that the Mortmain (or dead-hand) fortune, even though lost, is still a barrier between them. Note that the Fitzgerald hero is not attracted by the fortune in itself. He is not seeking money so much as position at the peak of the social hierarchy and the girl becomes the symbol of that position, the embodiment of its mysterious power. That is Daisy Buchanan's charm for the great Gatsby and it is the reason why he directs his whole life toward winning back her love.

"She's got an indiscreet voice," Nick Carraway says of her. "It's full of –" and he hesitates.

"Her voice is full of money," Gatsby says suddenly.

And Nick, the narrator, says to himself, "That was it. I'd never understood before. It was full of money – that was the inexhaustible charm that rose and fell in it, the jingle of it, the cymbals' song of it. . . . High in a white palace the king's daughter, the golden girl. . . ."

In Fitzgerald's stories a love affair is like secret negotiations between the diplomats of two countries which are not at peace and not quite at war. For a moment they forget their hostility, find it transformed into mutual curiosity, attraction, even passion (though the passion is not physical); but the hostility will survive even in marriage, if marriage is to be their future. I called the lovers diplomats, ambassadors, and that is another way of saying that they are representatives. When they meet it is as if they were leaning toward each other from separate high platforms – the man from a platform built up of his former poverty, his ambition, his competitive triumphs, his ability to earn and spend always more, more; the girl from another platform covered with cloth of gold and feather fans of many colors, but beneath them a sturdy pile of stock certificates representing the ownership of mines, forests, factories, and villages – all of Candy Town.

She is the incarnate spirit of wealth, as can clearly be seen in one of the best of Fitzgerald's early stories, "Winter Dreams." A rising young man named Dexter Green takes home the daughter of a millionaire for whom he used to be a caddy. She is Judy Jones, "a slender enameled doll in cloth of gold: gold in a band at her head, gold in two slipper points at her dress's hem." The rising young man stops his coupé, Fitzgerald says, "in front of the great white bulk of the Mortimer Jones house, somnolent, gorgeous, drenched with the splendor of the damp moonlight. Its solidity startled him. The strong walls, the steel of the girders, the breadth and beam and pomp of it were there only to bring out the contrast with the young beauty beside him. It was sturdy to accentuate her slightness –as if to show what a breeze could be generated by a butterfly's wing." Butterflies used to be taken as symbols of the soul. The

inference is clear that, holding Judy in his arms, Dexter is embracing the spirit of a great fortune.

Nicole Warren, the heroine of *Tender Is the Night,* is the spirit of an even greater fortune. Fitzgerald says of her:

> Nicole was the product of much ingenuity and toil. For her sake trains began their run at Chicago and traversed the round belly of the continent to California; chicle factories fumed and link belts grew link by link in factories; men mixed toothpaste in vats and drew mouthwash out of copper hogsheads; girls canned tomatoes quickly in August or worked rudely at the five-and-tens on Christmas Eve; half-breed Indians toiled on Brazilian coffee plantations and dreamers were muscled out of patent rights in new tractors–these were some of the people who gave a tithe to Nicole, and as the whole system swayed and thundered onward it lent a feverish bloom to such processes of hers as wholesale buying [of luxuries], like the flush of a fireman's face holding his post before a spreading blaze.

Sometimes Fitzgerald's heroines are candid, even brutal, about class relationships. "Let's start right," the heroine of "Winter Dreams" says to Dexter Green on the first evening they spend alone together. "Who are you?"

"I'm nobody," Dexter tells her, without adding that he had been her father's caddy. "My career is largely a matter of futures."

"Are you poor?"

"No," he says frankly, "I'm probably making more money than any man my age in the Northwest. I know that's an obnoxious remark, but you advised me to start right."

"There was a pause," Fitzgerald adds. "Then she smiled and the corners of her mouth drooped and an almost imperceptible sway brought her closer to him, looking up into his eyes." Money brings them together, but later they are separated by something undefined – a mere whim of Judy's, it seems on one's first reading of the story, through one comes to feel that the whim was based on her feeling that she should marry a man of her own caste. Dexter, as he goes East to earn a still larger income, is filled with regret for "the country of illusions, of youth, of the richness of life, where his winter dreams had flourished."

It seems likely that Judy Jones, like Josephine Perry in a series of later stories, was a character suggested by Fitzgerald's memories of a debutante with whom he was desperately in love during his first years at Princeton; afterward she made a more sensible marriage and Fitzgerald, too, regretted his winter dreams. As for the general attitude toward the rich that began to be expressed in the story, it is perhaps connected with his experiences in 1919, when Zelda broke off their engagement because they couldn't hope to live on his salary as a junior copywriter. "During a long summer of despair," he said years later, "I wrote a novel instead of letters, so it came out all right; but it came out all right for a different person. The man with the jingle of money in his pocket who married the girl a year later would always cherish an abiding distrust, an animosity, toward the leisure class – not the conviction of a revolutionist but the smoldering hatred of a peasant." He may for a time have regarded the hatred too, with the knowledge of class relations which it inspired, as being "essentially Marxian."

3.

Fitzgerald's mixture of feelings toward the very rich, which included curiosity and admiration as well as hatred, is revealed in his treatment of a basic situation that reappears in many of his stories. Of course he presented other situations which were not directly connected with the relationship between social classes. He wrote about the problem of adjusting oneself to life, which he thought was especially difficult in the case of self-indulgent American women. He wrote about the customs of flappers and slickers. He wrote engagingly about his own boyhood. He wrote about the attempt to recapture youthful dreams, about the patching up of broken marriages, about the contrast between Northern and Southern manners, about Americans going to pieces in Europe, about the self-tortures of gifted alcoholics, and in much of his later work – as notably in *The Last Tycoon* – he would be expressing his admiration for supremely great technicians, such as brain surgeons and movie directors. But a great number of his stories, especially the early ones, start with the basic situation I have mentioned: a young man of rising income in love with the daughter of a very rich family. (Sometimes the family is Southern, in which case it needn't be so rich, since Fitzgerald was essentially interested in high social status and since the status could exist in the South without great wealth.)

From that beginning the story may take any one of several turns. The hero may marry the girl, but only after she loses her fortune or (as in "Presumption" and "'The Sensible Thing'") he gains an income greater than hers. He may lose the girl (as in "Winter Dreams") and always remember that she represented his early aspirations. In "The Bridal Party" he resigns himself to the loss after being forced to recognize that the rich man she married is stronger and more capable than himself. In "More Than Just a House" he learns that the girl is empty and selfish and ends by marrying her good sister; in "The Rubber Check" he marries Ellen Mortmain's quiet cousin. There is, however, another development out of the Fitzgerald situation that comes

closer to revealing his ambiguous feeling toward the very rich. To state it simply – too simply – the rising young man wins the girl of established fortune and then is destroyed by her wealth or her relatives.

The plot appears for the first time in a fantasy, "The Diamond as Big as the Ritz," that Fitzgerald wrote in the winter of 1921-22. Like many other fantasies it reveals more of the author's mind than does his more realistic work of the same period. It recounts the adventure of a boy named John T. Unger (we might read "Hunger"), who was born in a town on the Mississippi called Hades, though it might also be called St. Paul. He is sent away to St. Midas', which is "the most expensive and most exclusive boys' preparatory school in the world," and there he meets a classmate named Percy Washington, who invites him to spend the summer at his home in the West. On the train Percy confides to him that his father is the richest man alive and owns a single diamond bigger than the Ritz-Carlton hotel (solid as opposed to fluid wealth).

The description of the Washington mansion, in its hidden valley that wasn't even shown on the maps of the U.S. Geodetic Survey, is fantasy mingled with burlesque; but then the familiar Fitzgerald note appears. John falls in love with Percy's younger sister, Kismine. After an idyllic summer Kismine tells him accidentally – she had meant to keep the secret – that he will very soon be murdered, like all the former guests of the Washingtons. "It was done very nicely." Kismine explains to him. "They were drugged while they were asleep – and their families were always told that they haddied of scarlet fever in Butte. . . . I shall probably have visitors too – I'll harden up to it. We can't let such an inevitable thing as death stand in the way of enjoying life while we have it. Think how lonesome it'd be out here if we never had *any*one. Why, father and mother have sacrificed some of their best friends just as we have."

"The Diamond as Big as the Ritz" can have a happy ending for the two lovers because it is a fantasy, but the same fable reappears in Fitzgerald's two best novels and there it is carried to its tragic conclusion. In *Tender Is the Night* the fable is a little hard to recognize, because in the finished book it is overlaid with other themes–for example, mental illness and the perils and charms of life on the Riviera–but it is much clearer in the "General Plan" for the book that was found among the author's papers. "The novel should do this," he wrote. "Show a man who is a natural idealist, a spoiled priest, giving in for various causes to the ideas of the haute bourgeoisie, and in his rise to the top of the social world losing his idealism, his talent and turning to drink and dissipation. Background one in which the leisure class is at their truly most brilliant and glamorous such as Murphys." Dr. Richard Diver gave in to the ideas of the *haute bourgeoisie* after marrying the fabulously rich Nicole Warren; that was the central cause of his ruin. In *The Great Gatsby* the fable retains its simple outlines, although Gatsby is presented as the archetype and tragic hero of a whole social class: they are the West Egg people, whose wealth is fluid income that might cease overnight. They have worked furiously to rise in the world, but for all the money they spend they will never live in East Egg among the possessors of solid fortunes; at most they can sit at the water's edge and look across the bay at the green light that shines and promises at the end of the Buchanans' dock. Gatsby almost crosses the bay; he almost wins back Daisy Buchanan, whom he had loved and possessed as a young army officer; but then Daisy forsakes him, her husband betrays him, and Gatsby is killed. It is the plot of "Young Lochinvar," but with another ending – as if fair Ellen's kinsmen had overtaken the pair and Ellen had refused to save her lover. It is also a fable that presents Fitzgerald's picture of his own life and the world in which he lived and inspired him to his best and truest writing.

−The Western Review, Summer, 1953

* * *

The Great Gatsby, Paramount, 1949

Richard Maibaum, producer and co-author of the screen play of "The Great Gatsby," wrote this article in advance of the release of the 1949 Paramount adaptation of Fitzgerald's novel.

The Question They Faced With 'Gatsby': Would Scott Approve?

The Daily Compass, 8 July 1949

Hollywood, July 7–Bringing the late F. Scott Fitzgerald's Jazz-Age novel, "The Great Gatsby," to the screen in 1949 presented a succession of problems much different from those usually encountered in the movies.

From first to last it called for making decisions we knew would certainly be challenged either by Fitzgerald devotees or by his detractors. He has both. The literary critic, Parrington, described him as 'a bad boy who loves to smash things to show how naughty he is . . . Precocious, ignorant–a short candle already burned out . . ." On the other hand, "The Great Gatsby," according to T. S. Eliot, represented "the first full step American fiction has taken since Henry James."

First and foremost was the problem of tackling the project at all. Was it timely? In 1931 Fitzgerald himself thought it too soon to write about the Jazz Age with perspective. But in 1946, when we went to work the

---

CAST

Jay Gatsby	ALAN LADD
Daisy Buchanan	BETTY FIELD
Nick Carraway	MACDONALD CAREY
Jordan Baker	RUTH HUSSEY
Tom Buchanan	BARRY SULLIVAN
Wilson	HOWARD DA SILVA
Myrtle Wilson	SHELLEY WINTERS
Dan Cody	HENRY HULL
Ella Cody	CAROLE MATHEWS
Myron Lupus	ED BEGLEY
Klipspringer	ELISHA COOK, JR.
The Guest	NICHOLAS JOY
Kinsella	WALTER GREAZA
Mavromichaelis	TITO VUOLO
Pamela	DIANE NANCE

CREDITS

Produced by . . . . Richard Maibaum
Directed by . . . . Elliott Nugent
Screenplay by,
       Cyril Hume and Richard Maibaun
From the novel by,
       F. Scott Fitzgerald and the play by Owen Davis
Director of Photography,
       John F. Seitz, A.S.C.
Art Direction,
       Han Dreier and Roland Anderson
Special Photographic Effects,
       Gordon Jennings, A.S.C., Jan Domela,
         and Irmin Roberts, A.S.C.
Process Photography,
       Farciot Edouart, A.S.C.
Set Decoration,
       Sam Comer and Ray Moyer
Costumes . . . . Edith Head
Edited by . . . . Ellsworth Hoagland
Makeup Supervision . . . . Wally Westmore
Assistant Director . . . . William H. Coleman
Sound Recording by,
       Hugo Grenzbach and Walter Oberst
Music Score . . . . Robert Emmett Dolan
       Western Electric Recording

---

sight lines were longer, and the Jazz Age appeared as a post-war era with a direct bearing upon the present.

The decision to produce the picture having been made, the usual problem of choosing a writer became particularly important. The project needed experienced craftsmanship to solidify Fitzgerald's often ambiguous and always oblique style to serve the simpler, clearer, more obvious requirements of the screen. Above all, it needed the feel of Fitzgerald and the flavor of the period without losing the moral implications of the theme. Cyril Hume, a personal friend of Fitzgerald, has been writing screenplays for almost 20 years. We went to work with Mr. Hume's query, "Would Scott approve?" the yardstick for all we did.

"Would Scott approve?" was not always easy to answer. He himself once wrote to a friend, "You are right about Gatsby being patchy and blurred. I never at any one time saw him clear myself . . ." We tried very hard to "see him clear," but, as Fitzgerald wrote him, Gatsby is an enigmatic personality who has baffled a good many people.

"Of all the reviews," wrote Fitzgerald, "even the most enthusiastic, not one has the slightest idea what the book was about."

So Mr. Hume and I started out to "clarify" Gatsby. We added material not in the novel dealing with his early career, which, incidentally, we later discovered had been suggested to Fitzgerald by the novelist, Edith Wharton. And we took one whopping license. We gave Gatsby an awareness at the end which he never achieved in the book. We "disenchanted" him, and shot him down at the moment of his awakening. Rightly or wrongly, we felt this was the only way to give him tragic stature.

Then came the toughest problem of all—censorship. I hasten to add that the Johnston Office, and Joseph Breen in particular, was most sympathetic. But it was obvious we could not put "The Great Gatsby" on the screen as we had written it. It dealt with unpunished adultery, unpunished manslaughter, and an unpunished moral accessory to a murder. And yet "The Great Gatsby" is in essence a modern morality play depicting irresponsibility leading to catastrophe. This thought was our solution. With the consent of the Johnston Office we enclosed the picture in a "frame." We created a prologue in which Nick and Jordan, in the present, look back at the '20s and at Gatsby, they themselves, like the country, having come through the debacle to become decent, humbled and worthy. And we placed on Gatsby's tombstone Proverbs 14:12: "There is a way which seemeth right unto a man, but the end thereof are the ways of death."

"Would Scott approve?" Frankly, we didn't know, but in a way it gave us the very sense of perspective he felt was lacking in 1931.

So much for script problems. Next came casting. In Alan Ladd we had an actor I personally believe was born to play Gatsby. Inwardly youthful, genuine, vital, idealistic, but with the ability to assume the nouveau riche aspects of Gatsby's exterior personality, he was Gatsby. Moreover, he was desperately interested in the project and in no small measure responsible for it.

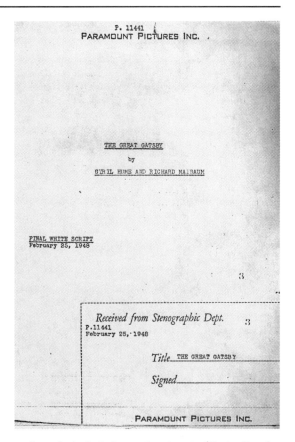

Cover of script for the first sound movie version (Matthew J. and Arlyn Bruccoli Collection, University of South Carolina)

It was "Daisy" that caused us the sleepless nights. Actually an unsympathetic role, she yet had to be played to make understandable Gatsby's unusual devotion. Although beauty was important, beauty alone, we decided, was not enough. What was more essential was the ability of the actress to project the carelessness, the vagueness, the erratic bursts of emotion, the charm and the sadness of the "'disenchanted'" high society female of the 20's.

We chose Betty Field because we decided her quality and her ability were more important than any other factors involved. We could think of no other actress who could manage what one of the London critics has called the "disharmonic chatter" so typical of the period.

The Two Staring Eyes

Our difficulties did not end with production. After the first sneak preview it was necessary to go back and establish the 20's much more vividly. The kids were too young to remember and the older people had to be reminded. Unless the audience understood the era the characters were incomprehensible. So we

Lobby poster for the 1949 production (Matthew J. and Arlyn Bruccoli Collection, University of South Carolina)

Cover of publicity book (Matthew J. and Arlyn Bruccoli Collection, University of South Carolina)

introduced them at the start to the jazz and the dancing, the Flaming Youth, the bootlegger, the gang wars, and the wild, uncontrolled stock market boom. "Would Scott approve?" I wish he were alive to tell us.

And I wish I could ask him one question. In the book he describes a weather-beaten sign, and advertisement for an oculist—one Dr. T. J. Eckleburg. It consists of two staring eyes that gaze dispassionately at the comic-tragedy played out beneath them. What do they mean? Are they the eyes of history? of fate? of eternity? What? One of our characters describes them tentatively, "Like God bought himself a pair of eyeglasses so he could watch us better!" As with all else in the motion picture "The Great Gatsby," we hope devoutly that "Scott approves."

* * *

'The Great Gatsby,' Based on Novel of F. Scott Fitzgerald, Opens at the Paramount
Bosley Crowther
The New York Times, 14 July 1949

F. Scott Fitzgerald's classic story of the "prohibition crowd," which he told with real irony and pity in "'The Great Gatsby" back in 1925, has been brought to the screen by Paramount with particular emphasis upon the aspects of the sentimental romance that formed the thread of the novel's fragile plot. Except for a few pictorial tracings of parties and brittle high-life, the flavor of the Prohibition era is barely reflected in this new film at the Paramount.

Indeed, there are reasons for suspecting that Paramount selected this old tale primarily as a standard conveyance for the image of its charm boy, Alan Ladd. For most of the tragic implications and bitter ironies of Mr. Fitzgerald's work have gone by the board in allowing for the generous exhibition of Mr. Ladd.

To the circle of his admirers, that will seem a respectable cause, since the gentleman is shown to full advantage as a wistful, heroic type. Solemnly representing Gatsby, he gives us a long and lingering look at a patient and saturnine fellow who is plagued by a desperate love. And for eighty-odd minutes we behold him moving quietly and supremely toward the fate which the author conveniently concocted to round out his dark and rueful tale.

But somehow he does not present us with the picture of a strangely self-made man exposed as the pitiful victim of the times and his own expansive greed. The period of the Nineteen Twenties is briefly and inadequately sketched with a jumble of gay Long Island parties, old clothes, old songs and old cars. The baneful influence of prohibition and the disillusionment of post-World War I are not in the least integrated into the projection of the man.

Blame this in part on a weak script. Cyril Hume and Richard Maibaum have achieved a dutiful plotting of the novel without the substance of life that made it stick. Blame it too, upon direction; Elliott Nugent's handling of the cast and of supposedly significant behavior is completely artificial and stiff. And blame it, at last, on the manner in which Mr. Ladd always acts. His portrait is quite in accordance with that stock character he usually plays.

A bit of illumination of the brittle and faithless jazz-age type is delivered in irritating snatches by our old friend, Betty Field, playing the married woman whom Gatsby loves in vain. And Barry Sullivan turns in a moderately sturdy account of the lady's Yale-man husband who is rotten at the core. As the pious observer and narrator of all that happens in this film, Macdonald Carey does a fair imitation of a youthful Father Time, and Ruth Hussey is mainly scenery as a wise-cracking golfing champ. Howard da Silva, Shelley Winters and Elisha Cook Jr. have secondary roles which they fill without any distinction or significance to the Fitzgerald tale.

* * *

The party scene (Matthew J. and Arlyn Bruccoli Collection, University of South Carolina)

Betty Field, Alan Ladd, Barry Sullivan (Matthew J. and Arlyn Bruccoli Collection, University of South Carolina)

Ed Begley, Elisha Cook, Alan Ladd, Howard Da Silva, and Shelley Winters (Matthew J. and Arlyn Bruccoli Collection, University of South Carolina)

Films

Manny Farber

The Nation, 13 August 1949

While *The Great Gatsby* is a limp translation of Fitzgerald's novel about the tasteless twenties, magical mid-Westerners on Long Island, and the champion torch-bearing hero in American literature, it captures just enough of the original to make it worth your while and rekindle admiration for a wonderful book. Its characters are like great lumps of oatmeal maneuvering at random around each other, but it tepidly catches the wistful tragedy of a jilted soldier (Alan Ladd) who climbs the highest mountains of racketeering and becomes an untalented socialite, trying to win back his Daisy (Betty Field) from a hulking snob and libertine (Barry Sullivan). Etched in old MGM-Renaissance style Fitzgerald's panorama of the twenties takes on the heavy, washed-out, inaccurate dedication-to-the-past quality of a Radio City mural. Save for an occasional shot—the rear of a Long Island estate studded

with country-club architecture and the bulky town cars—that shrieks of the period, the movie has little to offer of Fitzgerald's glory-struck but acrid perceptions of the period, place, and East Egg society. The cottage scene, with an added touch of Booth Tarkington, talks and moves, as little else of the movie does, with some complication and emotional development.

Director [Elliott] Nugent's forte is the country-club set tinkling delicately against each other amidst stupified living-room furniture, but it only appears in the scenes at Daisy's and the Plaza, which have a timeless aura and show the leisure class at customary half-mast—summary weather a glitter due to Betty Field's delight with her role, and tasteful, knee-waisted dresses. The crucial lack is that Gatsby, Daisy, the cynical Jordan, don't have enough charm to explain the story; in fact, they don't have much more than the wary hulks that are currently beached on Long Island. Owing to a tired director who, however, knows the book with uncommon shrewdness, and Fitzgerald's inspired dialogue combined with slow, conservative movie images this peculiarly mixed movie draws the most vociferous, uneasy audience response.

It would take a Von Stroheim to cast Fitzgerald's characters, each as fabulous as Babe Ruth, but rendered with the fragmentary touches of a Cezanne watercolor, the cast is routine for Paramount (Ladd, Da Silva, Macdonald Carey–Frank Faylen, a studio perennial, must have been sick) and inspired only in the case of Betty Field, whose uninhibited, morbid-toned art blows a movie apart. Ladd might have solved the role of Gatsby if he had consisted, as his normal role does, of shocking, constant movement, no acting, and trench coats. An electric, gaudily graceful figure in action movies, here he has to stand still and project turbulent feeling, succeeding chiefly in giving the impression of an isinglass baby-face in the process of melting. He seems to be constantly in pain, and this, occasionally, as in the touching cottage scene, coincides with Gatsby's. As a matter of fact, he gives a pretty good impression of Gatsby's depressed, non-public moments. Barry Sullivan streamlines the aging (30) football player ("if we don't look out the white race will be—will be utterly submerged. It's all scientific stuff") into a decent, restless gentleman whose nostrils constantly seem horrified. For a dismal C-Western star, Sullivan is surprisingly deft and subtle in a role that has become meaningless without the sentimentality, fears, and shockingly comic scenes with Myrtle's circle (probably dropped because they were too cinematic).

Betty Field is no more marked by Southern aristocracy than a cheese blintz, but she plays Daisy with her usual incredible daring and instinctive understanding. She hits the role (compulsive, musical voice; scared sophistication) so hard, giving Daisy a confused, ineffectual intensity, missing some of the scintillating charm, that her creation is a realistic version of the character Fitzgerald set up simply as a symbol for Gatsby to dream about. The music of the period, when it is played right, is heartbreaking, and Elisha Cook captures this nostalgia for a few minutes at Gatsby's grand piano.

Academic Broadway veteran that he is, Elliott Nugent implies in his direction that the period and terrain—so consistently primary and wondrous to Fitzgerald—are simply a backdrop. In place of the wasteland of ashes that surrounds Wilson's garage, morbidly counterpointing the story's death-ridden conclusion, there are fleeting glimpses of a humdrum dumping ground. The huge, chaotic parties are a dispiriting blur of Arthur Murray dancing,

Muzak orchestrations, stock drunks with one individualized detail (the stridently sequined stage twins) in place of the dozen needed to build the atmosphere that draws New York's night life to Gatsby's door. Fitzgerald's broken story structure has been straightened so that the movie flows slowly without break through routine stage sets. In the occasional place where a contrasting shot is slashed into "Old Man River" development, the strategy, because of its rarity, produces more excitement than the image warrants—the oculist's billboard, with the enormous spectacled eyes, steals the movie.

* * *

BECOMING A CLASSIC: REPRINTINGS, TRANSLATIONS, REAPPRAISALS

The novel was serialized in five 1926 issues after book publication (Matthew J. and Arlyn Bruccoli Collection, University of South Carolina).

246

EDITIONS OF *THE GREAT GATSBY*

Sales of this inexpensive reprint published in 1934 did not warrant keeping the volume in print (Matthew J. and Arlyn Bruccoli Collection, University of South Carolina).

The Modern Library Reprint

A11.1.d
Fourth printing (Modern Library)
[within double-rule frame] THE | GREAT GATSBY | [rule] | BY | F. SCOTT FITZGERALD | [rule] | WITH A NEW INTRODUCTION | BY | F. SCOTT FITZGERALD | [rule] | [four-line verse epigraph] –THOMAS PARKE D'INVILLIERS. | [device] | [rule] | BENNETT A. CERF • DONALD S. KLOPPER | THE MODERN LIBRARY | NEW YORK
Copyright page: 'First Modern Library Edition | 1934.'

Binding: Noted in blue, green, brown, or red cloth; gold-stamped.

Dust jacket: Some jackets are stamped in ink 'DISCONTINUED TITLE'.

Publication: One Modern Library printing only. Probably 5,000 copies. Published 13 September 1934. 95¢. First publication of Fitzgerald's introduction, pp. vii–xi.

* * *

The Great Gatsby *was included in the Modern Library series in 1934–the first reprinting of the book in the U.S. after 1925. Fitzgerald was paid fifty dollars for his introduction, which he labored over. But when the book was published Fitzgerald asked for the chance to rewrite the introduction at his own expense for the anticipated next printing: "I do not like the Preface. Reading it over it seems to have both flipness and incoherance, two qualities which the story that succeeds it manages to avoid." The reprint failed to sell at ninety-five cents and was discontinued by the publisher.*

The published introduction, written after the bitterly disappointing reception of Tender Is the Night, *provides Fitzgerald's response to the critics of both novels, without mentioning the later one. His declaration, "But, my God! it was my material and it was all I had to deal with" constitutes Fitzgerald's defense of his career–of every writer's career.*

Modern Library Introduction

To one who has spent his professional life in the world of fiction the request to "write an introduction" offers many facets of temptation. The present writer succumbs to one of them; with as much equanimity as he can muster, he will discuss the critics among us, trying to revolve as centripetally as possible about the novel which comes hereafter in this volume.

To begin with, I must say that I have no cause to grumble about the "press" of any book of mine. If Jack (who liked my last book) didn't like this one–well then John (who despised my last book) *did* like it; so it all mounts up to the same total. But I think the writers of my time were spoiled in that regard, living in generous days when there was plenty of space on the page for endless ratiocination about fiction–a space largely created by Mencken because of his disgust for what passed as criticism before he arrived and made his public. They were encouraged by his bravery and his tremendous and profound love of letters. In his case, the jackals are already tearing at what they imprudently regard as a moribund lion, but I don't think many men of my age can regard him without reverence, nor fail to regret that he got off the train. To any new effort by a new man he brought an attitude; he made many mistakes–such as his early undervaluation of Hemingway–but he came equipped; he never had to go back for his tools.

And now that he has abandoned American fiction to its own devices, there is no one to take his place. If the present writer had seriously to attend some of the efforts of political diehards to tell him the values of a métier he has practised since boyhood—well, then, babies, you can take this number out and shoot him at dawn.

But all that is less discouraging, in the last few years, than the growing cowardice of the reviewers. Underpaid and overworked, they seem not to care for books, and it has been saddening recently to see young talents in fiction expire from sheer lack of a stage to act on: West,† McHugh‡ and many others.

I'm circling closer to my theme song, which is: that I'd like to communicate to such of them who read this novel a healthy cynicism toward contemporary reviews. Without undue vanity one can permit oneself a suit of chain mail in any profession. Your pride is all you have, and if you let it be tampered with by a man who has a dozen prides to tamper with before lunch, you are promising yourself a lot of disappointments that a hardboiled professional has learned to spare himself.

This novel is a case in point. Because the pages weren't loaded with big names of big things and the subject not concerned with farmers (who were the heroes of the moment), there was easy judgment exercised that had nothing to do with criticism but was simply an attempt on the part of men who had few chances of self-expression to express themselves. How anyone could take up the responsibility of being a novelist without a sharp and concise attitude about life is a puzzle to me. How a critic could assume a point of view which included twelve variant aspects of the social scene in a few hours seems something too dinosaurean to loom over the awful loneliness of a young author.

To circle nearer to this book, one woman, who could hardly have written a coherent letter in English, described it as a book that one read only as one goes to the movies around the corner. That type of criticism is what a lot of young writers are being greeted with, instead of any appreciation of the world of imagination in which they (the writers) have been trying, with greater or lesser success, to live—the world that Mencken made stable in the days when he was watching over us.

Now that this book is being reissued, the author would like to say that never before did one try to keep his artistic conscience as pure as during the ten months put into doing it. Reading it over one can see how it could have been improved—yet without feeling guilty of any discrepancy from the truth, as far as I saw it; truth or rather the *equivalent* of the truth, the attempt at honesty of imagination. I had just re-read Conrad's preface to *The Nigger,* and I had recently been kidded half haywire by critics who felt that my material was such as to preclude all dealing with mature persons

in a mature world. But, my God! it was my material, and it was all I had to deal with.

What I cut out of it both physically and emotionally would make another novel!

I think it is an honest book, that is to say, that one used none of one's virtuosity to get an effect, and, to boast again, one soft-pedalled the emotional side to avoid the tears leaking from the socket of the left eye, or the large false face peering around the corner of a character's head.

If there is a clear conscience, a book can survive—at least in one's feelings about it. On the contrary, if one has a guilty conscience, one reads what one wants to hear out of reviews. In addition, if one is young and willing to learn, almost all reviews have a value, even the ones that seem unfair.

The present writer has always been a "natural" for his profession, in so much that he can think of nothing he could have done as efficiently as to have lived deeply in the world of imagination. There are plenty other people constituted as he is, for giving expression to intimate explorations, the:

—Look—this is here!

—I saw this under my eyes.

—*This* is the way it was!

—No, it was like this.

"Look, Here is that drop of blood I told you about."

—"Stop everything! Here is the flash of that girl's eyes, here is the reflection that will always come back to me from the memory of her eyes.

—"If one chooses to find that face again in the non-refracting surface of a washbowl, if one chooses to make the image more obscure with a little sweat, it should be the business of the critic to recognize the intention.

—"No one felt like this before—says the young writer—but *I* felt like this; I have a pride akin to a soldier going into battle; without knowing whether there will be anybody there, to distribute medals or even to record it."

But remember, also, young man: you are not the first person who has ever been alone and alone.

F. SCOTT FITZGERALD

Baltimore, Md.

August, 1934.

† Nathanael West (1903-1940), novelist who had published *The Dream Life of Balso Snell* (1931), *Miss Lonelyhearts* (1933), and *A Cool Million* (1934).

‡ Vincent McHugh (1904–1983), author of the 1933 novel *Sing Before Breakfast.*

* * *

THE SUNDAY NOVEL ... COMPLETE IN THIS ISSUE

Herald Examiner
SUNDAY, MAY 23, 1937

THE GREAT
GATSBY By F. Scott Fitzgerald

IN MY younger and more vulnerable years my father gave me some advice that I've been turning over in my mind ever since.

"Whenever you feel like criticising anyone," he told me, "just remember that all the people in this world haven't had the advantages that you've had."

I'm inclined to reserve all judgments, a habit that has opened up many curious natures to me and also made me the victim of not a few veteran bores.

Only Gatsby, the man who gives his name to this book, was exempt from my reaction—Gatsby, who represented everything for which I have an unaffected scorn. If personality is an unbroken series of successful gestures, then there was something gorgeous about him, some heightened sensitivity to the promises of life, as if he were related to one of those intricate machines that register earthquakes ten thousand miles away. This responsiveness had nothing to do with that flabby impressionability which is dignified under the name of the "creative temperament"—it was an extraordinary gift for hope, a romantic readiness such as I have never found in any other person and which is not likely I shall ever find again.

My family have been prominent, well-to-do people in this Middle-Western city for three generations. The Carraways are something of a clan, and we have a tradition that we're descended

A cut text of the novel appeared in newspaper supplements (Matthew J. and Arlyn Bruccoli Collection, University of South Carolina).

The Great Gatsby *was reprinted in a single issue of this British pulp magazine in August 1937 (Matthew J. and Arlyn Bruccoli Collection, University of South Carolina).*

Posthumously Published Editions of *The Great Gatsby,* 1941–1999

A11.1.e
Fifth printing: New York: Scribners, 1942. Published August 1942. Probably 260 copies. Location: MJB.

A11.1.f
Sixth printing: New York: New Directions, [1946]. New Classics, #9. $1.00. Introduction by Lionel Trilling. Published December 1945.

A11.1.g
Seventh printing: New York: Grosset & Dunlap, [1949]. Gray or light blue paper-covered boards. $1.49. Probably reprinted. Dust jacket has wraparound band advertising the 1949 Paramount movie.

A11.1.h
Eighth printing: New York: Scribners, [1989]. Facsimile of the first printing in dust jacket; with Introduction by Charles Scribner III. Copyright page: "This edition, limited to three thousand copies, is published by arrangement with Charles Scribner's Sons, a division of Macmillan Publishing Com-

pany. This editon is for promotional use by Scribner's Bookstores and is not for resale."

A11.1.i
Ninth printing: New York: Scribners, 1925 [1991]. Facsimile of the first printing in dust jacket and box. Copyright page: "The facsimile of the first edition of this work is published by Collectors Reprints, Inc. N.Y., N.Y. . . ."

A11.1.j
Tenth printing: Tokyo: Hon-No-Tomosha, 1996. Volume 6 of 9-volume set of facsimiles of *The Selected Works of F. Scott Fitzgerald.*

A11.2.a
Second edition

The Last Tycoon . . . Together With the Great Gatsby and Selected Stories. New York: Scribners, 1941.

The text of *GG* was silently emended by Edmund Wilson; the alteration of *orgastic* to *orgiastic* in the penultimate paragraph first appeared in this edition.

The Armed Services editions were distributed to members of the military during WWII. Many readers were introduced to Fitzgerald and The Great Gatsby *by this massive literary give-away endeavor (Matthew J. and Arlyn Bruccoli Collection, University of South Carolina).*

A11.2.b
Modern Standard Authors Three Novels of F. Scott Fitzgerald. New York: Scribners, [1953].

A11.3
Third edition (Armed Services)

[within double-rule frame] [to the left of a vertical rule] PUBLISHED BY ARRANGEMENT WITH | CHARLES SCRIBNER'S SONS, NEW YORK | COPYRIGHT, 1925, | BY CHARLES SCRIBNER'S SONS | [to the right of a vertical rule; the first three lines in script] The | Great Gatsby | by | F. SCOTT FITZGER-ALD | *Editions for the Armed Services, Inc.* | A NON-PROFIT ORGANIZATION ESTABLISHED BY | THE COUNCIL ON BOOKS IN WARTIME, NEW YORK | [outside frame] 862

Probably distributed in 1945. 154,663 copies. Not for sale. Locations: LC (received 16 April 1946); MJB. See *Editions*

for the Armed Services, Inc. A History (New York: Editions for the Armed Services, n.d.).

A11.4
Fourth edition (Portable)

The Portable F. Scott Fitzgerald, selected by Dorothy Parker and with an introduction by John O'Hara. New York: Viking, 1945. Reprinted 1945, 1949. Also published as *The Indispensable F. Scott Fitzgerald* (New York: The Book Society, 1949 and 1951).

A11.5
Fifth edition

[within double-rule frame] THE GREAT | GATSBY | F. SCOTT FITZGERALD | [four-line verse epigraph] | –Thomas Parke D'Invilliers | [rooster] | New York | BANTAM BOOKS

Cover of the first paperback edition, #8 in the first set of Bantams (Matthew J. and Arlyn Bruccoli Collection, University of South Carolina)

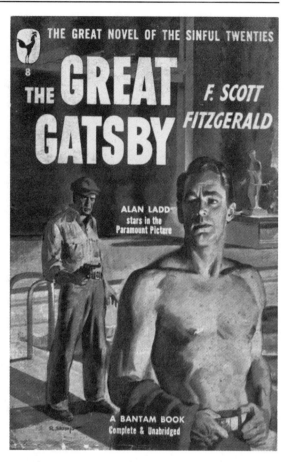

This dust jacket was placed on unsold copies as a movie tie-in Matthew J. and Arlyn Bruccoli Collection, University of South Carolina).

1945. #8. Wrappers. 25¢. Published November 1945. Reprinted January 1946, March 1946, March 1951, March 1952, March 1954. In 1949 a dust jacket was put on this edition, showing Alan Ladd in a scene from the Paramount movie.

A11.6
Sixth edition

[first two lines in swash] Great American | Short Novels | EDITED BY | WILLIAM PHILLIPS | [swash] A Permanent Library Book | [line of decorations with seal in center] | 1946 | DIAL PRESS: *NEW YORK*

1950 fifth printing and undated sixth printing noted. Includes *GG*, pp. 453–575.

A11.7
First English edition

F. SCOTT FITZGERALD | [star] | The Great | GATSBY | [star] | THE GREY WALLS PRESS

London, 1948. 8/6. Reprinted 1949.

A.11.8
Second English edition

THE GREAT GATSBY | [tapered rule with decoration in middle] | *F. Scott Fitzgerald* | PENGUIN BOOKS | HARMONDSWORTH • MIDDLESEX

1950. #746. Wrappers. 1/6. Reprinted 1954, 1958, 1961, 1962, 1963, 1964, 1966, 1967, 1968 (twice), 1969 (twice), 1970, 1971 (twice), 1972, 1973 (twice), 1974 (three times), 1975, 1976, 1977, 1978 (twice),

Dust jacket with wraparound band for the first English resetting, published by Grey Walls Press in 1948 (Matthew J. and Arlyn Bruccoli Collection, University of South Carolina)

Dust jacket with wraparound band for the 1949 Grosset & Dunlap reprint (Matthew J. and Arlyn Bruccoli Collection, University of South Carolina)

1979 (twice), 1980, 1981 (twice), 1982 (three times), 1983, 1984 (three times), 1985.

A11.9
English-language Swedish edition

[within single-rule frame] F. SCOTT FITZGER-ALD | *The Great* | *Gatsby* | [tapered rule] | THE POLYGLOT CLUB | STOCKHOLM | 1950

English text with Swedish gloss. Wrappers. Location: MJB.

A11.10.a
Student's Edition

The Great Gatsby | BY | F. SCOTT FITZGERALD | [four-line verse epigraph] | –THOMAS PARKE

D'INVILLIERS | *CHARLES SCRIBNER'S SONS* | New York

1957. Wrappers. On copyright page of first printing: 'A-8.57 [C]'. Reprint noted: 'B-1.58[C]'.

A11.10.b
Scribner Library

In 1960 the Student's Edition was incorporated into the Scribner Library (SL#1): 'A-1.60[C]'. Reprints noted: 'D-3.61[C]'. 'F-8.62[Col]'. 'G-4.63[Col]'; 'H-10.63[Col]'; 'J-9.64 [Col]'; 'J-2.65[Col]'; 'N-8.68[Col]'; 'O-5.69 [C]'; 'P-9.69[C]'; 'R-10.70[C]'; 'S-3.71 [C]'. Latest reprint noted: '39 Y/P 40 38. Also clothbound: 'C-7.59[H]'.

A11.10.c
New York: Scribners, [1979]. Contemporary Classics/Scribner Library #SL884. Wrappers (rack

size). $2.25. ISBN #0-684-16325-X. On copyright page: '1 [. . .] 19 A/P 20 [. . .] 2'.

A11.10.d
New York: Scribners, [1981]. Hudson River Editions. ISBN #0-684-16498-1. Reprint noted: '5 [. . .] 19 Q/C 20 [. . .] 6'.

Reprinted 1990 as part of 4-volume set of Fitzgerald novels distributed by the Book-of-the-Month Club.

A11.11
THE BODLEY HEAD | SCOTT | FITZGERALD | WITH AN INTRODUCTION BY | J. B. PRIESTLEY | VOL. I | THE GREAT GATSBY | THE LAST TYCOON, AND SOME | SHORTER PIECES | THE BODLEY HEAD | LONDON

1958. 5.

A11.12

English-language Japanese edition

[rule] | *Kairyudo's Mentor Library No. 11* | [rule] | F. SCOTT FITZGERALD | THE GREAT GATSBY | Edited and Annotated | by | NAOTARO TATSUNOKUCHI | and | NOBUYUKI KIUCHI | KAIRYUDO |TOKYO

1960. Wrappers.

A11.13
THE | *Great Gatsby* | [decoration] | BY F. SCOTT FITZGERALD | [four-line verse epigraph] | –THOMAS PARKE D'INVILLIERS | CHARLES SCRIBNER'S SONS | *597 Fifth Avenue, New York 17, New York*

1961. Scribner School Edition with foreword and study guide by Albert K. Ridout. On copyright page: 'A-9.61 [V]'. Reprint noted: 'A-6.68[MCOL]'. On copyright page of latest observed clothbound printing:

5 [. . .] 19 MC/C 20 [. . .] 4'

Reprinted as Scribner School Paperbacks: 'A–1.68[M]'. Also reprinted by Caves Books (Taipei, 1976?).

A11.14
The | FITZGERALD | *Reader* | Edited by ARTHUR MIZENER | Charles Scribner's Sons | *New York*

Cover of the first Penguin paperback, 1950 (Matthew J. and Arlyn Bruccoli Collection, University of South Carolina). It became the most widely distributed edition in the English-speaking world.

1963. On copyright page: '3.63 [H]'. Includes *GG*, pp. 105–238.

A11.15
A QUARTO | OF MODERN | LITERATURE | *Edited by* | LEONARD BROWN | *FIFTH EDITION* | CHARLES SCRIBNER'S SONS *New York*

1964. On copyright page: 'A-3.64 [V]'. Includes *GG*, pp. 212–267.

A11.16
[two-page title; the following on the left page] Three | Great | American | Novels |[the following on the right page] The Great Gatsby | F. SCOTT FITZGERALD | WITH AN INTRODUCTION BY MALCOLM COWLEY | [six lines of type] |

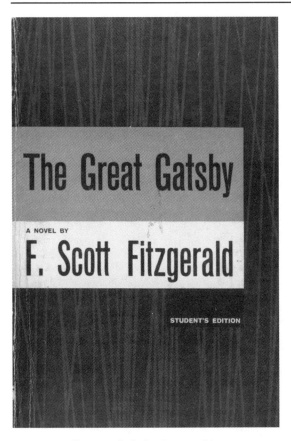

Front cover for the first classroom edition

MODERN STANDARD AUTHORS | CHARLES SCRIBNER'S SONS | NEW YORK

1967. On copyright page: 'A-9.67 [c]'.

A11.17
THE BODLEY HEAD SERIES | The | Great Gatsby | F. SCOTT FITZGERALD | *with commentary* | *and notes by* | J. F. WYATT | M.A. | THE BODLEY HEAD | LONDON SYDNEY | TORONTO

1967.

A11.18
THE GREAT GATSBY | F. SCOTT FITZGER-ALD | ILLUSTRATIONS BY CHARLES RAY-MOND | [rule] | THE FOLIO SOCIETY • LONDON • 1968

Introduction by Tim Andrews.

A11.19
The Great Gatsby | BY | F. SCOTT FITZGERALD | [four-line verse epigraph] | –THOMAS PARKE D'INVILLIERS | *CHARLES SCRIBNER'S SONS* | *New York*

1968. Scribners Large Type Edition. On copyright page: 'A-5.68 [C]'.

A11.20
HENRY DAN PIPER | Southern Illinois University, Carbondale | FITZGERALD'S *The Great Gatsby:* | The Novel, The Critics, The Background | [lamp] SCRIBNER | RESEARCH | ANTHOLO-GIES | CHARLES SCRIBNER'S SONS | New York

1970. On copyright page: 'A-3.70 [H]'.

A11.21
THE | GREAT GATSBY | BY | F. SCOTT FITZGERALD | [four-line verse epigraph] | –THO-MAS PARKE D'INVILLIERS | CHARLES SCRIBNER'S SONS | *New York*

1970. Part of a four-volume set (with *TSOP, TITN, LT*) distributed by The Literary Guild of America and its associated book clubs.

A11.22
THE GREAT GATSBY | BY | F. SCOTT FITZGERALD | [four-line verse epigraph] | –THO-MAS PARKE D'INVILLIERS | [around Bantam device] • BANTAM BOOKS • LONDON TOR-ONTO NEW YORK

1974. #T7448. Wrappers. $1.50. 12 printings, March–July 1974.

A11.23
[on white panel within decorated frame surrounded by gray] [script] The | [roman] GREAT | GATSBY | [script] by | [roman] F. SCOTT FITZGERALD | A Limited Edition | [leaf] | THE FRANKLIN LIBRARY | Franklin Center, Pennsylvania | 1974

On p. v: 'This limited edition of | THE GREAT GATSBY | is published exclusively for | subscribers to | The Franklin Library | collection | The 100 Greatest Books of All Time'.

A11.24
The Great Gatsby | BY | F. SCOTT FITZGERALD | [four-line verse epigraph] | –THOMAS PARKE

D'INVILLIERS | *CHARLES SCRIBNER'S SONS* | *New York*

1975. Contemporary Classics/Scribner Library #SL1. Wrappers. $2.25. ISBN #0–684–71760–3. [i–vi] 1–121 [122]
On copyright page of latest observed printing: '37 39 M/P 40 38 36'

See Margaret M. Duggan, "Editorial," *Fitzgerald/Hemingway Annual 1976*, p. 303.

A11.25
THE GREAT GATSBY | F. Scott Fitzgerald | [device] | LYTHWAY PRESS | BATH

1975. Large-print edition. Reprinted in wrappers, 1977.

A11.26
The | Great Gatsby | *and* | The | Last Tycoon | [rule] | SCOTT FITZGERALD | *with an Introduction* | *by* | J. B. PRIESTLEY | BOOK CLUB ASSOCIATES LONDON

1977. Reprint from Bodley Head plates.

A11.27
English-language Italian edition

FRANCIS SCOTT FITZGERALD | the great gatsby | edited with an introduction and notes | by Luigi Castigliano | EDIZIONI [device] | SCHOLASTICHE | BRUNO MONDADORI

1977. Wrappers.

A11.28
THE | SCRIBNER | QUARTO | OF MODERN | LITERATURE | Edited by | A. WALTON LITZ | CHARLES SCRIBNER'S SONS | NEW YORK

1978. Includes *GG*, pp. 208–264.

A11.29
[within double-rule blue frame] F. Scott Fitzgerald | [swash title] The | Great Gatsby | *Illustrated by Chuck Wilkinson* | [blue decoration] | *A Limited Edition* | THE FRANKLIN LIBRARY | Franklin Center, Pennsylvania | 1980

P. vii: 'THE 100 GREATEST MASTERPIECES | OF AMERICAN LITERATURE | a limited edition collection | is published under the auspices of | The

American Revolution | Bicentennial Administration | [seal]'.

A11.30
F. SCOTT FITZGERALD | *The Great Gatsby* | [silver-gray] *WITH AN INTRODUCTION BY* | [black] *Charles Scribner III* | [silver-gray] *AND ILLUSTRATIONS BY* | [black] *Fred Meyer* | [silver-gray] *PRINTED FOR MEMBERS OF* | [black] THE LIMITED EDITIONS CLUB

1980. 2,000 numbered copies signed by Meyer and Scribner.

A11.31
American Literature Texts | THE GREAT | GATSBY | F. Scott-Fitzgerald | With an Introduction, Notes and Bibliography by | M. Sivaramkrishna | Reader, Department of English | Osmania University | DELHI | OXFORD UNIVERSITY PRESS | BOMBAY CALCUTTA MADRAS | 1981

Wrappers.

A11.32a
[all within gray single-rule frame decorated at top] [black] F. Scott Fitzgerald | [red] THE | GREAT | GATSBY | [black] Illustrated by Bruce Dean | THE FRANKLIN LIBRARY | Franklin Center, Pennsylvania

1982.

A11.32.b
[all within single-rule frame decorated at top] The Oxford Library of | the World's Great Books | F. Scott Fitzgerald | THE | GREAT | GATSBY | Illustrated by | Bruce Dean | OXFORD UNIVERSITY PRESS

1982.

A11.33
THE | GREAT | GATSBY | F. Scott Fitzgerald

London: Viaduct Publications, 1982. Magazine format. Complete Bestsellers, II, #6. 95 pence.

A11.34
THE | GREAT | [blue-green] GATSBY | [black] By | F. SCOTT FITZGERALD | Illustrated by | MICHAEL GRAVES | THE ARION PRESS | SAN FRANCISCO | 1984

350 copies signed by Graves. Also 50 copies in "a green cloth box with a recessed lid displaying a spe-

cially cast sculptural relief, designed by Michael Graves, of a three-dimensional site plan for Gatsby's estate"—with two of the original drawings for the book.

A11.35
TEXTS FOR ENGLISH AND AMERICAN STUDIES | *edited by* | Peter Freese | 14 | F. Scott Fitzgerald | *The Great Gatsby* | *edited and annotated by* | *Dagmar Pohlenz* | *and* | *Richard Martin* | [boxed] STUDENTS' BOOK | Ferdinand Schöningh | 41091

Paderborn, 1984. Wrappers. Accompanied by Pohlenz and Martin's *Teacher's Book* (Paderborn: Schöningh, 1986).

A11.36
T·H·E | GREAT | GATSBY | F. Scott Fitzgerald

London: Marshall Cavendish, 1988. The Great Writers library #37. Published with magazine-format guide: *The Great Writers, Their Lives, works and inspiration . . . The Great Gatsby.*

A11.37
Fremdsprachentexte | [rule] | *F. Scott Fitzgerald* | *The Great Gatsby* | Herausgegeben von | Susanne Lenz | Philipp Reclam jun. Stuttgart

1989.

A11.38
THE GREAT GATSBY | [tapered rule] | *F. Scott Fitzgerald* | [penguin within oval] | PENGUIN BOOKS

London, 1990. With Introduction by Tony Tanner and Notes. ISBN 0–14–018067–2.

Text only reprinted by Penguin. ISBN 0–14–027413–8. In the 1999 reprinting of the copyright page stipulates: '70 . . . 68.'

A11.39
F. Scott Fitzgerald | [double rule] | MANUSCRIPTS III | [double rule] | *The Great Gatsby* | THE REVISED AND REWRITTEN GALLEYS | INTRODUCED AND ARRANGED BY | Matthew J. Bruccoli | Jefferies Professor of English, University of South Carolina | GARLAND PUBLISHING, INC. | New York & London, 1990

Part of 18-volume set.

"Now we have an American masterpiece in its final form: the original crystal has shaped itself into the true diamond. This is the novel as Fitzgerald wished it to be, and so it is what we have dreamed of, sleeping and waking."

—James Dickey
on the Cambridge University Press edition

A11.40
THE GREAT GATSBY | *** | F. SCOTT FITZGERALD | Edited by MATTHEW J. BRUCCOLI | Textual Consultant | FREDSON BOWERS | [open book] | CAMBRIDGE UNIVERSITY PRESS | *Cambridge* | *New York* | *Port Chester* | *Melbourne Sidney*

Copyright page: 'First published 1991'. ISBN: 0–521–40230.
21.16 retinas
54.24; 97.29   Astoria

Reprinted 1992, 1993 (twice), 1994, 1995, 1996.

Seventh printing
21.16 irises
54.24; 97.29 Long Island City

A11.41
THE | GREAT GATSBY | [rule] | [diamond] | F. Scott Fitzgerald | With an Introduction by | Matthew J. Bruccoli | [underlined: Scribners]

London: Macdonald, 1991. ISBN 0–356–19694 1. With "Winter Dreams."

Reprinted under Abacus imprint: London: Little, Brown, 1992. ISBN 0–349–10330–5.

A11.42
[within triple-rules frame] THE GREAT | GATSBY | [rule] F. Scott Fitzgerald | *with an Introduction by Charles Scribner III* | and Illustrations by Fred Meyer | COLLECTOR'S EDITION | *Bound in Genuine Leather* | [device] | [script: the Easton Press] | NORWALK, CONNECTICUT

1991

New series

THE CAMBRIDGE EDITION OF THE WORKS OF F. SCOTT FITZGERALD

General Editor: MATTHEW J. BRUCCOLI, Jefferies Professor of English, University of South Carolina

F. Scott Fitzgerald is among the foremost American writers of the twentieth century, but there is still no accurate and authoritative edition of his works. The *Cambridge Edition* removes the house-styling imposed by Maxwell Perkins and other Scribner's editors and realises a text that is singularly Fitzgerald's. The edition is supplemented by full introductions, textual apparatus, and helpful explanatory notes.

The edition will consist of twelve volumes in all. Forthcoming titles include *The Last Tycoon* and *Tender is the Night.*

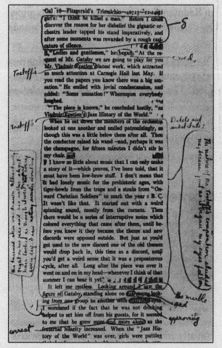

Author corrected proofs of *The Great Gatsby*

F. Scott Fitzgerald: *The Great Gatsby*

Edited by MATTHEW J. BRUCCOLI, Jefferies Professor of English, University of South Carolina

Since its publication in 1925, *The Great Gatsby*, F. Scott Fitzgerald's account of the American dream gone awry, has established itself as one of the most popular and widely read novels in the English language. Until now, however, no edition has printed the novel exactly as Fitzgerald himself wrote it. From its first publication onward, the text has been subject to a rigorous house-styling that has distorted the characteristic rhythms and structure of his sentences. This critical edition draws on the manuscript and surviving proofs of the novel, together with Fitzgerald's subsequent revisions to key passages, to provide the first authoritative text of *The Great Gatsby*.

The Cambridge Edition of the Works of F. Scott Fitzgerald

1991   216 x 138 mm   276pp.
0 521 40230 1   Hardback   £25.00   net

Catalogue entry for the first volume of the first Fitzgerald critical edition

A11.43

F. Scott Fitzgerald | [decorated rule] | THE GREAT GATSBY | Preface by MATTHEW J. BRUCCOLI | SCRIBNER CLASSICS

1992. Copyright page: 1 . . . 2. ISBN:0–684–83042–6. By 1999 this edition was in its 7th printing.

A11.44a

THE GREAT | GATSBY | [rule] | [diamond] | F. Scott Fitzgerald | Preface and notes | by Matthew J. Bruccoli | *A Scribner Classic* | COLLIER BOOKS | Macmillan Publishing Company | New York | MAXWELL MAC-MILLAN CANADA | *Toronto* | MAXWELL MAC-MILLAN INTERNATIONAL | *New York Oxford Singapore Sidney*

1992. Copyright page: First Collier Books Edition 1992 | 10 . . . 1'. ISBN 0–02–019881–7.
27.17 retinas
72.24; Astoria
132.3 Long Island City

A11.44b

[rule] F. SCOTT | FITZGERALD | [rule] | THE GREAT | GATSBY | [decoration] | Preface and notes | by Matthew J. Bruccoli | SCRIBNER PAPERBACK FICTION | PUBLISHED BY SIMON & SCHUSTER | NEW YORK LONDON TORONTO TOKYO SINGAPORE

1995. Copyright page: 'First Scribner Paperback Fiction Edition 1995'. ISBN 0–684–80152–3. By 1999 this paperback was in its 9th printing.

A11.45

THE GREAT GATSBY | F. SCOTT FITZGERALD | EDITED BY DAVID CRYSTAL AND DEREK STRANGE | WITH AN INTRODUCTION BY | ANTHONY BURGESS | PENGUIN ENGLISH

London: Penguin, 1992. Copyright page: '1 . . . 2'. "Penguin Authentic Texts" series.

A11.46

THE GREAT GATSBY | [decorated rule] | F. Scott Fitzgerald | [decoration] | WORDSWORTH CLASSICS

Ware, Hertfordshire: Wordsworth, 1993. ISBN 185326 041 X

A11.47

[rule] The Great Gatsby | [4 lines of verse] | THOMAS PARKE D'INVILLIERS | [underlined: Cornelsen]

Berlin, 1993. ISBN 3–464–6801–3

A11.48

F. Scott Fitzgerald | The Great Gatsby | Notes by Rudolph F. Rau | Ernst Klett Schulbuchverlag | Stuttgart Düsseldorf | Berlin | Leipzig

1994. Copyright page: '1. Auflage 1 . . . 94.' ISBN 3–12–577680–5. New edition of the CUP text.

A11.49

F. SCOTT | FITZGERALD | [rule] | *The Great* | *Gatsby* | [following two lines decorated with stars and B] BLOOMSBURY | CLASSICS

London, 1994. Copyright page: '10 . . . 1'. ISBN 0–7475–17665.

A11.50

The | Great Gatsby | F. Scott Fitzgerald | [decorated rule] | Edited by Ken Bush | Series Editor: Judith Baxter | [to right of seal] CAMBRIDGE | UNIVERSITY PRESS

1995. ISBN 0–521–48547–9 paperback.
Text varies from the CUP critical edition.

Reprint.
Delhi: Published by Manas Saikia for Foundation Books, 1998.

Copyright page: 'Special Edition for sale in South Asia only. | Not for export elsewhere.'

A11.51

THE GREAT GATSBY | [decorated rule] | F. Scott Fitzgerald | Thorndike, Maine: G. K. Hall; Bath: Chivers, 1995. Large-print edition.

A11.52

OXFORD WORLD'S CLASSICS | [two short rules] | F. SCOTT FITZGERALD | *The Great Gatsby* | [two short rules] | *Edited with an Introduction and Notes by* | RUTH PRIGOZY | Oxford New York | OXFORD UNIVERSITY PRESS | 1998

Copyright page: '1 . . . 2'. ISBN 0–19–283269–7

* * *

TRANSLATIONS OF *THE GREAT GATSBY*: 1926–1998

A Checklist compiled by Lisa Kerr

Arabic
[*The Great Gatsby*]. Baghdad: Haider Al Jawady, 1962.

Basque
GATSBY HANDIU. Iruñea: Iglea, 1990.

Bengali
[*The Great Gatsby*]. Pakistan: M/S Bright Book House, 1971.

Croatian translation (Matthew J. and Arlyn Bruccoli Collection, University of South Carolina)

Bulgarian
VELIKIJAT GETSBI. Bulgaria: Nar. Kultura, 1966.

Catalan
EL GRAN GATSBY. Barcelona: Edicions 62, 1967.

Chinese
TA HENG HSIAO CHUAN. Tapei: Chengchung Shu Chü, 1954.
YUNG HÊNG CHIH LÜAN. Tapei: Chengchung Shu Chü, 1954.
TA TSAL! KAI SHIH PI. Tainan: Chung Hua Pub. Ser., 1969.
TA HENG HSIAO CHUAN. Hsiang-kang: Chin Jih Shih Chieh She, 1971.
[*The Great Gatsby*]. Hong Kong: World Today Press, 1971.
Hsiang Kang: Chin Jih 'ch 'u Pan She, 1974.
Tapei: Yüan Ching Ch 'u Pan Shih Yeh Kung Ssu, 1982.
Tapei: Shu Hua Ch'u Pan Shih Yeh yu hsien kung ssu, 1986, 1994.
Tapei: Wan hsiang t 'u Shu Ku Fen Yu Hsien Kung Ssu, 1995.

Czech
VELKÝ GATSBY. Prague: Statní Nakladatelství Krásné Literotury, Hudby a Umeni, 1960.

Croation
VELIKI GETSBI I CETIRI PRICE. Beograd: Jugo-slavija, 1967.

Danish
DEN STORE GATSBY. Copenhagen: Thaning & Appel, 1948.
Copenhagen: Glydendal, 1960, 1971, 1974.
Copenhagen: Glydendals Bogklub, 1971.
Copenhagen: A&K, 1974.

Dutch
DE GROTE GATSBY. Amsterdam: G.A. Van Oorsr-chot, 1948.
Amersterdam: Contact, 1968, 1973.
Weesp: Agathon, 1985.

Estonian
SUUR GATSBY. Tallinn, USSR: Ëesti Raamat, 1966.

Finnish
KULTAHATTU. Helsinki: Otava, 1959, 1987.
Helsinki: Suuri Suomalainen Kirjakerho, 1974.

Danish translation (Matthew J. and Arlyn Bruccoli Collection, University of South Carolina)

French translation (Matthew J. and Arlyn Bruccoli Collection, University of South Carolina)

French
GATSBY LE MAGNIFIQUE. Paris: Collection Europeene, Kra Edit, 1926.
Paris: Sagittaire, 1946.
Paris: Le Club Francais du Livre, 1952, 1959.
Paris: Livre de Poche, 1962.
Paris: Bernard Grasset, 1962, 1968, 1976, 1996.
Paris: Editions Rombaldi, 1969.
Paris: Le Club de la Femme, 1969.
Paris: France Loisirs, 1974.
Geneva: Famot, 1976.
Paris: Grands Ecrivains, 1985.
Paris: Hachette, 1985.
Lausanne: L' Age d'Homme, 1995.

German
DER GROSSE GATSBY. Berlin: Knaur, 1928, 1932.
Berlin: Blanvalet, 1953.
Frankfurt: Büchergilde Gutenberg, 1958.
Berlin: Aufbau-Verlag, 1968.
Zurich: Diogenes, 1974.

In his 9 December 1928 letter to Fitzgerald, Victor Llona, who translated The Great Gatsby *into French, quoted a letter he had received from Jean Cocteau:*

"Voulez-vous faire savoir à F. Scott Fitzgerald que son livre m'a permis de passer de heures très dures (je suis dans une clinique). C'est un livre céleste: chose la plus rare du monde."

("Would you let Fitzgerald know that his book enabled me to pass some very difficult hours (I was in a clinic)? It's a heavenly book, the rarest thing in the world.")

Greek
GOTSBY O MAGHAS. Athens: Oi Filoi Tis Loghotechnias, 1955.
GATSBY HO MEGAS. Athens: Philio T-es Logotechnias, 1955.

Hebrew translation (Matthew J. and Arlyn Bruccoli Collection,
University of South Carolina)

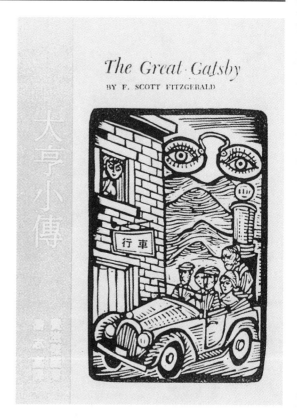

Japanese translation (Matthew J. and Arlyn Bruccoli Collection,
University of South Carolina)

Hebrew
GATSBY HAGADOL. Tel Aviv: Matzpen, 1962.
Tel Aviv: Sifre Siman Kri'a, Mif'alim Universita'iyim
le-Hoza'a La'or, 1974.
GATSBY HAGADIK. Tel Aviv: Mifalim Universitaim
Lehoza Leor, B.M., 1974.

Hindi
LALASA. Dehli, India: Rajpal, 1969.

Hungarian
A NAGY GATSBY. Budapest: Szépirodalmi Könyvki-
ado, 1953.
ÚJRA BABILONBAN [with stories and other writ-
ings]. Budapest: Magveto Könyvkiadó, 1962.

Italian
IL GRANDE GATSBY. Milano and Verona: Monda-
dori, 1950, 1958, 1961, 1964, 1965.
Verona: Mondadori, 1958, 1963, 1970.

Milano: Club degli Editori, 1976.
Milano: Narrativa Club, 1982.
Novara: Mondadori-De Agostino, 1986.

Japanese
IDAINARU GATSBY [with stories]. Tokyo: Ken-
kyû-sha, 1957.
YUME AWAKI SEISHUN. Kadokawa Shoten, 1957.
GURETO GYATSUBI. Tokyo: Shinchosa, 1974.
KAREINARU GYATSUBII. Tokyo: Shinchosa, 1974.

Korean
WI'DAE'HAN GATSBY. Seoul: Sin'yang'sa, 1959.
WIDAEHAN KAECH 'UBI. Soul: Kumsong Ch 'ulp
'ansa, 1982 [with *The Last Tycoon*].
Soul: Pomusa, 1988.
Soul: Sisa Yongosa, 1988, 1998.
Soul: Sodam Ch 'ulp 'ansa, 1997.

Lithuanian
DIDYSIS GETSBIS. Vilnius, USSR: Vaga, 1967.

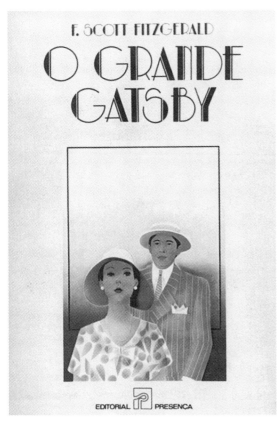

Portuguese translations (Matthew J. and Arlyn Bruccoli Collection, University of South Carolina)

Macedonian
GOLEMIOT GEJTZBI. Yugoslavia: Kočo Racin, 1965.

Malayasian
TUAN GATSBY. Kuala Lumpur: Dewan Bahasa dan Pustaka, 1988.

Norwegian
DEN GULE BIL. Oslo: Gyldendal Norsk Forlag, 1927.
DEN STORE GATSBY. Oslo: Gyldendal Norsk Forlag, 1951.
Oslo: Glydendal Norsk Forlag, 1965.

Persian
TALA VA KHASKISTAR: Gatsbi-yi buzurg. Teheran: Shirkat-i Siruyd, 1965.
[The Great Gatsby]. Teheran: Sherkat Saroid, 1966.

Polish
WIELKI GATSBY. Warsaw: Czytelnik, 1962, 1964, 1973.
Warsaw: Ksiazki Wiedza, 1962, 1982, 1990.

Warsaw: Comfort, 1991.
Poznan: SAWW, 1994.

Portuguese
O GRANDE GATSBY. Lisbon: Portugália, 1960, 1962.
São Paulo: Círculo de Livro, 1977.
Lisbon: Editorial Presença, 1986.
Lisbon: Círculo de Leitores, 1987.

Romanian
MARELE GATSBY. Bucharest: Editura Pentru Literatură Universală, 1967.
Timisoara: Editura Excelsior, 1991.

Russian
VELIKII GÉTSBI. Moscow: Izdatel'stvo "Khudozhestvennaia Literatura," 1965.
Moscow: "Khudozhestvenn ia Lit-ra," 1965.
VELIKII GÉTSBI. Moscow: Hudož, 1966.
VELIKII GÉTSBI. Minsk: "Mastatskara literatura," 1987 [includes *Tender is the Night*].
Kiev: "Vyshcha shkola," 1990.

Moscow: Sovetskii Pisatel, 1992
Saint Petersburg, 1992, 1993 [includes *This Side of Paradise*].
ROMANY [includes *The Great Gatsby*]. Saint Petersburg: Kristall: Respeks, 1998.

Serbo-Croation
SNAGA LJUBAVI. Sarajevo: Džepna Knjiga, 1956.
VELIKI GATSBY. Zagreb, Yugoslavia: Zora, 1959.
Belgrad: Izdavacko Preduzece "Rad," 1963.
Belgrade: "Rad," 1964, 1968.
Belgrade: Jugoslavija, 1967 [with stories].

Slovak
VEL'KY GATSBY. Bratislava: Slovensky Spisovatel, 1970.

Slovene
VELIKI GATSBY. Ljubljana: Mladinska Knjiga, 1961.
Yugoslavia: Cankarjeva Založba, 1970.
Ljubljana: CGP Delo, 1976.

Spanish
EL GRAN GATSBY. Barcelona: Edicions 62, 1925, 1982.
Buenos Aires: Futuro, 1946.
Barcelona: Plaza & Janés, 1953, 1960, 1979, 1980, 1994, 1995, 1997.
Mexico: Plaza &Janés, 1960, 1986.
Havana: Editorial Nacional de Cuba, 1965.
Barcelona: Ediciones Orbis 1970, 1983, 1985, 1987.
Mexico: Promexa, 1979.
Madrid: Alfaguara, 1983.
Santiago: Editorial Andrés Bello, 1984.
Barcelona: Circulo de Lectures, 1988.
Madrid: Alfaguara, 1990.
Bogotá: Grupo Editorial Norma, 1993.
Quito: Libresa, 1995.

Swedish
UN MAN UTAN SKRUPLER. Stockholm: Wahlström & Widstrand, 1928.
DEN STORE GATSBY. Stockholm: Bonnier, 1946, 1955, 1963.
[The Great Gatsby]. Stockholm: Polyglot Club [Seelig], 1950.
Stockholm: A. Bonniers Förlag, 1955.
Stockholm: Aldus/Bonniers, 1963.

Turkish
MUHTEŞM GATSBY. Istanbul: Ağaoğlu Yayinevi, 1964.
MUHTESEM GATSBY. Istanbul: Adam Yayincilik, 1982.

F. SCOTT FITZGERALD
EN MAN
UTAN SKRUPLER
WAHLSTRÖM & WIDSTRAND/STOCKHOLM

Swedish translation (Matthew J. and Arlyn Bruccoli Collection, University of South Carolina)

* * *

Reappraisals

Scott Fitzgerald's Fable of East and West
Robert Ornstein

He felt then that if the pilgrimage eastward of the rare poisonous flower of his race was the end of the adventure which had started westward three hundred years ago, if the long serpent of the curiosity had turned too sharp upon itself, cramping its bowels, bursting its shining skin, at least there had been a journey; like to the satisfaction of a man coming to die—one of those human things that one can never understand unless one has made such a journey and heard the man give thanks with the husbanded breath. The frontiers were gone—there were no more barbarians. The short gallop of the last great race, the polyglot, the hated and the despised, the crass and scorned, had gone—at least it was not a meaningless extinction up an alley. (*The Crack-Up,* p. 199)

After a brief revival, the novels of Scott Fitzgerald seem destined again for obscurity, labled this time, by their most recent critics, as darkly pessimistic studies of America's spiritual and ideological failures. *The Great Gatsby,* we are now told, is not simply a chronicle of the Jazz Age but rather a dramatization of the betrayal of the naive American dream in a corrupt society.[1] I would agree that in *Gatsby* Fitzgerald did create a myth with the imaginative sweep of America's historical adventure across an untamed continent. But his fable of East and West is little concerned with twentieth century materialism and moral anarchy, for its theme is the unending quest of the romantic dream, which is forever betrayed in fact and yet redeemed in men's minds.

From the start, Fitzgerald's personal dreams of romance contained the seeds of their own destruction. In his earliest works, his optimistic sense of the value of experience is overshadowed by a personal intuition of tragedy; his capacity for naive wonder is chastened by satire and ironic insights which make surrender to the romantic impulse incomplete. Though able to idealize the sensuous excitement of an exclusive party or a lovely face, Fitzgerald could not ignore the speciousity inherent in the romantic stimuli of his social world—in the unhurried gracious poise that money can buy. Invariably he studied what fascinated him so acutely that he could give at times a clinical report on the very rich, whose world seemed to hold the own imagination (and therefore incapable of self-deception), he peopled extravagant phantasy with superbly real "denizens of Broadway." The result in the earlier novels is not so much an uncertainty of tone as a curious alternation of satiric and romantic moments—a breathless adoration of flapper heroines whose passionate kisses are tinged with frigidity and whose daring freedom masks an adolescent desire for the reputation rather than the reality of experience.

The haunting tone of *Gatsby* is more than a skilful fusion of Fitzgerald's satiric and romantic contrarieties. Nick Carraway, simultaneously enchanted and repelled by the variety of life, attains Fitzgerald's mature realization that the protective enchantment of the romantic ideal lies in its remoteness from actuality. He knows the fascination of yellow windows high above the city streets even as he looks down from Myrtle Wilson's gaudy, smoke-filled apartment. He still remembers the initial wonder of Gatsby's parties long after he is sickened by familiarity with Gatsby's uninvited guests. In one summer Nick discovers a profoundly melancholy aesthetic truth: that romance belongs not to the present but to a past transfigured by imagined memory and to the illusory promise of an unrealizable future. Gatsby, less wise than Nick, destroys himself in an attempt to seize the green light in his own fingers.

At the same time that Fitzgerald perceived the melancholy nature of romantic illusion, his attitude towards the very rich crystalized. In *Gatsby* we see that the charming irresponsibility of the flapper has developed into the criminal amorality of Daisy Buchanan, and that the smug conceit of the Rich Boy has hardened into Tom Buchanan's arrogant cruelty. We know in retrospect that Anthony Patch's tragedy was not his "poverty," but his possession of the weakness and purposelessness of the very rich without their protective armor of wealth.

The thirst for money is a crucial motive in *Gatsby* as in Fitzgerald's other novels, and yet none of his major characters are materialists, for money is never their final goal. The rich are too accustomed to money to covet it. It is simply the badge of their "superiority" and the justification of their consuming snobberies. For those who are not very rich—for the Myrtle Wilsons as well as the Jay Gatsbys—it is the alchemic reagent that transmutes the ordinary worthlessness of life. Money is the demiurgos of Jimmy Gatz's Platonic universe, and the proof, in "Babylon Revisited," of the unreality of reality (". . . the snow of twenty-nine wasn't real snow. If you didn't want it to be snow, you just paid some money"). Even before *Gatsby,* in "The Rich Boy," Fitzgerald had defined the original sin of the very rich: They do not worship material gods, but they "possess and enjoy early, and it does something to them, makes them soft where we are hard, and cynical where we are trustful. . . ." surrounded from childhood by the artificial security of wealth, accustomed to owning rather than wanting, they lack anxiety or illusion, frustration or fulfillment. Their romantic dreams are rooted in the adolescence from which they never completely escape—in the excitement of the prom or petting party, the reputation of being fast on the college gridiron or the college weekend.

Inevitably, then, Fitzgerald saw his romantic dream threaded by a double irony. Those who possess the necessary means lack the will, motive, or promises of life have it because they are the disinherited, forever barred from the white palace where "the king's daughter, the golden girl" awaits "safe and proud above the struggles of the poor." Amory Blaine loses his girl writing advertising copy at ninety a month. Anthony Patch loses his mind after an abortive attempt to recoup his fortune peddling bonds. Jay Gatsby loses his life even though he makes his millions because they are not the kind of safe, respectable money that echoes in Daisy's lovely voice. The successful entrepreneurs of Gatsby's age are the panderers to vulgar tastes, the high pressure salesmen, and, of course, the bootleggers. Yet ounce, Fitzgerald suggests, there had been opportunity commensurate with aspiration, an unexplored and unexploited frontier where great fortunes had been made or at least romantically stolen. And out of the shifting of opportunities from the West to Wall Street, he creates an American fable which redeems as well as explains romantic failure.

But how is one to accept, even in fable, a West characterized by the dull rectitude of Minnesota villages and an East epitomized by the sophisticated dissipation of Long Island society? The answer is perhaps that Fitzgerald's dichotomy of East and West has the poetic truth of James's antithesis of provincial American virtue and refined European sensibility. Like *The Portrait of a Lady* and *The Amabassadors, Gatsby* is a story of "displaced persons" who have journeyed eastward in search of a larger experience of life. To James this reverse migration from the New to the Old World has in itself no special significance. To Fitzgerald, however, the lure of the East represents a profound displacement of the American dream, a turning back upon itself of the historic pilgrimage towards the frontier which had, in fact, created and sustained that dream. In *Gatsby* the once limitless western horizon is circumscribed by the "bored, sprawling, swollen towns beyond the Ohio, with their interminable inquisitions which spared only the children and the very old." The virgin territories of the frontiersman have been appropriated by the immigrant families, the diligent Swedes—the unimaginative, impoverished German farmers like Henry Gatz. Thus after a restless nomadic existence, the Buchanans settle "permanently" on Long Island because Tom would be "a God damned fool to live anywhere else." Thus Nick comes to New York with a dozen volumes on finance which promise "to unfold the shining secrets that only Midas, Morgan and Maecenas knew." Gatsby's green light, of course, shines in only one direction—from the East across the Continent to Minnesota, from the East across the bay to his imitation mansion in West Egg.

Lying in the moonlight on Gatsby's deserved beach, Nick realizes at the close just how lost a pilgrimage Gatsby's had been:

> . . . I became aware of the old island here that had flowered once for Dutch sailors' eyes—a fresh, green breast of the new world. Its vanished trees, the trees that had made way for Gatsby's house, had once pandered in whispers to the last and greatest of all human dreams; for a transitory moment man must have held his breath in the presence of this continent, compelled into an aesthetic contemplation he neither understood nor desired, face to face for the last time in history with something commensurate to his capacity for wonder.

Gatsby is the spiritual descendant of these Dutch sailors. Like them, he set out for gold and stumbled on a dream. But he journeys in the wrong direction in time as well as space. The transitory enchanted moment has come and gone for him and for the others, making the romantic promise of the future an illusory reflection of the past. Nick still carries with him a restlessness born of the war's excitement; Daisy silently mourns the romantic adventure of her "white" girlhood; Tom seeks the thrill of a vanished football game. Gatsby devotes his life to recapturing a love lost five years before. When the present offers nothing commensurate with man's capacity for wonder, the romantic credo is the belief—Gatsby's belief—in the ability to repeat the disembodied past. Each step towards the green light, however, shadows some part of Gatsby's grandiose achievement. With Daisy's disapproval the spectroscopic parties cease. To preserve her reputation Gatsby empties his mansion of lights and servants. And finally only darkness and ghostly memories tenant the deserted house as Gatsby relives his romantic past for Nick after the accident.

Like his romantic dream Jay Gatsby belongs to a vanished past. His career began when he met Dan Cody, a debauched relic of an earlier America who made his millions in the copper strikes. From Cody he received an education in ruthlessness which he applied when the accident of the war brought him to the beautiful house of Daisy Fay. In the tradition of Cody's frontier, he "took what he could get, ravenously and unscrupulously," but in taking Daisy he fell in love with her. "She vanished into her rich house, into her rich full life, leaving Gatsby—nothing. He felt married to her, that was all."

"He felt married to her"—here is the reaction of bourgeois conscience, not of calculating amibition. But then Gatsby is not really Cody's protégé. Jimmy Gatz inherited an attenuated version of the Amercian dream of success, a more moral and genteel dream suited to a nation arriving at the respectability of established wealth and class. Respectability demands that avarice be masked with virtue, that personal aggrandisement pose as self-improvement. Success is no longer to the cutthroat or the ruthless but to the diligent and the industrious, to the boy who scribbles naive resolves on the flyleaf of *Hopalong Cassidy*. Fabricated of pulp fiction clichés (the impoverished materials of an extraordinary imagination), Gatsby's dream of self-improvement blossoms into a preposterous tale of ancestral wealth and culture. And his dream is incorruptible because his great enterprise is not side-street "drugstores," or stolen bonds, but himself, his fictional past, his mansion and his gaudy entertainments. Through it all he moves alone and mansion and his gaudy entertainments. Through it all he moves alone and untouched; he is the impresario, the creator, not the enjoyer of a riotous venture dedicated to an impossible goal.

It may seem ironic that Gatsby's dreams of self-improvement is realized through partnership with Meyer Wolfsheim, but Wolfsheim is merely the post-war succesor to Dan Cody and to the ruthlessness and greed that once exploited a virgin West. He is the fabulous manipulator of bootleg gin rather than of copper, the modern man of legendary accomplishment "who fixed the World's Series back in 1919." The racketeer, Fitzgerald suggests, is the last great folk hero, the Paul Bunyan of an age in which romantic wonder surrounds underworld "gonnegtions" instead of raw courage or physical strength. And actually Gatsby is destroyed not by Wolfsheim, or association with him, but by the provincial squeamishness which makes all the Westerners in the novel unadaptable to life in the East.

Despite her facile cynicism and claim to sophistication, Daisy is still the "nice" girl who grew up in Louisville in a beautiful house with a wicker settee on the porch. She remains "spotless," still immaculately dressed in white and capable of a hundred whimsical, vaporous enthusiasms. She has assimilated the urbane ethic of the East which allows a bored wife a casual discreet affair. But she cannot, like Gatsby's uninvited guests, wink at the illegal and the criminal. When Tom begins to unfold the sordid details of Gatsby's career, she shrinks away; she never intended to leave her husband, but now even an affair is impossible. Tom's provinciality is more boorish than genteel. He has assumed the role of Long Island country gentleman who keeps a mistress in a midtown apartment. But with Myrtle Wilson by his side he turns the role into a ludicrous travesty. By nature a libertine, by upbring a prig, Tom shatters Gatsby's facade in order to preserve his "gentleman's" conception of womanly virtue and of the sanctity of his marriage.

Ultimately, however, Gatsby is the victim of his own small-town notions of virtue and chivalry. "He would never so much as look at a friend's wife"—or at least he would never try to steal her in her husband's house. He wants Daisy to say that she never loved Tom because only in this way can the sacrament of Gatsby's "marriage" to her in Louisville—his prior claim—be recognized. Not content merely to repeat the past, he must also eradicate the years in which his dream lost its reality. But the dream, like the vanished frontier which it almost comes to represent, is lost forever "somewhere back in that vast obscurity beyond the city, where the dark field of the republic rolled on under the night."

After Gatsby's death Nick prepares to return to his Minnesota home, a place of warmth and enduring stability, carrying with him a surrealistic night vision of the debauchery of the East. Yet his return is not a positive rediscovery of the well-springs of American life. Instead it seems a melancholy retreat from the ruined promise of the East, from the empty present to the childhood memory of the past. Indeed, it is this childhood memory, not the reality of the West which Nick cherishes. For he still thinks the East, despite its nightmarish aspect, superior to the stultifying small-town dullness from which he fled. And by the close of *Gatsby* it is unmistakably clear that the East does not symbolize contemporary decadence and the West the pristine virtues of an earlier America. Fitzgerald does not contrast Gatsby's criminality with his father's unspoiled rustic strength and dignity. He contrasts rather Henry Gatz's dull, grey, almost insentient existence, "a meaningless extinction up an alley," with Gatsby's pilgrimage Eastward, which, though hopeless and corrupting, was at least a journey of life and hope—an escape from the "vast obscurity" of the West that once spawned and then swallowed the American dream. Into this vast obscurity the Buchanans finally disappear. They are not Westerners any longer, or Easterners, but merely two of the very rich, who in the end represent nothing but themselves. They are careless people, Tom and Daisy, selfish, destructive, capable of anything except human sympathy, and yet not sophisticated enough to be really decadent. Their irresponsibility, Nick realizes, is that of pampered children, who smash up "things and creatures . . . and let other people clean up the mess." They live in the eternal moral adolescence which only wealth can produce and protect.

By ignoring its context one can perhaps make much of Nick's indictment of the Buchanans. One can even say that in *The Great Gatsby* Fitzgerald adumbrated the coming tragedy of a nation grown decadent without achieving maturity—a nation that possessed and enjoyed early, and in its arrogant assumption of superiority lost sight of the dream that had created it. But is it not absurd to interpret Gatsby as a mythic Spenglerian anti-hero? Gatsby is great, because his dream, however naive, gaudy, and unattainable is one of the grand illusions of the race which keep men from becoming too old or too wise or too cynical of their human limitations. Scott Fitzgerald's fable of East and West does not lament the decline of American civilization. It mourns the eternal lateness of the present hour suspended between the past of romantic memory and the future of romantic promise which ever recedes before us.

—*College English,* December 1956, pp. 139–143.

1. See Edwin Fussell, "Fitzgerald's Brave New World," *ELH,* 19 (December 1952), 291–306; Marius Bewley, "Scott Fitzgerald's Criticism of America," *Sewanee Review,* 62 (Spring 1954), 223–246; John W. Bicknell, "The Wasteland of F. Scott Fitzgerald," *VQR,* 30 (Autumn 1954). A somewhat different but equality negative interpretation is R. W. Stallman's "Gatsby and the Hole in Time." *Modern Fiction Studies,* 1 (Nov, 1955), 1–15.

* * *

Dust jacket for the 1966 novel drawn from The Great Gatsby

Kenneth Millar (Ross Macdonald) based his 1966 novel Black Money on The Great Gatsby, *as he acknowledged in a 28 October 1968 letter to Donald Davie:*

Nor, for what I consider good reason, did I mention Gatsby; though of course I wrote the book, <u>Black Money,</u> in an effort to tell that all-American story differently; and your close detailed grasp of the difference (you omitted only to mention that my poor hero had Negro blood as well as French and Indian) makes me believe that it met with some success, often over a decade of planning. My reasons for not mentioning Gatsby right out are that it is not a literary introduction, really; some readers would think I was boasting; others that I was confessing; the rest, the few rest, don't need to be told.

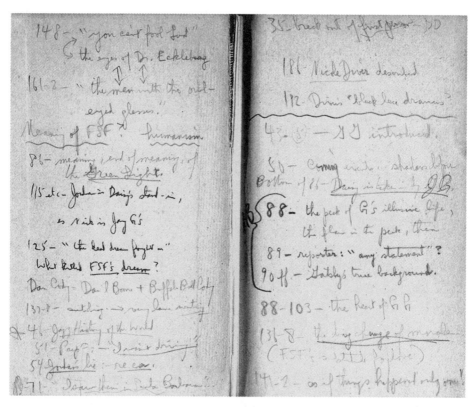

Kenneth Millar's Gatsby *notes on the endpapers of his copy of* The Portable F. Scott Fitzgerald *(Matthew J. Bruccoli Collection)*

F. Scott Fitzgerald's *The Great Gatsby:* Legendary Bases and Allegorical Significances

John Henry Raleigh

F. Scott Fitzgerald's character Gatsby, as has often been said, represents the irony of American history and the corruption of the American dream. While this certainly is true, yet even here, with this general legend, Fitzgerald has rung in his own characteristic changes, doubling and redoubling ironies. At the center of the legend proper there is the relationship between Europe and America and the ambiguous interaction between the contradictory impulses of Europe that led to the original settling of America and its subsequent development: mercantilism and idealism. At either end of American history, and all the way through, the two impulses have a way of being both radically exclusive and mutually confusing, the one melting into the other: the human faculty of wonder, on the one hand, and the power and beauty of things, on the other.

The Great Gatsby dramatizes this continuing ambiguity directly in the life of Gatsby and retrospectively by a glance at history at the end of the novel. Especially does it do so in the two passages in the novel of what might be called the ecstatic moment, the moment when the human imagination seems to be on the verge of entering the earthly paradise. The two passages are (1) the real Gatsby looking on the real Daisy, and (2) the imaginary Dutchmen, whom Nick conjures up at the end of the novel, looking on the "green breast" of Long Island.

Here is the description of Gatsby and Daisy:

> Out of the corner of his eye Gatsby saw that the blocks of the sidewalks really formed a ladder and mounted to a secret place above the trees–he could climb to it, if he climbed alone, and once there he could suck on the pap of life, gulp down the incomparable milk of wonder.
>
> His heart beat faster as Daisy's white face came up to his own. He knew that when he kissed this girl, and forever wed his unutterable visions to her perishable breath, his mind would never romp again like the mind of God. So he waited, listening for a moment longer to the tuning-fork that had been struck upon a star. Then he kissed her. At his lips' touch she blossomed for him like a flower and the incarnation was complete.

And below is Nick's imaginative reconstruction of the legendary Dutchman. He is sprawled on the sand at night, with Gatsby's mansion behind him and Long Island Sound in front of him:

> And as the moon rose higher the inessential houses began to melt away until gradually I became aware of the old Island that flowered once for Dutch eyes–a fresh green breast of the new world. Its vanished trees,

the trees that had made way for Gatsby's house, had once pandered in whispers to the last and greatest of all human dreams; for a transitory enchanted moment man must have held his breath in the presence of this continent, compelled into an aesthetic contemplation he neither understood nor desired, face to face for the last time in history with something commensurate to his capacity for wonder.[1]

The repetition in the two passages of the words "wonder" and "flower" hardly need comment, or the sexuality, illicit in the Dutchmen's and both infantile and mature in Gatsby's–or the star-lit, moon-lit setting in both. For these are the central symbols in the book: the boundless imagination trying to transfigure under the stars the endlessly beautifully object. Now, of course, the Dutchmen and Gatsby are utterly different types of being and going in different directions. The Dutchmen are pure matter, momentarily and unwillingly raised into the realms of the spirit, while Gatsby is pure spirit coming down to earth. They pass one another, so to speak, at the moment when ideal and reality seem about to converge. Historically, the Dutch, legendarily stolid, pursued their mercantile ways and produced finally a Tom Buchanan but also, it should be remembered, a Nick Carraway. But their ecstatic moment hung on in the air, like an aroma, intoxicating prophets, sages, poets, even poor farm boys in twentieth-century Dakota. The heady insubstantiability of the dream and the heavy intractability of the reality were expressed by Van Wyck Brooks (who could well have been Fitzgerald's philosopher in these matters) in his *The Wine of the Puritans* as follows:

> You put the old wine [Europeans] into new bottles [American continent] . . . and when the explosion results, one may say, the aroma passes into the air and the wine spills on the floor. The aroma or the ideal, turns into transcendentalism and the wine or the real, becomes commercialism.

No one knew better than Gatsby that nothing could finally match the splendors of his own imagination, and the novel would suggest finally that not only had the American dream been corrupted but that it was, in part anyway, necessarily corrupted, for it asked too much. Nothing of this earth, even the most beautiful of earthly objects, could be anything but a perversion of it.

The Great Gatsby, then, begins in a dramatization, as suggested, of the basic thesis of the early Van Wyck Brooks: that America had produced an idealism so impalpable that it had lost touch with reality (Gatsby) and a materialism so heavy that it was inhuman (Tom Buchanan). The novel as a whole is another turn of the screw on this legend, with the impossible idealism try-

> Nobody'll ever know America completely because nobody ever knew Gatsby, I guess.
>
> –Jack Kerouac,
> *Life,* 29 June 1962

ing to realize itself, to its utter destruction, in the gross materiality. As Nick says of Gatsby at the end of the novel:

> . . . his dream must have seemed so close that he could hardly fail to grasp it. He did not know that it was already behind him somewhere back in that vast obscurity beyond the city, where the dark fields of the republic rolled on under the night.

Yet he imagines too that Gatsby, before his moment of death, must have had his "realization" of the intractable brutishness of matter:

> . . . he must have felt that he had lost the old warm world, paid a high price for living too long with a single dream. He must have looked up at an unfamiliar sky through frightening leaves and shivered as he found what a grotesque thing a rose is and how raw the sunlight was upon the scarcely created grass.

Thus Fitzgerald multiplies the ironies of the whole legend: that the mercantile Dutchmen should have been seduced into the esthetic; that Gatsby's wondrous aspirations should attach themselves to a Southern belle and that in pursuit of her he should become a gangster's lieutenant; that young Englishmen ("agonizingly aware of the easy money in the vicinity") should scramble for crumbs at Gatsby's grandiose parties (the Dutchmen once more); that idealism, beauty, power, money should get all mixed up; that history should be a kind of parody of itself, as with the case of the early Dutch and the contemporary English explorers.

Still *The Great Gatsby* would finally suggest, at a level beyond all its legends and in the realm of the properly tragic, that it is right and fitting that the Jay Gatzes of the world should ask for the impossible, even when they do so as pathetically and ludicrously as does Gatsby himself. Writing to Fitzgerald about his novel, Maxwell Perkins, after enumerating some specific virtues, said:

> . . . these are such things as make a man famous. And all the things, the whole pathetic episode, you have given a place in time and space, for with the help of T. J.

Eckleburg, and by an occasional glance at the sky, or the city, you have imparted a sort of sense of eternity.

A "sense of eternity"–this is indeed high praise, but I think that Perkins, as he often was, was right.

For at its highest level *The Great Gatsby* does not deal with local customs or even national and international legends but with the permanent realities of existence. On this level nothing or nobody is to blame, and people are what they are and life is what it is, just as, in Bishop Butler's words, "things are what they are." At this level, too, most people don't count; they are merely a higher form of animality living out its mundane existence: the Tom Buchanans, the Jordan Bakers, the Daisy Fays. Only Nick and Gatsby count. For Gatsby, with all his absurdities and his short, sad, pathetic life, is still valuable; in Nick's parting words to him: "You're worth the whole damn bunch put together." Nick, who in his way is as much of this world as Daisy is in hers, still sees, obscurely, the significance of Gatsby. And although he knows that the content of Gatsby's dream is corrupt, he senses that its form is pristine. For, in his own fumbling, often gross way, Gatsby was obsessed with the wonder of human life and driven by the search to make that wonder actual. It is the same urge that motivates visionaires and prophets, the urge to make the facts of life measure up to the splendors of the human imagination, but it is utterly pathetic in Gatsby's case because he is trying to do it so subjectively and so uncouthly, and with dollar bills. Still Nick's obscure instinct that Gatsby is essentially all right is sound. It often seems as if the novel is about the contrast between the two, but the bond between them reveals that they are not opposites but rather complements, opposed together, to all the other characters in the novel.

Taken together they contain most of the essential polarities that go to make up the human mind and its existence. Allegorically considered, Nick is reason, experience, waking, reality, and history, while Gatsby is imagination, innocence, sleeping, dream, and eternity. Nick is like Wordworth listening to "the still sad music of humanity," while Gatsby is like Blake seeing hosts of angels in the sun. The one can only look at the facts and see them as tragic; the other tries to transform the facts by an act of the imagination. Nick's mind is conservative and historical, as is his lineage; Gatsby's is radical and apocalyptic–as rootless as his heritage. Nick is too much immersed in time and in reality; Gatsby is hopelessly out of it. Nick is always withdrawing, while Gatsby pursues the green light. Nick can't be hurt, but neither can he be happy. Gatsby can experience ecstasy, but his fate is necessarily tragic. They are generally two of the best types of humanity: the moralist and the radical.

One may well ask why, if their mental horizons are so lofty, is one a bond salesman and the other a gangster's lieutenant, whose whole existence is devoted to a love affair that has about it the unmistakeable stamp of adolescence? The answer is, I think, that Fitzgerald did not know enough of what a philosopher or revolutionary might really be like, that at this point in his life he must have always thought of love in terms of a Princeton Prom, and that, writing in the twenties, a bond salesman and a gangster's functionary would seem more representative anyway. Van Wyck Brooks might have said, at one time, that his culture gave him nothing more to work with. A lesser writer might have attempted to make Nick a literal sage and Gatsby a literal prophet. But it is certain that such a thought would never have entered Fitzgerald's head, as he was only dramatizing the morals and manners of the life he knew. The genius of the novel consists precisely in the fact that, while using only the stuff, one might better say the froth and flotsam of its own limited time and place, it has managed to suggest, as Perkins said, a sense of eternity.

—*University of Kansas City Review,* October 1957, pp. 55–58.

* * *

Fitzgerald reached a large public with *This Side of Paradise* (1920); an adolescent collegiate best-seller influenced by Rupert Brooke and Compton Mackenzie. It is all the more to his credit that he should have moved on to this light-hearted masterpiece of the boom years (one of the half-dozen best American novels) which won the instant acclaim of Eliot. There is evidence of weakness and there are shifts of emphasis in 'Gatsby', but it remains a prose poem of delight and sadness which has by now introduced two generations to the romance of America, as *Huckleberry Finn* and *Leaves of Grass* introduced those before it.

—Cyril Connolly, *The Modern Movement* (1965)

The Great Gatsby: Fitzgerald's Meditation on American History
Kermit W. Moyer

In a letter to Maxwell Perkins written in April of 1924, Fitzgerald said: "I feel I have an enormous power in me now, more than I've ever had in a way. . . ." He had just begun work on his third novel. "This book," he told Perkins, "will be a consciously artistic achievement and must depend on that as the first books did not."[1] Some four and a half months later, when he had nearly completed a first draft, Fitzgerald wrote Perkins again: "I think my novel is about the best American novel ever written," he said.[2] The only thing he was really unsure of was a title, but by the time the book appeared in April, 1925, Fitzgerald had decided to call it *The Great Gatsby.*

Gatsby has since become the Fitzgerald novel everyone agrees on—the book that assures Fitzgerald his place in the first rank. It is the novel that in 1925 T. S. Eliot called "the first step that American fiction has taken since Henry James."[3] *Gatsby* is so good, in fact, that critics tend to confront it with a hint of grateful incredulity; as if Fitzgerald simply couldn't have gone *that* far in the five years that separate *Gatsby* from *This Side of Paradise.*

There is also, among recent critics at least, a strong consensus that *The Great Gatsby* must be understood as a meditation on American history. As early as 1937, John Peale Bishop recognized in Jay Gatsby "the Emersonian man brought to completion and eventually to failure."[4] In an influential essay written less than a decade later, Lionel Trilling maintained that "Gatsby, divided between power and dream, comes inevitably to stand for America itself."[5] Trilling insisted that when Jay Gatsby is described first as springing "from his Platonic conception of himself" and then as a son of God whose business is "the service of a vast, vulgar, and meretricious beauty," Fitzgerald's clear intention is "that our mind should turn to the thought of the nation that has sprung from its 'Platonic conception' of itself."[6] A few years later Edwin Fussell based a strongly persuasive interpretation of the novel on the "connection between Gatsby's individual tragedy and the tragedy of American civilization."[7] Fussell claimed that "Roughly speaking Fitzgerald's basic plot is the history of the New World . . . more precisely, of the human imagination in the New World."[8] Fitzgerald's subject in *The Great Gatsby,* Fussell insisted, is not the Jazz Age or the Lost Generation, "but the whole of American civilization as it culminated in his own time."[9] This sort of historical approach to the novel has since become more or less standard. In 1954 Marius Bewley praised *Gatsby* as "an evocative and an exact description" of the violation of American "aspiration and vision" by "the conditions of American history."[10] Three years later, James E. Miller, Jr., talked about "the gradual expansion of the significance of Gatsby's dream," an expansion which Miller saw as finally encompassing "the dream of those who discovered and settled the American continent."[11] In 1958 another Fitzgerald scholar, John R. Kuehl, described *The Great Gatsby* as "a sort of cultural-historical allegory."[12] Still more recently, Richard Lehan has claimed that in *The Great Gatsby* "We move from a personal sphere (a story of unrequited love), to a historical level (the hope and idealism of the frontier and of democracy in conflict with a rapacious and destructive materialism)."[13] Finally, Robert Sklar maintains that "the whole of American experience takes on the character of Gatsby's romantic quest and tragic failure; the history of a continent finds expression in the transcendent images of felicity man made from the beauty of its mocking nature."[14] But despite critical agreement on the profound importance of the historical perspective in The Great Gatsby, we still lack a reading of the novel which clearly and concisely articulates the way Fitzgerald has worked out his historical theme. This essay is an attempt at such a reading.[15]

Fitzgerald originally conceived of *Gatsby* as an historical novel set in the Gilded Age: "its locale," he wrote Maxwell Perkins, "will be the middle west and New York of 1885 I think."[16] The story "Absolution" seems to derive from this first conception of the novel. Although the book that Fitzgerald finally wrote is contemporary in setting, the historical approach that seems to have informed his original conception was not discarded: *The Great Gatsby* is a profoundly historical novel.

Gatsby is really an extended flashback: events are narrated by Nick Carraway some two years after they have occurred. This technique gives the novel a formal circularity (starting at the end, we move to the beginning and proceed back to the end) which reflects structurally a series of circular movements within the story itself (circles of movement traced from West Egg to East Egg and back, from Long Island to Manhattan and back, from East to West and back). The image of the circle is perhaps most obviously apparent in the egg-shaped geography (hence the name) of East and West Egg. Ultimately this circularity reiterates the novel's perspective upon American history; and since that perspective is contained in Gatsby's personal history, it is perhaps inevitable that in death Gatsby describe with his own life's blood "a thin red circle" in the water of his swimming pool.[17]

Gatsby's romantic quest for Daisy Fay is circular in essence: his sustained and single-minded thrust into the future is an attempt to recapture, not merely Daisy, but *that moment of wonder which she had once inspired*. For Gatsby, the future has become simply an avenue leading back to the past—or, more specifically, leading back to the glittering possibilities the past once seemed to offer. It isn't enough that he have Daisy, he must have her as she was five years ago, before she married Tom Buchanan; he must recapture the romantic texture of that ecstatic instant when she suddenly embodied for him all of life's wonder and possibility, that moment when he exchanged forever the riotous tumult in his imagination for the vision of her white face and the enchantment of her silvery voice.

"And she doesn't understand," he said. "She used to be able to understand. We'd sit for hours—"

He broke off and began to walk up and down a desolate path of fruit rinds and discarded favors and crushed flowers.

"I wouldn't ask too much of her," I ventured. "You can't repeat the past."

"Can't repeat the past?" he cried incredulously. "Why of course you can!"

He looked around him wildly, as if the past were lurking here in the shadow of his house, just out of reach of his hand.

"I'm going to fix everything just the way it was before," he said, nodding determinedly. "She'll see."

He talked a lot about the past, and I gathered that he wanted to recover something, some idea of himself perhaps, that had gone into loving Daisy. His life had been confused and disordered since then, but if he could once return to a certain starting place and go over it all slowly, he could find out what that thing was. . . . (p. 86)

Gatsby's urge is transcendental: his vision of life acknowledges neither time nor limit. But throughout this passage an image of discarded favors and crushed flowers reminds us of the irrevocability of time and of the fatal materiality of the terms of Gatsby's transcendentalism. One autumn night five years before, he had "forever wed his unutterable visions to her *perishable* breath" (p. 112; my emphasis). He had kissed Daisy, and "At his lips' touch *she blossomed for him like a flower* and the incarnation was complete" (p. 112; my emphasis). Now the crushed flowers at his feet comment ironically upon the tragic terms of Gatsby's transcendental vision, and we suddenly realize why the girl who has given focus to that vision is named Daisy.

Throughout the novel, then, a flower metaphor reveals the essential materiality at the core of Gatsby's transcendentalism. In "Winter Dreams," a story universally recognized as a precursor to *The Great Gatsby*, Fitzgerald had also worked with this theme. Dexter Green's lavish dreams are also undermined by the mutability of their material terms (a mutability suggested by Dexter's surname and underscored by the seasonal emphasis of the title). The quality in Judy Jones upon which Dexter's dream of imaginative fulfillment depends is time-bound, transient; her particular beauty is characterized by "a sort of fluctuating and feverish warmth, so shaded that it seemed at any moment it would recede and disappear. This color and the mobility of her mouth gave a continual impression of flux, of intense life, of passionate vitality. . . ."[18] When time destroys Judy's fragile beauty, Dexter's dreams dissolve too. The dreams were winter dreams after all—they were tied to time from the outset, as transient as any green bud, as fugitive as any daisy. Gatsby's transcendentalism, of course, is not only tainted by materialism, it is revealed as disastrously circular since it seeks by embracing the *future* to regain and freeze that instant in the *past* when Daisy seemed equal to the demands of Gatsby's transcendental imagination. In the meantime, the present doesn't count: the present is simply the ground upon which Gatsby stands while looking to the future where he sees the past; the present is carelessly exploited (serving also as a dumping ground for the detritus of that exploitation) in order to feed the impassioned thrust into the future. Appropriately, Gatsby first appears in the novel frozen in a pose which exactly represents this circular transcendentalism: facing the green light at the end of Daisy's dock, Gatsby stands with arms outstretched, as if by somehow embracing that green light and possessing the "orgastic future" it represents (p. 141), he could regain that time five years before when he had kissed Daisy and she had "blossomed for him like a flower."

Throughout the novel, Fitzgerald underscores the transcendental nature of Gatsby's love for Daisy. To repeat, it is not just Daisy Gatsby wants but something *beyond* her: he wants that moment when life seemed equal to his extraordinary capacity for wonder, and that moment is indissoluably wedded to Daisy herself, to materiality. When Gatsby explains to Nick that any love Daisy may have felt for her husband was "just personal," Nick realizes that Gatsby's conception of the affair possesses an intensity that can't be measured (p. 152). Like Braddock Washington in "The Diamond as Big as the Ritz," Gatsby combines transcendental imagination with time-enthralled materialism (both heroes also try to control the future by buying back the past); and like the story of Braddock Washington's family, Gatsby's story is a mirror which reflects an image of American history.

After Gatsby reveals to Carraway his astonishing belief that the past can be repeated, that one can retrieve and sustain that moment when reality promised to realize the ideal, Nick remarks:

> Through all he said, even through his appalling sentimentality, I was reminded of something—an elusive rhythm, a fragment of lost words, that I had heard somewhere a long time ago. For a moment a phrase tried to take shape in my mouth and my lips parted like a dumb man's, as though there was more struggling upon them than a wisp of startled air. But they made no sound, and what I had almost remembered was uncommunicable forever. (p. 87)

Gatsby's story, his peculiar and naive audacity, his intense idealism, have evoked a resonance that goes beyond himself. By the end of the novel it becomes clear that the elusive rhythm Nick is here unable to articulate is the rhythm of American history, a rhythm created by man's headlong pursuit of a dream all the way across a continent and back again. Fitzgerald makes this parallel between Gatsby's history and America's history explicit on the last page of the novel.

> Most of the big shore places were closed now and there were hardly any lights except the shadowy, moving glow of a ferryboat across the Sound. And as the moon rose higher the inessential houses began to melt away until gradually I became aware of the old island here *that flowered once for Dutch sailors' eyes*—a fresh, green breast of the new world. Its vanished trees, the trees that had made way for Gatsby's house, had once pandered in whispers to the last and greatest of all human dreams; for a transitory enchanted moment man must have held his breath in the presence of this continent, compelled into an aesthetic contemplation he neither understood nor desired, face to face for the last time in history with something commensurate to his capacity for wonder. (p. 140; my emphasis)

Just as Daisy flowered for Gatsby, so the new world flowered for the Europeans who touched her shore; in both cases, for one electric moment, the material world promised to fulfill the imagination's deepest longings. Fitzgerald goes on to link the wonder evoked by Daisy's green dock light with the wonder evoked by the green breast of the new world: "And as I sat there brooding on the old, unknown world, I thought of Gatsby's wonder when he first picked out the green light at the end of Daisy's dock (p. 141). By association with the green trees *which have now vanished*, the green light is included in the flower metaphor which Fitzgerald has used to underscore the essential transiency of the materiality which Gatsby and the Dutch sailors before him have invested with spiritual value. The parallel between the wonder evoked in Gatsby by Daisy and the wonder inspired by the new world is reinforced through Fitzgerald's use of erotic imagery to describe the Dutch sailors' response to the new land: they are arrested by the "fresh, green *breast*" of America, and the trees *pander* to their insatiable dreams. The word "pandered" also suggests the essential meretriciousness of the new world's spiritual and imaginative appeal. We already know by this time that the promise embodied in Daisy is meretricious. The passage goes on to compete the link between Gatsby's pursuit of Daisy and America's historical pursuit of an ever-receding frontier:

> He had come a long way to this blue lawn, and his dream must have seemed so close that he could hardly fail to grasp it. He did not know that it was already behind him, somewhere back in that obscurity beyond the city, where the dark fields of the republic rolled on under the night. (p. 141)

Gatsby's dream, the dream inspired by Daisy, is here identified with the dream which pushed the frontier ever westward. The assumption contained in this identification is that, like Gatsby's history, American history has been the record of a futile attempt to retrieve and sustain a moment of imaginative intensity and promise. By reaching into the future, by pushing continually up against the receding frontier, we have tried to recapture that original sense of wonder evoked when the whole continent was a frontier–that original sense of wonder which soured because its evocation was essentially meretricious, a reading of spiritual, transcendental promise into mere materiality. So we struggle on against the current of time only to be "borne back ceaselessly into the past" (p. 141): our vain effort to seize the lost moment of promise by reaching for the future creates the fabric of our history.

This is an outline of the historical perspective which informs *The Great Gatsby* and which, to some extent, probably derived from Fitzgerald's discovery in Conrad of a kind of hero (Mr. Kurtz) who embraces cultural contradictions. But there are several other important aspects of the novel which must now be explored in terms of this perspective–specifically, Fitzgerald's treatment of Tom Buchanan and the Wilsons; his portrait of Gatsby's early mentor, Dan Cody; the significance of the "waste land" and the eyes of Doctor T. J. Eckleburg which preside over it; Nick Carraway's implicit contrast of East and West; and the role of World War I, which casts a kind of shadow over the events of the whole novel.

The Buchanans are obviously meant to represent an American class. When, at the end of the novel, Nick Carraway says, "They were careless people, Tom and Daisy–they smashed up things and creatures and then retreated back into their money or their vast carelessness, or whatever it was that kept them together, and let other people clean up the mess they had made" (p. 139), we realize that Nick's judgment is generic rather than individual in application. Before moving to East Egg, the Buchanans "had spent a year in France for no particular reason, and then drifted here and there unrestfully wherever people played polo and were rich together" (pp. 8–9). The Buchanans, standing for the modern American upper class, embody a materialism which is totally cynical, undirected by idealism or transcendental hope. Tom Buchanan's chief characteristic is his harsh *physicality*: his orientation is intensely physical at the expense of the mental, the spiritual, and the social. He is described as arrogant, aggressive, powerful: " . . . he seemed to fill those glistening boots until he strained the top lacing, and you could see a great pack of muscle shifting when his shoulder moved under his thin coat. It was a body capable of enormous leverage–

a cruel body" (p. 9). Even his past accomplishments are physical: he had been one of the most powerful ends ever to play football at Yale, and Gatsby introduces Tom to his party guests as "the polo player" (p. 82). Jordan Baker, also a representative of this class, mirrors Tom's materialist orientation and consequent athleticism as well as his dishonesty: "She was incurably dishonest. She wasn't able to endure being at a disadvantage and, given this unwillingness, I suppose she had begun dealing in subterfuges when she was very young in order to keep that cool, insolent smile turned to the world and yet satisfy the demands of her hard, jaunty body" (pp. 47–48). Appropriately enough, Jordan is a tournament golfer who cheats. Daisy's role, as we have seen, is more complicated than either Jordan's or Tom's, but the imagery surrounding her is loaded with materialistic associations: she is described continually in terms of silver and gold and her magical voice is "full of money" (p. 94). Daisy represents the materialism of her class as well as the materialism at the core of Gatsby's transcendental idealism. The class to which Daisy and Tom and Jordan Baker belong, the class represented in somewhat broader terms by East Egg itself, has completely lost touch with the transcendental spirit which once shaped American history and which renders Gatsby's materialism tragic rather than shallow. Although Nick deeply disapproves of Gatsby, a sense of the transcendental emotion at the bottom of Gatsby's materialism makes Nick stop, turn, and call out: "They're a rotten crowd . . . You're worth the whole damn bunch put together" (p. 120). Even Daisy senses the tragic nature of Gatsby's impossible transcendental-materialism when he displays his shirts for her, heaping them in a luxurious pile until she cries because she has "never seen such–such beautiful shirts before" (p. 73), moved not so much by the shirts themselves as by the intense emotion with which Gatsby has invested them.

The Buchanans and their class represent an historical dead end. In his own inarticulate way, Tom Buchanan senses this. He clumsily recommends Nick to read " 'The Rise of the Colored Empires' by this man Goddard" (p. 14), a reference–characteristic of Tom in its inaccuracy–to Theodore Lothrop Stoddard's *The Rising Tide of Color Against White World-Supremacy* (1920). "Civilization's going to pieces," Tom explains. "The idea is if we don't look out the white race will be–will be utterly submerged. It's all scientific stuff; it's been proved" (p. 14). Tom goes on: "This idea is that we're Nordics. . . . And we've produced all the things that go to make civilization–oh, science and art, and all that. Do you see?" (p. 14). Nick perceives that "Something was making [Tom] nibble at the edge of stale ideas as if his sturdy physical egotism no longer nourished his peremptory heart" (p. 19). Nick, of course, is right: Tom's panic over civilization's decay is symptomatic—standing at the end of an historical alley, Tom feels the wall against his back. In the light of Fitzgerald's historical perspective in this novel, the dead end was inevitable from the start: as the frontier disappeared, as the possibility of making the virgin land fulfill its first intense promise passed, American materialism increasingly became just that—simple, spiritless materialism, unregenerative and omnivorous. Gatsby (embodying the complete historical progression) inevitably arrived at this dead end himself. Near the close of the novel, Gatsby waits amidst shattered hopes for Daisy's telephone call, the call that never comes, and Carraway guesses that perhaps Gatsby no longer even cared.

> If that was true he must have felt that he had lost the old warm world, paid a high price for living too long with a single dream. He must have looked up at an unfamiliar sky through frightening leaves and shivered as he found what a grotesque thing a rose is and how raw the sunlight was upon the scarcely created grass. A new world, *material without being real.* . . . (p. 126; my emphasis)

This new world is mere materiality, no longer transformed by the transcendental vision which had given it its meaning and therefore its reality. Kismine Washington had felt the same sense of frightening materiality when, at the end of "The Diamond as Big as the Ritz," she could no longer think of the stars as "great big diamonds that belonged to some one."[19]

It was the American pioneer who carried the burden of this historical progression into the twentieth century. The American pioneer was the proper heir of those Dutch sailors; he inherited their transcendental spark and the promise of the frontier kept the spark alive; but after pursuing that promise all the way to the Pacific ocean, he discovered that it had somehow eluded him, and he was left with nothing but the material which had fed the flame. He was rich but that was all: direction was gone, meaning was gone; the dream began to turn back upon itself. Gatsby is the adoptive son of such a pioneer—a pioneer with the prototypal name of Dan Cody. The succession is almost apostolic, but (as in *The Beautiful and Damned*) the inheritance is essentially empty.[20] Cody has become "a gray, florid man with a hard, empty face" (p. 78) who continually circles the continent in his yacht, the *Tuolomee,* as though looking for something lost. Cody is a millionaire many times over, "a product of the Nevada silver fields, of the Yukon, of every rush for metal since seventy-five" (p. 77). His yacht is named after the gold fields of northern California—a name which manages to suggest both the frontier's end and the avid materialism to which the frontier gave way.[21] Jay Gatsby was born the moment James Gatz, idly searching for his destiny along the beaches of Lake Superior, saw Cody's yacht drop anchor in the dangerous waters of Little Girl Bay, a name which ironically foreshadows the direction of Gatsby's fate.

Given such a vision of American history, it is not surprising to find a theme of material and spiritual waste running through the novel. The famous description of the "valley of ashes" which opens Chapter II strongly echoes the description of the village of Fish which opens the second part of "The Diamond as Big as the Ritz." The barren little village and the valley of ashes are both rather obvious metaphors of American spiritual desiccation.[22] The waste land between West Egg and New York, in fact, comes to resemble a microcosm of America itself; it is a vision of an America made of dust:

> This is a valley of ashes—a fantastic farm where ashes grow like wheat into ridges and hills and grotesque gardens; where ashes take the forms of house and chimneys and rising smoke and, finally, with a transcendent effort, of men who move dimly and already crumbling through the powdery air. (p. 21)

It is a "gray land" and "spasms of bleak dust . . . drift endlessly over it." This description echoes a judgment Nick Carraway had made on the second page of the novel: "Gatsby turned out all right at the end; it is what preyed on Gatsby, *what foul dust floated in the wake of his dreams* that temporarily closed out my interest in the abortive sorrows and short-winded elations of men" (my emphasis). That dust actually becomes tangible toward the end of the novel. Wandering with Gatsby through the echoing emptiness of Gatsby's colossal mansion on the night of Myrtle Wilson's death and Daisy's defection, Nick had noticed that "There was an inexplicable amount of dust everywhere" (p. 115). The foul dust that floats in the wake of America's dreams: the waste of material resources exploited in a desperate effort to sustain that impossible and disastrously circular thrust into the future and the waste of spiritual resources exploited in "the service of a vast, vulgar, and meretricious beauty" (p. 77). The foul dust is the corruptive materialism, like a worm in an apple, at the center of the transcendental dream.

In the meantime, as though in eternal mourning, the gigantic billboard eyes of Doctor T. J. Eckleburg,[23] "dimmed a little by many paintless days, under sun and rain, brook on over the solemn dumping ground" (p. 21). George Wilson confuses those faded eyes with the eyes of God, a confusion which, like, the desolate village of Fish with its twelve ghostly inhabitants, suggests that in twentieth-century America God has become a thing of cardboard, ineffectual and passive, robbed of power by a short-sighted, materialistic displacement of spiritual values. This displacement is only underscored by the fact that Eckleburg's enormous, spectacled eyes are in actuality an oculist's abandoned roadside advertisement.

George Wilson and his wife are themselves closely associated with this metaphor of waste and spiritual anemia. The Wilsons live in "a small block of yellow brick" which sits on the very edge of the waste land, "a sort of compact Main Street ministering to it, and contiguous to absolutely nothing" (p. 22). The image suggests the exploited and wasted character of the American middle class (or "Main Street") from which the Wilsons derive. The Wilsons represent the resources of human energy and hope that are drained in order to feed the materialistic orgy which American transcendentalism has inevitably become. George Wilson is already a wasted man. He works sporadically on a "dust-covered wreck of a Ford" and first appears "wiping his hands on a piece of waste" (p. 22). He is described as "a blond, spiritless man, anaemic, and faintly handsome" (p. 22) and his dark suit is veiled by "white ashen dust" (p. 23). Wilson owns a failing garage. In the course of the novel, the automobile becomes an important symbol for the superficial and dangerous beauty of materiality—dangerous because its glitter conceals a vast, destructive power.[24] So it is appropriate that Wilson spend his energy feeding the automobile of the wealthy, of those who make the circular journey from New York to East or West Egg and back again. One of those automobiles destroys his wife. If George Wilson is a man already wasted, Myrtle Wilson still possesses a great reservoir of vitality. Nick Carraway described her as a woman whose fact "contained no facet or gleam of beauty, but there was an immediately perceptible vitality about her as if the nerves of her body were continually smouldering" (p. 23). It is Myrtle's vitality, of course, which attracts Tom Buchanan: the upper class, locked into its historical dead end, depends upon the energies of the aspiring middle class to sustain itself; the middle class, in turn, wastes its energy in fruitless pursuit of that materialistic and meretricious beauty embodied most completely in the upper class. Myrtle is killed in a desperately foolish attempt to intercept Gatsby's car; she is destroyed by the class (Daisy) and the materiality (the yellow car) she had so fervently pursued. Finally, Myrtle's death becomes a metaphor for human resources wasted in pursuit of and exploited by unregenerative materialism. Lying dead immediately adjacent to the valley of ashes, Myrtle mingles "her thick dark blood with the dust," her mouth "wide open and ripped at the corners, as though she had choked a little in

giving up the tremendous vitality she had stored so long" (p. 107). Fitzgerald had used this theme before, of course: the decay of Gloria Gilbert's vitality in *The Beautiful and Damned* had also stood for the waste of human resources in America, and Gloria had also been identified with the middle class.[25]

The one character in the novel who is able to understand the historical process in which they are all trapped is Nick Carraway. Carraway has been called "the historical voice of the book"; he has a sense of history which separates him from everyone else.[26] This is not to say that Carraway has escaped the trap—he simply understands it. Like all the characters in the novel, Carraway has come from the Midwest to the East—an inversion of the earlier, westward movement. The total progression implied here is, once again, circular: beginning in the East, America pushed westward, pursuing the frontier to California, and then turned back upon itself. The ultimate dead end of that historical thrust lay not in California then but in East Egg, at the original point of departure: it is there that the circle closes. "[T]he pilgrimage eastward of the rare poisonous flower of his race," Fitzgerald once wrote, "was the end of the adventure which had started westward three hundred years ago. . . ." And Fitzgerald compared that circular movement to a serpent turning back upon itself, "cramping it bowels, bursting it shining skin."[27] In line with this metaphor of reversed migration, of the East-as-inverted-frontier, Carraway, newly arrived in New York, thinks of himself as a "a guide, a pathfinder, an original settler" (p. 7). Driving across Manhattan on a warm summer afternoon, Nick finds the atmosphere so pastoral that he "wouldn't have been surprised to see a great flock of white sheep turn the corner" (p. 25).

America's migratory pilgrimage had begun to really circle back upon itself during "that delayed Teutonic migration known as the Great War" (p. 6). Nick confesses that he had returned from the war feeling "restless":[28] "Instead of being the warm centre of the world, the Middle West now seemed like the ragged edge of the universe—so I decided to go East and learn the bond business" (p. 6). Gatsby had also been overseas during the war; in fact, Nick's first conversation with Gatsby concerns their having been in the same Division. This reverse migration, moving from the New World back to the Old World, is further suggested by Gatsby's having spent some time at Oxford after the war and by the fact that Gatsby's lavish West Egg mansion is "a factual imitation of the Hôtel de Ville in Normandy" (p. 8).

If the war stands as a fulcrum in this radical shift which has brought Nick Carraway to the East, Nick's nostalgia is not for any factual Midwest, but for the *pre-war* world of his childhood—a world as yet untouched by the moral anarchy and inarticulate panic Nick finds in the dead end of the East. "That's my middle-west." Nick says, "not the wheat or the prairies or the lost Swede towns, but the thrilling returning trains of my youth" (p. 137).

The novel concludes on this note of irretrievable loss, of inchoate nostalgia for a past which no longer exists. The wheel of American history has revolved full circle, and the end is in the beginning. It is as if Nick and Gatsby and America itself, carrying still a burden of tarnished wonder and languishing hope, had gone East in a last, tired effort to deposit the burden, to find a lodging place for the fevered imagination, and had found instead—a dead end, a wrong address. The East, Nick says, still figures in his dreams:

> I see it as a night scene by El Greco: a hundred houses, at once conventional and grotesque, crouching under a sullen, overhanging sky and a lustreless moon. In the foreground four solemn men in dress suits are walking along the sidewalk with a stretcher on which lies a drunken woman in a white evening dress. Her hand, which dangles over the side, sparkles cold with jewels. Gravely the men turn in at a house—the wrong house. But no one knows the woman's name, and no one cares. (p. 137)

—Reprinted from *Fitzgerald/Hemingway Annual 1972* (Washington, D.C.: Bruccoli Clark/NCR, 1973)

Notes

1. F. Scott Fitzgerald, *The Letters of F. Scott Fitzgerald*, ed. Andrew Turnbull (New York: Scribners's, 1963), p. 163.

2. *Ibid.*, p. 166.

3. Reprinted in *The Crack-Up*, ed. Edmund Wilson (New York: New Directions, 1945), p. 310.

4. John Peale Bishop, "The Missing All," *Virginia Quarterly Review*, 13 (1937), 115.

5. Lionel Trilling, "F. Scott Fitzgerald," in his *The Liberal Imagination: Essays on Literature and Society* (New York: Viking, 1950), p. 251; appeared originally in Trilling's "Introduction" to *The Great Gatsby* (New York: New Directions, 1945).

6. *Ibid.*

7. Edwin S. Fussell, "Fitzgerald's Brave New World," in *F. Scott Fitzgerald: A Collection of Critical Essays*, ed., Arthur Mizener (Englewood Cliffs: Prentice-Hall, 1963), p. 48; appeared originally in slightly different form in *ELH*, 19 (1952), 297.

8. *Ibid.*, p. 43; original, 291.

9. *Ibid.*, p. 49; original, 297.

10. Marius Bewley, "Scott Fitzgerald's Criticism of America," *Sewanee Review*, 62 (1954), 225; reprinted in Bewley's "Scott Fitzgerald and the Collapse of the American Dream," in his *The Eccentric Design: Form in the Classic American Novel* (New York: Columbia University Press, 1959), p. 270.

11. James E. Miller, Jr., *The Fictional Technique of Scott Fitzgerald* (The Hague: M. Nijhoff, 1957), p. 105; reprinted in Miller's *F. Scott Fitzgerald: His Art and His Technique* (New York: New York University Press, 1964), pp. 122–123.

12. John R. Kuehl, "Scott Fitzgerald: Romantic and Realist," an unpublished dissertation (Columbia University, 1958), p. 144.

13. Richard Lehan, *F. Scott Fitzgerald and the Craft of Fiction* (Carbondale: Southern Illinois University Press, 1966), p. 118.

14. Robert Sklar, F. Scott Fitzgerald: *The Last Laocoön* (New York: Oxford University Press, 1967), p. 195.

15. Since finishing this essay, I have discovered that Milton R. Stern's long, informative, richly diffuse chapter on *The Great Gatsby* in his recently published *The Golden Moment: The Novels of F. Scott Fitzgerald* (Urbana: University of Illinois Press, 1970) confirms some of my conclusions. We have worked from similar assumptions about Fitzgerald's historical preoccupations; and this has led us, I think, to complementary, rather than identical, insights.

16. Fitzgerald in a letter to Maxwell Perkins, as quoted by Henry Dan Piper, *F. Scott Fitzgerald: A Critical Portrait* (New York: Holt, Rinehart and Winston, 1965), p. 101.

17. F. Scott Fitzgerald, *The Great Gatsby* (New York: Scribner's, 1925), p. 126, hereafter cited in the text.

18. F. Scott Fitzgerald, *All the Sad Young Men* (New York: Scribner's, 1926), p. 66.

19. F. Scott Fitzgerald, *Tales of the Jazz Age* (New York: Scribner's, 1922). p. 191.

20. Frederick Hoffman notes that, in his role as Gatsby's mentor, Meyer Wolfshiem can be seen as Cody's successor and that "the difference between the two masters suggests clearly the story of several decades of exploitation and money-gathering in the American world" (*The Twenties: American Writing in the Post-War Decade* [New York: Viking, 1955], p. 115). Cody is not the only prototypal American figure to whom Gatsby is linked; he is also linked, through his childhood "Schedule" and "General Resolves," to Benjamin Franklin. See Floyd C. Watkins, "Fitzgerald's Jay Gatz and Young Ben Franklin," *New England Quarterly*, 27 (1954), 249–252.

21. Robert Emmet Long suggests a similar interpretation of *Tuolomee*: "Cody's yacht, the *Tuolomee*, is named after the gold fields in northern California, and underlies the idea of grandiose promise betrayed by brutalized reality" ("The Great Gatsby and the Tradition of Joseph Conrad—Part I," *Texas Studies in Literature and Language*, 8 [1966], 262).

22. Although T. S. Eliot's *The Waste Land* almost certainly influenced Fitzgerald's conception of "the valley of ashes," the fact that Fitzgerald had used a similar "waste land" metaphor in "The Diamond as Big as the Ritz" (published four months before *The Waste Land*) should caution us against interpreting Gatsby completely in terms of Eliot's poem. Nevertheless, it is possible to see *Gatsby* as a novel concerning "a grail quest in a waste land, over which presides a deity-like figure" (Wilfred Louis Guerin, "Christian Myth and Naturalistic Deity: *The Great Gatsby*," *Renascence*, 14 [1962], p. 80). In other words, Fitzgerald, like Eliot, may be working with a set of symbols deriving from the Fisher King/Grail legends described in Jessie L. Weston's *From Ritual to Romance* (1920). Besides Mr. Guerin's article, see John W. Bicknell, "The Waste Land of F. Scott Fitzgerald," *Virginia Quarterly Review*, 30 (1954), 556–72 and Philip Young, "Scott Fitzgerald's Waste Land," *Kansas Magazine*, 23 (1956), 73–77.

23. Lottie R. Crim and Neal B. Houston note that the name Eckleburg seems to be a play on two German words ("ekel" and "burg") which taken together suggest "loath-

some town." It is therefore possible to see in the name an implicit judgment upon New York and, by extension, upon the East itself. See Crim and Houston, "The Catalogue of Names in *The Great Gatsby*," *Research Studies*, 36 (June 1968), p. 117.

24. The role of the automobile in *Gatsby* has been discussed elsewhere. See Sklar, *F. Scott Fitzgerald: The Last Laocoön*, pp. 180–182, and Leo Marx, *The Machine in the Garden* (New York: Oxford University Press, 1964), p. 358.

25. At a middle class nightclub in New York—the sort of place frequented by "the little troubled men who are pictured in the comics as 'the Consumer' or 'the Public'"—Gloria murmurs "I belong here . . . I'm like these people" (F. Scott Fitzgerald, *The Beautiful and Damned* [New York: Scribner's, 1922], pp. 69, 72).

26. Alan Trachtenberg, "The Journey Back: Myth and History in *Tender Is the Night*," in *Experience in the Novel: Selected Papers from the English Institute*, ed. Roy Harvey Pearce (New York: Columbia University Press, 1968), p. 136. Trachtenberg also notes that lack of historical sense which underlies Gatsby's tragic attempt to recover the past is parodied in the novel's other characters:

> The frenzy in the life surrounding Gatsby enacts the quest for recovery as parody. Like its elegant roughneck hero, the book's world has deprived itself of conscious historical experience—it prefers

the "sensation" of "Vladimir Tostoff's *Jazz History of the World*," or furniture like Myrtle's, tapestried with "scenes of ladies swinging in the garden of Versailles"–in order to pursue one or another debased version of the dream of incarnation.

Trachtenberg might have included here Carraway's sense that "Tom would drift on forever seeking, a little wistfully, for the dramatic turbulence of some irrecoverable football game." This lack of historical consciousness, of course, is a fundamental part of the circular transcendentalism I have already discussed.

27. Fitzgerald, "The Note-Books," in *The Crack-Up*, p. 199.

28. This restlessness is shared by all the novel's characters. The Buchanans drift "here and there unrestfully," Jordan Baker has a "wan, charming, discontented face" and a body that asserts itself with "a restless movement"; Gatsby's nervous physical energy is "continually breaking through his punctilious manner in the shape of restlessness."

* * *

The legend of a lost silent movie of The Great Gatsby *became so powerful that Jack Finney invented the cast in his 1973 novel* Marion's Wall *(Simon and Schuster).*

Dust jacket for the novel in which the lost silent movie version of The Great Gatsby *is discovered*

And then I found it. Walking past the second drawer labeled ERNST LUBITSCH, a corner of my eye caught a title on the label, and from that bin I brought out the picture I knew I had to see, the long-lost silent version of *The Great Gatsby*. At least I thought it must be, and I took the first reel out to the table to check the credits. The worktable was crowded with the film we'd opened, which bothered me; I'm sure it wasn't customary with this collection. But although it looked helter-skelter, winding lengths of film curling out of the open cans, it wasn't. No film tangled with any other; each can lay in a little space of its own. I had to make room for *The Great Gatsby* but I moved the other film carefully, clearing a little space for this. Then I uncoiled the leader from the outer edge of the big fat disk of wound film, found the cast listing, and held it to the light.

And there in tiny white letters on the black background of each of the frames stretched between my two hands was the incredible cast: Rudolph Valentino as Gatsby himself . . . Gloria Swanson as Daisy Buchanan . . . Greta Garbo as Jordan Baker . . . John Gilbert as Carraway . . . Mae West as Myrtle, her only silent role, I was almost sure . . . George O'Brien as Tom Buchanan . . . Harry Langdon, in his only serious role, that I did know, as Myrtle's husband . . .

Ted was standing beside me peering up at my film, and I said, "Isn't this the one with the party sequence at Gatsby's estate?"

"Yes, with Gilda Gray, Chaplin, and F. Scott Fitzgerald himself as part of the crowd."

from paramount pictures

HANDBOOK OF PRODUCTION INFORMATION
****

PARAMOUNT PICTURES PRESENTS

A DAVID MERRICK PRODUCTION

Starring

ROBERT REDFORD

MIA FARROW

in

A JACK CLAYTON FILM OF

"THE GREAT GATSBY"

KAREN BLACK
SCOTT WILSON
SAM WATERSTON
LOIS CHILES
and
BRUCE DERN as Tom
with
HOWARD DA SILVA
TOM EWELL
ROBERTS BLOSSOM
EDWARD HERRMANN
ELLIOT SULLIVAN

Director of Photography DOUGLAS SLOCOMBE	Production Designer JOHN BOX	Music Supervised by NELSON RIDDLE
Costumes by THEONI V. ALDREDGE	Associate Producer HANK MOONJEAN	Based on the Novel by F. SCOTT FITZGERALD

Screenplay by FRANCIS FORD COPPOLA

Produced by
DAVID MERRICK

Directed by
JACK CLAYTON

PARAMOUNT PICTURES CORPORATION 1 GULF + WESTERN PLAZA NEW YORK N.Y. 10023

Press book (Matthew J. and Arlyn Bruccoli Collection, University of South Carolina)

I lowered the film and stood staring up at the empty screen for a moment. Not only had this incredible picture been lost for decades, it had never even been *shown;* suppressed by Gloria Swanson, supposedly, because Lubitsch had given too much footage to Garbo and West. I turned to Ted. "This is the one," I said. "This is the one I want to see." Then, from inside the vault, Marion gave a little scream.

* * *

THE THIRD MOVIE (1974) AND THE COMMERCIALIZATION OF *GATSBY*

The Great Gatsby, Paramount, 1974

A Lavish 'Gatsby' Loses Book's Spirit
Vincent Canby
The New York Times, 28 March 1974

The newest, biggest, most expensive and longest screen version of "The Great Gatsby," which had its premiere here last night, moves spaniel-like through F. Scott Fitzgerald's text, sniffing and staring at events and objects very close up with wide, mopey eyes, seeing almost everything and comprehending practically nothing. The film begins its regular engagement at four theatres today.

The language is right, even the chunks of exposition that have sometimes been turned into dialogue. The sets and costumes and most of the performances are exceptionally good, but the movie itself is as lifeless as a body that's been too long at the bottom of a swimming pool.

Francis Ford Coppola, who wrote the screenplay, and Jack Clayton, the director, have treated the book as if it were an illustrated encyclopedia of the manners and morals of the nineteen-twenties instead of a short, elegiacal romantic novel whose idiosyncratic beat demands something more perceptive form the moviemakers than mere fidelity to plot.

"The Great Gatsby" has been filmed twice before, first with Warner Baxter and Lois Wilson in 1926, the year after it was published. It was done again in 1949 with Alan Ladd playing the title role, the elegant young roughneck, Jay Gatsby, a part-time bootlegger and swindler whose smile according to Fitzgerald, possessed the quality of "eternal reassurance," and with Betty Field as Daisy Buchanan, the pretty, easily distracted rich girl who became for Gatsby, all there was to hope for in the American Dream.

Though I didn't see the first version and remember very little of the second, I can't imagine that either

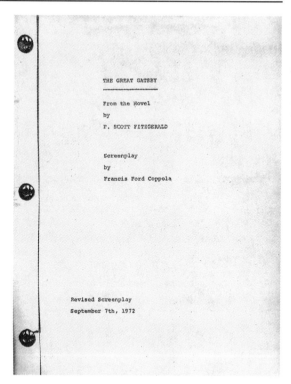

Several writers worked on the screenplay; Coppola received the screen credit (Matthew J. and Arlyn Bruccoli Collection, University of South Carolina).

could have been conceived with the care that went into this production. Why, then, should this "Gatsby" be so lugubrious, threatening at times to turn into the longest movie ever made?

The answer I suspect, is the all-too-reverential attitude. It completely mistakes the essence of Fitzgerald's novel, which is not in its story but in his headlong, elliptical literary style that dazzles us by the *manner* in which it evokes character and event, rather than with the characters and events themselves.

Nothing that Mr. Clayton does with the actors or with the camera comes close to catching the spirit of Fitzgerald's impatient brilliance. The film transforms "Gatsby" into a period love story that seems to take itself as solemnly as "Romeo and Juliet." The plot has been dismantled like an antique engine and photographed, piece by piece, preserved in lots of pretty, glistening images that bathe the film in nostalgia as thick as axle grease.

If reverence is one part of the problem, the other part is a stunning lack of cinematic imagination. The film's big set pieces—the wild parties at Gatsby's Long Island mansion—are almost embarrassingly awkward in

The casting of Robert Redford and Mia Farrow was not successful (Matthew J. and Arlyn Bruccoli Collection, University of South Carolina)

Daisy and Tom Buchanan, before moving to Long Island that fatal summer, had "drifted here and there unrestfully, wherever people played polo and were rich together."

Although Robert Redford is hardly an ideal choice to play Gatsby—he looks so Ivy League its difficult to believe that he didn't prep at Choate—he's a good enough actor to carry the role without damaging the film. He'd make a much better Dick Diver in "Tender Is the Night."

Mia Farrow is lovely, eccentric and unfathomable as Daisy, which may be an impossible role, one that is much more easily accepted on the page than on the screen. I also like Bruce Dern as her husband, a guy so securely rich and well-born he can be a slob, Mr. Waterston as Nick who, like Gatsby, remains an outsider in the society he inhabits, and Karen Black and Scott Wilson, as Myrtle and George Wilson, whose lives, like Gatsby's are so casually destroyed by the Buchanans.

As Fitzgerald wrote it, "The Great Gatsby" is good deal more than an ill-fated love story about the cruelties of the idle rich. Though set in Long Island, it is very much about the Middle West. All of its major characters have moved east, from Minnesota (Gatsby), from Chicago (Nick and Tom), from Louisville (Daisy), literally reversing the direction of the migrations that established the American civilization, thus marking its doom. The movie can't see this through all its giant closeups of pretty knees and dancing feet. It's frivolous without being much fun.

* * *

Great Gatsby: Flack or Fiction?
Sally Quinn
Washington Post (29 March 1974)

New York—Robert Redford is a New York Knicks freak.

Last year, when his movie, "The Way We Were," with Barbara Streisand, opened in New York, the Knicks were playing at Madison Square Garden. Redford had thought about going to the screening, but because he had had altercations with Ray Stark, producer of "The Way We Were" and Streisand's guru, and because he hates the promotion number and the publicity hype, he decided to go to the basketball game instead of the premiere.

He and his wife, Lola, got in a cab and told the driver to take them to the Garden. The driver went down Broadway. Just as the klieg lights began to pull up in front of Loew's II and the mobs began to scream "We want Redford"—his cab got stuck immediately in front of the theater.

their staging, the flappers and their beaux always caught doing their Charlestons at the same orgiastic pitch, like the figures on some complicated wind-up Bavarian toy.

Some of the movie's best moments are hardly more than recitations, as when the narrator, Nick Carraway (Sam Waterston), opens the film with a soundtrack exposition that sets the time, place and characters. This includes the marvelous line in which Nick tells us how

Redford threw himself on the floor of the cab and, while hot noses pressed themselves against the windows in desperate search of celebrity, he huddled at his wife's feet undiscovered until the traffic loosened up and his cab could pull away.

Wednesday night was the opening of Redford's latest movie, "The Great Gatsby," or, as some of the film's detractors are wont to call it, "The Great Ghastly." Once again, the star, Robert Redford, toyed with the idea of attending. After all his co-star, Mia Farrow, who plays Daisy, was recuperating from a cesarean delivery of her baby two weeks ago and couldn't possibly fly over from London. And he had promised Paramount's production chief Bob Evans (the former husband of Ali McGraw, who was first cast as Daisy) he would come. Evans even bought him a dinner jacket for the event.

At first, Paramount Pictures said Redford was coming, then, at the last minute, they said they weren't sure.

But Redford didn't even stick around town long enough to see his idol Dave DeBusschere's final regular-season game with the Knicks at Madison Square Garden on Tuesday night.

By Wednesday night, he was back at home in Sundance, Utah, with his family.

So the screaming, swelling, semihysterical mobs outside Loew's II would have to be content with the lesser luminaries Sam Waterston, Lois Chiles and Bruce Dern. They could chant "We want Redford" all night.

Redford wasn't coming.

"Certainly not," said his publicity agent Lois Smith, "not after he'd seen the film."

———

Everybody's heard by now about "The Great Gatsby," the newest film version of F. Scott Fitzgerald's novella of the '20s. Everybody's either seen the ads for it or gotten a Gatsby haircut, or a Gatsby "look," a Gatsby Arrow shirt, or a Gatsby bottle of Ballantine.

The production of "The Great Gatsby" which has been festering for over a year has been one of the most extraordinary hard sells Hollywood has ever seen.

It has permeated the lifestyles of the country. It has seeped into our pores, until some things have begun to look slightly gauzy. The entire nation has been, as Paramount wanted, "Gatsbyized."

"The promotion," said one proud publicity agent, was a work of art. In fact, he leaned forward and confided, "it was more of a work of art than the film."

"Next year," complained another, "at the Academy Awards, they're going to give an Oscar for the best promotion."

Despite much free promotion and advertising, the 1974 movie was not a box-office winner.

You can almost see it; the tearful flack, clutching the golden statuette and choking, "I couldn't have done it without those wonderful Teflon ads. . . ."

The culmination of all the publicity was the premiere Wednesday night. The usual theater scene, the usual charity benefits, the usual celebrities and semicelebrities and would-be celebrities, the questionable socialities, the unquestionable social climbers, the gays, the flacks, the crashers . . . and the usual party. Only the party at the Waldorf after the premiere wasn't all that usual. Certainly not in terms of money spent.

Three thousand white roses imported from as far as the Canary Islands, 250 potted palms, tables each draped with 12 yards of ecru plush velvet, five armed silver "candelabras" (sic), etc., the promo sheet bragged. And that was only the decoration.

Waiters in white tie and tails, with red sash and white gloves, served the 800 guests more than 100 pounds of Beluga caviar, iced vodka, pate de foie gras Strasborug with champagne, breast of pheasant with wild rice, salsify saute and hot apple Charlotte au Chantilly en flambe.

With the addition of Peter Duchin and his orchestra playing for dancing, 25 roving violonists did their numbers during intermission, serenading, even from the balconies.

The party, brought the cost of the promotion to "a little less than what we spent on the film," said Paramount publicist Mike Beiner. They spent $6.5 million on the film.

And the party just didn't make it.

For one thing, the premiere bit is getting a little old and it takes a lot to drag people out for one of these things. The press has gotten particularly hostile and aggressive, to the point that when Mike Nichols got out of his limousine at the theater, he was literally attacked by a large group of cameras and reporters. Nichols ran with his head down, as though under fire, for the inside, chased all the way by hungry reporters, half for a story, half just because it's getting kind of fun to hassle the celebrities.

For that reason, because of the undignified circumstances and circus-like atmosphere and because of the enormous and flagrant waste at these hotel brawls, the big celebrities just won't go. Fewer and fewer premieres feature their big stars any more, and even the minor "sparklies" are dropping out.

"The Great Gatsby" premiere was no exception. The only thing that made it interesting was the intense circulation of dirt, gossip, intrigues and hostilities that had built up to a fever pitch before the opening and all of which came to a climax of oozing bitterness and resentment as the evening and the Dom Perignon flowed on.

———

Here's a brief outline of who hated who or what and why:

Robert Redford couldn't stand the movie, according to his agent. Apparently he felt that British director Jack Clayton ("Room at the Top," "The Pumpkin Eater") hadn't spent enough time with the actors and that his character–Gatsby–hadn't been well enough developed.

Redford was also disgusted by the "super-hype," believed that the promotion for Gatsby had been tasteless and vulgar, and he felt, and rightly so, that there was no way the film or the actors could live up to the reputation being built.

Nobody in the cast thought Mia Farrow was any good. Bruce Dern, who played Tom, Daisy's husband, was alleged to have said that Gatsby may have wanted to build a castle for Daisy but nobody would build an A-frame for Mia Farrow. Robert Evans had wanted Ali McGraw because it was her idea in the first place, but then she ran off with Steve McQueen and he lost interest. Then he said he liked Mia Farrow but now apparently doesn't.

Lois Chiles, his next girl friend, was cast by Evans in the role of Jordan Baker. Clayton finally accepted her. It seems she was not good so they had to cut out some of her scenes with Redford, which made everybody furious because some were important to the movie.

Supporting actress Karen Black dropped out of the premiere at the last minute. They said she was on location in Los Angeles. No dirt about her.

The most celebrated clashes were, however, between producer David Merrick, Paramount production chief Evans, Paramount president Frank Yablans and director Clayton. It was all very confusing.

Briefly, Merrick was furious at Evans for taking complete control and acing him out of the picture. Evans was furious at Merrick for trying to take control, even though he lost, and for knowing before he did himself, that Ali McGraw was having an affair with Steve McQueen. When everyone else knew, Evans was still suggesting that McQueen play Gatsby to McGraw's Daisy. Yablans was "reportedly" upset that Evans was trying to take all the credit for the picture. And Clayton was furious with them all for the enormous publicity buildup which he felt only hurt the picture.

And he was right. A week before the premiere, a private screening was held for all the critics and press in New York. And they were out for blood. They hissed and laughed and catcalled and jeered throughout the movie, breaking all traditions of protocol at New York press screenings. But by sunup the next morning, as one critic put it, "everyone from Pearl's to Elaine's had heard the movie was a great big "yawn."

From then on out the principals began falling all over each other to give "credit" to their colleagues for the picture.

There's more.

It all came out at the party.

———

The theater scene was somehow without oomph. Studio heads arrived with unidentified women on their arms, "Harpers Bazaar models," someone said "A very big night for models." And most of the actresses arrived with their hairdressers. "A very big night for hairdressers," someone said.

Arrivals did include Jean Kennedy Smith, Julie Newmar, Mr. and Mrs. Hugh D. Auchincloss (Jacqueline Onassis' mother), Mike Nichols, Robert Goulet, Marion Javits, Paulette Goddard, Rep. and Mrs. Barry Goldwater Jr., Christina Ford, a lot of designers. And with Fitzgerald's daughter Scottie Lanahan Smith's party came Cornelia Wallace and Sheilah Graham, movie columnist and Fitzgerald's great friend.

Evans was the first celebrity to arrive at the Waldorf for the party. He was dressed in midnight blue velvet and he looked simply divine. He was with Lisa Taylor, someone he

Robert Redford, Mia Farrow, and Sam Waterston in the reunion scene (Matthew J. and Arlyn Bruccoli Collection, University of South Carolina)

identified as not an actress, not a model, "a girl around town." After they posed willingly for several minutes of photographs, whispering and sipping champagne, someone congratulated Evans on the movie. "I think it's the most impeccably made film we've ever done. But any project is a collabration," he said quickly. "The director should get the credit or the blame. I'm just the production head of the company."

Evans felt the hype "did the picture good, but maybe not from an artistic standpoint. But nothing ever lives up to its expectation if its been built up the way this had. From our stand point, though, it doesn't do any harm, it does good."

What did he think about the fact, that Redford didn't like the film? "I couldn't care less. He's lucky he was in it. Redford resented the Time magazine cover story because it wasn't about him. He loved the Newsweek cover because it has just his picture on it. That's how upset he is about the hype. Get it?"

Evans if one of Henry Kissinger's closest friends and Kissinger stays with Evans when he is in Hollywood.

And Evans fixes Kissinger up with the starlets he is seen with on the West Coast. Kissinger was invited but of course he couldn't come, said Evans. "But he was very

kind. He sent me caviar and champagne at the hotel with a note, 'I wish I could be with you and best of luck, Henry.' Now is that a friend?"

Just then Merrick arrived. Just then Evans moved off. "I think it's a very beautiful picture," Merrick said. "Even though I was supposed to be the producer they didn't let me have anything to do with it. But these guys like Evans are moguls and all moguls are the same, not just at Paramount. The last book they probably all read was 'Black Beauty.' One of the producer's chief jobs is defending the product against the moguls. So I think Bob Evans produced a very beautiful picture and I hope they make a lot of money with it."

Inside the ballroom, a rather contrived "happy" scene was revving up reminiscent of the forced gaiety of Gatsby's party scene in the film. A few women were dressed with feathers and chiffon a la Gatsby but a surprising number in just plain old dresses.

As Peter Duchin was about to play and the strings were positioning on the balcony, Yablans, who had only recently arrived, got up on the stage and made an announcement. It was a heartwarming announcement about how there'd been all this awful publicity, see, about him and Evans and how they were both fighting to be the head of Paramount, when really they were very close, loved each other like brothers and both were total equals at Paramount and both had equally large egos.

Evans was called to the stage. He concurred. They put their arms around each other and hugged in the glare of the spotlights and flashing cameras. Then Evans congratulated director Clayton who blew kisses to the stage.

Next Merrick was called up. "I would like to thank Bob Evans' assistant for putting it all together," he said.

"You're welcome," said Evans.

"Thanks for your warmth, David," said Yablans.

The evening wore on, the champagne and caviar and pheasants were rolled out and the strolling strings serenaded the celebrities, surrounding Evans with a rendition of the theme from 'Love Story.'"

Late in the evening, on the side of the ballroom away from the celebrities, Scottie Smith and her party of family, old Vassar roommates, Washington friends, Cornelia Wallace, Sheilah Graham and 22 of Scott Fitzgerald's family from Norfolk, were having a grand time. Scottie was trying graciously to be neither a flack for the movie nor to put it down. A difficult position. But she did say:

"I think it's the closest anyone has ever come to what my father was trying to do. I only wish Jack Clayton, the director, had had a couple more weeks to do the cutting he wanted to do. But he wasn't allowed to by Paramount because of all the publicity and the promotion."

Clayton, the only one from the "star" side of the room to venture over to Scottie's side for a chat, was probably the least happy person there. He had the flu and a temperature of 103 and came "out of duty." It was he who would suffer the most from the reviews.

"I hope the public likes it because I do. I do," he said emphatically. "The promotion was horrible, it was never meant to be that kind of picture. But wait a few weeks for the spite to die down, then see how people like it."

What did Clayton thinkg about the crowd at Paramount and all their infighting? "F——— them all," he said.

And the party was over.

* * *

Courtly Love's Last Throw of the Dice
Penelope Gilliatt
The New Yorker, 50 (1 April 1974), 93–98

LAST throw of the dice, last fling. Jack Clayton's slow, graceful film of F. Scott Fitzgerald's novel "The Great Gatsby" (1925) has a peculiar blurring and rallentando about it. Both qualities are in the book, as if the last Charleston were being danced by people making an inhuman effort. The picture upholds Scott Fitzgerald's discovery that when he wrote truthfully about his own dreams and misfortunes and discoveries, other people recognized themselves. At Princeton (with, among oth-

ers, Edmund Wilson, his great accomplice in gaiety, practical jokes, drinking, misadventures, hard times, and hatred of the shrill or redundant in literature), he must have had his characters' ardor. Fellow-Princetonians of the time remember that he had visions of being a football hero, and that in the First World War he dreamed of behaving with patriotic dash and courage; and later of winning what his contemporaries always called "the top girl." All typical ambitions of his lot. But it has probably been taken too much for granted that he was simply a reporter of his age. The beautiful, saddened prose is deceptive: it is homesick for a more serious future, if anything, not for a doomed time already so soaked in nostalgia that it could seem a lost past if the characters were drunk enough. Though his steely distance from his age is not obvious, in low times later his obdurate judgment of the epoch he lived through as a young man declined to indulge regret. When the gate clanged, he heard it first.

"The Great Gatsby" is an account of the lives rich Midwesterners come East, and of equally rich Easterners. They spend summers at the book's great fictional colonies on Long Island, the metaphorically named West Egg and East Egg. The Midwesterners who have enough self-knowledge not to try to change themselves stay at West Egg, which is less florid. The established families of rich Easterners live at East Egg but flock eagerly to the colossal parties of the *nouveau riche* millionaire and Midwesterner Gatsby. On days when boredom between parties becomes acute, or thoughts of what on earth to do next intrude, the inhabitants pour into a New York where it always seems to be time for iced tea or midnight sprees, which is something that Clayton's film acutely records. The sweating Beautiful People in pale suits and light, floating dresses are given a curious look of children in unexplored bays cloaked in mist. Even Fifth Avenue seems aquatic, and the Plaza Hotel; one would not be the least bit surprised to see a shoal of mermaids swimming through the traffic. But there are enough notes of sharp humor in the film to make one remember that Scott Fitzgerald never lost sight of the fact that, as he said in a letter, one side of his own family was "straight potato-famine Irish." Writing in an age when wisdom about consequences was out of fashion, he was not really in step at all. This is one of the moral underpinnings of his work. It has made it endure. He saw quite critically that this was a special time–probably before an economic crash, certainly a reaction to the First World War–and that the gulf was not between intellectuals and illiterate but between privileged and poor, boring (non-flamboyant) and amusing (if corrupt, no matter). President Harding, though old, behaved in the spirit of the young when he notoriously played poker with tycoon party-supporters. In general, though, the attitude of the rich young ghetto round Gatsby is to let the old keep to themselves. The past generation is tossed aside as the one that was in the World War, discredited for it, and impeached except for the procedure of appearances, and of colorful rumors bruited about which are never sworn to be untrue. The condemned rich would die out. The instinctive conviction of the characters is to adhere to the nineteenth century's theories of natural social evolution. They share appreciations of beauty in women, exoticism, breaking the rules of Prohibition, and free-wheeling ability: the people around Gatsby are always attracted by simple truthfulness, with the paradox that fibbing by the rich is regarded more as a splash of vividness than as a moral failure. Why not? is the reigning mood. Why not lovers, why not wear out a hundred pairs of slippers dancing, as Daisy in the film so eagerly says she has done? The manly ideal if a sort of combination of Darwin and Don Giovanni. Most of the girls seem to want to be loaded and free-loving Madonnas, equipped with a zoo of pampered pets and well-staffed nursery. Their swoops of passionate love at pretty dogs and carefully laundered children are overpowering and clownishly saintly, in the film as in the book.

Like Fitzgerald's "Winter Dreams" (the short story that was a preparation for "Gatsby"), the novel–and Francis Ford Coppola's film script–is a plethora of small incidents. They seem at first to amount only to a story about Jay Gatsby (Robert Redford), long since jilted by his shimmering Daisy (Mia Farrow) for a hulking, wealthy man with a touch of effete swank named Tom Buchanan (Bruce Dern). She threw aside her promise to wait for Gatsby when he was in the war and too far away for the satisfaction of her empty little head. The onlooker and confidant–technically replacing the first-person narrative of the book–is Daisy's second cousin once removed, called Nick (Sam Waterston). The tiny story and its fragile, sunny elements–nothing is irrelevant if the writer's mood is happy, as H. G. Wells wrote in "The Contemporary Novel," published in a 1911 *Fortnightly Review*–gradually balloon out like the muslin curtains of the Buchanans' house, and the lounging girls' soft, pale skirts, in a hot breeze at the beginning of the film. The unrequited-love story swells into a fable about a very rich man who seems to be his own creation, driven by a bitter disappointment that he has never stopped trying to heal, living in an illusion of company alone in an enormous mansion, and giving huge parties that he never attends but only scans from his window upstairs, because the hundreds of rich marauders are his diluted single hope of ever finding the girl he lost. The green light at the end of her dock blinks at him across the bay as soon as night falls. One

evening, alone, he raises his arm to it in a swift, odd gesture, half reaching, half benedictive.

Edmund Wilson once recalled that Scott Fitzgerald had looked into Emily Post's "Etiquette" and been inspired with the idea of a play in which all the motivations would consist in trying to do the right thing. The characters in "Gatsby" often do something very nearly as hilarious as that, though the narrative is mixed with rushes of violence, rudeness, danger, and tragedy. The eloquent film is not quite speedy enough to reproduce the movement of the book, which has life's birdlike fluttering. But Clayton is a very serious filmmaker, with a shapely comprehension of an author's intelligence. He makes one know that these Midwesterners in the East are hellbent on display and carnival partly because they are exiles who pay no heed. Like the people in "The Beautiful and Damned," they are self-consigned to an opportunist background that they will not admit to be alien. They take refuge in noise, secret crime, any disguise. The Easterners here are parasites they are proud to support, though Scott Fitzgerald himself never forgot that he was out of place in the East. He was a Celt among unromantics, and a non-practicing Catholic to boot, steeped in what he called in an ironic letter "my romantic Chestertonian orthodoxy." In another letter, he says, quite gaily, "I am ashamed to say that my Catholicism is scarcely more than a memory–no, that's wrong, it's more than that; at any rate, I go not to the church nor mumble stray nothings over crystalline beads." Some strain of Midwestern Irish always remained. He loathed French literature for its technical quarrels rehashed. He liked imagining arid future professors of literature relegating his early-twenties' work to his "second," or "neo-flapper," period. It fell, of course, as things turned out, in the middle of a pitifully short and harried writing life–he died at forty-four–in which he was perpetually concerned with the consequences of richness and carelessness. He wrote with magic felicity about a hellhole of a world, and about characters in paradisiacal captivity seen without lamps. "They were careless people, Tom and Daisy–they smashed up things and creatures and then retreated back into their money or their vast carelessness, or whatever it was that kept them together, and let other people clean up the mess they had made. . ." Nick narrates in the book and the film. Their career is the pursuit of the hectic. Jazz is always to move to, not to listen to. It is the jungle drum of the new, of the perilous but promising. People go to parties too much and stay up too late. The unseen work too much, especially the hideously misled garageman Wilson (marvellously played by Scott Wilson, of Richard Brooks' "In Cold Blood" and Norman Jewison's "In the Heat of the Night"). Everything deserves the same energy of the rich,

Bruce Dern, Sam Waterston, Mia Farrow, Robert Redford, and Lois Chiles in the Plaza Hotel confrontation

whether it is gadgets, polo-playing, or bigoted racial theories learned from suspect books about the natural supremacy of the Nordic peoples.

The film is the story of one short, hot summer of elation, an interlude of borrowed nobility. Fitzgerald wrote as if he were in a room full of motor horns and sailing times. He could catch the tinge of a year, feeling himself in the workhouse when others were in mansions on Long Island looking forward excitedly, like Daisy, to the longest day. The film's attitude toward romanticism is there in its attitude toward Daisy, the inexpressibly lovely girl who creates misery for a great number of men. She brings with her a satiety that will paradoxically always demand more. She fits perfectly into this society of casual trespassers on Gatsby's territory, vagrants who will last out the summer and then wonder where to go. "Gatsby" has the same notion of rich people's cruelty and casualness in love as Fitzgerald's "The Diamond as Big as the Ritz" (1922), in which a middle-class boy falls in love with the heiress to a great fortune and she returns his love; their plan to marry, though, is foiled by her family's jealous guard over the money, and the young pair can only be together later in poverty, when fortune and parents have been mythically incinerated and reduced to

exploding char. "Gatsby," book and film, is a story of luxe blown up to the bursting point, so that lives are damaged by the flying splinters. In Fitzgerald's story "The Rich Boy," he writes, "Let me tell you about the very rich. They are different from you and me. They possess and enjoy early, and it does something to them, makes them soft where we are hard, and cynical where we are trustful, in a way that, unless you were born rich, it is very difficult to understand." In "Gatsby," Daisy explains her action in jilting the then poor Gatsby, whose name had been Gatz: "Rich girls don't marry poor boys." Determination to have her at all costs has driven him to defeat the freezing axiom and turn himself into a millionaire. And then, after all that, Daisy's greatest award to him—truly the best she can do—is her unshared but real joy over his shirts, which are the most *beautiful* she has ever seen, and *hand-picked* for him in *England!*

The reigning idea in Fitzgerald, and especially in "Gatsby" as Clayton grasps it, is the law of chivalry and the terrible effects that can flow from transgressions: here, two deaths among the underprivileged and one among the rich upstarts. The opiate happiness of the heat suddenly turns into hysteria. Before this, Daisy's troubled notion of romantic behavior has been shaken by knowing of her husband's affair with the garage proprietor's wife, but even the flimsy idea of chivalry held by the aerial Daisy doesn't allow her to lie to her husband in revenge about her vow long ago to Gatsby, whose motive in getting her cousin Nick to come to his parties is obviously to have some contact with her. Having lovers doesn't quite count as infidelity in this world, though split marriages are as bad as lost chances. Marriages are approached with a practicality that strikes no one as repulsive: generally for money. "Imagine marrying *anybody* in this heat," says an idyllic-looking rich girl in a lilac dress, so lightly that all her rich friends agree. Gatsby, not guilty, is killed in his own swimming pool through a terrible act of misapprehended chivalry on the part of the cuckolded and now bereaved garageman, who walks dazedly into the grounds clutching a pistol in a crumpled paper bag that might be holding a workman's lunch sandwich.

The stately film has much kindness and beauty, but some works of art have their truest condensed existence only in the original form, perhaps. Fitzgerald's short novel could only be stretched out into this mistakenly lengthy film by the use of repeated views, shots sometimes held too long for the matter, tracking shots untrue to the terseness of Fitzgerald, and explanations in Fitzgerald voice-over dialogue of what has already been fully shown in visual incident. One of the best things about it is the performance by Mia Farrow as Daisy, Louisville-born, bastard product of East Egg sophistication. The character's deftness in manipulation and in pretty agitation is cloaked in a docile, talkative lyricism, with a suggested heritage of suitors stretching back to times when her ancestors might have ordered slaves around and shrivelled outsiders. She speaks in a sorcerous murmur that melts into the balmy evenings. She seems a true type of the courtesan, and a child of sophistication dropping back into the savage. She appropriates every emergency as confronting her, and ignores all other suffering and peril. When a man with a pistol threatens, she abandons her husband, clasps her hands to her pretty, quivering mouth, and runs to clutch her three-year-old daughter to her, who grumbles about having to wear oyster pink, which happens to be the same color as her mother's dress and as the drawing room where they are. "Beautiful little fools can wear whatever colors they want," murmurs Daisy. Beautiful little fools, she has been schooled to believe, are rich girls' best thing to be. The part is one of the most nearly perfect examples of women-as-toys in modern filmmaking. Feather-light though Mia Farrow makes the character seem, she also gives her a shivery cynicism about love. Knowing that her husband has just been on the phone to his mistress, Daisy turns away and talks about how romantic the birds look on the lawn. Knowing that Gatsby is again waiting for her and the he will count on her coming this time, she holds hands with her husband at breakfast and doesn't rock the boat. It is a performance that exquisitely mixes beauty, frailty, and instincts of the most perfidious sort. It makes you sense that her decision to marry Tom Buchanan might have been inspired by something as silly as Gatsby's future lack of a dashing uniform when he someday came back from the war. The choice certainly had to do with Gatsby's poverty, and it reminds one of Scott Fitzgerald's heartache when his fiancée, Zelda, who became his wife after he hit it rich, broke off their earlier engagement because she had decided he wasn't earning enough to keep them both. Bruce Dern as Tom, the only coward in the story, wears a narrow toothbrush mustache and acutely plays him with a touch of the brazen nitwit covering a peremptory heart. But the character can still stir Daisy, who, like her cousin Nick, finds almost any exhibition of self-reliance fit for worship. Tom's thick embrace of the virtue of being Nordic gives him a well-guarded moat around himself against, for instance, recognition of the racism in him—which certainly strikes Nick, who attends quietly to every glance and sees every hypocrisy and idle insult. Nick has the role of the go-between for Gatsby and Daisy; Same Waterston gives the Pandarus part, which could be grovelling, an alertness and nobility that recognize Gatsby to be worth the whole hungry crowd of his guests, none of whom turn up at his funeral, apart from one latecomer. The party has vanished because the money has died. The great Gatsby—rumored to be related to Kaiser Wilhelm, or to own oil, or to be something high up in the World War, with an implication that he was on the German side; but actually a bootlegger, gambler, and associate of a fixer of the World Series—dies too soon to know that his future is already behind him. Only Nick comprehends it. Without the film's sage use of Nick to stand in for Fitzgerald's first-person narrative—a device that always presents technical problems in literature, though it prevents the omniscient eyes of the author from peering round the back of his character's heads—the action might be preposterous. As it is, and in spite of ponderous moments, there is much beauty and thoughtfulness in the film. It is marvellously cast and acted, from the waiting, watchful performance by Redford down to Elliot Sullivan in the small part of a man desperately looking up churches in the telephone directory to comfort the garageman, whose wife has been killed by a hit-and-run car.

Gatsby, the self-created man, who seems to have been his own parents, was forever making lists of how to improve himself, even as a child. His father arrives after his murder, unshaven and has one of them with

Bookstore poster for the movie tie-in edition (Matthew J. and Arlyn Bruccoli Collection, University of South Carolina)

him: "Practice elocution, poise and how to attain it. Study needed inventions. . . . Save five [crossed out] three dollars per week." The coffin is lowered into the turf. What shall we do next, the absent habitual guests wonder. It will be fall soon. We have no plan. What shall we plan? The sometimes drowsy film pierces, with Fitzgerald's moral breeding, to the weakness in the society's fabric: lack of intelligence and resolve going unperceived, like lack of heart. All admiration in the East Egg crowd is still given to gusto and achievement, even after terrible toll has been taken. Meanwhile, mist swirls around Gatsby's empty mansion like the scarf that choked Isadora Duncan to death.

* * *

Ballantine's Scotch, Glemby Haircuts, White Suits, and White Teflon: Gatsby 1974
Janet Maslin

I still recall vividly the big New York unveiling of Jack Clayton's *The Great Gatsby*. Everyone was there–from Liz Smith to Andy Warhol. And everyone seemed to be having the same reactions. There was a moment when an impeccable Robert Redford turned to fact the camera, delivered his first line and then smiled–separating his gestures like an escapee from a Swiss clock–that elicited startled but still vaguely admiring gasps from us all. There was another moment, when Mia Farrow first opened her mouth, that elicited gasps of a different order. Than there was the scene where Sam Waterston and Lois Chiles stopped in the valley of ashes to buy gas from Scott Wilson and it only cost 40 cents to fill their tank; coming as it did in the middle of a collossal fuel crisis, the transaction provoked a reasonably amiable guffaw. But the real laughter was reserved for the latter part of the picture, most notably for the scene in which Farrow and Redford kiss and their images are studiously reflected in a pool stocked with expensive Japanese goldfish. *That* moment launched something noisy enough to qualify as The Snicker Heard 'Round the World.

Big studio previews are usually packed with friends of the studio, who usually lead the applause at screening's end. This time it was hard to hear the ovation, if indeed there even was one, over the din of studio friends exiting before the credits were over. Outside the theater, the pavement was littered with crumpled-up programs that looked as if they'd been thrown rather than dropped. The audience straggled away looking resentful, confused and—above all else—miserably betrayed.

I saw *The Great Gatsby* again two years later in a small, grimy, and underpopulated revival house. And I was surprised to note that, while the opus hadn't exactly improved with age, at least it didn't feel like such an affront any more. For one thing, I was no longer going for blood by making line-by-line comparisons with Fitzgerald's novel. For another, Paramount's promotional hoopla (Ballantine's scotch? Glemby haircuts? White suits? White *teflon*?) was no longer enough of an irritant to obscure the picture's few minor merits. Mia Farrow's performance, while still nightmarish, at least made more sense this time; the edge of hysteria she had tried to lend Daisy might, if better developed, have provided that character with the sense of genuine frustration, and hence the human complexity, that Fitzgerald denied her in the novel. And the film wasn't as sluggish as it had initially seemed; though whatever momentum it did possess was strictly the story-line's doing and certainly not attributable to Francis Ford Coppola's tin-eared screenplay or Clayton's moribund direction. The single most intriguing aspect of the movie remained its maverick stupidity; the film is neither faithful enough to qualify as even a run-of-the-mill screen adaptation, nor is it guided by even the faintest glimmer of adaptive imagination.

The former point can be readily attested to by anyone with an emotional stake in (and an accordingly dog-eared copy of) Fitzgerald's compact, obsessively romantic masterpiece. As for the latter one, it's odd that neither the film's director nor its screenwriter seems, on the evidence of the finished product, to have given much thought to the various adaptive options open to them. They might, for example, have elected to treat the story as psychodrama and stay relatively close to the dynamics of the novel, making up in character what they sacrificed in atmosphere and thus piquing the interest of Fitzgerald devotees. Or they could have gone the all-out glamour route, even if that meant deliberately cheapening their material, suffering a barrage of bad reviews and losing the literati. They could even have stumbled onto a successful approach by coming up with a bad film whose very garishness inadvertently evoked Jazz Age attitudes. In any case, they ultimately opted for nothing more complex than one-note sobriety, committing *Gatsby* to the screen in much the same way that an elegantly boxed corpse is committed to its burial ground.

The Great Gatsby is admittedly a very difficult work to film. It is also, I think, one of the two great American romances, the other being *Gone with the Wind* (1936). The two novels are hardly comparable in terms of style or quality, but their authors shared a number of similar values and an incontrovertible flair for storytelling. Both works have an extraordinary capacity for engaging their readers' emotions; both are set in tumultuous historical periods and draw cultural tension from geographical polarities—North/South in Margaret Mitchell's case, East/West in Fitzgerald's. Most importantly, both books understand that the eroticism of wealth is a crucial ingredient in American daydreams about love and seduction.

Each novel, of course, also creates a pair of incomparably high-spirited sparring partners whose differences can never be reconciled, couples whose illusions about one another are both their drama and their eventual undoing. Taken on their own, Scarlett, Rhett, Daisy, and Gatsy are all great and singularly American characters—but because Scarlett and Rhett stand out in such sharp counterpoint to their surroundings, they make for great dramatic roles as well. Gatsby and Daisy are more closely interwoven with the culture they inhabit, and as such they make for potentially poor dramatic material, since their efficacy depends almost entirely on how well their surroundings are drawn. The most basic and insidious of the filmed *Gatsby's* many flaws is thus its absolute failure to create a believable Jazz Age ambience.

The human backdrop of the story, the carousers who come to Gatsby's parties and fritter their lives away, represented (in the novel) a dubious, *nouveau-riche* "Broadway" element, people so brash in their hedonism that they actively offend old-money types like Tom and Daisy. But Clayton clearly misunderstands the character of the guests and the nature of their boozy jubilation: he populates his party scenes with an impossible blend of dusty Newport bluebloods and hyperthyroid New York hoofers. The same two-dozen trained danc-

Despite the efforts of clothing manufacturers, the 1974 movie had little effect on men's fashions

ers are in the foreground of virtually every mass-revelry shot, yet if you glance behind them you'll make out a wall of immobile, aristocratic stiffs.

And Jazz Age elegance presupposes not just fashion-plate airs but also the inclination to raise hell without worrying about getting one's dress dirty—so when Clayton shoots a tableful of guests sitting primly at a party, each one carefully enunciating his or her remark in turn, he demolishes the whole feeling of an era in only fifteen seconds. Worst of all, even *Gatsby's* stylishness winds up working against it, as the characters positively suffocate in their coordinated pastels. It's too pretty, stultifyingly so, and seventies-pretty at that; *Gatsby's* brand of airless affluence is so anachronistic that whatever social commentary Clayton may have set out to make is lost in a flurry of voile and tulle. The picture has a cold, narcissistic beauty, admiring its own image without any real sense of enjoyment.

Clayton's ideas about the women who prompt the plot's romantic machinations only add to the pervasive chill. Farrow's Daisy is as dry as a dowager, with a voice about two octaves higher than the "thrilling murmur" Fitzgerald so lovingly described. (The basic unattractiveness of Farrow's screechy, brittle-wigged Daisy makes Nick, who is expected to cast admiring glances her way throughout their first few scenes together, seem all the

more nonsensical.) And Farrow, unlike the somewhat underrated Redford, is unable to deliver her character's most famous lines casually; instead she giver her readings a *Bartlett's Book of Familiar Quotations* ring, forever pausing in search of the right word when the audience knows full well what that word will be. Still, she is the most bearable, even the most sympathetic of the story's three central women; if Lois Chiles's Jordan is no livelier than a mannequin, Karen Black's repellent Myrtle unfortunately fills the breach. Black is at fever pitch in a role that doesn't demand even half the histrionics, and Clayton's idea of helping her out involves accentuating the sweat of her upper lip (this is *Gatsby's* closest brush with sensuality), muting the background sound during her embarrassingly breathy monologue about first meeting Tom and, on one ignominious occasion, having her smash her hand through a window and then enthusiastically suck her own blood. None of the three, who give far worse performances than their male counterparts, seems to have been given any idea of how she fit into the film's overall scheme.

Mia Farrow violently overreacts to Clayton's and Coppola's reshaping of Gatsby's entire obsession around the dubious (and certainly incomprehensible, at least for the audience) force of Daisy's allure. In their hands, Gatsby's unattainable dream becomes literal, earthbound, and sometimes (as when Redford is seen flexing his fist in the direction of the Buchanans' green light across the bay) just plain silly. The photo in Gatsby's bedroom is now of Daisy, not of his bourgeois mentor Dan Cody; Gatsby's romanticism has been cut down from a grand illusion to simple unrequited love.

To see what the film does to perhaps the book's greatest passage is to weep: Gatsby's "wed[ding] his unutterable visions to Daisy's perishable breath" as he "saw that the blocks of the sidewalks really formed a ladder . . . to a secret place about the trees" has been reduced to a simple ten-second flashback of a kiss, including a voice-over of Farrow whispering "I love you, Jay." Taken at face value, such moments suggest that Daisy alone, rather than the whole set of values she has come to represent, has been enough to drive Gatsby to scale such dizzying capitalist heights. And taking these touches literally is almost inevitable, because Clayton seems every bit as awestruck by Gatsby's opulence as the character is himself. He turns his star filter on every available scrap of silver or cystal, and his reverence lingers on even after Gatsby is gone. The boys who defile Gatsby's mansion after his murder scrawl their obscenities in the neatest, most respectful manner imaginable.

Never lending the film a discernible viewpoint of their own, Clayton and Coppola compound the problem by doing away with that of Nick Carraway, through whose eyes Fitzgerald's story was originally filtered. First of all, Nick is robbed of his engaging stodginess (when Gatsby of the novel tells Nick about sealing–or decreeing–his own fate with that one irrevocable kiss in Louisville, Nick silently condemns his friend's "appalling sentimentality" yet is "reminded of something–an elusive rhythm, a fragment of lost words, that [he] had heard somewhere a long time ago.") Even worse, Fitzgerald's wry, level-headed narrator has been turned into something of a portentous windbag. Coppola's three-week-wonder of a script demonstrates an appalling insensitivity to normal speech patterns, forcing Nick and others to stumble over descriptive passages from the novel that were never meant to be delivered in conversation.

The screenplay is worse than merely clumsy; it deals the film a death-blow by making an excruciating miscalculation. Coppola pieced together details about Daisy's and Gatsby's early courtship, added a "Kiss me" or an "I love the way you love me" here and there, and slapped together a series of interchanges we were never meant to see. The novel very deliberately avoids invading the couple's privacy, once they have been reunited, and it does so for reasons more important than mere tact. The whole point, the whole agonizing irreconcilability of the story, grows out of the fact that Daisy and Gatsby never do understand one another– they *can't*. Daisy is an icon to her lover, not a real woman; she herself is so ethereally drawn that it's hard to imagine what Gatsby means to her, except perhaps some vaguely bitter memory of a chance not taken. But whatever they see in one another, they don't see eye to eye; their accounts of the reunion, if stated, would certainly and tragically differ. Yet Coppola makes the incredible gaffe of trying to objectify these moments, of trying to satisfy his audience's voyeurism instead of acknowledging the lovers' heartbreaking misapprehensions.

Filling in those blanks may have been more of a business decision than an aesthetic one; audiences don't come to see an airy, expensive love story without expecting an airy, expensive clinch or two. But the change completely violates the novel, and the only consoling thing about it is that it doesn't work. Redford and Farrow never for one minute give the impression of being in love, and that's the film's single most astonishing shortcoming. When the two of them run off conspiratorially during a huge gala, Clayton fills the moment with absurd sexual innuendo, even though Farrow is so overdressed it's impossible to imagine her taking off that diamond headgear for the sake of a mere tryst. The book handles the same moment infinitely more gently; we sense that the two of them have already tacitly re-established their physical relationship,

and that they're so close all they really *need* to do right then is talk.

Ordinarily, when a novel is adapted for the screen, readers of the book have a slight edge over patrons who have simply wandered in off the street; if you've read the book, you can overcome some of the movie's inadequacies by filling in details from memory. *The Great Gatsby* expects the viewer to do a little legwork–how does Nick know the oculist is called Dr. T. J. Eckleburg, for instance, when half the billboard bearing his name is rotted away in the name of Atmosphere? But the film doesn't play fair with the viewer's instinct to fill in the blanks; it falls back on the text whimsically, unevenly, expecting the audience's help, yet playing havoc with its sense of the original meaning. Crucial images linger on, but with a slightly distorted import; in the film, the green light across the bay still exists as a symbol of Gatsby's indefatigable vision, but it has also been turned into a ring that he gives to Daisy, that Daisy then returns to him, and that Gatsby wears when he dies. Whatever else that little alternation may hint at, it certainly suggests that Coppola and Clayton sorely needed some guiding beacon of their own.

–*The Classic American Novel and the Movies*, edited by Gerald Peary and Roger Shatzkin (New York: Frederick Ungar, 1977), pp. 261–267

* * *

This article by an important English drama critic coincided with the release of the movie but does not mention it.

Gatsby and the American Dream
Kenneth Tynan

There is no mystery about the causes of nostalgia, whether it be for the twenties, thirties, forties, fifties or sixties, each of which now has its commercially thriving cultlet. The simple truth is that we are nostalgic for these periods mainly because science has given us the capacity to resurrect them. We can take them off the shelf and replay them at the touch of a button–their films, their newsreels, their speeches and songs.

If we are particularly nostalgic for the twenties, it is because they are the earliest period to which we have such intimate and exhaustive access. (The twenties, themselves, of course, had no such opportunities for nostalgia. They lacked the technology to re-create, say, the sounds and movements of the nineties. Noël Coward was right when he told me: 'There's nothing more modern than nostalgia. That's why I shall always be up to date.')

But why the special passion for 'The Great Gatsby'? How does Scott Fitzgerald's novel–published in 1925, once dramatized, thrice filmed, endlessly reprinted–work its steady, implacable magic? T. S. Eliot called it the first step forward that American fiction had taken since Henry James: yet it is not easy, even after a third or fourth reading, to say precisely what is so great about 'Gatsby.' Briefly described, it is a very long short story about a self-made man, 'an elegant young roughneck' in his early thirties, who owns a vast house on Long Island where he gives, and is lonely at, vast parties; who loves Daisy Buchanan, a rich girl he first met in 1917, when he was a penniless Army officer and she had not yet married wealthy Tom Buchanan; and who, in a final rush of violent incident, is pointlessly murdered.

What has happened is that Tom Buchanan has a mistress who is killed by Daisy's hit-and-run driving; the dead woman's husband, wrongly convinced that Gatsby is the killer, tracks him down and shoots him. With Gatsby out of the way, Tom and Daisy retreat 'back into their money or their vast carelessness, or whatever it was that kept them together. . . .' Thus condensed, the book sounds like a pulp novelette. Compression dispels the aura of tragic mystery in which Fitzgerald envelops his hero.

His portrait of Gatsby–'Mr. Nobody from Nowhere,' as Tom Buchanan contemptuously calls him–is made up of hints and counter-hints, rumour and innuendo, implausible truth and persuasive lie. It's whispered that he is 'a nephew or cousin of Kaiser Wilhelm's,' possibly related to Hindenburg, perhaps even 'second cousin to the devil.' Once we hear that he was a German spy, often that he is a bootlegger, repeatedly that he 'killed a man.' By his own account, his parents were 'wealthy people in the Middle West'; during the war he was a major, much decorated for valour; and after going to Oxford he toured the capitals of Europe, took up painting, collected jewels and hunted big game. He says he lost his inheritance in what he vaguely describes as 'the big panic–the panic of the war,' and claims to have made money since in drugstores and oil: 'But I'm not in either one now.'

Some of this, we later discover, is true. He was indeed a war hero; did indeed go to Oxford (though only for five months, on some kind of ex-Service grant); was indeed an owner of drugstores. But his sponsor in the latter enterprise was a crooked gambler with whom he may or may not have conspired to fix the World Series of 1919; and what they sold in their drugstores was illicit grain alcohol. Whether or not he actually killed anyone is never established, though it seems probable.

He was born James Gatz in North Dakota, the son of 'shiftless and unsuccessful farm people.' He was 17 years old, scraping a living as a salmon fisherman on the shore of Lake Superior, when he introduced himself to a drunken copper millionaire on a passing yacht, and started to claw his way to the top. Out of all the lies and confusions a single resounding truth emerges:–

> The truth was that Jay Gatsby of West Egg, Long Island, sprang from his Platonic conception of himself.

Like Orson Welles's Charles Foster Kane–another fictional embodiment of America's boom period, conceived in the year Fitzgerald died–Gatsby is a self-invented man. The epitaph spoken by his father

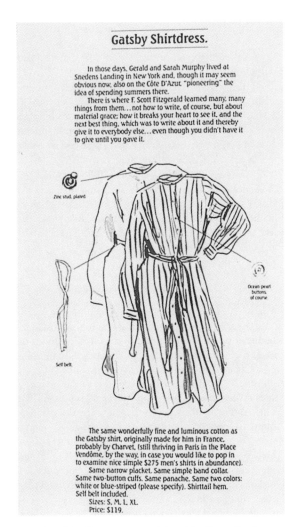

Gatsby Shirtdress.

In those days, Gerald and Sarah Murphy lived at Snedens Landing in New York and, though it may seem obvious now, also on the Côte D'Azur, "pioneering" the idea of spending summers there.

There is where F. Scott Fitzgerald learned many, many things from them... not how to write, of course, but about material grace: how it breaks your heart to see it, and the next best thing, which was to write about it and thereby give it to everybody else... even though you didn't have it to give until you gave it.

Zinc stud, plated

Ocean pearl buttons, of course

Self belt

The same wonderfully fine and luminous cotton as the Gatsby shirt, originally made for him in France, probably by Charvet, (still thriving in Paris in the Place Vendôme, by the way, in case you would like to pop in to examine nice simple $275 men's shirts in abundance). Same narrow placket. Same simple band collar. Same two-button cuffs. Same panache. Same two colors: white or blue-striped (please specify). Shirttail hem. Self belt included.
Sizes: S, M, L, XL.
Price: $119.

One of the sillier attempts to cash in on The Great Gatsby
(Peterman catalogue)

after the murder is not ironically intended. 'If he'd of lived,' the old man says, 'he'd of been a great man. . . . He'd of helped build up the country.'

At the heart of a corrupt and corrupting way of life, Gatsby–like his creator–retains his innocence. Technically no doubt a criminal, he remains to the end an obsessed, impenitent romantic, driven and sustained by his love for Daisy, by what Fitzgerald calls 'the colossal vitality of his illusion,' and finally paying, with not the slightest regret, 'a high price for living too long with a single dream.' Within the gangster there is a poet: and Fitzgerald conveys this by taking great literary risks. Gatsby says little, and what little he says is boyish, shy to the point of curtness, and punctuated, when he is addressing men, by the incongruous slang phrase 'old sport,' perhaps a souvenir of his Oxford days. Nor does Fitzgerald show him in action, except to comment on his physical restlessness–'that resourcefulness of movement that is so peculiarly American'–and on his smile, which must have resembled Fitzgerald's own:–

It was one of those rare smiles with a quality of eternal reassurance in it, that you may come across four or five times in life. . . . It understand you just as far as you wanted to be understood, believed in you as you would like to believe in yourself, and assured you that it had precisely the impression of you that, at your best, you hoped to convey.

In order to persuade us that Gatsby is a man of poetic sensibility, Fitzgerald takes the dangerous, no-hands course of simply *saying so,* in language we cannot resist. There was 'something gorgeous about him, some heightened sensitivity to the promises of life, as if he were related to one of those intricate machines that register earthquakes ten thousand miles away.' Again, as the narrator Nick Carraway tells us, he had 'an extraordinary gift for hope, a romantic readiness such as I have never found in any other person. . . .' He believed, Nick says in the great coda that rounds off the book, in 'the orgiastic future that year by year recedes before us. It eluded us then, but that's no matter–tomorrow we will run faster, stretch out our arms farther. . . . And one fine morning–'

It's no wonder that Nick, taking leave of Gatsby for the last time and comparing him to the people around him, who cannot go for a 30-minute drive without taking a quart of Scotch for the journey, turns back to shout: 'They're a rotten crowd. . . .You're worth the whole damn bunch put together.'

But it is not merely Gatsby, the self-created aristocrat, who possesses this sensitivity, this hope, this faith in the future. It is surely Fitzgerald too, speaking as he so often does to the self-dramatist in all of us–Fitzgerald

the indigent Army officer who met a high-born local *belle* (named Zelda) and devoted his life to her; chasing the orgiastic future from St. Paul, Minnesota, to St. Paul de Vence; already oppressed, and soon to be immobilised, by his knowledge of the gulf between what he ought to have been and what he was; an instinctive moralist, crippled by his own self-accusing morality; a romantic hemmed in, like Gatsby, by unromantic circumstance. But there is, as I hope to show, far more than Fitzgerald in Gatsby.

In 1929 Fitzgerald wrote a short story that contained a passage about leaving New York on the 'Majestic':–

The best of America was the best of the world. . . . France was a land, England was a people, but America, having about it still that quality of the idea, was harder to utter. . . . It was a willingness of the heart.

In a letter written near the end of his life, he said of his country's past:–

I think it is the most beautiful history in the world. . . . And if I came here yesterday like Sheilah [Graham, his mistress], I should still think so. It is the history of all aspiration–not just the American dream but the human dream, and if I came at the end of it that too is a place in the line of the pioneers.

'At the end of it'–here is a clue to follow up. Fitzgerald venerated America, and it was in his work that his patriotism found its last refuge and supreme expression. On the last page of 'Gatsby' Nick imagines what the early settlers must have felt as they surveyed the coastline of the New World:–

. . . for a transitory enchanted moment man must have held his breath in the presence of this continent, compelled into an aesthetic contemplation he neither understood nor desired, face to face for the last time in history with something commensurate to his capacity for wonder.

The people in 'Gatsby' are not Europeanised Americans, not Eastern Seaboarders, not Henry James's Bostonians. Nor are they rural-regional, like Tom Sawyer and Huck Finn. They are the middle-American people about whom Hemingway might have written if he had ever written a novel about America; and I suspect that Hemingway, although he later declared that he 'never thought so much of Gatsby,' privately envied Fitzgerald for having beaten him to the post and written what may be credibly defined as the Great American Novel. 'I see now,' says Nick, 'that this has been a story of the West after all–Tom and Gatsby, Daisy and Jordan and I were all Westerners, and perhaps we possessed

One of several references to Jay Gatsby in Peanuts *(by permission of Charles Schulz)*

some deficiency in common which made us subtly unadaptable to Eastern life.'

So who is Gatsby? What does he stand for? Let us look at him in context. The war is over and won. Wall Street will not crash for at least half a decade. The plush life on Long Island Sound can be honestly mirrored in prose like this:—

> Slowly the white wings of the boat moved against the blue cool limit of the sky. Ahead lay the scalloped ocean and the abounding blessed isles.

It is prose of a kind seldom heard nowadays except, carefully vulgarised, in commercials for semi-sweet aperitifs. Against this glittering background stands a cool and classless figure, seemingly from nowhere, with no verifiable roots, though he eventually proves to be rural transplanted to urban. He is a reader, in youth, of Hopalong Cassidy, who sets himself a schedule of study and self-improvement, and who ends up a wealthy criminal. The guests at his parties, listed in one of the most breathtaking cadenzas in American literature, are mostly not old money but new rich:—

> . . . the Catlips and the Bembergs and G. Earl Muldoon, brother to that Muldoon who afterwards strangled his wife . . . the Dewers and the Scullys and S. W. Belcher and the Smirkes and the young Quinns, divorced now, and Henry L. Palmetto, who killed himself by jumping in front of a subway train in Times Square. Benny McClenahan arrived always with four girls. . . . In addition to all these I can remember that Faustina O'Brien came there at least once, and the Baedeker girls and young Brewer, who had his nose shot off in the war, and Mr Albrucksburger and Miss Haag, his fiancée, and Ardita Fitz Peters and Mr P. Jewett, once head of the American legion, and Miss Claudia Hip, with a man reputed to be her chauffer. . . . All these people came to Gatsby's house in the summer.

And Gatsby represents all their aspirations. He represents a nation at the peak of its pride and self-confidence, tainted by corruption but still reaching for the stars. He stands for everything that is uniquely and glamorously American. He is the national flowering, the genius of the place: he is, in short, the ideal and exemplary American hero.

His spell is potent beyond the shores and borders of America because, for those who live in the Western world, this is the American century. A book like 'Gatsby,' thrown off the very crest of the American wave, has for us an instant and durable appeal. Its sense of *lacrimae rerum,* of grief over doomed innocence, is timeless; but this sense is all the stronger, all the more sharply focused, because it comes out of the last era in which innocence was an integral part of the American psyche.

After 1929, as we know, the sweet dream curdled and the innocence fled. The collapse of the economy undermined the golden vision. The Depression wiped the smile off the face of high American culture for good and all. It turned out, in William Saroyan's phrase, that there was 'no foundation, all the way down the line.' The crook with the soul of a poet ceased to exist; perhaps, outside Fitzgerald's imagination, he had never exited.

In the thirties and afterwards, the protagonists of serious American novels and plays tend to be brutalised and embittered by the life around them. They are usually destroyed by it, whether they are farm labourers from the Middle West like the Joads in 'The Grapes of Wrath,' patricians from the South like Blanche DuBois in 'A Streetcar Named Desire,' or salesmen from the East like Arthur Miller's Willy Loman. Since Gatsby, American fiction has produced no heroes who are worldly-wise without cynicism—unless we count, a quarter of a century after Fitzgerald's novel, Holden Caulfield in 'The Catcher in the Rye.' This is why Gatsby, who died with his dream intact, continues to haunt us, stirring in us an unappeasable desire to find out what went wrong, how the gaudy dream was shipwrecked into nightmare.

'In the midst of prosperity, people look as if they had been robbed.' I wrote that about the citizens of New York in 1960, and anyone who knows America will recognise what I meant. Everywhere in the streets—and above all among the poor—you see the faces of people whose history promised them fulfilment, but whose hopes have been shortchanged with frustration. Even their smiles are somehow bruised; and their characteristic expression, even in moments of celebration, retains about it something sour and suspicious, permanently cheated. It is the look of post-Gatsby America.

—The Observer, 14 April 1974, p. 25

* * *

THE GREAT AMERICAN NOVEL

A "Perfect Novel"
Louis Auchincloss

In *The Great Gatsby* Scott Fitzgerald makes a hero out of a kind of monster. Jay Gatsby, born James Gatz, acquires a fortune, or at least what appears to be one, by the age of thirty, by means that are far from clear but that are certainly dishonest. He starts with bootlegging, but in the end he seems to be engaged in the theft or embezzlement of securities. As Henry James leaves to our imagination how his heroes made their money (because he did not really know), so Fitzgerald allows us to make up our own crimes for Gatsby. But there is no doubt that he is a crook and a tough one, too. He has no friends, only hangers-on, no intellectual interests, no real concern for people. His entire heart and imagination are utterly consumed with his romantic image of Daisy Buchanan, a selfish, silly, giddy creature, who turns in the end into a remorseless hit-and-run driver. What seems to attract him to Daisy is the sense of financial security that she emanates: she has always been, and somehow always will be, abundantly, aboundingly rich. She is the tinselly department store window at Christmastime to the urchin in the street. Her very laugh, as one character puts it, sounds like money.

Fitzgerald is a courageous author. For what is Daisy, dreadful Daisy, but his dream and the American dream at that? He seems to make no bones about it. Vapid, vain, heartless, self-absorbed, she is still able to

Louis Auchincloss

dispel a charm the effect of which on Gatsby is simply to transform him into a romantic hero. The American dream, then, is an illusion? Certainly. It is all gush and tinkle. But nonetheless its effect on a sentient observer is about all life has to offer.

Is Fitzgerald then seriously telling us that to fall in love with a beautiful heiress with a monied laugh, even if she's superficial, selfish and gutless, is a fitting goal for a man's life, and one to justify years of criminal activity? Perhaps not quite. What he may be telling us is that he, the author, by creating the illusion of that illusion, may be doing the only thing worth doing in this vale of constant disillusionment.

To create his illusion of illusion Fitzgerald must set down the dismal atmosphere of Gatsby's life: the senseless, drunken parties, the dull, hard people, the inane conversations, the curious juxtaposition of the luxury of West Egg with the huge garbage dumps of Flushing—and yet make the whole gleam with a hard brittle beauty. It is difficult to see just how he does it, but he does. It is a book of beautiful sentences. Consider this passage in the epilogue:

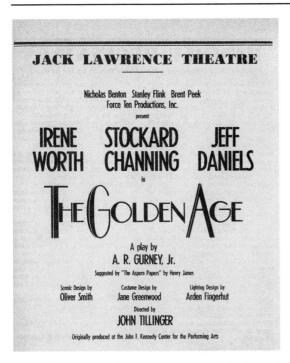

Program for a 1984 play about the attempt to recover the lost chapter of
The Great Gatsby

Most of the big shore places were closed now and there were hardly any lights except the shadowy, moving glow of a ferryboat across the Sound. And as the moon rose higher the inessential houses began to melt away until gradually I became aware of the old island here that flowered once for Dutch sailors' eyes—a fresh, green breast of the new world. Its vanished trees, the trees that had made way for Gatsby's house, had once pandered in whispers to the last and greatest of all human dreams; for a transitory enchanted moment man must have held his breath in the presence of this continent, compelled into an aesthetic contemplation he neither understood nor desired, face to face for the last time in history with something commensurate to his capacity for wonder.

To me there is much in common between Fitzgerald's prose and the paintings of Edward Hopper. Hopper selects dull houses, drab streets, plain people, and invests them with a glow that is actually romantic. No matter what we think of Jay Gatsby and the trivality of his dream, it is impossible not to see what he sees and even feel a bit what he feels. I find myself almost embarrassed, in the end of the book, at regretting his sorry death. As one character says, "he had it coming to him." He certainly did. But Fitzgerald has caught the magic as well as the folly of Gatsby's dream.

There is a peculiar power in these three novels that may stem from the isolation of their protagonists. Hester lives in a world that is consistently cruel to her. Even those who care about her treat her harshly: her husband tortures her; her lover allows her to be punished alone. Heathcliff lives in a world that hates him and that he despises. Gatsby lives in a world where nobody understands him, except, in the very end, the narrator. Yet Nick Carraway's ultimate understanding of his friend costs him his own romance with Jordan Baker. He perceives at last that with *her* he does not even have the short-lived hope that Gatsby had of sharing with Daisy a perfect life.

The reader's experience with these three lonely characters is itself a lonely one. It is difficult to say just why one's reaction is so intense. Sometimes I think it is only self-pity. One likes to identify with a person as unjustly treated as Hester; it makes one feel the single sensitive soul in a world of horrid gaolers, and hence something finer than the world. One likes to identify with a dreamer like Gatsby whose dreams are better than anyone else's. Or even with Heathcliff, who revenges himself on a world that has mistreated him and then throws that world away. But the term "self-pity" may be simply denigrating. The business of living is a lonely one for all of us, and these novels repeat, embellish and illuminate our own inner feelings.

—From an address delivered at the Pierpont Morgan Library, New York City, 15 January 1981 and published in *Three "Perfect Novels" and What They Have in Common* (Columbia, S.C.: Bruccoli Clark Layman, 1981)

* * *

Fire and Freshness: A Matter of Style in *The Great Gatsby*
George Garrett

I have never yet known, or, indeed known of, a contemporary American writer who did not admire *The Great Gatsby*. This evidence, admittedly and purely anecdotal, is, also in my experience, unique. I know of no other twentieth-century masterpiece in our language or, for that matter, in our Western tradition about which this can be said. Let it be said again as simply as possible: I have never know an American writer, of my generation or of the older and younger generations, who has not placed *Gatsby* among the rare unarguable masterpieces of our times. In some cases this admiration is frankly surprising, because *Gatsby* seems to be, in form and content, so different from what has otherwise engaged the passions and commitment of one writer and the other. It really has not seemed to matter very much which side of the (aesthetic) tracks the writer came from or what side of the street the writer is working. In an era of increasingly specialized special interests, it does not seem to be a matter defined or limited by race, creed, color, gender, or country of national origin. And strangely, in an age when we have become so politicized that even the toothpaste one uses becomes, like it or not, a political statement, writers of all political stripes and persuasions seem to admire *Gatsby,* even as, inevitably, they describe the characters and the story in somewhat different terms.

Finally, it doesn't even seem to matter very much if the writer in question holds any positive feelings about the life and (other) works of F. Scott Fitzgerald. Many did not admire him in his lifetime—although it is clear that he was much envied from time to time. Many do not have feelings one way or the other, nothing beyond a polite shrug, even now. But *Gatsby* itself stands by itself—a permanent monument of our literature, a national treasure. And I share the consensual wisdom, although not without a willingness to question it, if only to ask where it comes from. In part perversely, because I have always been automatically contemptuous of trends and fashions, especially *intellectual* trends, which seem to be a contradiction in terms (like the concept of military justice), I have always preferred *Tender Is the Night.* It was always my favorite among the Fitzgerald novels, since I read them, back to back, for the first time, to the best of my recollection, in the summer of 1948 in Princeton. *Gatsby* was assigned reading in a summer school course, the first time Fitzgerald was ever read at Princeton as part of an official course. It was, in fact, the first time at Princeton that any American writers beyond the life and time of Henry James were allowed to be part of the authorized academic curriculum. The course was new and different, a departure. It was an altogether stunning, unforgettable experience to "discover" William Faulkner (*The Sound and the Fury*) and Ernest Hemingway (*The Sun Also Rises*) in the summer. But it was very heaven to be in Princeton reading *The Great Gatsby,* as a class assignment, and then finding, in the stacks of the brand new Firestone Library, the stories and *This Side of Paradise* and *Tender Is the Night* and the others. And over at the U-Store you could buy, and I did, *The Last Tycoon* and *The Crack-Up,* edited by Edmund Wilson.

All of us that summer planned to be the next F. Scott Fitzgerald. We have all come a distance, a far piece, since then, swept by waves of unimaginable change, until, surfacing nearly a half century later, it seems that almost everything has changed beyond memory or repair. One of the things that has not changed, however, that still shines with authentic inner light, is *Gatsby.* That it has this same glowing effect on writers young enough to be my sons and daughters,

George Garrett

new enough not to care a serious hoot about Old Nassau, I find an absolutely fascinating phenomenon.

To a certain extent, it may be a matter of historical content and the long, attractive shadows of nostalgia, but that cannot explain the depth of the novel's lasting appeal. Much of the context and content is lost now in the present. Clearly, only a modest handful of American writers and critics alive now, of any age (and forget the foreigners, even the English, who haven't a real clue), possess by birth, education, and experience the assumed knowledge and the imagination to understand the very subtle social implications and ambiguities that lie at the center, the very heart, of the story of *Gatsby.* Even at the time, the delicacy of Fitzgerald's sensitive recording of a specific and special world, as envisioned and judged by a particular and special intelligence, Nick Carraway, must have escaped many of his contemporaries. Significantly, the letters about *Gatsby* he savored from prominent writers he admired—for example, the letters from Gertrude Stein, Edith Wharton, and T. S. Eliot—stress and praise aspects of form as much as content. Each differently, they see *Gatsby* as advancing the art of the novel not so much from what it talks about as in the interesting ways and means of its making. As for us, it is very hard now to unlearn all that has happened since 1925; difficult, if not impossible, to imagine ourselves safely on the other side of the Great Depression and World War II and all the wars since then.

In one respect, then, contemporary interest in and excitement about the subjects and content of *Gatsby* derive from its odd prescience. Ash heap and eyeglasses, sordid orgy and casual accident, murder and suicide, lust and unrequited love—these are literary signs we have come to live among as if they had always been there, inherent in any conventional literary picture of modern American life. There is, in fact, a direct line of influence and authority running from *Gatsby* to a great many of our most prominent contemporary literary artists, both popular and serious. The signs and portents of Joan Didion, for example, or of Renata Adler, are rooted in Fitzgerald's acres of ashes in *Gatsby,* as are the economic minimalism of Raymond Carver, the half-stoned nihilism that pervades the stories of Ann Beattie, the lyrical ambiance of the novels and stories of Richard Yates. Gore Vidal, not deeply sympathetic to Fitzgerald, is nevertheless clearly admiring of the "small but perfect operation" of *Gatsby.* Of all these, and so many others, by the way, only the quirky Vidal has the depth and subtlety, rooted in old American experience, to understand some of what was eccentric and original about *Gatsby.* At any rate, American writers of all stripes and stamps, from Marxists to reactionaries, seem to be at home with the apparent content of *Gatsby,* to believe in its world, to take it for granted.

It is worth remembering that the down side of the Jazz Age, namely, the Depression, was several years beyond the horizon in 1925 and that the main line of action in the story of *Gatsby,* the summer of 1922, was firmly set in the booming post-World War I years. Worth keeping in mind that prophets of doom seemed more outrageous and eccentric then than they would a decade later. It is part of Tom Buchanan's foolishness that he sees doom and trouble ahead. Worth recalling that popular fiction in which crimes could be allowed to go without punishment (if only by fate and bad luck) was very rare. After all, in American films and television, as late as the 1960s there was a serious problem of getting Code approval for a story in which vice was not punished in some way. It was startling in 1925 to let the Buchanans off the hook with a brief judgmental aside by the narrator: "They were careless people, Tom and Daisy—they smashed up things and creatures and then retreated back into their money or their vast carelessness, or whatever it was that kept them together, and let other people clean up the mess they had made" (p. 139). That they have done what they have done and can walk away from it safely and cheerfully enough, with nobody but the reader and the narrator any the wiser, was as daring as it was remarkable.

There are other things, qualities of which our own ignorance and lack of imagination now deprive us. There is so much drinking in *Gatsby,* and, of course, Fitzgerald was such a heavy drinker at times (and we know all about that now), that it is tricky to keep in mind the fact that both the story and the telling of it are deep in the heart of Prohibition. Which was, as a constitutional amendment, very much the law of the land. And which was not yet, either by Fitzgerald or others, seen as coming to an easy end either soon or painlessly. Time has turned the underworld and internecine wars, the blood and savagery that accompanied Prohibition, into something close to comedy, perhaps musical comedy. But Fitzgerald knew very well the shock value he gained by having so much drinking in his novel. (As did Hemingway in *The Sun Also Rises,* although that story was conveniently set in Europe.) It is significant that Jay Gatsby and Daisy Buchanan meet again, tentative and a little shy at first, in the proper atmosphere of an intimate and wonderfully awkward little tea party at Carraway's cottage. And, in accuracy and fairness, we have to recognize that, daring as he was, Fitzgerald carefully demonstrates throughout the book the bad results that inevitably follow from excessive drinking. Jay Gatsby is self-disciplined and abstemious; this is a rhetorical plus. The fact that Daisy does not drink is viewed ambiguously, more a matter of "an absolutely perfect reputation" (p. 61) than, perhaps, a sign of virtue.

Just so, adulterous affairs and, indeed, even premarital sex were still to be viewed as essentially criminal vices in polite society; and, to an extent, the views of polite society were confirmed by the law. Tom's affair with Myrtle (and the fact that she would dare to call him at home!), together with the absence of any apparently serious consequences, to himself at least, coming from it were conceived as shocking elements in the novel. Tom's promiscuity is rhetorically presented, and so intended to be taken, as wickedness rather than a "problem" or a bad habit. Gatsby's lifetime obsession with the image and reality of Daisy may be more than a little crazy and more than a little vulgar in its material manifestations—the extraordinary house, the parties, the fancy yellow car, and the piles of gorgeous shirts over which Daisy wept; but his dedication to her (including even the folly of asking "too much" (pp. 86, 103) of Daisy, asking her to confess that she had never loved anyone else but him) and his love for her were morally solid and appropriate for their time. Knowing better, even knowing why he was doing it, Gatsby had been Daisy's lover. "He took what he could get, ravenously and unscrupulously–eventually he took Daisy one still October night, took her because he had no real right to touch her hand" (p. 116). After which–"He felt married to her, that was all" (p. 117)–he always wanted to do the right thing. Buchanan, from a good family and background, has criminal vices. Gatsby, although a technical criminal of sorts and a man who mingles with strange and exotic types–the mysterious Jew Wolfsheim, show business types, flotsam and jetsam of society–possesses the best American middle-class standards of the time.

Only a few can still believe, still fewer remember, that there was a time not so long ago when celebrity of any kind, even the kind of celebrity Fitzgerald himself had acquired by the time he came to write *Gatsby,* had a chilling effect upon one's social position. The "best people" never appeared in the press except, perhaps, on the occasion of a wedding or funeral. The "best people" did not, beyond the wild-oats days of youth, mingle with celebrities and show business types, famous opera stars sometimes excepted. It is not quite true that American society despised the lively arts, but it is certainly true that most artists of all kinds, even those from good family, were somewhat suspect and a little bit déclassé. The Homeric list of Gatsby's guests from East Egg and West Egg is monumental in its witty snobbery. And as for Jews (the sinister and shady, two-dimensional Wolfsheim) or ethnics (the pathetic Henry C. Gatz, Gatsby's father, "a solemn old man, very helpless and dismayed, bundled up in a long cheap ulster against the warm September day" [p. 130]), these are not people one might have met except on some most unusual occasion or in the pages of a novel. To understand the prevalent attitude toward the very idea or image of the Jew at that time, one can take quite seriously the stance of Eliot in his early poems. Or one can turn to Edith Wharton's letter of congratulations in which she asserts, "it's enough to make this reader happy to have met your *perfect* Jew, & the limp Wilson, & assisted at that seedy orgy in the Buchanan flat, with the dazed puppy looking on."[1] The truth is, as both Fitzgerald and Edith Wharton knew (both in Europe at the time), the nineteenth century had not yet ended, socially at least, in America. For a moment of almost surreal social topsy-turvy, consider Nick's celebrated drive with Jay Gatsby into New York, over the Queensboro Bridge:

> A dead man passed us in a hearse heaped with blooms, followed by two carriages with drawn blinds, and by more cheerful carriages for friends. The friends looked out at us with the tragic eyes and short upper lips of southeastern Europe, and I was glad that the sight of Gatsby's splendid car was included in their sombre holiday. As we crossed Blackwell's Island a limousine passed us, driven by a white chauffeur, in which sat three modish negroes, two bucks and a girl. I laughed aloud as the yolks of their eyeballs rolled toward us in haughty rivalry. (pp. 55)

No comment is necessary. Except, perhaps, to point out that the language, and the reactions of the narrator and the anticipated reader, were not only neutral but decently appropriate for the time. Which was almost the last time they would be so in serious American literature. Popular narrative was (to an extent remains) slow to change and follow. Perhaps it should be noted, however, that the *author's* intention in this brief sight gag was clearly to show Carraway's modernity, his openness to and delight in the otherwise shocking (to the reader) confusions of order in America.

All of this is stated only to make the point that in many ways we are far removed, as Americans, and as writers and readers as well, from the content and context of *Gatsby*. The old social guidelines have vanished.

If it is hard for us to imagine and to reconstruct the world Fitzgerald wrote about and out of, it is only fair to remind ourselves that, some extraordinary prescience aside, our world was beyond his imagining as well. He could not, for example, possibly have conceived of a time when this novel's art might be submitted to the scrutiny and judgment of literary critics and historians, preservers of the totems of the American tribe, who might themselves be ethnic or Jewish or black. That is to say, even as he felt the end of something and sensed many changes, Fitzgerald could not imagine the end of society as he know it, except by an apocalypse.

In stressing what might be called the societal inaccessibility of *The Great Gatsby* to the contemporary reader, there is another social note worth mentioning. It happens to be something Nick Carraway mentions to us, a point *he* wants to make. Although there are fine-tuned differences and distinctions among all of the principals, there is one common bond. They are one and all outsiders. As Carraway points out in the final chapter: "I see now that this has been a story of the West, after all–Tom and Gatsby, Daisy and Jordan and I, were all Westerners, and perhaps we possessed some deficiency in common which made us subtly unadaptable to Eastern life" (p. 137). That remark, like many others made by Carraway, is layered in irony, more than a little ambiguous. But it does carefully call to mind, in case anyone had missed the fact, that nobody at all from the *real* society of the East even appears in this story. Some of the dregs of that society do, indeed, show up at Gatsby's parties; but in truth the whole story is a playing out, on foreign territory as it were, as alien and exotic as the France and Spain of *The Sun Also Rises,* of a story of love and death among expatriates.

I think it can be convincingly argued that we are by now far removed, imaginatively and in fact, from at least the *rhetorical social world of Gatsby*. And a case can be made, persuasively I believe, that precisely because Fitzgerald was so sensitively attuned to that world, and because that world was created and dramatized through the words and consciousness of a single character, Nick Carraway, we are no more likely to find out what Fitzgerald "really felt" about that world, from the text, than we are ever likely to know the views of our language's preeminent anonymous artist. That is, we know much about Elizabethan attitudes and prejudices, and we know much of this from the plays of Shakespeare. But we know precious little about what Shakespeare felt or thought, if anything, *except as an Elizabethan*. In some ways the world of *Gatsby*, although deceptively tricked out with things we know of and can believe in, is as foreign to us as Elizabethan and Jacobean England. And yet there stands this particular novel, by acclamation taken as nearly perfect in all detail, by example taken by writers, and thus readers, as admirable and enormously influential. If it is not really a matter of content or context, then it is, I believe, a matter of form that makes it so. Finally it is, then, a matter of style, an imperishable style, that has made *Gatsby* a permanent experience.

Briefer than it seems to be—for there are any number of adroitly used literary devices in *Gatsby* that are associated with a much more leisurely, old-fashioned kind of storytelling, giving a serious impression of much more abundance than is, in truth, the case—*Gatsby* is also much more complex in its method of presentation than the luminous clarity of its language implies. Most of the critics have taken due note of the influence of Joseph Conrad on the novel's strategy, particularly insofar as the story is filtered through the consciousness of an alert and sensitive first-person narrator who stands as a witness to the main thrust of the central action even as he works out a knotty story, with its particular and pressing problems, of his own. Carraway's story of that summer is important to himself. He loses in the game of love, turns thirty, loses, too, in his choice of work and place to be, and by the end (which is in fact the beginning of the telling of this story) has turned his back on all that and gone home for good. Yet the main thing that happens to Carraway, from the reader's point of view, is his fascination and involvement with his neighbor—Gatsby. The character of Carraway, as he presents himself, is complex and not entirely relevant to the subject of style. But it needs to be noted that he is an ambiguous character, one about whom the reader is intended to have mixed feelings; that these mixed, sometimes distinctly contradictory feelings give him more weight and solidity as a character than most witness-narrators; that

these mixed feelings add more suspense and mystery to the elements of the story he relates and the ways he chooses to relate them.

However, to deal, in partial abstraction, with the matter of form and style, it is necessary to simplify, perhaps to oversimplify, what is naturally complex. All first-person narratives are presumed, by inference at the very least, to be either directly told to us, that is, spoken, or written; in the latter case, shaped into the form of a manuscript. "Heart of Darkness" is a story presumed to be told aloud to a small group of witnesses (including the original narrator) on a becalmed boat waiting for the tide to turn. "The Turn of the Screw," on the other hand, presents a speaking narrator who kindly allows us to read a written manuscript (written by somebody else) over his shoulder. Both of the effects, although equally strong in original authenticity, as is the case of any good first-person story, at least at its beginning, are also oddly and deliberately distanced from the events that make up the story. That is to say, by definition, from the beginning and for as long as the narrator is both engaging and apparently trustworthy, the principal action (event) of any given first-person story is the telling of the story itself. That is all that is really presumed to be happening—a story is being told. Sometimes it is written; sometimes it is spoken; sometimes, for the sake of celebrating the spoken vernacular, it is, as in *Huckleberry Finn*, assumed to be dictated, as it were, by a narrator and corrected by the author. Third-person stories, by their very different stances, pretend to emphasize events directly rather than the ways and means of telling a tale. It becomes very important, then, for writer and reader of a first-person story to negotiate early on and to determine two related conditions: (1) is the story considered to be mainly written or spoken? And (2) where is the narrator now, and how much time has passed since the events here recounted have transpired?

Gatsby is barely underway before we learn (in the fourth paragraph) that this is intended as a written rather than a spoken version of the tale, and, indeed, that it is a *book*, presumably the same book that we are here and now reading: "Gatsby, the man who gives his name to this book" (p. 5). This assumption raises another question, one whose resolution is held in abeyance (suspense) for quite some time. As far as the narrator is concerned, as stated clearly in the opening paragraphs, the events of the story are all over and done with. Things have happened. The teller has experienced them, reacted to them, and in some ways been changed by them. It is all after the fact. But there are various elements of the telling of the story that are clearly in the present tense. Some are merely aphoristic, reactions that have become generalizations and link the time of telling directly with the time of happening:

In 1991 the Japanese Takarazuka Opera Company produced a musical version of The Great Gatsby *with a female cast.*

ジェイ・ギャツビー　杜けあき

"Again a sort of apology arose to my lips. Almost any exhibition of complete self-sufficiency draws a stunned tribute from me" (p. 11). Or (for instance): "There is no confusion like the confusion of a simple mind, and as we drove away Tom was feeling the hot whips of panic" (p. 97). There are many of these present judgments of past actions. And there are other occasions, at regular intervals throughout, when the narrator interrupts past action to assert an act of present memory: "Among the broken fragments of the last five minutes at table I remember the candles being lit again, pointlessly, and I was conscious of wanting to look squarely at every one, and yet to avoid all eyes" (p. 16). Or: "I think [*now*, evidently and distinctly from *then*] he'd tanked up a good deal at luncheon, and his determination to have my company bordered on violence" (p. 22). And: "But I am slow-thinking and full of interior rules that act as brakes on my desires, and I knew that first I had to get myself definitely out of that tangle back home" (p. 48).

At the risk of being crudely obvious, I call attention to two elements above and beyond the functional value that these recurring time shifts—between the time of the events described and the time of the composition of their description—have, by keeping the reader conscious of the two separate but simultaneous time schemes. The first of these is to focus our attention on aftermath, to emphasize reaction more than action. The second characteristic is to set in some sense of tension, if not conflict, often within the same sentence, the qualities of the spoken versus the written American language.

Gatsby is a marvelous experiment, a triumph of the *written* American vernacular, the range, suppleness, and eloquence of it. But for the written vernacular language of the times to be fully explored, it was necessary to set it in direct contrast to the spoken language, not only in the contrast between credible dialogue in the dramatic scenes, but, occasionally and within limits, in the narration itself: thus "out of that tangle back home" and "I think he'd tanked up a good deal at luncheon. . . ." In other words, the written narration, this *book* by Nick Carraway, has to touch, however briefly, on the level of spoken narration in order to define itself clearly. Moreover, this capability is necessary if full use is to be made of the spoken vernacular in dramatic and satirical scenes. The overall effect, the created language of this book, Nick Carraway's language, offers up a full range between lyrical evocation and depths of feeling at one end and casual, if hard-knuckled, matters of fact. It allows for the poetry of intense perception to live simultaneously and at ease with a hard-edged, implacable vulgarity. Each draws strength from the conflict with the other.

This same tension of time and language is at the center of Carraway's point of view and is expressed early on in Chapter 2 as Carraway, drunk, imagines himself as a stranger capable of including even Carraway as an object in his speculative vision: "Yet high over the city our line of yellow windows must have contributed their share of human secrecy to the casual watcher in the darkening streets, and I was him too, looking up and wondering. I was within and without, simultaneously enchanted and repelled by the inexhaustible variety of life" (p. 30). *I was within and without. . . . Gatsby* becomes an intricate demonstration of that kind of complex double vision, of the *process* of it. We are not far into the story (Chapter 3) before we discover that the "book" Nick Carraway mentioned at the outset, the book that, completed, will turn out to be *The Great Gatsby,* is not yet finished, is in the process of being written. "Reading over what I have written so far, I see I have given the impression that the events of three nights several weeks apart were all that absorbed me" (p. 46). This additional sense of time (narrator pauses to reread what he has written so far) almost, not quite, allows for another kind of time level—the time of revision. At least it asserts that what is being reported has been carefully thought about and can be corrected if need be. And at the least, it makes the time of the composition of the story closely parallel to the reader's left-to-right, chronological adventure.

A bit later, in a number of ways, we are encouraged to *participate* actively in the narrative process as, for example in Chapter six, where Carraway explains and defends a narrative choice:

> He told me all this very much later, but I've put it down here with the idea of exploding those first wild rumors about his antecedents, which weren't even faintly true. Moreover he told it to me at a time of confusion, when I had reached the point of believing everything and nothing about him. So I take advantage of this short halt, while Gatsby, so to speak, caught his breath, to clear this set of misconceptions away. (p. 79)

Here the focus is so clearly on the process of making and of the free, if pragmatic, choices involved that the reader is strongly reminded of the story as artifact, although, ironically, it is Carraway's selective virtuosity that at once supersedes and disguises Fitzgerald's.

Meanwhile, narrative virtuosity becomes increasingly various and complex as we move deeper into the story. In Chapter 4 we are given a first-person narration, in her own words, by Jordan Baker, "sitting up very straight on a straight chair in the tea-garden at the Plaza Hotel" (p. 59), concerning Daisy and Gatsby in 1917. This is told in a credible and appropriate vernacular for Jordan Baker—as recalled, of course, by Carraway. More romantic and lyrical by far is Gatsby's own story, which is told (out of sequence) in indirect discourse. Carraway finds a third-person high style appropriate to the inner mystery and turmoil of the young (and mostly nonverbal) Gatsby.

By this time, Carraway so dominates the material of the story (even his speculation and tentativeness can be taken as the authority of integrity) that he is capable of creating a language that can dramatize in rhythmic images the inward and spiritual condition of Gatsby as a young man:

> But his heart was in a constant, turbulent riot. The most grotesque and fantastic conceits haunted him in his bed at night. A universe of ineffable gaudiness spun itself out in his brain while the clock ticked on the washstand and the moon soaked with wet light his tangled clothes upon the floor. Each night he added to the pattern of his fancies until drowsiness closed down upon some vivid scene with an oblivious embrace. For a while these reveries provided an outlet for his imagination; they were a satisfactory hint of the unreality of reality, a promise that the rock of the world was founded securely on a fairy's wing. (p. 77)

In Chapter 7, another form of indirect discourse, this time a third-person account of the death of Myrtle Wilson, matter of fact and vaguely journalistic (as if, as is later implied, its source were indeed the newspapers), is employed. "The young Greek, Michaelis, who ran the coffee joint beside the ashheaps was the principal witness at the inquest. He had slept through the heat until after five, when he strolled over to the garage, and found George Wilson sick in his office—really sick, pale as his own pale hair and shaking all over" (p. 106). Carraway returns to this place—"Now I want to go back a little and tell what happened at the garage after we left there the night before" (p. 122)—out of chronological sequence, in Chapter 8, with an almost purely dramatic third-person omniscient scene, which, in any literal sense, has to be wholly *imagined* by Carraway, but which offers brief moments of sensory perception and thought by both Michaelis and George Wilson. Stylistically, this unit is quite distinct, as is Carraway's imagined version of Gatsby's last moments, here quite candidly blending overt speculation with an implausible certainty to form a single poetic vision:

> He must have looked up at an unfamiliar sky through frightening leaves and shivered as he found what a grotesque thing a rose is and how raw the sunlight was upon the scarcely created grass. A new world, material without being real, where poor ghosts, breathing dreams like air, drifted fortuitously about . . . like that ashen, fantastic figure gliding toward him through the amorphous trees. (p. 126)

This high moment is a direct reversal of the more usual pattern of perception in the book, in which the sight of the ashen figure (Wilson) might have led him next to react with a generalized vision of "poor ghosts, breathing dreams like air." Here, at the last moment of his life, Gatsby, as conceived and imagined by Carraway reverses reality and unreality, just as Carraway himself had done earlier, imagining himself as a stranger in the street staring up at lit windows and wondering. The result of the reversal is something close to prescience, certainly something stronger than premonition.

Finally, this extension of style to the extreme, almost absurd edge of narrative credibility allows Carraway the indulgence of imagining direct, and quite vernacular, dialogue from the dead Gatsby:

> But, as they drew back the sheet and looked at Gatsby with unmoved eyes, his protest continued in my brain:
> "Look here, old sport, you've got to get somebody for me. You've got to try hard. I can't go through this alone." (p. 128)

In point of fact, stylistically *Gatsby* is a complicated composite of several distinct kinds of prose, set within the boundaries of a written narration, a composite style whose chief demonstrable point appears to be the inadequacy of any single style (or single means of perception, point of view) by itself to do justice to the story. Which is a story of a world not so much in transition as falling apart without realizing it. New and old clash continually, violently. It is shown to be impossible to escape the one by embracing the other. Carraway, as is his habit, finds an aphorism for precisely this paradox, seeking to explain "the colossal vitality" of Gatsby's illusion: "No amount of fire or freshness can challenge what a man will store up in his ghostly heart" (p. 75).

Nick Carraway's authority, and his insistence on telling his own story together with Gatsby's—and it should be remembered that it is Carraway who gets the last aphoristic and poetic word, who presents the haunting image of "the green light, the orgastic future that year by year recedes before us" even as we are swept backward like "boats against the current, borne back ceaselessly into the past" (p. 141)—is to establish a powerful, if illusory, sense of unity that tends to camouflage the variety and complexity of the narration. French critic André Le Vot, in the chapters of his recent biography of Fitzgerald that deal with *Gatsby,* creates an elegant and impressive paradigm of the use of color symbolism and the constant use of light and dark in the story, contrived to hold the discrete parts of the story, in the subtext at least, in a conventional unified coherence. These things seem to work well for that purpose; and there are other elements and patterns that tend to serve roughly the same purpose, all adding up to an impression of unified style. Beneath the surface, however, *Gatsby* is boiling with conflict—chiefly the conflict of new and old, the inadequacy of the old ways and means to deal with the new world of the twentieth century.

The only ballet production based on the novel premiered in 1996; it was well received and continues to be performed.

Thus, behind its seemingly bland and polite surface, *Gatsby* is, in many ways, a wildly experimental novel, a trying out of what would become familiar, if more varied, strategies of our serious literature and, especially, of the range of our literary language.

With all of its apparent acknowledgment of the power of the past, *Gatsby* is a leap toward the future, the invention of new styles, therefore the dead end of something else. Those wonderful letters the young Fitzgerald received from literary dignitaries at the time are explicit in announcing this. "You are creating the contemporary world much as Thackery did in *Pendennis* and *Vanity Fair*," Gertrude Stein wrote, "and this isn't a bad compliment."[2] T. S. Eliot called it, accurately, "the first step that American fiction has taken since Henry James."[3] And Edith Wharton, wisely, felt threatened. She had a minor criticism, based on traditional practices: "My present quarrel with you is only this: that to make Gatsby really Great, you ought to have given us his early career . . . instead of a short

résumé of it. That would have situated him, & made his final tragedy a tragedy instead of a 'fait divers' for the morning papers.

"But you'll tell me that's the old way, & consequently not *your* way."[4]

In terms of form, then, more than anything else, in terms of *style*, *Gatsby* is a pioneering novel. Other masters of the first half of this century may have done more radical and extraordinary things with the novel's shape and substance, but, by and large, these other great books were (are), at the least, inimitable. With *Gatsby*, Fitzgerald advanced the form of the American novel for the benefit of all American novelists who have followed after him, whether they know it or not. They seem to sense this, to bear witness to it, in their continuing admiration for *Gatsby*. For youthful romance, it is hard to beat *This Side of Paradise*. For the purity of nostalgia and the evocation of a period, an era, there is always my old favorite, *Tender Is the Night*. But in *Gatsby*, which pretends to be a little of both,

THE RARE-BOOK MARKET

The Great Gatsby in dust jacket has become the most notable twentieth-century American book. Depending on condition, a copy of the first printing without dust jacket brings $500–$1000; a copy in the dust jacket brings $25,000–$35,000.

27,600

•22

FITZGERALD, F. SCOTT. The Great Gatsby. New York: Scribner's 1925. *8vo, original green cloth*, PICTORIAL DUST JACKET *after F. Cugat (frayed at heel of spine, light wear at front bottom edge and front fore-edge)*. FIRST EDITION, FIRST PRINTING of text and of dust jacket (the lower case "j" at rear hand-corrected in ink). Bruccoli A11.1.a; Connolly, *The Modern Movement* 48: "...a prose poem of delight and sadness which has by now introduced two generations to the romance of America, as *Huckleberry Finn* and *Leaves of Grass* introduced those before it." A very good, bright dust jacket.

Estimate: $20,000–30,000

Christie's Catalogue, *8 November 1996. The $27,600 paid for this copy at auction was mostly for the value of the jacket.*

34   FITZGERALD, F. SCOTT. *The Great Gatsby*, Charles Scribner's Sons, New York, 1925. First issue. A very good copy in the first state dustwrapper, with some restoration at head of spine and foot of lower panel, but altogether fresh and bright.

Bruccoli A11.1.a. Connolly, *Modern Movement*, 48.   *£12500*

R. A. Gekoski Catalogue 23 *(1997). The price is about $21,000.*

An Inscribed "Gatsby" in Dust Jacket

100. FITZGERALD, F. SCOTT. *The Great Gatsby*. New York: Scribner, 1925. First Edition, second printing in the second issue dust jacket with the "J" in "Jay Gatsby" corrected in type. Signed presentation copy to his friend, Hollywood screenwriter Hugo Butler, inscribed, "For Hugo Butler, with apologies that in writing this story of his life I had to leave out so much for which the public is not yet 'ready' - and feeling that in dedicating the proceeds to his speedy release I will make those days in St [San] Quentin pass more swiftly for him. From his old buddy in cell block 3. F. Scott Fitzgerald. Hollywood-on the-Square, August 1938." "Cell block 3" is a reference to the portion of the Irving Thalberg Building at the MGM studios where Butler and Fitzgerald were screenwriters together. Hugo Butler wrote such notable films as the Jean Renoir directed *The Southerner, Young Tom Edison, Lassie Come Home, The Adventures of Huckleberry Finn*, and *A Christmas Carol*. Front hinge professionally repaired. Near fine in a completely unrestored dust jacket with a few small chips at the extremeties and some tears. $35,000.00

Peter Stern Catalogue 28 *(1997). $35,000 is more than Fitzgerald earned from his novel during his lifetime.*

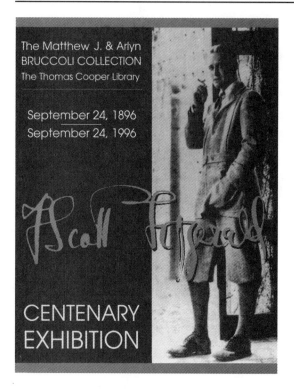

Cover of the catalogue compiled by graduate students at the University of
South Carolina

Keepsake produced by the Columbia, S.C., postmaster to celebrate the
F. Scott Fitzgerald stamp

youthful romance and nostalgic period piece, it is a matter of style; and that style is for all our bitter seasons.

–from *New Essays on The Great Gatsby,*
edited by Matthew J. Bruccoli
(Cambridge & New York: Cambridge University Press,
1985), pp. 101–116

Notes

1. "Three Letters about *The Great Gatsby*," *The Crack-Up,* ed.
   Edmund Wilson (New York: New Directions, 1945), p.
   309.
2. Ibid., p. 308.
3. Ibid., p. 310.
4. Ibid., p. 309.

* * *

Centenary Tributes

From F. Scott Fitzgerald . . . Centenary Celebration
*(Columbia: Thomas Cooper Library, University of South Caro-
lina, 1996).*

The Great Gatsby is a perfect book–what the Norwe-
gians call "an egg of a book."

–*Margaret Atwood*

I first read *The Great Gatsby* as a high school student
more than thirty years ago, and even now I don't think I
have fully recovered from the experience. Fitzgerald's
book is not like other books. It does more than just tell a
story–it cuts to the heart of storytelling itself–and the
result is a work of such simplicity, power, and beauty that
one is marked by it forever. I realize that I am not alone in
my opinion, but I can't think of another twentieth-century
American novel that has meant as much to me.

–*Paul Auster*

I reread Fitzgerald perhaps more often than any other
writer, and one of the saddest things I know of is the letter to
Perkins, where he speaks of himself in the past tense: "In my
own way I was an original." My God, that always makes
me hurt. How much he would have reveled in the history of

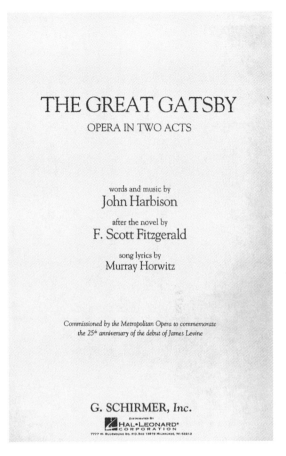

THE GREAT GATSBY

OPERA IN TWO ACTS

words and music by
John Harbison

after the novel by
F. Scott Fitzgerald

song lyrics by
Murray Horwitz

Commissioned by the Metropolitan Opera to commemorate
the 25th anniversary of the debut of James Levine

G. SCHIRMER, Inc.

DISTRIBUTED BY
HAL•LEONARD®
CORPORATION
7777 W. BLUEMOUND RD. P.O. Box 13819 MILWAUKEE, WI 53213

Playbill and libretto for the first American opera production based on the novel

World Premiere
December 20, 1999

The Great Gatsby

Music and Libretto by John Harbison
With popular song lyrics by
Murray Horwitz

Opera based on the novel by
F. Scott Fitzgerald

Conductor: James Levine
Production: Mark Lamos
Set Designer: Michael Yeargan
Costume Designer: Milena Canonero
Lighting Designer: Duane Schuler
Choreographer: Robert LaFosse
Fight Director: B.H. Barry

Dawn Upshaw, Susan Graham, Lorraine Hunt*/Victoria Livengood,
Jerry Hadley, Mark Baker, Dwayne Croft, Richard Paul Fink

World War I was over and the Roaring Twenties had begun. It was
a time of enormous change in the moral and social fabric of our
country. F. Scott Fitzgerald's great American Jazz Age novel is a
fable evoking the spirit of those times — a spirit recaptured today
by composer John Harbison in his score for this World Premiere,
specially commissioned by The Metropolitan Opera.

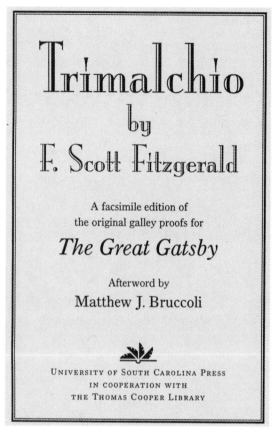

Trimalchio
by
F. Scott Fitzgerald

A facsimile edition of
the original galley proofs for

The Great Gatsby

Afterword by
Matthew J. Bruccoli

UNIVERSITY OF SOUTH CAROLINA PRESS
IN COOPERATION WITH
THE THOMAS COOPER LIBRARY

Title page for the reproduction of the unrevised galleys, published in 2000

ably, mislaid all memory of the mixture of the comic and the touching in the scene in which Klipspringer is summoned by Gatsby to play the piano for Daisy on her tour of the mansion, and the song he performs on Gatsby's special request is "Ain't We Got Fun," a vivacious tune with somewhat cynical lyrics that, though I was an infant when the novel was published, was still around when I was old enough to listen to it during the Great Depression that, so to speak, put paid to the era with which Fitzgerald is peculiarly associated, the one towards which, having been born just before its midpoint, I feel proprietary.

—*Thomas Berger*

After many seasons of occasional reflection it begins increasingly to seem to me that the power of Fitzgerald's work to fascinate is the product of the destructive paradox that *The Great Gatsby* captures so nearly perfectly. The only means Gatsby has to create the grand illusion of his shining romance with Daisy is his loot, its origin as corrupt as the carefree world where she lives with Tom. The existence of the romance requires first the corruption that creates the wealth, and then the denial that the corruption took place—which assures the demolition of the romance. The enduring congruent power of Fitzgerald's life to fascinate, and sadden, is the result of his disastrous insistence upon making it a looking-glass of the lethal paradox he wrote about, so that if his life was to reflect truly the romance he wished to live, it too had to be destroyed. He was too good an artist for his own good; he saw the necessity for the fatal symmetry, however reluctantly or imperfectly, and he attended to it.

—*George V. Higgins*

From my sense of the attitude to life which irradiates his work, I regard Scott Fitzgerald as the most generous, and the most grateful of American writers. And *The Great Gatsby* still strikes me as the most perfectly crafted work of fiction to have come from America.

—*Tony Tanner*

his work, though, and *Gatsby* stands right up there with the best of everything. This slender volume that manages to be inclusive, and to express the peculiarly cruel effects of our oddly materialistic brand of optimism, better than so many tomes, so many roundhouse attempts to be as big as the country. I hope there is a writers' heaven, and that he's sitting on a bar stool there, toasting, as he would be, everybody who sold him short.

—*Richard Bausch*

The Great Gatsby is as nearly perfect as a novel can be, with not a word, not an emotion, not an idea in excess or lacking or misplaced or corrupted. On each rereading I am prepared to find on almost every page gems previously overlooked or perhaps once noticed but temporarily forgotten: e.g., the character Klipspringer, a career houseguest, who after Gatsby's death telephones the house not to ask when to come for the funeral but rather to request that his tennis shoes be forwarded to the address of his new host—I had only half-recalled that his first name (Ewing) is as wondrously right as the last, but until recently I had, unaccount-

Professionally, I know, the next move must come from me. Would the 25 cent press keep <u>Gatsby</u> in the public eye—or <u>is the book unpopular.</u> Has it <u>had</u> its chance? Would a popular reissue in that series with a preface <u>not</u> by me but by one of its admirers—I can maybe pick one—make it a favorite with class rooms, profs, lovers of English prose—anybody. But to die, so completely and unjustly after having given so much. Even now there is little published in Americn fiction that doesn't slightly bare my stamp—in a <u>small</u> way I was an original. . . .

—Fitzgerald to Maxwell Perkins, 20 May 1940

Checklist of Further Reading

Mary Jo Tate and Lisa Kerr

Fitzgerald's Publications

Books

Fie! Fie! Fi-Fi! Cincinnati, New York & London: The John Church Co., 1914. Seventeen song lyrics.

The Evil Eye. Cincinnati, New York & London: The John Church Co., 1915. Seventeen song lyrics.

Safety First. Cincinnati, New York & London: The John Church Co., 1916. Twenty-one song lyrics.

This Side of Paradise. New York: Scribners, 1920; London: Collins, 1921. Novel.

Flappers and Philosophers. New York: Scribners, 1920; London: Collins, 1922. Stories.

The Beautiful and Damned. New York: Scribners, 1922; London: Collins, 1922. Novel.

Tales of the Jazz Age. New York: Scribners, 1922; London: Collins, 1923. Stories.

The Vegetable. New York: Scribners, 1923. Play.

The Great Gatsby. New York: Scribners, 1925; London: Chatto & Windus, 1926. Novel.

All the Sad Young Men. New York: Scribners, 1926. Stories.

John Jackson's Arcady, arranged for public reading by Lilian Holmes Strack. Boston: Baker, 1928. Story.

Tender Is the Night. New York: Scribners, 1934; London: Chatto & Windus, 1934. *Tender Is the Night,* "With the Author's Final Revisions." Ed. with intro. by Malcolm Cowley. New York: Scribners, 1951; London: Grey Walls, 1953. Novel.

Taps at Reveille. New York: Scribners, 1935. Stories.

The Last Tycoon. Ed. with intro. by Edmund Wilson. New York: Scribners, 1941; London: Grey Walls, 1949. Unfinished novel. With *The Great Gatsby* and 5 stories.

The Crack-Up. Ed. with intro. by Edmund Wilson. New York: New Directions, 1945; Harmondsworth, U.K.: Penguin, 1965. Essays, selections from the notebooks and letters.

The Stories of F. Scott Fitzgerald. Ed. with intro. by Malcolm Cowley. New York: Scribners, 1951.

Afternoon of an Author. Ed. with intro. by Arthur Mizener. Princeton, N.J.: Princeton University Library, 1957; New York: Scribners, 1958; London: Bodley Head, 1958. Stories and essays.

The Pat Hobby Stories. Ed. with intro. by Arnold Gingrich. New York: Scribners, 1962; Harmondsworth, U.K.: Penguin, 1967.

The Apprentice Fiction of F. Scott Fitzgerald, 1909–1917. Ed. with intro. by John Kuehl. New Brunswick, N.J.: Rutgers University Press, 1965.

Dearly Beloved. Iowa City, Iowa: Windhover Press, 1970. Story.

F. Scott Fitzgerald In His Own Time: A Miscellany. Ed. with intro. by Matthew J. Bruccoli and Jackson R. Bryer. Kent, Ohio: Kent State University Press, 1971.

Three Hours Between Planes. Agincourt, Ontario: The Book Society of Canada Limited, 1970. Story.

The Basil and Josephine Stories. Ed. with intro. by Jackson R. Bryer and John Kuehl. New York: Scribners, 1973.

Bits of Paradise. Selected by Scottie Fitzgerald Smith and Matthew J. Bruccoli, with foreword by Smith and preface by Bruccoli. London: Bodley Head, 1973; New York: Scribners, 1974. Stories by Fitzgerald and 10 stories by Zelda Fitzgerald.

F. Scott Fitzgerald's Preface to This Side of Paradise. Ed. John R. Hopkins. Iowa City, Iowa: Windhover Press/Bruccoli Clark, 1975.

The Cruise of the Rolling Junk. Intro. by Matthew J. Bruccoli. Bloomfield Hills, Mich. & Columbia, S.C.: Bruccoli Clark, 1976. Three travel articles.

F. Scott Fitzgerald's Screenplay for Three Comrades by Erich Maria Remarque. Ed. with afterword by Matthew J. Bruccoli. Carbondale & Edwardsville, Ill.: Southern Illinois University Press, 1978.

F. Scott Fitzgerald's St. Paul Plays, 1911–1914. Ed. with intro. by Alan Margolies. Princeton, N.J.: Princeton University Library, 1978.

The Price Was High. Ed. with intro. by Matthew J. Bruccoli. New York & London: Harcourt Brace Jovanovich/Bruccoli Clark, 1979; London: Quartet, 1979. Stories.

Checklist of Further Reading

Poems 1911–1940. Ed. Matthew J. Bruccoli; intro. by James Dickey. Bloomfield Hills, Mich. & Columbia, S.C.: Bruccoli Clark, 1981.

Babylon Revisited: The Screenplay. Intro. by Budd Schulberg. New York: Carroll & Graf, 1993.

Letters, Diaries, Notebooks

The Letters of F. Scott Fitzgerald. Ed. with intro. by Andrew Turnbull. New York: Scribners, 1963; London: Bodley Head, 1964.

Thoughtbook of Francis Scott Key Fitzgerald. Intro. by John Kuehl. Princeton, N.J.: Princeton University Library, 1965.

Dear Scott/Dear Max: The Fitzgerald-Perkins Correspondence. Ed. with intro. by John Kuehl and Jackson R. Bryer. New York: Scribners, 1971; London: Cassell, 1973.

As Ever, Scott Fitz–. Ed. with intro. by Matthew J. Bruccoli and Jennifer M. Atkinson, with foreword by Scottie Fitzgerald Smith. Philadelphia & New York: J. B. Lippincott, 1972; London: Woburn, 1973. The Fitzgerald/Harold Ober correspondence.

F. Scott Fitzgerald's Ledger: A Facsimile. Intro. by Matthew J. Bruccoli. Washington: NCR Microcard Books/Bruccoli Clark, 1978.

The Notebooks of F. Scott Fitzgerald. Ed. with intro. by Matthew J. Bruccoli. New York & London: Harcourt Brace Jovanovich/Bruccoli Clark, 1978.

Correspondence of F. Scott Fitzgerald. Ed. with intro. by Matthew J. Bruccoli and Margaret M. Duggan, with Susan Walker. New York: Random House, 1980.

F. Scott Fitzgerald: A Life in Letters. Ed. with intro. by Matthew J. Bruccoli, with Judith S. Baughman. New York: Scribners, 1994.

Editions and Collections

The Portable F. Scott Fitzgerald. Ed. Dorothy Parker; intro. by John O'Hara. New York: Viking, 1945.

The Bodley Head F. Scott Fitzgerald, 6 vols. London: Bodley Head, 1958–1963.

The Stories of F. Scott Fitzgerald, 5 vols. Harmondsworth, U.K.: Penguin, 1962–1968.

F. Scott Fitzgerald on Writing. Ed. Larry W. Phillips. New York: Scribners, 1985.

The Short Stories of F. Scott Fitzgerald. Ed. with preface by Matthew J. Bruccoli. New York: Scribners, 1989; London: Scribners, 1991.

The Cambridge Edition of the Works of F. Scott Fitzgerald. Cambridge: Cambridge University Press, 1991– . *The Great Gatsby,* ed. with intro. by Matthew J. Bruccoli, 1991; *The Love of the Last Tycoon: A Western,* ed. with intro. by Bruccoli, 1993.

Tender Is the Night. Ed. Matthew J. Bruccoli. London: Samuel Johnson, 1995. Facsimile of Bruccoli's emended copy of the first printing.

Tender Is the Night, Centennial Edition. Ed. with intro. and notes by Matthew J. Bruccoli. London: Everyman, 1996.

F. Scott Fitzgerald on Authorship. Ed. Matthew J. Bruccoli, with Judith S. Baughman. Columbia: University of South Carolina Press, 1996.

F. Scott Fitzgerald: The Jazz Age. Intro. by E. L. Doctorow. New York: New Directions, 1996.

Facsimiles

The Great Gatsby: A Facsimile of the Manuscript. Ed. with intro. by Matthew J. Bruccoli. Washington: Bruccoli Clark/NCR Microcard Books, 1973.

F. Scott Fitzgerald: Inscriptions. Columbia, S.C.: Matthew J. Bruccoli, 1988.

F. Scott Fitzgerald Manuscripts. Ed. Matthew J. Bruccoli. New York & London: Garland, 1990–1991. 18 vols: *This Side of Paradise, The Beautiful and Damned, The Great Gatsby* galleys, *Tender Is the Night, The Last Tycoon, The Vegetable,* stories, and articles.

Fie! Fie! Fi-Fi! Intro. by Matthew J. Bruccoli. Columbia: University of South Carolina Press for the Thomas Cooper Library, 1996. Music score and previously unpublished acting script.

Trimalchio. Ed. with intro. by Matthew J. Bruccoli. Columbia: University of South Carolina Press, 2000.

Stories and Plays

First periodical appearance and first publication in a Fitzgerald collection.

"The Mystery of the Raymond Mortgage," *The St. Paul Academy Now and Then,* 2 (October 1909), 4–8; *Apprentice Fiction.*

"Reade, Substitute Right Half," *The St. Paul Academy Now and Then,* 2 (February 1910), 10–11; *Apprentice Fiction.*

"A Debt of Honor," *The St. Paul Academy Now and Then,* 2 (March 1910), 9–11; *Apprentice Fiction.*

"The Room with the Green Blinds," *The St. Paul Academy Now and Then,* 3 (June 1911), 6–9; *Apprentice Fiction.*

"A Luckless Santa Claus," *The Newman News,* 9 (Christmas 1912), 1–7; *Apprentice Fiction.*

"Pain and the Scientist," *The Newman News* (1913), 5–10; *Apprentice Fiction.*

"The Trail of the Duke," *The Newman News,* 9 (June 1913), 5–9; *Apprentice Fiction.*

"Shadow Laurels," *The Nassau Literary Magazine,* 71 (April 1915), 1–10; *Apprentice Fiction.*

"The Ordeal," *The Nassau Literary Magazine,* 71 (June 1915), 153–159; *Apprentice Fiction.*

"The Debutante," *The Nassau Literary Magazine,* 72 (January 1917), 241–252; *The Smart Set,* 60 (November 1919), 85–96; *Apprentice Fiction.*

"The Spire and the Gargoyle," *The Nassau Literary Magazine,* 72 (February 1917), 297–307; *Apprentice Fiction.*

"Tarquin of Cheepside," *The Nassau Literary Magazine,* 73 (April 1917), 13–18; *Apprentice Fiction.* Revised and expanded as "Tarquin of Cheapside," *The Smart Set,* 64 (February 1921), 43–46; *TJA.*

"Babes in the Woods," *The Nassau Literary Magazine,* 73 (May 1917), 55–64; *The Smart Set,* 60 (September 1919), 67–71; *Apprentice Fiction.*

"Sentiment–And the Use of Rouge," *The Nassau Literary Magazine,* 73 (June 1917), 107–123; *Apprentice Fiction.*

"The Pierian Springs and the Last Straw," *The Nassau Literary Magazine,* 73 (October 1917), 173–185; *Apprentice Fiction.*

"Porcelain and Pink (A One-Act Play)," *The Smart Set,* 61 (January 1920), 77–85; *TJA.*

"Benediction," *The Smart Set,* 61 (February 1920), 35–44; *F&P.*

"Dalyrimple Goes Wrong," *The Smart Set,* 61 (February 1920), 107–116; *F&P.*

"Head and Shoulders," *The Saturday Evening Post,* 192 (February 21, 1920), 16–17, 81–82, 85–86; *F&P.*

"Mister Icky The Quintessence of Quaintness in One Act," *The Smart Set,* 61 (March 1920), 93–98; *TJA.*

"Myra Meets His Family," *The Saturday Evening Post,* 192 (March 20, 1920), 40, 42, 44, 46, 49–50, 53; *Price.*

"The Camel's Back," *The Saturday Evening Post,* 192 (April 24, 1920), 16–17, 157, 161, 165; *TJA.*

"The Cut-Glass Bowl," *Scribner's Magazine,* 67 (May 1920), 582–592; *F&P.*

"Bernice Bobs Her Hair," *The Saturday Evening Post,* 192 (May 1, 1920), 14–15, 159, 163, 167; *F&P.*

"The Ice Palace," *The Saturday Evening Post,* 192 (May 22, 1920), 18–19, 163, 167, 170; *F&P.*

"The Offshore Pirate," *The Saturday Evening Post,* 192 (May 29, 1920), 10–11, 99, 101–102, 106, 109; *F&P.*

"The Four Fists," *Scribner's Magazine,* 67 (June 1920), 669–680; *F&P.*

"The Smilers," *The Smart Set,* 62 (June 1920), 107–111; *Price.*

"May Day," *The Smart Set,* 62 (July 1920), 3–32; *TJA.*

"The Jelly-Bean," *Metropolitan Magazine,* 52 (October 1920), 15–16, 63–67; *TJA.*

"The Lees of Happiness," *Chicago Sunday Tribune* (December 12, 1920), Blue Ribbon Fiction Section, 1, 3, 7; *TJA.*

"His Russet Witch," *Metropolitan Magazine,* 53 (February 1921), 11–13, 46–51; in *TJA* as "'O Russet Witch!'"

"The Far Seeing Skeptics," *The Smart Set,* 67 (February 1922), 48.

"The Popular Girl," *The Saturday Evening Post,* 194 (February 11 & 18, 1922), 3–5, 82, 84, 86, 89; 18–19, 105–106, 109–110; *Bits.*

"Two for a Cent," *Metropolitan Magazine,* 55 (April 1922), 23–26, 93–95; *Price.*

"The Curious Case of Benjamin Button," *Collier's,* 69 (May 27, 1922), 5–6, 22–28; *TJA.*

"The Diamond as Big as the Ritz," *The Smart Set,* 68 (June 1922), 5–29; *TJA.*

"Winter Dreams," *Metropolitan Magazine,* 56 (December 1922), 11–15, 98, 100–102, 104–107; *ASYM.*

"Dice, Brass Knuckles & Guitar," *Hearst's International,* 43 (May 1923), 8–13, 145–149; *Price.*

"Hot & Cold Blood," *Hearst's International,* 64 (August 1923), 80–84, 150–151; *ASYM.*

"Gretchen's Forty Winks," *The Saturday Evening Post,* 196 (March 15, 1924), 14–15, 128, 130, 132; *ASYM.*

"Diamond Dick and the First Law of Woman," *Hearst's International,* 45 (April 1924), 58–63, 134, 136; *Price.*

"The Third Casket," *The Saturday Evening Post,* 196 (May 31, 1924), 8–9, 78; *Price.*

"Absolution," *The American Mercury,* 2 (June 1924), 141–149; *ASYM.*

"Rags Martin-Jones and the Pr-nce of W-les," *McCall's,* 51 (July 1924), 6–7, 32, 48, 50; *ASYM.*

"'The Sensible Thing,'" *Liberty,* 1 (July 5, 1924), 10–14; *ASYM.*

"The Unspeakable Egg," *The Saturday Evening Post,* 197 (July 12, 1924), 12–13, 125–126, 129; *Price.*

"John Jackson's Arcady," *The Saturday Evening Post,* 197 (July 26, 1924), 8–9, 100, 102, 105; *Price.*

"The Baby Party," *Hearst's International,* 47 (February 1925), 32–37; *ASYM.*

"The Pusher-in-the-Face," *Woman's Home Companion,* 52 (February 1925), 27–28, 143–144; *Price.*

"Love in the Night," *The Saturday Evening Post,* 197 (March 14, 1925), 18–19, 68, 70; *Bits.*

"One of My Oldest Friends," *Woman's Home Companion,* 52 (September 1925), 7–8, 120, 122; *Price.*

"The Adjuster," *Redbook,* 45 (September 1925), 47–51, 144–148; *ASYM.*

"A Penny Spent," *The Saturday Evening Post,* 198 (October 10, 1925), 8–9, 160, 164, 166; *Bits.*

"Not in the Guidebook," *Woman's Home Companion,* 52 (November 1925), 9–11, 135–136; *Price.*

"The Rich Boy," *Redbook,* 46 (January & February 1926), 27–32, 144, 146; 75–79, 122, 124–126; *ASYM.*

"Presumption," *The Saturday Evening Post,* 198 (January 9, 1926), 3–5, 226, 228–229, 233–234; *Price.*

"The Adolescent Marriage," *The Saturday Evening Post,* 198 (March 6, 1926), 6–7, 229–230, 233–234; *Price.*

"The Dance," *Redbook,* 47 (June 1926), 39–43, 134, 136, 138; *Bits.*

Checklist of Further Reading

"Your Way and Mine," *Woman's Home Companion,* 54 (May 1927), 7–8, 61, 64, 67, 68; *Price.*

"Jacob's Ladder," *The Saturday Evening Post,* 200 (August 20, 1927), 3–5, 57–58, 63–64; *Bits.*

"The Love Boat," *The Saturday Evening Post,* 200 (October 8, 1927), 8–9, 134, 139, 141; *Price.*

"A Short Trip Home," *The Saturday Evening Post,* 200 (December 17, 1927), 6–7, 55, 57–58; *TAR.*

"The Bowl," *The Saturday Evening Post,* 200 (January 21, 1928), 6–7, 93–94, 97, 100; *Price.*

"Magnetism," *The Saturday Evening Post,* 200 (March 3, 1928), 5–7, 74, 76, 78; *Stories.*

"The Scandal Detectives," *The Saturday Evening Post,* 200 (April 28, 1928), 3–4, 178, 181–182, 185; *TAR; B&J.*

"A Night at the Fair," *The Saturday Evening Post,* 201 (July 21, 1928), 8–9, 129–130, 133; *B&J.*

"The Freshest Boy," *The Saturday Evening Post,* 201 (July 28, 1928), 6–7, 68, 70, 73; *TAR; B&J.*

"He Thinks He's Wonderful," *The Saturday Evening Post,* 201 (September 29, 1928), 6–7, 117–118, 121; *TAR; B&J.*

"Outside the Cabinet-Maker's," *Century Magazine,* 117 (December 1928), 241–244.

"The Captured Shadows," *The Saturday Evening Post,* 201 (December 29, 1928), 12–13, 48, 51; *TAR; B&J.*

"The Perfect Life," *The Saturday Evening Post,* 201 (January 5, 1929), 8–9, 113, 115, 118; *TAR; B&J.*

"The Last of the Belles," *The Saturday Evening Post,* 201 (March 2, 1929), 18–19, 75, 78; *TAR.*

"Forging Ahead," *The Saturday Evening Post,* 201 (March 30, 1929), 12–13, 101, 105; *B&J.*

"Basil and Cleopatra," *The Saturday Evening Post,* 201 (April 27, 1929), 14–15, 166, 170, 173; *AOAA; B&J.*

"The Rough Crossing," *The Saturday Evening Post,* 201 (June 8, 1929), 12–13, 66, 70, 75; *Stories.*

"Majesty," *The Saturday Evening Post,* 202 (July 13, 1929), 6–7, 57–58, 61–62; *TAR.*

"At Your Age," *The Saturday Evening Post,* 202 (August 17, 1929), 6–7, 79–80; *Price.*

"The Swimmers," *The Saturday Evening Post,* 202 (October 19, 1929), 12–13, 150, 152, 154; *Bits.*

"Two Wrongs," *The Saturday Evening Post,* 202 (January 18, 1930), 8–9, 107, 109, 113; *TAR.*

"First Blood," *The Saturday Evening Post,* 202 (April 5, 1930), 8–9, 81, 84; *TAR; B&J.*

"A Nice Quiet Place," *The Saturday Evening Post,* 202 (May 31, 1930), 8–9, 96, 101, 103; *TAR; B&J.*

"The Bridal Party," *The Saturday Evening Post,* 203 (August 9, 1930), 10–11, 109–110, 112, 114; *Stories.*

"A Woman with a Past," *The Saturday Evening Post,* 203 (September 6, 1930), 8–9, 133–134, 137; *TAR; B&J.*

"One Trip Abroad," *The Saturday Evening Post,* 203 (October 11, 1930), 6–7, 48, 51, 53–54, 56; *AOAA.*

"A Snobbish Story," *The Saturday Evening Post,* 203 (November 29, 1930), 6–7, 36, 38, 40, 42; *B&J.*

"The Hotel Child," *The Saturday Evening Post,* 203 (January 31, 1931), 8–9, 69, 72, 75; *Bits.*

"Babylon Revisited," *The Saturday Evening Post,* 203 (February 21, 1931), 3–5, 82–84; *TAR.*

"Indecision," *The Saturday Evening Post,* 203 (May 16, 1931), 12–13, 56, 59, 62; *Price.*

"A New Leaf," *The Saturday Evening Post,* 204 (July 4, 1931), 12–13, 90–91; *Bits.*

"Emotional Bankruptcy," *The Saturday Evening Post,* 204 (August 15, 1931), 8–9, 60, 65; *B&J.*

"Between Three and Four," *The Saturday Evening Post,* 204 (September 5, 1931), 8–9, 69, 72; *Price.*

"A Change of Class," *The Saturday Evening Post,* 204 (September 26, 1931), 6–7, 37–38, 41; *Price.*

"A Freeze-Out," *The Saturday Evening Post,* 204 (December 19, 1931), 6–7, 84–85, 88–89; *Price.*

"Six of One–," *Redbook,* 58 (February 1932), 22–25, 84, 86, 88; *Price.*

"Diagnosis," *The Saturday Evening Post,* 204 (February 20, 1932), 18–19, 90, 92; *Price.*

"Flight and Pursuit," *The Saturday Evening Post,* 204 (May 14, 1932), 16–17, 53, 57; *Price.*

"Family in the Wind," *The Saturday Evening Post,* 204 (June 4, 1932), 3–5, 71–73; *TAR.*

"The Rubber Check," *The Saturday Evening Post,* 205 (August 6, 1932), 6–7, 41–42, 44–45; *Price.*

"What a Handsome Pair!" *The Saturday Evening Post,* 205 (August 27, 1932), 16–17, 61, 63–64; *Price.*

"Crazy Sunday," *The American Mercury,* 27 (October 1932), 209–220; *TAR.*

"One Interne," *The Saturday Evening Post,* 205 (November 5, 1932), 6–7, 86, 88–90; *TAR.*

"On Schedule," *The Saturday Evening Post,* 205 (March 18, 1933), 16, 17, 71, 74, 77, 79; *Price.*

"More Than Just a House," *The Saturday Evening Post,* 205 (June 24, 1933), 8–9, 27, 30, 34; *Price.*

"I Got Shoes," *The Saturday Evening Post,* 206 (September 23, 1933), 14–15, 56, 58; *Price.*

"The Family Bus," *The Saturday Evening Post,* 206 (November 4, 1933), 8–9, 57, 61–62, 65–66; *Price.*

"No Flowers," *The Saturday Evening Post,* 207 (July 21, 1934), 10–11, 57–58, 60; *Price.*

"New Types," *The Saturday Evening Post,* 207 (September 22, 1934), 16–17, 74, 76, 78–79, 81; *Price.*

"In the Darkest Hour," *Redbook,* 63 (October 1934), 15–19, 94–98; *Price.*

"Her Last Case," *The Saturday Evening Post,* 207 (November 3, 1934), 10–11, 59, 61–62, 64; *Price.*

"The Fiend," *Esquire,* 3 (January 1935), 23, 173–174; *TAR.*

"The Night before Chancellorsville," *Esquire,* 3 (February 1935), 24, 165; *TAR.*

"Shaggy's Morning," *Esquire*, 3 (May 1935), 26, 160.

"The Count of Darkness," *Redbook*, 65 (June 1935), 20–23, 68, 70, 72.

"The Intimate Strangers," *McCall's*, 62 (June 1935), 12–14, 36, 38, 40, 42, 44; *Price*.

"The Passionate Eskimo," *Liberty*, 12 (June 8, 1935), 10–14, 17–18.

"Zone of Accident," *The Saturday Evening Post*, 208 (July 13, 1935), 8–9, 47, 49, 51–52; *Price*.

"The Kingdom in the Dark," *Redbook*, 65 (August 1935), 58–62, 64, 66–68.

"Fate in Her Hands," *American Magazine*, 121 (April 1936), 56–59, 168–172; *Price*.

"Image on the Heart," *McCall's*, 63 (April 1936), 7–9, 52, 54, 57–58, 62; *Price*.

"Too Cute for Words," *The Saturday Evening Post*, 208 (April 18, 1936), 16–18, 87, 90, 93; *Price*.

"Three Acts of Music," *Esquire*, 5 (May 1936), 39, 210; *Price*.

"The Ants at Princeton," *Esquire*, 5 (June 1936), 35, 210.

"Inside the House," *The Saturday Evening Post*, 208 (June 13, 1936), 18–19, 32, 34, 36; *Price*.

"An Author's Mother," *Esquire*, 6 (September 1936), 36; *Price*.

"'I Didn't Get Over,'" *Esquire*, 6 (October 1936), 45, 194–195; *AOAA*.

"'Send Me In, Coach,'" *Esquire*, 6 (November 1936), 55, 218–221.

"An Alcoholic Case," *Esquire*, 6 [7] (February 1937), 32, 109; *Stories*.

"'Trouble,'" *The Saturday Evening Post*, 209 (March 6, 1937), 14–15, 81, 84, 86, 88–89; *Price*.

"The Honor of the Goon," *Esquire*, 7 (June 1937), 53, 216.

"The Long Way Out," *Esquire*, 8 (September 1937), 45, 193; *Stories*.

"The Guest in Room Nineteen," *Esquire*, 8 (October 1937), 56, 209; *Price*.

"In the Holidays," *Esquire*, 8 (December 1937), 82, 184, 186; *Price*.

"Financing Finnegan," *Esquire*, 9 (January 1938), 41, 180, 182, 184; *Stories*.

"Design in Plaster," *Esquire*, 12 (November 1939), 51, 169; *AOAA*.

"The Lost Decade," *Esquire*, 12 (December 1939), 113, 228; *Stories*.

"Strange Sanctuary," *Liberty*, 16 (December 9, 1939), 15–20.

"Pat Hobby's Christmas Wish," *Esquire*, 13 (January 1940), 45, 170–172; *PH*.

"A Man in the Way," *Esquire*, 13 (February 1940), 40, 109; *PH*.

"'Boil Some Water–Lots of It,'" *Esquire*, 13 (March 1940), 30, 145, 147; *PH*.

"Teamed with Genius," *Esquire*, 13 (April 1940), 44, 195–197; *PH*.

"Pat Hobby and Orson Welles," *Esquire*, 13 (May 1940), 38, 198–199; *PH*.

"Pat Hobby's Secret," *Esquire*, 13 (June 1940), 30, 107; *PH*.

"The End of Hate," *Collier's*, 105 (June 22, 1940), 9–10, 63–64; *Price*.

"Pat Hobby, Putative Father," *Esquire*, 14 (July 1940), 36, 172–174; *PH*.

"The Homes of the Stars," *Esquire*, 14 (August 1940), 28, 120–121; *PH*.

"Pat Hobby Does His Bit," *Esquire*, 14 (September 1940), 41, 104; *PH*.

"Pat Hobby's Preview," *Esquire*, 14 (October 1940), 30, 118, 120; *PH*.

"No Harm Trying," *Esquire*, 14 (November 1940), 30, 151–153; *PH*.

"A Patriotic Short," *Esquire*, 14 (December 1940), 62, 269; *PH*.

"On the Trail of Pat Hobby," *Esquire*, 15 (January 1941), 35, 126; *PH*.

"Fun in an Artist's Studio," *Esquire*, 15 (February 1941), 64, 112; *PH*.

Elgin, Paul [pseud.]. "On an Ocean Wave," *Esquire*, 15 (February 1941), 59, 141; *Price*.

"Two Old-Timers," *Esquire*, 15 (March 1941), 53, 143; *PH*.

"Mightier Than the Sword," *Esquire*, 15 (April 1941), 36, 183; *PH*.

"Pat Hobby's College Days," *Esquire*, 15 (May 1941), 55, 168–169; *PH*.

"The Woman from Twenty-One," *Esquire*, 15 (June 1941), 29, 164; *Price*.

"Three Hours Between Planes," *Esquire*, 16 (July 1941), 41, 138–139; *Stories*.

"Gods of Darkness," *Redbook*, 78 (November 1941), 30–33, 88–91.

"The Broadcast We Almost Heard Last September," *Furioso*, 3 (Fall 1947), 8–10.

"News of Paris–Fifteen Years Ago," *Furioso*, 3 (Winter 1947), 5–10; *AOAA*.

"Discard," *Harper's Bazaar*, 82 (January 1948), 103, 143–144, 146, 148–149; *Price*.

"The World's Fair," *The Kenyon Review*, 10 (Autumn 1948), 567–568.

"Last Kiss," *Collier's*, 123 (April 16, 1949), 16–17, 34, 38, 41, 43–44; *Bits*.

"That Kind of Party," *The Princeton University Library Chronicle*, 12 (Summer 1951), 167–180; *B&J*.

"Dearly Beloved," *Fitzgerald/Hemingway Annual* (1969), pp. 1–3; *Bits*.

"Lo, the Poor Peacock!" *Esquire,* 76 (September 1971), 154–158; *Price.*

"On Your Own," *Esquire,* 91 (January 30, 1979), 55–67; *Price.*

"A Full Life," *The Princeton University Library Chronicle,* 49 (Winter 1988), 167–172.

Articles and Essays

First periodical appearance and first publication in a Fitzgerald collection.

"S.P.A. Men in College Athletics," *The St. Paul Academy Now and Then,* 3 (December 1910), 7.

Untitled news feature about school election, *The Newman News* (1912), 18.

Untitled news feature about school dance, *The Newman News* (1913), 18.

"Who's Who–and Why." *The Saturday Evening Post,* 193 (September 18, 1920), 42, 61; *AOAA.*

"Three Cities," *Brentano's Book Chat,* 1 (September–October 1921), 15, 28; *In His Own Time.*

"What I Think and Feel at Twenty-five," *American Magazine,* 94 (September 1922), 16, 17, 136–140; *In His Own Time.*

"How I Would Sell My Book If I Were a Bookseller," *Bookseller and Stationer,* 18 (January 15, 1923), 8; *In His Own Time.*

"10 Best Books I Have Read," *Jersey City Evening Journal* (April 24, 1923), 9.

"Imagination–and a Few Mothers," *Ladies' Home Journal,* 40 (June 1923), 21, 80–81.

"The Cruise of the Rolling Junk," *Motor,* 41 (February, March, April 1924), 24–25, 58, 62, 64, 66; 42–43, 58, 72, 74, 76; 40–41, 58, 66, 68, 70.

"'Why Blame It on the Poor Kiss If the Girl Veteran of Many Petting Parties Is Prone to Affairs After Marriage?'" *New York American,* (February 24, 1924), LII-3; *In His Own Time.*

"Does a Moment of Revolt Come Sometime to Every Married Man?" *McCall's,* 51 (March 1924), 21, 36; *In His Own Time.*

"What Kind of Husbands Do 'Jimmies' Make?" *Baltimore American,* (March 30, 1924), ME-7; *In His Own Time.*

"How to Live on $36,000 a Year," *The Saturday Evening Post,* 196 (April 5, 1924), 22, 94, 97; *AOAA.*

"Wait Till You Have Children of Your Own!'" *Woman's Home Companion,* 51 (July 1924), 13, 105; *In His Own Time.*

"How to Live on Practically Nothing a Year," *The Saturday Evening Post,* 197 (September 20, 1924), 17, 165–166, 169–170; *AOAA.*

"Our Young Rich Boys," *McCall's,* 53 (October 1925), 12, 42, 69; *In His Own Time.*

"How to Waste Material A Note on My Generation," *The Bookman,* 63 (May 1926), 262–265; *AOAA.*

"Princeton," *College Humor,* 13 (December 1927), 28–29, 130–131; *AOAA.*

"Ten Years in the Advertising Business," *The Princeton Alumni Weekly,* 29 (February 22, 1929), 585; *AOAA.*

"A Short Autobiography (With Acknowledgments to Nathan)," *The New Yorker,* 5 (May 25, 1929), 22–23; *In His Own Time.*

"Girls Believe in Girls," *Liberty,* 7 (February 8, 1930), 22–24; *In His Own Time.*

"Echoes of the Jazz Age," *Scribner's Magazine,* 90 (November 1931), 459–465; *CU.*

"One Hundred False Starts," *The Saturday Evening Post,* 205 (March 4, 1933), 13, 65–66; *AOAA.*

"Ring," *The New Republic,* 76 (October 11, 1933), 254–255; *CU.*

"My Ten Favorite Plays," *New York Sun* (September 10, 1934), 19; *FSF on Authorship.*

"Introduction," *The Great Gatsby.* New York: Modern Library, 1934; *In His Own Time.*

"Sleeping and Waking," *Esquire,* 2 (December 1934), 34, 159–160; *CU.*

"The Crack-Up," *Esquire,* 5 (February 1936), 41, 164; *CU.*

"Pasting It Together," *Esquire,* 5 (March 1936), 35, 182–183; *CU.*

"Handle with Care," *Esquire,* 5 (April 1936), 39, 202; *CU.*

"Author's House," *Esquire,* 6 (July 1936), 40, 108; *AOAA.*

"Afternoon of an Author," *Esquire,* 6 (August 1936), 35, 170; *AOAA.*

"Early Success," *American Cavalcade,* 1 (October 1937), 74–79; *CU.*

"Foreword," *Colonial and Historical Homes of Maryland,* by Don Swann. Baltimore: Etchcrafters Art Guild, 1939; *In His Own Time.*

"The High Cost of Macaroni," *Interim,* 4, nos. 1–2, (1954), 6–15.

"My Generation," *Esquire,* 70 (October 1968), 119, 121, 123; *Profile of F. Scott Fitzgerald.*

Selected Works about Fitzgerald and *The Great Gatsby*

Bibliographies and Catalogues

Bruccoli, Matthew J. *F. Scott Fitzgerald: A Descriptive Bibliography.* Revised and augmented edition. Pittsburgh: University of Pittsburgh Press, 1987. Primary.

Bryer, Jackson R. *The Critical Reputation of F. Scott Fitzgerald.* Hamden, Conn.: Archon, 1967. Secondary.

Bryer. *The Critical Reputation of F. Scott Fitzgerald: Supplement through 1981.* Hamden, Conn.: Archon, 1984. Secondary.

Bucker, Park S., ed. *Catalogue of the Matthew J. and Arlyn Bruccoli F. Scott Fitzgerald Collection at the Thomas Cooper Library, The University of South Carolina.* Columbia, S.C.: MJB, 1997.

F. Scott Fitzgerald Centenary Exhibition. Columbia, S.C.: University of South Carolina Press for the Thomas Cooper Library, 1996. Catalogue.

Stanley, Linda C. *The Foreign Critical Reputation of F. Scott Fitzgerald.* Westport, Conn.: Greenwood Press, 1980. Secondary.

Biographies and Memoirs

Books

Bruccoli, Matthew J. *Scott and Ernest: The Authority of Failure and the Authority of Success.* New York: Random House, 1978. Revised as *Fitzgerald and Hemingway: A Dangerous Friendship.* New York: Carroll & Graf, 1994; London: André Deutsch, 1995.

Bruccoli. *Some Sort of Epic Grandeur.* San Diego: Harcourt Brace Jovanovich, 1981; London: Hodder & Stoughton. Revised edition, London: Cardinal, 1991; New York: Carroll & Graf, 1993.

Graham, Sheilah, and Gerold Frank. *Beloved Infidel.* New York: Holt, Rinehart & Winston, 1958.

Graham. *College of One.* New York: Viking, 1967.

Lanahan, Eleanor, ed. *Zelda, An Illustrated Life: The Private World of Zelda Fitzgerald.* New York: Harry N. Abrams, 1996.

Mellow, James R. *Invented Lives.* Boston: Houghton Mifflin, 1984.

Meyers, Jeffrey. *Scott Fitzgerald: A Biography.* New York: HarperCollins, 1994.

Milford, Nancy. *Zelda.* New York: Harper & Row, 1970.

Mizener, Arthur. *The Far Side of Paradise.* Boston: Houghton Mifflin, 1951. Revised, 1965.

Mizener. *Scott Fitzgerald and His World.* New York: Putnam, 1972.

Smith, Scottie Fitzgerald, Matthew J. Bruccoli, and Joan P. Kerr, eds. *The Romantic Egoists: A Pictorial Autobiography from the Scrapbooks and Albums of F. Scott Fitzgerald and Zelda Fitzgerald.* New York: Scribners, 1974.

Turnbull, Andrew. *Scott Fitzgerald.* New York: Scribners, 1962; London: Bodley Head, 1962.

Book Sections and Articles

Hemingway, Ernest. "Scott Fitzgerald," "Hawks Do Not Share," "A Matter of Measurements." *A Moveable Feast* (New York: Scribners, 1964), 147–163.

Lanahan, Francis Fitzgerald. Introduction. *Six Tales of the Jazz Age and Other Stories* by F. Scott Fitzgerald (New York: Scribners, 1960), 5–11.

Meyers, Jeffrey. "Scott Fitzgerald and Edmund Wilson: A Troubled Friendship." *American Scholar,* 61 (Summer 1992), 375–388.

Critical Studies

Baughman, Judith S., with Matthew J. Bruccoli. *F. Scott Fitzgerald Gale Study Guide.* Detroit: Manly/Gale, 2000.

Berman, Ronald. *The Great Gatsby and Fitzgerald's World of Ideas.* Tuscaloosa, Ala.: 1997.

Berman. *The Great Gatsby and Modern Times.* Urbana, Ill.: University of Illinois Press, 1994.

Bruccoli, Matthew J. *"The Last of the Novelists": F. Scott Fitzgerald and The Last Tycoon.* Carbondale & Edwardsville, Ill.: Southern Illinois University Press, 1977.

Bruccoli, with Judith S. Baughman. *Reader's Companion to F. Scott Fitzgerald's Tender is the Night.* Columbia, S.C.: University of South Carolina Press, 1996.

Callahan, John. *The Illusions of a Nation.* Urbana, Ill.: University of Illinois Press, 1972.

Chambers, John B. *The Novels of F. Scott Fitzgerald.* London: Macmillan/New York: St. Martin's Press, 1989.

Crosland, Andrew T. *A Concordance to F. Scott Fitzgerald's The Great Gatsby.* Detroit, Mich.: Bruccoli Clark/Gale Research, 1975.

Cross, K. G. W. *Scott Fitzgerald.* New York: Grove, 1964.

Eble, Kenneth. *F. Scott Fitzgerald.* New York: Twayne, 1963. Revised, 1977.

Fahey, William A. *F. Scott Fitzgerald and the American Dream.* New York: Crowell, 1973.

Fryer, Sarah Beebe. *Fitzgerald's New Women: Harbingers of Change.* Ann Arbor, Mich.: UMI, 1988.

Gallo, Rose A. *F. Scott Fitzgerald.* New York: Ungar, 1978.

Goldhurst, William. *F. Scott Fitzgerald and His Contemporaries.* Cleveland & New York: World, 1963.

Gross, Dalton and Mary Jean. *Understanding the Great Gatsby.* Westport, Conn.: Greenwood Press, 1998.

Higgins, John A. *F. Scott Fitzgerald: A Study of the Stories.* New York: St. John's University Press, 1971.

Hook, Andrew. *F. Scott Fitzgerald.* London & New York: Arnold, 1992.

Lehan, Richard D. *F. Scott Fitzgerald and the Craft of Fiction.* Carbondale, Ill.: Southern Illinois University Press, 1966.

Lehan. *The Great Gatsby: The Limits of Wonder.* Boston: Twayne, 1990.

Long, Robert Emmett. *The Achieving of The Great Gatsby.* Lewisburg, Pa.: Bucknell University Press, 1979.

Mangum, Bryant. *A Fortune Yet: Money in the Art of F. Scott Fitzgerald's Short Stories*. New York: Garland, 1991.

Matterson, Stephen. *The Great Gatsby and the Critics*. London: Macmillan, 1990.

Miller, James E., Jr. *F. Scott Fitzgerald: His Art and His Technique*. New York: New York University Press, 1964. Revised as *The Fictional Technique of Scott Fitzgerald*. Folcroft, Pa.: Folcroft Press, 1974.

Moseley, Edwin. *F. Scott Fitzgerald*. Grand Rapids, Mich.: Eerdmans, 1967.

Parkinson, Kathleen. *F. Scott Fitzgerald: The Great Gatsby*. Harmondsworth, U.K.: Penguin, 1987.

Pendleton, Thomas A. *I'm Sorry About the Clock: Chronology, Composition, and Narrative Technique in The Great Gatsby*. Selinsgrove, Pa.: Susquehanna University Press, 1993.

Perosa, Sergio. *The Art of F. Scott Fitzgerald*. Ann Arbor, Mich.: University of Michigan Press, 1965.

Petry, Alice Hall. *Fitzgerald's Craft of Short Fiction: The Collected Stories*. Ann Arbor, Mich.: UMI, 1989.

Piper, Henry Dan. *F. Scott Fitzgerald: A Critical Portrait*. New York: Holt, Rinehart & Winston, 1965.

Seiters, Dan. *Image Patterns in the Novels of F. Scott Fitzgerald*. Ann Arbor, Mich.: UMI, 1986.

Shain, Charles E. *F. Scott Fitzgerald*. Minneapolis, Minn.: University of Minnesota Press, 1967.

Sklar, Robert. *F. Scott Fitzgerald: The Last Lacoön*. New York: Oxford University Press, 1967.

Stavola, Thomas J. *Scott Fitzgerald: Crisis in an American Identity*. New York: Barnes & Noble, 1979.

Stern, Milton R. *The Golden Moment: The Novels of F. Scott Fitzgerald*. Urbana, Ill.: University of Illinois Press, 1970.

Way, Brian. *F. Scott Fitzgerald and the Art of Social Fiction*. London: Arnold, 1980; New York: St. Martin's Press, 1980.

Whitley, John S. *F. Scott Fitzgerald: The Great Gatsby*. London: Arnold, 1976.

Collections of Essays

Bloom, Harold, ed. with intro. *F. Scott Fitzgerald*. New York: Chelsea House, 1985.

Bloom, ed. with intro. *F. Scott Fitzgerald's The Great Gatsby*. New York: Chelsea House, 1986.

Bloom, ed. with intro. *Gatsby*. New York: Chelsea House, 1991.

Bruccoli, Matthew J., ed. *Profile of F. Scott Fitzgerald*. Columbus, Ohio: Merrill, 1971.

Bruccoli, ed. with intro. *New Essays on The Great Gatsby*. Cambridge: Cambridge University Press, 1985.

Bryer, Jackson R., ed. *F. Scott Fitzgerald: The Critical Reception*. New York: Burt Franklin, 1978. Contemporary reviews of Fitzgerald's novels and short-story collections.

Bryer, ed. *The Short Stories of F. Scott Fitzgerald: New Approaches in Criticism*. Madison: University of Wisconsin Press, 1982.

Bryer, ed. *New Essays on F. Scott Fitzgerald's Neglected Stories*. Columbia: University of Missouri Press, 1996.

Claridge, Henry, ed. *F. Scott Fitzgerald: Critical Assessments*. 4 vols. Near Robertsbridge, East Sussex, U.K.: Helm Information, 1991. Contents: 226 essays. Volume I: Fitzgerald in Context, Memories and Reminiscences, Contemporary Critical Opinion; Volume II: Early Writings, *TSOP, B&D, The Vegetable,* and *GG;* Volume III: *TITN, LT, The Crack-Up,* and the Short Stories; Volume IV: General Perspectives, Fitzgerald and Other Writers.

De Koster, Katie, ed. *Readings on The Great Gatsby*. San Diego, Cal.: Greenhaven Press, 1998.

Donaldson, Scott, ed. with intro. *Critical Essays on F. Scott Fitzgerald's The Great Gatsby*. Boston: Hall, 1984.

Eble, Kenneth, ed. with intro. *F. Scott Fitzgerald: A Collection of Criticism*. New York: McGraw-Hill, 1973.

Hoffman, Frederick J., ed. with intro. *The Great Gatsby: A Study*. New York: Scribners, 1962.

Kazin, Alfred, ed. with intro. *F. Scott Fitzgerald: The Man and His Work*. Cleveland: World, 1951.

Lee, A. Robert, ed. with intro. *Scott Fitzgerald: The Promises of Life*. London: Vision / New York: St. Martin's, 1989.

Lockridge, Ernest, ed.with intro. *Twentieth Century Interpretations of The Great Gatsby*. Englewood Cliffs, N.J.: Prentice-Hall, 1968.

Mandal, Somdatta, ed. *F. Scott Fitzgerald: A Centenary Tribute*. 2 vols. New Dehli: Prestige, 1997.

Mizener, Arthur, ed. with intro. *F. Scott Fitzgerald: A Collection of Critical Essays*. Englewood Cliffs, N.J.: Prentice-Hall, 1963.

Piper, Henry Dan, ed. with intro. *Fitzgerald's The Great Gatsby: The Novel, The Critics, The Background*. New York: Scribners, 1970.

Journals

Fitzgerald Newsletter (quarterly, 1958–68). Reprinted Washington, D.C.: NCR Microcard Books, 1969. Includes checklists.

Fitzgerald/Hemingway Annual (1969–79). Washington, D.C.: NCR Microcard Books, 1969–73. Englewood, Colo.: Information Handling Services, 1974–76; Detroit: Gale Research, 1977–79. Includes checklists.

F. Scott Fitzgerald Collection Notes. Columbia, S.C.: Thomas Cooper Library, University of South Carolina, 1995–
.

Book Sections and Articles

Atkinson, Jennifer. "Fitzgerald's Marked Copy of *The Great Gatsby*." *Fitzgerald/Hemingway Annual* (1970), 28–33.

Berryman, John. "F. Scott Fitzgerald." *The Kenyon Review,* 8 (Winter 1946), 103–112.

Bewley, Marius. "Scott Fitzgerald's Criticism of America." *Sewanee Review,* 62 (Spring 1954), 223–246. Expanded as "Scott Fitzgerald and the Collapse of the American Dream." *The Eccentric Design* by Bewley. (New York: Columbia University Press, 1959).

Bicknell, John W. "The Waste Land of FSF." *Virginia Quarterly Review,* 30 (Autumn 1954), 556–572.

Bigsby, C. W. E. "The Two Identities of F. Scott Fitzgerald." *The American Novel and the Nineteen Twenties.* ed. Malcolm Bradbury and David Palmer (London: Arnold, 1971), 129–149.

Birkets, Sven. "A Gatsby for Today." *Atlantic Monthly,* 271 (March 1993), 122–126.

Bishop, John Peale. "The Missing All." *Virginia Quarterly Review,* 13 (Winter 1937), 106–121.

Bruccoli, Matthew J. "Getting It Right: The Publishing Process and the Correction of Factual Errors—with Reference to *The Great Gatsby,*" *Essays in Honor of William B. Todd,* comp. Warner Barnes and Larry Carver (Austin: Harry Ransom Humanities Research Center, The University of Texas, 1991), 40–59; revised edition separately published (Columbia, S.C.: Privately printed, 1994).

Bufkin, E. C. "A Pattern of Parallel and Double: The Function of Myrtle in *The Great Gatsby.*" *Modern Fiction Studies,* 15 (Winter 1969–1970), 517–524.

Chase, Richard. "*The Great Gatsby.*" *The American Novel and Its Traditions* (Garden City, N.Y.: Doubleday, 1957), 162–167.

Corso, Joseph. "One Not-Forgotten Summer Night: Sources for Fictional Symbols of American Character in *The Great Gatsby.*" *Fitzgerald/Hemingway Annual* (1976), 9–34.

Cowley, Malcolm. "The Scott Fitzgerald Story." *New Republic,* 124 (February 12, 1951), 17–20.

Cowley. "Fitzgerald: The Double Man." *Saturday Review of Literature,* 34 (February 24, 1951), 9–10, 42–44.

Cowley. "F. Scott Fitzgerald: The Romance of Money." *Western Review,* 17 (Summer 1953), 245–255.

Dos Passos, John. "Fitzgerald and the Press." *New Republic,* 104 (February 17, 1941), 213.

Doyno, Victor A. "Patterns in *The Great Gatsby.*" *Modern Fiction Studies,* 12 (Winter 1966–67), 415–426.

Eble, Kenneth. "The Craft of Revision: *The Great Gatsby.*" *American Literature,* 36 (Autumn 1964), 315–326.

Emmitt, Robert J. "Love, Death and Resurrection in *The Great Gatsby.*" *Aeolian Harps,* ed. Donna G. and Douglas C. Fricke (Bowling Green, Ohio: Bowling Green University Press, 1976), 273–289.

Friedrich, Otto. "Reappraisals—F. Scott Fitzgerald: Money, Money, Money." *American Scholar,* 29 (Summer 1960), 392–405.

Fuson, Barbara. "'And How Shall I Begin?' The Example of *The Great Gatsby.*" *Literature and Writing,* 3 (November 1989), 12–14.

Fussell, Edwin S. "Fitzgerald's Brave New World." *ELH,* 19 (December 1952), 291–306.

Geismar, Maxwell. "F. Scott Fitzgerald: Orestes at the Ritz." *The Last of the Provincials* (Boston: Houghton Mifflin, 1943), 287–352.

Gervais, Ronald J. "The Socialist and the Silk Stockings: Fitzgerald's Double Allegiance." *Mosaic,* 15 (June 1982), 79–92.

Hanzo, Thomas A. "The Theme and Narrator of *The Great Gatsby.*" *Modern Fiction Studies,* 2 (Winter 1956–57), 183–190.

Harding, D. W. "Scott Fitzgerald." *Scrutiny,* 18 (Winter 1951–52), 166–174.

Harvey, W. J. "Theme and Texture in *The Great Gatsby.*" *English Studies,* 38 (1957), 12–20.

Hildebrand, William H. "*The Great Gatsby* and 'Utter Synthesis.'" *Serif,* 2 (March 1965), 19–26.

Irish, Carol. "The Myth of Success in Fitzgerald's Boyhood." *Studies in American Fiction,* 1 (Autumn 1973), 176–187.

Ishikaway, Akiko. "From Winter Dreams to *The Great Gatsby.*" *Persica,* 5 (January 1978), 79–92.

Kruse, Horst Hermann. "Gatsby and Gadsby." *Modern Fiction Studies,* 15 (Winter 1969–1970), 539–541.

Kuehl, John. "Scott Fitzgerald: Romantic and Realist." *Texas Studies in Literature and Language,* 1 (Autumn 1959), 412–426.

Kuehl. "Scott Fitzgerald's Reading." *Princeton University Library Chronicle,* 22 (Winter 1961), 58–89.

Kuehl. "Scott Fitzgerald's Critical Opinions." *Modern Fiction Studies,* 7 (Spring 1961), 3–18.

Kuhnle, John H. "*The Great Gatsby* as Pastoral Elegy." *Fitzgerald/Hemingway Annual* (1978), 141–154.

MacKendrick, Paul L. "The Great Gatsby and Trimalchio." *Classical Journal,* 45 (April 1950), 307–314.

McCall, Dan. "The Self-Same Song That Found a Path: Keats and *The Great Gatsby.*" *American Literature,* 42 (January 1971), 521–530.

Moyer, Kermit W. "*The Great Gatsby:* Fitzgerald's Meditation on American History." *Fitzgerald/Hemingway Annual* (1972), 43–58.

Mulford, Carla. "Fitzgerald, Perkins, and *The Great Gatsby.*" *Journal of Narrative Technique,* 12 (Fall 1982), 210–220.

O'Hara, John. "On F. Scott Fitzgerald." *"An Artist Is His Own Fault": John O'Hara on Writers and Writing,* ed. Matthew J. Bruccoli (Carbondale, Ill.: Southern Illinois University Press, 1977), 135–154.

Checklist of Further Reading

Ornstein, Robert. "Scott Fitzgerald's Fable of East and West." *College English,* 18 (December 1956), 139–143.

Parr, Susan Resneck. "Individual Responsibility in *The Great Gatsby.*" *Virginia Quarterly Review,* 57 (Autumn 1981), 662–680.

Person, Leland S. "Herstory and Daisy Buchanan." *American Literature,* 50 (May 1978), 250–257.

Podis, Leonard A. "The Unreality of Reality: Metaphor in *The Great Gatsby.*" *Style,* 11 (Winter 1977), 56–72.

Quirk, Tom. "Fitzgerald and Cather: *The Great Gatsby.*" *American Literature,* 54 (December 1982), 576–591.

Raleigh, John Henry. "F. Scott Fitzgerald's *The Great Gatsby:* Legendary Bases and Allegorical Significance." *University of Kansas City Review,* 24 (Autumn 1957), 55–58.

Rosenfeld, Paul. "F. Scott Fitzgerald." *Men Seen* (New York: Dial, 1925), 215–224.

Samuels, Charles T. "The Greatness of 'Gatsby.'" *Massachusetts Review,* 7 (Autumn 1966), 783–794.

Sanders, Barbara G. "Structural Imagery in *The Great Gatsby:* Metaphor and Matrix." *Linguistics in Literature,* 1 (1975), 53–75.

Savage, D. S. "The Significance of F. Scott Fitzgerald." *Arizona Quarterly,* 8 (Autumn 1952), 197–210.

Schwartz, Delmore. "The Dark Night of F. Scott Fitzgerald." *The Nation,* 172 (February 24, 1951), 180–182.

Scribner, Charles, III. "Celestial Eyes: From Metamorphosis to Masterpiece." *Princeton University Library Chronicle,* 53 (Winter 1992), 140–155.

Scrimgeour, Gary J. "Against *The Great Gatsby.*" *Criticism,* 8 (Winter 1966), 75–86.

Settle, Glen. "Fitzgerald's Daisy: The Siren Voice." *American Literature,* 57 (March 1985), 115–124.

Stallman, R. W. "Conrad and *The Great Gatsby.*" *Twentieth Century Literature,* 1 (April 1955), 5–12.

Stark, Bruce R. "The Intricate Pattern in *The Great Gatsby.*" *Fitzgerald/Hemingway Annual* (1974), 51–61.

Steinbrink, Jeffrey. "'Boats Against the Current': Mortality and the Myth of Renewal in *The Great Gatsby.*" *Twentieth Century Literature,* 26 (Summer 1980), 157–170.

Tanselle, G. Thomas and Jackson R. Bryer. "*The Great Gatsby:* A Study in Literary Reputation." *New Mexico Quarterly,* 33 (Winter 1963–64), 409–425.

Trilling, Lionel. "F. Scott Fitzgerald," *The Liberal Imagination* (New York: Viking, 1950), 243–254.

Troy, William. "Scott Fitzgerald–The Authority of Failure." *Accent,* 6 (Autumn 1945), 56–60.

Turlish, Lewis Afton. "The Rising Tide of Color: A Note on the Historicism of *The Great Gatsby.*" *American Literature,* 43 (November 1971), 442–443.

Watkins, Floyd C. "Fitzgerald's Jay Gatz and Young Ben Franklin." *New England Quarterly,* 27 (June 1954), 249–252.

Wescott, Glenway. "The Moral of Scott Fitzgerald." *The New Republic,* 104 (February 17, 1941), 213–217.

Wilson, Edmund. "The Literary Spotlight–VI: F. Scott Fitzgerald." *The Bookman,* 55 (March 1922), 20–25.

Study Guides

Altena, I. *Notes on Scott Fitzgerald's The Great Gatsby.* London: Methuen Educational, 1976.

Bloom, Harold, ed. with intro. *Bloom's Reviews: F. Scott Fitzgerald's The Great Gatsby.* Broomall, Pa.: Chelsea House Publishers, 1996.

Cooperman. *F. Scott Fitzgerald's The Great Gatsby (A Critical Commentary)* New York: Monarch, 1965.

De Lathbury, Roger. *The Great Gatsby Gale Study Guide.* Detroit: Manly/Gale, 2000.

F. Scott Fitzgerald: The Great Gatsby Notes. Toronto: Coles, 1983.

Fowler, Austin. *F. Scott Fitzgerald's The Great Gatsby: A Critical Analysis in Depth.* New York: Barrister, 1966.

Goethals, Thomas R. *A Critical Commentary: The Great Gatsby.* Study Master, New York: American R. D. M. Corporation, 1963.

Handley, Graham. *Brodie's Notes on F. Scott Fitzgerald's The Great Gatsby.* London: Pan, 1978.

Northman, Phillip. *The Great Gatsby Notes.* Lincoln, Neb.: Cliffs Notes, 1966, 1996.

Ping, Tang Soo. *Notes on The Great Gatsby: F. Scott Fitzgerald.* London & Beirut: Longman/York Press, 1980.

Pohlenz, Dagmar and Richard Martin. *The Great Gatsby by F. Scott Fitzgerald: Interpretations and Suggestions for Teaching.* Paderborn: Ferdinand Schöningh, 1986.

Taylor, Douglas R. *A Comprehensive Outline of The Great Gatsby.* East Longmeadow, Mass.: Harvard Outline Company, 1965.

Taylor, Douglas. *The Great Gatsby: Review Notes.* Boston: Ivy Notes, 1966.

White, Sidney Howard. *Barron's Simplified Approach to Fitzgerald: The Great Gatsby.* Woodbury, N.Y.: Barron's Educational Series, 1968.

Audiorecordings

"A Study Guide to F. Scott Fitzgerald's *The Great Gatsby.*" Narr. Lawrence Pressman. Time Warner, 1994.

Videorecordings

Bruccoli, Matthew J. *An Introduction to F. Scott Fitzgerald's Fiction.* Modern American Literature–Eminent Scholar/Teachers Series, Detroit: Omnigraphics, 1988.

Bruccoli. *Reading F. Scott Fitzgerald's The Great Gatsby*. Modern American Literature–Eminent Scholar/Teachers Series, Detroit: Omnigraphics, 1988.

Discovery Channel & Summer Productions. *Great Books: The Great Gatsby*. Bethesda, Md.: Discovery Channel Education, 1997.

Engel, Elliot. *The Greatness of The Great Gatsby*. United States: E. Engel, 1994.

Klise, Thomas S. *Gatsby, An American Myth*. New York: Thomas S. Klise Company, 1993.

Klise, Thomas S. *Gatsby, The American Myth Filmstrip*. Peoria, Ill.: Thomas S. Klise Company, 1970.

Selected Websites

Pioneer Press. *Fitzgerald Childhood Home Tour*. 1996. http://www.pioneerplanet.com/archive/fitzgerald/stories/fitztour10.htm.

The Great Gatsby, A Beginner's Guide. 1996. http://www.geocities.com/BourbonStreet/3844/.

USC: F. Scott Fitzgerald Centenary Home Page. University of South Carolina. December 1997. http://www.csd.edu/fitzgerald/index.html.

Literary and Social-History Backgrounds

Baughman, Judith S., ed. *American Decades: 1920–1929*. Detroit: Manly/Gale, 1995.

Baxter, John. *Hollywood in the Thirties*. London: Tantivy Press, 1968.

Beach, Sylvia. *Shakespeare & Company*. New York: Harcourt, Brace, 1959.

Berg, Scott. *Max Perkins: Editor of Genius*. New York: Congdon/Dutton, 1978.

Bondi, Victor, ed. *American Decades: 1930–1939*. Detroit: Manly/Gale, 1995.

Bruccoli, Matthew J., ed., with Robert W. Trogdon. *The Only Thing That Counts: The Ernest Hemingway/Maxwell Perkins Correspondence*. New York: Scribners, 1996.

Bruccoli, Matthew J., and Robert W. Trogdon, eds. *American Expatriate Writers: Paris in the Twenties* (Detroit: Bruccoli Clark Layman/Gale Research, 1997). Dictionary of Literary Biography Documentary Series 15.

Cowley, Malcolm. *Exile's Return: A Literary Odyssey of the 1920s*. New York: Norton, 1934. Revised edition, New York: Viking, 1951.

Cowley. *A Second Flowering: Works and Days of the Last Generation*. New York: Viking, 1973.

Cowley. *Unshaken Friend: A Profile of Maxwell Perkins*. Boulder, Colo.: Roberts Rinehart, 1985.

Cowley, Malcolm, and Robert Cowley, eds. *Fitzgerald and the Jazz Age*. New York: Scribners, 1966.

Delaney, John, ed. *The House of Scribner, 1905–1930* (Detroit: Bruccoli Clark Layman/Gale Research, 1997). Dictionary of Literary Biography Documentary Series 16.

Hoffman, Frederick J. *The Twenties: American Writing in the Postwar Decade*. Revised edition, New York: Collier, 1962.

Meyers, Jeffrey. *Edmund Wilson: A Biography*. Boston: Houghton Mifflin, 1995.

Reynolds, Michael. *Hemingway: The Paris Years*. Oxford & New York: Basil Blackwell, 1989.

Rood, Karen Lane, ed., with foreword by Malcolm Cowley. *American Writers in Paris, 1920–1939; Dictionary of Literary Biography*, vol. 4. Detroit: Bruccoli Clark/Gale, 1980.

Spindler, Elizabeth Carroll. *John Peale Bishop: A Biography*. Morgantown: West Virginia University Library, 1980.

Wheelock, John Hall, ed. *Editor to Author: The Letters of Maxwell Perkins*. New York: Scribners, 1979.

Wilson, Edmund. *The Shores of Light*. New York: Farrar, Straus and Young, 1952.

Wilson. *The Twenties*, ed. Leon Edel. New York: Farrar, Straus and Giroux, 1975.

Wilson. *The Thirties: From Notebooks and Diaries of the Period*. New York: Farrar, Straus and Giroux, 1980.

Yardley, Jonathan. *Ring: A Biography of Ring Lardner*. New York: Random House, 1977.

Index

Index

Index